T0320918

Business and Human Rights
Ethical, Legal, and Managerial Perspectives

The first of its kind, this comprehensive interdisciplinary textbook in
Business and Human Rights (BHR) connects and integrates themes,
discussions, and issues in BHR from both legal and non-legal
perspectives, and provides a solid foundation for cross-disciplinary
conversations. It equips students, teachers, and scholars with the
necessary knowledge to navigate and advance evolving BHR debates,
and fosters a thorough understanding of the academic foundations,
evolving policy spaces, and practical approaches in BHR. Short cases
throughout translate conceptual insights into practical solutions.
Study, reflection, and discussion questions help readers to consolidate
and synthesize their understanding of the material and provide
stimulating frameworks for debate in the classroom and beyond.
The book features a collection of online resources to support students
and instructors in their preparation for courses and assignments.

Florian Wettstein is a professor of business ethics and Director of
the Institute for Business Ethics at the University of St. Gallen in
Switzerland. Florian has published widely on topics at the intersection
of corporate responsibility, business ethics, and business and human
rights, and has been involved in numerous practical and policy
initiatives and projects on those topics. He is the author of
*Multinational Corporations and Global Justice: Human Rights
Obligations of a Quasi-Governmental Institution* (2009) and editor-in-
chief of the *Business and Human Rights Journal* (*BHRJ*).

Business and Human Rights
Ethical, Legal, and Managerial Perspectives

Florian Wettstein

University of St. Gallen, Switzerland

CAMBRIDGE
UNIVERSITY PRESS

CAMBRIDGE
UNIVERSITY PRESS

University Printing House, Cambridge CB2 8BS, United Kingdom

One Liberty Plaza, 20th Floor, New York, NY 10006, USA

477 Williamstown Road, Port Melbourne, VIC 3207, Australia

314–321, 3rd Floor, Plot 3, Splendor Forum, Jasola District Centre, New Delhi – 110025, India

103 Penang Road, #05-06/07, Visioncrest Commercial, Singapore 238467

Cambridge University Press is part of the University of Cambridge.

It furthers the University's mission by disseminating knowledge in the pursuit of education, learning, and research at the highest international levels of excellence.

www.cambridge.org
Information on this title: www.cambridge.org/highereducation/isbn/9781009158381
DOI: 10.1017/9781009158374

First published 2022

Printed in the United Kingdom by TJ Books Limited, Padstow, Cornwall 2022

A catalogue record for this publication is available from the British Library.

Library of Congress Cataloging-in-Publication Data
Names: Wettstein, Florian, author.
Title: Business and human rights : ethical, legal, and managerial perspectives / Florian Wettstein,
   Universität St. Gallen, Switzerland.
Description: Cambridge, United Kingdom ; New York, NY : Cambridge University Press, 2022. | Includes
   bibliographical references and index.
Identifiers: LCCN 2021046666 (print) | LCCN 2021046667 (ebook) | ISBN 9781009158381 (hardback) |
   ISBN 9781009158398 (paperback) | ISBN 9781009158374 (epub)
Subjects: LCSH: Social responsibility of business. | Corporate governance. | Human rights.
Classification: LCC HD60 .W468 2022 (print) | LCC HD60 (ebook) | DDC 658.4/08–dc23
LC record available at https://lccn.loc.gov/2021046666
LC ebook record available at https://lccn.loc.gov/2021046667

ISBN 978-1-009-15838-1 Hardback
ISBN 978-1-009-15839-8 Paperback
Additional resources for this publication at www.cambridge.org/wettstein

Brief Contents

List of Boxes   *page* xv
Preface   xvii

1   Introduction: Learning and Unlearning Business and
    Human Rights   1

Part I Foundations

2   BHR: Emergence and History of a Movement   11

3   A Brief Introduction to Human Rights   25

Part II Setting the Scene

4   Corporate Human Rights Violations: Direct and Indirect   65

5   Corporate Human Rights Violations: Overview of Issues   77

Part III Corporate Human Rights Responsibility

6   Justification of Corporate Human Rights Responsibility   103

7   Nature and Extent of Corporate Human Rights Responsibility   126

8   Operationalizing and Implementing Human Rights
    Responsibility at the Corporate Level   142

Part IV Corporate Human Rights Accountability

9   Transnational Governance and Corporate Human Rights
    Accountability: Preliminary Questions and Foundational Issues   171

10 The UN Guiding Principles on BHR: Foundations,
    Contemplations, Critique   185

11 Further International Soft-Law Standards and
    Voluntary Initiatives   206

12 **Home-State Solutions**   226

13 **International Law-Based Solutions**   298

Part V Selected Industries and Emerging Discussions

14 **Industry-Specific Issues and Challenges**   317

15 **Emerging Discussions and Narratives**   348

16 **Conclusion: Building Back Better**   364

Helpful Online Resources and Blogs on BHR   368
References of Court Cases   370
Glossary   372
References   375
Index   413

Contents

List of Boxes		*page* xv
Preface		xvii

1 Introduction: Learning and Unlearning Business and Human Rights — 1

1.1 Unlearning Human Rights: Challenging Traditional Human Rights Thinking — 1

1.2 Unlearning Business: Challenging Corporate Social Responsibility — 2

1.3 Learning BHR: The Human Rights Perspective on Corporate Responsibility — 4

1.4 Rationale and Structure of the Book — 6

Part I Foundations

2 BHR: Emergence and History of a Movement — 11

2.1 Precursors (1945–1995) — 11

2.2 The Beginnings (1995–2005) — 15

2.3 The Formative Years (2005–2011) — 18

2.4 Maturing of the BHR Movement (2011–ongoing) — 19

2.5 BHR in the Academic Discourse: Emergence of a New Field — 21

3 A Brief Introduction to Human Rights — 25

3.1 Philosophy of Human Rights — 25

  3.1.1 A Brief History of Thought on Human Rights — 26

  3.1.2 Elements of Human Rights — 30

  3.1.3 Universalism v. Relativism — 31

    3.1.3.1 Absolutism — 32

    3.1.3.2 Relativism — 32

    3.1.3.3 Universalism — 33

    3.1.3.4 Are Human Rights Western? — 35

  3.1.4 Foundation and Justification of Human Rights — 38

    3.1.4.1 Foundationalist Accounts of Human Rights — 38

    3.1.4.2 Non-Foundationalist Accounts of Human Rights — 42

    3.1.4.3 Reconciliation of Different Approaches — 45

3.2 International Human Rights System   46
   3.2.1 UN Human Rights Bodies and Agencies   46
   3.2.2 Other Human Rights Bodies and Agencies   49
3.3 International Human Rights Law   52
   3.3.1 Kinds of Human Rights   53
   3.3.2 Sources of International Human Rights Law   54
   3.3.3 International Bill of Human Rights   56
   3.3.4 Core Human Rights Treaties   58
   3.3.5 Regional Human Rights Conventions   60

Part II Setting the Scene

4 Corporate Human Rights Violations: Direct and Indirect   65
4.1 A Note on Terminology: Impact v. Violation   65
4.2 Direct Human Rights Violations   66
4.3 Indirect Human Rights Violations   67
   4.3.1 Active Complicity   70
   4.3.2 Passive Complicity   71
   4.3.3 Moral and Legal Elements of Complicity   72

5 Corporate Human Rights Violations: Overview of Issues   77
5.1 Employment Relations   77
   5.1.1 Discrimination and Harassment   77
   5.1.2 Monitoring and Privacy   78
5.2 Workers in the Supply Chain   80
   5.2.1 Child Labor   80
   5.2.2 Exploitation and Sweatshop Labor   82
   5.2.3 Forced Labor and Modern Slavery   82
5.3 Affected Communities   83
   5.3.1 Land-Grabbing and Displacement   83
   5.3.2 Security and Protest   85
   5.3.3 Conflict   85
5.4 Environment   87
   5.4.1 Contamination of Air, Soil, and Water   88
   5.4.2 Deforestation   90
5.5 Vulnerable Groups   91
   5.5.1 Indigenous Communities and Free, Prior, and Informed
       Consent   92
   5.5.2 Migrant Workers   94
   5.5.3 Human Rights Defenders   95

Part III Corporate Human Rights Responsibility

6   Justification of Corporate Human Rights Responsibility   103
   6.1 Human Rights as Ethical Obligations of Business   103
      6.1.1 Ethical Obligations of Business: Beyond Profit-Maximization   103
      6.1.2 Human Rights as Ethical Imperatives of Business:
         Two Approaches   106
      6.1.3 Corporate Power and Authority   107
   6.2 Human Rights as Legal Obligations of Business   110
      6.2.1 Legal Personhood at the National Level   110
      6.2.2 Legal Personhood at the International Level   112
      6.2.3 Human Rights as Legal Imperatives of Business   113
   6.3 Pragmatic Perspectives on Human Rights Obligations
      of Business   116
      6.3.1 The Social License to Operate   117
      6.3.2 The Business Case for Corporate Human Rights Responsibility   118
   6.4 Common Objections   122

7   Nature and Extent of Corporate Human Rights Responsibility   126
   7.1 Basic Obligation Types   126
   7.2 Human Rights Obligations in Particular   128
   7.3 Corporate Obligations to Respect, Protect, and Fulfil
      Human Rights?   129
      7.3.1 The Corporate Obligation to Respect Human Rights   129
      7.3.2 The Corporate Obligation to Protect Human Rights   131
         7.3.2.1 Direct Protection: Relational Contexts   133
         7.3.2.2 Indirect Protection: Structural Contexts   136
      7.3.3 The Corporate Obligation to Fulfil Human Rights   138

**8   Operationalizing and Implementing Human Rights Responsibility
   at the Corporate Level**   142
   8.1 Managing Impacts: Human Rights Due Diligence   142
      8.1.1 Human Rights Due Diligence in Law   142
      8.1.2 Human Rights Due Diligence in Business Practice   144
      8.1.3 Human Rights Due Diligence Process   145
         8.1.3.1 Committing to Human Rights: Human Rights
            Policy Statement   145
         8.1.3.2 Identifying Impacts: Human Rights
            Impact Assessments   147
         8.1.3.3 Responding to Human Rights Impacts: Operational-level
            Grievance Mechanisms   148

8.1.3.4 Tracking Responses: Human Rights Performance Indicators 151

8.1.3.5 Communicating Responses: Human Rights Reporting 153

8.1.4 Remedying Adverse Human Rights Impacts 154

8.1.5 Implementation Challenges 159

8.1.5.1 Industry and Company-Specificity 160

8.1.5.2 Dedicated v. Non-Specific Human Rights Processes 160

8.1.5.3 Prioritization and Weighing of Risks and Impacts 161

8.1.5.4 Community Engagement 162

8.1.5.5 Effective Collaborations 162

8.1.5.6 Supplier Engagement and Audits 163

8.1.6 Critique of Human Rights Due Diligence 163

8.2 Beyond Managing Impacts: Organizing for Human Rights 165

Part IV Corporate Human Rights Accountability

9   **Transnational Governance and Corporate Human Rights Accountability: Preliminary Questions and Foundational Issues** 171

9.1 International and Domestic Approaches 172

9.2 Public and Private Approaches 174

9.3 Hard and Soft Approaches 176

9.4 Soft Accountability Mechanisms: Certification, Labels, and Stakeholder Pressure 178

9.4.1 Consumers: Certification and Labels 178

9.4.2 Investors: ESG Investment 180

9.4.3 Civil Society: Naming and Shaming 182

10 **The UN Guiding Principles on BHR: Foundations, Contemplations, Critique** 185

10.1 The UN Protect, Respect, and Remedy Framework 185

10.1.1 Pillar One: The State Duty to Protect Human Rights 187

10.1.2 Pillar Two: The Corporate Responsibility to Respect Human Rights 188

10.1.3 Pillar Three: Access to Remedy 191

10.2 The UN Guiding Principles on BHR 192

10.2.1 Content of the UNGPs 193

10.2.2 Accountability Regime of the UNGPs 196

10.3 Critical Assessment 197

10.3.1 Key Achievements 198

10.3.2 Main Criticism 199

10.3.2.1 Principled Pragmatism: Accommodating Business to Achieve Consensus? 199

　　　　10.3.2.2 Normative Foundation: Social Expectations or
　　　　　　　　Ethical Principles?   200
　　　　10.3.2.3 Enforcement Mechanisms: Hard Duties or Soft
　　　　　　　　Responsibilities?   201
　　　　10.3.2.4 Distribution of Roles and Responsibilities: Clear
　　　　　　　　Division or Blurred Lines?   202

**11 Further International Soft-Law Standards and
Voluntary Initiatives**   206
11.1 OECD Guidelines for Multinational Enterprises   206
　　　11.1.1 Content   207
　　　11.1.2 Accountability Regime   208
　　　11.1.3 Critique   209
11.2 UN Global Compact   211
　　　11.2.1 Content   211
　　　11.2.2 Accountability Regime   215
　　　11.2.3 Critique   216
11.3 ISO 26000   218
　　　11.3.1 Content   218
　　　11.3.2 Accountability Regime   220
　　　11.3.3 Critique   221
11.4 The Role and Purpose of Multi-stakeholder Initiatives   221

12 Home-State Solutions   226
12.1 The State Duty to Protect Human Rights   227
12.2 Extraterritorial Obligations   229
12.3 Policy Measures   233
　　　12.3.1 National Action Plans on BHR   233
　　　12.3.2 Public Procurement   235
　　　12.3.3 Export Credit and Investment Guarantees   238
12.4 Legislative Measures   240
　　　12.4.1 Accountability by Reporting: Transparency and
　　　　　　 Disclosure Legislation   241
　　　　　　12.4.1.1 UK Modern Slavery Act and Australian Modern
　　　　　　　　　　 Slavery Act   242
　　　　　　12.4.1.2 California Transparency in Supply
　　　　　　　　　　 Chains Act   244
　　　　　　12.4.1.3 EU Non-Financial Reporting Directive   246
　　　12.4.2 Accountability by Process: Disclosure and Mandatory
　　　　　　 Human Rights Due Diligence Legislation   248

12.4.2.1 Dodd-Frank Act, Section 1502 and EU Conflict
Minerals Regulation   248
12.4.2.2 Dutch Child Labor Due Diligence Law   251
12.4.3 Accountability by Impact: Mandatory Human Rights Due
Diligence and Liability Legislation   254
12.4.3.1 French Duty of Vigilance Law   254
12.5 Adjudicative Measures: Foreign Direct Liability   259
12.5.1 Reasons for Human Rights Litigation against Parent
Companies   260
12.5.2 Common Characteristics and Challenges   261
12.5.2.1 Jurisdiction   261
12.5.2.2 Forum Non Conveniens   262
12.5.2.3 Choice of Law   264
12.5.2.4 Attribution   266
12.5.3 US: Alien Tort Claims Act   269
12.5.3.1 Main Features   269
12.5.3.2 *Curtailing ATCA I: Kiobel* v. *Royal Dutch Petroleum Co.*   272
12.5.3.3 *Curtailing ATCA II: Jesner* v. *Arab Bank*   274
12.5.4 UK: Common Law Duty of Care   274
12.5.4.1 *Vedanta Resources Plc* v. *Lungowe*   276
12.5.4.2 *Okpabi* v. *Royal Dutch Shell Plc*   279
12.5.5 Canada: Duty of Care Liability Continued   281
12.5.5.1 *Araya* v. *Nevsun Resources*   282
12.5.6 Various Civil Law Jurisdictions   285
12.5.6.1 The Netherlands   285
12.5.6.2 Germany   288
12.5.6.3 Italy   289
12.5.7 Corporate Criminal Liability   290
12.6 Home-State Solutions: Criticisms and Responses   292
12.6.1 Imperialism   292
12.6.2 Unintended Consequences   293
12.6.3 Compliance over Engagement   294
12.6.4 Frivolous Litigation   295

13 **International Law-Based Solutions**   298
13.1 International Investment Law and International Arbitration 298
13.1.1 Integrating Human Rights into International
Investment Agreements   300
13.1.2 Human Rights Compatible Investor–State Dispute
Settlement Mechanisms   301

        13.1.3 Arbitration for BHR Disputes Beyond Investor–State
                Dispute Settlement Mechanisms   304
    13.2 Toward a Binding Treaty on BHR   305
        13.2.1 Elements of a Binding Treaty on BHR   306
            13.2.1.1 Scope   306
            13.2.1.2 Sanctions and Enforcement   308
        13.2.2 Arguments For and Against a Binding Treaty on BHR   310
        13.2.3 Outlook and Prospect of (Current) Treaty Negotiations 312

Part V Selected Industries and Emerging Discussions

14 **Industry-Specific Issues and Challenges**   317
    14.1 Extractive Sector   317
        14.1.1 Issues and Challenges   318
        14.1.2 Sector-Specific Standards and Initiatives   319
        14.1.3 Solutions and Best Practice   320
    14.2 Finance and Banking Sector   322
        14.2.1 Issues and Challenges   323
        14.2.2 Sector-Specific Standards and Initiatives   324
        14.2.3 Solutions and Best Practice   327
    14.3 Information and Communication Technology Sector   328
        14.3.1 Issues and Challenges   329
        14.3.2 Sector-Specific Standards and Initiatives   332
        14.3.3 Solutions and Best Practice   334
    14.4 Garment and Footwear Sector   335
        14.4.1 Issues and Challenges   336
        14.4.2 Sector-Specific Standards and Initiatives   339
        14.4.3 Solutions and Best Practice   340
    14.5 Food, Beverage, and Agribusiness Sector   341
        14.5.1 Issues and Challenges   342
        14.5.2 Sector-Specific Standards and Initiatives   344
        14.5.3 Solutions and Best Practice   345

15 **Emerging Discussions and Narratives**   348
    15.1 BHR and the UN Sustainable Development Goals   348
    15.2 BHR and Climate Change   352
    15.3 Gender Perspectives on BHR   356
    15.4 BHR in (Post-) Conflict and Transitional Justice Contexts 358

16 Conclusion: Building Back Better   364

Helpful Online Resources and Blogs on BHR   368
References of Court Cases   370
Glossary   372
References   375
Index   413

Boxes

2.1 The Sullivan Principles of 1977	*page* 13
2.2 John Gerard Ruggie	17
2.3 The Bhopal gas disaster	22
3.1 Legal positivism	26
3.2 IKEA and Starbucks: Gender equality in Saudi Arabia	37
3.3 James Griffin's account of "normative agency" and human rights	41
3.4 Thirty articles of the Universal Declaration of Human Rights	57
4.1 Child labor on Côte d'Ivoire's cocoa farms	69
4.2 Doing business in Xinjiang	74
5.1 Workplace surveillance	79
5.2 The 'Marikana massacre'	86
5.3 Trafigura's toxic waste dumping	89
5.4 2022 FIFA World Cup in Qatar	96
5.5 Berta Cáceres	98
6.1 Nike's path from worst to best case in supply chain responsibility	121
7.1 Google in China	132
8.1 Effectiveness criteria for non-state-based non-judicial remedy mechanisms according to Principle 31 of the UNGPs	150
8.2 Remediation at Barrick Gold's Porgera Mine	158
9.1 BlackRock's new human rights approach	181
10.1 Artisanal mining in the DRC: engage or disengage?	190
11.1 Ten principles of the UN Global Compact	212
11.2 Precautionary principle	215
12.1 Practical guidance on NAPs	236
12.2 German Supply Chain Act	253
12.3 French Duty of Vigilance Law litigation cases against Total SA	257
12.4 Swiss Responsible Business Initiative	258
12.5 Brussels I Regulation (EC Regulation No. 44/2001)	264
12.6 Rome II Regulation (EC Regulation No. 864/2007)	265
12.7 *Garcia* v. *Tahoe Resources and Choc* v. *Hudbay Minerals*	283
12.8 *Lliuya* v. *RWE AG*	289
12.9 Lafarge in Syria	291
13.1 *Urbaser* v. *Argentina*	303

13.2 Toward a World Court of Human Rights?   309
14.1 Formalizing artisanal mining in the DRC: Entreprise Générale
      du Cobalt   321
14.2 Financing the Dakota Access Pipeline   325
14.3 Principles for Responsible Investment   327
14.4 Global Network Initiative Principles   333
14.5 Rana Plaza factory collapse   337
15.1 Seventeen Sustainable Development Goals   349

Preface

Over the course of roughly three decades, business and human rights has evolved from a niche discussion to an interdisciplinary scholarly field studied by a well-connected global community of scholars, featuring its own dedicated journal, its own association, and an annual event – the UN Forum on Business and Human Rights – which gathers some 2,500 business and human rights practitioners, advocates, policy-makers and academics at the UN's Palais des Nations in Geneva every year. Business and human rights courses have proliferated at law schools, business schools, and in public policy and political science programs across the world. The number of business and human rights courses is increasing rapidly and so are extracurricular summer and winter schools, seminar and lecture series, and training programs. The Teaching Business and Human Rights Forum, a global platform for multidisciplinary collaboration among BHR teachers, unites over 350 individuals teaching business and human rights at more than 200 institutions in 45 countries on all continents (Ewing 2021). While most established courses are still found at institutions in North America and Western Europe, business and human rights is quickly entering the classrooms also in other parts of the world. This trend will continue over the coming years since business and human rights has also been gaining importance and influence in the international policy sphere.

What is still missing in this fast-evolving field of study is a "classic" comprehensive textbook. The book at hand is trying to fill this gap by providing a systematic interdisciplinary introduction to the field of business and human rights. Conversations that draw on insights from various disciplines are still a major challenge in this field. In this regard, business and human rights is no different than other fields of study. When highly technical analyses of human rights litigation meet pragmatic considerations on human rights management, for example, it can feel like two entirely separate and disconnected conversations. This translates seamlessly into business and human rights classrooms. What is being taught at law schools tends to have little in common with how the subject is taught at management schools. As a result, business and human rights students are trained without a common language.

Those of us who have taught interdisciplinary courses on business and human rights have experienced both the challenge of bringing students from different disciplines together in conversation with each other and the extraordinary rewards of successfully doing so. Classroom conversations are richer, more holistic, and cut deeper if students of various disciplinary backgrounds find a common language in which to talk, work, and collaborate together. The presupposition of such conversations and collaboration is that students understand where their peers from other disciplines are coming from and that they grasp in a basic sense the foundational concepts and ideas that drive the discussion on business and human rights in those disciplines.

This is where this textbook is meant to make its contribution: Its *intention* is to provide a common foundation that allows us to approach business and human rights conversations from a multidisciplinary and interdisciplinary angle. It shows the key questions raised from different disciplinary perspectives on business and human rights and connects them to each other across disciplinary boundaries. Its *aim and ambition* is to provide a teaching and learning resource that can be used wherever business and human rights courses are being taught: in business schools, law schools, or schools of public policy. The book is not meant to provide a resource only for interdisciplinary courses; perhaps even more importantly, it offers a comprehensive perspective on business and human rights particularly for courses that are taught *within* the various disciplines, in order to enable students to generate a more holistic understanding of the field. It is clear that such courses need to drill deeper on certain topics; it is impossible for an interdisciplinary introduction to cover all discussions in the various disciplines in detail. Hence, teachers are invited to complement the content of this book and add to it where they deem appropriate with regard to the emphases of their own courses and disciplinary specializations. The underlying *hope* is to contribute to teaching a generation of business and human rights students who will be able to converse across the boundaries of their respective disciplines. Years from now, when those students lead the way in business and human rights practice, policy, and scholarship, their ability to speak different business and human rights "languages" will translate into better solutions for those who matter the most: the people on the ground whose rights are impacted and violated by business operations.

Writing this book has not only served to address a glaring gap in the business and human rights field but has also provided an opportunity for me personally to reflect upon and "consolidate" almost twenty years of scholarship and teaching in this exciting field. Throughout those two decades I have met countless brilliant and exceptionally dedicated scholars, practitioners, civil servants, and advocates who have put their work at the service of human rights protection and invested much of their time and energy in building this field. Many of the conversations I have had over the years are reflected in this book. Knowledge is always generated collectively and so I collectively thank all those people who have shared their insights and expertise and who continue to impress me with their wisdom, work, and dedication, for being the source of inspiration and knowledge that any such book project depends and thrives on.

Special recognition is due to some of the junior and senior researchers at the Institute for Business Ethics at the University of St. Gallen in Switzerland, which has been my intellectual home base for much of my academic life. Laura Neufeldt-Schoeller provided outstanding research assistance during earlier phases of the writing process. When the submission drew closer and pressure was rising, I was fortunate to be able to rely on the truly exceptional work and help of Catherine McDonald and Stefania Marasco. Their heavy lifting enabled me to bring the project across the finish line. I am also grateful to Wangui Kimotho and Kebene Wodajo for their concise commenting on some of the more legalistic parts of the book.

The professionalism of Cambridge University Press, which I have experienced in the past years as a co-editor of the *Business and Human Rights Journal* and which seamlessly translated into this book project, cannot be stressed enough. I owe particular gratitude to Valerie Appleby for her trust in this project, for her guidance and commitment, and, not least, for her understanding and seemingly stoic patience in the face of pandemic-induced schedule changes and moving deadlines.

1 Introduction: Learning and Unlearning Business and Human Rights

Until recently, human rights and business were perceived as two separate domains. Human rights, traditionally understood as a shield and protection for human beings against the abuse of governmental power and discretion, were seen as having few direct implications for business. As a consequence, private actors like corporations were not on the radar of human rights scholars. At the same time, those concerned with corporations and corporate responsibility, both in practice and in theory, hardly adopted a human rights perspective. Human rights, for them, were a part of the larger legal, regulatory, and policy frame within which corporate practices were taking place, but they were not themselves a part of corporate responsibility engagements. Hence, bringing business and human rights together was intuitive neither for human rights scholars nor for corporate responsibility researchers. Accordingly, and somewhat paradoxically, learning "business and human rights" (BHR) actually means unlearning both business and human rights, at least to some degree. For a certain taken-for-grantedness of "business as usual" often provides fertile ground for corporate human rights violations and the inadequacies of the current international legal system offer the shield for these violations to be carried out with impunity. Opening a space for a conversation, let alone a theorization, of BHR requires us to look beyond the confines of established doctrines. To develop an understanding of what is possible and to break free from the limits of conventional thinking, we need not only to learn but also at times to unlearn particularly paradigmatic knowledge, in order to make space for new, innovative, and perhaps even revolutionary ideas.

1.1 Unlearning Human Rights: Challenging Traditional Human Rights Thinking

Traditional human rights thinking has revolved around the state as the main guarantor and provider of human rights. The conceptual and doctrinal rootedness of this state-centrism was for a long time too strong for a broader and more systematic discussion on BHR to emerge. Such a discussion would have gone against the very definition and foundations of human rights. However, the neoliberal global expansion of markets, which set in during the 1970s, accelerated throughout the 1980s, and reached its peak in the 1990s, put the certainties of the Westphalian state-based international order into question and profoundly reshuffled power relations in the transnational economic and political arena (Chapter 9). The promise of growth and prosperity led governments to deregulate and liberalize their domestic economies, making them fit for participation in global markets. Relinquishing some of their policy autonomy was the price governments had to pay in order for their domestic economies to be competitive in the global market place. At the same time, global markets created unprecedented opportunities for multinational corporations to expand their reach and grow in size and power. Once firmly subject to the tight grip of governmental regulation, global businesses increasingly escaped governmental controls. Thus, economic globalization created so-called governance gaps – which multinational corporations, with their transnational organization and agility, were able to exploit. Governance gaps can be defined as spaces that are beyond the reach and control of public regulatory authority and in which the activities of private actors remain unchecked and transgressions of any kind often remain largely unaccounted for. John Ruggie (Box 2.2), who became the United Nations Special Representative on the Issue of Human Rights and Transnational Corporations and Other Business Enterprises (SRSG) in 2005 (Chapter 2), as well as the BHR literature more generally (see e.g. Simons & Macklin 2014), later denoted such governance gaps as the very root cause of the "business and human rights predicament" (Ruggie 2008: 3).

Hence, BHR as a discussion that addresses these emerging new global constellations requires us to think anew about both the role of business in our global society and the notion of human rights as ethical and legal principles with relevance not only for governments but also for non-governmental actors, and particularly business. The challenge BHR students and scholars face is thus not only learning new approaches but also unlearning some of the "certainties" that have traditionally obstructed our view to include business in the human rights discourse. In this vein, this textbook provides guidance both in learning and unlearning human rights.

1.2   Unlearning Business: Challenging Corporate Social Responsibility

BHR as a new discussion at the intersection of human rights and corporate responsibility not only challenges traditional human rights thinking but also confronts more conventional notions of corporate responsibility. Much of the theory and practice of corporate responsibility over the past five decades has taken place under the banner of corporate social responsibility (CSR). The idea of CSR as a more or less distinct corporate practice and as a field of scholarly inquiry started to emerge in the 1950s and thus is much older and more established than BHR. It has traditionally served as an "umbrella term" (Jonker 2005: 20; Scherer & Palazzo 2007: 1096) for a variety of issues and questions discussed in connection with corporate responsibility. Accordingly, it is of little surprise that BHR is often perceived as a "subset of CSR" or just another "CSR issue" – or even as one and the same thing. However, equating the two discussions or reducing BHR to "merely" a dimension of CSR is both conceptually and historically flawed.

1. *Conceptually*, human rights have not played a prominent role in the long-standing discussion of CSR. While the CSR discussion has certainly dealt with issues and problems that can essentially be characterized as human rights challenges at their core – examples include sweatshop labor, clinical trials, or the invasion of privacy in recruiting and hiring processes – it has rarely addressed them as actual human rights issues. This is no coincidence. Traditionally, CSR has been viewed essentially as private responsibility, that is, as a sort of voluntary, residual responsibility within a given framework of state regulation (Wettstein 2020). Such an understanding is based on "a clear line between private economic activities on the one hand and public political activities on the other" (Scherer & Palazzo 2007: 1106). According to this model, governments alone are in charge of the public domain of which human rights are seen to be a part. While this does not give corporations a free pass to do as they please within the private space provided by the state, they are not generally seen to have any responsibility for broader public concerns. From this point of view, human rights are not commonly perceived to be a part of the private responsibilities of businesses in CSR theorizations.

2. *Historically*, the emergence of BHR in the 1990s coincided with the internationalization of the CSR discussion and an expansion of its focus on related issues such as sweatshops and child labor. Nevertheless, despite this overlap, BHR did not emerge as a logical extension of CSR. Rather, as will be shown in Chapter 2, BHR was introduced as a new and separate discussion, whose precursors are found outside of CSR and which evolved in parallel rather than as an integral part of CSR. More concretely, while the CSR discourse is rooted in management and business scholarship in a broad sense, BHR by and large originated in legal scholarship. Accordingly, the BHR discussion has traditionally involved different actors – both as a social movement and as an academic discussion – and followed a different logic than CSR. In particular, BHR tends to focus much more on accountability mechanisms and particularly on the role of binding regulation, while CSR has become almost synonymous with voluntary, business-led initiatives for the promotion of responsible business practices:

> Corporate Social Responsibility (CSR) and Business and Human Rights (BHR) are like two close cousins—they are intertwined concepts focused on companies engaging in responsible and socially beneficial activities—but both concepts have key differences and hence distinct identities based on their origins. They are in essence two different but overlapping discourses: CSR growing out of scholarship from the business academy and BHR emerging from the work of legal academics and human rights advocates focused on formalistic notions of rights and remedies (Ramasastry 2015: 237).

It is against the background of these profound differences between a BHR and a CSR perspective that BHR has been viewed not as a subset or an issue of CSR, but rather as its critique. CSR has come under increasing criticism for its soft and voluntary approach, its lack of force, and a resulting lack of impact in regard to the transformation of business practices. BHR, with its focus on accountability and binding measures, has been characterized much more as a confrontation of and challenge to this CSR paradigm and thus as an alternative approach to corporate responsibility.

1.3   Learning BHR: The Human Rights Perspective on Corporate Responsibility

In the assumption of CSR as essentially a private responsibility, we find the basic chasm between conventional CSR approaches and BHR also from a normative perspective. While a CSR perspective on corporate human rights responsibility implies their shift into the realm of private responsibility, a BHR perspective would advocate for a shift in the opposite direction – that is, for an extension of corporate responsibility into the public realm and thus for a reinterpretation of corporate responsibility as inherently political in nature. As public or political responsibilities, corporate human rights responsibilities will differ in a number of ways from the conventional understanding of CSR as private responsibility (Wettstein et al. 2019).

First, human rights entail a different normativity than we commonly associate with private responsibility. As mentioned above, CSR has traditionally been perceived as voluntary or optional, as praiseworthy corporate goodwill beyond the call of duty. This view was defining for CSR in the 1970s and 1980s when CSR was often equated with charitable donations by companies to good causes. While CSR has evolved dramatically since then, such perceptions still linger and remain widespread today (McCorquodale 2009: 391; Kolk 2016; Bansal & Song 2017), particularly among companies themselves (Obara & Peattie 2018). In contrast to this perspective, human rights responsibilities are not a voluntary, discretionary, or subjective matter. The very point of rights, as Chapter 3.1 will show, is that they can be claimed; respecting human rights is not a charitable act, but owed to the rights-holders. Addressing human rights claims as a private responsibility risks emptying them of their essential character as rights and turning them into a function of mere corporate goodwill.

Second, public responsibility entails a strong call for public accountability. It is not a coincidence that BHR scholars tend to favor a much stronger and more interventionist role of the law and of governments than scholars in the CSR field (Wettstein 2016). They tend to call for a more rigid enforcement of responsibility through legal and policy means rather than emphasizing the alleged benefits of more flexible, private initiatives in coping with managerial "realities" on the ground. Again, this is a direct reflection of the different roots of the two fields, with BHR being shaped predominantly by legal disciplines, which focus not only on prescribing but also on enforcing the respective responsibilities (Wettstein 2016). Against this background, Ramasastry (2015) has characterized the shift of perspective from CSR to BHR as one from responsibility to accountability.

Third, human rights are commonly seen as unconditional, universal, and equal rights (Chapter 3.1.2). All human beings have them equally and at all times, merely by virtue of being human. Accordingly, at least the most fundamental responsibility to respect these rights is also unconditional. Most importantly, this responsibility holds irrespective of what domestic laws say. Human rights, and the respective responsibilities, cannot simply be legislated away by law and policy-makers. For companies this means that they are responsible to observe human rights, even if doing so conflicts with the laws of the country in which they operate. The reference to national laws has long served as an excuse for companies to justify low and often untenable social, labor, and environmental standards in their operations. This is no longer an option with reference to human rights. The most authoritative policy framework in the BHR space, the UN Guiding Principles on Business and Human Rights (UNGPs) (Chapter 10), leave no doubt about the hierarchy between national laws and human rights norms: "The responsibility to respect human rights ... exists over and above compliance with national laws and regulations" (Ruggie 2011a: 13).

Fourth, and directly related to the previous point, human rights provide a strong and universal reference point for responsible corporate conduct (Giuliani, Macchi, & Fiaschi 2014; Ramasastry 2015). The focus of CSR has traditionally been less defined, allowing for wide variation in form and content of respective initiatives and instruments. Therefore, CSR tends to be more susceptible to moral relativism (Chapter 3.1.3.2) that can potentially undermine, rather than advance, responsible business in foreign contexts. Thus, at least conceptually, the reference to an internationally agreed normative framework is one of the perceived strengths of BHR, because it leaves less room for corporations to use discretion in the interpretation of their own responsibilities (Giuliani, Santangelo, & Wettstein 2016; Nieri & Giuliani, 2018).

1.4   Rationale and Structure of the Book

Learning BHR requires us not only to break free from the doctrines that have traditionally obscured the intersection between corporate responsibility and human rights but also to transcend the boundaries of disciplinary silos. By its very nature, BHR spans different disciplines. Therefore, having a basic understanding of how different disciplines approach the field and of the key questions and issues raised by them, is essential to gain a truly holistic understanding of BHR. However, the reality often looks different. Conversations in the different disciplines, despite all belonging to and exploring different aspects of BHR, often share little common ground. They look at different issues, from different perspectives, and address them with different language. The rationale of this textbook is to overcome such disciplinary silos by providing a common foundation to build on. This will not necessarily change the conversations in the different disciplines. But it opens them up to other disciplinary perspectives and thereby enables BHR students and scholars to better access, understand, and contribute to the conversations in other disciplines. In short, the goal is to provide the common foundation that is necessary to have a truly interdisciplinary conversation about BHR.

The book integrates legal, ethical, and managerial insights on BHR. *Legal perspectives* deal with the role and applications of laws and jurisprudence in and for BHR, both in the domestic and international arenas. *Ethical perspectives*, at their core, are concerned with the application of normative theory to the BHR domain. They are commonly grounded in moral and political philosophy, but they naturally depend also on social, cultural, and political contexts. *Managerial perspectives* entail a more pragmatic implementation view, which takes into consideration the managerial realities and contexts in which such implementation occurs and the obstacles and constraints that managerial conditions often impose. While these are the three dominant perspectives that inform the book, insights from other disciplines such as political science, international relations, and social sciences more generally, are relevant and included in the book as well. Importantly, the book is not structured along disciplinary perspectives. Hence, there is not a legal, an ethical, and a managerial part of the book. Rather, all three perspectives tend to be present throughout the entire book. The goal is integration rather than separation of the different disciplinary perspectives. However, it is unavoidable that certain perspectives are dominant in some chapters, particularly when some of the disciplinary foundations are laid. That said, all these chapters also contain reflection, critique, and complementary insights from the other disciplines.

Each chapter in this book contains a variety of "textbook features" designed to support the process of studying and learning BHR:

- *Cross-references*: Whenever the book touches on content that is elaborated in-depth elsewhere, readers will find cross-references to navigate easily and conveniently to this elaboration.
- *Contextual boxes*: There are text boxes throughout the book that provide further contextual information on selected content. Such information is not critical to understanding the core BHR content, but is rather aimed at broadening readers' understanding of BHR. Some contextual boxes contain discussion questions to further reflect on the content.
- *Short cases*: The book features multiple short cases, outlining and discussing specific BHR challenges. The short cases have been selected to illustrate specific content discussed in the chapters. The cases contain a number of discussion questions at the end to guide readers' reflection and deliberation and animate classroom discussions on them.
- *Study and reflection questions*: At the end of each chapter there are two sets of review questions. Study questions are designed to quiz readers on the contents of the chapter. Reflection questions aim at motivating readers to reflect beyond the immediate contents of the chapter by pointing to some broader implications and challenges deriving from them.
- *Internet sources*: At the end of the book, readers will find a collection of blogs and helpful internet resources and websites in the BHR domain. These websites provide useful information, tools, and guidance on a variety of BHR-related contents. The collection contains resources featuring general BHR-related information, as well as more specific information relating to BHR practice and BHR accountability.

The book is divided in five main parts and 16 chapters. Part I provides some basic foundational knowledge to prepare readers for a deeper exploration of BHR in the subsequent parts. It consists of chapters 2 and 3. Chapter 2 provides a brief overview of the history of BHR as a movement and an academic field. The goal of this historical overview is to provide readers with a sense of the emergence, evolution, and basic shape of the field, in order to enable them to better see how the different parts and chapters of the book fit within a broader overall outlook on the field. Chapter 3 gives a basic introduction to human rights, both from legal and non-legal perspectives. Understanding different and sometimes conflicting approaches to human rights is of critical importance not least because different takes on BHR are often rooted in deviating underlying accounts of human rights.

Part II sets the scene by taking a preliminary look at the intersection between business conduct and human rights. Chapter 4 looks at how business can be implicated in human rights violations in a conceptual sense. It introduces an important distinction between direct and indirect corporate human rights violations and distinguishes between various forms of corporate complicity. Subsequently,

Chapter 5 provides a more issue-centered overview of various corporate involvements in human rights abuse. It aims to give a sense of the breadth and complexity of the BHR challenge.

Part III engages with the foundations of corporate human rights responsibility. At the center of this part of the book is the question of how such responsibility can be justified. Chapter 6 explores this question from the three constitutive perspectives of the book, analyzing ethical, legal, and pragmatic foundations to ground corporate human rights obligations. Subsequently, Chapter 7 assesses the nature of such obligations, how extensive they are, and what they entail. This chapter is approached predominantly from an ethical perspective. Chapter 8 concludes the third part of the book with a close look at how companies tend to implement their human rights responsibilities and what challenges typically arise.

Part IV is concerned with questions related to holding companies accountable for their human rights responsibilities. Chapter 9 introduces corporate human rights accountability conceptually in the broader context of global governance. In doing so, it provides a frame for the different accountability mechanisms that are discussed in the subsequent chapters. Chapter 10 is devoted to the UNGPs and their foundation, the UN Protect, Respect and Remedy Framework (UN Framework). The UNGPs are the authoritative global BHR standard, which is why they warrant a special assessment in this book. Chapter 11 complements this perspective on the UNGPs with an evaluation of a number of other international soft-law standards and initiatives in the BHR domain. The subsequent two chapters look at hard law and policy solutions. Chapter 12 does so at the domestic level. It focuses specifically on policies and laws with extraterritorial effects as well as on so-called foreign direct liability. Foreign direct liability denotes the attempt to hold corporations liable in the domestic courts of their home states for human rights violations committed abroad. Chapter 13 looks at hard law solutions at the international level. In particular, it assesses international investment law and arbitration as well as the potential of a new international treaty on BHR as possible avenues of corporate human rights accountability.

Part V concludes the book by reflecting on BHR from more context-specific perspectives. Chapter 14 puts the focus on a number of industries and displays their respective industry-specific BHR issues, challenges, and solutions. Chapter 15 explores four emerging discussions in the BHR field and thus provides indications of some future key trends in BHR. Finally, Chapter 16 concludes the book with a brief reflection on the future of BHR in and for a post-pandemic world after COVID-19.

PART I
Foundations

2 | BHR: Emergence and History of a Movement

The term BHR commonly refers to the international discourse and movement as it has evolved since the mid-1990s. However, history is always interpreted through the definitions, concepts, perspectives, and labels we use to access and address it. Thus, depending on the prism through which we look at the history of BHR, we might perceive its starting point earlier or later and emphasize different events, actors, and developments as historically significant. This chapter outlines the evolution of BHR since the 1990s in three stages: beginnings, growth phase, and consolidation. Before doing so, it touches on a number of significant precursors that are often overlooked in more cursory historical accounts of the BHR movement. As a "tour d'horizon" of BHR, this chapter naturally touches on certain issues only in passing. However, many of those topics and issues will be discussed in more depth throughout this book and are cross-referenced accordingly.

2.1 Precursors (1945–1995)

BHR did not emerge out of the blue. There are a number of discussions and events that proved significant in the lead-up to the emergence of BHR as a movement and field of study. Three of them will be briefly pointed out in this section: the Nuremberg trials after World War II, the role played by businesses during the apartheid era in South Africa, and the struggles of the Ogoni population against international oil companies in Nigeria.

Nuremberg trials: At the end of World War II, the Allied powers formed special tribunals to bring those involved in the Nazi atrocities to justice. These are known as the Nuremberg trials. Three of those trials were against German industrialists from the three companies I.G. Farben, Flick, and Krupp (Ramasastry 2002: 105). They were charged with using and abusing war prisoners and concentration camp inmates for forced and slave labor as well as other war crimes and crimes against humanity. The Nuremberg trials serve as an important precursor for the modern BHR discussion for two reasons: (1) They asserted that individuals bear direct obligations under international law for certain egregious violations alongside governments. Forced and slave labor are among such violations for which individuals can be prosecuted, as are piracy, aircraft hijacking, genocide, war crimes, and crimes against humanity (Ramasastry 2002: 100). (2) While the trials and verdicts concerned individuals, rather than corporations, the decisions contain extensive explications that attribute many of the offenses and violations directly to the corporations as the actual perpetrators (Ramasastry 2002: 108). Thus, while the trials did not explicitly attribute responsibility to the companies, they foreshadowed the extension of responsibility from natural to legal persons in their decisions in important ways. Much later, in 1999, a US district court made this extension explicit. In a decision on forced labor lawsuits against Ford and its subsidiary Ford Werke A.G. on the basis of the Alien Tort Claims Act (ATCA) (Chapter 12.5.3), it held that slave trading was among a handful of crimes for which customary international law attributed responsibility not only to states but also to private actors such as Ford (Ramasastry 2002: 125). Even though this case, and many others that followed suit, were ultimately dismissed by the court, it clarified "that legal persons have the same obligations as natural persons when it comes to certain egregious violations of international law norms, at least for purposes of ATCA jurisdiction" (Ramasastry 2002: 130).

Apartheid South Africa: During the apartheid era in South Africa, businesses were forced by law to discriminate against their black employees – for example, in regard to the kind of work they were allowed to do, the remuneration and benefits attached to it, or the facilities and spaces they were allowed to use. By doing so, Western companies inevitably became complicit in the systematic abuse of human rights by the South African government. Western governments were reluctant to put pressure on South Africa, given its strategic importance for resource access and sea trade – and, not least, as a Cold War ally against communism in the East. As a consequence, activists demanding a tougher stance by their governments eventually shifted their focus onto Western companies doing business in South Africa, calling on them to use their economic clout to oppose the apartheid regime (Kline 2010: 50). Of particular importance and prominence was Reverend Leon Sullivan, a Baptist minister and the first Black member of the board of the then largest company in the world, General Motors. Leon Sullivan lobbied for US companies to take a forceful stand against the apartheid regime. For this purpose, he drafted the so-called Sullivan Principles, a set of norms that he urged companies to follow when doing business in South Africa (Box 2.1). By calling on businesses to engage in civil disobedience and even to work actively toward the abolishment of all apartheid laws and the demise of the regime, the Sullivan Principles foreshadowed two core insights that characterize today's BHR discussion: (1) They mirror the view purported today by the UNGPs (Chapter 10) that business ought to uphold human rights even, or perhaps particularly, in cases in which they conflict with domestic laws. Human rights take precedence over local laws and customs for corporate compliance. (2) They foreshadowed one of the recurring, perhaps most controversial,

BOX 2.1 (Context) The Sullivan Principles of 1977

In 1977, Reverend Leon Sullivan issued the so-called Sullivan Principles to urge all American companies doing business in South Africa to engage in passive resistance and refuse to abide by discriminatory apartheid laws. There were originally six principles, but in 1984 he added a seventh that called on companies to engage in active resistance in order to increase the pressure on the apartheid regime.

(1) Nonsegregation of the races in all eating, comfort, and work facilities.
(2) Equal and fair employment practices for all employees.
(3) Equal pay for all employees doing equal or comparable work for the same period of time.
(4) Initiation of and development of training programs that will prepare, in substantial numbers, blacks and other nonwhites for supervisory, administrative, clerical, and technical jobs.
(5) Increasing the number of blacks and other nonwhites in management and supervisory positions.
(6) Improving the quality of life for blacks and other nonwhites outside the work environment in such areas as housing, transportation, school, recreation, and health facilities.
(7) Working to eliminate laws and customs that impede social, economic, and political justice.

(Added in 1984)

questions relating to BHR today, which is whether and to what extent it is appropriate for corporations to assume political roles in opposition to government for the sake of actively promoting and protecting human rights (Chapter 7.3). By 1980, almost half of all US firms invested in South Africa had signed the Sullivan Principles (Kline 2010: 55). However, dissatisfied with the progress made, Sullivan eventually called on the signatory companies to pull out of South Africa altogether. His call ended up being followed by more than 100 companies.

Oil extraction in Nigeria: The escalation of conflicts between the local Ogoni population and the central government in Nigeria in the mid-1990s over oil extraction in the Niger Delta is commonly viewed as the beginning of the BHR discussion. The struggles of the local people against environmental destruction caused by oil extraction can be traced back at least to the 1970s. Extraction of oil was by far the most important revenue source for Nigeria, making up about 80 percent of government revenue and 90 percent of foreign exchange during the 1980s and 1990s

(Kline 2010: 68–69). But those revenues hardly found their way to the local communities and were syphoned off by the corrupt authoritarian regime around the Nigerian dictator Sani Abacha. Thus, local populations had to live with very serious environmental destruction but had little to show for it. With soil, water, and air severely impacted by oil spills and gas flares, many lost their livelihoods, which were based on fishing and agriculture. While oil companies profited, the local communities suffered poverty and declining well-being. As a result, they engaged in protests, but kidnappings and sabotage were among the means of resistance as well. Such protests were often brutally silenced by government forces, leaving scores of people dead and injured, villages destroyed, and families displaced over the years. At the center of these protests was the Western oil company Shell, which was the largest oil producer in Nigeria at the time. Shell was not a mere bystander to the conflicts, but reportedly played active roles in calling police forces in to protect their employees and facilities and to avoid interruptions to their operations. In 1995, in the process of suppressing protest and dissent, the celebrated playwright, activist, and head of the local nonviolent resistance movement Movement for the Survival of the Ogoni People (MOSOP), Ken Saro-Wiwa, and eight of his followers were rounded up by government forces, arrested, and ultimately sentenced to death by a specially convened tribunal. Shell faced international criticism for not denouncing the trial and for failing to put pressure on the Abacha regime to release the nine activists. Shell's official response was that it was not for private companies to get involved in Nigerian politics, though it did emerge later that some attempts were made behind closed doors on the part of Shell to request the release of Saro-Wiwa (Kline 2010: 71). It was to no avail; Ken Saro-Wiwa and his followers were executed on November 10, 1995. The international outcry over the executions and over the role of Shell would eventually lead to the emergence of the BHR discussion as we know it today. However, the case makes it clear that BHR was not a new issue, but had lingered in local struggles long before the Shell case brought it to international attention in 1995. The struggles of local populations against destructive business practices reach far back, but such struggles often occurred off the radar of public and policy discussion in the West. A proper understanding of BHR cannot ignore the diverse and local histories of abuse and resistance that led up to the international discussion starting in the mid-1990s.

Early attempts to regulate the investment activities of multinational companies reach back to the 1970s, too. In response to the increasing concerns of developing nations over the rising power of multinational companies, the UN created a new Center on Transnational Corporations in 1977, whose main task was to come up with a comprehensive code of conduct for multinational corporations (Ramasastry 2013: 165). Among other things, the draft code asked multinational companies to "respect human rights and fundamental freedoms in the countries in which they operate," to foster equal opportunity and treatment, and to abstain from any kind of discrimination. However, in the face of opposition from Western governments and the multinational corporations themselves, the draft code project was abandoned and the center dissolved some two decades later, in 1992.

Around the same time, in 1976, the Organisation for Economic Co-operation and Development (OECD) launched the well-known OECD Guidelines for Multinational Enterprises (Chapter 11.1). Designed as a voluntary alternative addressing states rather than corporations directly, it proved more viable than the UN's binding approach. The first iteration of the OECD Guidelines contained one lone paragraph on the human rights responsibilities of corporations, which over the years developed into a major section aligned with the UNGPs after 2011. Today, the OECD Guidelines have become an important soft-law instrument within the broader governance of multinational corporations (Chapter 9.3) and particularly its complaint and mediation procedure, based on so-called National Contact Points (NCPs), is gaining significance in the struggle for accountability within the broader BHR movement (Chapter 11.1.2).

2.2　The Beginnings (1995–2005)

Ken Saro-Wiwa's death and the ensuing international protests marked the starting point of a more coordinated international discussion on BHR. Prominent human rights NGOs, such as Human Rights Watch and Amnesty International, started to engage more systematically with BHR issues and published high-profile reports on the complicity of Western companies with rights-violating regimes (see e.g. Human Rights Watch 1999a; 1999b). They built capacity and expertise and some launched teams and divisions with a specific focus on BHR, such as the Amnesty International Business Group in the UK, which had a lasting impact in shaping the early debate. The launch of the Business & Human Rights Resource Centre (BHRRC) in 2002 marked another critical milestone in the institutionalization of the movement. BHRRC would later turn into the most important information hub and thematic news source for the BHR field and one of the trendsetters in shaping the debate for years to come.

At the same time judicial developments, particularly in the United States, paved the way to bring lawsuits against corporations to domestic courts for their involvement in human rights violations abroad. Some high-profile "pilot" cases involving prominent companies such as Chiquita, Unocal, and particularly Shell – for its links to the murder of Ken Saro-Wiwa and his followers – brought further attention to BHR during the late 1990s and early 2000s.

Both NGO campaigns and the increasing risks of human rights litigation have played important roles in compelling companies to start adopting explicit human rights policies, signing up to and participating in voluntary multi-stakeholder initiatives (MSIs) (Chapter 11.4), or addressing human rights in their sustainability or CSR reporting (Schrempf-Stirling & Wettstein 2017). Marked by its experiences in

Nigeria and the resulting global backlash against its brand, Shell became one of the first companies to formally adopt a human rights policy around that time. Other companies would follow suit.

Two prominent global initiatives were of particular significance for the BHR movement during these early years.

UN Global Compact (UNGC): In 2000 the then Secretary-General of the United Nations, Kofi Annan, launched the UNGC. With more than 13,000 signatory companies in 2021, the UNGC is often seen as the most successful international soft-law initiative for sustainable business. Its aspiration at the turn of the millennium was to give a human face to global capitalism by committing corporations to initially nine and later ten broad normative principles, ranging from respecting human rights, to ensuring decent labor conditions, protecting the environment, and combating corruption (Box 11.1). By devoting principles 1 and 2 squarely to human rights, the UNGC was the first global code of major significance that put corporate human rights responsibility at its very core. Doing so, it had an important signaling effect for the broader BHR movement: Not only was the UN ready and willing to engage businesses on their social and environmental impacts, but it also recognized corporations' relevance in relation to human rights. This makes the UNGC a key initiative in the historic development of the BHR discussion, despite its impact and legacy being frequently contested. Chapter 11.2 will discuss the UNGC, its content and impact, and critique it in more detail and depth.

Norms on the Responsibility of Transnational Corporations and Other Business Enterprises with Regard to Human Rights (UN Draft Norms): Two years before the UNGC, in 1998, the UN Sub-Commission on Human Rights initiated the drafting of a set of human rights norms for business, which, in stark contrast to the UNGC, were meant to be the basis of what was to become a legally binding global framework on corporate human rights responsibility (Weissbrodt & Kruger 2003; Weissbrodt 2005). Given the fate of the earlier draft code, which was abandoned by the UN in the 1990s, the UN Draft Norms were always likely to be met with opposition. In contrast to the non-binding UNGC, an instrument mandating corporate human rights responsibilities was not likely to garner broad support in the business community. Predictably, most companies fiercely opposed the UN Draft Norms, branding them a "legal error" and a "privatization of human rights." They were joined in this response by the governments of the Global North, where most multinational companies were based. Going up against the innovative, highly successful, and newly founded UNGC as an alternative, the UN Draft Norms were doomed to fail almost from the start. Therefore, this renewed attempt for a binding solution was shelved in 2003 and later abandoned completely. The UN Commission of Human Rights rebuked the Sub-Commission harshly for pursuing this project in the first place, pointing out that it had never asked for such a binding instrument to be drafted and, accordingly, that it did not have legal standing.

The UN Draft Norms were the first comprehensive BHR initiative at a global level. While the UNGC put human rights center stage, it was always meant to be broader in its scope and focus and non-binding in its nature and approach. The UN Draft Norms, on the other hand, were designed to address corporate human rights responsibility in an exclusive manner and by means of international law. The contest between these two initiatives within the very same organization can be seen as almost paradigmatic for how the BHR discussion would evolve over the coming fifteen years. That is, it modeled the ensuing oscillation between binding and non-binding initiatives and drew the lines between supporting and opposing stakeholder groups.

In the heyday of neoliberal globalization, opposition against a binding human rights framework for corporations proved too powerful to overcome. However, the intensity of debate that led up to the failure of the UN Draft Norms demonstrated the relevance of the issue at hand while opening deep rifts between the different parties dealing with it. Thus it became clear that the discussion on BHR could not be laid to rest along with the UN Draft Norms; there was a clear need to move the debate forward by other means and the UN was committed to continue to facilitate this discourse. As a consequence, on April 20, 2005, the UN Commission on Human Rights (2005) adopted a resolution asking the Secretary-General to appoint a SRSG. Harvard professor John Ruggie was subsequently appointed as the SRSG and his work shaped the BHR movement decisively during its formative years.

BOX 2.2 (Context) John Gerard Ruggie

John Gerard Ruggie (1944–2021) was the Berthold Beitz Professor in Human Rights and International Affairs at Harvard University's John F. Kennedy School of Government and Affiliated Professor in International Legal Studies at Harvard Law. Ruggie was trained as a political scientist and held a PhD from the University of California, Berkeley. In 2005, Ruggie was appointed SRSG. He held the mandate for six years until 2011. During his tenure as the SRSG, he authored the influential UN Guiding Principles on Business and Human Rights (UNGPs). When John Ruggie was appointed SRSG, he was no newcomer to the UN. From 1997 until 2001, he served as the UN Assistant Secretary-General for Strategic Planning. In this role, he assisted the then Secretary-General Kofi Annan in establishing and overseeing the UN Global Compact (Chapter 11.2) and in proposing and gaining General Assembly approval for the Millennium Development Goals (Chapter 15.1). John Ruggie's voice remained influential in the BHR discussion until his passing in 2021. Among other things, he chaired the board of the New York-based NGO Shift, and advised governments, companies, and civil society organizations on the implementation of the UNGPs.

2.3   The Formative Years (2005–2011)

The formative years of the BHR discussion were shaped by the mandate of the SRSG. John Ruggie's appointment was initially meant to last three years, but it was extended for a further three-year period in 2008. Hence, the mandate was characterized by two major phases, which each concluded with a major report that proved to be of seminal significance for the BHR movement.

Phase 1 (2005–2008): The SRSG was initially tasked with taking stock and bringing more clarity to the BHR debate. In particular, he was asked to identify and clarify standards of corporate responsibility and accountability with regard to human rights; to clarify also the role of the state in regulating and adjudicating the role of business with regard to human rights; to clarify the meaning and implications of key concepts such as "complicity" or "sphere of influence"; to provide guidance with regard to human rights impact assessments of corporate activity; and to compile and assess best practices both of corporations and states in regard to BHR. The SRSG concluded the first phase of his mandate with a much-anticipated report, which has come to be known as the UN Protect, Respect and Remedy Framework (UN Framework) (Ruggie 2008). The UN Framework clarifies the conceptual relation between the human rights responsibilities of corporations and governments. More specifically, it outlines the state duty to protect human rights against violations of third parties, including business, which is grounded in international law (Pillar I); it establishes a corporate responsibility to respect human rights, which is non-binding and based on social expectations (Pillar II); and it calls for improved access to remedy for victims of human rights abuse, which is interpreted as a part both of the state duty to protect and of the corporate responsibility to respect human rights (Pillar III). At the conclusion of the three-year mandate, the UN Human Rights Council (HRC) (2008) issued another resolution extending its duration for three more years, asking the SRSG to operationalize the UN Framework (UN Human Rights Council 2008).

Phase 2 (2008–2011): In addition to providing guidance on the practical realization and operationalization of the three pillars of the UN Framework, the resolution tasked the SRSG with the elaboration of a gender perspective on BHR (Chapter 15.3) and with paying special attention to vulnerable groups (Chapter 5.5), including children. The SRSG was also asked to deepen his collaboration with other UN and non-UN bodies operating in the BHR space as well as to continue his efforts to integrate a full range of stakeholders into the process. In 2011 the SRSG presented the anticipated operationalization of the UN Framework, the UNGPs (Chapter 10). In an unprecedented move, the UNGPs were endorsed unanimously by the HRC in June 2011, which marked the conclusion of the six-year mandate of the SRSG. It was the first time ever that a normative document, which was not negotiated by governments, was endorsed without opposition by the HRC. Following this endorsement, other existing standards and codes for responsible business such as the OECD Guidelines (Chapter 11.1) or ISO 26000 (Chapter 11.3) started to integrate new human rights provisions or align their existing ones with the UNGPs. As such, they contributed to the success and broad influence that the UNGPs would have over subsequent years.

The publication of the UNGPs in June 2011 meant that for the first time there was an agreed global standard that spelled out conceptually and practically the responsibilities of both states and corporations in regard to the identification, mitigation, and remediation of corporate human rights impacts. At this critical moment in the history of BHR, one of the main concerns was to maintain this momentum to start implementing the UNGPs broadly. For this purpose, the HRC established a working group on the issue of human rights and transnational corporations and other business enterprises (UNWG), which has spearheaded and supported the dissemination and implementation process to this day.

2.4   Maturing of the BHR Movement (2011–ongoing)

While all eyes were on the mandate of the SRSG between 2005 and 2011, the third wave has brought further developments that will likely end up being of momentous implication for the future of the BHR movement. Many of these developments have emerged as a direct response to the UNGPs, both as a matter of their realization and implementation (e.g. home-state regulatory approaches – see Chapter 12.4) and as a matter of compensating for their limitations (e.g. treaty discussions – see Chapter 13.2). The following paragraphs will briefly touch on some of the key developments at the global and domestic levels.

Global level: The UNWG has been a key player in defining and shaping the agenda of the maturing BHR movement. The UNWG's mandate was initially set to run for three years starting in June 2011, but has been periodically extended since. Its mandate has been to promote the dissemination and implementation of the UNGPs; to consult, assess, inform, and make recommendations on good practices, policy, and legislation; and to promote and lead the dialogue, effective collaboration and coordination on BHR issues both within and outside of the UN at domestic, regional, and global levels (UN Human Rights Council 2011). Importantly, the UNWG convenes the annual UN Forum on BHR in Geneva, which brings together around 2,500 BHR professionals from government, practice, civil society, and academia every year and has become the most important annual gathering and a key fixture in the BHR space.

The push for implementation of the UNGPs has further led to the emergence of a plethora of BHR-specific organizations in the civil society space. While many of them fulfil more classic think-tank functions (e.g. the Institute for Human Rights and Business in London), others have offered detailed guidance and practical consulting services aimed at the implementation of the UNGPs in practice (e.g. the New York-based NGO Shift). Such organizations have been at the forefront of setting the agenda for the ongoing BHR discussion and have had a growing influence on the trajectory of the field since the publication of the UNGPs.

In line with the oscillating history of BHR between binding and non-binding approaches and initiatives, it did not take long after the publication of the non-binding UNGPs for the pendulum to swing back once again to a push for a binding regulatory framework for corporate human rights responsibility. Ten years after the definitive failure of the UN Draft Norms and with the implementation phase of the UNGPs in full swing, a new attempt to start negotiations on a binding treaty on BHR at the UN level was launched. After a resolution to this end passed the HRC, an open-ended intergovernmental working group was put in place and treaty discussions started in 2015 (Chapter 13.2.3).

Domestic level: By 2021, some two dozen governments had released so-called National Action Plans (NAPs) on BHR and many more are in the process of doing so or have considered first steps in that direction (Chapter 12.3.1). NAPs express the commitment of governments to fostering and advancing business respect for human rights by means outlined in the plans. While most NAPs so far have been criticized for being vague and non-committal, they do express the increasing significance of BHR in the policy agenda of governments. BHR has seen significant developments also in the legislative arena, both domestic and regional. A number of countries have adopted landmark BHR legislation in recent years. Most significantly, France passed a groundbreaking piece of legislation, the so-called French Duty of Vigilance Law, which renders conducting human rights due diligence (HRDD) mandatory for the largest companies in the country (Chapter 12.4.3.1). Furthermore, the Netherlands have adopted a similar law, but limited to the issue of child labor (Chapter 12.4.2.2), while the UK has set a precedent for other countries with its UK Modern Slavery Act, which is a mandatory reporting scheme aimed at rooting out trafficking and modern slavery (Chapter 12.4.1.1). The United States, as a part of the Dodd-Frank Act, has established mandatory due diligence in connection with the import of conflict minerals (Chapter 12.4.2.1); a similar provision was recently adopted also by the European Union (Chapter 12.4.2.1). However, this development has not come without setbacks. Most momentous among them, perhaps, are two verdicts of the US Supreme Court on *Kiobel* v. *Shell* and *Jesner* v. *Arab Bank*, respectively (Chapter 12.5.3.2 and Chapter 12.5.3.3). The two decisions limited the scope and application of the ATCA significantly, establishing a presumption against its extraterritorial application and making it impossible to sue foreign companies under the ATCA. Thus, while the United States has taken a step backward on corporate accountability based on the

ATCA, various other countries are in the process of expanding home-state measures to hold multinational companies to account for their human rights impacts. It is to be expected that this discussion on home-state solutions will evolve significantly in the near future.

2.5   BHR in the Academic Discourse: Emergence of a New Field

The emergence and evolution of the academic discourse on BHR largely parallels that of the broader BHR movement. In fact, the porous, if not fluid, boundaries between the academic discourse and the broader movement can be seen as one of the distinct characteristics of the BHR field. This may be owed to the subject matter: Most scholars doing research at the intersection of corporate responsibility and human rights are driven by the desire to improve corporate human rights responsibility and accountability. Thus, they view their research as a contribution to advancing the discussion and to changing the status quo. The strong normativity inherent to human rights certainly also impacts scholarship in the human rights space: It seems to be impossible to conduct research in the face of human rights abuse without at least an implicit claim that such abuse is to be avoided and redressed.

This normativity of human rights was identified earlier as one of the reasons why the BHR discourse ought to be distinguished from the broader discussion on CSR (Chapter 1.2). Thus, while the history of BHR may overlap with the history of CSR, it is not congruent with it. Academic writing on BHR has different roots and started later than scholarship on CSR. While early works in CSR can be traced back to the 1950s and 1960s, scholarship with a focus on the human rights responsibilities of corporations emerged in the mid- to late 1980s. It was the Bhopal tragedy of 1984 (Box 2.3) and the above-discussed context of businesses operating in apartheid South Africa that triggered some of the first BHR-specific academic contributions both in law and non-law. For example, Upendra Baxi's early writing on the Bhopal disaster provided some important legal groundwork for the exploration of corporate impunity for human rights violations (Baxi 1986a; 1986b; Baxi & Dhanda 1986). Tom Donaldson's seminal book *Ethics of International Business* (Donaldson 1989), on the other hand, was one of the first non-law academic works on corporate responsibility to refer directly to human rights in a foundational sense. The book was influenced, if not inspired, by the events unfolding in South Africa at that time. A number of other contributions at the intersection of corporate responsibility and human rights took place around the same time, but scholarly research on BHR more generally remained scant and isolated throughout the 1970s and 1980s and only started to gain traction toward the end of the 1990s.

BOX 2.3 (Short case) The Bhopal gas disaster

On December 3, 1984, a gas leak in a factory of Union Carbide India Ltd. (UCIL), which was owned by the American-based company Union Carbide Corporation (UCC) at the time, released 47 tons of highly toxic methyl isocyanate gas into the night air of the densely populated Bhopal area in the Indian state Madhya Pradesh. The incident, in which several thousand people lost their lives and hundreds of thousands others were left with lasting health damage, counts as the largest industrial disaster in history. It was followed by a decades-long struggle for justice by victims and their families, which continues to this day (Baxi 2016).
A lawsuit against the UCC in a US court was dismissed in 1986 on the grounds of *forum non conveniens* (Chapter 12.5.2.1). After legal proceedings continued in India, a settlement was approved by the Indian Supreme Court in 1989 of more than $470 million, payable by UCC to the Indian government (Deva 2016: 23). Given the long-term health damage to hundreds of thousands of people and the lasting large-scale contamination of soil and water in the region, this settlement was widely decried as scandalous. In comparison, the damage claims by the Indian Union before the courts amounted to more than $3 billion (Baxi 2016: 29). Furthermore, the burden of proof for victims to access the settlement money has been so high that many of them have been left with little or no compensation (Baxi 2016: 30). The second part of the settlement deal, which would have granted UCC and UCI immunity from all further criminal and civil proceedings, was later reversed. However, it was not until 2010 – twenty-six years after the catastrophe – that an Indian court found UCIL and seven of its executives guilty of criminal negligence (Deva 2016: 23). To this day, the disaster area remains contaminated and UCC has evaded accounatability altogether. A lawsuit in US courts addressing the damage resulting from environmental contamination was rejected in 2016 after several appeals (BHRRC n.d. (j)). Dow Chemical, which acquired UCC in 2001, has staunchly denied any responsibility for Bhopal (Deva 2016: 24). Thus, more than three decades later, victims have still not been adequately compensated and the responsible have still not been held to account. Hence the Bhopal gas disaster has become an historical reference point for the modern BHR movement, a frequently raised reminder of the real and often insurmountable obstacles that multinational corporate structures pose for corporate accountability, even in the most blatant and devastating cases of corporate abuse.

Discussion Questions

(1) What do you think are the reasons why it is so difficult for victims to finally receive justice in the Bhopal case? How do the structures of the multinational

corporation and of the international legal system counteract the victims' efforts to claim their rights?

(2) Dow Chemical acquired UCC in 2001. Do you think by doing so the company also acquired a responsibility to provide remedy for the victims of the Bhopal disaster, despite being unconnected to the event? What should the company do, more than thirty-five years after the catastrophe?

Thus it was not until the late 1990s and early 2000s that a more systematic academic discourse on the topic started to emerge. Historically, BHR emanated from legal scholarship, particularly as it pertains to international human rights law, rather than from managerial CSR scholarship. This is not a coincidence; the struggle of victims of corporate human rights abuse has been about legal redress and access to justice all along. Thus, driven by the growing movement advocating corporate accountability in this regard, academic lawyers began to look into and conceptualize the relation between companies and international human rights law. Accordingly, the early discussion on BHR focused heavily on the fundamental question as to whether or not international law indeed gives rise to corporate human rights obligations or what it would take to make such an argument (see e.g. Frey 1997; Muchlinski 2001; Ratner 2001). The publication of the UN Framework and later the UNGPs started both to broaden the discussion in terms of interdisciplinarity and to narrow it in terms of its focus on the implications of these instruments. While legal scholars have remained the dominant force in the academic discussion to this day, the field became more interdisciplinary around that time, attracting scholarship from various related areas such as CSR, business ethics, or international relations.

The academic discussion on BHR has not only grown significantly both by number of contributions and scholars involved but also made significant strides toward institutionalization as an academic field since the publication of the UNGPs. The foundation of dedicated BHR centers by universities (e.g. NYU Stern School of Business's Center for Business and Human Rights) and the creation of designated faculty positions are concrete manifestations of this development. A number of journals launched special issues on the topic and increasingly there was a need and demand for a more dedicated publication platform for the evolving BHR field. This void was filled by the *Business and Human Rights Journal* (BHRJ), which was launched in 2015 and aims at offering a publication platform for the entire interdisciplinary BHR community, rather than addressing only specific, disciplinary subsets thereof. The foundation of the Global Business and Human Rights Scholars Association in 2017 marks the latest step in the institutionalization of BHR as an academic field.

STUDY QUESTIONS

1. Why were the Nuremberg trials important for BHR? How can they be understood as a part of BHR? How are they different to BHR?
2. What are the UN Draft Norms? Why were they important for the history of BHR despite being abandoned in 2003?
3. What is the UNGC and why do you think it is so successful? Why does it prove attractive for companies?
4. Name the pillars of the UN Protect, Respect and Remedy Framework. Which one of the three is most important?
5. What is the UNWG and what is its role in and for the BHR movement?
6. What happened in the Bhopal gas disaster and why is this case of particular importance for the BHR movement and discussion?

REFLECTION QUESTIONS

1. Shell faced international criticism for not intervening to save Ken Saro-Wiwa and eight other activists. Do you think this criticism was justified? If you had been a Shell manager, what would you have advised the company to do? Is it a company's role to get involved in a host country's internal affairs?
2. What are the merits of voluntary regulations and what are the merits of binding regulations? In your opinion, is there a need for a binding international framework on BHR? Do you foresee the BHR field leaning toward one or the other in the future, or maintaining the need for both?
3. Will the UNGPs remain important for the BHR field in the long run? What will be their legacy if we look back fifty years from now?
4. Given the role of international organizations such as the UN and the OECD in the field of BHR, how do you foresee their roles in the future? Do you believe that governments will play a larger role in regulation, that international organizations must lead the agenda, or that the private sector should take initiative? Do you think the UN, in particular, will keep its leading role in shaping the BHR agenda?

3 | A Brief Introduction to Human Rights

In order to understand the key questions and issues surrounding BHR, a basic understanding of human rights more generally is necessary. Since BHR is an interdisciplinary field, it is important to gain an understanding both of the legal and non-legal dimensions of human rights. This chapter will first provide a brief introduction to the philosophy of human rights and some of the key discussions that derive therefrom. It will then take a look at the main human rights bodies that institutionalize human rights in the international and regional context. Finally, the chapter will provide a brief introduction to international human rights law.

3.1 Philosophy of Human Rights

For legal positivists, human rights exist because they are stipulated in international law and supported by an international and domestic institutional infrastructure. For them, there is no foundation outside of the law that would justify human rights (Box 3.1). However, the thought that our human rights depend solely on their institutionalization seems troubling. Laws and institutions help us express and claim such rights; they protect them and help us realize them in practice. But is it plausible to say that we would not have human rights at all, if not for such laws and institutions? Many of us would intuitively argue that we have human rights no matter what, simply by virtue of being human (Griffin 2008: 2). In fact, there is a long philosophical tradition arguing along those lines.

This chapter will first provide a brief and necessarily non-comprehensive overview of this long history of thought on human rights. It will then define and analyze the moral character of human rights further. One defining element will be of particular interest: the universality of human rights. There have been contentious discussions not only about whether human rights can and ought to claim universal validity but also about the proper understanding of universalism to begin with. This is not an abstract discussion relevant only for philosophers, but similarly concerns BHR scholars and practitioners. After all, should managers and businesses operating in foreign contexts adhere blindly to local laws and customs? Should they follow the proverb "When in Rome, do as the Romans do," or can they refuse to follow

BOX 3.1 (Context) Legal positivism

Legal positivism expresses the view that law and ethics are two separate domains with very little or no overlap. For legal positivists, the validity of the law does not depend on moral criteria, such as whether it is morally just or good, but solely on its constitution through an authoritative process and its factual acceptance by society. Thus, the validity of the law depends entirely on observable facts, rather than on its moral normativity. Accordingly, legal positivists do not believe the law does or should aspire to serve a higher aim or purpose such as justice, but simply see it as an expression of the will of society or a legitimate authority. For them, moral considerations do not play and ought not to play any role in interpreting the law. Anti-positivists, on the other hand, hold that legal validity depends on moral considerations. There are different interpretations of legal positivism, from more "radical" views that reject any overlap between legal validity and morality to "weaker" forms, which accept the relevance of moral considerations in certain cases (Himma 2002; Marmor 2002).

practices they deem problematic with reference to universal ethical principles and values? In order to build a foundation for such decisions, the chapter will provide insight on the controversy between universalism on the one side and relativism on the other. This will set the ground for a discussion of the possible justifications and foundations of human rights in the concluding section of this chapter.

3.1.1 A Brief History of Thought on Human Rights

The idea that people have "natural" rights that protect their basic human condition is almost as old as philosophy itself. Early antecedents of such "natural law" thinking can be found in Greek and Roman antiquity. Aristotle already promoted the idea that governments should prevent encroachments upon the conditions that help human beings flourish and realize their potential. Perhaps the most direct precursor to the theorization of universal rights can be found in the philosophy of the Stoics (Cranston 1983: 3). Particularly in its global, cosmopolitan outlook on the dignity and equality of all human beings, its view on global citizenship, and its allegiance to a moral community of all human beings we find early, visionary antecedents of modern human rights thinking. However, the specific notion of a "right" did not enter the Western philosophical vocabulary until the Middle Ages (MacIntyre 1981: 67)

Natural law is the idea that there is a moral law above and beyond the positive laws put in place by rulers or legislators. It is based on the assumption that human beings possess something like moral rights in an a priori manner, irrespective of whether or not such rights have been recognized by written laws or formal institutions. Initially, such arguments had theological roots. Such conceptions of natural law and natural rights were perceived to be bestowed on human beings by God. They first appeared in the late Middle Ages (Griffin 2008: 1), most notably in the philosophy and theology of Thomas Aquinas, whose own thinking was influenced heavily by Aristotle. Later on, during the Enlightenment period of the seventeenth and eighteenth centuries, natural law thinking became progressively secularized and detached from its religious roots; reason started to take the place of divine revelation. Nevertheless, the term and idea of a "natural" law and of "natural" rights remained common and dominant until the mid-twentieth century, when the actual notion of "human rights" started to gain broad currency (Griffin 2008: 7).

Political philosophers of the Enlightenment period argued that both the lawmaking and executive powers of rulers were bound by natural rights. In his famous work *Leviathan*, the influential English philosopher Thomas Hobbes argued that in a state of nature, without government, human beings would find themselves in a permanent state of war and insecurity. Therefore, they would enter a social contract, in which they all freely abandon some of their liberties in return for the protection and security provided by the state. The idea of an implicit social contract between free and equal human beings, that is, an implicit, hypothetical agreement, in which they grant each other certain rights and accept certain obligations, was influential among Enlightenment philosophers to build a rational foundation for their claims and it still provides the grounds for various contemporary human rights theories today.

Another key natural rights and social contract theorist of the Enlightenment period was John Locke. Locke's philosophy is often credited with providing the key foundation and impetus for the emergence of human rights thinking and practice. Going beyond Hobbes' idea of people surrendering their liberties for the protection of security, Locke argued that our natural rights to life, liberty, and property put absolute constraints on legitimate government. In other words, in Locke's view, government can never be absolute. It finds its limits in the fundamental rights of the people subjected to its authority. Locke's thinking and work was very influential in the changing Western world of that time. It directly influenced the English Revolution of 1688 and is reflected in the subsequent Bill of Rights enacted by the English Parliament in 1689. The Bill of Rights proclaimed life, liberty, and property as innate rights of all, along with a right to fair and public trial by jury and a prohibition on excessive fines and cruel and unusual punishment (Cranston 1983: 1). The profound transformations in the Western world during the subsequent century, which were manifested in the form of the Declaration of Independence of 1776 in the United States or the Declaration of the Rights of Man and the Citizen (*La déclaration des droits de l'homme et du citoyen*) of 1789 in France, were carried by Locke's theory, his idea of innate human rights, and his rejection of absolutism

(Cranston 1983: 1). The Declaration of Independence and the subsequent American Constitution of 1787 decisively inspired the modern human rights movement in Europe (Fremuth 2015: 78). The American Bill of Rights, which was added to the Constitution in 1789, guarantees freedom of religion, of opinion, of the press, and of association, as well as the protection of the person and of property among other things (Fremuth 2015: 78).

Like the influential Locke, most moral and political philosophers of the Enlightenment period grappled with (natural) rights in their philosophies. Many of them saw natural rights as the parameters that delimit legitimate government. However, some visionaries among them already saw that the implications of such natural rights thinking were truly global. The seventeenth-century Dutch philosopher Hugo Grotius, who is often referred to as the "father of international law" today, argued that in addition to protecting the natural rights of people, states should enter agreements among each other to provide a stable and secure international order. For Grotius, a just society was one that strives for the equal fulfilment of basic entitlements, which he derived from the inherent dignity and sociability of human nature (Nussbaum 2006: 36–37). The French political philosopher Montesquieu embraced the idea of an international law and of people as citizens of the universe (Haas 2014: 29), while the German moral philosopher Immanuel Kant also formulated such a vision in his essay on eternal peace.

Kant's philosophy provides an important foundation for the modern idea of human rights as universal, inalienable entitlements of all human beings. Kant viewed human beings as rational, autonomous creatures, who are inherently capable of giving purpose and meaning to their lives from within. That is, the purpose of a human life is not imposed on people from outside, but set by each human being individually. As such, Kant proclaimed human beings as ends in themselves, as parts of what he called the "kingdom of ends." Consistent with and as a consequence of this view, one version of Kant's famous Categorical Imperative states that human beings are always to be respected as ends in themselves and should never be treated merely as means for some other purpose. This non-instrumentalization formula can be seen as the very essence of contemporary understandings of human rights.

However, there were also staunch critics of the idea of moral and natural rights among Enlightenment philosophers. Jeremy Bentham, the English philosopher and founder of utilitarianism, was one of the fiercest and perhaps best-known critics in this regard. Only a few years after the French Revolution, Bentham derided the idea of natural rights and thus the French Declaration of Rights as pure "rhetorical nonsense" – worse even, as "nonsense upon stilts." Real rights, Bentham proclaimed, can be derived only from real laws, while from imaginary – that is, natural – laws, only come imaginary rights. For Bentham, proclaiming natural rights was no more than a grand gesture, aimed at deflecting attention from achieving real reform by putting in place actual laws. In his view, only real, positive laws could give rise to real rights. And such laws had to correspond to his utilitarian ideal of benefitting – in the sense of providing utility to – a majority of people, rather than protect some imaginary natural rights of a minority. This proposition was rejected by one of the most influential liberal thinkers of the time, John Stuart Mill. While sharing with Bentham the utilitarian worldview, Mill thought of moral rights and liberty for all not as opposites but essential presuppositions to achieving utilitarian ideals.

A criticism similar to Bentham's was voiced also by the contemporary Scottish philosopher Alasdair McIntyre, who compared human rights to witches and unicorns. While witches and unicorns may well exist, no one has ever succeeded in proving their existence; similarly, he claimed, Enlightenment philosophers have not successfully proven that human rights, which were originally based on theological claims, can be justified also on secular grounds. Unlike Bentham, conservative skeptics such as Edmund Burke or David Hume did not criticize natural rights talk on the grounds that it was empty rhetoric; instead, they were afraid of the revolutionary and agitative potential of such bold proclamations (Cranston 1983: 4). Burke, in particular, was afraid that the example of the French Revolution could lead to a similar uprising against the British aristocracy. The criticism voiced by a growing community of skeptics discredited natural rights thinking throughout much of the nineteenth century and all the way through the rise and fall of fascism in the lead-up to and throughout World War II, when the real and devastating consequences of the denial of such rights became painfully manifest.

Emerging from the rubble of World War II, the newly founded United Nations organization (UN), which succeeded the former League of Nations, set out to build and ensure peace by forming a functioning international political community. A crucial element of the project was the construction of an international human rights infrastructure, consisting of a body of international human rights law and the respective institutions to promote and assert the laws. A critical first step in this process was made in 1948 with the adoption of the Universal Declaration of Human Rights (UDHR), which laid the foundations for continuous expansion of human rights law over the coming decades (Chapter 3.3). Thus, the foundation of the UN was the decisive step in the establishment of human rights as a truly international concern and for the subsequent expansion of an international human rights system (Chapter 3.2) (Fremuth 2015: 82). While this body of international law rests on the same idea of inherent human dignity, the function of human rights was transformed under the aegis of the UN: the new purpose that human rights were to serve was the "regulation of the global order" (Griffin 2012: 14). As such, a political rather than a moral understanding of human rights took hold (Chapter 3.1.4.2). Thus, the truly momentous developments in the evolution of human rights after the philosophically formative Enlightenment period occurred not in the philosophical but in the political realm during the second half of the twentieth century. Chapter 3.2 will take a closer look at the evolving international human rights infrastructure.

3.1.2   Elements of Human Rights

Human rights, as this brief history of human rights thinking has shown, are "primarily ethical demands" rather than legal manifestations (Sen 2004: 321). Of course, as ethical claims human rights may, and indeed have, inspired legislation – but, as Sen (2004: 319) notes, "this is a further fact, rather than a constitutive characteristic of human rights." Human rights, from this point of view, are "normative considerations whose existence is independent of law and social practice" (Tasioulas 2012: 37).

What makes a right a right, in this moral sense, is that it is owed to us; and what is owed to us can be claimed. Rather than being dependent on the charity of others, rights-holders can demand their due.

> Rights are not mere gifts or favors, motivated by love or pity, for which gratitude is the sole fitting response. A right is something that can be demanded or insisted upon without embarrassment or shame (Feinberg 1973: 58–59).

Thus, an essential characteristic of a right is that it empowers the right-holder. This is essentially what distinguishes a right from other moral considerations such as "mere" priorities, wishes, or expectations: rights obligate. Where there is a right, there must be obligations. As such, rights – and human rights, in particular – take precedence over other (ethical) considerations of lesser weight, such as considerations of general welfare.

For rights to qualify as human rights, they must be of particularly fundamental nature (Feinberg, 1973: 85). Human rights address the very conditions of a life worth being lived by human beings. They protect the basic possibility of living a human life in dignity. Martha C. Nussbaum defines a human right as "an especially urgent and morally justified claim that a person has, simply in virtue of being a human adult, and independently of membership in a particular nation, class, sex, or ethnic, religious or sexual group" (Nussbaum 2002: 135). Human rights, thus understood, can be specified further, as universal, equal, indivisible, and inalienable rights.

Universal: Human rights are often thought to be universal. For some, universality is the very essence and core of human rights. However, this has always been a contested and controversial claim and there is an ongoing discussion as to how universal human rights truly are. Different positions on this derive from different understandings of the foundations and justification of human rights. An overview of such understandings will be provided in Chapter 3.1.4. However, there is a broader discussion on universalism and relativism in ethics, which is directly relevant also for human rights. This discussion will be addressed in Chapter 3.1.3.

Equal: Human rights are unconditional and therefore equal rights. They apply equally and to the same extent to all human beings.

> The possession of a human right cannot be conditional on some conduct or achievement of the right-holder, a relationship to which they belong, or their membership of a particular community or group. Instead, human rights are rights possessed by all human beings (however properly characterized) in all or certain generally specified socio-historical conditions simply in virtue of being. (Tasioulas 2012: 37)

Amid all the pluralism and diversity that characterize humanity, we are all of equal moral worth. This assumption of equality in difference is the very presupposition and foundation of pluralism and diversity among human beings.

Indivisible: All human rights play their part in protecting our dignity as human beings. They are interdependent insofar as the violation of one human right tends to affect the enjoyment of many other human rights. The indivisibility and interdependence of human rights is of particular importance in regard to the perceived separation of civil and political rights on the one hand and economic, social and cultural rights on the other (Chapter 3.3.1). There is no hierarchy between them and they are of equal importance for a life in dignity. The enjoyment of one human right always presupposes the realization of other human rights. For example, a person living in poverty and without adequate shelter lacks the condition to make full use of their civil liberties. A life in freedom is an illusion under such circumstances.

Inalienable: Human rights can be denied and infringed, but they can never be taken away from us. We cannot lose them, forfeit them, or trade them in. The reasoning behind this is as simple as it is plausible: Because we cannot lose or give away our humanity as such, we must, logically, retain our human rights. This does not mean that human rights cannot be restricted where justified and proportional. For example, certain rights, such as the right to free movement, may be restricted temporarily in order to respond to a health crisis, as experienced, for example, in the context of the global COVID-19 pandemic. Alternatively, dangerous criminals may be put behind bars to protect the public; but they do not lose their human rights as such and they ought still to be treated humanely and with dignity under conditions of incarceration. Only very few human rights, such as the right not to be tortured, are generally considered absolute. As such, they must not be restricted under any circumstances (Chapter 3.3.1).

3.1.3   Universalism v. Relativism

There has been a long-standing discussion on the universality of ethical norms, which relates directly to the question of whether or not human rights are universal. This discussion is commonly framed as the clash between two positions, with universalists on one side and so-called relativists on the other. However, this controversy often confuses universalism with a strict form of absolutism and perceives relativism as uncompromising subjectivism. Understood in less radical terms, the differences between universalism and relativism may not always be insurmountable. This section will first juxtapose absolutism with various interpretations of relativism and subsequently introduce a "well-understood" account of universalism as a mediating middle ground between the two polar opposites.

3.1.3.1   Absolutism

Universalism does not imply absolutism. Absolutism is the belief that there is an objective moral truth – that is, an objective right and wrong that can and must be acknowledged and adhered to by everyone. From such a point of view, there is one "correct" morality, which ought to claim superiority over all other moral systems and traditions, which, as a consequence, are to be considered and rejected as incorrect and inferior. Thus, absolutism is a form of dogmatism, which does not actually believe in or strive for universal justification of moral norms. Rather it ideologically proclaims one particular moral point of view as per se valid and superior to all others.

An absolutist view of human rights would thus hold that there is one correct view of human rights, which ought to be valid for everyone – without exception or room for interpretation. Whether such a view can be justified on universal grounds is of little importance or relevance to absolutists, as long as it is consistent with their own moral point of view.

3.1.3.2   Relativism

Relativists do not believe that there are any universal, let alone, absolute moral norms. Generally, we can distinguish between two different kinds of relativism, one descriptive and one normative. Descriptive relativism is a less far-reaching type of relativism often referred to as "cultural relativism." Normative relativism is a more uncompromising type of relativism, generally referred to as "ethical relativism."

- *Descriptive or cultural relativism* is based on the observation that we are living in a diverse and pluralistic world, characterized by countless different and at times competing and conflicting cultural and moral traditions. It is a proven fact that people with different cultural backgrounds may hold divergent moral views on a variety of issues (DeGeorge 2010: 26). In such a world, it may not be intuitively evident that there are, or ought to be, certain moral claims and norms of universal validity. As a consequence, human rights may not appeal to all such moral traditions equally, or at all. Such empirical relativism does not entail a normative qualification; it does not say that human rights ought or ought not to claim universal validity, but it simply observes that de facto human rights do not hold equal currency in different cultural settings and, therefore, that we should be cautious in claiming universality when reality, in fact, tells a different story.

- *Normative or ethical relativism* goes further than descriptive relativism. It not only points to existing differences between moral systems and traditions but also denies the existence and desirability of any universally justifiable norms and principles at the same time. For normative relativists, ethics itself is inherently relative. There is no standpoint outside of the cultural setting in which we are embedded and perhaps not even outside of our own personal backgrounds from which to assess and judge our norms and actions. Therefore, ethics is seen as inherently subjective and it provides no grounds for generalization or universalization of any moral claims. Thus, if one person or society holds one moral view and another person or society holds another, potentially conflicting view, there is no way to assess who is right and who is wrong. From this point of view, there are no human rights that can be justified universally. If one society deems the violation of what another society holds to be human rights as unproblematic, it must simply be accepted as a different moral view of equal validity.

3.1.3.3 Universalism

Neither absolutism nor a strong ethical relativism seem plausible and ultimately tenable positions. Particularly when invoked in defense of human rights, an absolutist position amounts to ethical ethnocentrism that runs counter to the very idea of human rights. Similarly, a strong ethical relativism seems a rather implausible position to hold. A variety of arguments speak against such ethical relativism. One of the key arguments of relativists is that as a matter of respect and tolerance toward other cultures, we ought not to judge local moral views and traditions by reference to universal principles. However, it is precisely by invoking principles like respect for other cultures, pluralism, and tolerance that such relativist positions ultimately revert back to relying on the very universalism they set out to reject. Furthermore, as the British philosopher Mary Midgley (1981: 69–75) argued so eloquently, we cannot respect other cultures without judging them, since respect itself is based on a favorable judgment. Midgley goes even further: if we follow the advice of relativists not to judge and form opinions about the morality of others, we lose the means to judge ourselves. For critically assessing our own behavior, both positive or negative, requires a mirror, which we often find in the way that others conduct themselves. This is why this sort of moral isolationism, as Midgley (1981: 71) explains, ultimately leads to "a general ban on moral reasoning" as such.

Emerging from the rejection of both absolutism and ethical relativism is a well-understood universalism that not only respects difference and pluralism, but is the very foundation and presupposition of it. For acknowledging and respecting our cultural variety and individual uniqueness presupposes that we first accept our fundamental moral equality. We can be different and unique precisely because we are all equal in our moral worth as human beings. This is the core of the universality of human rights. It is not a set list of norms that ought to be proclaimed universal, but the underlying principle of equal moral worth on which the idea and concept of human rights as such is based. Again, we can distinguish between two kinds of universalism, one descriptive and one normative.

- *Descriptive universalism* argues that amid all the differences we can find commonalities and overlaps between different cultural and moral traditions. Thus, descriptive universalism believes that there is what John Rawls called an "overlapping consensus" on certain ethical principles or values that are shared by all cultures, religions and moral traditions. The Golden Rule – treat others the way you would want to be treated yourself – may be such a norm. Its specific form and interpretation may vary, but its core has been shown to be a part of most if not all moral codes across the globe (Donaldson 1996: 53).
- *Normative universalism*, on the other hand, believes that there are certain ethical principles that are universally justifiable, irrespective of whether we can indeed find them in all moral traditions. It is the general belief in the possibility of universal justification that characterizes this position. Normative universalists may not claim to know what those universal principles look like, but merely argue for the general possibility of such principles. It is not an objective universal morality itself, but rather the idea of the possibility of an intersubjective, universal discourse on morality that builds the core of such an understanding of morality. As the eminent American business ethicist Richard DeGeorge (2010: 31) puts it:

> There is an alternative to absolutism, however, which does not fall into the category of relativism. The position claims that morality is not eternal. Rather, it is an attempt by human beings to adopt principles to govern human society and the lives of those within society, principles that will help people live together and abide by rules that all of them, in their reasonable and objective moments, would accept. Unlike the absolutist, someone holding this position need not claim that some final, ultimate, and eternal moral principle exists somewhere – for instance, in the mind of God. He need only claim that the idea of such a principle forms an ideal toward which ethics strives.

Hence, it is the idea of the universal justifiability of our moral claims as such that provides the universal normative ideal. What drives normative universalists is the idea that our conduct and behavior per se ought to be critically assessed and continuously justified against the reasoned objections of all those who may be affected by it. In accordance with this insight, Amartya Sen (2004: 320) sums up the essence of the universality of human rights as follows: "The universality of human rights relates to the idea of survivability in unobstructed discussion – open to participation by persons across national boundaries."

Indeed, if we give up on the idea of universality of human rights and thus of the demand to justify in a basic sense our conduct toward other people and cultures, we adopt indifference instead of concern as our basic outlook on the world and ourselves and thus open the doors for barbarism and human atrocities (Ulrich 2008: 29)

3.1.3.4   Are Human Rights Western?

Human rights are often seen as the quintessential manifestation of ethical universalism. However, while some praise them as the core of a global ethical framework, others deride them as an instrument of Western imperialism and neocolonialism. In order to come to a well-founded position on this divide, we must carefully delineate what in fact we are talking about. Most importantly, perhaps, we need to distinguish between the real manifestation and institutionalization of human rights and the underlying ethical idea or concept.

Often, the criticism of human rights as imperialist addresses the concrete legal and institutional human rights infrastructure that is currently in place. The UDHR is indeed based on and compiled from pre-existing human rights provisions in the constitutions of predominantly Western liberal countries (Chapter 3.3.3). Furthermore, it is often pointed out by critics that the working group that drafted the instrument was far from representative in regard to non-Western cultural and geographical regions, although it was similarly far from representing a unified Western view on the subject. However, others argue that what counts is not who drafted the instrument but the fact that it achieved near universal adoption. Furthermore, it was first and foremost non-Western nations whose advocacy, based on the UDHR, advanced the further institutionalization and codification of human rights (Joas 2015: 75). Latin American governments as well as newly independent African nations, in particular, were the most dedicated supporters and advocates of human rights, while Western governments tended to be skeptical. Particularly in former colonies, human rights were seen as a tool to promote the liberation and self-determination of nations against the imperial West. These national liberation movements and the struggle for development and self-determination often bred their own kind of ruthless authoritarianism, which had little regard for the human rights of the people they were supposed to liberate (Osiatynski 2016: 13).

However, some critics see the very idea of human rights as based on Western values and as incompatible with non-Western cultures and moral traditions. In this vein, they often point to the perceived incompatibility of human rights with what has been called "Asian values" (Sen 1997), which are often said to give community, order, discipline, and loyalty to family and to the state priority over individual freedoms. Based on this, critics often point to authoritarian governments as a symptom and manifestation of such values and of the disregard for individual rights and freedoms. What they tend to ignore, however, are the human rights practices and movements that emerge even in such political contexts and despite the great risk and danger faced by those who are driving them. Such practices and movements at the grassroots can be viewed as a significant reflection of the emerging universality of human rights, even in the presence of authoritarian regimes that try to undermine them. Furthermore, as Amartya Sen points out, the very term "Asian values" is misleading. Asia, with its vast population, is highly diverse and across this diversity the theorization of tolerance and freedom is just as important a part of many traditions as order and discipline (Sen 1997). Perhaps, then, the very claim that human rights, in their essence, are based on distinctly Western values that are now imposed on other parts of the world, is itself a manifestation of the imperialist mindset, a kind of "Western triumphalism" (Joas 2015: 79) that this critique of human rights is supposed to reject. As Amartya Sen (1997: 30) goes on:

> I have disputed the usefulness of a grand contrast between Asian and European values. There is a lot we can learn from studies of values in Asia and Europe, but they do not support or sustain the thesis of a grand dichotomy. Contemporary ideas of political and personal liberty and rights have taken their present form relatively recently, and it is hard to see them as "traditional" commitments of Western cultures. There are important antecedents of these commitments in the form of the advocacy of tolerance and individual freedoms, but those antecedents can be found plentifully in Asian as well as Western cultures.

The German sociologist Hans Joas has made a similar argument, but rather than pointing to the positive antecedents of human rights such as freedom and tolerance in non-Western cultures, he emphasizes that human rights-opposing values were as common in Western cultures as they were in non-Western ones. After all, the West not only has a centuries-long history of slavery but also one of justifying it, based on European values. Even liberal thinkers such as Locke or Hobbes, who laid the foundation for modern human rights thinking, engaged in the justification of slavery at the very same time (Joas 2015: 44–45). It was precisely during the advent of Western liberalism in the late eighteenth century that Western slave trade reached its peak (Joas 2015: 45). Similarly, colonial violence – torture, rape, abductions – remained an inherent part of Western nations' colonial rule long after they abolished such practices for their own citizens and even while they advocated for human rights in Europe (Joas 2015: 59–65). To this day, the human rights project is far from completed in the West, with clear tendencies to backslide in many areas.

BOX 3.2 (Short case) IKEA and Starbucks: Gender equality in Saudi Arabia

In 2012, the Swedish furniture giant IKEA came under fire when news broke that it had edited the Saudi Arabia edition of its catalogue to remove all women from the photographs. The company did so even though depicting women in marketing materials is not prohibited by law in Saudi Arabia. The company publishes 200 million copies of its catalogue in sixty-two slightly different versions globally. The bulk of the catalogue is the same, but certain adjustments are commonly made to account for cultural differences in styles and tastes. The version produced for Saudi Arabia was by and large identical with the global standard version, with the exception that women were removed from the pictures. The company later apologized and acknowledged that removing women from the catalogue was in conflict with its values (Molin 2012).

A somewhat similar incident in 2016 involved the American coffee chain Starbucks. Their stores in Saudi Arabia feature separate entrances and service areas for men and women. After a separation wall collapsed in one of their stores, Starbucks responded by banning women from entering the store, thus only serving men for the time of rebuilding the wall. As *The Independent* newspaper reported at the time: "Gender segregation is widespread in Saudi Arabia, with women requiring male permission to work, travel, study, marry or even access healthcare. They are also unable to drive or open a bank account, and must be accompanied by a male chaperone on shopping trips" (Matharu 2016). Nevertheless, Starbuck's ban on women was widely criticized and reported on in the West. The company issued the following response: "Starbucks in Saudi Arabia adheres to the local customs by providing separate entrances for families as well as single people. All our stores provide equal amenities, service, menu, and seating to men, women and families. We are working as quickly as possible as we refurbish our Jarir store, so that we may again welcome all customers in accordance with local customs" (Rose 2016).

Discussion Questions

(1) Was the criticism of IKEA and Starbucks justified? Were they not just trying to be responsive to local norms and customs? Can we blame them for adjusting their standards to the Saudi Arabian context?

(2) What might have been the driver(s) behind IKEA's and Starbuck's actions in those incidents? How could the companies have acted differently? What would have been a better solution in each case that did not have adverse impacts on human rights?

3.1.4   Foundation and Justification of Human Rights

Closely associated with the more general discussion on universalism and relativism, there are two basic camps concerning the foundation of human rights. Foundationalists believe that human rights can be justified independently by philosophical means and that such justifications can achieve universal appeal. Non-foundationalists doubt that such universal justifications are available, nor do they believe that seeking them would be desirable. For them, human rights emerge through political and social practices and fulfil social and political functions that are historically, geographically, and culturally contingent.

3.1.4.1   Foundationalist Accounts of Human Rights

Foundationalists commonly start with the assumption that human rights are rooted in and derive from some essential and defining features of human beings or a human life. For if human rights are rights that human beings have simply by virtue of being human, the key question that needs to be answered from a philosophical point of view is: what defines us and our lives as uniquely human?

The concept of human dignity has traditionally played a key role for grounding human rights, from both a legal and a philosophical perspective. In fact, dignity is where philosophical and legal accounts of human rights converge. Most international legal human rights instruments rely on our human dignity as a source and foundation of human rights protection and refer to the concept also in relation to the interpretation of specific rights; so do most regional human rights instruments and also human rights tribunals have a long history of referring to dignity in their jurisprudence (Shelton 2014: 7–13). Most famously, perhaps, the UDHR (Chapter 3.3.3) refers to dignity twice in its preamble and again in the very first one of its thirty articles. The preambles of the two international covenants (Chapter 3.3.3) even state explicitly that "these rights derive from the inherent dignity of the human person." Other conventions, such as, for example, the Convention against Torture or the Anti-Discrimination Conventions, have adopted this wording and/or have integrated similar references to dignity (Shelton 2014: 8).

From the perspective of ethics, there are two basic approaches, which provide two alternative justifications of human rights, both tied closely to human dignity as a basic defining concept for human beings and the lives they pursue. First, there are teleological or consequentialist accounts, which ground human rights in a conception of the good human life. Second, there are deontological accounts of human rights, which are based on the autonomy of human beings. A third, rationalist, account aims at justifying human rights from a purely rational or logical point of view. However, substantively, rationalist accounts tend to be rooted in either teleological or deontological thinking, which is why they will be touched on only very briefly in addition to some more extensive elaborations of teleological and deontological accounts.

1. *Teleological accounts:* The term "teleological" derives from the Greek *telos*, which means goal or objective. Accordingly, teleological accounts define certain goals or outcomes as universally desirable and, consequently, derive human rights from such objectives. In other words, human rights are based on distinct conceptions of the "good," that is, of some ideal or desirable state or end that we strive to achieve. From an individual perspective, this may be a conception of the "good," dignified life or of human well-being that is perceived as universally desirable. From a collective perspective, it is the idea of the "common good" that is at the center of attention. Such ethics is also called consequentialist, because it suggests that we should evaluate our actions and decisions based on how their consequences contribute to the achievement of such an ideal state.

   Two well-known teleological approaches are interest-based and needs-based conceptions of human rights. Such accounts perceive a good human life to depend on the fulfilment of certain basic interests or needs, which are universally shared. Such interests or needs are seen as so fundamental that they give rise to actual rights. For example, one could define good health as a universal human interest, which is critical to human well-being in a wide-ranging sense (Tasioulas 2012: 21). The same can be said for certain fundamental needs like food, water, or the need for shelter from harsh conditions.

   That teleological accounts have to assume some substantive, universal idea of a good life or a common good from which to derive human rights has been one of the main points of critique against them. The more pluralistic our societies become, the more difficult it seems to make general assumptions about what constitutes a good life, worthwhile interests, or universal needs. The critique from a deontological point of view is that if we hold that people are free and autonomous, we cannot define for them what a good life ought to look like. Living in freedom means that each individual can and ought to decide for themselves what ideals to pursue and what kind of (good) life to strive for, as long as they respect that same freedom for everyone else.

2. *Deontological accounts*: Deontological accounts, as opposed to teleological ones, do not prescribe or presuppose a particular idea of a good human life or of a "common good." For them, human beings ought to be free to choose what kind of life they want to live. However, their freedom to choose is necessarily limited by the same freedom of everyone else. Human rights are seen as fundamental moral norms that define both this freedom and the limits that ought not to be infringed upon in the pursuit of one's own idea of a good life. Thus, in deontological ethics more generally, the moral quality of an action or decision does not derive from its consequences and how it contributes to a good life, as in teleological thinking. Rather, what makes a choice or action right is its conformity with a moral norm (Alexander & Moore 2020).

Deontology means "duty-based." Hence, it is the fulfilment and violation of obligations that is at the center of deontological ethics and that determines the moral quality of actions and decisions. In other words, the "right" has priority over the "good"; one cannot justify harm by the pursuit of a certain worthy end.

At the core of such deontological accounts is an idea of human beings as autonomous. What defines them is their intentionality – that is, their capacity to reasonably weigh, contemplate, and choose among different alternative ways of living their lives and to pursue the chosen conception in a deliberate manner within the boundaries of respecting the same right of all others. This capacity is called agency or personhood. An agent is someone who acts with a purpose and based on reasoned intention. Thus, it is the conditions that enable human beings' agency that human rights ought to protect and, hence, their capacity to live autonomous, intentional, and reasoned lives (Box 3.3). Deontological accounts attach human dignity to human beings' autonomy and intentionality to choose a good life, but they abstain from developing a substantive account of what such a life ought to look like.

It is important to emphasize this reference to human beings' *capacity* to live autonomously and intentionally. It does not mean that we always act on good reasons or that we always choose our objectives wisely. As human beings we are defined not least by our fallibility and we often act counter to what good faith and reason would demand – this is one of the very reasons for why a discourse on human rights protection is necessary in the first place. For human agency renders us not only capable but also inherently vulnerable at the same time. The fact that we can act intentionally, that we can set our own goals, that we pursue wishes and dreams that provide meaning to our lives also means that those possibilities can be denied to us, that we can be instrumentalized, diminished, hurt, and humiliated at the core of what defines us as human beings. It is this distinct vulnerability to have our autonomy undermined and taken away that derives from our status as moral persons and that grounds the claim for human rights.

While deontological accounts do not fall into the trap of being overly prescriptive in terms of what kind of life human beings ought to live, they are often criticized for being too abstract and too removed from the lived reality of human beings. This is where pragmatic accounts of human rights come in (Chapter 3.1.4.2). In order to achieve relevance for our daily lives, as they argue, we need to start with how human rights are expressed and pursued through our daily practices and routines, rather than with idealized justificatory or foundational discourses that provide little guidance on how to live our lives.

BOX 3.3 (Context) James Griffin's account of "normative agency" and human rights

One of the best-known "agentic accounts" (Arnold 2010) of human rights was developed by the late University of Oxford philosopher James Griffin (1933–2019). Griffin grounds human rights in personhood and, at the heart of it, in what he calls the "normative agency" of human beings. Agency is normative because it is a specific kind of agency that underlies human rights: the agency involved in living a worthwhile life. Furthermore it is not the fact of such agency that gives rise to human rights, but rather the normative importance that we attach to it (Griffin 2008: 44–48).

Living a worthwhile human life thus means both having certain capacities of agency and being able to exercise them (Griffin 2008: 47). Accordingly, three conditions must be fulfilled to realize "normative agency" (Griffin 2008: 33). The first condition is autonomy. Autonomy means that human beings are free to pursue their own goals and ideas of what a good life ought to look like, rather than being controlled by something or someone external. The second condition is choice. One must have real options to choose from in regard to the kind of life one wants to live and people must have the capabilities necessary to act upon their choices (otherwise they are not real choices). People living in severe poverty, for example, lack the freedom to choose and their lives are often determined by the harsh circumstances they live under. Similarly, choices need to be informed and based on a minimum amount of education to be deliberate and intentional. Hence, according to Griffin, one must have at least a minimum provision of resources and capabilities to act on one's choices. The third condition is liberty. One must not forcibly be stopped or interfered with in the pursuit of such life choices.

The three conditions for agency are normative, because they give rise to obligations to respect, protect, and realize these conditions. Hence, it is these conditions for normative agency that human rights ought to protect.

3. *Rationalist accounts*: Rationalist accounts attempt to make a case for human rights based solely on a logical argument. Their attempt is to formulate a rational argument in favor of human rights that cannot be denied by anyone without contradiction. Ethical theorist Alan Gewirth (1996) formulates such a rationalist argument, which in a somewhat simplified version goes as follows. He starts with the claim that every agent must logically presume that he or she has rights to freedom and well-being, since without it, no intentional and autonomous action would be possible, and this would negate the very agency status of the agent.

Thus, as rational agents, we must presuppose a basic right to freedom and well-being so we can act. But if that is the case, the agent cannot rationally deny the same rights for all other agents, without giving up on his or her own claim for such rights. The point here is that by trying to rationally deny the rights of others, you cannot but presuppose their capacity to understand your rational argument. In other words, you presuppose their equal agency. But if your argument must, by matter of contradiction, presume other people's equality in their agency, you must at the same time recognize that they have the same rights, which protect their agency, that you claim for yourself. "If any agent holds that he has the generic rights because he is a prospective purposive agent, then he also logically must hold that every prospective purposive agent has the generic rights" (Gewirth 1996: 18).

3.1.4.2 Non-Foundationalist Accounts of Human Rights

Non-foundationalists are skeptical about the quest to find a philosophical foundation for human rights that can truly claim universal validity. It does not mean that they reject human rights across the board. However, they tend to see them as contingent and grounded more in our everyday practices. In their view, human rights do not hinge on an ultimate foundation. In fact, they perceive the pursuit of such a foundation more as a distraction and as counter-productive to the plausibility of human rights. For the sake of this brief overview two kinds of non-foundationalist accounts can be distinguished: Political or realist accounts of human rights on the one hand and constructivist or pragmatist accounts on the other.

1. *Political or realist accounts:* A political view of human rights, as opposed to the moral or philosophical one, assumes that a distinct political function is what defines human rights at their core. Such accounts are sometimes called "functional accounts" instead. Hence, those advocating for such political or functional conceptions of human rights do not believe that human rights derive from certain essential features of humanity as such; or at least they do not believe that this is what ultimately makes them human rights. Rather, they perceive them as political constructs that emerge from political discourse and practice and are promoted by political institutions for a particular political purpose (Schaber 2012: 61). The best-known advocates of political conceptions of human rights include John Rawls, Joseph Raz, and Charles Beitz.

   While for the philosophical view it is the foundation and justification of human rights that counts, rather than any particular set or list of rights, the political view does not perceive justification to be of primary or any importance, but rather a (politically) agreed upon set of rights. This is not to say that advocates of such political conceptions deny that there is something like human dignity or that they are necessarily opposed to the idea that our dignity gives rise to certain obligations for decent treatment. However, they are skeptical that human dignity provides a sufficient ground from which to derive human rights (Raz 2010). For them, foundationalist accounts of human rights are based on an error that confuses important values with the distinct nature of (human) rights. If we want to understand the nature and purpose of human rights, as they argue, we need to look at the international political discourse and practice on human rights and at the institutional human rights infrastructure as it has emerged and evolved since 1945 (Chapter 3.2). It is thus the idea of human rights as tools for the regulation of the global order, and more specifically, as limits to state autonomy and sovereignty, which started to emerged in the post-World War II political system, that is at the core of most political conceptions of human rights today.

At the center of that institutional infrastructure and the discourse and practice surrounding it has arguably been the state, which has been defined as the central actor in terms of the violation as well as the protection and realization of human rights. Therefore, the very nature of human rights in such accounts has been defined in and through their relation to the state. Two main political functions are commonly distinguished to be of defining importance for human rights with the second one perhaps being *the* key idea behind modern political thinking on human rights. First, human rights define the limits of the *internal autonomy* of the state (Schaber 2012: 61). They put boundaries on the legitimate use of power and force and prevent the abuse of authority. Thus, human rights constrain the right to rule of the state and other political institutions and ensure the kind of conditions under which the subjects of state authority can lend legitimacy to state rule by obeying freely; second, they define the limits of the *external sovereignty* of the state. They are the limits to what states can legitimately view as purely domestic affairs. The violation of human rights can provide a justified reason for international concern and critique and potentially even for intervention by the international community. There is a broad range of possible and appropriate types of outside intervention in the case of systematic human rights violations, ranging from reprimands to sanctions and all the way to military options.

Human rights discourse, against the background of those particular political functions, only makes sense within a system of states. Thus, political or institutional conceptions of human rights have been informed by a statist perspective by definition. From the vantage point of such accounts, it is a defining feature and "in the very nature" (Tasioulas 2012: 45) of human rights that the primary responsibility for compliance rests with the state. All other agents and agencies may only have secondary and indirect responsibilities for human rights – for example, if the state delegates or mandates such responsibilities, or fails to properly meet its own, leaving a responsibility void that others may have to fill.

From the point of view of such accounts, a human rights violation can logically only occur if the perpetrator is the state, since the very definition of human rights is based on state responsibility.

The relevance of such political views for the BHR discussion is evident. If human rights are seen primarily as rights with the function to define and limit state autonomy and sovereignty and if their very nature and definition hinges on state responsibility, then it is not intuitively evident why and on what grounds they ought to give rise to obligations for any other agents than the state and its representatives. The very reason there has been a BHR discussion in the first place, and a controversial one at that, is the kind of state-centrism or statism that such political or institutional conceptions of human rights are based on. Bringing in companies and other non-state actors as direct responsibility-bearers thus goes against a, or perhaps *the*, constitutive foundational view of political conceptions of human rights; it denotes nothing short of a paradigm change.

2. *Constructivist or pragmatist accounts:* Constructivist or pragmatist accounts do not believe that human rights are grounded in universal normative principles. Such foundationalism, as they criticize it, does not adequately consider and engage with the cultural, social, and historical origins of morality and thus of human rights (Fagan 2014: 17). At the same time, such accounts do not believe in the formalism of legal or political accounts of human rights, either. For them, human rights do not predominantly emerge through law or political institutionalization, but instead they are grounded and enacted in social and cultural practices, "in social struggles, which are as necessary as they are perennial" (Dembour 2010: 3). Thus, while political accounts tend to look toward political processes and practices as a source and enactor of human rights, constructivist or pragmatist accounts are interested in social and cultural practices and discourses more broadly:

> Normativism and institutionalism neglect what can be termed the socio-cultural substance of these rights, that is to say, how they are put into practice by persons and groups engaged in performing collective rituals and beliefs that cannot be reduced to normative principles and may not seek official institutional recognition or juridical inscription. Hence, formalism poorly grasps the cultural processes and forms of social interaction that are at the core of human rights, which become meaningful realities for ordinary persons through what are frequently non-legal, extra-institutional discourses, claims, and actions … To insist that human rights are either ontological attributes of persons (as per natural law theory) or institutionally derived entitlements is to miss their existence as forms of social labor that agents invest with meaning through their performance and capacities that they exercise when confronted with structural obstacles that compromise human dignity and equality (Kurasawa 2014: 156, 160).

Hence, constructivists or pragmatists see human rights not so much as individual entitlements, as rights that we have simply by virtue of being human, but rather as a "project always in the making (and reversible)" (Dembour 2010: 3). Their concrete manifestation occurs within social and cultural practices, human rights struggles and campaigns that enact and provide meaning to them (Kurasawa 2014: 156). At the core of the pragmatist perspective is not the "formalization" but the "informalization" of human rights within intersubjective processes and various forms of social interaction as well as in alternative arenas and spaces of public debates – such as art, film, music, literature, protest, etc. (Kurasawa 2014: 157). Accordingly, pragmatist accounts cast the net of relevant participants in the shaping of human rights much more widely and, indeed, put their main emphasis beyond formal institutions on a plethora of actors from all domains of civil society (Kurasawa 2014: 160).

3.1.4.3   Reconciliation of Different Approaches

Despite the fundamental differences in outlook of foundational and non-foundational accounts, we may not need to pit them against each other, but rather put the best of both accounts at the service of human rights. Disagreeing with the quest for an ultimate foundation does not require the rejection of human rights philosophy across the board. On the contrary, engaging with human rights philosophy helps one to spot the weaknesses and shortcomings of one's own approach. The value of foundationalist philosophies is perhaps less in the proposed foundations themselves than in the philosophical pursuit of them – that is, in the deep philosophical engagement with human rights. On the other hand, foundationalist philosophy can never be entirely disconnected and detached from contemporary practices and human beings' lived reality, for otherwise it would lose its practical value, relevance, and plausibility. Thus, a deep understanding of human rights practice is essential for any meaningful human rights philosophy. Human rights philosophy and human rights practice are codependent in any plausible project to theorize human rights, whether foundational or non-foundational.

This being said, it is evident that a significant part of disagreements on BHR can be traced to conflicting accounts and differing understandings of human rights. Those who hold political views on human rights tend to see fundamental obstacles in extending human rights obligations to business. Those adhering to a view of human rights as applying to all of us simply by virtue of being human tend to perceive it as intuitive that they obligate not only states, but everyone, including corporations. It is perhaps one of the more significant shortcomings of the current BHR discussion that it hardly engages with the foundations of human rights. Doing so would go a long way in fostering common ground to stand upon when deliberating on the responsibilities of business.

3.2   International Human Rights System

The UN stands at the core of the international human rights system. It was founded in 1945 as a response to the atrocities committed in World War II. The hope was that it would prevent the world from similar devastation in the future. It replaced the League of Nations, which was put in place after World War I and was considered to have failed. The founding document of the UN, the UN Charter, outlines three basic purposes of the organization. Those are the promotion of peace, development, and human rights. Hence, the key role of the UN in the promotion of human rights is one of the very founding purposes of the organization. In order to pursue this purpose, the UN's Economic and Social Council created a commission for the promotion of human rights in 1946 (Osiatynski 2016: 10). The commission has become well known for its drafting of the UDHR. Its first chair and most famous member was human and civil rights activist and former First Lady of the United States, Eleanor Roosevelt, who became an icon of the international human rights movement more generally. The UN organization has since deepened and expanded its efforts to advance and promote human rights and has become the core institution and platform for the creation of international human rights law. This section provides a brief overview of the main international human rights bodies both within and outside of the UN. Subsequently, Chapter 3.3 will take a closer look particularly at human rights law.

3.2.1   UN Human Rights Bodies and Agencies

The UN consists of main organs, subsidiary organs, and specialized agencies. The UN's main organs are the General Assembly, the Security Council, the Economic and Social Council, the Trusteeship Council, the International Court of Justice (ICJ), and the UN Secretariat. Subsidiary organs include a variety of different boards, commissions, councils, committees, and working groups. The HRC, which will be discussed below, is a subsidiary body of the UN. Specialized agencies are autonomous UN-affiliated intergovernmental organizations including, among others, the International Labour Organization (ILO), the UN Development Program (UNDP), the UN Children's Fund (UNICEF), the UN Educational, Scientific and Cultural Organization (UNESCO) and the World Health Organization (WHO) (Shelton 2014: 56). A number of those different organs and agencies deal directly with the protection and promotion of human rights.

The International Court of Justice: Located at the Peace Palace in the Hague, the ICJ was established under the UN Charter in 1945 as a successor to the Permanent Court of International Justice, which was established by the League of Nations in 1921 (Kolb 2013: v; Thirlway 2016: 3). The ICJ is the oldest and the most important judicial organ of the UN (Kolb 2013: v) and one of the UN's main bodies. Although not a human rights court, the ICJ acts as a mechanism in accordance with international law for the peaceful settlement of disputes between states that arise due to differing opinions on their obligations, conduct or interests, and may include cases with human rights components (Kolb 2013: 1). Most cases before the court deal with the demarcation of borders between countries. About a quarter of cases involve human rights issues (Haas 2014: 278). However, the ICJ does not have jurisdiction over human rights claims brought by individuals. The court can make three types of decisions: it can issue binding rulings when all parties accept its jurisdiction in advance; it can issue advisory opinions to clarify legal issues; and it can engage in mediation and dispute resolution (Haas 2014: 277). The ICJ is comprised of fifteen judges, who are elected separately by the Security Council and the General Assembly for terms of office of nine years (International Court of Justice n.d.; Thirlway 2016: 4).

Human Rights Council: The HRC was initially called the Commission on Human Rights and grew out of the drafting commission of the UDHR. The Commission on Human Rights initially comprised government representatives of eighteen states (including the five permanent members of the Security Council) and grew to fifty-three members by 2006. In 2006, it was replaced by the HRC and its membership was reduced to forty-seven states. The HRC reports directly to the General Assembly (Fremuth 2015: 150), which is the organ of the highest rank within the UN. It holds three regular sessions per year but can call special sessions in order to react swiftly to emerging human rights crises. The HRC conducts so-called universal periodic reviews, through which it assesses the human rights situation and the compliance with human rights obligations of all member countries every four years. It then issues recommendations for improvement. Furthermore, civil society organizations or individuals can file complaints with the HRC in case of systematic and severe violations of human rights. If a complaint is approved, the HRC will issue a report with recommendations or initiate further investigation or support through the Office of the High Commissioner for Human Rights (OHCHR) for the improvement of the situation (Fremuth 2015: 154–155). Finally, the HRC can initiate so-called special procedures. Within such special procedures, the HRC can mandate independent experts, special rapporteurs, or working groups to report and advise on specific human rights issues (Fremuth 2015: 155–156). The UNWG is a special procedure of the HRC.

Office of the High Commissioner for Human Rights: The OHCHR was established by the UN General Assembly in June 1993. It is a part of the UN Secretariat and represents the leading entity within the UN for the promotion and protection of all human rights. Specifically, it provides technical and advisory services to member states, coordinates the information and education programs on human rights within the UN, facilitates and maintains a dialogue with all governments about their implementation of human rights standards, facilitates international cooperation in regard to the protection of human rights, engages in standard-setting and monitoring, coordinates and mainstreams human rights within all UN programmes, and enhances their efficiency and effectiveness (Fremuth 2015: 159). It also provides secretariat services to the HRC, the special procedures, and the treaty bodies (Shelton 2014: 46). It supports the HRC's Universal Periodic Reviews, publishes reports, comments and speaks out objectively on human rights violations around the world, and provides a forum for engagement on human rights issues (Fremuth 2015: 160). The OHCHR is headed by the High Commissioner for Human Rights. The High Commissioner is an independent official with a mandate to act on behalf of the UN and to lead the OHCHR (Shelton 2014: 46). He or she is elected by the General Assembly for a maximum of two terms of four years.

International Labour Organization: The ILO was created in 1919 as part of the Treaty of Versailles following World War I. Following the creation of the UN in 1945, the ILO became the first specialized agency of the UN (International Labour Organization n.d. (a)). Its mandate is to promote decent work and human rights, including, among others, the right to form trade unions, the right to strike, the right to be free from slavery and forced labor, the right to safe and healthy working conditions and equal employment opportunities. ILO standards also focus on the protection of especially vulnerable groups, addressing child labor, migrant labor, and employment of women or Indigenous peoples (Shelton 2014: 57). The ILO operates through a unique tripartite structure in which each member state's delegation consists of government representatives as well as delegates from employers' and workers' organizations (Shelton 2014: 57; International Labour Organization n.d. (b)). It consists of three main bodies, namely: the International Labour Conference, which sets the standards and policies of the ILO; the ILO's Governing Body, which acts as an executive council for issues related to the organization's programme and budget; and the International Labour Office, which is the permanent secretariat of the ILO and acts as the focal point for the organization's activities (International Labour Organization n.d. (b)). The ILO can enact conventions, which are binding on the member states that ratify them. Examples include the Convention on Forced Labor (1930) and the Convention on Freedom of Association and Protection of the Right to Organize (1949). The implementation of ILO conventions and recommendations is monitored by a twenty-member independent ILO Committee of Experts (Shelton 2014: 58).

Treaty bodies: The human rights core treaties establish so-called treaty bodies, which are committees of up to twenty-five international experts who monitor the implementation and compliance of states with the respective treaty provisions. The human rights treaty bodies act as plenary bodies and receive secretarial resources and support from the OHCHR (Keller & Ulfstein 2012: 3). The following ten treaty bodies have been established: the Committee on the Elimination of Racial Discrimination (CERD); the Committee on Economic, Social and Cultural Rights

(CESCR); the Human Rights Committee (CCPR); the Committee on the Elimination of Discrimination Against Women (CEDAW); the Committee Against Torture (CAT); the Committee on the Rights of the Child (CRC); the Committee on Migrant Workers (CMW); the Subcommittee on Prevention of Torture (SPT); the Committee on the Rights of Persons with Disabilities (CRPD); and the Committee on Enforced Disappearances (CED) (OHCHR n.d. (a)). Within their mandate to monitor state compliance, treaty bodies can generally make use of a number of instruments. These include assessing the periodic reporting of state parties on their compliance with the respective treaty; adjudicating complaints by either individuals or other states about potential treaty violations by state parties; and launching investigations on egregious violations of treaty provisions (Fremuth 2015: 162–166; Mason Meier & Brás Gomes 2018; Carraro 2019). Of particular importance is the treaty bodies' power to issue interpretations and specifications of treaty provisions through so-called general comments. While the General Comments are not legally binding, they are widely noted as authoritative statements of human rights law and, as such, can achieve significant weight (Fremuth 2015: 167; Shelton 2014: 55).

3.2.2 Other Human Rights Bodies and Agencies

In addition to the UN entities described above, there are a number of bodies and institutions that fulfil important functions in the international human rights infrastructure without being formally affiliated with the UN. Among the most important are the International Criminal Court (ICC) and three regional human rights courts – the European Court of Human Rights, the Inter-American Court of Human Rights along with the Inter-American Commission on Human Rights, and the African Court of Human and Peoples' Rights along with the African Commission on Human and Peoples' Rights.

International Criminal Court: The ICC was established in 2002 and is based in The Hague. It is based on the Rome Statute of the ICC, which was adopted in 1998 by 120 states (Haas 2014: 300; Shelton 2014: 206). Currently, 123 countries are ICC members. Among those that have not signed or ratified the statute are, for example, the United States and China (Human Rights Watch 2020; International Criminal Court n.d. (a)). The establishment of the ICC was built on other historical precedents in international law, including the Nuremberg trials and the Tokyo War Crimes Tribunal, as well as the International Criminal Tribunals for the Former Yugoslavia and for Rwanda (Schabas 2011: 12). The growing number of such ad hoc tribunals showed the need for a permanent criminal court (Shelton 2014: 206). The ICC acts as an independent and permanent judicial institution, with the jurisdiction to investigate and prosecute any of the following four crimes, if they occurred on or after July 1, 2002: 1) the crime of genocide, 2) crimes against humanity, 3) war crimes resulting from a breach of the Geneva conventions in the context of armed conflict, and 4) the crime of aggression, or the use of armed force by a state against the sovereignty, integrity, or independence of another state (Human Rights Watch 2020). The ICC may exercise jurisdiction if an alleged crime was either committed in the territory of a state that is party to the statute or was committed by a national of such a state (Shelton 2014: 207). Importantly, the ICC prosecutes individuals, rather than states. Cases can be referred by the UN Security Council, by individual states, or by the ICC Prosecutor. The ICC aims to act in a complementary manner with national criminal systems, meaning that it will pursue a case only if the state concerned is unable or unwilling to investigate or prosecute the crime, or if it is acting in bad faith (Shelton 2014: 207). It cooperates worldwide with countries in order to make arrests, transfer arrested individuals to the ICC detention center, freeze the assets of suspects, and enforce sentences (International Criminal Court n.d. (b)).

European Court of Human Rights: The European Court of Human Rights, which is based in Strasbourg, was established in 1959 in order to put force behind the European Convention on Human Rights (ECHR) (Merrills 1993: 1). It is a main organ of the Council of Europe (not to be confused with the European Union) and the longest-standing human rights tribunal in the world (Haas 2014: 372). The Court acts as a regional full-time court, to which individuals or member states can apply directly if human rights have been violated and domestic mechanisms have been exhausted. By 2012, the Court had made decisions or judgments on more than 17,000 cases (Haas 2014: 373). Because its decisions are legally binding and override domestic law, the rulings of the Court frequently lead to changes of domestic practices and laws (Haas 2014: 372–374). Furthermore, the Court can mandate compensation of victims, providing them with an effective means to access remedy (De Schutter 2014: 983). The Court is made up of full-time professional judges, who are elected by the Parliamentary Assembly of the Council of Europe for non-renewable terms of nine years. They do not represent their respective states, but rather act as independent individuals (Shelton 2014: 62).

Inter-American Commission on Human Rights and Inter-American Court of Human Rights: The Inter-American Commission on Human Rights and the Inter-American Court of Human Rights are the two main human rights bodies within the Inter-American human rights system, which are empowered by the American Convention on Human Rights (Pasqualucci 2013: 5). The Inter-American Commission on Human Rights was created in Washington, D.C., in 1959, and acts as a principal and autonomous organ of the Organization of American States (OAS) to promote and protect human rights in the American hemisphere (Organization of American States n.d.). The Commission engages in activities in three broad areas: first, it runs an individual petition system; second, it monitors the human rights situation in member states; third, it can devote attention to specific thematic areas that require investigation and awareness (Organization of American States n.d.). More specific activities include the drafting of declarations and treaties, monitoring of human rights situations, publishing of country and thematic reports, responding to complaints, making country visits, and issuing recommendations and precautionary measures (Haas 2014: 417). The Commission can also refer cases to the Inter-American Court of Human Rights for judgments (Haas 2014: 417).

The Inter-American Court of Human Rights was established by the American Convention on Human Rights in 1978 in order to uphold, apply, and interpret the Convention (Buergenthal 1982: 231). It is an autonomous judicial institution based in San José, Costa Rica. Cases can be filed with the Court by the Inter-American Commission on Human Rights or by ratifying governments. For example, a member state can challenge the Commission's attribution of responsibility by submitting a case to the Court (Pasqualucci 2013: 6). However, as opposed to the European Court of Human Rights, for example, the Court does not take direct complaints by individuals. Instead, they have to file their cases with the Commission, which can then refer them to the Court (Haas 2014: 420). Judges of the court can be elected for up to two terms of six years (Buergenthal 1982: 231). The Court is composed of seven judges who are nationals of OAS member states. They act independently, in an individual capacity (Buergenthal 1982: 231).

African Commission on Human and Peoples' Rights and African Court of Human and Peoples' Rights: Two bodies are tasked with the protection of human rights within the regional African human rights system. The African Commission on Human and Peoples' Rights was established in 1986, once the African Charter on Human and Peoples' Rights came into force (Haas 2014: 450). Among the Commission's functions are informing, educating, and awareness-raising on human rights, handling of complaints from individuals and organizations about alleged Charter violations, interpreting the Charter as well as monitoring Charter implementation by member states. It can also appoint special rapporteurs for the investigation of specific thematic issues (Haas 2014: 450). The Commission is not a judicial body, which means that it cannot issue binding rulings and interpretations (Haas 2014: 450).

The Protocol on the Establishment of an African Court on Human and Peoples' Rights was adopted in 1998 and came into effect in 2004. As one of the three regional human rights courts globally, the Court is permanently based in Arusha, Tanzania. It consists of eleven independent judges on six-year terms. Cases can be referred to the Court by the African Commission on Human and Peoples' Rights, other African intergovernmental bodies, international NGOs that have observer status with the Commission, states that have ratified the Protocol, and individuals in those states (Haas 2014: 452). The Court can refer cases to the Commission, order provisional measures, push for amicable settlements, or issue decisions on cases (Haas 2014: 452). In 2008 the African Union adopted a Protocol on merging the Court with the African Court of Justice to build a new African Court of Justice and Human Rights. However, to date, the Protocol has not been ratified by the required minimum of fifteen states and thus has not entered into force. The Court of Justice and Human Rights is not yet operational as a result (Open Society Justice Initiative 2013).

The Protocol on the Statute of the African Court of Justice and Human Rights was further amended by the adoption of the so-called Malabo Protocol by the African Union Assembly of Heads of State in 2014. The Malabo Protocol extends the jurisdiction of the yet-to-be-established Court of Justice and Human Rights to cover crimes under international law and transnational crimes, giving the court competence to investigate and try fourteen international, transnational, and other crimes (Amnesty International 2016a: 5). The Malabo Protocol is unique among regional courts. It would establish "the first regional criminal jurisdiction capable of prosecuting serious crimes condemned by international law such as genocide, the crime of aggression, war crimes and crimes against humanity" (Jalloh, Clarke, & Nmehielle 2019: xx). Thus, the criminal law section of the Court will essentially operate as a regional criminal court akin to the ICC, but with a limited geographical scope and based on an expanded list of crimes. Similar to the Protocol on the Statute of the African Court of Justice and Human Rights, the Malabo Protocol has not yet achieved the minimum number of ratifications either (Amnesty International 2016a: 5).

3.3   International Human Rights Law

The philosophy of human rights is centuries old and its institutionalization at the domestic level reaches as far back as to the 1776 Declaration of Independence in the United States as well as to the French Revolution some ten years later in 1789 (Chapter 3.1.1). Compared to that, human rights have a rather short history as a part of international law, starting with the adoption of the UDHR in 1948. Since then, international human rights law has progressively developed and expanded. Human rights law has a special place in the body of international law for two reasons. First, while international law generally regulates the relationship between states, human rights law regulates the relationship between states and the individuals under their jurisdiction (De Schutter 2014: 13). Second, while international law traditionally served to protect state sovereignty, human rights law establishes limits to it. An important aspect of human rights law is precisely to delineate the boundaries of what ought to be considered the internal affairs of sovereign states: human rights cannot simply be disregarded or legislated away simply by reference to states' sovereignty. Some scholars also perceive human rights to be establishing a hierarchy in international law, regarding human rights as superior to other international legal norms. One argument in favor of such a hierarchy is that the UN Charter itself establishes the protection of human rights as one of the purposes of the UN

(De Schutter 2014: 72–73). At least where we deal with *jus cogens* (Chapter 3.3.2) norms, from which states are not allowed to derogate under any circumstances, such a hierarchy seems implied.

The following paragraphs will provide a brief overview of the sources and the main instruments of international human rights law. At the heart of international human rights law is what we call the International Bill of Human Rights. It is complemented by several core human rights treaties. Furthermore, three regional human rights regimes specify and complement the provisions of the International Bill of Human Rights for their respective regional contexts. Finally, the ILO Conventions, while not a part of international human rights law in a narrow sense, bear special relevance for BHR.

3.3.1 Kinds of Human Rights

Human rights can be classified along different parameters, such as their emergence, their force, or the kind of entitlement they give rise to (Fremuth 2015: 53).

Generations of human rights: Human rights are often clustered along so-called generations of human rights (Haas 2014: 5). The first generation consists of civil and political rights, which protect our most basic freedoms and liberties. Examples include the right to life, the right to free expression and opinion, and the right not to be subjected to torture. Civil and political rights are codified in the International Covenant for Civil and Political Rights (ICCPR) (Chapter 3.3.3 and Chapter 3.3.4). The second generation comprises economic, social, and cultural rights, which provide for an equal standard of a dignified life for all human beings. Examples of such rights include the right to subsistence, the right to an adequate standard of health and education, and the right to adequate shelter. Human rights of the second generation are codified in the International Covenant on Economic, Social and Cultural Rights (ICESCR) (Chapter 3.3.3 and Chapter 3.3.4). The third generation contains a wider range of issues, which tend to address the rights of collectives, rather than of individuals. Such rights include, for example, the right to an intact environment, the right to development and self-determination, and the right to peace. Some regional human rights charters (Chapter 3.3.5) contain third-generation rights, while at the international level they can mostly be found in non-binding declarations and resolutions (Fremuth 2015: 67). The classification in generations refers to the historical emergence and evolution of the respective rights and is not meant to imply a hierarchy between them.

Absolute and relative human rights (Fremuth 2015: 58–62): We can further classify human rights according to their force – that is, with regard to the extent to which they can be legitimately restricted. Absolute rights are human rights that do not allow for any restrictions under any circumstances. They are considered so fundamental that every infringement denotes an untenable assault on the dignity of human beings. There is only a small number of such rights for which any restriction must be considered disproportionate. The prime example is the right not to be tortured. Most human rights are relative rights, which can be restricted if the restriction is justified by a strong and urgent public interest, such as public health or public security, and is necessary and adequate for and proportionate to the satisfaction of that interest.

Negative and positive rights: Human rights are often classified according to the nature of their entitlement. Negative rights protect our liberty from undue interference; they are rights to prevent harm. Civil and political rights are commonly viewed as negative rights. Positive rights, on the other hand, are rights for a particular provision by the duty-bearer. In other words, the duty-bearer is not merely obligated to abstain from certain harmful conduct or actions, but to actively contribute to and provide the substance of the right. For example, in order to fulfil the right to education, the state must not only abstain from interference with people's right to seek education, but also ought to provide an infrastructure of schools, teachers, quality controls, and so on that enables them to do so. Economic, social, and cultural rights are commonly understood to be positive rights. A slightly more differentiated tripartite distinction of liberty rights (equivalent to negative rights), welfare rights (equivalent to positive rights), and participation rights is sometimes used as well (see e.g. Fremuth 2015: 62–67). However, while the distinction between positive and negative rights is still common, it has been discredited as largely inadequate. Notably Henry Shue (1996) showed that all rights have both positive and negative dimensions. For example, the right to physical security does not merely require non-interference, but entails a claim for protection that calls for "a wide range of positive actions" (Shue 1996: 37). What some may perceive simply – or simplistically – as merely a right to be left alone, in fact necessitates an entire system of police forces, court systems, penitentiaries, schools for the training of lawyers and police officers, and not least a system of taxation that allows for the maintenance of adequate institutions and processes for the prevention, detection, and punishment of violations (Shue 1996: 37–38). Similarly, social and economic rights, such as the right to subsistence, give rise not only to positive obligations but also to negative ones, such as the obligation not to participate in unjust institutional schemes and structures, which perpetuate and compound, rather than remedy poverty and existing inequalities (Pogge 2002: 70). Hence, rather than defining rights themselves as positive or negative, it is the correlating obligations that can be of positive or negative character (Chapter 7.1). All rights correlate with both types of obligations (Chapter 7.2).

3.3.2   Sources of International Human Rights Law

We can distinguish three kinds of binding international law, according to their respective legal sources: treaty law, customary law including *jus cogens*, and general principles of law.

Treaty law emerges from a formal treaty process, adoption of the resulting binding document and ratification of the treaty by national governments. Treaties are bilateral (between only two parties) or multilateral (between a larger number of parties) contracts between states. Thus, treaty law is codified, written international law. Human rights treaties may also come with different designations, such as conventions, covenants, or protocols (Shelton 2014: 74). Treaty law must be distinguished from softer provisions contained, for example, in formal declarations, resolutions, or the concluding texts of international conferences. Such instruments are not legally binding and thus count as a part of international "soft law" (Chapter 9.3). They are normally tied to strong expectations of compliance and often also come with certain sanctions and political consequences in the case of non-compliance (Shelton 2014: 80–81).

Customary law is not codified. It emerges from custom, understood as the general and consistent practice of states (Joseph 2004: 23), rather than from a formal treaty process. Broadly, custom can be defined as "international practices that traditionally govern relations between states without being encoded in treaty form" (Haas 2014: 109). As such, customary law does not require formal adoption or ratification. Ordinary customary law binds all states, with the exception of those who have persistently objected to its validity and application (Joseph 2004: 23). Accordingly, two elements specify custom, one objective and one subjective (Clapham 2006: 86; Shelton 2014: 77). The objective criterion is "state practice": the norm must have been practiced by a state in an unambiguous and consistent manner; the second criterion is what lawyers call *opinio juris*: the state must have practiced that norm out of a sense of legal obligation. In other words, states must believe that the practice is rendered obligatory by a rule of law, rather than being a matter of courtesy or discretion (De Schutter 2014: 63; Shelton 2014: 77). The evident open question is, at what point a practice turns into custom – that is, for how long it must have been practiced and how widespread that practice must be (Shelton 2014: 77). Typically, customary law norms do not emerge from nowhere, but are proclaimed in international instruments that are widely adhered to, such as the UDHR. However, the reverse process is possible, as well, meaning that such proclamations or declarations may only specify and put in writing what has previously emerged as custom. Accordingly, most provisions of the UDHR are considered customary and thus binding in international law, despite the non-binding character of the UDHR itself (Clapham 2006: 86; De Schutter 2014: 18, 63; Frey 1997: 161; Shelton 2014: 77).

Jus cogens, or peremptory norms, are a part of customary law, too. *Jus cogens* consists of those customary international norms that are deemed so essential by the international community that they are binding on all states without exception and from which no derogation is permitted (Shelton 2014: 84). *Jus cogens* obligations are so-called obligations *erga omnes* - that is, they are owed to the international community as a whole. Whether or not all human rights obligations more generally are to be considered *erga omnes* is still an open discussion (De Schutter 2014: 114). Concordantly, as opposed to general customary international law, *jus cogens* norms merely need to be accepted by the international community of states as a whole; whether individual states practice them out of a sense of obligation is irrelevant for their validity (Clapham 2006: 87). Even state practice as such is far less important for *jus cogens* than for general custom (De Schutter 2014: 87). Therefore, the list of norms that may qualify as peremptory is in constant evolution. However, a number of norms are generally agreed to belong to *jus cogens*. Among them are the prohibition of aggression, slavery and the slave trade, genocide, racial discrimination, apartheid, and torture; the basic rules of international humanitarian law applicable in armed conflict; and the right to self-determination (De Schutter 2014: 87–88). Whereas there is significant disagreement about the existence of international human rights law obligations for non-state actors (Chapter 6.2), *jus cogens* norms are generally perceived to apply to individuals and potentially to other non-state actors, as well (Clapham 2006: 90).

General principles of law are well-recognized principles on which international law is based and which are considered sources of binding obligations, as well. Examples include the principle of good faith, or equality of the parties to a dispute (Shelton 2014: 78). It is often argued that at least certain human rights are to be considered among such principles, which is not least evidenced by the fact that countless states have implemented or incorporated the UDHR into their national constitutions (De Schutter 2014: 67). What this means is that at least a number of human rights might be considered binding on all nations, even if they have not ratified the respective treaties.

3.3.3 International Bill of Human Rights

The International Bill of Human Rights builds the core of international human rights law and provides the basis for most BHR instruments, such as the UNGPs. It consists of the UDHR and the two binding covenants, i.e. the ICCPR and the ICESCR, including the respective optional protocols.

The UDHR is the centerpiece of international human rights law. Adopted by the UN General Assembly in 1948, it stipulates thirty fundamental principles of human rights (Box 3.4). Like all UN declarations, the UDHR is non-binding and non-enforceable and can therefore be considered a part of international "soft law" (Chapter 9.3). Nevertheless, as a formal declaration, the UDHR signals a strong expectation that member states should adhere to it (Shelton 2014: 81). Accordingly, after adoption of the UDHR, many states started to incorporate human rights provisions modeled after the UDHR into their constitutions (Haas 2014: 92). That being said, many of the rights in the UDHR were already linked to or derived from provisions in the constitutions of the then fifty-five UN member states (De Schutter 2014: 36; Shelton 2014: 78). Furthermore, there is a growing consensus

BOX 3.4 (Context) Thirty articles of the Universal Declaration of Human Rights

Accepted by the United Nations General Assembly in Paris on December 10, 1948, the UDHR paved the way for the adoption of more than seventy human rights treaties, and has been translated into over 500 languages (United Nations n.d.). The following is an abbreviated version of the UDHR's thirty articles (Flowers n.d.):

Article 1   Right to Equality
Article 2   Freedom from Discrimination
Article 3   Right to Life, Liberty, Personal Security
Article 4   Freedom from Slavery
Article 5   Freedom from Torture and Degrading Treatment
Article 6   Right to Recognition as a Person before the Law
Article 7   Right to Equality before the Law
Article 8   Right to Remedy by Competent Tribunal
Article 9   Freedom from Arbitrary Arrest and Exile
Article 10   Right to Fair Public Hearing
Article 11   Right to be Considered Innocent until Proven Guilty
Article 12   Freedom from Interference with Privacy, Family, Home and
              Correspondence
Article 13   Right to Free Movement in and out of the Country
Article 14   Right to Asylum in other Countries from Persecution
Article 15   Right to a Nationality and the Freedom to Change It
Article 16   Right to Marriage and Family
Article 17   Right to Own Property
Article 18   Freedom of Belief and Religion
Article 19   Freedom of Opinion and Information
Article 20   Right of Peaceful Assembly and Association
Article 21   Right to Participate in Government and in Free Elections
Article 22   Right to Social Security
Article 23   Right to Desirable Work and to Join Trade Unions
Article 24   Right to Rest and Leisure
Article 25   Right to Adequate Standard of Living
Article 26   Right to Education
Article 27   Right to Participate in the Cultural Life of Community
Article 28   Right to a Social Order that Articulates this Document
Article 29   Community Duties Essential to Free and Full Development
Article 30   Freedom from State or Personal Interference in the above Rights

that most, if not all, of the rights stipulated in the UDHR can be viewed as a part of binding customary international law (Chapter 3.3.2) today (De Schutter 2014: 63). Also, all states have a general duty to respect and promote human rights, which the UDHR specifies. Article 56 of the UN Charter obligates all states to work toward the achievement of the purposes of the UN, which is specified in Article 55 to be the promotion of, universal respect for and observance of human rights (De Schutter 2014: 63). Finally, the provisions of the UDHR were specified and rendered binding in the two international covenants, which are a part of the International Bill of Human Rights, as well as in a number of further international human rights treaties (Chapter 3.3.4). The covenants were adopted in 1967 after lengthy negotiations and put into force in 1976, after being ratified by a sufficient number of states.

The ICCPR specifies the civil and political rights of the UDHR and codifies them in binding international law. Civil and political rights protect our basic liberties from interference. Among the rights protected by the ICCPR are: the right to life; the right to be protected from slavery and slave trade and from inhumane or cruel punishment; the right to freedom of religion, conscience or thought and expression; and the right to privacy, among many others. Initially, a draft for a single convention included both civil and political as well as economic, social, and cultural rights. However, the views of states on how much attention to give to these different categories of rights differed profoundly and stalled the project. While Western nations tended to prioritize civil and political rights, the Soviet bloc in particular emphasized economic, social, and cultural rights, while being skeptical of civil liberties and the prospect of their international enforcement. In 1951, the General Assembly approved the drafting of two separate treaties to break free of the impasse (Haas 2014: 93).

The ICESCR codifies the economic, social, and cultural rights stipulated in the UDHR in binding international law. Social, economic, and cultural rights protect the material and non-material basis on which the pursuit of meaningful life goals becomes thinkable and possible. Among the rights codified in the ICESCR are the right to work, to education, to health, and to adequate food, clothing, and housing.

Along with the two international covenants, a number of other human rights treaties make up the core of international human rights law. The following section will briefly touch on those treaties.

3.3.4   Core Human Rights Treaties

International human rights law is commonly said to consist of nine core treaties, including the two international covenants. They are all based on the UDHR. The development of these treaties is a reflection not least of an increasing awareness of a need for better protection of the rights of vulnerable and marginalized groups such as women, children, migrant workers, or persons with disabilities. The following paragraphs briefly address the nine core human rights treaties in chronological order.

- *International Convention on the Elimination of All Forms of Racial Discrimination (1969)*: This treaty aims to prevent distinction, exclusion, restriction, or preference based on race, color, descent, and national or ethnic origin, which can nullify or impair the equal enjoyment of human rights and fundamental freedoms. Additionally, the purpose of this treaty is to ensure equality between ethnicities, by abolishing racial segregation and racial discrimination.

- *International Covenant on Economic, Social and Cultural Rights (1976)*: The ICESCR aims to grant economic, social, and cultural rights to all individuals, including, among others, the right to self-determination, the right to health, labor rights, the right to education, and the right to an adequate standard of living.

- *International Covenant on Civil and Political Rights (1976)*: The ICCPR aims at the recognition of and respect for the inherent dignity of each individual, and at the promotion of conditions within member states that allow for the enjoyment of civil and political rights, such as, for example, the right to life, freedom of expression, and the right to freedom of religion.

- *Convention on the Elimination of All Forms of Discrimination against Women (1981)*: This treaty focuses on the human rights concerns of women. The Convention defines equality between men and women, and addresses their civil rights, legal status, labor rights, reproductive rights, and the impact of cultural factors on gender relations, specifically those pertaining to marriage and family relations.

- *Convention against Torture and Other Cruel, Inhuman or Degrading Treatment or Punishment (1987)*: This treaty aims to prevent and prohibit torture, as well as other acts of cruel, inhuman, or degrading punishment or treatment regardless of jurisdiction or circumstance (including war, armed conflict, terrorism, or public emergencies). Additionally, the Convention prohibits parties from returning, extraditing, or refouling an individual to a state in which he or she may be at risk of torture or similar treatment, and requires parties to the Convention to train and educate their legal, medical, civilian, and military personnel on the prevention of torture.

- *Convention on the Rights of the Child (1990)*: This treaty aims to protect and uphold four core principles, namely: non-discrimination; devotion to the best interests of the child; the right to life, survival and development; and respect for the views of the child. Additionally, minimum entitlements and freedoms are outlined by the Convention, setting standards for children's rights to a safe environment and health care and education, as well as to legal, civil, and social services.

- *International Convention on the Protection of the Rights of All Migrant Workers and Members of their Families (2003)*: This treaty aims to protect migrant workers and their family members by ensuring their freedom of movement, conditions of labor (especially with regards to the prevention of forced or compulsory labor and slavery or servitude), freedom of thought and religion, and the right to fair, equal, and established legal proceedings.

- *Convention on the Rights of Persons with Disabilities (2008)*: This treaty aims to protect the rights and dignity of individuals with disabilities, to ensure that they are consulted with and respected, and treated equally before the law and within society, regardless of their gender, age, or impairment. The Convention also aims to protect their health, safety, education, employment, accessibility, and privacy, as well as to ensure their freedom from punishment, torture, violence, abuse, or exploitation.
- *International Convention for the Protection of All Persons from Enforced Disappearance (2010)*: This treaty aims to protect individuals from enforced disappearances, and to ensure that all states party to the Convention take the necessary measures to hold those involved criminally responsible and to enforce the appropriate penalties, resulting from fair legal proceedings.

In addition to the nine core treaties, there are a number of other treaties that can be considered human rights treaties (De Schutter 2014: 21). They include, for example, the Convention on the Prevention and Punishment of the Crime of Genocide (1948), the Convention on the Non-Applicability of Statutory Limitations of War Crimes and Crimes against Humanity (1968), and the International Convention on the Suppression and Punishment of the Crime of Apartheid (1973).

3.3.5 Regional Human Rights Conventions

In addition to the international human rights system, there are regional human rights systems, which specify and, in some instances, expand international human rights. Each regional system tends to be established by a regional human rights convention. They consist of certain monitoring bodies and, as in the case of Europe, the Americas, and Africa, of a regional human rights court (Chapter 3.2.2). This section briefly introduces the five existing regional systems, with a focus specifically on the respective conventions.

Europe: In 1950, the Council of Europe adopted the Convention for the Protection of Human Rights and Fundamental Freedoms, better known today as the ECHR. The ECHR further established the European Commission on Human Rights as well as the European Court of Human Rights (Chapter 3.2.2). The ECHR entered into force in 1953 and, hence, was the first legally binding human rights treaty worldwide (Fremuth 2015: 181). The ECHR is unique insofar as it provides people with the right to call on the European Court of Human Rights in case their human rights are violated by their governments (Fremuth 2015: 182). While the ECHR focuses predominantly on civil and political rights, economic, social, and cultural rights are covered in the European Social Charter, which came into force in 1965. Besides the ECHR and the European Social Charter, which are the main instruments for the protection of human rights in Europe, there are other more specific conventions such as the European Convention for the Prevention of Torture and Inhuman or Degrading Treatment or Punishment (De Schutter 2014: 23–25).

The Americas: In 1948, the Ninth International Conference of American States established the OAS (formerly the Pan American Union) and adopted the American Declaration on the Rights and Duties of Man at the same time. In 1959, the Inter-American Commission on Human Rights was established. While the Declaration was non-binding (though applied by the Inter-American Commission to all member states), the binding American Convention on Human Rights was adopted in 1969 and came into force in 1978, along with the Inter-American Court of Human Rights, which has jurisdiction over it (Chapter 3.2.2). The Convention is comparable to the ECHR in terms of content and substance (Fremuth 2015: 188). Ten members of the Organization of American States have not ratified the Convention, among them the United States and Canada. In 1988, the Convention was complemented by an additional protocol covering economic, social, and cultural rights. Besides the American Convention on Human Rights as the main regional instrument for the protection of human rights of the Americas, a number of other conventions were adopted in the human rights realm, such as, for example, the Inter-American Convention to Prevent and Punish Torture (De Schutter 2014: 25–31).

Africa: The African Charter on Human and Peoples' Rights was adopted in 1981 by the Organization of African Unity, which is now the African Union, and came into force in 1986. In 1998, the African Court on Human and Peoples' Rights was established and came into force in 2004 (Chapter 3.2.2). The African Charter deviates from the other regional conventions in its attempt to interpret human rights at least partly in light of the traditions and values of African cultures, which leads to a number of specificities of the Charter. For example, alongside individual rights, the Charter also contains provision on individual duties. Furthermore, a number of economic and social rights are treated as equivalent to civil and political rights in terms of their justiciability. Finally, it gives high importance to collective rights (De Schutter 2014: 31–32). On the other hand, the Charter has been criticized for not mentioning certain other rights, such as the right to subsistence or privacy rights (Fremuth 2015: 189).

Arab states: In 2004, the Council of the League of Arab States adopted the Arab Charter of Human Rights, which came into force in 2008, after it was ratified by the required minimum of seven states. The Charter also establishes the Arab Human Rights Committee, which examines the reports that member states have to periodically submit. However, the Charter has been widely criticized, among others by the UN High Commissioner on Human Rights, for its apparent incompatibilities with the International Bill of Human Rights, particularly as it pertains to its approach to the death penalty for children, the protection of women's rights, and the rights of non-citizens (De Schutter 2014: 33).

South-East Asian states: In 2009, the Association of South-East Asian Nations (ASEAN) established the ASEAN Intergovernmental Commission on Human Rights, a human rights body with very limited, consultative powers. In 2012, the ASEAN Heads of State and Governments further adopted the ASEAN Human Rights Declaration. The Declaration was criticized for its selective and potentially relativistic approach to human rights (De Schutter 2014: 34–35).

STUDY QUESTIONS

1. What are four defining elements of human rights?
2. What is the difference between universalism and absolutism? What is the difference between descriptive and normative universalism? What is Mary Midgley's argument against relativism?
3. What is the difference between foundationalist and non-foundationalist accounts of human rights? Why does this distinction matter from a BHR perspective?
4. What is the difference between natural and positive law? And why is this distinction important with regard to human rights? What is the key "innovation" of Enlightenment philosophers with regard to human rights?
5. What is the International Bill of Human Rights? What else is part of international human rights law beyond the International Bill of Human Rights?
6. What are the three most advanced regional human rights systems? What can such regional systems contribute in addition to the international one?

REFLECTION QUESTIONS

1. Historically, there have been concerns surrounding human rights as instruments of Western imperialism and neocolonialism. How can we ensure that human rights are universal and reflective of other cultures globally?
2. Human rights are often said to derive from and protect human dignity. What does human dignity mean to you? How does a teleological account of dignity differ from a deontologial one? Which one is more plausible to you?
3. Can human rights claim universal validity?
4. In your opinion, what are the strengths of the current international human rights system? What are its weaknesses? How could international protection of human rights be improved?

PART II
Setting the Scene

4 Corporate Human Rights Violations: Direct and Indirect

Corporations can be implicated in human rights violations in direct and indirect ways. Direct violations are caused by corporations through their own activities. Indirect violations are violations caused by third parties but to which corporations contribute indirectly. This chapter looks in more detail at this important distinction between direct and indirect human rights violations, presents a common typology of different kinds of complicity, and contrasts some legal and non-legal implications deriving therefrom. Before that, some critical reflection on terminology is provided, particularly as it pertains to the notions of human rights impacts and human rights violations.

4.1 A Note on Terminology: Impact v. Violation

The publication of the UNGPs (Chapter 10) in 2011 caused a number of shifts in the larger BHR discourse. One was that the focus on corporate human rights impacts moved to the center of attention. The terminology of human rights violations, on the other hand, largely disappeared. The UNGPs do not contain a single reference to corporate human rights violations. Instead, they speak of negative human rights impacts. This is not a coincidence and though it seems that the two notions largely address the same thing, they have different connotations, as defined below.

Human rights violations: Generally, a violation occurs if a valid norm is being breached. The norm establishes the standard for legitimate action and thus an obligation to conform. A violation implies the breach of that obligation (Deva 2013: 97). Accordingly, speaking of corporate human rights violations presupposes human rights as valid norms for business, which give rise to respective obligations for companies. Therefore, there is a strong normativity connected to the terminology of violation, which is not the case if we "merely" speak of human rights impacts.

Human rights impacts: Anyone can impact human rights through their actions, independently of whether they do or do not have any human rights obligations. Thus, it is not the breach of a norm that is of interest but rather all actions which may have negative consequences for the enjoyment of human rights. In their interpretive guide on the corporate responsibility to respect human rights, the OHCHR defines an "adverse human rights impact" as an impact that "occurs when an action removes or reduces the ability of an individual to enjoy his or her human rights" (OHCHR 2012: 5). Whether such an action conflicts with a valid norm is irrelevant. Thus, a focus on impacts casts the net wider in terms of the kind of behavior and actions that are addressed, but it does so with lower normativity and authority: "'Impact' is a term with a much wider scope, but lesser rigour than 'violation'" (Deva 2013: 98).

The two views correspond to what has been introduced earlier as deontological and teleological or consequentialist perspectives on human rights (Chapter 3.1.4.1). A deontological perspective emphasizes the responsibility of actors to conform with moral norms and principles. Consequentialism, on the other hand, assesses actions based on whether they result in more good than harm for society.

For Deva (2013: 97), the terminological shift from "violation" to "impact" has the potential to undermine human rights as norms. Impact, as he notes, "appears to devalue both the importance attached to human rights and the consequence of their violation on victims" (Deva 2013: 97). Symptomatically, the UNGPs do not refer to "victims" either, but address them as "adversely affected stakeholders." On the other hand, a consequentialist view of human rights *impacts* expands the range of human rights-relevant corporate behavior and may find fault with certain actions that would not reach the deontological threshold of an actual violation of human rights. Nevertheless, Deva (2013: 97) rightly points out that the focus on impacts perpetuates the "state-centric human rights ideology under which non-state actors such as companies cannot ordinarily have human rights obligations." However, such state-centric views on human rights responsibility are at least contested. This question will be explored in Chapter 6.

4.2   Direct Human Rights Violations

Direct human rights violations occur if companies are immediately responsible for the actions that cause the violation. In such scenarios, the primary perpetrators, are companies who cause the abuse with their own actions or omissions.

According to a 2008 survey conducted in the context of John Ruggie's mandate as the former SRSG (Box 2.2), nearly 60 percent of corporate human rights violations qualified as direct (Wright 2008; see also Ruggie 2013: 23–29). Of these direct cases, 34 percent were connected to the rights of employees and workers. Examples include discrimination of all sorts, but mobbing, harassment, and infringements on privacy are also all frequent occurrences in the workplace (Chapter 5.1). Another 50 percent of direct cases concerned the rights of affected communities, of which the majority occurred as a result of environmental pollution and degradation

(Chapter 5.4). As Chapter 5.3 will show, local communities, with which corporations share space and resources, can be affected by the conduct of corporations in manifold ways. They often are impacted by so-called "externalities" of corporate activity. Externalities are costs that corporations "externalize" in the process of value creation. This means that such costs are not borne by the corporation itself, but by its external environment. As a consequence, such costs are not factored into the prices of the company's goods and services, which results in overconsumption relative to the external burden that they produce. An example is environmental pollution, which can affect the health and livelihoods of people living in the vicinity of the corporation's facilities (Chapter 5.4). If, for example, airlines fail to "internalize" the cost of pollution into their pricing of tickets, airfares will remain artificially low and demand for air travel will go up. This, in turn, results in even more pollution and increases the external burden further. The remaining 16 percent of direct cases in the SRSG's study consisted of negative impacts on end users. Almost all of these cases were related to access to essential medicine. In such cases, prohibitive costs and patent restrictions prevent people from accessing drugs that are critical for their health and sometimes survival. Examples are HIV/AIDS or cancer treatment drugs.

One quintessential BHR challenge surfaces between the lines of the SRSG's study and concerns the relation between parent companies and their subsidiaries and how to account for them in regard to human rights violations. If a corporation does business with an independent supplier that commits human rights violations – for example, by maintaining sweatshop conditions in its factories (Chapter 5.2.2) – this would qualify as an indirect human rights violation, as the corporation contributes to the violation of the supplier through its business relationship, without itself being the cause of the violation. In contrast, if such transgressions are committed by fully owned subsidiaries of the corporation, we tend to look at them as direct violations. For example, if a subsidiary of Nestlé commits human rights violations in Colombia, we tend to look at it as a violation by Nestlé more generally. However, things are not that clear-cut when looking at the scenario from a legal perspective. Even fully owned subsidiaries are considered separate legal entities from the parent company. Therefore, their actions and potential wrongdoing cannot readily be attributed to the parent company, which is one of the reasons why it has proven to be exceedingly difficult for victims of human rights abuse to bring lawsuits against parent companies in order to hold them liable for human rights violations committed by their subsidiaries. Such cases of foreign direct liability will be dealt with in Chapter 12.5.

4.3   Indirect Human Rights Violations

Indirect violations of human rights occur if corporations become implicated in human rights violations committed by a third party. This can happen if a company is involved in, contributes to, or is linked with human rights abuse through its activities and business relations (Ruggie 2011a). In such scenarios, corporations do not cause the violations themselves, but contribute to or are associated with them through their conduct or business relationships.

Indirect human rights violations are often referred to as cases of complicity. More narrowly, complicity means if companies aid and abet human rights violations committed by third parties. Early writings on complicity made reference to the concept only in relation to the state as the primary perpetrator (see e.g. Clapham & Jerbi 2001; Ramasastry 2002). The rationale was that for a company to become complicit, there must be a third party that violated human rights norms and in traditional human rights thinking such a party can only be the state. However, particularly since the UNGPs have recognized corporate human rights responsibility in principle, the concept has been used more broadly, referring also to other institutions such as suppliers, strategic partners, or international organizations as potential primary violators of human rights with whom a company can be complicit.

According to the SRSG's survey (Ruggie 2013: 23-29), some 41 percent of reported human rights abuses were of indirect nature, 44 percent of which (18 percent across all – direct and indirect – violations) occurred in the supply chains of multinational companies. For example, if child labor is detected on cocoa farms from which large food and beverage companies are sourcing, such companies are linked to those violations through maintaining direct or indirect business relationships with them. Human rights violations indeed often occur deep in the multilayered supply chains of multinationals. Accordingly, overseeing and controlling such long and complex supply chains poses a tremendous challenge and can make the prevention of human rights violations a daunting task.

The remaining proportion of indirect cases – roughly 56 percent (23 percent overall) – were connected to human rights violations committed by various other agents, such as governments or arms of governments, individuals, or other business enterprises outside of a company's value chain. For example, such violations can occur if extractive companies hire security guards to protect their facilities and operations. Security personnel are indispensable in the often volatile contexts in which such companies operate. Yet they frequently use excessive force and violence against protesters or unwelcome trespassers, which can result in the abuse of human rights (Chapter 5.3.2).

As the above examples illustrate, there are different ways in which a company can become complicit in human rights violations. Commonly, four main types of complicity are distinguished, which can be clustered as active and passive kinds of complicity. While active complicity implies an active involvement or contribution on the part of the company, passive complicity is based on omissions, that is, on a corporation's failure to act in the face of ongoing human rights abuse.

BOX 4.1 (Short case) Child labor on Côte d'Ivoire's cocoa farms

Almost half of the global supply of cocoa is produced in Côte d'Ivoire. Two thirds come from West Africa. Accordingly, most of the world's largest and most prominent chocolate manufacturers – among them Nestlé, Cargill, Barry Callebaut, Mars, Olam, Ferrero, Hershey, and Mondelēz – are sourcing cocoa in the region (Whoriskey & Siegel 2019; Balch 2021). The workforce on the cocoa farms in West Africa consists in large part of migrant workers, many of them children, sometimes as young as ten years of age. It is estimated that more than 2 million children are engaged in dangerous and hazardous work on West Africa's cocoa farms (Whoriskey & Siegel 2019). The children are often unaccompanied by parents, trafficked across the border from Burkina Faso, and exposed to agro-chemical products, lifting of heavy loads, or using sharp tools to harvest the cocoa beans – activities that frequently cause accidents. Many of the children are undernourished and lack safe and sanitary living conditions and access to school.

In 2001, the world's largest chocolate manufacturers such as Nestlé, Mars, and Hershey pledged to establish a certification system and eradicate the worst form of child labor from their cocoa supply chains by signing the so-called Harking-Engel Protocol. The Protocol specified 2005 as the deadline to achieve this goal. In return, chocolate manufacturers would avoid binding regulation. However, twenty years after signing the pledge and fifteen years past the original deadline, the companies are still far from meeting the agreement, despite having spent more than $180 million on the issue across the industry (Whoriskey & Siegel 2019). Child labor is still rampant on cocoa farms in West Africa and the companies are often still in the dark about the sources of their cocoa. Controlling hundreds of thousands of cocoa farms in the remote forests of West Africa is a daunting, if not impossible, task. Mars is currently able to trace 25 percent of its cocoa to the individual farm level; Hershey and Nestlé manage to trace about half of their cocoa to their source (Whoriskey & Siegel 2019). Accordingly, none of them is able to guarantee that its products – examples include M&M's, Snickers, and Toblerone – are free of child labor.

In February 2021, eight former child laborers launched a lawsuit in Washington, DC, against some of the largest chocolate brands on the basis of the Trafficking Victims Protection Reauthorization Act of 2017. The lawsuit alleges complicity of the corporations in the illegal enslavement of "thousands" of children on cocoa farms. The lawsuit also alleges that the companies have actively misled the public about their commitment to the 2001 Harkin-Engel Protocol (Balch 2021). Another lawsuit against Nestlé and Cargill that was targeting child slavery in their cocoa supply chains was brought under the Alien Tort Claims Act (ATCA) in 2005 (Chapter 14.5.1). However, the lawsuit was dismissed by the US Supreme Court in June 2021 based on the presumption against extraterritoriality (Chapter 12.5.3.2).

Discussion Questions

(1) Over the last twenty years, the chocolate industry has spent more than $180 million on the eradication of child labor in their cocoa supply chains. By comparison, it collected $103 billion in sales of its chocolate products. Are the companies allocating sufficient priority and resources to addressing the issue, in your opinion?

(2) Are lawsuits against the chocolate companies an effective means to pressure them to do more toward the eradication of child labor in their supply chains?

(3) Controlling hundreds of thousands of small cocoa farms seems an almost impossible task. Against this background, did the chocolate companies make an unachievable commitment back in 2001? If you were a human rights manager at one of those companies, how would you suggest going about effectively implementing the agreement? What actions would you take to work toward fulfilling the commitment?

(4) Can and should multinational chocolate manufacturers be blamed for the child labor situation on Côte d'Ivoire's cocoa farms? What is the state's and what is the companies' responsibility? As the human rights manager of such a company, on what government measures would you insist in order to make your own efforts more effective?

4.3.1 Active Complicity

There are two variations of active complicity, one direct and one indirect. Some commentators and most international standards such as the UNGC or the UNGPs deal with them together under the heading of direct complicity. However, for the sake of a better and more differentiated understanding, they are listed separately here. As mentioned above, active complicity requires an active contribution by the company. Such a contribution can happen either as direct involvement or indirect facilitation.

- *Direct complicity* refers to a corporation's direct involvement in and contribution to specific human rights violations committed by a third party. For example, a company may provide equipment such as vehicles or helicopters to local police or security forces, which are then used to violently suppress the protests of local populations, or it may offer up its facilities for such forces to detain, mistreat, or even torture people.

- *Indirect complicity* does not require a company's direct contribution, but rather an indirect facilitation of human rights violations. A corporation that partners up and does business with regimes that are notorious for systematically violating human rights may not contribute to such violations in direct and causal ways. Yet, the business relationships bolster the economic position and viability of the regime and thus facilitate the continuation of such harmful policies and practices.

Even skeptics of corporate human rights responsibility may find some plausibility in cases of active complicity, at least as they pertain to governments as primary perpetrators. In such cases, one can see fault with the involvement of corporations even without acknowledging any particular human rights responsibility of companies and without abandoning the state-centrism that underlies traditional human rights thinking. The actual violation in such a scenario is committed by a government and it seems wrong, whether we do or do not acknowledge any human rights responsibility for corporations themselves, to aid and abet such violations.

4.3.2 Passive Complicity

Passive complicity does not derive from specific actions of corporations, but rather from their omission to act. In other words, the corporation remains passive when it should be responding actively to human rights violations. Two types of passive complicity are commonly distinguished: beneficial and silent complicity.

- *Beneficial complicity* occurs if a corporation benefits directly from ongoing and systematic human rights violations. It is commonly agreed that two conditions need to be fulfilled in order for benefit to turn into complicity: First, the corporation is receiving benefits from systematic and ongoing human rights violations over an extended period of time. Hence, beneficial complicity is not about more or less coincidental, one-off benefits that corporations may gain from isolated human rights violations. Rather, it is about cases in which companies knowingly benefit from violations on an ongoing basis. Second, the corporation remains passive in the face of such benefit. It is content reaping the benefits without changing anything about the situation. For example, the ongoing suppression of local dissent and protests by public security forces may allow extractive businesses to keep operating without major disruptions. Even if the company is otherwise not connected to the acts of such security forces, it nevertheless benefits directly from their ongoing acts of oppression.
- *Silent complicity* is similar to beneficial complicity but without the requirement of benefit. Thus, silent complicity occurs if a company that is in a position to prevent, mitigate, or stop systematic and ongoing human rights

violations, fails to do so, and instead silently tolerates and condones the abuse that occurs in its vicinity. Hence, companies that have little influence and leverage over the perpetrator and may not be in a position to effectively oppose its human rights violations may not qualify as complicit if they remain silent. Shell's passive stance toward the arrest and execution of Ken Saro-Wiwa in Nigeria in 1995 (Chapter 2.1) is often referred to as an example of silent complicity. Commentators generally agree that as one of the most powerful companies in the country, Shell would have had the power to exert at least some pressure and influence on the Nigerian government to drop charges against Saro-Wiwa and his followers. Instead, the company decided not to interfere and remained silent.

It is important to note that the claim inherent in both beneficial and silent complicity is not merely that it is morally wrong to benefit or remain silent in the face of human rights violations. Instead, the claim is that silence and benefit can turn companies into actual accomplices and thus into parties, rather than mere bystanders, to the violation. Both benefit and silence can be expressions of moral support and thus serve to legitimize the violation and encourage the perpetrator to continue or even expand the harmful practices. Such moral support can then be interpreted as a contribution, albeit a passive one, to the human rights violation. Again, this legitimizing effect of a corporation's silence increases, the more powerful the corporation is and the more extensive its possibilities would be to counteract the violations (Wettstein 2010; 2012c).

The claim underlying such passive complicity is arguably quite far-reaching, since, as we will see, it implies corporate human rights obligations of the positive kind (Chapter 7.3.2). However, it is noteworthy that all major international policy and soft-law instruments in the BHR domain, such as the UNGPs, the UNGC, or the OECD Guidelines for Multinational Enterprises, expressly accept and include silence and benefit as parameters of corporate complicity. They do so for good reason; the silent condonement of human rights abuse by actors in positions of power and authority (Chapter 6.1.3) can be instrumental in creating and fostering an environment in which human rights abuse is rampant and goes unchallenged.

4.3.3 Moral and Legal Elements of Complicity

Complicity, as it is used in the BHR discussion and elsewhere, is informed essentially by international criminal law. Lawyers commonly distinguish between a material (*actus reus*) and a mental (*mens rea*) requirement that must be met or fulfilled in order to establish a case of complicity. These are essential elements also for an ethical qualification of complicity; however, as we will see, an assessment from an ethical perspective differs from a legal one.

- *Actus reus*: The material element of complicity refers to the kind of assistance that the corporation has provided in the commission of a human rights violation. Lawyers commonly argue that a company's aiding and abetting must have a substantial effect on the human rights violation in order to be of legal relevance. However, substantiality does not necessarily mean indispensability; it is not required that a violation would not have taken place at all if not for the contribution of the corporation, but merely that it would not have taken place in the same way and to the same extent. Neither does substantiality necessarily require concrete, tangible actions of great magnitude and scope. Rather, it may "accumulate" over time if a company provides ongoing support over an extended duration (Ramasastry 2002: 150; Clapham 2004: 63f).
- *Mens rea*: It is generally agreed that the necessary mental element of complicity cases is knowledge. A corporation can become complicit in human rights abuse if it knows or should know (can reasonably be expected to know) that its conduct may contribute to the violation of human rights. From this point of view, complicity does not presuppose intent to do harm or ill will on the part of the corporation. It is not necessary that the corporation shares the intention of the perpetrator or otherwise intended or wanted to commit an offense. However, particularly with a view on complicity liability, it is unclear what the required standard is under international criminal law (Bernaz 2017: 271–274). For example, the statute of the ICC establishes criminal complicity if a person aids and abets "for the purpose of facilitating the commission of [such] a crime" (United Nations 2002: Article 25 (3) (c)), implying that mere knowledge is not sufficient. Accordingly, some domestic courts have applied such a purpose test in ATCA litigation, thereby raising the bar substantially for victims of corporate human rights abuse to get justice.

The threshold to make a legal case for complicity is thus quite high. However, the absence of a legal case does not imply that there cannot be moral blame. An ethical assessment is prone to set the bar lower, since it tends to emphasize only one of the two elements, while giving less importance to the respective other one. Thereby, whether contribution or mental state is emphasized, depends again on whether we adopt a deontological or a more consequentialist perspective on the issue.

A deontological perspective tends to prioritize the mental state of a corporation. What counts is not whether a contribution is substantial, but rather whether the corporation knowingly breached a moral or social norm. Hence, a deontological perspective would suggest that any kind of association with or contribution to a human rights violation is subject to blameworthiness, even if it is rather insignificant in terms of substantiality. Blameworthiness derives from the sheer willingness of the corporation to knowingly conduct its business in ways that are linked to human rights violations.

BOX 4.2 (Short case) Doing business in Xinjiang

Xinjiang is a large autonomous region in north-western China which is inhabited by about 12 million Uyghurs and other Muslim minority groups. Relations between the region and China have been tense since the 1990s and the rise of separatist movements in the area. Under the pretext of protecting national security and fighting terrorism, the Chinese government gradually increased repression of the Muslim population in Xinjiang, subjected them to constant surveillance, and forced them to abandon their religion, cultural practices, and local languages (Amnesty International 2021; BBC 2021). As a part of the repressive measures, the government arbitrarily detained hundreds of thousands of Uyghurs both in prisons and in internment camps. These camps are officially defined as "re-education camps." However, witness testimonies point to the systematic use of torture, violence, and degrading and dehumanizing treatment of detainees (Amnesty International 2021; BBC 2021).

The fate and whereabouts of detainees is often unknown. Thousands end up in forced labor settings in the production of cotton, yarn, shoes, solar panels, and various other sectors. With China being the largest cotton producer in the world and 84 percent of its cotton coming from the Xinjiang region, it is estimated that as many as one in five cotton products worldwide contain forced labor from the Xinjiang region, as many of the leading global fashion and clothing brands continue to source from there (Kelly 2020). The Australian Strategic Policy Institute has identified countless supply chains that may be affected by Uyghur forced labor, including those of at least 82 major global brands, such as Nike, Amazon, Apple, and H&M (Xu et al. 2020). Many companies have publicly raised concerns about the ongoing human rights violations and labor abuses, and international pressure on China has been mounting. As a reaction to the increased international pressure, some Western brands have faced consumer boycotts by the Chinese public and the Chinese government has signaled clearly to Western companies that it does not tolerate any criticism from them.

Discussion Questions

(1) Are Western clothing brands complicit in the human rights violations committed against the Uyghur population? What types of complicity, if any, do you identify?

(2) Are we as consumers complicit? What is our role and responsibility with regard to the situation in Xinjiang?

(3) You are the human rights manager of a Western company manufacturing sewing machines. Your company has production facilities in Xinjiang. In what ways do you risk becoming implicated in the ongoing human rights violations in the area?

(4) Knowing the risk of becoming complicit in the widespread abuse, should you close down your factory in Xinjiang? Even if your company may not be directly contributing to the human rights violations, should you speak out against the abuse? If so, how would you go about it?

A teleological perspective would assess these elements precisely the other way around. The mental state of the corporation is of secondary importance. Rather, what counts is whether the practical assistance provided had a significant, or substantial, impact on the human rights violation. Whether such impacts derived from knowingly negligent or even intentional action on the part of the company is of less concern from a consequentialist perspective.

STUDY QUESTIONS

1. What is the difference between a "human rights violation" and a "human rights impact"? Why does it matter what terminology we use with regard to corporate conduct?

2. What is the difference between direct and indirect human rights violations? Why is it important to differentiate between the two?

3. What are the two types of active and the two types of passive complicity? Provide examples of each and explain how they differ from one another.

4. What are externalities? Name three instances in which externalities can occur.

REFLECTION QUESTIONS

1. Reflect on deontological and consequentialist perspectives as they relate to corporate complicity. In your personal opinion, which do you believe to be more plausible?

2. Under what circumstances can the silence of companies and their benefitting from human rights violations turn them into actual accomplices and thus parties to the violations? Is it appropriate to consider a company to be an accomplice of a human rights violation for the mere fact that it benefits from it or does not try to stop it?

3. How far do companies have to go to avoid silent complicity? What is required of them to prevent, mitigate, or stop human rights violations in their proximity?

4. "Human rights violations often occur deep in the multilayered supply chains of multinationals. Overseeing and controlling such long and complex value chains is a big challenge and can make the prevention of human rights violations a daunting task." What can companies do? Name some ideas of how to oversee and control such long and complex value chains and some mechanisms for doing this.

5 Corporate Human Rights Violations: Overview of Issues

When John Ruggie took over as the SRSG in 2005, he criticized the recently abandoned UN Draft Norms on various grounds and made it clear that his mandate would pursue a different approach. One particular criticism was that the UN Draft Norms did not cover the full spectrum of human rights. Ruggie was convinced that corporate activities can impact all human rights in various ways, which is why it is important not to exclude any of them at the outset by drawing the list too narrowly. This section will provide a brief overview of some of the more common human rights violations with corporate involvement. The non-exhaustive overview aims at providing some first insights into how corporate conduct can affect and impact human rights and at showing the breadth of issues that fall under a BHR lens. Hence, the focus of this section is on problems, rather than on solutions. The issues and violations dealt with were selected as they pertain particularly to multinational corporations and they are cross-cutting – that is, not specific to one particular industry. Industry-specific issues and challenges will be dealt with in Chapter 14. Together, this chapter and Chapter 14 will provide an extensive collection of the most pertinent BHR issues.

5.1 Employment Relations

This section looks at the direct relations of multinational corporations with their own employees and human rights issues that can arise within such relations. However, it does not deal with labor conditions in the facilities of suppliers along the value chain, which will be dealt with in the subsequent section.

5.1.1 Discrimination and Harassment

Within formal employment relations, discrimination and harassment are among the most frequent human rights issues and they occur at every stage of the employment process, from recruitment to termination. Discrimination occurs if people are systematically excluded from work-related benefits, such as employment, promotion, and training based on arbitrary criteria, which are unrelated to their qualifications, work performance, or other functional requirements that would justify such an exclusion. The most relevant and frequent kinds of discrimination in human rights terms concern gender, race, sexual orientation, religion, disability, age, and body type. Frequently, business also provides a context not only for work-related discrimination against certain groups of people, but also for broader social exclusion, mobbing, and harassment. Such types of harassment can range from sexual harassment all the way to homophobic or racist abuse.

Many global brands have stepped up their efforts in fostering pluralistic and diverse business cultures in recent years. They have not only become less lenient in sanctioning discriminatory and abusive behavior, but have also proactively implemented affirmative action measures and progressive policies on equal treatment in a variety of domains. An example is the recent movement to install separate bathrooms for non-binary and transgender people at the workplace. Businesses have been at the forefront in pushing progressive policies on equal treatment and diversity not only in their own facilities but also beyond their own business in society at large. Nevertheless, particularly in terms of equal representation of diverse groups on the boards and in the top management of companies, much more needs to be done even in the most progressive countries to date.

5.1.2   Monitoring and Privacy

The success of a business depends on the performance of its employees. Against this background, it seems only natural that companies put certain systems in place to make sure that employees indeed meet the expectations or at least do not use their paid worktime to perform tasks that are unrelated to their job. But how far can such monitoring systems go and at what point do they start to illegitimately infringe on the privacy of the employees? What is a company allowed to know about its employees and what information should be protected as private? In particular, the rapid development of new technologies has dramatically enhanced the possibilities for employers to monitor their employees, who are sometimes put under almost complete surveillance. Often there are laws that prohibit such extensive surveillance. But the more advanced technological surveillance instruments become, the more we are moving beyond existing regulation and into grey zones of responsible conduct.

Gaining private information about employees by accessing e-mails and social media accounts, testing for drugs and other substances, screening health, or tracking internet use, among other things, can also set the grounds for subsequent discriminatory practices by the employer. Thus, the infringement of privacy rights may lead to further violations of the right to equal treatment.

BOX 5.1 (Short case) Workplace Surveillance

Employee performance tracking and surveillance has increased at an exponential rate and become more invasive in recent years (Benson 2018). The problem has been compounded by the COVID-19 pandemic, during which millions of employees worked remotely from home and employers intensified their efforts to keep a level of control over their work performance (O'Flaherty 2020). In this context, Microsoft introduced a new tool for employers called "Productivity Score" in the fall of 2020. The tool allowed employers to closely track all Office 365 activity of their employees and thus to monitor in what way and for how long they use services like Teams, Outlook, SharePoint, and OneDrive or software such as Word, Excel, or PowerPoint and on what device (O'Flaherty 2020). Microsoft insisted that the tool was meant to provide IT administrators insight about infrastructure and technology usage in their company, but it quickly faced a firestorm of outrage by privacy advocates who criticized the tool's large potential to be misused for surveillance purposes. They were worried not only about the privacy infringement as such but also about the psychological effects that constant workplace surveillance can have on employees. Being under surveillance can cause stress and anxiety, which can impact the well-being and health of employees and, ultimately, backfire also in terms of decreasing, rather than increasing, productivity (Benson 2018; O'Flaherty 2020). In response to the widespread outrage, Microsoft ended up changing the user interface and removed individual user names from the tracking tool. Instead, metrics will be aggregated across the company, in order to prevent employers from using the tool to surveil individual employees (O'Flaherty 2020; Sandler 2020).

Many other companies have intensified their efforts to track and monitor employees (Benson 2018). Amazon, for example, closely tracks the productivity of its warehouse workers and generates automated warnings or even terminations if productivity slips below certain thresholds (Jee 2021). The delivery service UPS collects extensive data on the performance of its drivers, recording by the second, for example, when truck doors are opened and closed, when seat belts are buckled, when the engine is started and turned off, and how many times their drivers are backing up during the day and at what speed (Goldstein 2014; Benson 2018). The company justifies such practices with hard numbers: A productivity loss of one minute per driver per day over a year costs the company $14.5 million (Goldstein 2014). Hence, optimizing delivery times down to the second saves the company millions across its whole fleet.

Furthermore, as a result of such optimization, the number of daily deliveries per driver has gone up substantially and, as a consequence in some cases, driver remuneration also (Goldstein 2014).

Discussion Questions

(1) How far can employers legitimately go in tracking the performance of their employees? How would you define the line between a justified concern about a justified monitoring of employees' performance and an unjustified infringement of their privacy? What are relevant criteria that define that line?

(2) Microsoft altered the features of its Performance Score product in response to criticism. Is it really Microsoft's responsibility to make sure that employers do not use the product for illegitimate purposes? As the Microsoft product manager, how would you have responded to the backlash?

(3) As a concerned employer who is hesitant to use such tracking technology on your employees, what possibilities and alternatives do you have to make sure your employees perform well in remote work settings?

5.2 Workers in the Supply Chain

Modern multinational companies often maintain large webs of sometimes thousands of suppliers and sub-suppliers that extend into remote corners of the world. Needless to say, keeping oversight, let alone adequate governance, over these countless tiers is a formidable challenge. Accordingly, many of the human rights violations that we commonly perceive as "typical" of the corporate context occur within the value chains of multinationals and often concern the treatment and conditions of low-wage workers.

5.2.1 Child Labor

Child labor is still a common occurrence and one of the main BHR problems in a number of sectors such as agriculture, mining, and the garment and footwear industry. It is often connected to contexts of poverty. While the number of child laborers has declined significantly since the turn of the millennium, around 152 million children still are engaged in child labor worldwide (International Labour Office 2017: 5). Child labor is prohibited by a number of international legal instruments, such as the UN Convention on the Rights of the Child (UNCRC), as well as the ILO Minimum Age Convention (No. 138), and the ILO Worst Forms of Child Labour Convention (No. 182). In 2020, Convention No. 182 became the first ILO convention in history to achieve universal ratification from all 187 member countries (UN News

2020). This international treaty protects children from slavery, forced labor, trafficking, recruitment for armed conflict, prostitution, pornography, illicit activities, and hazardous work. It requires ratifying countries to take immediate action to prohibit and eliminate any work that is harmful by its nature to the health, safety, or morals of children (International Labour Organization 1999).

Not all forms of work by children qualify as prohibited child labor. Children and adolescents engage in many different kinds of work such as helping in family businesses and earning money outside of the school hours. As long as this does not negatively affect their health and personal development and does not interfere with their education, it is commonly not seen as concerning and sometimes even qualified as positive (International Labour Office 2004: 14). Accordingly, child labor is commonly defined as work that deprives children of their childhood, their potential and their dignity, and that is harmful to their physical and mental development (International Labour Office 2004: 14). Prohibited is work that is mentally, physically, socially, or morally dangerous and harmful to children, and interferes with their schooling, meaning that it deprives them of the opportunity to attend school, forces them to leave school prematurely, or requires them to attempt to combine school attendance with excessively long and heavy work (International Labour Office 2004: 14). ILO Convention No. 138 puts the minimum age for children to work at fifteen years, but leaves the possibility to reduce it to fourteen years for countries that lack appropriate economic and educational infrastructure. For light work that does not interfere with a child's education, the minimum age is thirteen years and this can be reduced to twelve years for countries lacking adequate educational and economic facilities. Hazardous work is prohibited under the age of eighteen years in any case. As the International Labour Office (2004: 14) points out:

> Whether or not particular forms of 'work' can be called 'child labour' depends on the child's age, the type and hours of work performed, the conditions under which it is performed and the objectives pursued by individual countries. The answer varies from country to country, as well as among sectors within countries.

One of the main drivers of child labor is poverty. Poor families, particularly in the Global South, often have no other option than to put their children to work in order to survive. According to the International Labour Organization and United Nations Children's Fund (2020: 8), a one percentage point rise in poverty can lead to "at least a 0.7 per cent increase in child labour." Accordingly, there are no easy solutions to this problem. It is commonly agreed that simply banning child labor across the board will achieve little and risks making the situation worse for the affected families. Rather, adequate solutions must aim at the elimination of the problematic, harmful features of the respective work (Chapter 14.5.3 and Box 4.1).

5.2.2   Exploitation and Sweatshop Labor

The term sweatshop work is commonly used for notoriously precarious, unsafe, unsanitary, and unhealthy working conditions. Workers in sweatshop conditions are often exploited, work long hours for little pay, and are frequently exposed to harassment and abuse. They may not be allowed to take any breaks, sometimes not even to use bathrooms. Factory doors are often locked during working hours, to prevent workers from leaving their workplace, which can have devastating consequences in case of factory fires or building collapses (Box 6.1 and Box 14.5).

Defenders of sweatshop labor commonly argue that such working conditions are a necessary stage on the path to prosperity and that economic development will eventually lead to improvements of workers' rights. After all, the West went through the same issues in its development trajectory. They also tend to point to the fact that workers often subject themselves to such working conditions voluntarily. No one forces them to work in such factories, but they do so anyway, because, for them, such work is still better than no work at all. In other words, if such factories were to be shut down, the workers would be out of work and even worse off than they are now. Opponents of this position, on the other hand, argue that in today's day and age there would be means available to prevent such exploitation by holding multinational companies accountable for the governance of their value chains. For them, the violation of workers' rights does not need to be an inevitable part of economic development. Furthermore, it is deceptive to speak of free choice of work if the dire living conditions of the workers force them to subject themselves to exploitation and abuse in order to survive. It is correct that simply shutting down such factories is not the solution. If multinational companies respond to such conditions by dropping suppliers altogether, the situation for the workers will likely worsen. Therefore, multinational companies should collaborate with their suppliers and invest in building capacity for the long-term improvement of working conditions (Chapter 14.4.3).

5.2.3   Forced Labor and Modern Slavery

Slavery is not a thing of the past. Roughly 40 million men, women, and children were victims of modern slavery in 2016, including around 25 million people in forced labor (International Labour Office & Walk Free Foundation 2017: 5; Walk Free Foundation 2018: 10); 71 percent of modern slavery victims were women and girls (International Labour Office & Walk Free Foundation 2017: 5). According to the International Labour Office (2014), a total of $150 billion is generated annually worldwide through forced labor. The term "modern slavery" is often used as a non-legal umbrella term for situations in which men, women, and children are forced to work as a result of intimidation or violence (LeBaron 2020: 7; Scarpa 2018: 6; Walk Free Foundation 2018: 7). In essence, modern slavery can be seen as the systemic and severe exploitation of labor (LeBaron 2020: 9), often connected with human trafficking, debt bondage, and sexual exploitation.

Most forms of modern slavery are covered by the ILO's definition of forced labor, which the Forced Labour Convention (No. 29) of 1930 defines as involuntary work or service performed under threat of punishment. The interpretation by the ILO's Committee of Experts (International Labour Office 2007: 20–21) includes physical, financial, and psychological coercion, but expressly excludes economic coercion. This has been criticized by LeBaron et al. (2018: 10), who emphasize that people across the world routinely submit themselves to exploitative labor relationships as "doing so represents their best or only available option." In spite of international legal commitments to prohibit various forms of modern slavery, many countries still have not criminalized forced labor (Schwarz & Allain 2020: 8). However, a number of countries such as the UK, Australia, and Canada have recently enacted modern slavery legislation, or are in the process of doing so (Chapter 12.4.1.1).

Modern slavery and forced labor are widespread in a number of industries such as food and beverage (Chapter 14.5) or the garment and footwear sector (Chapter 14.4). Trafficking is endemic in the sex industry; but housekeeping and building maintenance, construction and the global hotel industry have also been shown to be intimately connected to modern slavery. One reason for such sectors to be susceptible to forced labor and modern slavery is that they deal with and employ people who experience more structural disadvantages in regard to market access and thus face an increased risk of labor exploitation. Women, youth, or migrant workers in particular are among such groups (Minderoo Foundation et al. 2019: 8). Furthermore, such vulnerable groups often work in relatively low skilled jobs that are often outsourced to companies that operate in relative obscurity and thus increase the risk of exploitation even further. Examples of such outsourced work in the hotel sector are cleaning and housekeeping, shuttle and bus drivers, or tourist guides (Minderoo Foundation et al. 2019: 9).

5.3 Affected Communities

Business activities not only affect the rights of employees and workers along the supply chain but can also have adverse impacts on the communities in which they are embedded or in whose proximity they operate.

5.3.1 Land-Grabbing and Displacement

Land grabbing occurs when private and sometimes public investors take control of often large areas of land in order to benefit from its use and exploitation. For example, agricultural companies require massive amounts of land to build large monocultures for the production of palm oil and biofuels. Likewise, large development projects, for example dams or wind farms, require large areas of land, as do the operations of extractive companies mining for copper, zinc, and other metals and minerals. For such companies, land and the raw materials, water, and other benefits the land offers, are key components of their business models. Accordingly, they are willing to invest large amounts of capital to gain control over such land.

Land grabs can occur legally or illegally, but often happen in grey zones of the law. Such land deals are often lacking in transparency and adequate assessments of social, environmental, and economic impacts. Accordingly, they may not contain any clear and binding commitments regarding the sharing of benefits with local communities and the mitigation of adverse impacts (International Land Coalition 2011). Hence the acquisition of land by investors often comes at the expense of peasant farmers and local communities, whose rights are violated in the process, and of biodiversity more generally (Borras Jr. et al. 2012: 851; TNI Agrarian Justice Programme 2013: 3; Baker-Smith & Miklos Attila 2016: 15). Land grabs can be made by any person or entity (public or private, foreign or domestic) through ownership, lease, concession, contracts, quotas, or general power (Baker-Smith & Miklos Attila 2016: 15). The focus is commonly on large land deals made by foreign investors, but land grabs are also made by domestic actors and are often connected to corruption and bribery (Hall 2011). Land deals are often obscure, and their extent worldwide is difficult to estimate. However, the prominent example of the South Korean Daewoo conglomerate in Madagascar reveals the dimensions of some land grabs. In 2008, Daewoo leased 1.3 million hectares of land in Madagascar for food cultivation; this amounted to about half of the island's agricultural land (Ouma 2012: 171). This led to nationwide unrest and ultimately to the overthrow of Madagascar's president (Vinciguerra 2011). As a result, the new government cancelled the contract with Daewoo.

A consequence of land grabs is that local communities are sometimes forced to leave their lands and relocate. In other instances, they may remain on their lands, but are cut off from vital waterways, lose large chunks of grazing grounds for their cattle, or are otherwise negatively affected by the externalities of the land use. It is not uncommon that such communities are not, or not adequately, consulted by the government before it strikes such land deals with investors and the rights of community members are not considered sufficiently. Thus, the requirement of obtaining free, prior, and informed consent (FPIC) (Chapter 5.5.1) from local populations is often disregarded. As a consequence, local communities may face forceful removal and displacement from their lands to make space for the planned projects or business operations and they are often not adequately compensated for their losses. They may be relocated to areas with less fertile agricultural land that lack access to fishing grounds or have inadequate access to water or other natural resources. Thus, besides losing their homes and ancestral lands, such communities often are threatened with losing their livelihoods and may slide even deeper into poverty and despair. While there is no internationally recognized human right to land as such, land grabbing, particularly if it is connected to the forceful eviction of local people from their homes, affects a variety of other human rights such as the right to food, water, health, or basic subsistence (Cotula 2014: 17).

5.3.2   Security and Protest

Some of the most egregious business-related human rights violations are connected to the provision of security. Particularly in contexts of high volatility, conflict, and weak institutions, it is common, sometimes essential, for businesses to secure their premises and operations from trespassers, vandalism, or sabotage. Particularly in the extractive industries, arrangements with private or public security forces for this purpose are a regular part of doing business. Unfortunately, the use of force and violence is similarly common among such security personnel to keep intruders off company premises and human rights violations are a frequent result of that. Furthermore, the power differential between the security personnel and those affected by the business operations can lead to abuse and exploitation. Human Rights violations in such contexts can range from harassment to physical abuse, torture, and rape, all the way to killings (Box 5.2). The responses of security and police forces to protests against business operations can be similarly brutal. In order to protect businesses from disruptions, protests are frequently crushed by excessive force and violence, and by arbitrary detentions and arrests.

5.3.3   Conflict

Businesses that operate in contexts of conflict often face a particular challenge with regard to the prevention of negative human rights impacts. Companies can provide stability and development and can be a force for peace in such contexts (Katsos 2020). However, they can also contribute to and exacerbate conflicts and they can get drawn into becoming a party to egregious human rights abuses if they fail to implement adequate precautions (Ruggie 2013: 29). For example, companies may trade minerals and precious metals from mines under the control of armed groups, with the revenues then being used to finance the conflict. Or they may directly pay money to the parties in conflict in order to protect their personnel and to make sure they can keep operating without major disruptions. But such payments contribute to the funding of the parties in conflict and thus to prolonging the conflict and the violence. The case of Chiquita Brands in Colombia is now well documented. Between 1997 and 2004, Chiquita made payments to paramilitary groups on both sides of the conflict in order to keep its employees safe. However, by doing so, the company itself was drawn ever deeper into the conflict. As a consequence and in addition to a criminal complaint that the company settled for $25 million with the US government, the families of victims of the conflict brought a case against the company for complicity in extrajudicial killings, torture, forced disappearances, crimes against humanity, and war crimes under the ATCA (Chapter 12.5.3) in

BOX 5.2 (Short case) The 'Marikana massacre'

On August 16, 2012, the South African Police Service opened fire on striking platinum miners at the Marikana mine, which was owned by the British mining company Lonmin and located 80 miles (130 km) north of Johannesburg, South Africa. The shooting killed thirty-four and injured seventy-eight people, in an event that came to be known as the Marikana massacre (Alexander 2013: 608; Davies 2015). The Marikana massacre was the culmination of a week-long strike in which workers protested low pay, long shifts of twelve hours a day or more, and unsafe and precarious working and living conditions (Alexander 2013: 608). Violence during the week ahead of the massacre left ten people dead, which put the total death toll at 44.

While in the aftermath of the massacre much of the focus was on the excessive force applied by police forces, an inquiry commission set up by the government was critical also of the role that the company played in the lead-up to the incident. The commission argued that Lonmin failed to engage in the resolution of the disputes to the best of its abilities and to respond appropriately to the threat and outbreak of violence (Marikana Commission of Inquiry 2015). Lonmin had earlier agreed to a legally binding commitment to provide 5,500 housing units for workers, but failed to keep its promise and instead left its workers to live in substandard informal settlements (Hamann 2019). The failure to live up to such commitments was found to have contributed to "an environment conducive to the creation of tension, labor unrest, disunity among its employees or other harmful conduct" (Marikana Commission of Inquiry 2015: 542). Furthermore, the company is said to have provided critical logistical support for the police, including access to over 200 security cameras, helicopters ambulances, and a detention center, as well as intelligence collected by security personnel, and offices, food, and transport for police forces (Alexander 2013: 609).

The company itself, despite being praised for engaging in a number of remedy initiatives, such as the design of a memorial site and setting up a trust fund for victims and their families (Yeomans 2017), has staunchly denied any responsibility for the incident, blaming it on a fallout between rival unions instead.

Discussion Questions

(1) Private security contractors and police forces are often used in contexts of high volatility, conflict, and weak institutions in order to secure premises from vandalism, trespassers, and sabotage. Yet there remain many instances, as described above, in which they commit egregious human rights abuses. In your opinion, how can the tension between the protection of property and the protection of human rights be resolved?

(2) Beyond the shooting incident, many commentators have pointed to the structural roots of the Marikana massacre. What might they be referring to when they speak of structural causes of the incident? If we understand BHR as a structural issue, what would have to be done in order to prevent such incidents from happening again? What do governments need to do? What is the responsibility of companies?

(3) How do you make sense of the company's empathic and proactive engagement in remedial mechanisms on the one hand and its unwillingness to acknowledge any responsibility for the incident on the other? How can these two "faces" of the company be reconciled?

2007 (Ruggie 2013: 29–30; BHRRC, n.d. (a)). However, the case was ultimately thrown out by the US Supreme Court in 2014, which, in the aftermath of the seminal *Kiobel* ruling (Chapter 12.5.3.2), argued that the case lacked a substantial connection to the US (BHRRC, n.d. (a)). Nevertheless, a number of new class action lawsuits have been filed in US courts against the company since then (BHRRC, n.d. (a)). Another more recent case involves the French-Swiss cement producer LafargeHolcim. In order to keep operations in their Syrian plant going during the civil war in that country, the company made payments of €13 million to terrorist groups in 2013 and 2014. A criminal case against the company is currently pending (Box 12.9).

5.4 Environment

While environmental degradation and pollution have long been viewed as separate from human rights issues and have therefore not featured prominently in BHR, there has been a more recent push to analyze the specific human rights impacts that emanate from the destruction of the environment and thus to integrate these issues as genuine human rights issues into the BHR discussion. Various scholars have even presented arguments as to why actual environmental rights – that is, rights to an intact and safe environment – are to feature among human rights and a variety of international accords referenced environmental rights as third-generation human rights (Chapter 3.3.1) held by all human beings (Hiskes 2014: 399). Such movements and theories that explore and advocate for the link between the environment, its use and destruction, and the various positive and negative impacts on people that emanate from it often are subsumed under the label of "environmental justice."

Similar connections have recently been drawn between BHR and climate change. Climate change will be taken up separately as an emerging discussion in the BHR field in Chapter 15.2.

5.4.1   Contamination of Air, Soil, and Water

Pollution is one of the most persistent problems connected to business activity per se and it can affect human rights directly and immediately. The pollution of the air through particulate matter can lead to severe respiratory problems for people living near cement plants, for example. Residues of pesticides used by agribusinesses can stay in the ground for years and contaminate drinking water. Toxic waste from the extraction process in the mining industry frequently pollutes rivers and agricultural land. Similarly, bleach and other chemicals used in the garment industry often pollute and contaminate soil and water. Oil spills have caused environmental disasters across the world and gas flares are a major source of emissions in the oil and gas industry. As mentioned in Chapter 2, the environmental toll and the resulting human rights impacts created by oil extraction in the Niger Delta and the subsequent violent crackdown on the resulting protests of the local Ogoni population was one of the defining incidents that gave rise to the BHR movement in the 1990s.

Environmental degradation and pollution affect a number of human rights such as the right to clean water, the right to food, the right to health, and not least the right to life itself. Because a clean and healthy environment is the presupposition of our enjoyment of many if not all other human rights, the calls for formal recognition of the human right to a healthy environment have become louder and more frequent in recent years. In a report on the subject, the former UN Special Rapporteur on Human Rights and the Environment, John H. Knox, recalled that the right to a healthy environment is widely recognized by a majority of states in their domestic legislations and constitutions. As a consequence, the HRC formally recognized access to a clean and healthy environment as a fundamental human right in October 2021. Nevertheless, there are still severe gaps in the international infrastructure aimed at the protection of the environment. Knox's report addresses not only the role of states in regard to the protection of the environment, but also of corporations. Referencing the UNGPs (Chapter 10), the report calls for the responsibility of business enterprises to respect human rights by addressing their environmental footprint. This "includes the responsibility to avoid causing or contributing to adverse human rights impacts through environmental harm, to address such impacts when they occur and to seek to prevent or mitigate adverse human rights impacts that are directly linked to their operations, products or services by their business relationships" (Knox 2018: 18).

BOX 5.3 (Short case): Trafigura's toxic waste dumping

On August 19, 2006, the cargo ship *Probo Koala*, belonging to the Anglo-Dutch (later Swiss) commodity trading company Trafigura, discharged approximately 500 tons of toxic waste in Abidjan, Côte d'Ivoire (OHCHR 2016). Trafigura initially wanted to dispose of the waste at the port of Amsterdam, but abstained from doing so due to the high cost. Instead, Trafigura reached an agreement with Compagnie Tommy, a recently licensed local operator in Abidjan, Côte d'Ivoire, to dispose of the waste for $17,000; it rejected a similar offer by a Dutch waste disposal company to properly dispose of the waste for $620,000 (OHCHR 2016; Amnesty International 2016b).

Lacking any facilities to properly dispose of the waste, Compagnie Tommy dumped the waste at approximately 18 locations around Abidjan, causing a range of health problems including headaches, skin irritations, and breathing problems for tens of thousands of people in Abidjan (Amnesty International 2016b). Official estimates recorded fifteen deaths, sixty-nine hospitalizations, and more than 108,000 instances of people seeking medical treatment (OHCHR 2016). Ten years after the incident countless residents still suffered from the health consequences of the waste dumping (OHCHR 2016). Trafigura argued that it had no responsibility for the incident since it had outsourced waste disposal to Compagnie Tommy, who dumped the waste of its own accord. Trafigura maintained that it believed Compagnie Tommy would dispose of the waste in a lawful and safe manner (Amnesty International 2016b).

The incident sparked a long list of legal proceedings against Trafigura. In 2007, after the arrest of two company executives in Côte d'Ivoire, the company reached a settlement with the government amounting to $195 million. In return, the government would drop all prosecutions and legal proceedings against Trafigura then and in the future (BHRRC n.d. (k)). Victims were not consulted ahead of the settlement and by 2016, only 63 percent of them had been able to access compensation from the settlement money (OHCHR 2016). In 2008, a Dutch court fined Trafigura €1 million for illegally exporting toxic waste from the Netherlands (Amnesty International 2016b). Another settlement was reached in 2009 in the UK to compensate 30,000 claimants with about $1500 each (BHRRC n.d. (k)). In 2015 and 2016 respectively, two new liability claims were brought forward to the Amsterdam District Court, representing more than 100,000 Ivorian claimants each. Trafigura is considering appealing one of them in the Dutch Supreme Court (Trafigura n.d. (a)).

In November 2015, the government of Côte d'Ivoire announced that it had completed the decontamination of all of the dumpsites, and the United Nations Environment Programme (UNEP) verified their decontamination through an environmental audit in July 2016 (OHCHR 2016).

Discussion Questions

(1) Trafigura has vehemently denied responsibility for the Probo Koala incident, stating that it believed Compagnie Tommy would dispose of the waste legally. In your opinion, what is the role of companies in ensuring the proper conduct of contracted suppliers, with regards to human rights issues? How would you answer the question after reading Chapter 10?

(2) Trafigura reached a number of settlements with the authorities of Côte d'Ivoire, the Netherlands and the UK. Do these settlements really "settle" the issue, in your opinion? What would adequate remedy look like in this case?

(3) Ten years after the Probo Koala incident, many victims remained without compensation and treatment, and long-lasting environmental and health effects persisted. Reflecting on the role of the law, both national and international, where do you spot gaps in holding companies accountable for such incidents? What should be improved? How would you answer the question after reading Chapter 12?

5.4.2   Deforestation

Roughly 30 percent of the world's land masses are covered with forests, but trees are being cut down at an alarming rate and speed. In 2019, the world lost thirty soccer fields of tropical rain forest per minute to deforestation and illegal logging. Estimates by the World Bank show that 502,000 square miles (1.3 million square kilometers) of forest were lost between 1990 and 2016, which equals an area larger than South Africa (Khokhar & Eshragh-Tabary 2016). The main cause of forest deterioration is agricultural land use, but also forest products and paper, the planning and building of infrastructure such as roads, and mining for precious metals and minerals are frequent causes. In the Amazon, 17 percent of forests were lost between 1970 and 2020, predominantly due to forest conversion for cattle ranching (WWF, n.d.). Overall, Latin America and the Caribbean, which hold one-quarter of the world's total forest area, lost 10 percent of it between 1990 and 2016 (Khokhar & Eshragh-Tabary 2016).

Deforestation affects human rights in direct and indirect ways. Forests are directly linked to the livelihoods of millions of people. An estimated one-fifth of the world's population derive benefits in the form of employment, income, forest products (such as timber), and contributions to livelihood from forests. About 300–350 million, of which half are Indigenous peoples, depend almost entirely on forests for their subsistence (World Bank 2016). Furthermore, forested watersheds and wetlands supply 75 percent of the world's accessible fresh water and we all depend on forests as natural filters for clean air (World Bank 2016). But deforestation not only threatens and affects such direct benefits of forests; it is also a major driver of climate change and its consequences. Forests store massive amounts of carbon. When they are cut down, they release large quantities of carbon dioxide and other greenhouse gases into the atmosphere and thus contribute to climate change, which, as shown in Chapter 15.2, has manifold impacts on human rights (World Bank 2016). Furthermore, where fire is used to clear forests, the pollution of the air can reach alarming levels and severely affect the health of people sometimes even hundreds of kilometers away. For example, the toxic haze from slash-and-burn methods of clearing land in Indonesia has affected millions of people across Indonesia, Singapore, Malaysia, and even the Philippines and Thailand (Mohan 2017: 325). In 2015, air quality in Singapore dropped to such dangerous levels that schools, hotels, and tourist attractions had to be temporarily closed (Mohan 2017: 325). Furthermore, the daily levels of greenhouse emissions through the fires were higher than those of all the member states of the European Union put together (Mohan 2017: 325).

5.5   Vulnerable Groups

Certain groups of people are particularly exposed to the negative impacts of corporate activities and thus may be at risk of having their human rights violated more acutely than others. Therefore, companies ought to operate with heightened sensitivity toward the specific vulnerabilities of such groups and put in place specific and tailored measures to prevent and mitigate negative impacts on them. People with disabilities, for example, suffer from general marginalization and a lack of protection in society and are vulnerable to business-related discrimination and exploitation. Children are inherently vulnerable and in need of special protection from social and economic exploitation and abuse. Women, too, are commonly listed as a vulnerable group, due to their often weak socioeconomic status and position and the historically perpetuated patriarchal oppression that can lead to disproportional exposure to negative impacts of corporate activities. This section will take a brief look at corporate human rights impacts on three particular groups of special vulnerability. Those are Indigenous communities, migrant workers, and human rights defenders (HRDs). In addition, we have elaborated on the exposure of children particularly in regard to the use of child labor in corporate value chains in Chapter 5.2.1 and will touch on the impacts on women more extensively in Chapter 15.3.

5.5.1   Indigenous Communities and Free, Prior, and Informed Consent

There are about 370 million Indigenous people across 90 countries in the world (UN Permanent Forum on Indigenous Issues 2015: 2). The UN system has abstained from adopting an official definition of Indigenous peoples due to their diversity. Instead, it relies on an understanding based on a number of broad characteristics: Indigenous communities show historical continuity with pre-colonial and/or pre-settler societies; they have a strong link to territories and surrounding natural resources; they maintain distinct social, economic, or political systems; they have distinct language, culture, and beliefs; they form non-dominant groups in society; and they resolve to maintain and reproduce their ancestral environments and systems as distinctive peoples and communities. Thus, Indigenous communities practice unique traditions and retain social, cultural, economic, and political characteristics that are distinct from those of the societies in which they live. However, more important than an actual "objective" definition is their self-identification as Indigenous peoples (UN Permanent Forum on Indigenous Issues n.d.; see also UN Permanent Forum on Indigenous Issues 2015: 3–4).

Indigenous communities are among the most severely impacted by corporate activities. Among the "typical" human rights violations in this regard are forced evictions from ancestral lands, violence and intimidation, and pollution and contamination of soil and water. The violation of land rights often weighs particularly heavily on Indigenous communities, which have inhabited their land for centuries and not only depend on the land for their livelihoods but also have a close spiritual connection to it. Their Indigenous culture is often intimately tied to the land, and its destruction and exploitation can be a deep assault to the very fabric of the communities.

Their special vulnerability to such abuse derives from their historical oppression, marginalization, and exploitation. Despite the historic possession of their ancestral land and their often close and spiritual connection to it, they often are not recognized as legal landholders and thus receive very weak protections. With large-scale development projects, energy, agricultural, and extractive operations claiming ever larger areas of land, Indigenous lands are increasingly being contested and the communities are being pushed out of their historical territories. As the Rights and Resource Initiative (2015: 1) states:

> When local communities and Indigenous Peoples lack formal, legal recognition of their land rights, they are vulnerable to dispossession and loss of their identities, livelihoods, and cultures. Pressures are increasing as governments issue concessions for forestry, industrial agriculture, large-scale mining, and oil and gas production on community lands. Disputes over land and natural resources are also a contributing cause of armed conflict.

Furthermore, their social, political, and cultural marginalization and isolation often leads to precarious socioeconomic positions. Indigenous communities are often among the poorest populations and tend to suffer from neglect due to limited access to public goods, services, and amenities. Ill health in particular remains a critical challenge for Indigenous communities. Among others, the destruction of their lands, territories, and resources, which are critical to their survival, and various obstacles to accessing health services such as lack of health facilities in Indigenous communities, the absence of adequate health insurance, poverty as well as illiteracy and language issues contribute to the precarious health situation of Indigenous communities (UN Permanent Forum on Indigenous Issues 2015: 3). Those factors are often compounded by racist and discriminatory attitudes toward Indigenous peoples and often a lack of cultural understanding and sensitivity (Hongbo 2015: IV).

The UN has had the protection of Indigenous peoples on the agenda since the 1950s. In 1957, the ILO adopted ILO Convention 107 on Indigenous and Tribal Populations and in 1986 ILO Convention No. 169 concerning Indigenous and Tribal Peoples in Independent States. In 2000, the UN established the Permanent Forum on Indigenous Issues (UNPFII) and one year later appointed the first Special Rapporteur on the Human Rights and Fundamental Freedoms of Indigenous People. A further, major achievement was the adoption of the UN Declaration on the Rights of Indigenous Peoples in the year 2007.

One of the most important concepts advanced particularly by the UN Declaration on the Rights of Indigenous Peoples is the requirement of FPIC. According to Article 19 of the Declaration, states must consult and cooperate in good faith with Indigenous communities in order to obtain their FPIC before taking administrative or legislative measures or undertaking projects that adversely affect them. In particular, Indigenous communities must not be forcibly removed from their territories and no relocation must be conducted without their FPIC and without an agreement on just and fair compensation and, if possible, with an option to return (Article 10). This is of importance also to companies that sign contracts and concessions with governments to engage in development or mining projects, for example. They must make sure that those governments obtained FPIC and compensated the affected communities accordingly. The International Finance Corporation's (IFC) Performance Standard No. 7 (Chapter 14.2.2) defines FPIC as a requirement and best practice also for private actors that are tasked with the implementation of projects financed by the World Bank. Such companies must make sure that FPIC is obtained in the case of adverse impacts on Indigenous lands and resources, relocation of Indigenous people from their lands, or impacts on critical cultural heritage of Indigenous peoples. The IFC performance standards can and frequently are used also as a best practice benchmark for corporate conduct beyond World Bank-financed projects. Generally, whether applied to governments or companies, FPIC is not merely about consulting with communities or providing them with proper information. It goes beyond what is often less ambitiously understood as "stakeholder engagement." The key element of FPIC is that the communities can freely agree or disagree with the proposed measures and that their agreement or disagreement has direct impact on whether a project or measure is being implemented and in what way. For this purpose, Indigenous communities must receive full information and negotiations must be had before a project or a specific measure is put in place.

5.5.2 Migrant Workers

There are about 150 million migrant workers in the global workforce (IHRB 2016). Many of them leave their country out of desperation and a lack of opportunity at home, with the goal of pursuing a life without economic hardship or sending money to support their families and communities back home. Such people often end up in inherently vulnerable positions, in which they depend fully on their employer, in a system that is foreign and often offers little protection to outsiders and in places where they have no social connections and networks. This makes migrant laborers particularly vulnerable to exploitation and trafficking as well as bonded and forced labor.

The special vulnerability of migrant workers is acknowledged in the International Convention on the Protection of the Rights of All Migrant Workers and Members of their Families, which was adopted in 1990 and went into force in 2003 (Chapter 3.3.4). The Convention establishes minimum standards that all states that are party to it are obliged to respect, protect, and fulfil. It is directly relevant to documented and undocumented migrant workers and members of their families (Asia Pacific Forum of National Human Rights Institutions 2012: 12). Furthermore, a couple of ILO conventions address the situation of migrant workers, namely the Migration for Employment Convention of 1949 (No. 97), which focuses on the recruitment of migrants and conditions of work in the host country, and the Migrant Workers (Supplementary Provisions) Convention of 1975 (No. 143), which was the first treaty to deal directly with the rights of migrants workers in irregular, that is illegal and abusive, situations (Asia Pacific Forum of National Human Rights Institutions 2012: 8).

Bonded and forced labor, as well as trafficking, are particular concerns for migrant workers, with recruitment fees playing a particularly problematic role. Migrant workers often have to rely on recruitment agencies to not only find them jobs abroad but also to support their visa process, travel arrangements, and other services. For such services, migrants are often charged substantial recruitment and placement fees directly or indirectly (e.g. through the prospective employer). Since they often cannot afford such fees, they tend to be set up as loans, which often incur high interest. This pushes the laborers into debt, which can be used to trap them into low-paying and exploitative working conditions. Being in a position of debt erodes their bargaining power and renders them acutely dependent on the work, no matter the circumstances and conditions in which they find themselves (IHRB 2016). This is why recruitment fees are one of the key indicators for modern slavery and forced labor in supply chains and why ILO Convention No. 181 on Private Employment Agencies prohibits private employment agencies charging workers any fees or costs. In order to combat the exploitation of migrant labor in supply chains, multinational companies thus ought to put policies and systems in place that ban the charging of recruitment fees to workers and effectively detect such practices among the suppliers and agencies with which they work (IHRB 2016).

Besides pushing migrant workers into debt, there are other tactics that are used to exploit their vulnerability. For example, employers frequently confiscate passports, which means workers are unable to leave, are placed in a vulnerable position, and are subject to further pressure from employers, particularly in cases where workers' immigration status may be problematic. Furthermore, in many Middle Eastern states, the relation between employers and migrant labor is regulated by the so-called *kafala* system, which is a sponsorship system that essentially delegates overseeing workers' immigration and work status to employers.

> Under *kafala*, a migrant worker's immigration and legal residency status is tied to an individual sponsor (*kafeel*) throughout his or her contract period in such a way that the migrant worker cannot typically enter the country, resign from a job, transfer employment, nor leave the country without first obtaining explicit permission from his or her employer. This is distinct from most other sponsorship regimes, where only the migrant worker's employment status is determined by the employer at the time of entering the country, and where there is more flexibility in being able to switch employers without losing immigration status (International Labour Organization, Regional Office for Arab States 2017: 3).

In recent years, a number of Gulf states have loosened or abolished the *kafala* system, both to achieve higher labor productivity and to counteract labor abuse. However, it is still in place, in part or full, in many Middle Eastern nations.

5.5.3 Human Rights Defenders

HRDs can be defined as "individuals or groups that, in their personal or professional capacity and in a peaceful manner, strive to protect and promote human rights" (Forst 2017: 5). They can be members of affected communities, civil society organizations, journalists, academics, lawyers, government officials, company employees, or members of the public. The role of HRDs is of critical importance, particularly in the BHR space, since many human rights violations, especially in remote areas of the world, would never be exposed and reported without their work. However, because of this role, HRDs often face great personal risk when confronting human rights abuse connected to powerful business interests. They frequently face

BOX 5.4 (Short case) 2022 FIFA World Cup in Qatar

Mega sporting events such as the Olympics or the World Cup in soccer are tremendous commercial undertakings and countless businesses are involved in, contribute to, and benefit from them in various roles and capacities. Also, such events frequently raise human rights-related questions and issues. A recurring controversy has been whether or not they should be hosted by and thus provide a prestigious platform for countries with a record of widespread, systematic, and egregious abuse of human rights. The 2022 soccer World Cup in Qatar is a case in point. For this small country in the Arabian peninsula to host the World Cup requires substantial new infrastructure, including new state-of-the-art stadiums, a new airport, roads, and hotels. The workforce needed for such construction projects consists largely of migrant workers from countries such as Nepal, Pakistan, India, Bangladesh, Sri Lanka, the Philippines, and Kenya (Pattison et al. 2021). The roughly 2 million migrant laborers in the Gulf state are subject to the *kafala* system and vulnerable to exploitation and abuse, from unsafe and dangerous conditions of work and accommodation to the charging of expensive recruitment fees, to forced labor settings (Amnesty International n.d.).

With the international spotlight on Qatar and pressure rising, the country vowed to improve the situation of its migrant labor force. In 2020, it announced a substantial loosening of its *kafala* rules, allowing foreign workers to quit their jobs or change employers without fear of deportation. It also raised the minimum wage for migrant laborers. However, implementation of these protections take time and abuses still occur frequently (*The Economist*, 2021). By 2021, an estimated 6,500 migrant workers had lost their lives on the construction sites in the lead-up to the World Cup since 2010 (Pattison et al. 2021).

Some national teams made use of the official start of the qualification games for the World Cup in 2021 to raise awareness about the human rights situation of migrant workers in Qatar. Some of them even contemplated boycotting the World Cup. The influential human rights organization Amnesty International, on the other hand, vowed to use the momentum for constructive engagement rather than boycotting the event altogether.

Discussion Questions

(1) Should countries' human rights records be a part of the selection criteria of sports organizations like FIFA when awarding them mega sporting events? How would you define such a requirement? What other human rights responsibilities do large sports organizations such as FIFA have?

(2) What should be the role and responsibility of international construction companies building the infrastructure in Qatar in the lead-up to the World Cup? If you were a human rights consultant, what would you advise they should do? What mechanisms should businesses have in place to make sure they do not get implicated in human rights abuses? How would you answer the question after reading Chapter 10 on the UNGPs?

(3) What should be the role and responsibility of international sponsors of the World Cup? Should they try to use their influence to press for change? If so, how should they go about it? What is your opinion on this question after reading Chapter 10 on the UNGPs?

(4) What should be the role and responsibility of soccer clubs and national teams? Should they get involved in the discussion or ought they remain "apolitical"?

retaliation in the form of criminalization, intimidation, harassment, violence, and even death. The UN Special Rapporteur on the situation of human rights defenders has frequently pointed to the complicity of business actors in human rights violations against HRDs and has called HRDs in the BHR space as among the most vulnerable groups of defenders (Forst 2017: 3). Generally, the environment has become more hostile toward HRDs in recent years as governments around the world have engaged in the shrinking of civic space by enacting legislation aimed at curtailing the activities of civil society and taking measures to restrict the freedoms of expression, assembly, and association (Forst 2017: 3–4).

The BHRRC has reported more than 2,000 attacks on HRDs, who raised concerns about business-related human rights abuses only in the short timespan between 2015 and 2019; 572 of those attacks happened in 2019 alone. Such attacks have ranged from frivolous lawsuits, to arbitrary arrests and detention, to physical violence, all the way to killings. Land-intensive sectors such as agribusiness and mining were most frequently connected to attacks on HRDs and a majority of such attacks occur in Latin America (BHRRC, n.d. (b)). Violent attacks occur most frequently against defenders of environmental and land rights. In 2016, 185 land and environmental rights defenders were murdered, of whom 40 percent were Indigenous persons (Global Witness 2016: 4). Thus, the risk of being harmed and silenced when standing up against mining and agricultural operations has been most acute for members of local and Indigenous communities, not least due to their geographic isolation and their weak land rights (Global Witness 2016: 4). Women also face heightened risks of attacks, which can involve threats against their families (Forst 2017: 6). Various industries also have long histories of intimidation and attacks against union members who defend workers' rights.

BOX 5.5 (Context) Berta Cáceres

Berta Cáceres was a Lenca Indigenous woman and a prominent human and environmental rights defender. For more than twenty years, she defended the territory and the rights of the Indigenous Lenca people in Honduras (Front Line Defenders n.d.). For this purpose, she co-founded the Consejo Cívico de Organizaciones Populares e Indígenas de Honduras (Civic Council of Popular and Indigenous Organizations of Honduras; COPINH), in 1993 (Front Line Defenders n.d.). In 2015, she was recognized for her environmental activism with the prestigious Goldman Prize (NPR 2021).

On March 3, 2016, Berta Cáceres was murdered by unidentified gunmen in her home after having received threats in the previous days (Front Line Defenders n.d.). In November 2018, the Honduran National Criminal Court convicted seven men of her murder, among them the former security chief and the environment manager of Desarrollos Energéticos SA (Desa), a company constructing a dam in indigenous Lenca territory, against which COPINH was campaigning (Front Line Defenders n.d.). The $50 million Agua Zarca hydroelectric dam project was being built without proper consultation with the Indigenous community (UNEP n.d. (b)). The Court found that the men had been hired by executives of Desa, who feared financial losses resulting from Cáceres's activism in the region (Front Line Defenders n.d.). The protests against the dams led to a temporary halt of construction work in 2013 and to the withdrawal of international investors (UNEP n.d. (b)). In July 2021, Roberto David Castillo, the former head of Desa, was convicted of being co-collaborator in ordering the murder of Cáceres (Lakhani 2021). Cáceres was forty-four years old at the time of her death.

Criminalization has become a widespread tactic to silence HRDs, who frequently face criminal prosecution or are drawn into frivolous defamation lawsuits as a means of intimidation, of draining their finances, and of tying up their resources. Companies have increasingly made use of such tactics against NGOs, journalists, academics, and other HRDs. Such lawsuits have become known as Strategic Lawsuits Against Public Participation (SLAPPs) (Chapter 12.6.4). As the BHRRC reports, pressing criminal charges and filing lawsuits became the most common type of attack against HRDs in 2019; in fact, almost half of all reported attacks on HRDs in 2019 were related to judicial harassment, according to the BHRRC (n.d. (b)).

The UN Declaration on the Right and Responsibility of Individuals, Groups and Organs of Society to Promote and Protect Universally Recognized Human Rights and Fundamental Freedoms recognizes and protects the critical role of HRDs in the promotion and protection of human rights. Furthermore, the UN maintains the position of a Special Rapporteur on the situation of human rights defenders to assess and raise awareness of the critical importance of and worsening situation for HRDs. The UNGPs (Chapter 10) also address the role of HRDs explicitly, asking businesses to engage with HRDs as critical sources of information in the context of human rights impact assessments (Principle 18) and governments to make sure that the legitimate activities of HRDs are not obstructed (Principle 26). However, increasingly, BHR advocates have called on businesses to adopt specific policies on HRDs and to take a proactive stance in supporting and protecting them by engaging in constructive dialogues and speaking out against the abuse of the rights of HRDs. Concordantly, there have been growing efforts by a number of civil society organizations and by the UNWG to issue specific guidance for states and companies in regard to providing better protection to HRDs.

STUDY QUESTIONS

1. What is land grabbing and how can it affect local communities?
2. What is FPIC and when is it required? Can you give an example?
3. How are human rights and environmental issues linked?
4. Why are migrant workers particularly vulnerable to exploitation and human rights abuse?
5. What are human rights defenders and why are they important for BHR?

REFLECTION QUESTIONS

1. How far can and should employee performance monitoring systems go and at what point do they start to illegitimately infringe on the privacy of the employees? What is a company allowed to know about its employees and what information should be protected as private?
2. What is discrimination and how should companies address it? What policies should a company have in place to combat discrimination? Is discrimination only an internal matter for companies, or should they take a stand also in the public discussion?
3. Defenders of sweatshop labor commonly argue that such working conditions are a necessary stage on the path to development and prosperity, and that economic development will eventually lead to improvements of workers' rights. Do you believe that developing countries can "leapfrog" over this stage, and if so, what

would be the necessary conditions or policies required to do so? How can and should businesses support this process?

4. Some of the most egregious corporate-related human rights violations occur in contexts of conflict. Therefore, should companies operate in conflict-affected settings at all? What are the arguments for and against it?

PART III
Corporate Human Rights Responsibility

....

6 Justification of Corporate Human Rights Responsibility

The question of whether corporations have or ought to have human rights responsibilities is not intuitive. After all, human rights have traditionally been viewed as being of concern only to governments. The BHR discussion challenges this traditional, state-centric view and provides reasons why businesses ought to have human rights responsibilities, too. Such reasons or justifications can be formulated from an ethical, legal, or more pragmatic, managerial point of view. In the following, all three perspectives will be assessed in more detail.

6.1 Human Rights as Ethical Obligations of Business

Whether businesses ought to have human rights obligations is first and foremost an ethical question. As such, it is about assessing the normative grounds on which to extend human rights obligations to business. However, before we can do so, we must first reflect on the question of whether business entities can and ought to be bearers of any ethical obligations in the first place.

6.1.1 Ethical Obligations of Business: Beyond Profit-Maximization

Extending human rights responsibilities to business presupposes that corporations can be bearers of ethical obligations more generally and that such obligations entail more than merely to maximize profits.

Three conditions are commonly seen as relevant in order for responsibility to be attributed to any actor or agent. They can be traced all the way back to the ancient Greek philosopher Aristotle. First, agents must act *intentionally and voluntarily*. The cause of action must be internal to the agents and based on free will, rather than being forced on them from outside. Second, the agents must be – or can reasonably be expected to be – aware of and *knowledgeable* about the consequences of their actions. Third, they must *understand* the implications of those outcomes for those affected by them. In other words, they must have the capacity to discern the knowledge about the consequences of their actions and have a degree of empathy and rationality to understand the point of view of those affected by them. Actors who meet these requirements are what we call moral agents; moral agency is thus the condition for attribution of responsibility.

Whether corporations, as entities, possess moral agency, has been the subject of a lively discussion in the business ethics field that reaches back to the 1970s. This discussion has produced a whole spectrum of positions in many different shades. However, two broad types of arguments can be distinguished, one broadly characterizing opponents' view on corporate moral agency and the other representing the perspective of proponents.

Opponents of corporate moral agency argue that only human beings possess the moral capacities to have moral responsibility (Velasquez 1983). Accordingly, it is not the corporation as an entity, but the individuals within it who are the bearers of responsibility. Corporations, for these opponents, are no more than aggregates or collections of individuals, and all corporate acts can ultimately be traced and broken down to the acts and intentions of individuals within the company (Werhane 2015: 13). In their view, there is no such thing as corporate intentionality, which could give rise to moral agency of corporations. Besides such conceptual objections against corporate moral agency, there are more practical concerns about assigning responsibility to corporations, as well. Some opponents have argued that focusing on corporate responsibility would distract from holding to account the individuals who were in charge of decision-making within the company. The corporate structure could be used as a shield to evade individual accountability. The global financial crisis of 2008 is a case in point. While the risk-taking behavior and greed of company executives led the world into an unprecedented financial crisis that caused financial, economic, and social damage of unseen proportions, those responsible by and large evaded accountability and only a handful of executives ended up facing prosecution.

Proponents of corporate moral agency, on the other hand, generally argue that groups of people can have collective responsibilities *as groups*, which may not be congruent with the sum of the individual responsibilities of its members. For example, if a group of people witnesses an assault on an innocent person, they may have a responsibility to confront the perpetrator as a group. However, no one individual member of the group may have that same responsibility on their own, since it may be too dangerous to act alone. Peter French (1979: 212), who pioneered scholarship on collective and organizational responsibility, argued that a group of people can have such responsibilities, if it is minimally organized. It is minimally organized if it possesses an internal decision-making structure. In other words, such minimally organized groups can acquire moral agency by virtue of their internal decision-making structures. Such structures enable organizations to act based on organizational reasons, which are distinct from and irreducible to the reasons of individual members. Based on these insights, corporations qualify as moral agents, whose corporate decisions are morally relevant and thus give rise to moral responsibility. While the scholarly discussion on the moral nature of corporations is ongoing today, there is a broad consensus that corporations are moral agents that do acquire certain moral responsibilities through their business conduct. This leads to the question: What should they be responsible for?

The renowned economist Milton Friedman (1962; 1970) famously proclaimed in the 1960s and 1970s that the only social responsibility of business was to maximize its profits, "so long as it stays within the rules of the game, which is to say, engages in open and free competition without deception or fraud" (Friedman 1970) As economic institutions, corporations ought not to be burdened with any broader social responsibilities. In fact, it would be counterproductive to give them such responsibilities, since this would reduce their productivity, lower their performance and output, and ultimately result in a reduction of general welfare. Friedman's view corresponds to what we call shareholder primacy today. This position holds that a corporation's first allegiance is to its owners, the shareholders, and thus their primary responsibility is to maximize the return on the shareholders' investment. By maximizing shareholders' returns, corporations are seen to contribute most effectively to a successful and growing economy and thus to the general prosperity of society at the same time.

However, as Chapter 5 has shown, a company's success does not necessarily benefit all of society and it often comes at the expense of others. Thus, adopting a purely economic perspective of the corporation proves too narrow; we cannot assess companies merely by how much they contribute to economic growth through their profits and investments. For some economists, corporations are not more than a nexus of contracts, whose purpose it is to reduce transaction costs and thus to increase the efficiency of organizing economic relations (Coase 1937). But corporations are also social communities that interact with the "outside" world in many different ways and which consist of individuals from all spheres and walks of life. Rather than being merely a nexus of contracts, corporations consist of countless personal and social relationships. Together, those relationships and personalities build unique corporate cultures, which are shaped not merely by economic laws and necessities, but also by social and cultural values, norms, and conventions. Accordingly, corporate activities are not just economic transactions; they are loaded with social and cultural meaning and symbolism, too. Managers of companies need to be aware of their company's social and cultural significance and to integrate such considerations into their management decisions and leadership.

Finally, corporations are not only economic and social but also political actors. They are deeply involved in activities and tasks that are public in nature and formerly thought to be the exclusive domain of governments (see e.g. Matten & Crane 2005; Scherer & Palazzo 2007; 2011). Large-scale global problems – so-called "grand challenges" such as poverty, massive inequalities, or climate change – require political solutions, which ought to involve actors from different sectors, including corporations. Corporations have become important actors in regard to the governance of a variety of issues, particularly those that are of a transnational character. This is due not least to the limited capacity of governments to deal with global issues on their own. A political view of corporations stresses their responsibility not only for their private business affairs and conduct but also to contribute in a much broader way to the provision of public goods and services, including governance tasks. While scholarship on corporations as political actors has proliferated in recent years, such views are not new. Peter Drucker elaborated on the political nature of the modern (American) corporation as early as 1946. For Drucker, the corporation "sets the standard for the way of life and the mode of living of our citizens," it "leads, molds and directs," and it "determines our perspective on our own society." As a consequence, for Drucker it was increasingly the modern corporation, rather than the state, "around which crystallize our social problems and to which we look for their solutions" (Drucker 1993 [1946]: 6). Two decades later, Dow Votaw, one of the early thinkers on corporate responsibility, concluded:

> Only if we have a thorough familiarity with the corporation as a political institution, as well as an economic and social one, can we hope even to recognize the effects that it has had and will have on the rest of society (Votaw 1961: 106).

Thus, corporations are complex economic, social, and political constructs, rather than one-dimensional economic entities. Their purpose and function, as well as their impact and responsibilities, reach far beyond the laws of supply and demand of the market. If and to what degree such responsibility extends to and includes human rights will be assessed in the following section.

6.1.2   Human Rights as Ethical Imperatives of Business: Two Approaches

There are two basic types of ethical arguments in favor of corporate human rights responsibility: a moral rights approach and an institutional rights approach. As their names indicate, they differ mainly in terms of their underlying understanding of human rights and the implications deriving from those, as discussed in Chapter 3.

Moral rights approach: For those embracing an understanding of human rights as primarily ethical articulations or so-called moral rights (Chapter 3.1.2), arguing for corporate human rights obligations seems natural. If we embrace the idea of corporations having any moral responsibilities beyond making a profit, it seems intuitive that such responsibilities must include human rights as the most fundamental moral claims of human beings. Indeed, from this perspective, all actors and agents necessarily have human rights responsibilities and it would be incoherent to argue that corporations ought to be an exception in this regard. Thus, from a foundational perspective, there may be nothing particularly unique or different about arguing for corporate human rights responsibility in comparison to other moral and social responsibilities of business, although human rights responsibilities may differ, for example, in terms of the urgency with which they need to be addressed. Hence, for those adhering to a moral rights approach to corporate human rights responsibility, the challenge of BHR is not so much about justifying corporate human rights responsibility; it would seem more challenging for opponents to present a plausible case as to why corporations should be unique in not having any human rights responsibility. Rather, the challenge is about defining the *extent* of such responsibility, as well as in fleshing out the conceptual, normative, and not least practical and managerial implications of framing corporate responsibility in human rights terms.

Institutional rights approach: Those adhering to a political or institutional view of human rights (Chapter 3.1.4.2) may not be satisfied with the justification that the moral rights approach provides. For them, human rights are not merely fundamental ethical demands but rather institutional rights that define the boundaries of legitimate government authority. From that perspective, arguing for corporate human rights responsibility is not simply an extension of a more general argument in favor of businesses having ethical obligations; rather, it involves making a special case as to why such rights, which are designed specifically to limit the authority of governments, should be of relevance also for private companies. Supporters of a political or institutional view of human rights may not deny that businesses have ethical responsibilities to avoid discrimination, to provide decent working conditions, or to consult with communities affected by their operations. They may even argue that such responsibilities are congruent with what others call "human rights responsibilities." However, they perceive them as general ethical responsibilities aligned with, but not grounded in, human rights (Hsieh 2015; 2017). In order to make a case for corporate human rights responsibility on these grounds, one would have to show that they, too, operate in positions of authority akin to governments, which similarly require to be curtailed and thus legitimized by human rights. In other words, an ethical argument for corporate human rights responsibility from the perspective of an institutional rights approach must be grounded in corporate power and authority. Therefore, the following section will engage with the nature of corporate power in more depth.

6.1.3   Corporate Power and Authority

There has been a long-standing discussion of the nature and extent of corporate power, but BHR scholars have engaged surprisingly little with it so far. Corporations have long been recognized as institutions of exceptional power. Back in the sixteenth and seventeenth centuries, the precursors of the modern stock company, the chartered trading companies with their telling names such as East India Company or South Sea Company were colonial superpowers, holding monopolies on entire trade routes, maintaining armies, and fighting wars for their governments. Later on, far into the age of the modern stock company in the first half of the twentieth century, the critical US Supreme Court Justice Louis Brandeis called corporations "Frankenstein monsters," alluding to a situation in which they threatened to become too big and too powerful to be controlled even by their very creators (quoted in Drucker 1993: 223). Brandeis was echoed by Peter Drucker, who, as mentioned earlier, saw the modern American company as the main institution of his time; an institution that was increasingly at the forefront of determining not only the economic but also the social and political prospects of society. Many would argue that this situation has not changed to this day, and perhaps become even more pronounced. Moreover, what some might have perceived to be a uniquely American problem – that is, the emergence of what American sociologist Charles Derber (1998) called a "corporation nation" – can increasingly be observed on a global scale today. The spread of neoliberal economic policies across the globe freed corporations from many constraints and enhanced their global mobility, which enabled them to evade the reach of domestic regulations. The turn of the millennium brought a revelation. For the first time, large corporations had surpassed nation-states in size and power. Based on a comparison between corporate revenues and national GDPs, a majority of the world's largest economies were now corporate entities (Anderson & Cavanagh 2000).

The amount of a corporation's revenues, of course, is not necessarily a good approximation of corporate power. While it may be one indicator among many, defining and understanding the nature and extent of corporate power is a more complex matter. In its most basic sense, power denotes the ability to shape and affect outcomes in such a way that one's own preferences take precedence over the preferences of others (Strange 1996: 17). Based on this, we commonly distinguish two kinds of power: direct, relational power, and more indirect, structural power.

- *Relational power* means the exercise of power within direct relationships between actors. It is the expression of the classic Weberian definition of power as the ability of one actor to get another actor to do something that they would not otherwise do – that is, to influence, force, or coerce someone to work toward someone else's preferences, possibly by going against their own interests. Relational power is the most directly visible expression of corporations' power. A glaring example is corporate lobbying. Corporations are overwhelmingly successful in their attempts to influence and sway politicians to adopt business-friendly positions and to ease their regulatory burden. This kind of power has also been called "instrumental power," alluding to the direct and targeted use of resources as a means of influencing relationships in order to exert one's preferences over those of others (Fuchs 2007; Ruggie 2017).

- *Structural power* is positional, rather than instrumental. It derives not primarily from the direct, relational use of resources, but from corporations' positions within (global) structures, which cater to the interests and work for the benefit of those corporations. Susan Strange (1988), in particular, argued that we must understand power as the ability to control and shape the structures within which other participants, including states, operate and interact. One example is multinational corporations' positions within global tax structures, which allow them to evade billions by shifting their profits between different tax regimes. Similarly, by means of internalization, multinationals have withdrawn a large part of international trade from effective governance by public institutions and instead acquired a great deal of control over global trade structures themselves (Ruggie 2017: 8–9).

Beyond relational and structural power, corporations exert what some have called discursive power (Fuchs 2007; Ruggie 2017).

- *Discursive power* is a more subtle but all the more pervasive form of power. It is the power to influence public discourse, promote ideas, shape perceptions and identities, set social and cultural norms and expectations, and indeed determine what is being perceived as within the range of the socially acceptable and normal. Not least through their powerful public relations and marketing machinery, corporations have successfully promoted cultures of materialism and consumerism, within which corporate influence is gradually normalized. Charles Derber (1998: 119) called this the "corporate mystique," which is a set of "cherished beliefs and illusions" or an "ideology" that both disguises and venerates corporate power. This process transforms corporate power into corporate authority. Authority more generally is commonly defined as the legitimate exercise of power (Wettstein 2009). If power goes largely unchallenged, it can become legitimized tacitly by the apathy of the people subject to it. The normalization of corporate power in today's society has led to a situation in which corporations can be said to increasingly operate in positions of de facto authority (Wettstein 2009).

With corporations exerting power in a relational, structural, and discursive manner, it is evident that such power is no longer merely economic but also political and social. In other words, corporations have become not only economically but also politically and socially powerful actors. There is a mismatch today between this apparent power and authority of corporations and still perceiving them as essentially private institutions with largely discretionary private responsibilities (Chapter 1.2). A change of perspective is required that conceptualizes them as what they truly represent: political actors with public responsibilities. Identifying them as such puts them squarely in the space in which human rights have validity also from an institutional rights perspective. From this view it can be argued that corporations ought to observe human rights just as other institutions in positions of power and authority – among them, most prominently, governments.

The argument formulated here is a philosophical one, based on a notion of corporate power rooted in social science. As such, it differs particularly from the notion of control as it pertains to human rights litigation cases. Especially the question of attribution in parent company liability cases hinges on whether the parent company exerted effective control over a subsidiary, which is said to have violated human rights (Chapter 12.5.2.3). Responsibility for the subsidiary's transgression tends to be attributed to the parent company only if it had effective control over the operations of the subsidiary. Whether or not courts perceive this to be the case, however, may have very little to do with the overall power of a multinational company. As many such liability cases show, even for the most powerful multinationals it is frequently possible to argue that they lacked a sufficient degree of influence and control over their subsidiary in order to mitigate the effects of a human rights violation or prevent it occurring.

6.2 Human Rights as Legal Obligations of Business

The previous subsection has outlined ethical arguments for corporate human rights obligations. However, one of the core concerns particularly of the early BHR discussion has always been to assess whether there are sufficient legal grounds on which to extend human rights obligations to business. Just as the attribution of moral obligations requires moral agency, so assigning legal obligations presupposes a certain legal standing of the respective actors. More specifically, corporate legal responsibility presupposes that corporations are recognized as legal persons in law. The meaning and interpretation of corporate legal personhood is subject to ongoing discussion among legal scholars with different theories being developed as a result of it (Blair 2013). The following paragraphs will provide a brief introduction to those discussions on corporate legal personhood both at the national and international levels.

6.2.1 Legal Personhood at the National Level

Similar to an understanding of corporations as moral agents, corporate legal personhood means that corporations are recognized by law as persons, which are independent from natural individuals, such as the employees, managers, or owners, who are part of the corporate entity. This allows those individuals who form the corporation to act as one entity or one legal person (Blair 2013: 789). The practice of recognizing and treating certain collectivities or "group agents" as legal persons is nothing new, dating back to ancient Roman Law (Garthoff 2019). It remained common and indeed was strengthened and expanded during the medieval period and the treatment of churches, monasteries, municipalities, or universities, among others, as legal persons. This allowed those institutions to hold property, operate as separate entities, and prevent their assets from being transferred to the heirs of those who operated and controlled them (Blair 2013: 789). Thus, legal personhood allowed for "perpetual succession" (Blair 2013: 789), that is, to continue to exist beyond the death or replacement of the individuals who once were in charge of those organizations. A further expansion occurred throughout the seventeenth, eighteenth, and nineteenth centuries (Garthoff 2019). It included the emergence of chartered trading companies and their evolution and eventual transformation into modern stock companies (Blair 2013; Garthoff 2019), leading up to *Santa Clara* v. *Southern Pacific* in 1886, in which the American Supreme Court argued that the protection of "persons" under the Fourteenth Amendment was to apply also to corporations (Blair 2015: 421). This trend of strengthening corporations' standing as legal persons has continued to this day. A most dramatic recent expansion occurred in the United States in a 2010 Supreme Court judgment on the *Citizens United* case, which struck down as unconstitutional any spending limits for corporations on political speech. This essentially means that companies can spend as much on political advertising and other forms of political expression (but not on direct contributions to political campaigns) as they please, despite the highly distorting effects this may have on democratic processes.

The upshot of legal personhood is that corporations have certain rights and duties under law, analogous to natural persons. They are, on the one hand, subject to law and legal authority and thus subject to liability, which means that they can be sued under law. On the other hand, they are also protected by law (Garthoff 2019), which means that they have certain rights that they can claim and which ought to be protected, such as the right to own property or to enter and enforce contracts. However, as legal persons, corporations remain "artificial" persons. They clearly lack some of the defining characteristics of natural persons, such as the capacity to suffer pain or to feel emotions, which is why their moral standing and thus the protection granted to them must be different from that of human beings. Four central functions of corporate legal personhood can be distinguished (Blair 2013: 785): First, corporate personhood provides continuity by making sure that contract relations as well as property are tied to the corporation as an entity, rather than to specific individuals, and can thus continue seamlessly even amidst fluctuation of personnel. Second, it serves to create identification among internal and external stakeholders. It generates an "identifiable persona," which can be the bearer of important intangible assets such as goodwill, reputation, and brand (Blair 2013: 798). Third, it serves to separate pools of assets belonging to the corporation from those belonging to the individuals participating in it. Fourth, it provides a framework for self-governance of certain business or commercial activities.

Similar to corporate moral agency, the function, form, and nature of corporate legal personality remains subject to ongoing discussion and critique. When human rights obligations are extended to business, things become even more complicated, since corporations' status as legal persons is relevant not only under national but also under international law.

6.2.2   Legal Personhood at the International Level

Similar to the role of corporate legal personhood for the recognition of rights and duties under domestic law, there is an ongoing discussion about the status of corporations under international law. More specifically, the question is whether in addition to legal personhood at the domestic level, (multinational) corporations also have international legal personality and thus whether they are subjects of international law, as well. International law can only impose duties on entities that have international legal personality. Conversely, any entity on which international law imposes duties has to be considered a subject of international law (Gaja 2003). Hence, international legal personality would enable corporations to acquire duties under international law.

Who is or can be subjects of international law besides nation states has been part of a controversial discussion. Traditionally, the function of international law was to govern the relationships between states. Accordingly, states have been seen as the only subjects of international law (Bernaz 2017: 86).

> International human rights law has developed in a way that technically makes states
> the only duty-bearers of human rights obligations. Those obligations derive from
> treaty law and from customary international law. Under a conservative reading of
> the system, corporations, even multinational corporations are not subjects of international
> human rights law and therefore are under no legal obligation to abide by human rights
> treaties (Bernaz 2017: 81).

More recently, it has come to be accepted that the UN is also a subject of international law with international legal personality, since otherwise it could not fulfil its mandate. A similar case can be made for the International Committee of the Red Cross (ICRC) and perhaps some other international organizations. Furthermore, individuals have international legal personality, as well.

One reason for the hesitancy to expand the category of international legal persons recognized under international law is the fear that this will "lead to an expansion of the possible authors of international law" (Clapham 2006: 58). Accordingly, there has been strong resistance against the idea of including multinational corporations among those entities with international legal personality (Clapham 2006: 76). Nevertheless, some commentators have argued that the rights and obligations that multinationals have already under existing international treaties may actually suggest "sufficient international legal personality to bear obligations, as much as to exercise rights" (Kinley & Tadaki 2004: 947). Clapham proposed to solve the dilemma by recognizing what he calls "limited international legal personality" for multinational companies.

These concerns lose much of their sting when one reorientates the issue and simply asserts that corporations have limited international legal personality rather than pretending that multinationals are proper/primary subjects of international law with the "status" that implies. As long as we admit that individuals have rights and duties under customary international human rights law and international humanitarian law, we have to admit that legal persons may also possess the international legal personality necessary to enjoy some of these rights, and conversely to be prosecuted or held accountable for violations of the relevant international duties (Clapham 2006: 79).

This discussion of corporations' potential international legal personality is clearly relevant to the BHR discussion, which can be approached from two slightly different perspectives. One approach is to argue that multinational corporations are among those entities that *ought* to be considered subjects of international law. Based on this, one can then spell out what their human rights obligations ought to be. The alternative approach is to show that multinational companies have already acquired human rights obligations under international law, which means that their international legal personality is implied to begin with. Most of the discussion of BHR presupposes this second approach. Hence, the question of whether multinationals are subjects of international law is less of constitutive than of derivative relevance to BHR. This is why BHR scholars do not commonly start their analyses with lengthy elaborations on why multinational corporations ought to be considered subjects of international law. More generally, it is increasingly acknowledged that the lines between the subjects and objects of international law are permeable and fluid, which makes the very separation of these categories appear increasingly unhelpful and insignificant (Clapham 2006: 62): "Scholars are increasingly rejecting the whole notion of subjects, and exposing the fact that there seem to be no agreed rules for determining who can be classed a subject." As an alternative, some scholars have proposed to focus not on subjectivity, but on *participation* in international law (Bernaz 2017: 87). In sum, while these discussions are ongoing and far from settled, merely pointing to multinational corporations' alleged lack of international legal personality is no longer a valid argument anymore against BHR. The variety of positions on international legal personhood in general and on the international legal personhood of corporations in particular leaves ample room for diverse theorizations of corporations as bearers of human rights obligations.

6.2.3 Human Rights as Legal Imperatives of Business

The question whether or not corporations do or can have international legal personality resembles a chicken-and-egg conundrum: Some argue that because corporations do not have international legal personality, international law cannot be interpreted as favoring corporate human rights obligations; but others argue that because international law includes the basis on which human rights responsibility should be ascribed to corporations, they must as a consequence be attributed international legal personality, at least in a limited sense. This section dwells on the second line of argument. It is interested in the respective foundations that international law may already offer to assign human rights responsibility to corporations. For Andrew Clapham (2006:28–29) "one can accept that international law is mostly generated by accepted processes between nation states, but still reject the prevalent assumptions that . . . the bearers of international obligations are limited to presumed, so called, 'subjects' of international law." This reinforces the point that the very discussion about whether or not corporations have international legal personality is losing significance altogether.

The state-centeredness of international (human rights) law does not imply that international law is blind to the fact that corporations can and do violate human rights. Rather, it has traditionally perceived such violations not as being of direct and primary concern for the corporations themselves but rather as a failure of states to meet their own human rights obligations under international law to protect human beings from abusive conduct by corporations. States have to make sure, by means of domestic policy, legislation and regulation, that companies do not interfere with the enjoyment of human rights at least on their own territory (Joseph 2004: 9). Thus, international law has influence on the conduct of third parties at least indirectly, which is known as the concept of *Drittwirkung* (Bernaz 2017: 93). According to this logic, then, corporations can be said to have at least indirect human rights responsibilities implied by international law. Such a "horizontal" application of international human rights is expressly stated in a number of treaties, as well as supported by various court cases (Joseph 2004: 9; Bernaz 2017: 94–95) and reiterated in the UNGPs (Chapter 10). Whether the state duty to protect human rights extends also to the extraterritorial conduct of corporations is controversial and will be discussed later (Chapter 12.2).

As a response to the state duty to protect human rights, most domestic jurisdictions have implemented various human rights provisions in their national legislation and regulations concerning companies. Examples include worker protections for health and safety, product safety and liability, and anti-discrimination laws. Some commentators have even interpreted the state's duty to protect human rights from corporate abuse as implying – or being close to implying (Kamminga & Zia-Zarifi 2000) – a derivative direct corporate obligation to respect human rights, which is similarly rooted in international law (Ratner 2001; Bilchitz 2013: 112).

However, within the dominant state-centric doctrine, corporations are thought to have only very limited, if any, human rights obligations that can be derived directly from international law. At best, they have an obligation based on customary international law and certain treaties not to commit violations amounting to international crimes as defined by the Statute of the ICC (Chapter 3.2.2) (Joseph 2004: 9; Bernaz 2017: 81). It is commonly agreed that at least in connection with such violations of the most egregious kind – including slavery, war crimes, geno-cide, crimes against humanity, disappearances, and torture – individuals are also subject to respective international obligations (Clapham 2006: 29). Whether the inclusion of individuals extends to *legal* persons as well is unclear and subject to discussion. However, while such an extension to corporations may not be immedi-ately evident, neither is denying the possibility to do so.

The real controversy regarding the extension of direct human rights obligations to corporations is not in relation to international crimes, but rather occurs in relation to more "ordinary" human rights violations. However, a more progressive interpretation of international human rights law can offer possibilities to extend obligations to corporations also in a more general sense. Advocates for corporate human rights obligations like to point to the preamble of the UDHR, which expressly points out that not only states but "every individual and every organ of society shall strive... to promote respect for these rights." Businesses are thus not excluded from such a responsibility. The UDHR is not a binding instrument, but it does at the very least provide a foundation to question whether overly narrow state-centric inter-pretations adequately capture the spirit and original intention of the international human rights regime. Furthermore, in Article 30 the UDHR states that "Nothing in this Declaration may be interpreted as implying *for any State, group or person* any right to engage in any activity or perform any act aimed at the destruction of any of the rights and freedoms set forth herein" (emphasis added). This phrasing is con-tained with minor amendments also in Article 5 of both binding international covenants. The non-binding preambles of the two covenants, in addition, reiterate that not only states but also "the individual, having duties to other individuals and to the community to which he belongs, is under a responsibility to strive for the promotion and observance of the rights recognized in the present Covenant." Thus, the UDHR is concerned, overall, less with defining a particular relation between individuals and the state than with proclaiming the inherent rights belonging to all individuals. Most human rights stipulated in the UDHR are not defined with regard to a specific duty-bearer (Clapham 2006: 34).

> Some may say it is obvious that human rights are defined as rights exclusively
> applicable against the state, but no international definition states this in these terms. In
> fact ... the Universal Declaration was carefully drafted to avoid suggesting that the state
> has specific duties, the rights are written in the form of 'everyone has the right to...'. The
> focus is on the inherent possession of the right, and references to duties can be found to
> society, the state, groups, and individuals (Clapham 2006: 40).

Such an argument is similar to the moral rights-based ethical argument outlined above: If we understand human rights first and foremost as fundamental (ethical) entitlements of all human beings, it seems inevitable that they give rise to obliga-tions for everyone, rather than merely for governments. Accordingly, corresponding to this logic, some legal commentators have argued all along that corporations do have a duty also under the International Bill of Human Rights to respect human rights (Frey 1997: 163).

The state-centric paradigm underlying conventional interpretations of international (human rights) law is perhaps less intuitive than is commonly perceived. At the very least, it is not absolute and leaves room for non-state actors, among them business corporations, to assume human rights responsibilities in specific contexts and circumstances. While the international legal foundations of corporate human rights responsibility are neither clear-cut nor uncontroversial, there are plausible arguments that support their existence. Thus, the question of corporate human rights responsibility is one of extent, rather than of existence per se. In addition, there have been frequent attempts to create and spell out the foundations of such responsibility in international law by working toward specific binding instruments and frameworks (Chapter 2). In its latest attempt to do so, the HRC started new negotiations for a treaty on BHR in 2015 (Chapter 13.2.3). Furthermore, a variety of domestic legal initiatives have recently aimed at legislating human rights responsibility for companies, often with direct reference to international human rights law (Chapter 12.4). Hence, the basis on which human rights obligations are extended to business continue to develop both at the international and the national levels.

6.3 Pragmatic Perspectives on Human Rights Obligations of Business

While scholars may still be dwelling – and disagreeing – on the conceptual grounds and nuances of human rights responsibility, it has become commonplace in the broader public to use human rights terminology in direct relation to corporate conduct and responsibility. This changing public discourse on corporations and human rights coincides with a host of civil society organizations increasingly advocating for corporate human rights responsibility, various international corporate responsibility standards and initiatives incorporating human rights requirements, and not least increasing numbers of corporations framing corporate responsibility in human rights terms and adopting human rights policies and processes within their operations. Hence, while there may not necessarily be agreement on the ethical and legal foundations of human rights responsibility, human rights practice in connection with corporate conduct is changing rapidly. As Clapham notes:

> Of course, *claiming* a human rights abuse does not generate a human rights duty in law; but the term "human rights" has generated meanings and significance beyond the realm of international legal obligations owed by states ... Some governments may wish to restrict the meaning or understanding of the term "human rights", but excluding any obligations

for non-state actors through appeals to the "definition'", "essence", or "original sense" of the term "human rights" are unconvincing. (Clapham 2006: 41)

With human rights practice increasingly treating corporations as relevant actors in the human rights arena, more pragmatic arguments for corporate human rights responsibility have gained currency as of late. Such pragmatic arguments refer to and cater for the changing discourse in civil society, as well as in business itself. Arguments based on the changing public discourse stress the so-called "social license to operate" as the reference point for corporate human rights responsibility, while arguments appealing to the managerial discourse in the private sector refer to the so-called "business case" for corporate human rights responsibility. The following paragraphs will explore the two lines of argumentation in some more depth.

6.3.1   The Social License to Operate

When the former SRSG John Ruggie (Box 2.2) developed the UN Framework and the UNGPs, he did not look to the law or to ethics as a foundation for the corporate responsibility to respect human rights. Rather, he derived it from the changing social expectations toward business. The responsibility to respect human rights, according to Ruggie (2008: 5), is "the basic expectation society has of business." Respecting human rights has turned into a social norm, understood as a collective sense of what constitutes appropriate and expected conduct of a social actor (Ruggie 2013: 92). Thus, as Ruggie goes on, "the broader scope of the responsibility to respect is defined by social expectations – as part of what is sometimes called a company's social license to operate" (Ruggie 2008: 17).

The term and idea of a "social license to operate" has its origins in business practice and has been used particularly, although not only, in connection with the mining sector, whose operations often have direct adverse impacts on local communities. As a consequence, corporate-community relationships have often been tense or even confrontational in the sector. The term alludes to the tacit consent and acceptance a company enjoys for its activities in the wider community in which it is embedded. As such, it expresses the broader social legitimacy of corporate activities (Demuijnck & Fasterling 2016: 675). A company that fails to work in line with established social norms and to live up to its expected conduct – for example, by polluting the environment, wasting scarce resources, annexing communal land, or being unresponsive to community concerns – may sooner or later lose that acceptance and be faced with active resistance and opposition, which can lead to protests, civil unrest, conflict, and violence. Despite still holding a legal license issued by the authorities to continue its business operations, such a company is said to have lost its *social* license to operate and thus its legitimacy and approval among the people who are affected by its operations. The social license to operate, in the words of Ruggie (2008: 16), is withdrawn not in actual courts, but in the "courts of public opinion."

Pragmatic arguments invoking the social license to operate can be situated, conceptually, between genuine ethical arguments and a more narrow "business case" for corporate human rights responsibility (Chapter 6.3.2). The reference to social expectations and legitimacy places social license arguments clearly beyond the purely strategic considerations of business. As opposed to "business case" arguments, it implies that businesses ought to conform to social norms and expectations even if no immediate business benefit derives from such conformity.

Moral legitimacy, on the other hand, deviates from social legitimacy insofar as it subjects social expectations to ethical scrutiny, rather than accepting them as an unquestioned reference point from which to derive acceptable conduct. The UNGPs in particular have been criticized from an ethical perspective for their sole reliance on social expectations as a grounding for the corporate responsibility to respect human rights (Chapter 10.3.2.2). Social expectations have been criticized as normatively vague and indeterminate. What, after all, constitutes and who represents "society," and how do we measure what its expectations are (Deva 2014: 109–110)? How do we deal with conflicting or ill-informed expectations in this regard? And what if certain practices enjoy broad social acceptance despite conflicting with most basic ethical standards, as we have seen happen repeatedly throughout history? Finally, philosophers and economists have pointed to the related problem of adaptive preferences (Sen 1985). Human beings tend to adapt their expectations to the circumstances and contexts in which they live. Those living in abject poverty may thus have lower expectations toward business and other actors than those enjoying a higher standard of living. What is considered appropriate conduct may thus vary and exploitation and abuse by businesses may become socially acceptable under circumstances of despair. Furthermore, in many parts of the world, expectations toward corporate conduct may be low to begin with, based on past experiences with poor track records of such companies (Bilchitz 2013: 123). This, however, does not make such conduct ethically justifiable by any means. In sum, while references to the social license to operate have become a powerful argument to advance corporate respect for human rights, particularly where legal force is lacking, they must be used with caution. Especially in contexts in which discrimination, marginalization, and systematic human rights violations against minorities are endemic and widespread, the reliance on social acceptance may bolster, rather than expose such harmful practices.

6.3.2   The Business Case for Corporate Human Rights Responsibility

The second pragmatic perspective aims at showing the compatibility of corporate human rights responsibility with the dominant business rationale of pursuing profits. Foundational discourses may prove counterproductive to advancing corporate human rights responsibility in practice, since both moral and legal arguments may run counter to the dominant mode of business operations. As a consequence, businesses may react defensively or ignore them altogether. Therefore, such goes the argument, if real progress is to be made in practice, corporate human rights responsibility ought to be reframed in business terms and appeal to the underlying logic of costs and benefits. Thus, by "business case" we mean arguments as to why businesses should embrace human rights responsibility not for moral or legal reasons but for their own economic benefit. We can distinguish a positive and a negative business case for corporate human rights responsibility (Paine 2000). The positive argument stresses the possibility that respecting human rights may increase profits. The negative argument stresses the costs and risks associated with the potential violation of human rights.

Negative business case: Reputational considerations are perhaps the most common way to frame the business case for corporate human rights responsibility. Indeed, there is positive potential as well as negative reputational risks connected to corporate human rights conduct. However, in reputational terms, there is perhaps more to lose for corporations that violate human rights than there is to gain for those who promote human rights in exemplary ways. Companies' failure to uphold human rights standards – for example, in relation to workers and employees or communities affected by business operations – is often condemned widely, vigorously, and publicly by advocacy groups and NGOs and often generates public disapproval and backlash against the companies. This can directly reduce the value of companies, impact their market capitalization, and, for those serving consumer markets, lead to a decline in sales and thus profitability. Even for companies not tied directly to consumer markets, the consequences of bad human rights records can be damaging, economically. At least since the publication of the UNGPs, some governments have started to integrate corporate human rights responsibility into their procurement policies (Chapter 12.3.2). This means that corporations risk being excluded from lucrative procurement bids if they fail to effectively implement a corporate human rights policy and human rights due diligence procedures. This trend will likely continue in the future, which means that for corporations not actively concerned with their human rights conduct, it will become increasingly difficult to secure procurement contracts. In a variety of sectors, in which public authorities are the principal buyers, the impact of such exclusions can be severe. Examples include energy, transport, waste management, social protection, and the provision of health or education services (Baglayan et al. 2018).

Another cluster of arguments supporting the negative business case relates closely to this last point about procurement. In order to comply with their duty to protect human rights, governments have started to implement binding human rights legislation for corporations headquartered in their jurisdictions (Chapter 12.4). Corporations that fail to address this growing trend sufficiently early on will fall behind and incur increasing adjustment costs later on when such legislation becomes standard. Related to this is the growing litigation risk for corporations involved in human rights violations. The past two decades have heralded a steadily increasing number of home-state litigation cases in an expanding number of jurisdictions against parent companies whose foreign subsidiaries were allegedly involved in the violation of human rights (Chapter 12.5).

Positive business case: As pointed out above, in reputational terms, the negative consequences of violating human rights may outweigh the positive potential of leading with exemplary human rights conduct. After all, while human rights violations by corporations are often highly publicized, exemplary conduct often goes unnoticed publicly. Nevertheless, there are positive economic arguments for human rights responsibility as well and their significance may increase in the future. One major reason for this is the immanent generational shift as the so-called millennials are becoming an ever more important force within the key stakeholder groups of corporations. Millennials were born between 1980 and 2000 and count for 27 percent of the world population. They are generally perceived to be a generation with a heightened commitment to value and purpose not only in their private but also in their professional lives. Sustainability, responsibility, and not least human rights considerations are thus a much more significant part of their agenda than for previous generations. Accordingly, nine out of ten millennials believe that business success cannot be measured in terms of financial performance alone (Deloitte 2016). Thus, corporations will have to address the implications of this shift, as this generation makes up a growing part of the consumer, investor, and workforce base on which they inevitably depend. Looking at the future investment pool illustrates this generational shift clearly: Calculations indicate that an estimated $24 trillion will be passed on to millennials by 2020, representing one of the largest and most rapid intergenerational transfers of wealth ever (Haefele et al. 2017). However, not only in terms of investment but also in regard to the workforce, catering to millennials will be decisive in the future. It is estimated that by 2025, millennials will account for 75 percent of the global workforce (Winograd & Hais 2014). Generally, the fluctuation rate among millennials is high. Accordingly, it is getting more difficult for companies to retain their employees. This indicates that millennials are less willing to compromise on their values, for example, for a well-paid job. According to a large-scale research study, 56 percent of surveyed millennials stated that they would not work for an organization with poor values or standards of conduct. Furthermore, 49 percent are willing and ready to refuse undertaking particular tasks within companies, if they go against their personal values or ethics (Deloitte 2016). Thus, increasingly, companies pay for their poor human rights records in terms of heightened fluctuation rates and decreasing productivity (Baglayan et al. 2018).

Such economic arguments have provided the main motivation and rationale for corporations and governments alike to address BHR more seriously. For some, this renders the search for ethical and legal foundations and indeed the very question of

BOX 6.1 (Short case) Nike's path from worst to best case in supply chain responsibility

Building on the foundations of Blue Ribbon Sports, Nike was founded in 1971. The company pioneered a new globalized business model; while its competitors such as Adidas and Puma manufactured their shoes in Europe, Nike outsourced production to a network of independent suppliers in Asian countries with low labor costs (Hsieh, Toffel, & Hull 2019: 3).

The business model proved highly successful, but in the 1990s critics started to publicize images and reports of substandard working conditions in the factories of Nike's suppliers and their subcontractors. In 1996, *Life* magazine published an article featuring an image of a child stitching footballs with the Nike logo. The article prompted enormous public backlash and Nike became the symbol for globalized exploitation and workers' rights abuse, with then CEO and founder of Nike, Phil Knight, noting: "the Nike product has become synonymous with slave wages, forced overtime and arbitrary abuse" (Baker 2016). With its strong international brand, the company became one of the primary targets of the early anti-sweatshop movement, facing protests and consumer boycotts. In response, the company began to make efforts towards building a more responsible supply chain. Nike was the first company to publish a complete list of its suppliers; it established a suppliers' code of engagement and built a factory monitoring system (Baker 2016; Hsieh, Toffel, & Hull 2019: 4). Between 2002 and 2004 it conducted more than 600 factory audits (Nisen 2013). Eventually it reduced the number of suppliers and switched to a model that built on long-term relationships rather than on short-term transactions (Hsieh, Toffel, & Hull 2019: 8–9). This does not mean that the company did not experience any further setbacks over time. A similar incidence to the one in 1996 cost the company $100 million in recalling soccer balls in 2006. But it also showed that the company was ready to put principles over profits when it mattered. Today, Nike is widely seen as a leader in responsible sourcing and ranks consistently among the top performers in responsibility rankings (Baker 2016).

Discussion Questions

(1) Targeted NGO campaigns and resulting consumer backlash were decisive factors in Nike's turnaround from laggard to leader in corporate human rights responsibility. What is the potential of such "naming and shaming" campaigns (Chapter 9.4.3) in creating a business case for human rights responsibility more generally? What are their limitations? What other potential factors may have contributed to Nike's "success story"?

(2) Nike's switch from transactional relationships with many suppliers to long-term engagement of a smaller number of suppliers is a key component of its supply-chain responsibility strategy. What advantages do you see in such a strategy? What are its risks? You will find some insight on this question in Chapter 14.4.3.

(3) One important element of Nike's turnaround was to publicly acknowledge rather than to deny the challenges they faced in their factories (Nisen 2013). Why do you think such public acknowledgment is still rare today? What could be done to change this?

whether or not businesses have human rights responsibilities in the first place, a moot exercise. However, there are clear pitfalls to trusting blindly in the business case for corporate human rights responsibility. Most importantly, any such approach implies, advertently or inadvertently, that human rights responsibilities ought to be taken into consideration by companies only if they are consistent with the profit maximization aim (Garriga & Melé 2004). Many studies have tried to prove a causal link between social responsibility and increasing financial returns and indeed a whole subfield has emerged under the label of corporate social performance, which has centered on precisely this link between corporate financial and corporate social performance. However, the evidence provided by those studies has been mixed (see e.g. Orlitzky, Schmidt, & Rynes 2003; Rost & Ehrmann 2017) and the methodology and general conceptual soundness of such correlations has frequently been questioned (see e.g. Vogel 2005). Even where the numbers speak a clear language such as in the case of public procurement, such business case arguments are highly context-dependent (Paine 2000). As pointed out above, while public procurement is of essential importance in some sectors, others are less dependent on it. Similarly, litigation risk is significant in the extractive sector, while other sectors remain off the public radar despite dismal human rights records. Thus, while business case arguments may be highly effective in addressing corporate human rights conduct in some contexts, they hardly work across the board and thus cannot serve as a replacement for a thorough discourse on the foundations and justification of corporate human rights responsibility. For replacing foundational discourses risks leaving unaddressed all those pressing BHR issues that may not readily be translated into business opportunities.

6.4 Common Objections

Despite the idea of extending human rights responsibility to corporations being rooted in ethical, legal, and pragmatic arguments, not everyone agrees with it.

Therefore, this chapter concludes with a series of common, interconnected objections and possible responses to them.

Duplicating responsibility: States have a duty to protect human rights, which includes a duty to make sure that private actors, such as corporations, do not act in ways that prevent or diminish the opportunity of individuals to enjoy those rights. Thus, one could argue that if states met their own duty to protect human rights, assigning a responsibility to respect human rights to corporations would be redundant. This represents the classic state-centric view on human rights responsibility. In an ideal world, states would perhaps indeed be able to protect everyone from human rights harm. However, unfortunately, the world is less than ideal, the power and reach of governments is limited, and human rights violations are a part of the daily reality of countless people. If we take into account not only how the world should be, ideally, but how it is in reality, relying on the state alone to protect human rights seems to be problematic. Furthermore, the duty of governments to protect human rights represents a standard of conduct, rather than of results. It obligates states to put adequate measures in place to protect human rights in the best possible way, but it does not require absolute protection. Hence, states have a certain leeway to decide what measures are appropriate to ensure a reasonable degree of protection. Indeed, the very ideal of full protection may run counter to the liberal idea of a free and open society since it would essentially imply a police state in which constant surveillance and the restriction of free movement and further limitations to our individual freedoms would be necessary means to keep us out of harm's way. The ideal world of full governmental protection appears to be not all that ideal after all. A non-ideal world, in which responsibility necessarily is shared, on the other hand, is one in which freedom becomes possible as a result.

Replacing governments: The second objection is closely related to the first one. If we expand human rights responsibility to corporations, this can lead to governments shirking their own. The more we hold corporations directly responsible for their human rights conduct, the more incentive we provide for governments to withdraw from certain areas of human rights protection. Thus, rather than shifting responsibility to corporations, the objection goes, we should focus on strengthening the enforcement regime underlying state obligations. This touches on a real concern, of course, since the enforcement regime underlying state obligations indeed is fraught with major gaps. However, three points can be made in response. First and as pointed out above, the state obligations, which ought to be better enforced, do entail a duty to protect from corporate abuse. Thus, such a regime would have to make sure that, within the scope of their own duty to protect human rights, states find ways to effectively hold corporations accountable for their human rights conduct. Hence, enforcing state obligations does not exclude but rather entails the idea of corporate human rights responsibility. Second, the claim to enhance the enforcement regime underlying state obligations does not in and of itself imply that we cannot work on also improving corporate accountability systems at the same time. It is not about improving either one or the other, but about improving both simultaneously. Third, many human rights challenges have become too big and too complex for any government to solve alone. Not only do such challenges depend on cooperation between governments, but also on the constructive collaboration between various actors of different sectors, including business. If we ought to solve the pressing human rights challenges we are faced with as a global society today, we cannot afford to keep one of the most powerful actors – business – out of the equation when it comes to finding holistic solutions. Thus, within such collaborative efforts, corporate human rights responsibility is not at all about replacing state action. On the contrary, it is about leveraging it.

Legitimizing corporate power: From a political view, one of the core functions of human rights is to legitimize state power (Chapter 3.1.4.2). Thus, some have argued that shifting human rights responsibility to corporations would similarly imply the legitimization and therefore consolidation of corporate power. This, too, is a valid concern. However, it is important to note that the BHR movement not only demands an expansion of human rights *responsibility* to corporations but also a strengthening of corporate *accountability* in this regard. Thus, while human rights may infer legitimacy, they are crucial limitations to power at the same time. As Clapham (2006: 53) notes: "We can also see that, to deny the applicability of human rights law to powerful non-state actors, is to deny the empowerment which accompanies human rights claims." Corporate power has become a reality in today's society. Not extending human rights responsibility to such powerful actors means shielding them from accountability and granting them impunity.

> If human rights once offered a shield from state oppression in the vertical relationship between the individual and the state, they now also represent a sword in the hands of victims of private human rights abuses. Perhaps we do have to pull human rights inside out and acknowledge that they can be used against other human rights holders (Clapham 2006: 56).

The controversy about the foundations and justification of extending human rights responsibility to private actors will likely continue for some time. However, as the world continues to change in the direction of multipolarity and states become but one among many actors involved in international politics and global governance (Chapter 9), the state-centric paradigm underlying the discourse on human rights will eventually weaken and assessing private actors based on human rights considerations will become the new normal.

STUDY QUESTIONS

1. What are the three conditions that must be met for responsibility to be attributed to corporations as moral agents?
2. What are the arguments cited by proponents and opponents on corporate moral agency?
3. What is legal personality? What does it mean to say that corporations are legal persons?
4. Does it matter from a BHR perspective whether corporations do or do not have international legal personality?
5. What is the social license to operate and how often does it need to be "renewed"? How is the concept different from a "business case" argument?
6. Why are the millennials becoming an ever more important force when it comes to corporate human rights responsibility? Can you give a few examples?

REFLECTION QUESTIONS

1. What is the difference between the negative and the positive business case for corporate human rights responsibility? How plausible are such business case arguments, in your opinion? How important are they to advance BHR?
2. Based on the introduction to moral agency, who should be held morally responsible – the company, the individual, or both? Is there a trade-off between the two?
3. "Corporations are political actors with public responsibilities." Do you agree or disagree with this perspective? What are arguments in favor and against such a position?
4. One of the objections against corporate human rights responsibility is that it may incentivize states to "outsource" their own responsibility to companies. What, in your opinion, can and should be done to prevent such a scenario from happening?

7 Nature and Extent of Corporate Human Rights Responsibility

Corporate human rights obligations were justified in general terms in the last chapter, and this chapter defines their nature and extent further. The question is approached, first, by distinguishing different obligation types in a general manner before zooming in on human rights obligations in particular. It will discuss in detail the tripartite duty structure correlating with human rights and how the three types of human rights obligations – the obligation to respect, protect, and fulfil human rights – may be interpreted to apply to corporations.

7.1 Basic Obligation Types

One of the essential features of rights is that they correlate with obligations. If someone has a right to something, someone else has an obligation toward that person. From an ethical perspective, this inseparability of rights and obligations is one of the main reasons why a BHR discourse is necessary in relation to more conventional CSR discourses. While CSR is often associated with voluntary action based on charity and goodwill, BHR is based on rights and obligations. Thus, there is a different, more demanding normativity underlying BHR thinking.

There are different types of obligations that correlate with rights. A classic distinction is between negative and positive obligations (Pogge 2002: 197; Wettstein 2012c: 41), based on the *type of demand* that is placed on the obligation-bearer:

- *Negative obligations* are obligations of non-violation or non-infringement. In this vein, a negative human rights obligation is an obligation not to violate human rights or, in more general terms, an obligation to do no harm. This is commonly equated with an obligation to respect human rights. The UN Framework and the UNGPs (Chapter 10) define the responsibility to respect human rights along the same lines as a responsibility "not to infringe on the rights of others," or "put simply, to do no harm" (Ruggie 2008: 9).
- *Positive obligations* are obligations to provide assistance or generally to do good and thus to improve a given state of affairs – as opposed to negative

obligations, which merely aim at not making a given state of affairs worse (i.e. not to cause harm). Thus, positive obligations always require the obligation-bearer to actively do or contribute something in order to meet his or her obligation. It is not sufficient to simply do no harm.

Along with positive and negative obligations, a further distinction is between active and passive obligations (Wettstein 2012c: 41). This distinction is based on the *type of action (or omission)* that is required in order to meet the obligation:

- *Passive obligations* require the obligation-bearer to refrain from certain harmful or damaging actions in order not to violate human rights. Typically, passive obligations are negative in nature. Passive negative obligations require the obligation-bearer to abstain from any activity that could result in causing harm.
- *Active obligations*, on the other hand, require the obligation-bearer to perform certain specific actions in order to meet his or her obligations. Active obligations can be negative or positive in nature. Active negative obligations require the obligation-bearer to engage in specific activities in order to prevent his or her actions from harming others. For example, a company might have to actively adjust its policies and processes in order to make sure its recruiting practices are non-discriminatory. Active positive obligations require an obligation-bearer to engage in specific activities to assist people or to improve the current state of affairs. For example, a company may put affirmative action policies in place in order to actively promote diversity beyond "mere" non-discrimination.

A further distinction separates obligation types based on the *scope and range of obligation-bearers* that they address:

- *General or universal obligations* apply to everyone equally and at all times. Negative obligations, at least of the passive kind, are typically general or universal obligations. Everyone can and is supposed to abstain from harmful action, unless specific circumstances would justify it in exceptional cases. Self-defense in situations in which one's life is acutely threatened is a classic example of such an exception.
- *Special or particular obligations* only apply to specific agents. Typically, such special obligations are of positive character, and they derive from the specific capacities or capabilities or the specific social or professional roles of such agents. For example, lawyers or doctors are obligated in their professional roles to work in and for the best interest of their clients. Similarly, parents owe an obligation of special protection to their children. However, certain circumstances call for special negative obligations, which can similarly be attached to specific social or professional roles. An example, again, are lawyers, who owe a special duty of confidentiality to their clients, which would not normally be owed outside of professional roles.

Finally, we can distinguish between perfect and imperfect obligations, a distinction that is commonly associated with Kant's (1996 [1797]) moral philosophy:

- *Perfect obligations*: An obligation is considered to be perfect, understood in the sense of "complete," if three defining elements are clearly identifiable. These are a) the substance of the obligation, b) the obligation-bearer, and c) the corresponding rights-holder as the addressee of the obligation. Perfect obligations typically are of the negative kind, but also include certain well-defined special obligations of the positive kind (Wettstein 2009: 124).
- *Imperfect obligations*: Obligations are imperfect, or incomplete, if one of the three elements mentioned above remains unspecified. Typically, imperfect obligations refer to situations in which it is unclear to whom an obligation is owed. Most common among such obligations are so-called duties of beneficence. For example, we may agree that a corporation has a duty of beneficence to contribute to poverty alleviation. However, because the company is hardly in a position to solve the problem singlehandedly, such an obligation can only be defined in very general terms; it is not owed to any specific individual, but rather to the poor overall or even to society as such. A slightly different interpretation derives from the perspective of rights-holders. Since their rights are violated, an obligation to remedy is owed to them. However, while the addressees of this obligation can be clearly identified, it is unclear who owes the obligation in the particular case. Rather than a duty of beneficence, we are dealing here with an imperfect obligation of justice (Wettstein 2009: 127–134).

Such general distinctions are important in order to make sense of and critically assess the human rights obligations of businesses. The following section will zoom in on three types of human rights obligations, which, in a further step, can then be analyzed from a specific BHR lens.

7.2 Human Rights Obligations in Particular

As argued in Chapter 3.3.1, the common distinction between positive and negative rights proves too simplistic. Instead, the complete fulfilment of each right always requires the performance of multiple kinds of duties of both positive and negative nature (Shue 1996: 52). Henry Shue, who famously rejected the dichotomy between positive and negative rights, proposed a tripartite typology of obligations, all of which correlate with each and every basic right ranging from classical "negative" liberty rights to "positive" socioeconomic rights:

- *The duty to avoid depriving* corresponds to the duty to respect, that is, not to violate human rights. The duty to respect human rights is a negative obligation.

Shue himself formulates it in passive form as "a duty simply not to take actions that deprive others of a means that, but for one's own harmful actions, would have satisfied their [subsistence] rights or enabled them to satisfy their own [subsistence] rights, where the actions are not necessary to the satisfaction of one's own basic rights and where the threatened means is the only realistic one" (Shue 1996: 55). As indicated in the previous section, negative duties can be either of passive or active nature.

- *The duty to protect from deprivation* corresponds to the duty to protect human rights. Human rights protection means to make sure that rights are not violated through the conduct of third parties. The duty to protect human rights is a positive duty, since it is not about the obligation-bearer's own conduct, but rather about the conduct of potential third-party perpetrators. According to Shue, the duty to protect involves two parts, one direct and one indirect: direct protection is relational in nature. It means directly stopping a perpetrator from causing harm. Indirect protection is structural in nature and involves indirectly designing and supporting structures and institutions that make it less likely that those operating in and through them violate human rights (Shue 1996: 60).
- *The duty to aid the deprived* corresponds to the obligation to fulfil human rights or remedy them (in case of a prior violation). The duty to fulfil or remedy human rights is a positive obligation, since it always requires certain measures to assist those in need and improve a given state of affairs.

Shue's tripartite model of obligations is reflected by and large also in the legal structure of human rights (Joseph 2004: 9) and it similarly underlies also the UN Framework and the UNGPs (Chapter 10), which have coined the BHR movement since their publication.

7.3 Corporate Obligations to Respect, Protect, and Fulfil Human Rights?

Chapter 6 showed more generally that corporations can be said to have human rights obligations based on ethical, legal, and pragmatic grounds. After establishing the tripartite character of human rights, the next step is to assess how the three categories of human rights obligations specifically relate and apply to corporations.

7.3.1 The Corporate Obligation to Respect Human Rights

The obligation to do no harm is a general obligation, which is owed to everyone, by everyone, and at all times. Such an obligation necessarily includes human rights, since human rights abuse is among the most fundamental harms that can be done to human beings. An obligation not to violate and thus to respect human rights entails both direct and indirect violations as outlined in Chapter 4. Furthermore, it entails passive abstinence from harmful activities, as well as, where necessary, the adoption of active precautionary measures to prevent potential human rights risks from materializing.

This is the least controversial category of corporate human rights obligations. As a general obligation, it ought to apply to anyone, including business. Recent years have heralded the emergence of a broad consensus that corporations ought to respect human rights at minimum. This emerging consensus has much to do with the publication of the UN Framework in 2008 and the UNGPs in 2011. The UNGPs, which have since become the authoritative and most widely acknowledged BHR standard globally, have clearly established a corporate responsibility to respect human rights. The unanimous endorsement of the UNGPs by the HRC shows the broad agreement among nations in regard to this most basic human rights responsibility of corporations.

Respecting human rights is at the very least an ethical obligation of businesses. The UNGPs ground such an obligation in social expectations, but they do not establish it as a legal norm. Whether such an obligation can be derived from or ought to be established by law, whether international or domestic or both, is more controversial. However, as a negative and general obligation, the obligation to respect human rights is the most likely candidate among the three categories to be put into law. Accordingly, the current push for direct regulation of corporate human rights conduct through domestic legislation and policies focuses predominantly, if not exclusively, at mandating corporations to respect human rights (Chapter 12.4). Expanding such mandates to include also positive obligations for business to protect, promote, and fulfil human rights, would likely provoke insurmountable resistance. This was illustrated by the discussion around the UN Draft Norms back in 2003, when an attempt to establish the full range of negative and positive human rights obligations for corporations was stonewalled by businesses and Western governments (Chapter 2.2). It was this very struggle around the UN Draft Norms that led John Ruggie to focus exclusively on a corporate responsibility to respect human rights when drafting the UN Framework and the UNGPs (Chapter 10.1).

Whatever perspective we adopt beyond a purely legal one, it seems hard to argue against a basic corporate obligation to do no harm and it is similarly evident that such harm includes the basic elements covered by human rights. To insist that such an obligation includes genuine human rights obligations matters for at least two reasons. **First**, there is a moral urgency attached to human rights, which other moral claims lack. While the responsibility to do no harm is never merely a matter of charity or philanthropy but rather an ethical obligation, such harm connected to our basic human dignity claims highest priority when it comes to providing adequate responses. **Second,** distinguishing an obligation to respect human rights from the more general duty to do no harm makes sense in regard to its interpretation and specification in the industry-specific contexts in which companies operate. What it means to do no harm may be clear in principle. However, within the complex, highly specific and ever-changing contexts of various industries it is often less evident what activities can cause or contribute to harm and in what ways. Take the example of Information and Communication Technology (ICT) companies such as Google. What it means to do no harm may be evident and clear for Google in its direct relationships with its employees. However, it may be less clear when it comes to the question of how internet usage today can be linked to harm and in what ways Google as an ICT company may be facilitating it. Thus, the complex and often evolving contexts in which businesses operate keep raising new, unexplored questions about the mechanisms that produce harm and how they are linked to the operations of businesses. From a moral point of view, a human rights framework helps to conceptualize new issues and problems that emerge from such contexts and for managers it can provide a frame for respective instruments to detect and qualify such harm and respond to it adequately.

7.3.2 The Corporate Obligation to Protect Human Rights

Protecting human rights means working towards preventing or stopping third parties from infringing on the rights of others. It is not about an agent's own harmful conduct, but about the harmful conduct of a third party. This makes the obligation to protect essentially a positive obligation. As a positive obligation, the obligation to protect is not a general but a particular obligation. It applies only to specific agents in specific roles and under specific circumstances. This section aims at spelling out some of the key parameters and contexts that give rise to such an obligation.

The obligation to protect human rights has commonly been associated exclusively with the state. Governments have such a duty by matter of international law and, as pointed out above, this duty includes a mandate to protect people also from harm committed by corporations. The UNGPs have reiterated this state duty to protect human rights, while at the same time limiting the responsibility of corporations to respecting human rights (Chapter 10). However, all of this does not mean that there are no plausible arguments for corporate human rights obligations beyond mere non-violation. While it may be prudent for policy-makers and legislators to focus on a more narrow, enforceable obligation to respect human rights, the demands of morality may well support broader obligations of business, including an obligation to protect human rights. In order to assess to what extent this is the case, Shue's distinction between direct and indirect protection is helpful; both of those categories of protection may indeed bear some relevance also for corporations.

BOX 7.1 (Short case) Google in China

Google runs the most widely used and most successful search engine globally. But not so in China, where the local internet service provider Baidu dominates the market. Up until 2006, Google could compete with Baidu only from afar; the company had no local presence, but instead ran a Chinese-language search engine from outside of China. However, the search engine was filtered by Chinese authorities, and certain types of content that were deemed disrupting and inappropriate were blocked; many international news sources, information on historical events, or the websites of human rights organizations are commonly not accessible from inside China. This slowed Google's service down and often the website was entirely unavailable to the Chinese users (Quelch & Jocz 2010: 3). Thus, in 2006, Google decided to build a presence inside China in order to be competitive in the vast and fast-growing Chinese internet market.

However, running a search engine inside China meant that Google would have to abide by Chinese censorship rules and self-censor its search results. While this would allow Google to operate its search engine at a competitive speed and reliability, becoming a part of the censorship system in China conflicted with its basic values and ran against its company mantra of "don't be evil." On the other hand, Google hoped that through providing higher-quality and more reliable service and providing better and more information than its competitors despite censorship, it would be able to enhance access to information for the Chinese people over time (Brenkert 2009: 461). This plan did not work out. In 2010, after a series of cyberattacks on the Gmail accounts of human rights activists, Google reassessed its 2006 decision and came to the conclusion that it had not succeeded in being a force for good in China; indeed, on the contrary, repression and internet censorship and surveillance had increased during the time of Google's presence. As a consequence, Google decided to confront the Chinese government on the issue, releasing the following statement: "We have decided we are no longer willing to continue censoring our results on Google.cn, and so over the next few weeks we will be discussing with the Chinese government the basis on which we could operate an unfiltered search engine within the law, if at all. We recognize that this may well mean having to shut down Google.cn and potentially our offices in China" (quoted in Quelch & Jocz 2010: 8). The Chinese government was not impressed by Google's attempt at confrontation. As a consequence, Google stopped its operations in 2010 and moved to Hong Kong, from where it could run an uncensored search engine, which, however, was filtered and at times blocked again by Chinese authorities.

Discussion Questions

(1) What is the core issue in this case, from a BHR perspective? Why is it problematic for Google to operate from within China? From a freedom of information perspective, is the result of operating from within or outside of China not exactly the same?

(2) In its decision to move into China in 2006, Google weighed its positive responsibility to contribute to internet freedom more highly than its negative responsibility not to contribute to harm, stating that the "belief that the benefits of increased access to information for people in China and a more open Internet outweighed our discomfort in agreeing to censor some results" (quoted in Quelch & Jocz 2010: 7). Do you think Google's decision was justified?

(3) Business ethicist George Brenkert argued that under specific circumstances, moral compromise is justifiable. Moral compromise "involves doing something one believes is wrong to do, but this may be morally permissible if it is outweighed by other considerations" (Brenkert 2009: 468). What would you consider necessary conditions for such a compromise to be justifiable and do you think such conditions were met in the case of Google? What has changed for Google to believe that it could not uphold the compromise anymore in 2010?

(4) Commentators viewed Google's confrontation with the Chinese government as a bold move. Do you think Google was justified in presenting an ultimatum to the government or did it overstep its role as a private company? Is it for a company like Google to tell China how to handle internet access?

7.3.2.1   Direct Protection: Relational Contexts

Direct protection occurs in relational contexts – that is, within direct relations between a (potential) perpetrator and the obligation-bearer. Thus, the obligation-bearer intervenes directly in the activities of third parties to prevent them from violating someone else's rights. There are numerous situations in which corporations may engage in such interventions in order to protect human rights. But do they have an obligation to do so and, if so, under what circumstances? For example, does a corporation have an obligation to protect its employees if they are targeted by paramilitary forces in contexts of conflict? Does it have an obligation to protect villagers in the vicinity of its operations from the violence of government forces? Does it have to protect people from human rights abuse on its doorstep even if such violations are entirely unconnected to its own business activities?

Most, if not all, international soft-law initiatives and standards in the BHR domain, including the UNGPs and the UNGC, agree that under some circumstances, inactivity by companies in the face of human rights violations can be problematic and render the company silently complicit with the abuse (Chapter 4.3.2). To avoid silent complicity, as these initiatives commonly advise, companies ought to "intervene with the authorities to try and prevent or stop the violations" (International Council on Human Rights Policy 2002: 133). However, trying to prevent and stop violations through intervening actively with the perpetrators is commonly associated with protecting, rather than merely respecting, human rights. Accordingly, silent complicity "suggests that a non-participant is aware of abusive action and, although possessing some degree of ability to act, chooses neither to help protect nor to assist victims of the abuse, remaining content to meet the minimal ethical requirement to do no (direct) harm" (Kline 2005: 79). Thus, circumstances of silent complicity occur if companies violate a duty to protect by not intervening with perpetrators even though they would be in a position to do so. This specific context of silent complicity shows that limiting corporate human rights obligations to negative non-violation at the outset is problematic. The UNGPs, which limit the corporate responsibility to respecting human rights while at the same time accepting silent complicity as a relevant offense applicable to corporations seem to be incoherent in this aspect (Wettstein 2013). The broad acceptance of silent complicity by most international policy instruments and soft-law initiatives seems to point at least implicitly to the existence of contexts in which corporations may incur certain obligations to (help) protect human rights.

Some scholars have defined such contexts in much broader terms. They contemplate an obligation to protect human rights as a possibility in potentially all situations in which corporations have a certain leverage or influence over the perpetrator. Whether or not one agrees, in principle, to a corporate obligation to protect human rights, it is clear that as a particular obligation, it is based and dependent on certain conditions being met. That is, it is always a *qualified* obligation. Commonly, those who argue in favor of a corporate obligation to protect human rights see, in various combinations, the following conditions as relevant (Santoro 2000, 2009, 2010; Wettstein 2010, 2012c; Wood 2012):

- *Power/Influence*: As opposed to an obligation not to violate human rights, which applies to any actor, whether weak or powerful, an obligation to protect can only be fulfilled by those with a sufficient degree of power and influence over the situation or the perpetrator to prevent or stop the abuse. Power is a necessary, but not sufficient, condition for an agent to have an obligation to protect human rights. It is not least due to this condition that conventional thinking on human rights assigns an obligation to protect exclusively to states. However, as seen in Chapter 6.1.3, corporations increasingly operate in positions of substantial political power and de facto authority, which may give rise to an obligation to protect human rights in particular contexts and circumstances.

- *Connection*: To argue that corporations ought to intervene and protect human rights wherever they have the possibility and power to do so would not only overburden them morally, but also threaten to undermine the very institutional purpose they are meant to fulfil. Thus, while an obligation to protect does not presuppose that a corporation is directly involved in or contributing to a human rights violation, there must be a morally significant connection to the victims, the perpetrator, or the harm that is being done, in order for such an obligation to exist. For example, the fact that Shell was at the very center of the protests that led to the arrest and execution of Ken Saro-Wiwa in 1995 (Chapter 2.1) inevitably links Shell in a morally significant way to the killing and might establish, along with the other conditions listed here, a duty to speak out against and intervene with Saro-Wiwa's arbitrary detention and killing.

- *Normative burden/reasonableness*: Any obligation must meet the condition of reasonableness. Fulfilling a potential obligation cannot come at unreasonable cost or even hardship for the obligation-bearer. What is to be considered reasonable or proportional is dependent not least on what is at stake. Arguing that rescuing someone from drowning would have destroyed one's new, expensive suit certainly is not acceptable as a sufficiently weighty reason. However, if rescuing another person puts one's own life in acute and serious danger, the sacrifice might become unreasonably high. Included in the question about normative burden is the risk of severe retaliation by a potential perpetrator. Those intervening with perpetrators to stop them from violating human rights risk that they will become a target of retaliation. Therefore, the ability to withstand or absorb potential retaliatory action is commonly seen as a part of the relevant conditions for an obligation to protect human rights (Santoro 2010; Wood 2012).

- *Egregiousness*: Those in support of a corporate obligation to protect tend to restrict the relevant contexts in which such an obligation arises to egregious and systematic human rights abuse (Wettstein 2012c; Wood 2012). Corporations lack democratic legitimacy, which makes interference with public institutions per se problematic. Therefore, they should use their influence and leverage only in regard to human rights violations that are widely condemned and in situations in which there is a broad social expectation that they do get involved. Furthermore, they ought to rely on adequate support from civil society organizations and other agents with relevant human rights expertise.

As this last point made clear, successful practical implementation of such an obligation to protect human rights crucially depends on partnership and cooperation. Corporations should operate in broad coalitions, whenever possible. Such coalitions should include other corporations facing this same issue, as well as civil society organizations with adequate expertise and a track record of action and advocacy on such issues. They should also be in close contact with their home government and their embassies in the respective countries. Acting in concert with other like-minded actors serves two purposes. First, it helps to build leverage over and increase pressure on the perpetrator and at the same time shields a company from the full force of potential retaliation. Second, the broader such a coalition becomes, particularly in regard to the inclusion of civil society actors, the higher the legitimacy of its actions. A corporation is not a human rights institution and may lack sufficient expertise to get such responses right when acting on its own. Basing such decisions and actions on the view of a broad and diverse coalition of actors from different sectors may not only provide reassurance but also garner support in society more broadly.

7.3.2.2   Indirect Protection: Structural Contexts

In an increasingly complex, globally interconnected world, an ever-growing part of human rights violations have structural root causes. They are the result of the complex interplay of a large number of structurally connected actors and not necessarily of targeted, malicious acts of more or less isolated and identifiable perpetrators. Examples include human rights violations linked to poverty, malnutrition, climate change and other grand challenges we are facing as a global society.

Those who knowingly participate in harmful structures can be said to be at least structurally complicit in such human rights violations (Wettstein 2009: 304–305). However, the causal chain between their own actions and the harm that results from unjust structures is often too complex and too obscure to determine the degree of responsibility of one particular actor, let alone to hold them accountable for it. Furthermore, particularly when looking at global economic processes or the causes of climate change, it may be impossible for any one actor to exit such structures altogether. Thus, a different approach to our thinking about responsibility under structural conditions is needed in order to tackle the resulting human rights violations.

One influential approach to conceptualize responsibility under conditions of structural harm is the late philosopher Iris Marion Young's (2006; 2011) "social connection model" of responsibility. In this model, Young argues that global obligations of justice arise based on the social connections between people that are rooted in such structural processes. The basic assumption underlying the social connection model is that all agents who participate in unjust global structures, and therefore contribute to the harm that results from those structures, have an obligation to work toward their transformation for the protection of those who are harmed by them. Since the degree of an agent's responsibility cannot be determined based on its causal contribution, Young advances four parameters, based on which the degree and kind of obligation can be assessed:

- *Power*: Power or influence is a defining factor also for the kind of structural responsibility advanced by Young. Young (2006: 127) states that "an agent's position within structural processes usually carries with it a specific degree of potential or actual power or influence over the processes that produce the outcomes." This is the essence of what was earlier denoted as structural power (Chapter 6.3.1). The responsibility to influence and change unjust structures lies predominantly with those who have the power to do so.
- *Privilege*: Structures that produce injustice on one side always also create privilege on the other. While some are harmed by the structural processes, others in more privileged positions benefit from them. It is safe to assume that current economic structures would not be in place if no one benefited substantially from them. Privilege often but not always coincides with power. For example, human rights violations are endemic in the structures of the apparel industry (Chapter 14.4). While informal low-wage workers in the Global South are often exploited, middle-class income consumers in the West benefit greatly (Young 2006: 128). However, while they are in privileged positions, they generally hold little power individually. Nevertheless, they may have a responsibility based on their relative privilege. As Young (2006: 128) concludes, "Persons who benefit relatively from structural injustices have special moral responsibilities to contribute to organized efforts to correct them, not because they are to blame, but because they are able to adapt to changed circumstances without suffering serious deprivation."
- *Interest*: This is the most controversial of Young's parameters for structural responsibility. It means that those with the greatest interest in structural change have a responsibility to work more forcefully towards it. Essentially, this means that the victims themselves have a responsibility to be involved and cooperate in the efforts of structural change, not least because much of the essential knowledge necessary for such undertakings is with the victims (Young 2006: 128). This parameter has often led to criticism. After all, the lack of involvement of victims' voices in remedy efforts has rarely been due to a lack of interest on the part of the victims, but rather to a lack of commitment to full or adequate representation on the part of those who control such processes.
- *Collective ability*: Since the transformation of unjust structures can only be achieved by collective action, agents' ability to organize and work collectively towards particular goals is a parameter in the responsibility equation, as well (Young 2006: 129). Those who are in positions to act swiftly, for example, because they have access to important networks whose organized support could make a real difference have a respective responsibility to make use of that possibility.

Based on these parameters, Young's social connection model is less interested in attributing blame and guilt and thus in backward-looking liability for structural harm than it is in assigning forward-looking responsibility for prevention and protection. Since such forward-looking responsibility requires collective organization and action, Young defines such responsibility as *political* responsibility. Hence, such an understanding of corporate human rights responsibility as political responsibility resonates with a view of corporations as economic, social, and political actors, as outlined earlier (Chapter 6.1.1).

7.3.3   The Corporate Obligation to Fulfil Human Rights

Corporations are operating in powerful positions and play key roles in the provision of some of the essential products and services to meet our basic needs. Think of the food and beverage industry, pharmaceuticals and healthcare, transportation, but also banking and insurance and many other sectors on which we rely daily. Such powerful positions come with respective responsibilities, which may reach beyond "merely" respecting and even beyond protecting human rights into the realm of human rights fulfilment. Human rights fulfilment means contributing to the realization of the rights and providing remedy where they have been violated.

The SRSG, who limited corporate human rights responsibility to the non-violation of human rights, acknowledged that "there are situations in which companies may have additional responsibilities – for example, where they perform certain public functions, or because they have undertaken additional commitments voluntarily" (Ruggie 2008: 9). However, he did not specify these responsibilities or the contexts in which they occur. At least three such contexts can be distinguished, ranging from specific to general and giving rise to respective corporate responsibilities in the domain of human rights fulfilment. However, it is important to emphasize that the three contexts merely raise the *possibility* of such obligations and that their existence is contested. Nevertheless, it seems essential for any account of BHR to contemplate if and under what circumstances businesses may indeed have such obligations to get involved in the proactive fulfilment of human rights. The three contexts are as follows.

- *Corporate obligation to rescue*: It is reasonable to argue that everyone has an obligation to come to the help of people in acute distress if such hardship is sufficiently weighty, if the people who can help are well-positioned to provide immediate help, and if there are no reasons of equal weight that prevent them from helping. Helping people in acute danger is even a legal obligation in many jurisdictions. Thus, the context of such an obligation to rescue are extraordinary and specific, but the duty is general: Everyone has such an obligation if the circumstances are met; corporations are no exception in this regard. Stepan Wood (2012: 79) outlines four conditions that must be met in order for such an obligation to rescue to arise: 1) *urgency*: the situation must be urgent, meaning that an important and basic interest must be acutely and severely threatened; 2) *ability*: the potential obligation-bearer must have the ability, that is, knowledge, capacity (including resources), and experience to help the person(s) in distress; 3) *opportunity*: the potential obligation-bearer must be well-positioned in the sense of being in the right place at the right time to provide help; 4) *affordability*: the potential obligation-bearer must be in a position to help without incurring unreasonable costs to him- or herself. While the situations in which such an obligation to rescue can indeed be consistently applied to corporations may be rare, they cannot be ruled out per se. Such situations provide a context in which arguing for corporate human rights obligations beyond do no harm seems plausible and conceptually coherent, no matter how frequent or infrequent they may occur in reality.

- *Corporations in public functions*: Particularly during the heyday of neoliberal globalization between the 1980s and the early 2000s, many of the essential public services, such as utilities – including water and electricity, healthcare, security, telecommunications, and transport – were handed over partly or fully to the private sector. The hope was that private companies would be able to deliver them more efficiently and less costly. Many of these services are intimately connected to the ability of people to meet basic needs and thus to their very human rights. For exactly that reason, their public provision has always been based on the principles of affordability and equal access. The mere involvement of private corporations and the hope for efficiency gains does not change the primacy of these principles. What we call "privatization" of such services does not mean that their provision ought to be subjected to the primacy of private gain, but rather that private companies are integrated into public provision and thus ought to observe the principles underlying it. As such, they naturally incur a public responsibility that is attached to the provision of such services. It seems hardly plausible to argue that all we expect from such companies is that they do no harm. Rather, they ought to work toward the progressive expansion of equal access to such services and thus toward the progressive fulfilment of human rights.

- *Collaborative obligations*: Governments have become increasingly dependent on other actors – international organizations, NGOs, and also corporations – for the fulfilment of human rights, not merely when it comes to the provision of "classic" public services. Corporations are highly specialized organizations that have resources, capabilities, expertise, networks, and outreach that can play critical roles in addressing persistent human rights problems. The same logic can be observed at the international level, where organizations like the UN or even the International Committee of the Red Cross (ICRC) have come to realize that the provision of holistic solutions for some of the most pressing human rights and humanitarian challenges the world faces requires the involvement of a variety of actors, including corporations. Such involvement of the private sector with organizations like the ICRC are often accompanied by criticism from civil society organizations, who fear that the private corporate interests may co-opt the public mission of such organizations. Thus, adequate safeguards to prevent such co-optation from happening must be in place for any such collaborative arrangement. However, there is broad acknowledgment that many of the problems and challenges that we face today have simply become too complex and multifaceted to be solved by any one actor alone; they require collaborative solutions, involving actors from all sectors. While such proactive corporate engagement can hardly be enforced by law, it has become a broad social expectation of business. As early as 2009, a survey by the Edelman Trust Barometer (Edelman 2009: 3) showed that two-thirds of people aged between twenty-five and sixty-four around the world believe that businesses should step up and partner with governments and other institutions to address global issues. Furthermore, as the report stated, "virtually no one believes that business has no role in addressing these challenges" (Edelman 2009: 3).

It is tempting to look at such proactive corporate engagement for the fulfilment of human rights merely as a "nice to have" on top of the more essential duty to do no harm. However, as Shue (1996: 62) pointed out, "it is duties to aid that often have the highest urgency, because they are often owed to persons who are suffering the consequences of failures to fulfil both duties to avoid and duties to protect." Thus, creating hierarchies between different duty categories may be of little help in developing a holistic understanding of corporate human rights obligations. Rather, we should get used to the idea that corporations may have equally important responsibilities in each of the three categories and meeting a responsibility in one category never absolves them of meeting the ones also in the other respective categories.

STUDY QUESTIONS

1. What are negative and positive obligations? What distinguishes them from each other? Can you add a practical example for each?
2. What are active and passive obligations? What distinguishes them from each other? Can you add a practical example for each?
3. What is the tripartite typology of obligations according to Henry Shue?
4. What conditions are commonly viewed as relevant when arguing in favor of a corporate obligation to protect human rights?
5. Why did Iris Marion Young reconceptualize responsibility in her "social connection model" ? What was the thinking behind her doing so? Why does

she call it a model of *political* responsibility? Can you name and explain the four parameters that are relevant to determine the agent's responsibility in her model?

REFLECTION QUESTIONS

1. Some multinational corporations have become exceptionally powerful institutions, sometimes even more powerful than nation-states. Should they use their power and influence to protect human rights? What benefits do you see and what risks may be associated with it?

2. In 1995, Shell was criticized for not taking position and intervening with the Nigerian government to ask for the release of Ken Saro-Wiwa and eight other Ogoni activists. Was this criticism justified, in your opinion? Did Shell have such a responsibility?

3. Can a corporate obligation to fulfil human rights be reconciled with the profit motive of business or are we asking companies to become philanthropic institutions by arguing for such an obligation?

4. Some critics fear that positive corporate human rights obligations may potentially become limitless, since there is always more that a corporation could do to help. Where can and should we draw the line for such obligations? Is Young's "social connection model" sufficient in specifying that line?

8 Operationalizing and Implementing Human Rights Responsibility at the Corporate Level

Arguing conceptually for corporate human rights responsibility is one thing. However, implementing it effectively in the operations of companies is quite another. Particularly after the publication of the UNGPs, implementation moved to the center of attention in the BHR field. The UNGPs suggest that companies conduct human rights due diligence (HRDD) to ensure respect for human rights. As a result, HRDD as promoted by the UNGPs has quickly turned into the standard and benchmark to assess corporations' implementation efforts. Nevertheless, while best practices clearly are oriented toward such approaches, HRDD alone will not suffice to make sure that human rights are not violated by corporations. This chapter will first look more thoroughly at HRDD as a standard tool to address corporate human rights responsibility and, second, reflect on what else corporations ought to do beyond HRDD to truly organize for human rights.

8.1 Managing Impacts: Human Rights Due Diligence

The core idea behind HRDD is that corporations ought to conduct their operations with due care for human rights. They ought to do what is reasonably possible and in their power to avoid infringing on human rights through their own actions or contributing to violations committed by others. They ought to do so, in a nutshell, by identifying, assessing, monitoring, and mitigating their human rights impacts (Fasterling & Demuijnck 2013: 801).

The UNGPs' rationale for introducing HRDD was that due diligence more generally was new neither to (international) law nor to corporate practice. New was "merely" its connection to human rights. Thus, the UNGPs put at their center a concept to which corporations as well as human rights lawyers and advocates could relate.

8.1.1 Human Rights Due Diligence in Law

In law, due diligence has its origins in Roman law and is commonly understood as a standard of conduct, which is closely related to the tort of negligence: Acting with diligence is the flip side of negligence (Bonnitcha & McCorquodale 2017: 903). Negligence means acting without the care or diligence that is called for to avoid harming others. Thus, there is an obligation to take reasonable precaution to anticipate, foresee, and avoid harm (Bonnitcha & McCorquodale 2017: 904). In its interpretive guide specifically on the UNGPs, the OHCHR defined due diligence in general and HRDD more specifically as follows:

> Such a measure of prudence, activity, or assiduity, as is properly to be expected from, and ordinarily exercised by, a reasonable and prudent [person or enterprise] under the particular circumstances; not measured by any absolute standard, but depending on the relative facts of the special case. In the context of the Guiding Principles, human rights due diligence comprises an ongoing management process that a reasonable and prudent enterprise needs to undertake, in light of its circumstances (including sector, operating context, size and similar factors) to meet its responsibility to respect human rights. (OHCHR 2012: 4)

Due diligence provisions aiming at corporate conduct more generally are well developed in many domestic systems as a part of corporate governance. They have their origins in securities law and can be traced back to financial regulation after the Great Depression in the United States (Martin-Ortega 2014: 51). In this commercial and financial context, due diligence aims to "confirm facts, data and representations involved in a commercial transaction in order to determine the value, price and risk of such transactions, including the risk of future litigation" (Martin-Ortega 2014: 51). Due diligence provisions are often used also as statutory defense for corporations. Under such provisions, corporations can defend themselves against lawsuits or criminal charges by showing that the alleged offenses happened despite them having done everything that could be reasonably expected to prevent such harm occurring (Fasterling & Demuijnck 2013: 806; McCorquodale et al. 2017: 203).

More recently, a number of domestic laws have included more specific HRDD provisions for corporations (Chapter 12.4). For example, in the United States, section 1502 of the US Dodd–Frank Wall Street Reform and Consumer Protection Act requires companies to report on their supply chain due diligence and disclose whether conflict minerals were sourced from the Democratic Republic of the Congo (DRC) and neighboring countries (Chapter 12.4.2.1). The California Supply Chain Transparency Act requires companies to show how they combat modern slavery and human trafficking in their supply chains (Chapter 12.4.1.2). Similarly, in the UK, the Modern Slavery Act requires companies to report on their measures to eliminate modern slavery in their operations and supply chains (Chapter 12.4.1.1). Under the French Duty of Vigilance Law, large companies have to publish their annual vigilance plans in order to avoid human rights violations in their operations and supply chains (Chapter 12.4.3.1).

Due diligence is an accepted standard of reasonable precaution also in international human rights law, where it has been used particularly as a standard to assess "State compliance with international human rights obligations when address-ing the conduct of non-State actors" (Martin-Ortega 2014: 45). Such due diligence standards to assess state responsibility in regard to the actions of non-state actors are common in other areas of international law as well (Martin-Ortega 2014: 53). States are to exercise due diligence to prevent, punish, investigate, or redress the harm caused by third parties. Thus, an act by a third party that violates human rights, even if not attributable to the state, can lead to international responsibility of a state if there was a lack of due diligence on the part of the state to prevent or respond to the violation (Martin-Ortega 2014: 54). However, in regard to the state's own actions, a breach of its obligations is not dependent on whether or not the state acted with due diligence (Bonnitcha & McCorquodale 2017).

8.1.2   Human Rights Due Diligence in Business Practice

In corporate practice, due diligence has a long history as a procedure and instrument to assess the risk of financial and commercial transactions (Martin-Ortega 2014: 49). It is best known as a risk assessment tool in the context of mergers and acquisitions. In such contexts, due diligence commonly requires a thorough vetting of the risks a new project, new business partner, or new acquisition may pose to a corporation's objectives. Thus, due diligence is commonly perceived as a risk management task (Fasterling 2017: 226), as a "process of investigation conducted by a business to identify and manage commercial risks" (Bonnitcha & McCorquodale 2017: 901).

Starting in the mid-1990s due diligence was increasingly used by – and required from – businesses to address broader concerns beyond narrow commercial or financial transactions, such as anti-corruption and anti-bribery efforts (Matin-Ortega 2014: 49–50). More recently, due diligence has been applied to non-financial areas of business, particularly as they pertain to sustainable management. Examples include social and environmental impact assessments or health impact assessments that companies conduct in order to understand the implications and risks emanat-ing, for example, from new projects (Götzmann 2017: 89). Finally, the UNGPs extended the application of due diligence procedures to human rights concerns, pointing to the similarity of such HRDD with existing risk assessment and manage-ment processes in companies. Thus, the UNGPs translated the familiar commercial interpretation of due diligence into the less familiar sphere of human rights (Martin-Ortega 2014: 51).

HRDD, as envisioned by the UNGPs, has much in common with more conven-tional enterprise risk management systems, particularly as they pertain to social and environmental risks (Fasterling 2017: 229). However, a decisive difference is that while conventional enterprise risk management systems are designed to identify and assess a company's vulnerabilities (Fasterling 2017: 230), HRDD addresses the vulnerabilities of affected rights-holders. This is one of three key characteristics of HRDD:

- *Risk to rights-holders*: While enterprise risk management systems commonly understand "social risk" as the risk for the company, which emanates from the social sphere (for example, reputational risks, or risks of operational disruption due to protests), human rights risk, as it pertains to HRDD, means the potential or actual adverse impacts of company operations on rights-holders (Fasterling 2017: 230–231). Hence, HRDD requires a change of perspective from "risk to the company" to "risk to the rights-holders." This insight is of key methodological importance, since it implies that HRDD processes differ from other types of due diligence and are not readily compatible with more conventional risk management systems (Fasterling 2017; McCorquodale et al. 2017). Chapter 8.1.5.2 will pick up on this point in more detail.
- *Actual and potential impacts*: HRDD is about the identification and mitigation of both actual and potential adverse human rights impacts resulting from business conduct. Where actual impacts are identified, the company ought to mitigate and eliminate them as well as respond with remedial action, if warranted. Where potential adverse impacts are identified, companies need to put adequate precautionary measures in place to make sure such impacts will not materialize.
- *Ongoing process*: Precisely because HRDD is also about potential impacts, it must be understood as an ongoing process rather than a one-off exercise. The circumstances and contexts in which businesses operate are constantly changing. This means also that the potential human rights impacts arising from business operations can change over time. Therefore, HRDD requires businesses to assess and address such potential impacts on an ongoing basis.

Having defined HRDD in basic terms and outlined some of its key features, the following section will now have a closer look at the main elements of an HRDD process as it is required by the UNGPs.

8.1.3 Human Rights Due Diligence Process

Standard HRDD processes as defined by the UNGPs consist of four consecutive steps. They are: 1) assessing actual and potential human rights impacts; 2) integrating and acting upon the findings; 3) tracking responses; and 4) communicating how impacts are addressed. Even prior to setting up an HRDD process, businesses ought to adopt an explicit human rights policy. Furthermore, where human rights have been violated, corporations must engage in providing adequate remedy. This subchapter outlines such an HRDD framework. However, the concrete implementation of such a process is necessarily specific to the industry in which a company operates (Chapter 8.1.5.1).

8.1.3.1 Committing to Human Rights: Human Rights Policy Statement

A human rights policy expresses a company's basic commitment to respect human rights in its operations. Such statements commonly outline the company's stance and interpretation of its human rights responsibility, along with the underlying rationale for this commitment. Some human rights policies include an endorsement of specific standards such as the UNGPs or the UNGC in order to provide more substance to the company's human rights commitment. Generally, human rights policies are broad, normative statements and do not commonly include any details on how respect for human rights ought to be or will be implemented by the company.

For companies aligning their human rights policies with the UNGPs, Principle 17 outlines five basic requirements for such a policy:

- *Top management endorsement*: A human rights policy statement should be approved and endorsed by the most senior level of management. After all, such a policy, if taken and implemented seriously, ought to change the very way a company conducts its business. However, such a far-reaching policy will only be taken and implemented seriously if its message is perceived to come straight from the top. Conversely, if a human rights policy is perceived as not having the support of top management, it will likely fail to have any real impact on the daily operations of the company.
- *Human rights expertise*: A human rights policy should be informed by relevant internal and/or external expertise. Drafting such a policy requires both business expertise and expertise in human rights. It is unlikely that there is an abundance of human rights expertise within companies at early stages of human rights engagement. Thus, most companies will be well advised to bring external experts into this process, as well.
- *Third-party expectations*: A human rights policy should not only outline the company's own commitment to human rights, but also its expectations of personnel, business partners, and other parties linked to it. A company cannot coherently commit to human rights and do business or partner up with other parties that fail to adhere to the same standards. Doing so would essentially mean that the company is not working toward the elimination of adverse human rights impacts, but is merely outsourcing it to third parties.
- *Public accountability*: A human rights policy should be made publicly available and communicated to all relevant parties both internally and externally. A company that states its human rights commitment and expectations publicly can be held to account for it by anyone interested in the company's conduct. Thus, a company that adopts a human rights policy statement will subject itself to public scrutiny and measures of its accountability.
- *Integration and implementation*: The commitments of the human rights policy ought to be integrated in operational policies and procedures and embedded and implemented throughout the enterprise. After all, for a policy to be brought to life, it must have an impact not only on what the company believes in but on what it *does*.

A human rights policy statement serves two important functions. On the one hand, it signals *internally* that human rights are to be taken seriously and integrated into the processes and daily operations of the business. On the other hand, it expresses *externally* that the company is ready to be measured by and held to account on its human rights commitment. Against this background, a policy statement can and perhaps should be ambitious and aspirational, but at the same time it needs to be realistic in terms of what a company is able to achieve. Nevertheless, it is evident that a human rights policy on its own will be of limited value. For it to be effective, a company needs to foster and ensure broad buy-in among its leadership and its employees and it must follow through in implementing and bringing it to life throughout the entire organization. An inclusive drafting and development process, in which both internal and external stakeholders are represented, can go a long way in achieving legitimacy, buy-in, and ownership for the policy. Furthermore, the process of developing a human rights policy is itself an important element in both fostering an internal conversation and engaging with external stakeholders on human rights. Thus, while the finalized policy is important, the process of getting there is of equal significance (GBI 2017a).

8.1.3.2   Identifying Impacts: Human Rights Impact Assessments

Identifying and assessing actual and potential human rights impacts is the first step of the HRDD process. A company can be involved with adverse human rights impacts either directly through its own activities or indirectly as a result of its business relationships. For this purpose, companies can and ought to conduct so-called human rights impact assessments (HRIAs).

Conducting an HRIA means to assess who is impacted by the corporations' operations and in what way, and how such actual and potential impacts relate to relevant human rights standards. HRIAs are still an emerging practice and there is less established knowledge on HRIAs compared to the practices of environmental or social impact assessments (Götzmann 2017: 88). Both environmental and social impact assessments have turned into key corporate risk management tools and in many jurisdictions environmental impact assessments in particular are even required by law for the approval of new large-scale projects (Götzmann 2017: 89–90).

Most companies conduct HRIAs in two phases (Graf & Iff 2017: 124). The first phase assesses the typical industry-related human rights risks as well as the human rights situation and context in a specific country or region of operation. There are a number of organizations, both profit and non-profit, that have specialized in providing such information for businesses. HRIAs should draw on such services as well as on available reports, academic writings, and other information to create a detailed human rights risk profile of the area in which a company is operating. This first step consists predominantly of desk research. The second phase deals with the identification and assessment of the concrete and specific human rights impacts of the company's operations on the ground. Here the company ought to engage directly with potentially affected stakeholders to gain a holistic understanding of what impacts its operations generate and for whom. There are two key requirements for such a process, which are specified directly in Principle 18 of the UNGPs:

1. *First*, HRIAs must be based on explicit human rights expertise. Where such expertise is available internally, companies should make use of it. However, it is preferable for companies also to draw on independent external expertise, not only to complement internal expertise but also to enhance the legitimacy of the process.

2. *Second*, where appropriate, companies should consult with affected groups and other relevant stakeholders in meaningful and constructive ways. HRIAs cannot be mere internal desk research exercises, but should involve direct investigation in the field and communication with a variety of external stakeholders. However, scholars have pointed out that the involvement particularly of rights-holders needs to go beyond mere consultation. HRIAs need to provide for actual inclusion and participation of rights-holders throughout the whole process, rather than perceive the consultation as just one stage of the process. Such comprehensive participation can ensure that rights-holders have real influence on the HRIA process itself, as well as on the results and implications derived from it. Such inclusive processes can mitigate the power differential between companies and affected communities, which may lead to biased results of such assessments (Götzmann 2017: 99–100). It requires adequate transparency and that the company grants access to relevant information to the rights-holders. This often involves overcoming language, literacy and educational challenges.

Against the background of the tripartite duty structure attached to (corporate) human rights responsibility (Chapter 7.2), it is important to point out that HRIAs focus on identifying and assessing (and later mitigating or remedying) *adverse* human rights impacts only. However, they are not about the generation or identification of *positive* impacts that corporations may have, let alone about assessing the balance of negative and positive impacts, which may involve the implicit offsetting of negative impacts in one area with positive ones in another (Götzmann 2017: 98).

8.1.3.3 Responding to Human Rights Impacts: Operational-level Grievance Mechanisms

The second step of the HRDD process as outlined above deals with the design and implementation of appropriate responses to the potential and actual impacts that were identified through the HRIAs. Depending on the kind of impact – potential or actual – there are three categories of possible responses: 1) companies should prevent identified potential impacts from materializing; 2) companies should mitigate the consequences of impacts that are occurring; and 3) companies should remedy adverse impacts that have occurred in the past. The third response – that is, remediation of past violations – will be dealt with separately in the subsequent subchapter (Chapter 8.1.4). Regarding the prevention and mitigation of impacts, the UNGPs remain vague. Principle 19 calls on companies to assign responsibility clearly within the organization and structure decision-making procedures, budget allocation, and oversight processes in a manner that enables the effective provision of appropriate responses.

So-called operational-level grievance mechanisms are one concrete instrument, commonly discussed under the umbrella of the HRDD process for the prevention and mitigation of adverse impacts. An operational-level grievance mechanism "is a formalized procedure administered by the business itself (alone or in collaboration with others) which addresses the grievances of individuals and communities that have been affected by their activities" (Thompson 2017: 56). They are designed as communication and dialogue channels established on site, which aim to enable affected stakeholders – workers, community members, and others affected by the company's operations – to voice their grievances and to prompt swift and effective responses by the company to address them (Kaufman & McDonnell 2015: 128). It is not always clear-cut where prevention and mitigation of impacts ends and actual remediation starts. Thus, there is considerable overlap between the discussion of measures for the prevention and mitigation of impacts and those for remediation. Tellingly, the UNGPs discuss operational-level grievance mechanisms in Principle 29, under the heading of remediation. However, they do point out that such mechanisms should allow for any complaint or grievance to be raised, even if they do not (yet) amount to actual human rights violations. It is the very point of such mechanisms to catch and address adverse impacts early, in order to avoid long and protracted remedy processes later on. This makes operational grievance mechanisms a preventative and mitigative measure, rather than a remedial one. in fact, they have often been criticized for paying little attention to concrete remedies (Kaufman & McDonnell 2015: 129).

Thus, the idea of such mechanisms is to address contentious issues before adverse impacts and potential conflicts escalate and much more complex, expensive, and cumbersome remedy processes have to be initiated (Graf & Iff 2017: 12). They aim at early-stage recourse and, possibly, resolution, where potential conflicts arise (Ruggie 2013: 116). There are countless ways in which corporations can organize such grievance mechanisms. For example, they can appoint community representatives as designated point-persons for complaints, create the position of a company ombudsperson, maintain independently administered phone hotlines, and establish other safe and effective communication channels. Whatever combination of channels a company implements, operational-level grievance mechanisms ought to meet a number of key requirements. These requirements are outlined in Principle 31 of the

> **BOX 8.1 (Context) Effectiveness criteria for non-state-based non-judicial remedy mechanisms according to Principle 31 of the UNGPs**
>
> (1) *Legitimate*: Enabling trust from the stakeholder groups for whose use they are intended, and being accountable for the fair conduct of grievance processes.
> (2) *Accessible*: Being known to all stakeholder groups for whose use they are intended and providing adequate assistance for those who may face particular barriers to access.
> (3) *Predictable*: Providing a clear and known procedure with an indicative time frame for each stage, and clarity on the types of process and outcome available and means of monitoring implementation.
> (4) *Equitable*: Seeking to ensure that aggrieved parties have reasonable access to sources of information, advice and expertise necessary to engage in a grievance process on fair, informed and respectful terms.
> (5) *Transparent*: Keeping parties to a grievance informed about its progress, and providing sufficient information about the mechanism's performance to build confidence in its effectiveness and meet any public interest at stake.
> (6) *Rights-compatible*: Ensuring that outcomes and remedies accord with internationally recognized human rights.
> (7) *A source of continuous learning*: Drawing on relevant measures to identify lessons for improving the mechanism and preventing future grievances and harms.
> (8) *Based on engagement and dialogue*: This requirement applies particularly to operational-level grievance mechanisms. Consulting the stakeholder groups for whose use they are intended on their design and performance, and focusing on dialogue as the means to address and resolve grievances.

UNGPs and apply to non-judicial remedy mechanisms more generally. They are summarized in Box 8.1.

Operational-level grievance mechanisms pose a number of practical challenges for companies. For example, leaflets and information sheets that communicate such mechanisms to affected rights-holders and communities will be ineffective if those addressed by them are illiterate or speak local languages for which translations are missing. Furthermore, depending on the design of the mechanisms, structural discrimination in communities may make it difficult, for example, for women to access the mechanisms or prevent them from benefiting from mitigation measures (Götzmann 2017: 100). Phone hotlines are of little help if affected workers do not have access to telecommunication services. Therefore, it is critical that companies make sure that there are multiple entry points to the grievance mechanisms as well as multiple pathways for resolution (Shift 2014: 9). They should pay specific attention to making such mechanisms accessible to particularly vulnerable and marginalized groups.

However, a larger issue is general distrust of affected rights-holders in mechanisms that are administered by the company itself. This can lead to affected rights-holders not making use of such mechanisms even when they are accessible in principle. Therefore, it is advisable that companies involve independent third parties and possibilities for recourse to external institutions in their grievance mechanisms (Shift 2014: 5). However, an opposite challenge can occur, as well: Grievance mechanisms may be overused and lead to an overburdening of corporations with complaints and grievances that would better be dealt with elsewhere. For example, if the company lacks a regular stakeholder engagement process, all stakeholder issues and concerns might ultimately end up being framed as grievances and channeled through the grievance mechanism (Shift 2014: 9). Thus, defining the scope of such mechanisms (who is eligible to bring what types of complaints?) and designing them accordingly is an important consideration when setting them up (Shift 2014: 7). For example, who is eligible to bring complaints; only directly affected individuals, or everyone? And what types of complaints can they bring: only human rights grievances or also commercial complaints (Shift 2014: 19)? In order to foster trust and effectiveness (Box 8.1), experts have called for "community-driven" grievance mechanisms. Such mechanisms ought to involve rights-holders early on in the very design of the process (Kaufman & McDonnell 2015: 128).

8.1.3.4   Tracking Responses: Human Rights Performance Indicators

The third step in the HRDD process, according to the UNGPs, requires tracking the effectiveness of the responses to the identified impacts. Such monitoring and assessing of responses can be done both through targeted evaluations of the specific measures that the company has adopted and as a part of updated HRIAs and of existing grievance mechanisms (Graf & Iff 2017: 129). Monitoring and assessing responses are not least reasons for why HRIAs are to be understood as continuous, ongoing processes. Where responses have been implemented, adverse human rights impacts and related grievances should decrease as a consequence. Ongoing HRIAs should thus account for such reduced impacts, unless the responses are not working as hoped for.

Principle 20 of the UNGPs asks companies to compile a set of appropriate qualitative and quantitative indicators to track the effectiveness of responses and get direct feedback from internal and external stakeholders, including those affected by corporate impacts. The UNWG reiterated the importance of BHR performance indicators:

[T]he development of performance indicators that can be used by stakeholders to encourage proper functioning of grievance mechanisms is important and can be used by stakeholders to understand how grievance mechanisms at the operational level are working and to hold business enterprises accountable. (UNWG 2013: 15)

There has been a growing practical and scholarly discussion on human rights indicators, measurement, and benchmarking in recent times, which aims not least at providing crucial information on corporate human rights performance for investors, consumers, advocacy groups, and other stakeholders wanting to hold corporations accountable by using their respective means to apply pressure on them (Chapter 9.4). Such indicators make it possible both to track a corporation's human rights performance over time and to make it comparable to its peers. However, the practice of measuring corporate human rights performance is in its infancy and caution is advised in general when relying on such performance indicators. Two main considerations are worth pointing out in this regard.

1. *Quality of data*: There are practical challenges in gathering the data necessary to measure human rights performance. For example, it is common for corporate human rights violations to go unreported due to the sometimes severe risks that victims, witnesses, and human rights defenders face when reporting such incidents (De Felice 2015a: 546). Thus, it may be difficult even for corporations themselves to get a clear picture of their own human rights situation in some contexts. Furthermore, the information that corporations can gather may be biased in some cases. For example, local representatives may indicate that they have consulted with all relevant stakeholders on a particular issue, but they may have biased views on who is and who is not relevant to the matter at hand. As a consequence, they may falsely qualify incomplete data as complete.

2. *Quality of approximations*: Measuring human rights performance is an attempt at making measurable what cannot actually be measured. Human rights fulfilment is a qualitative rather than a quantitative endeavor, which measurements can always only approximate to some degree. Thus, designing indicators in a way that they indeed measure what they are supposed to measure is a challenge per se. Accordingly, there are countless possibilities of how to frame quantitative and qualitative indicators. The number of grievances being voiced through grievance mechanisms is one possible quantitative indicator. The number of lawsuits brought against the company based on community and human rights abuses is another. Qualitative indicators can derive, for example, from community consultations on the effectiveness of responses. Thus, a company may conduct surveys and ask community members to rank certain initiatives by the company on a scale from 1 to 5. However, such examples already show some of the limitations that necessarily come with these types of measurements. For example, the number of grievances may be decreasing not because the company

is addressing its impacts effectively but because community members do not know existing grievance mechanisms or do not trust them. Lawsuits may be increasing not because a company's human rights record has become worse but because the judicial bases for bringing lawsuits to domestic courts may be improving. One danger that derives from such approximations through measurement was described as early as 1975 by management scholar Steven Kerr as the "the folly of rewarding A, while hoping for B" (Kerr 1975). A company that solely relies, for example, on the number of grievances as an indicator for measuring its human rights performance, may actually incentivize people within the organization to be complacent about improving accessibility of their grievance mechanisms, masking slowly decreasing human rights performance with a decline in grievances. Therefore, it is recommended to at least complement indicators always with contextual information in narrative form (De Felice 2015a: 542).

There are other challenges associated with the measurement of a company's human rights performance (see De Felice 2015a: 548–550). For example, when comparing scores on human rights performance indicators across industries, companies with a smaller number of violations may be viewed as "good performers," which implicitly leads to normalizing and condoning a low level of violations. A comparatively "good" score is taken to reflect "good" conduct (De Felice 2015a: 549). However, particularly when it comes to human rights, any adverse impact ought to be avoided. Furthermore, viewing human rights violations through the filter of quantitative indicators can lead to a desensitization toward the grave personal stories of harm and suffering behind the numbers and thus reduce, rather than increase, the sense of urgency in addressing them.

8.1.3.5 Communicating Responses: Human Rights Reporting

The fourth and final step of the HRDD process deals with the communication of impacts and the respective corporate responses. Principle 21 of the UNGPs asks companies to communicate externally how they address their human rights impacts in order to increase transparency and accountability. Such communication, according to the UNGPs, should be frequent and accessible; it ought to provide sufficient information for key stakeholders to evaluate the adequacy of the corporate responses; and it ought not to create further risks to affected stakeholders or conflict with the requirements of commercial confidentiality.

The UNGPs list a variety of possible communication channels and platforms. Among them are in-person meetings, online dialogues, consultations, and formal reporting. Thus, the reporting requirements of the UNGPs are rather weak and some BHR advocates have called for formal reporting as standard communication to include not only impacts and responses but also the entire process, its underlying methodology, and the findings that result from it (Götzmann 2017: 104). In this vein, corporate human rights reporting should at minimum (Mehra & Blackwell 2016: 281):

1. Describe how human rights are embedded within a company's operations, including who is responsible and who has oversight.
2. Cover both policies and practices, including a detailed account of HRDD.
3. Report outcomes and impacts that the company is causing and detail how it will prevent, mitigate, and address them.
4. Reveal what remedial measures are in place in case human rights violations do occur.

A number of initiatives provide guidance for the formal reporting of a company's human rights performance. The most established and well-known initiative in the non-financial reporting space is the Global Reporting Initiative (GRI). Founded in 1997, it is the most widely used global standard for sustainability reporting. While its general reporting standard does not include a specific lens on human rights, the GRI released a focused standard specifically on reporting human rights impacts in 2016.

In 2015, the Human Rights Reporting and Assurance Framework Initiative (RAFI), which is facilitated by Shift and Mazars, released the UN Guiding Principles Reporting Framework (RAFI 2015), which provides an even more tailored instrument to report according to the UNGPs. In three parts, consisting of a total of thirty-one targeted questions, the Framework asks companies to report on their governance structure in regard to respecting human rights (Part A), outline its salient human rights issues and other severe human rights impacts (Part B), and show how it addresses and manages those issues and impacts (Part C). The reporting framework is complemented with detailed explanations and definitions, as well as with an implementation guide.

A growing number of jurisdictions have introduced mandatory non-financial reporting requirements in recent years. For example, the European Union's 2014 Non-Financial Reporting Directive (Chapter 12.4.1.3) mandates corporations to disclose their HRDD and their consideration of human rights risks, consistent with the UNGPs (Ewing 2016: 288). Similarly, the Modern Slavery Acts both in the UK and in Australia (Chapter 12.4.1.1) as well as the French Duty of Vigilance Law (Chapter 12.4.3.1) require companies to report on their due diligence efforts in the human rights domain. However, while more and more countries adopt such legislation, the parameters of those mandatory reporting requirements still vary considerably (Ewing 2016: 284). We will engage further with human rights disclosure laws in Chapter 12.4.1.

8.1.4 Remedying Adverse Human Rights Impacts
According to the UDHR (Article 8) and the ICCPR (Article 2), as well as many other international human rights instruments, victims of human rights abuse have a right

to remedy (UNWG 2017a: 6). Thus, when comparing HRIAs to other types of impact assessments, such as environmental or social impact assessments, there is one decisive difference: Where human rights have been violated, remedy must be provided.

The UNGPs deal with access to remedy separately from the HRDD process, though it is understood to be a part of the corporate responsibility to respect human rights. As such, it can be perceived at least as an extension of addressing and responding to adverse impacts identified through HRIAs and operational-level grievance mechanisms. As pointed out earlier, the line between prevention and mitigation of adverse impacts and their remediation is fluid. For example, while some treat operational-level grievance mechanisms as an instrument for the prevention and mitigation of adverse impacts, others, and among them the UNGPs, deal with such mechanisms as a part of human rights remedies.

The goal of remedy provision is to restore victims of corporate human rights violations to the situation they would have been in if the adverse impact had not occurred or, in case this is not possible – which for human rights violations is the rule, rather than the exception – to compensate them accordingly through adequate means (Shift 2014). The UNGPs and the BHR discussion more generally distinguish between three different kinds of remedy mechanisms in case of corporate human rights violations, as displayed below:

1. *State-based judicial remedies*: States ought to make sure that victims have access to the judicial system in order for justice to be served. This includes, for example, the opportunity to bring lawsuits against corporations that have violated their human rights (Chapter 12.5).
2. *State-based non-judicial remedies*: Besides judicial remedies, states can offer other means and channels to address and provide remedy for victims of corporate human rights abuse. One example is the NCPs, which are based on the OECD Guidelines for Multinational Enterprises (Chapter 11.1).
3. *Non-state-based non-judicial remedies*: Remedy mechanisms can be provided and administered also below the state level, for example, by MSIs or by corporations themselves, in cases in which they were involved in or have contributed to human rights violations. For example, companies may provide compensation where access to more formal state-based mechanisms are blocked for victims or engage in broader community development projects as a part of wider remedy efforts.

The UNGPs deal with state-based remedy provision as a part of the state duty to protect human rights, while corporate-level remedy mechanisms are a part of the corporate responsibility to respect human rights (Chapter 10). This chapter specifically deals with non-state-based non-judicial remedies. Such remedies can complement state-based ones, but often serve the purpose to provide remedy where state-based and judicial alternatives are lacking entirely (Kaufman & McDonnell 2015: 128).

Remedies can take a wide range of forms. The commentary to Principle 25 of the UNGPs lists "apologies, restitution, rehabilitation, financial or non-financial compensation and punitive sanctions (whether criminal or administrative, such as fines), as well as the prevention of harm through, for example, injunctions or guarantees of non-repetition" as possible manifestations of remedy-provision. Thereby, it is not one or the other, but rather a combination of different remedy types – the UNWG has called this a "bouquet of remedies" – that allows for addressing harms fully (UNWG 2017a: 12). Not all of those can be provided by businesses themselves, of course. Some egregious violations and alleged international crimes call for access to courts and judicial remedies. However, in the commentary to Principle 22, the UNGPs explicitly call on businesses to support and cooperate with judicial mechanisms in such situations rather than potentially circumvent and substitute them.

The UNGPs not only call for companies to engage in remedy processes, but also for the provided remedies to be effective. Hence, it is not enough for companies to merely provide some remedy mechanism to meet their responsibility. They must also make sure that the mechanisms they put in place are effective. However, what constitutes "effectiveness" in regard to remedies has been subject to some discussion. What seems clear is that this question cannot be answered without including the voices of victims who are addressed by the remedies. Two broad procedural criteria for effective remedy provision derive from this insight:

1. *Victim participation*: Victims need to be involved both in the determination of adequate remedies and the design of the grievance and remedy process. Their involvement must include more than mere consultation; victims must have real influence on the process and the kind of remedies provided and the provision of such remedies must be based on consensual agreement between the two parties. However, victims' perceptions are also subjective and may not always hold up to an objective assessment of a situation. For example, it is well known that human beings tend to adapt their outlook and preferences to the contexts and situations in which they live. Thus, victims who have been living in contexts of repression, abject poverty, and other kinds of deprivation, may consent to remedies that are far below an objectively adequate standard. This leads to a second, complementary criterion.

2. *Independent third-party involvement*: Power differentials between the company and the victims are endemic to operational-level grievance and remedy mechanisms. This structural disadvantage of victims paired with the above problem of adaptive preferences and other obstacles – such as a potential lack of education about their own rights, or lacking access to key information, to

name but two examples – can result in the undercompensation of victims. In such situations, the lack of checks and balances within remedy mechanisms can lead to remedy schemes that are themselves hardly compatible with human rights. Therefore, it is critical for the legitimacy of such processes that independent third parties are involved for monitoring and mediation purposes.

Principle 31 of the UNGPs outlines a number of additional key criteria that need to be met in order for company-led remedy and grievance mechanisms to be considered legitimate and effective. Those criteria are outlined in Box 8.1.

A criticism of those criteria has been that with the exception of "rights-compatibility" they focus too much on process, while neglecting the substance of remedy outcomes. As the UNWG states in its 2017 report on access to remedy, "while there is a close correlation between the effectiveness of a remedial mechanism and obtaining an effective remedy, these are two separate aspects, because an effective process may not always result in an effective outcome" (UNWG 2017a: 4). Therefore, the UNWG has added two more substantive criteria that need to be considered, in addition to the ones outlined by the UNGPs:

1. *Sensitivity to diverse experiences of rights-holders*: The different experiences of harm of different, particularly vulnerable, stakeholder groups should be reflected in the kind of remedy that is provided. For example, Indigenous communities with deep ties to their ancestral lands may not perceive compensation or alternative land as an adequate remedy in the case of displacement even if such land may objectively be rated as more valuable than their old land (UNWG 2017a: 9–10)
2. *Accessible, affordable, adequate, and timely*: Not only the process but also the outcomes need to be accessible and affordable. For example, a relief fund will be of little use to victims, if the money is not accessible or if accessibility comes at an unreasonable cost to the victims. Furthermore, remedies need to be adequate. The UNWG stresses that adequate remedy should not only address the current situation but also keep in mind the victims' future long-term needs. Finally, it is critical that remedies are provided promptly and are not delayed, keeping in mind that timeliness is relative also to the complexity of the respective case (UNWG 2017a: 11).

Hence, there are both practical and inherent challenges connected to remedy provision at the operational level. However, if effectiveness and legitimacy criteria are observed adequately, operational-level grievance and remedy mechanisms can offer some distinct advantages, as well. One advantage is the speed with which remedies can be provided; victims do not have to go through lengthy and uncertain legal proceedings but rather can be compensated swiftly and directly. Related to

BOX 8.2 (Short case) Remediation at Barrick Gold's Porgera mine

The Canadian mining company Barrick Gold is the world's largest gold miner, operating mines around the globe. One large mine is the Porgera mine in Papua New Guinea, which Barrick Gold had operated since 2006. In 2010 the human rights organization Human Rights Watch uncovered that private security forces of Barrick Gold had systematically sexually assaulted, abused, and raped local women over years. Barrick Gold reacted to the incidents by setting up a remedy process. The process was run by an independent assessment team and processed a total of 125 claims, which led to reparation packages of more than $1 million. The remedy process was narrowly framed to address issues connected to sexual violence against women only; other potential human rights claims were not considered. The remedy packages offered consisted of different services (for example, medical care, school fees, or business training), as well as different possible items (such as chickens or clothes) from which victims could choose (Knuckey & Jenkin 2015: 809). The remedy efforts also included a community development program, through which 200 community relations specialists engaged in a wide variety of activities aimed at fostering gender equality and women's rights in the Porgera Valley (Henderson & Hsieh 2016: 11).

Some 90 percent of eligible women accepted the remedy packages offered (Henderson & Hsieh 2016: 11). However, not everyone was satisfied with the "standardized" remedies, arguing that experiences of harm are highly subjective and individualized and that the remedies did not reflect the severity of the violations in some cases (Knuckey & Jenkin 2015: 809). One reason why not all women accepted the remedy packages was that doing so included signing a waiver that they would not pursue any further legal action against the company. Eleven women proceeded to sue Barrick Gold instead of accepting a remedy package and eventually settled their claim outside of court. Later, it was reported that their settlement turned out to be ten times greater than what was awarded to the other women through the remedy mechanism. In response, the company subsequently increased the remedies for all women (Knuckey & Jenkin 2015: 809–810).

Discussion Questions

(1) The Porgera remedy program has been praised by some as one of the most comprehensive company-level remedy processes to date. Others have raised concerns about administering remediation of such serious violations outside of the judicial system. What is your opinion: Can it be legitimate to replace the judicial process by a company-based process? Under what circumstances? What do you think about the waiver of legal action that the women had to sign in order to access remedy packages?

(2) Imagine you are the manager in charge of designing the remedy process at the Porgera mine. How would you go about it? What are key considerations that you would include in the process? Who would you involve? What challenges and obstacles might you expect to run into while setting up the process?

(3) There was criticism that Barrick Gold did not provide sufficient opportunity for victims and local communities to get involved and that the process was fixed, rather than dialogical (Knuckey & Jenkin 2015: 805–807). At what stages of the process would you involve rights-holders and local representatives and how much decision-power would you give them?

(4) The root problem at Porgera was not least connected to weak institutions, such as corrupt and violent police forces, a broken prison system, and a weak judiciary (Henderson & Hsieh 2016). What, if anything, can and should Barrick Gold do to contribute to the improvement of such systems? Can you generate some ideas of how powerful companies like Barrick Gold can constructively engage without exerting undue influence or even completely taking over state functions?

this, operational-level remedy-provision is less costly compared to legal or administrative proceedings. In addition, corporate-level procedures can be more flexible when dealing with cross-border cases that require work across multiple jurisdictions – a challenge that frequently poses almost insurmountable obstacles in legal compensation cases (Chapter 12.4). Thus, there are distinct benefits with regard to the speed, cost, and efficiency of operational-level remedy mechanisms and the availability of operational-level remedy mechanisms is critical where state-based mechanisms are inaccessible, non-existent, or failing.

8.1.5 Implementation Challenges

Whether a corporation ends up respecting human rights depends not only on whether or not that corporation has a human rights policy and an HRDD process in place, but rather on how this policy and process are brought to life in its daily operations. Encouraging employees to adopt and execute policies in their daily work is identified as one of the biggest challenges in regard to companies' human rights commitment. Furthermore, ensuring consistency across multiple business units and in different countries and regions, as well as communicating the value of human rights to employees with different cultural backgrounds, education, values, skills, and capabilities exacerbates those difficulties for companies (Obara & Peattie 2018: 789). In addition, a number of further challenges are worth being elaborated on in some more depth in the following paragraphs.

8.1.5.1 Industry and Company-Specificity

The UNGPs outline the steps of a generic HRDD process. However, implementing such a process requires adaptation to the specificities of different industries and organizations. HRDD may look very different depending on whether it is conducted in the food and beverage industry or in the banking sector, for example. Different sectors and industries vary in regard to the typical human rights issues they face. Relevant stakeholder groups, the shape and complexity of supply chains, and the kinds of violations will also differ between sectors and industries (Chapter 14). Such differences must be accounted for and reflected in the tools and instruments designed to deal with human rights issues. For this purpose, various organizations have engaged in developing a growing number of industry-specific guidance materials. Well known examples are the EU sector guides on the oil and gas sector (Shift & Institute for Human Rights and Business [IHRB] 2013a), the ICT sector (Shift & IHRB 2013b), or the employment and recruitment sector (Shift & IHRB 2013c), all developed by the New York-based NGO Shift and the London-based Institute for Human Rights and Business (IHRB). A similar guide has been developed by IHRB for the commodity trading industry (IHRB 2018).

Notably, small and medium-sized enterprises (SMEs) face particular challenges in regard to the implementation of HRDD due to limited resources, expertise, and a lack of existing structures that would accommodate the implementation of such processes. Nevertheless, SMEs can violate human rights and are not excluded from human rights responsibility. The UNGPs are clear on the need to adapt requirements for SMEs but do not allow for an exception concerning their responsibility to respect human rights: "Small and medium-sized enterprises may have less capacity as well as more informal processes and management structures than larger companies, so their respective policies and processes will take on different forms. But some small and medium-sized enterprises can have severe human rights impacts, which will require corresponding measures regardless of their size." (Ruggie 2011a: 14)

8.1.5.2 Dedicated v. Non-Specific Human Rights Processes

HRDD processes can be and are often viewed as a part of enterprise risk management systems. Furthermore, HRIAs have much in common with environmental and social impact assessments, with which companies may be familiar. Thus, many companies have structures in place already, which align at least to some degree with HRDD processes. Therefore, a recurring question is whether companies should consider human rights through such existing structures, such as workplace safety or labor rights due diligence processes, rather than build new ones, specifically dedicated to human rights. As mentioned earlier, HRDD requires a change of perspective from standard due diligence or risk-management processes: While standard processes aim at assessing risk to the company, HRDD is primarily interested in the impacts on rights-holders. Given this crucial difference, HRDD may not be a matter simply of integrating human rights into existing due diligence or risk-management processes. Indeed a comparison between these two alternative approaches to HRDD makes this evident; companies with a dedicated HRDD process that addressed human rights directly and explicitly identified adverse impacts in about 80 percent of their assessments, while companies that merely considered human rights implicitly through existing processes only identified adverse impacts 20 percent of the time. Thus, where "dedicated HRDD is undertaken, human rights [impacts] are more likely to be detected than during non-specific human rights processes" (McCorquodale et al. 2017: 207).

Hence, human rights language matters decisively when it comes to effective implementation of HRDD. However, companies remain reluctant in using human rights language, particularly internally, due to its controversial and politicized character (Obara 2017; Obara & Peattie 2018). Related to language, involving human rights experts in the HRDD process is a critical factor, as well. While almost 95 percent of companies doing dedicated HRDD relied on internal and external human rights experts, only 25 percent of companies considering human rights only indirectly through existing processes did so (McCorquodale et al. 2017: 213).

In terms of institutional responsibility, most companies doing dedicated HRDD put their Corporate Social Responsibility (CSR) departments in charge of the process (McCorquodale et al. 2017: 209). Indeed, companies' CSR experience can be both a trigger and a catalyst for a company's human rights commitment and it can help a company in organizing, framing, and managing its human rights approach (Obara & Peattie 2018: 790). At the same time, and as pointed out earlier, such an approach is not entirely unproblematic, since it entails the danger that companies equate BHR with CSR or reduce it to merely one among many CSR issues. As a consequence, human rights language may indeed be avoided and human rights may not be treated with the normative importance necessary (Chapter 1.2).

8.1.5.3 Prioritization and Weighing of Risks and Impacts

Several multinational companies operate in many and varied countries through hundreds of subsidiaries and thousands of suppliers and contractors. This makes the sheer idea of comprehensive HRDD a daunting task. It is hardly possible for such companies to address all (potential) human rights issues simultaneously and with the same urgency. But where should a company's focus lie? And which impacts should a company address as a matter of priority? Generally, companies should prioritize high-risk areas for their due diligence efforts, meaning that they should first focus on areas in which human rights impacts are likely and potentially grave. According to Principle 17 of the UNGPs, the complexity of HRDD conducted by a company can vary with the size of the business enterprise, the risk of severe human rights impacts, and the nature and context of its operations. Where human rights risks are not imminent and impacts less likely to be severe, due diligence efforts may remain more cursory. Where HRIAs have identified adverse impacts on human rights, Principle 24 of the UNGPs asks companies to prioritize those impacts that are most severe or for which a delayed response would risk making them irremediable. However, despite allowing companies to prioritize their responses, the UNGPs are clear that all human rights impacts must be addressed eventually; this, again, is a direct consequence of victims' right to a remedy. Severity is defined by Principle 14 of the UNGPs as a function of the scope, extent, and irremediability of the impacts. Importantly, the determination of an impact's severity ought to include the perspective of the victims (Götzmann 2017: 105–106).

8.1.5.4 Community Engagement

HRDD critically depends on assessments and investigations on the ground, in and with the affected communities. It requires that company representatives go where potential human rights violations are occurring and that they talk to potential victims and get their perspective on company operations. However, such a process is fraught with challenges. Rights-holders and affected communities may not trust the company and may refuse to engage in such conversations altogether. There is a danger also of interpreting "community" as a monolithic concept and thus underestimating the complexity of ensuring representation. Designated spokespersons and leaders of communities may not adequately represent all voices within communities. As a consequence, impacts on marginalized groups within communities may not be identified adequately, responses to such impacts may be designed without having particularly vulnerable groups in mind, and remedies may never reach those people who need them the most. There is a risk also of stirring conflicts within the community when such constellations are not addressed properly. The most effective and perhaps only way to address such challenges is to collaborate with other stakeholders such as human rights groups and NGOs, who can provide insight, advice, and access.

8.1.5.5 Effective Collaborations

Effective collaborations, especially with civil society organizations, are key when it comes to assessing impacts, tracking responses, and engaging communities and workers more generally. Local organizations have established and trusted relationships with workers and communities and can provide expertise, knowledge and insights, and not least access that multinational companies may not have. A lack of trust among affected rights-holders and a refusal to engage can derail thorough impact assessments or effective grievance mechanisms if companies are trying to do it alone. Similarly, selection bias and certain blind spots of a corporate perspective on the issues more generally may lead to incomplete, biased, or distorted information and undermine a company's HRDD process. Building such partnerships and collaborations requires time and effort. The starting point of such efforts is often at home; strong partnerships with NGOs in a multinational company's home state often build the gateway to accessing and building relationships with potential local partners in host states. Collaboration at the industry level, and sometimes also across industries, is similarly important for companies, not least to set clear standards and expectations. Additionally, it can make use of synergies in regard to the access, creation, and distribution of information, and allow for the development of common tools and methodologies (GBI 2017b). Collaborating along the value chain can increase both the efficiency and the effectiveness of HRDD processes.

More generally, businesses may establish stakeholder panels and a network of external partners to test their thinking and receive periodic and regular feedback both on their usual activities and their handling of specific challenges (GBI 2017c). In sum, HRDD must be understood as a collaborative process at its very core. Without an international network of collaborators, the impact of HRDD exercises will necessarily remain modest. Multi-stakeholder collaboration more generally is a critical element in addressing corporate human rights challenges holistically.

8.1.5.6 Supplier Engagement and Audits

Auditing the factories and facilities of suppliers is a necessary part of making sure that human rights are being respected along a company's value chain. Such audits can also be important sources of information, for example, for impact assessments or grievance mechanisms. However, there are clear limitations of what audits can achieve and they have come under increasing criticism in recent years as a representation of an outdated "command and control" approach to managing relations with suppliers. There are numerous challenges associated with such audits. Even if audits are unannounced, suppliers are often tipped off and make sure that they present their factories in the best light; often auditors lack adequate qualifications and human rights expertise; and the sheer number of suppliers makes it impossible to maintain a schedule of regular visits. Critics have thus promoted more collaborative engagement models as promising alternatives. Such models build on the collaboration with, rather than control of, suppliers. For example, a company may provide assistance, resources, and know-how to suppliers to solve human rights issues in collaboration and with a view to building lasting partnerships with them for the long term.

8.1.6 Critique of Human Rights Due Diligence

HRDD, as it is outlined in the UNGPs, has turned into the standard way for companies to deal with their human rights responsibility. However, just as there are critical voices about the UNGPs (Chapter 10.3.2), so there is also a more critical discourse specifically on HRDD.

From a *legalistic point of view*, Bonnitcha and McCorquodale (2017) have argued that the UNGPs' reference to HRDD is inconsistent. More specifically, they have pointed out that the UNGPs use two different understandings of due diligence, without clarifying how they relate to each other. Lawyers commonly understand due diligence as a standard of (expected) conduct in order to discharge an obligation. From such a perspective, a company must conduct HRDD in order to meet its responsibility to respect human rights. For business people, on the other hand, due diligence "merely" represents a procedure to manage business risks. Respecting human rights, from this point of view, may presuppose a process of HRDD, but this may not be sufficient on its own. Thus, if violations do occur, a corporation cannot claim to have met its responsibility to respect human rights simply by pointing to its HRDD process. This is different if HRDD is interpreted as a standard of conduct and thus as a proxy for the responsibility to respect human rights. From this point of view, a company can be in violation of human rights without actually breaching its responsibility to respect them, as long as it has done proper HRDD. This leads to two problems related to the UNGPs. First, the confusion about the meaning of HRDD may reinforce the problematic view that conducting HRDD is sufficient for businesses to meet their responsibility to respect human rights. Related to this, and second, if businesses can infringe on human rights without actually breaching their responsibility to respect them, victims will be left without a valid claim for remedy in such situations. Therefore, and in accordance with the common use of due diligence in international law, Bonnitcha and McCorquodale (2017) argue that HRDD as a standard of conduct ought to apply only as it pertains to the conduct of third parties, whose actions cannot be attributed to the company itself. Since a company can never fully control the actions of third parties, all we can ask is that it operates with all due care when engaging with them. However, a company should be held strictly liable for its own actions and it ought to make up for the damage it causes, even if it claims to have acted with care.

A similar critique has been voiced also from an *ethical point of view*. The responsibility to respect human rights is a perfect obligation (Chapter 7.1), for which HRDD can always only be an insufficient approximation. HRDD, understood as a process of investigation, may be a suitable management tool for a company to support its responsibility to respect human rights. However, equating the two is problematic, not least because it is often difficult or even impossible in practice to assess the true effectiveness of HRDD measures, which opens a possibility for opportunistic corporations to discharge their responsibility to respect human rights by implementing rather lax due diligence standards. Fasterling and Demuijnck (2013) conclude from this that merely having an HRDD process in place and following it mechanistically does not suffice to ensure respect for human rights. What is needed is a deeper moral commitment to human rights in the company. Only such a commitment can make sure that the process does not exist merely on paper, but is also being taken seriously in the daily operations of the business. Therefore, companies must invest not only in designing adequate processes but also in fostering a climate and culture in which such processes indeed generate impact (Chapter 8.2).

Viewing HRDD as a risk management tool exacerbates the problem from a *managerial point of view*. As indicated above, the idea of enterprise risk management systems is not to prevent or mitigate risks to others, but to avoid or manage risks that can result in disadvantages for the corporation itself. While the UNGPs are clear about their focus on the risks to rights-holders, this change of perspective is not always applied consistently by corporations. The efforts to integrate HRDD mechanisms within existing risk management systems increases the danger of further weakening this primacy of risk to rights-holders. To be sure, risks to rights-holders may often also constitute business risks if they turn into protests, NGO campaigns, or legal action against the company. But such a business case for corporate human rights responsibility (Chapter 6.3.2) may not hold across the board. This would only be the case if respect for human rights was to be an actual corporate objective that determines a corporation's strategic concerns. In such a case, any risk to human rights would at the same time be a risk to meeting the company's objectives (Fasterling 2017).

8.2   Beyond Managing Impacts: Organizing for Human Rights

The critical remarks above should have made clear that HRDD alone will not suffice to ensure that companies respect human rights. On the one hand, there is a crucial difference between having an HRDD process on paper and implementing it effectively on the ground. On the other hand, even implementing it effectively depends on various other organizational factors, which must be in place.

One such key factor, as argued above, is a company's moral commitment; without it, HRDD will remain ineffective. This indicates that just as much as it is about the right tools and instruments, it is also about the right corporate culture and mindset. Thus, whether HRDD can become truly effective as an instrument and process to respect human rights depends a great deal on whether or not a company succeeds in building a culture of respect and integrity around such processes.

Culture is to an organization what character is to a person; it guides and constrains the behavior of the organization in subtle, often covert ways through the shared norms that are implicitly held within the organization or subsets thereof (Schein 2010: 14). The culture of the company is hidden and difficult to grasp. The "most intriguing aspect of culture as a concept," as the renowned expert on corporate culture Edgar Schein remarked, "is that it points us to phenomena that are below the surface, that are powerful in their impact but invisible and to a considerable degree unconscious" (Schein 2010: 14). He defines corporate culture as "a pattern of shared basic assumptions," which are perceived to be valid and seen as the "correct way to perceive, think, and feel" when approaching organizational challenges and problems (Schein 2010: 18).

Culture, according to Schein (2010: 23–33) happens at three levels, which range from tangible and overt manifestations to deeply embedded, unconscious basic assumptions. At the *first level* are what he calls "artifacts," which are phenomena that one can observe, hear, and feel – such as the language used in interactions and the myths and stories told about the company. Visible structures, organizational charts, and processes, including published value statements along with concrete patterns of behavior, rituals, and ceremonies, and even the architecture and style of the spaces in which members of the organization interact and the clothing they wear also comprise these "artifacts." At the *second level* are espoused and commonly explicitly articulated beliefs and values, including ideals, goals, and aspirations. They often become embodied in an ideology or organizational philosophy and lead to shared rationalizations. However, it is not uncommon that the values explicitly espoused by an organization do not reflect the actual behavior one can observe. In order to explain such discrepancies, one needs to dig to the *third level*, which is the level of basic underlying assumptions, that is, of unconscious, taken-for-granted beliefs and values that shape behavior, perceptions, thoughts, and feelings. Espoused values and beliefs can over time become normalized and deeply engrained at this third level. On the other hand, this also shows that transforming an organization's culture is a process that does not end with the adoption of a value statement, but will require a long-term, conscious effort to work toward internalizing change in the organization's mindset. This third level of underlying assumptions is the essence of a corporation's culture, in which the very identity of an organization is embodied.

Many of the factors that shape cultures have to do with the people working in and for the organization, such as the ways in which they think and behave, and the things they do or do not value. Thus, meeting the responsibility to respect human rights has much to do with how organizations select and hire their employees, how they lead them, and what kind of behavior they do or do not reward. Accordingly, some of the essential building blocks of a human rights-respecting corporate culture include the following elements.

Values and vision: A corporation's vision together with its foundational values build its core ideology (Waddock & Rasche 2012: 56). A company's vision provides meaning, purpose, and direction to those working for the company and its basic values build the foundation on which its purpose is pursued. Employees and other key stakeholders will be able to make sense of a mandate to respect human rights, if they perceive it to be consistent with the purpose and core values expressed by the company. If they perceive the core ideology to run counter the idea of respect for human rights, and the respective human rights policies and processes as alien to what the company stands for otherwise, there is little hope that they will seriously embrace and implement them into their daily work. On the other hand, merely having a rights-compatible vision and value statement will not transform an organization on its own.

It requires a conscious effort to embed and internalize these aspects in the daily activities and interactions of people. Leadership is a key element of doing so.

Responsible and authentic leadership: BHR starts and ends with leadership commitment. The message that human rights ought to be respected must come from the very top, not once but repeatedly. Thus, top management must walk the human rights talk and model and practice the values they preach. Authenticity is a key requirement for responsible leadership. A message alone will have little impact if employees notice that top management is not taking it seriously in their own actions. This insight has two specific implications. First, commitment is reflected in a respective allocation of resources. Human rights can only be prioritized in organizations if their budgets account for it accordingly and human rights-related projects are funded appropriately. Second, authentic leadership is displayed particularly in the tough decisions that managers make when human rights conflict with the financial goals of the organizations (Paine 1994: 112). These are the decisions through which the culture of an organization is both revealed and shaped.

Recruiting and training: A company's aspirations with regard to responsibility, integrity, and respect for human rights must also concern its recruiting practices. Building a culture of integrity necessitates hiring people who believe in those fundamental values and share the vision of the company. If a company keeps hiring employees mainly on the basis of their "functional" qualifications and competitiveness, it will have a hard time generating broad enough buy-in to transform its culture around ethical commitment. Similarly, as seen above, much of the HRDD process depends on the availability of human rights expertise, not only commissioned from the outside, but also fostered within the company. Accordingly, companies must actively engage in human rights training and capacity-building across the entire organization. In order to be effective, such training must be specific to the function of the trainees within the company and tailored to their daily activities. This illustrates the earlier point about resource allocation; human rights training, if taken seriously, requires not only financial resources but also organizational capacity and the availability of time resources. A company that is serious about its human rights commitment must be willing to invest substantially in such training efforts. In order to overcome the challenge of scale, some large companies first train a group of trainers or champions, who can then themselves lead such trainings with staff in their respective regions and parts of the business (GBI 2017d).

Incentives and remuneration: Too often still, companies implement human rights policies and processes without tying them to their reward and incentive systems. Such systems may not only be disconnected from human rights targets but may even run counter to them and undermine respect for human rights. For example, if procurement managers are rewarded based on indicators relating to low cost and fast turnaround, they will increase cost and time pressure on their suppliers, rather than putting adequate emphasis on HRDD, helping to build capacity, and creating the trusted long-term relationships that foster mutual investments into the improvement of working conditions. If a company wants its supply-chain managers to pay attention to human rights, they must be adequately incentivized by rewards that are at least partly based on human rights indicators. It is one thing to tell employees and managers to work toward respecting human rights, but another to make their performance reviews, their rewards, and bonuses dependent on it.

STUDY QUESTIONS

1. What are the five basic requirements for a human rights policy, as identified in Principle 17 of the UNGPs?
2. Define HRDD from both a legal and a business standpoint. How are the definitions similar and how do they differ?
3. Which four steps characterize the standard HRDD process?
4. What is the difference between HRDD and HRIAs?
5. Why is it important to make human rights measurable? And what are the risks associated with doing so?
6. What are four key aspects for corporations to consider when providing remedy according to the UNGPs and the UNWG?
7. Can you name and explain three criteria for effective remedy provision?

REFLECTION QUESTIONS

1. What are operational-level grievance mechanisms and what purpose do they serve? How can companies design such mechanisms that can effectively allow for true stakeholder engagement?
2. Conducting HRDD effectively hinges on a company's moral commitment to human rights. How can a company foster such commitment? What can and should companies do to build strong, human rights-respecting business cultures? How can you personally contribute to building such organizational cultures in your career? What concrete actions can you take?
3. Your company is an important player in the cocoa industry and importing chocolate. You are tasked with implementing a human rights assessment of your business activities. How do you proceed? Where should your company's focus lie? And which impacts should be addressed with priority?
4. Managing human rights responsibility for a multinational company, you know that it is critical that your suppliers adhere to the same standards as your own company. How do you engage with your suppliers on this question? How do you make sure they will adhere to the standards that you ask them to follow?

PART IV
Corporate Human Rights Accountability

Transnational Governance and Corporate Human Rights Accountability: Preliminary Questions and Foundational Issues

With the responsibility of corporations in relation to human rights clarified in the previous part of this book, this part deals with the possibility of holding them accountable and the tools for doing so. The chapter at hand will clarify some foundational questions relating to transnational governance and thus provide the context in which different accountability regimes are embedded. Chapters 10–13 will then deal with more concrete and specific accountability instruments and mechanisms.

The term "accountability" in this context derives from holding corporations to account and making them answerable for their actions and how they meet (or do not meet) their responsibilities. Hence, while the focus so far has been on corporate human rights responsibilities in principle, this part deals with how such responsibilities ought to be enforced and with the consequences that may follow if corporations fail to meet them. The law is one and perhaps the most obvious accountability mechanism. It can mandate corporate human rights responsibilities and define legal sanctions in case of non-compliance. But accountability pressure can emanate also from potential non-legal sources, often referred to as "soft" sources, such as customers' buying behavior, shareholders' investment decisions, or reputational risk.

The strong focus on accountability measures has always been a defining feature of the BHR discussion and has been identified as a key difference between BHR and the broader, more management-driven discussion on CSR (Ramasastry 2015) (Chapter 1.2). In fact, this chasm runs through the BHR discussion itself: While legal BHR scholars have traditionally focused on questions of accountability, non-legal BHR scholars have been concerned more with the underlying foundations of corporate human rights responsibility as well as with the operationalization and implementation of such responsibility within business organizations. This is one reason why legal and non-legal BHR scholars, despite belonging to the same field, often focus on very different issues and speak entirely different languages.

This chapter opens up the larger transnational governance context in which different accountability systems and mechanisms in BHR are embedded. It distinguishes between accountability approaches at the international and domestic levels, accountability approaches that are public and those that are private, as well as hard and soft approaches to corporate accountability. Finally, it will explore the role of some particular stakeholder groups in holding corporations to account for their human rights conduct.

9.1   International and Domestic Approaches

Since the emergence of the Peace of Westphalia in 1648, the Westphalian world order has revolved around sovereign states. It has been an order in which states exercise authority over their national territory and are at the same time the main and only relevant actors in the international sphere. In such a world order, states are in charge both of their domestic affairs and of their limited international exchanges. However, this worldview has changed profoundly in the last three or four decades. Accelerating globalization processes have heralded a transition to what some have called a "post-Westphalian" world order (Kobrin 2009; Santoro 2010), in which no single actor is fully in charge anymore. Within this process, national borders are becoming increasingly porous. They are not only crossed but transcended by a fast-rising number of transnational economic and social processes and structures. The *inter*national sphere is giving way to a *trans*national space in which states, while still powerful, have come to be just one of many relevant actors. A variety of non-governmental and supranational actors and organizations, among them multinational companies, are operating within this space and act with considerable autonomy beyond the full control of national governments. In the absence of a centralized global state, authority in this transnational space is fragmented among functional areas with a variety of different actors fulfilling various governance tasks alongside states. But state authority is challenged not only within the transnational space but also at the domestic level. While states remain in charge of their territory at least formally, their policy space – that is, their autonomy to regulate and govern their respective domestic spaces – has become ever-more constrained by transnational forces and interdependencies.

The regulation of multinational companies is a case in point. Their transnational structures have become increasingly difficult to regulate for states. Domestically, multinational companies have gained significant leverage to challenge and pressure governments to adopt policies favorable to the companies' business interests and abstain from putting new regulation in place. Such pressure often does not even have to be exerted overtly; the looming "exit threat," understood as the implicit danger that multinational companies could relocate their operations elsewhere, is commonly sufficient for states to be careful about adopting policies, for example, on taxation or on emission control, that may push the envelope too far. This holds both for host and home states. Host states, particularly in the Global South, often lack the capacity to regulate multinational companies and may be in harsh competition with other states that offer low wages and lax social and environmental regulation. At the home-state level, governments are similarly reluctant to regulate multinational groups, fearing that this would put "their" companies at a disadvantage relative to companies domiciled in other countries. Nevertheless, while there are clear limitations on what domestic regulation can achieve in a globalized world, it remains of utmost importance. This being said, its potential to enhance corporate accountability often remains untapped due to the constraining transnational forces on national governments.

A similar problem occurs at the global level. International law has been designed for a Westphalian, rather than a post-Westphalian world order, and in its current form is often insufficient and ill-equipped to regulate multinational companies (Chapter 6.2). New approaches to both domestic and international legislation are necessary to reflect today's transnational realities (Chapter 12). However, the repeated failure of the international community to adopt binding international frameworks to regulate corporations' human rights conduct as well as states' reluctance to extend the reach of domestic regulation toward "their" multinational companies beyond the boundaries of their own territory illustrates the magnitude of this challenge. A new attempt to negotiate a binding treaty on BHR started in 2015 in the HRC, but the prospects of it are highly uncertain once again (Chapter 13.2.3).

The post-Westphalian, transnational world order is characterized by what is often called polycentric governance, in which a variety of actors, both public and private, national and supranational, fulfil governance roles and different governance tasks at different levels of governance. Ideally, they do so in a complementary, synergistic, and coordinated manner. But in reality, gaps, incoherences, and even conflicts emerge between different governance levels and instruments. Such polycentric governance is both the root cause of and the solution to the BHR problem in a post-Westphalian world. The governance gaps that accompany the patchwork of different approaches and instruments have been identified as the key underlying cause of the BHR challenge by the former SRSG, John Ruggie (Chapter 1.1). At the same time, the most plausible solution to the problem lies not in abandoning, but in enhancing and strengthening the polycentric governance system. This does not mean abandoning the state altogether. On the contrary, governments will remain of critical importance for making polycentric governance effective. For example, the effective implementation of transnational standards by businesses and the impact that such standards can have on the ground is crucially dependent on a conducive context shaped by domestic legislation. Transnational governance will not make the state and domestic regulation irrelevant (Bartley 2018: 31). On the contrary, it underscores their continued importance.

Hence, within such multilevel and multiactor governance systems, mechanisms to ensure corporate accountability for human rights ought to be located both at the domestic and international levels. At the level of host states, this concerns the domestic regulation of local companies and of the subsidiaries of multinational companies. However, the more contentious question concerns home-state regulation of multinational companies' business activities abroad. The adoption of home-state measures to regulate the extraterritorial conduct of multinational companies has become one of the key discussions and controversies in BHR. Therefore, the focus on accountability measures at the state level will be on home-state solutions in the policy, legislative, and adjudicative spaces (Chapter 12). However, such measures must be complemented by international governance instruments with the aim of guiding, enhancing coherence, and increasing the comprehensiveness of the various domestic approaches. Such measures can be pursued in the domain of both private and public international soft standards and initiatives (Chapter 11) or based on international law (Chapter 13). This leads to the next crucial distinction of different governance approaches, which is the one between public and private governance.

9.2   Public and Private Approaches

Traditionally, governance tasks were predominantly, if not exclusively, seen as a public responsibility associated with the state. States had the exclusive authority to regulate the economy and its actors, by means of legislation, policy, or direct engagement. However, the global expansion of markets throughout the 1980s and 1990s was achieved not least by a shift of regulatory authority from public actors such as state agencies to private actors such as businesses and NGOs. Increasingly, markets were liberated from the constraints of governmental regulation with the expectation that industries and companies would fill the resulting regulatory voids through private governance schemes and self-regulation. "Private regulation refers to a structure of oversight in which non-state actors – whether for-profit companies, non-profit organizations, or a mix of the two – adopt and to some degree enforce rules for other organizations, such as their suppliers or clients" (Bartley 2018: 7). It is characteristic of private regulation schemes that they do not derive their force from state authority and that they are not accountable to the state, either. Private regulation employs a variety of different sanctioning mechanisms, such as the expulsion of actors from initiatives in case of non-compliance or through stakeholder pressure and naming-and-shaming. However, in some instances, such regulation is pursued on a purely voluntary basis. Hence, the mode of governance ranges from softer forms of coercion to entirely voluntary commitment.

Today's polycentric governance landscape in BHR is a mixture of public and private approaches. While public, state-based regulation is still dominant in the domestic realm, private and hybrid forms of governance, consisting of both public and private actors, have become dominant in transnational regulation. Hundreds of MSIs (Chapter 11.4) in particular address countless issues in both specific and general ways and often blur the lines between private and public governance. Such hybrid forms of public-private governance have become the dominant transnational governance approach with regard to many of the prevailing challenges and issues in the domain of corporate responsibility. Some industry-specific examples of such initiatives will be provided in Chapter 14.

The rapid increase of private governance, especially where it amounts to "mere" self-regulation of particular industries or companies, has been subject to critique. Critics lament that such regulation frequently caters too much to the interests of corporations, keeping standards low and enforcement and monitoring mechanisms weak. Further, they point to a lack of democratic legitimacy within such standards and argue that they may serve the mere purpose of pre-empting more extensive public regulation (Abbott 2012: 556). Thus, critics fear that state authority in public realms is being replaced by private authority without proper public accountability. Finally, the mushrooming of private standards and initiatives makes it increasingly difficult to keep oversight, both for companies, which are expected to support them, and for stakeholders and the public, who play a watchdog role in order to make sure that companies live up to their commitments and promises. Particularly for small suppliers that produce goods for numerous large brands, which potentially adhere to different standards and thus demand compliance with varying sets of requirements, the cost of doing business may become prohibitively high.

On the other hand, private regulation offers a few distinct advantages. First, private governance can address challenges and issue areas, for which it is difficult to negotiate public solutions. As such, it can fill governance gaps that may persist, for example, because interstate negotiations at the global level may be stalling (Abbott 2012: 543). Second, they often succeed in generating substantial buy-in from corporations, not least by "speaking their language" and better acknowledging and providing flexibility with regard to the often significant implementation challenges that companies face on the ground. Buy-in is critical for all forms of regulation, even if they are based on legal mandates. Laws, too, need to be able to generate a degree of intrinsic commitment from the regulated subjects to be effective, since otherwise compliance can turn into a pure tick-box exercise. Developing such commitment in a variety of actors is one decisive strength of private and hybrid regulatory schemes. Third, buy-in from corporations commonly also generates substantial resources and thus more leverage to achieve real impact through such initiatives. Fourth, private regulation can be highly particular and targeted with regard to specific issues or actors and it is readily adaptable to changing contexts and situations. Thus, private regulation tends to be more versatile than public regulation, which can be a key advantage in fast-changing environments.

Nevertheless, precisely because both private and public regulatory approaches offer distinct advantages and drawbacks, effective governance is less about whether to adopt one or the other approach, but rather about how to effectively combine the two. Research shows that the effectiveness of private regulation depends a great deal on the existence of strong and credible public institutions both at the domestic and international levels (Cafaggi 2011: 41). As mentioned above, both transnational and domestic and private and public regulation are inextricably interlinked and interdependent. An effective polycentric governance system must make the best possible use of their complementary and synergistic potential.

9.3 Hard and Soft Approaches

Related to the distinction between private and public governance is the one between hard and soft regulation. Hard regulation commonly means regulation that is mandated by use of "hard law." In a more general sense, it can refer to a wider spectrum of regulation, which is supported by strong enforcement and sanctioning mechanisms. Soft regulation, on the other hand, is regulation that is not or only minimally enforced and thus runs predominantly on the voluntary commitment of companies. A related, often-used term is "soft law." Soft laws are private or public lawlike instruments and rules that are non-binding in character and generally not based on governmental enforcement mechanisms (Abbott & Snidal 2000; Mena & Palazzo 2012: 528). There is a broad variety of soft-law instruments both at national and international levels. The UDHR is an example of public soft law. However, private standards and initiatives, which aim at regulating certain issue areas, are also commonly seen as a part of soft law.

Hard and soft-law approaches are often perceived as binary. As such, there has been a long-standing discussion, both in BHR and beyond, about which one of the two approaches is preferable to regulate business responsibility. Those favoring a hard-law approach emphasize its binding and enforceable character and the predictability and public legitimacy that derives from it. They criticize discretionary soft-law approaches for providing companies with a platform to showcase social and environmental commitment without forcing the companies to follow through and implement the commitment throughout their organization. Those favoring soft-law approaches, on the other hand, are commonly critical of companies adopting a merely cosmetic compliance focus on issues that are mandated by hard law. They allege that hard regulation can lead to companies being preoccupied with their compliance and draw attention away from engaging with the substance of the underlying issue. In other words, companies are merely making sure they tick all the necessary boxes to be compliant with a law in order not to risk any fines and the reputational cost of breaking the law, but lose sight of and focus on whether this actually has any positive impact on the ground. For example, a company may comply with an HRDD obligation by drawing up a human rights policy and a respective process, but without providing adequate resources, capacities, and training for their implementation throughout the organization. As a consequence, such processes may exist predominantly on paper without actually changing anything about how business is conducted within the organization. In contrast, soft law is seen to provide more flexibility in regard to implementation and thus as better suited to accommodate the different contexts and circumstances of various actors as well as their potentially diverging interests, preferences, and capacities (Abbott & Snidal 2000: 445).

Such concerns on both sides are justified at least to some degree. However, two considerations are important in response to them:

First, the choice between hard and soft approaches is not a binary one. Rather, there is a continuum consisting of countless approaches, with varying degrees of force and bindingness. Even "soft" approaches are often not entirely voluntary, but make use of a variety of accountability mechanisms to increase stakeholder pressure. On the other hand, not all "hard" laws are forceful in demanding compliance. Some laws lack monitoring and enforcement mechanisms altogether and thus may be softer in this regard than some of the more far-reaching soft-law standards (Chapter 12.4). Hence, any critique aimed at soft law or hard law per se is prone to miss the point, since its validity crucially depends on the shape and specification of the respective regulatory instrument in the concrete case.

Second, hard and soft approaches should not be seen as mutually exclusive. Both approaches fulfil specific functions that can be combined in complementary and mutually reinforcing ways to increase the accountability of companies. For example, hard regulation is often met with opposition and resistance by those who are subject to the regulation. It is easier to reach compromises on softer provisions (Abbott & Snidal 2000: 444–445) and once agreements are achieved, such soft-law instruments can pave the way for more binding rules down the road. Soft-law initiatives can foster acceptance for certain rules and standards and thereby shape the context in which hard regulation may become viable over time. A case in point of this "enabling function" (Schrempf-Stirling & Wettstein 2021) of soft law are the UNGPs (Chapter 10). The UNGPs have fostered broad acceptance of a corporate responsibility to respect human rights and established HRDD as the key instrument to meet such a responsibility. This has created an environment in which various civil society movements pushing for hard HRDD regulation were able to gain traction – their demands were not perceived as unreasonable anymore, but as well within the scope of what the UNGPs had established as the new normal. As a consequence, a growing number of countries have enacted hard regulation or are in the process of doing so (Chapter 12.4). On the other hand, states and international organizations can make soft laws more binding, by endorsing them and integrating them into policies and regulation, for example, relating to public procurement (Chapter 12.3.2). Hard regulation can reference or integrate existing soft provisions, thus rendering them indirectly binding, leading to increasing adherence to and compliance with those soft-law instruments. Many of the emerging laws mentioned above mandate HRDD generally or in connection with specific issues, such as child labor or conflict minerals. As such, they lead to what has been called a "hardening" of the UNGPs (Choudhury 2017; 2018), meaning that they render the UNGPs or parts thereof implicitly binding in those contexts.

9.4 Soft Accountability Mechanisms: Certification, Labels, and Stakeholder Pressure

Private and soft governance approaches are not based on hard legislation and thus are formally voluntary. However, they can nevertheless achieve a certain level of force by making use of alternative accountability mechanisms. Such mechanisms aim at generating pressure from various stakeholder groups by enhancing transparency around corporate conduct. While such mechanisms have proven to be effective in some instances, their potential is often limited. Thus, while they fulfil an important role in a holistic, polycentric governance system, it would be illusory to assume that respect for human rights by companies can be achieved solely by appealing to stakeholder pressure. As mentioned previously, it is the combination of hard and soft, private and public, and domestic and transnational forms of governance that ultimately leads to the most effective results. In the following, we will have a brief look at three key stakeholder groups and their potential to enhance corporate accountability through their own conduct.

9.4.1 Consumers: Certification and Labels

Consumers are a crucial stakeholder group that can contribute to holding corporations accountable for human rights conduct through their purchasing decisions. Two variables determine whether sufficient consumer pressure can be generated to push corporations to enhance their human rights record.

Conscious consumption: First, it depends on the "enlightened" mindset and behavior of consumers themselves. Consumers must both care about the human rights conduct of the companies behind the products they buy and their concern must be translated into actual purchasing behavior. While consumers have indeed become more reflective or conscious in recent years and tend to prefer sustainably produced goods over products with a more problematic footprint, their mindset does not always translate into their respective purchasing decisions. This has been called the intention-behavior gap. It means that even though consumers may voice the intention to buy responsibly, they may not always follow through with it in their actual buying decisions (Carrington, Neville, & Whitwell 2014). There are various reaons why such a gap exists. One may be price premiums for more sustainable and more responsible products. Consumers are generally willing to pay a small premium for responsibly produced goods, but their willingness and also their financial capacity to do so is limited. Another reason is consumers' general susceptibility to other external influences, such as discounts, the buying behavior of peers, fashion trends, and so on. While consumers may rationally support and prefer responsible products, their decision-making is often clouded by such influences and may lead to inconsistencies between their mindset and their buying behavior. Finally, consumers may not have sufficient knowledge and may be ill-informed about the products they buy. Thus, they might lack the information necessary to match their buying-decisions with their mindset. This brings us to the second variable.

Transparency: Second, responsible consumption crucially depends on transparency and adequate information on products and companies being available to consumers. Even if consumers are ready to shop responsibly, they will be severely constrained in their buying decisions if there is a lack of transparency and information on the products. As a result, private labelling and certification schemes have mushroomed in recent years. Their aim is to signal to consumers which products fulfil certain predefined responsibility and sustainability criteria and can therefore be "safely" bought by them. An example is the Marine Stewardship Council (MSC). The MSC certifies fisheries that operate according to the MSC standard, which addresses sustainability and overfishing in seafood production. Products from such fisheries are then eligible to carry the MSC label, signaling to conscious consumers that the product they buy is certified to correspond to the respective sustainability criteria.

Despite these efforts, many challenges remain. The lack of transparency is an enduring problem and keeping track of the sheer number of different labels, which signal adherence to different standards with different criteria and issued by a variety of different private organizations and initiatives, poses a challenge for consumers. They may lack an adequate overview of different labels and display label fatigue when it comes to researching and finding out what is behind the different certifications. The number of different standards and labels can lead also to a diffusion of consumer pressure and thus reduce, rather than increase, the force of consumer demand (Abbott 2012: 558). Furthermore, such labels – and certification and consumer power more generally – only work in industries that serve consumer markets. In other words, what works well for food and beverage markets may not work at all for the trade of commodities and raw materials, which are almost entirely business-to-business markets. Finally, even for industries, which do serve consumer markets, consumers tend to lack adequate organization and coordination, which means that their ability to develop targeted pressure is naturally limited. As a consequence, their demands often remain very general, providing companies with ample leeway to design "self-serving responses" (Abbott 2012: 557). While social media has certainly improved the possibilities for targeted consumer campaigns, there are still clear limits to what can be achieved solely by consumer pressure.

9.4.2   Investors: ESG Investment

The relevance of investors as a key stakeholder group in pressuring companies to respect human rights is increasing rapidly. The share of responsible investments has grown at a staggering rate, to become mainstream in recent years. Globally, managed assets that take into account environmental, social, and governance (ESG) criteria in some form have reached $31 trillion, which amounts to more than 25 percent of total assets under management (Ruggie 2021). In Europe, this share even amounts to 50 percent. This growth is likely to continue, as women make up a growing share of investors and up to $30 trillion of assets will be transferred to the generation of millennials over the coming decades (O'Connor & Labowitz 2017: 5). Both women and millennials (Chapter 6.3.2) are considered more environmentally and socially conscious investors (Rogers 2016).

While in the past the prospective lower return of sustainable investments was the main concern of mainstream investors, the expansion and diversification of responsible portfolios has all but eliminated that fear. Responsible investments have become competitive and today generally perform equally well, if not better than, conventional investments (Ruggie 2021). This is particularly so for investments with a long-term horizon (O'Connor & Labowitz 2017: 8). A larger concern from a BHR perspective is the current lack of uniform ESG criteria that different funds and asset managers apply. Critics warn that the mainstreaming of ESG investing inevitably comes with a certain watering down of standards. This discussion is not unique to the investment realm, but represents a common struggle and discussion connected to all domains of corporate responsibility and sustainability: Is it preferable to adhere to uncompromisingly high sustainability standards and keep sustainable and responsible business a niche phenomenon as a result, or should the benchmarks be lowered in order to achieve a critical mass for the mainstreaming of responsible business?

Initiatives like the Principles for Responsible Investment (PRI) (Chapter 14.2.2) have worked toward the harmonization of ESG investing, but much still needs to be done. The persistent lack of transparency with regard to ESG criteria and metrics and how they are used in investment decisions creates ample opportunity for greenwashing (Ruggie 2021). Furthermore, while human rights considerations are also on the rise in ESG investing, they are often addressed in incoherent ways (Ruggie 2021). A major gap to be addressed in this regard is the provison of adequate data and metrics based on human rights that investors can use to assess the human rights risks and performance of companies for their screening and investment decisions (O'Connor & Labowitz 2017: 2).

BOX 9.1 (Short case) BlackRock's new human rights approach

BlackRock is one of the world's largest asset managers, with assets under management (AUM) totaling nearly $9 trillion as of April 2021. It has a track record in in the area of responsible investment and in recent years has made some efforts to integrate ESG-related investment criteria in line with the UNGPs (Rogge 2021). In March 2021, BlackRock published a widely noted human rights policy, which highlights the organization's commitment and prioritization to engage critically with firms whose conduct has violated the UNGPs (BlackRock 2021). BlackRock holds at least a 5 percent stake in more than half of the firms in the S&P 500 index (Rogge 2021).

BlackRock's announcement is significant not only because it is the first time that an institutional investor of such size and prominence has put human rights and the UNGPs at the center of its responsible investment strategy but also because of the underlying message that this shift conveys. In the United States, as in many other countries, asset management firms are subject to fiduciary trust laws that oblige them to give primacy to creating value for investors (Rogge 2021). Thus, with its new policy, BlackRock makes it clear that it considers its engagement on human rights not as an addition or supplement to its "regular" investment activities, but as an integral part of its fiduciary duty and thus a key part of its mission to protect and create value for its clients (BlackRock 2021; Rogge 2021). For BlackRock, unmanaged potential and actual adverse human rights impacts can "expose a company to legal, regulatory, operational, and reputational risks," which "can materialize in a variety of ways, from fines and litigation to workforce and supply chain disruptions that may damage a company's standing with business partners, customers, and communities," and ultimately "call into question a company's social license to operate" (BlackRock 2021). This is why with its new policy, BlackRock "asks companies to implement processes to identify, manage, and prevent adverse human rights impacts that are material to their business, and provide robust disclosures on these practices" (BlackRock 2021). BlackRock announced that it would vote against directors of companies that fail to address or disclose human rights risks appropriately and engage in direct dialogue with company leadership on their human rights performance (BlackRock 2021).

Discussion Questions

(1) BlackRock has made sure that its human rights policy is aligned with its legal duties to abide by fiduciary trust laws. From a BHR perspective, where do you see the key limitations of such an approach? Where do you see its strengths?

(2) Rather than avoiding firms with problematic human rights records, BlackRock chooses to engage critically with them. How promising is this approach from a BHR perspective, in your opinion?

(3) Do you think BlackRock's approach could establish a new "standard" for other companies to follow suit? How significant a step is this in the quest for mainstreaming human rights concerns in investment decisions?

(4) How could BlackRock further advance its policy on human rights impacts, in order to ensure greater corporate accountability on these issues? What changes in the regulatory environment could facilitate such improvements?

In sum, recent years have heralded a major shift in ESG investing from a niche phenomenon to the investment mainstream. However, more needs to be done, particularly with regard to bringing human rights to the center of ESG investing. ESG investing has the potential to become a critical mechanism to ensure corporate accountability for human rights; large institutional investors and stock exchanges adopting respective listing requirements have a key role to play in this regard. However, to unlock the potential of ESG investing for BHR, the role of regulation will be of similar importance. For example, in many countries fiduciary investment laws are framed narrowly and allow for the consideration of human rights, if at all, only insofar as this is in investors' interest (Rogge 2021). However, there is a clear push in the direction of broadening such requirements. The PRI report that 44 percent of countries have existing or proposed regulation that will allow or even require pension funds to consider ESG criteria as a part of their fiduciary responsibilities (O'Connor & Labowitz 2017: 6). Furthermore, providing an adequate informational basis on ESG investing is crucially dependent on the disclosure of relevant information by companies. Hence, ESG investment as an accountability mechanism does not work in isolation of, but only in combination with public regulatory approaches.

9.4.3 Civil Society: Naming and Shaming

"Soft" accountability mechanisms hinge on publicity in order to generate pressure from key stakeholder groups. Civil society organizations play a critical role in generating such publicity through what are often called "naming and shaming" campaigns. Led by civil society organizations acting as watchdogs for soft accountability measures, these campaigns name and publicly reprimand companies that engage in misconduct or fall short of meeting the standards to which they have committed. As a result, such public campaigns can lead to reputational damage for companies, to consumer boycotts, or to their banishment from responsible investment funds, for example. Rebuilding a tarnished reputation is a costly, long, and uncertain process for companies. Therefore, naming and shaming campaigns can be highly successful instruments to put pressure on them, particularly on strong global brands, for whom reputation and image are key success factors.

However, similar to consumer and investor-based approaches, naming and shaming strategies also have clear limits. Such campaigns and the investigations on which they are based are time-, resource-, and cost-intensive for civil society organizations. In addition, there is always the risk that legal action is taken by the corporation to combat them. Being drawn into legal proceedings by corporate lawsuits can tie up such organizations' resources and, in some instances, threaten their very survival (Chapter 12.6.4). This means that there are clear and often hard limits with regard to how many campaigns such organizations can run and how extensive the campaigns can be. As a consequence, naming and shaming approaches generally only focus on a few exemplary and potentially high-profile cases at a time in order to increase public awareness and sensitivity for the larger underlying issues (Abbott 2012: 557). Furthermore, they necessarily focus on issues and industries with promising potential to catch the public spotlight and around which sufficient stakeholder pressure can be generated. In turn, many equally pressing issues may receive little attention and remain under the public radar. Thus, while naming and shaming campaigns address the tip of the iceberg effectively, a large part of corporate misconduct necessarily remains unaddressed. In sum, while civil society organizations can indeed play a critical role with regard to enhancing corporate accountability, outsourcing the entire accountability problem to them disregards the serious constraints under which they generally operate.

STUDY QUESTIONS

1. What does polycentric governance mean? Can you explain this system? What accountability approaches can be found in this system?
2. What is the difference between hard and soft law? When is each approach used and what is their relationship to each other?
3. To what extent are consumers a crucial stakeholder group when it comes to holding corporations accountable for their human rights conduct? What are the limitations of consumers' accountability pressure?
4. What is the "intention-behavior gap"? Can you provide an example of it by considering your own purchasing behavior?
5. What is "label fatigue"? How does it affect corporate human rights accountability?
6. What is ESG investing and how relevant is it to the BHR discussion?

REFLECTION QUESTIONS

1. Name at least two advantages and disadvantages for both private and public regulation, concerning their effectiveness to ensure corporate human rights accountability. In your opinion, what are the best ways to ensure corporate human rights responsibilities? Would you prefer a private or public regulatory approach or a mixture of both? Can you provide examples to support your argument?

2. What labels or certifications are you familiar with within the responsible business sphere? Choose one label and reflect on whether its requirements are sufficient to ensure corporate accountability. What are the strengths and the limitations of the chosen label?

3. Given the precarious working conditions in the textile industry, your friend asks you where they could purchase clothing that is responsibly made. What criteria would you suggest they look for, when considering companies? How do you go about shopping responsibly in your own role as a consumer?

4. From your perspective, is it preferable to adhere to uncompromisingly high sustainability standards and keep sustainable and responsible business a niche phenomenon as a result, or should the benchmarks be lowered to achieve a critical mass for the mainstreaming of responsible business?

The UN Guiding Principles on BHR: Foundations, Contemplations, Critique

The unanimous endorsement of the UNGPs by the HRC in June 2011 brought John Ruggie's mandate as the SRSG to an official conclusion. The form of his mandate and the rationale underlying it were covered in Chapter 2.3. The current chapter will engage with the content of the two main instruments resulting from it, namely the UN Protect, Respect and Remedy Framework and the UNGPs. The UN Framework was published in 2008 and develops the conceptual foundation upon which the UNGPs are built. The UNGPs, on the other hand, can be interpreted as the operationalization of the UN Framework. Or in the words of John Ruggie (2013: 81), "The Framework addresses *what* should be done; the Guiding Principles *how* to do it."

10.1 The UN Protect, Respect, and Remedy Framework

When John Ruggie took over as the SRSG in 2005, he wanted to start his mandate on a clean slate and thus declared the UN Draft Norms (Chapter 2.2) to have officially failed – a move later labeled "normicide" by his critics, who had hoped to see him revive, rather than "kill off" the UN Draft Norms. Three points of contention in particular led Ruggie to officially do away with the UN Draft Norms, one formal and two material.

First, Ruggie disagreed that a legally binding framework would be best suited to get businesses on board with the BHR agenda. For him, the failure of the UN Draft Norms showed that a more pragmatic approach was needed, particularly for creating sufficient buy-in from the business community. Ruggie was not against legislating BHR in principle. After all, the UNGPs themselves call on national governments to use their legislative means to mandate BHR provisions where necessary and feasible. Furthermore, Ruggie did not oppose the use of international law to advance the BHR agenda. However, he saw international law as unsuitable to establish an all-encompassing, overarching framework. Rather, he saw the role of binding treaties in legislating more narrowly defined, specific BHR issues and areas. Thus, Ruggie adopted a position of what he called "principled pragmatism" (Chapter 10.3.2.1) – principled in terms of an unwavering commitment to advance corporate respect of human rights, and pragmatic in terms of adopting a framework that would have substantial impact as quickly as possible and thus make a real difference in the lives of those whose rights are adversely affected by business activities.

The *second* point is a material one and concerns the content of the UN Draft Norms. In Ruggie's view, the UN Draft Norms defined the range of corporations' responsibility for human rights too extensively. "Within their respective spheres of activity and influence," as the UN Draft Norms stated, "transnational corporations and other business enterprises have the obligation to promote, secure the fulfilment of, respect, ensure respect of and protect human rights recognized in international as well as national law" (UN Sub-Commission on the Promotion and Protection of Human Rights 2013: 4). Thus, constrained only by their own sphere of influence, corporations were seen to have largely the same range of responsibilities for human rights as governments. However, corporations, as Ruggie was convinced, are "specialized economic organs" with "distinctive responsibilities," which "cannot and should not simply mirror the duties of States" (Ruggie 2008: 16). Accordingly, Ruggie aimed for a model in which the responsibilities of governments and those of corporations are "differentiated but complementary" (Ruggie 2008: 4) rather than overlapping, and in which the responsibility of companies is defined much more clearly and more narrowly.

Third, the UN Draft Norms defined a subset of distinct human rights, which they perceived as being particularly relevant for the business context. They included the right to equal opportunity and non-discriminatory treatment and specified rights of workers, among others. The scope of the UN Draft Norms was thus limited to those specific rights. Ruggie, on the other hand, argued that limiting the scope to only a subset of human rights might prove counterproductive. While some rights might indeed be particularly prone to being impacted in business contexts, corporate activity can affect all human rights in principle. Accordingly, none of them can be considered beyond the realm of corporate responsibility. Thus, Ruggie turned the logic of the UN Draft Norms inside out: Rather than presupposing expansive duties for a limited sample of human rights, he aimed at establishing a limited corporate responsibility, but for the full range of human rights.

In a nutshell, the UN Framework introduces a model of distribution of human rights responsibilities between states and corporations. It is based on three pillars, which mirror the tripartite duty structure of human rights (Chapter 7.2): The state duty to protect human rights builds the core and central pillar of the UN Framework; the corporate responsibility to respect human rights is known as "pillar two"; "pillar three" is a joint commitment to improved access to remedy for victims of corporate human rights abuse. The following paragraphs will briefly define and elaborate on the conceptual underpinnings of the three pillars.

10.1.1   Pillar One: The State Duty to Protect Human Rights

The central pillar of the UN Framework is the state duty to protect human rights against violations committed by third parties, including business. Thus, Ruggie did not abandon the state-centrism that characterizes traditional human rights thinking. However, while states remain the central duty-bearers, they are no longer seen as the only responsible actors.

The state duty to protect human rights is a legally binding duty that is firmly rooted in international law. Accordingly, this first pillar does not establish any new norms, but merely restates what is already well established. However, what exactly that duty means and entails in detail is not that clear; hence, the UN Framework and particularly the UNGPs aim at spelling that out. From a conceptual point of view, three points advanced by the UN Framework with regard to the state duty to protect are of particular relevance:

- *"Smart mix" of measures*: Generally, states are asked to make use of the full range of the policy, legislative, and judicial means available to them to ensure business respect for human rights (Chapter 12). The UNGPs later coined the notion of a "smart mix" of measures, meaning that states should combine voluntary and mandatory, policy and legislative means in complementary and mutually supportive ways in order to maximize the protection of human rights.
- *Extraterritorial regulation*: Both the UN Framework and the UNGPs avoid taking a clear position on whether or not the state duty to protect extends to the so-called extraterritorial activities and impacts of businesses and, hence, to potential violations that occur outside of the state's own territory. Instead, they adopt the rather vague position that based on international law, states are generally not obligated to regulate and adjudicate the extraterritorial activities of transnational companies, but neither are they prohibited from doing so. The question about extraterritorial regulation and jurisdiction has become a sticking point in current discussions on BHR and will be analyzed more thoroughly in Chapter 12.2.
- *Policy coherence*: BHR touches on a wide range of issues and raises challenges in a variety of different domains of state action. Accordingly, the state duty to protect human rights from corporate abuse does not concern one particular government department or ministry only, but must also inform a plethora of different policies across different departments. For this reason, it is critical that states adopt coherent approaches, both vertically across different policies in a particular department and also – and especially – horizontally, across different state divisions. For example, governments should make sure that bilateral investment and trade agreements do not run counter to the protection of human rights and do not provide spaces for corporations to circumvent the policies put

in place by other departments of the government. Hence, such trade and investment agreements should also proactively include BHR provisions, which are aligned with the state duty to protect human rights (Chapter 13.1.1).

While the state remains the primary duty-bearer in the UN Framework, its main innovation is that it assigns a responsibility also to corporations, which holds independently of the state duty to protect. The corporate responsibility to respect human rights is established and dealt with in the second pillar of the UN Framework, as seen below.

10.1.2   Pillar Two: The Corporate Responsibility to Respect Human Rights

The second pillar of the UN Framework covers the corporate responsibility to respect human rights. In an ideal world, in which states fully meet their duty to protect human rights from corporate abuse, there would be no need for such a responsibility. However, we do not live in a perfect world and both the capacity and at times the political will of governments to protect human rights adequately is lacking. Therefore, Ruggie defined the corporate responsibility to respect human rights as independent from governments' duty to protect human rights. This means that it holds irrespective of whether or not the state meets its own duty. For example, corporations may operate in contexts in which local laws are in conflict with human rights standards and where compliance with such laws inevitably results in human rights violations. Such contexts do not absolve the company from its responsibility to respect human rights. The responsibility to respect human rights holds "above and beyond compliance with laws and regulations" (Ruggie 2013: 91). Thus, meeting the responsibility to respect human rights in such contexts means either not entering these contexts at all or finding ways to eliminate such negative impacts.

Ruggie defines the corporate responsibility to respect human rights in terms of non-violation, in line with the common interpretation of the human rights discourse: "To respect rights essentially means not to infringe on the rights of others – put simply, to do no harm" (Ruggie 2008: 9). The responsibility to respect human rights is the baseline expectation, which holds for all companies in all situations (Ruggie 2008: 9; 2013: 95). Besides these definitional elements, a number of other aspects are important to understand the UN Framework's take on the corporate responsibility to respect human rights.

- *First*, the corporate responsibility to respect human rights is not grounded in international law. While for some egregious violations, companies may face lawsuits in domestic courts (Chapter 12.5), Ruggie sees the corporate responsibility to respect human rights first and foremost as a social norm grounded in social expectations. Social norms, according to Ruggie, express a "collective sense of 'oughtness' with regard to the expected conduct of social actors," asserting that the corporate responsibility to respect human rights has acquired near-universal recognition (Ruggie 2013: 92). Thus, in most cases, not meeting the responsibility to respect human rights will not have any legal repercussions for a company. But breaking social norms and disregarding social expectations can result in the erosion of trust and can, in Ruggie's (2008: 16) own words, "subject companies to the courts of public opinion." Eventually, this can end in the loss of the company's social license to operate (Chapter 6.3.1).

- *Second*, Ruggie differentiates the term "responsibility" from "duty" precisely to make the distinction between legal obligations and "mere" social expectations explicit. While states have a binding duty to protect human rights, which is grounded in international law, corporations "merely" have a responsibility to respect human rights, which derives from social norms and expectations.

- *Third*, in order to meet the responsibility to respect human rights, corporations are asked to conduct HRDD as a means and process to identify, address, and report on adverse impacts on human rights (Chapter 8.1). HRDD was introduced by the UN Framework as an alternative for the UN Draft Norms' reliance on the "sphere of influence" concept. The "sphere of influence" concept was first introduced to the BHR discussion by the UNGC. It builds on the understanding that a company's influence is like a set of concentric circles with decreasing influence toward the outside. As the influence decreases, the company's responsibility also becomes smaller. However, Ruggie held that the notion of influence was too "elusive and elastic" to serve as a foundation for corporate human rights responsibility (Ruggie 2013: 101). Ruggie feared that the concept would be prone to strategic gaming, which could lead states to shirk their responsibility at the cost of corporations having to step in. Also, insufficient and inadequate interpretations of influence could distort the view on corporate responsibility, such as when influence is perceived merely as a function of (geographic) proximity. After all, a corporation's influence is determined less and less by its spatial closeness. For example, internet providers and platforms can have large influence without any physical presence anywhere close to where a violation may occur. Thus, Ruggie argued that it is a company's human rights impacts, both actual and potential, direct and indirect, that should determine its responsibility, rather than its influence. In order to minimize their adverse impacts, corporations ought to be able to demonstrate that they act with reasonable care in all their endeavors.

In sum, the departure of the UN Framework from the UN Draft Norms becomes most obvious in this second pillar. While the UN Draft Norms defined corporate human rights responsibility extensively but limited it to corporations' sphere of influence, the UN Framework defines it narrowly in terms of non-violation but extends it to all of a corporation's actual or potential impacts.

BOX 10.1 (Short case) Artisanal mining in the DRC: engage or disengage?

Over the past decade, global cobalt consumption has tripled and is expected to grow fourfold by 2030, driven by the growing demand for consumer electronics and electric-battery vehicles (Baumann-Pauly 2020: 3; Calvão, McDonald, & Bolay 2021). The increased demand has brought heightened attention to the Democratic Republic of the Congo (DRC), which produces more than 70 percent of the world's cobalt. Approximately 20–30 percent of the cobalt currently exported from the DRC is extracted by artisanal miners (Baumann-Pauly 2020: 3; Nkumba 2020: 297).

Artisanal mining (ASM) is a critical livelihood source for more than 2 million Congolese (Baumann-Pauly 2020: 6). At the same time, it is notoriously unsafe, dangerous, and precarious work, rife with human rights risks, and often involving children (Chapter 14.1.1) (Nkumba 2020). Thus, with the supply chains of many of the world's most reputable electronics companies such as Apple and Samsung linked to cobalt mining in the DRC, the pressure particularly on cobalt trading companies to address the problem is increasing (Amnesty International & AfreWatch 2016).

In response to this pressure, Glencore, one of the world's largest mineral traders, decided to abandon the trade of ASM-extracted cobalt altogether and instead focus exclusively on industrially mined cobalt. While the company announced in August 2020 that it would support initiatives on the ground to make ASM safer, it has reiterated its stance not to source any ASM-extracted materials (Biesheuvel 2020).

Trafigura, another Swiss-based commodity trading company, chose a different path to manage ASM-related human rights risks. Together with the local mining company Chemaf, the ASM cooperative COMIAKOL, and the international NGO Pact, it developed a model site for safe and secure ASM at Chemaf's Mutoshi mine (Baumann-Pauly 2020; Nkumba 2020). On site, the roughly 5,000 registered miners have access to protective equipment, training, and are supported in maintaining safe working conditions. Child labor is eliminated on site by preventing workers under eighteen years of age from entering the premises (Calvão, McDonald, & Bolay 2021). The extracted cobalt is sold to Chemaf and kept separate from the industrially mined material in order to keep it traceable. However, in order to recoup some of the project costs, Chemaf's price is lower than that commonly paid by public depots (Baumann-Pauly 2020: 10).

Discussion Questions

(1) Why do you think Glencore initially chose an avoidance strategy? What parameters likely influenced its decision? Why did Trafigura choose a different strategy? What strategy would you pursue and why?

(2) If you were the manager of the Mutoshi ASM project, what additional measures would you put in place in order to minimize adverse human rights impacts on the miners and their families? What do the UNGPs say?

(3) Is engagement always better than avoidance? If not, under what conditions should companies pursue an avoidance strategy with regard to human rights risks? Can you support your argument by reference to the UNGPs?

(4) Do you think examples like the one of the Mutoshi mine are scalable or will they necessarily remain a niche occurrence without being broadly adopted? What would it take to "generalize" such projects and turn them into standard business practice?

10.1.3   Pillar Three: Access to Remedy

Both the state duty to protect and the corporate responsibility to respect human rights include the requirement to provide remedy where human rights violations have taken place.

> State regulation proscribing certain corporate conduct will have little impact without accompanying mechanisms to investigate, punish, and redress abuses. Equally, the corporate responsibility to respect requires a means for those who believe they have been harmed to bring this to the attention of the company and seek remediation, without prejudice to legal channels available (Ruggie 2008: 22).

Thus, both states and corporations, the latter to the extent that they were involved in and contributed to human rights violations, are required to engage in the provision of adequate and effective remedies. Accordingly, Chapter 8.1 defined remedy provision as an integral part of a corporate HRDD process.

The UN Framework's third pillar is built along the common distinction between state-based and non-state-based remedy mechanisms as introduced earlier (Chapter 8.1.4). Recalling this earlier distinction, state-based remedy mechanisms can be both judicial and non-judicial, while non-state-based mechanisms are always non-judicial.

The UN Framework refers to criminal and civil law as the avenues to provide judicial redress. Judicial institutions and mechanisms are often not well developed, particularly in countries where corporate-related human rights abuse occurs most frequently. As a consequence, victims of such abuse often do not have access to judicial or any remedy, be it because a legal basis is missing, because courts are lacking resources and enforcement power, or because broken institutional arrangements and corruption are undermining the independence of the judicial system. The lack of access to justice for victims in many host states raises the question of whether they should have access to courts in the home states of multinational parent companies. Thus, the question and challenge of extraterritorial jurisdiction becomes particularly relevant with regard to this third pillar. Victims still often face obstacles of a prohibitive nature when attempting to bring cases to the home states of multinational companies. The UN Framework encourages states to "address [such] obstacles to access to justice, including for foreign plaintiffs – especially where alleged abuses reach the level of widespread and systematic human rights violations" (Ruggie 2008: 23). Chapter 12.5 will deal with these questions separately and in more detail.

For state-based non-judicial remedy mechanisms, the UN Framework points to national human rights institutions or the NCPs of the OECD Guidelines, among other things. However, NCPs would have to be enhanced to fulfil such a role adequately; their processes and protocols are often inadequate to serve as a remedy mechanism, lacking not only sufficient funding and resources but also transparency, equitability and predictability (Chapter 11.1.3). As pointed out in Box 8.1, such considerations are among the key effectiveness criteria that non-judicial mechanisms ought to meet.

Where non-judicial mechanisms are provided by companies, it is critical that in addition to such general effectiveness criteria, both the remedy process and the particular remedy outcomes are based on dialogue and designed and overseen with the involvement of affected communities. The involvement of independent third parties can help make sure that the company is not simultaneously both defendant and judge (Ruggie 2008: 25).

10.2   The UN Guiding Principles on BHR

The UN Framework clarifies the basic nature and shape of the human rights responsibilities both of states and companies, as well as their relation to each other. However, it provides very limited guidance with regard to how both states and corporations ought to meet their respective responsibilities. Little information is provided about what each actor ought to do in order to prevent, mitigate, and remedy adverse impacts caused or contributed to by corporations and how they should go about doing this. In order to provide more specific guidance, the SRSG and his team made an effort to operationalize the UN Framework, which resulted in the publication of the UNGPs in June 2011. This being said, the SRSG was keen to stress that the UNGPs are not to be misunderstood as a "tool kit, simply to be taken off the shelf and plugged in" (Ruggie 2011a: 5). Their implementation still depends on the context and situation and requires industry- and company-specific interpretation.

Today, the BHR discussion commonly refers to the UNGPs alone, though the UN Framework, which builds their conceptual foundation, should always be understood as a part of such references, at least implicitly. Accordingly, the basic structure of the UNGPs mirrors that of the UN Framework. They are designed along the three pillars – protect, respect, and remedy. For each of the three pillars, the UNGPs formulate a number of principles, which provide more concrete guidance to governments and corporations about what their respective responsibilities entail and how to discharge them. Each pillar consists of "foundational principles" that outline the basic nature and direction of the respective responsibilities and "operational principles" that specify and concretize the responsibilities. Each principle is elaborated and clarified in a commentary within the document.

10.2.1 Content of the UNGPs

The *first pillar* consists of two foundational and eight operational principles. The foundational principles reiterate the state duty to protect human rights and ask governments to make use of the full range of permissible preventative and remedial measures in order to prevent, investigate, punish, and redress corporate human rights abuse and to voice their expectation that businesses domiciled in their territory respect human rights both at home and abroad. The UNGPs do not explicitly recommend the use of extraterritorial regulation and jurisdiction, but do point out its permissibility under international law. The commentary to Principle 2 distinguishes between domestic measures with extraterritorial implications and direct extraterritorial legislation and enforcement, as introduced in Chapter 12.2. The operational principles ask states to ensure that the laws aimed at business respect for human rights are adequate and properly enforced and that other laws do not compromise and undermine that agenda. Where governments own or control businesses or provide substantial support and assistance such as, for example, export credits, additional measures to ensure respect for human rights are warranted. This is because the state's own responsibility and its means to ensure respect for human rights are enhanced in such situations. Similarly, governments need to ensure protection of human rights when privatizing state functions or in their commercial transactions with the private sector. Particular attention is given to contexts of conflict as well as to policy coherence. Within conflict-affected contexts, states should take adequate measures to ensure that companies do not become complicit in gross human rights abuse. As for the latter aspect of policy coherence, governments ought to ensure consistency across governmental departments and agencies, and make sure that they retain adequate policy space to meet their human rights obligations, for example, when entering trade agreements with other states, as well as in their dealings as members of multilateral institutions.

The *second pillar* consists of five foundational and nine operational principles. The foundational principles reiterate the corporate responsibility not to infringe on human rights and to address negative impacts where they occur. Businesses should not only avoid causing or contributing to human rights violations through their own activities but also "seek to prevent or mitigate adverse human rights impacts that are directly linked to their operations, products or services by their business relationships, even if they have not contributed to those impacts" (Principle 13). The responsibility to respect human rights applies to all companies, be they small or large, national or multinational, and refers to human rights as established by the International Bill of Human Rights (Chapter 3.3.3) as well as the principles concerning fundamental rights set out in the ILO's Declaration on Fundamental Principles and Rights at Work. The operational principles specify the process by which companies ought to ensure respect for human rights. It outlines the modalities of an explicit policy commitment as well as of an HRDD process as addressed in Chapter 8.1.3. Large companies with long and complex value chains should prioritize high risk areas for their HRDD processes. Prioritizations with regard to responses to adverse human rights impacts should be based on the severity of the impacts and the urgency of the responses needed. Companies need to make sure they draw on adequate internal and external human rights expertise and consult with affected communities when assessing impacts and risks. Furthermore, they should assign responsibility for addressing adverse impacts to the appropriate level and function within their organization and make sure that internal decision-making, budget allocations, and oversight processes enable effective responses to such impacts. As a part of the HRDD process, they should track and communicate their responses and "provide for or cooperate in their remediation through legitimate processes" (Principle 22), as outlined in Chapter 8.1.3.

Principle 19 deserves particular mention. Where companies are not causing the adverse impacts themselves, but are contributing or linked to them through their business relationships, they ought to use their available leverage to stop or mitigate such impacts. Leverage, according to the UNGPs, "is considered to exist where the enterprise has the ability to effect change in the wrongful practices of an entity that causes a harm" (Ruggie 2011a: 18). A company whose orders make up for a large part of the annual revenue of a supplier may have considerable leverage to pressure a supplier into human rights compliance. For example, it can offer to help build capacity and, as a more confrontational measure, threaten to withdraw its business in case of non-compliance. Where companies do not have sufficient or any leverage, they should find ways to build and increase it. They can do so, for example, by partnering up with other companies in similar situations or with third parties willing to support them. Seeking independent expert advice in such situations is advisable in any case (Ruggie 2011a: 19), not least for the purpose of enhancing legitimacy for such measures. Where corporations are linked to human rights violations but lack both leverage over the wrongdoer and the possibility to build and increase it, the UNGPs suggest that they should consider ending a business relationship. Should they decide to do so, however, corporations must give due consideration to the human rights impacts that may derive from such a decision, for example, the effect on workers who may lose their employment and on the communities in which those workers live (Ruggie 2011a: 19).

The leverage provision in Principle 19 is a peculiar departure from the UN Framework, which took a fundamentally skeptical position toward leverage and influence as parameters for corporate responsibility. The UN Framework's position is that corporations cannot be held responsible for the impacts of other actors over which they have influence, since this would include cases in which they are not a causal agent in the harm (Ruggie 2008: 19–20). However, by extending leverage as a parameter of responsibility to cases in which corporations are merely linked to human rights violations, rather than causing or contributing to them, the UNGPs are doing just that – extending responsibility to cases in which corporations are not causal agents. It is, by any means, an important and warranted departure from the UN Framework, but one with potentially momentous implications both from a practical and an ethical perspective. Practically, it leads to questions of how to best use leverage and what the potential consequences or even ramifications may be if a company takes a position on contentious issues. After all, the UNGPs do not specify who the parties may be over which a corporation ought to exercise leverage. For example, there will be little controversy if a company puts pressure on one of its suppliers over human rights compliance. But what if it is about a host government instead? This is where some of the tricky ethical questions about the legitimate use and the limits of corporate influence emerge. We have touched on this issue in connection with silent complicity and a potential corporate responsibility to protect human rights earlier (Chapter 7.3.2). Relating to the tripartite duty structure of corporate human rights responsibility introduced in Chapter 7.2, the use of leverage particularly in situations in which a corporation is merely linked to human rights violations shows again that the lines between the responsibility to respect and the responsibility to protect are not clear-cut and that it may be difficult to limit corporate human rights responsibility to just one category, as the UNGPs suggest.

The *third pillar* consists of one foundational principle and six operational principles. The foundational principle defines access to remedy within the context of the state duty to protect human rights. The operational principles ask states to ensure the effectiveness of domestic judicial mechanisms as well as to reduce any obstacles and barriers that may prevent legitimate cases from being brought to court. The commentary to Principle 26 differentiates between legal barriers and practical and procedural barriers in this regard. As the commentary states, victims face legal barriers where they are denied "justice in a host State and cannot access home State courts regardless of the merits of the claim" (commentary to Principle 26). Thus, notwithstanding the vague position of the UNGPs on extraterritorial jurisdiction, they seem to perceive this issue as not entirely up to the discretion of the state after all. Ruggie's elaborations in his 2013 book *Just Business* on this particular issue prove instructive to understanding the position of the UNGPs on extraterritorial adjudication more generally:

> Nevertheless, having explored this challenge extensively and with a broad spectrum of governments, other stakeholders, and legal experts, I concluded that it was not possible to reach a consensus on it among governments at this time, and that my putting forward an overly prescriptive recommendation in the GPs could well jeopardize the entire initiative because the Human Rights Council process dictated that states either support or reject the GPs as a whole (Ruggie 2013: 117).

In other words, the vague position of the UNGPs on extraterritorial jurisdiction is based not on substantive reasons, but on predominantly pragmatic considerations in order to secure the endorsement of governments in the HRC. Practical and procedural barriers, on the other hand, can consist of prohibitive costs to access courts or of difficulties in securing legal representation among other things. Besides judicial mechanisms, states should also provide non-judicial grievance and remedy mechanisms. Even in systems with a well-functioning judicial apparatus, non-judicial mechanisms can play important roles in supplementing judicial ones. As for businesses, they should establish or participate in effective operational-level grievance mechanisms (Chapter 8.1.3.3). Such mechanisms often have the advantage of being cost-effective, transnational in reach, and fast in the provision of remedy. Importantly, operational-level grievance mechanisms are not meant merely for human rights claims. On the contrary, they should capture and deal with grievances at an early stage and ideally before they even turn into human rights issues. Furthermore, the commentary to Principle 29 states that operational-level grievance mechanisms can complement but not replace more general stakeholder and community engagement processes. Finally, Principle 31 contains the effectiveness criteria for non-judicial grievance mechanisms, as outlined in Box 8.1.

10.2.2   Accountability Regime of the UNGPs

The UNGPs are not a voluntary standard in the narrow sense of the UNGC. Companies are not merely bound by the principles if they explicitly sign on to them; rather, the UNGPs hold per se for all companies, whether they want it or not. Furthermore, at least with regard to the state duty to protect, the UNGPs reiterate what has already been established in international law. However, with regard to the corporate responsibility to respect, the UNGPs remain soft, lacking any direct enforcement mechanisms. Nevertheless, the UNGPs indirectly do contain at least a concept of accountability. More specifically, Ruggie delegates the enforcement quandary to governments themselves, rather than suggesting an international mechanism for it. The commentary of Principle 3 of the UNGPs suggests that states should "consider a smart mix of measures – national and international, mandatory and voluntary – to foster business respect for human rights," which includes that states "enforce existing laws that directly or indirectly regulate business respect for human rights," and that they "review whether these laws provide the necessary coverage in light of evolving circumstances." The idea of a smart mix of measures has shaped the implementation of the UNGPs considerably and it challenges those views that hold that the UNGPs are entirely voluntary. As Ruggie notes:

> The Guiding Principles take us beyond the stalemate induced by the mandatory-vs.-voluntary divide. They reaffirm that the state duty to protect human rights includes the creation of legally binding rules and the provision of effective judicial remedy (Ruggie 2013: 125).

This integration of the corporate responsibility to respect human rights and the state obligation to enforce it is one key innovation of the UN Framework and the UNGPs, respectively; no other corporate responsibility standard integrates corporate responsibility and state obligations in one and the same framework.

Nevertheless, what seems like a smart move on paper will also have to work out in practice. After all, there is a certain irony behind delegating the enforcement of corporate human rights responsibility to states, since it was precisely their inability and lack of political will to deal with such issues in the first place that led to the governance gaps that have come to facilitate the corporate human rights abuses the UNGPs are designed to address (Wettstein 2015). The question that remains with regard to the accountability regime underlying the UNGPs is whether governments are able and willing to use their legislative, policy, and adjudicative means to enforce corporate respect for human rights; where they fail to do so, the UNGPs risk remaining one of many soft-law initiatives without real teeth.

10.3 Critical Assessment

Hardly anyone would deny today that John Ruggie moved the BHR debate forward decisively during his mandate as the SRSG. However, there was also criticism of the process, form, and particularly content of the UNGPs. Thus, this section will briefly reflect on the work of the SRSG, particularly as it pertains to the UNGPs in light of both the praise and the criticism that has been voiced.

10.3.1   Key Achievements

The impact of the SRSG's mandate on the BHR discussion was significant. His achievements were many, though this brief assessment will focus on three specific points.

First, when John Ruggie took over as the SRSG in 2005, the BHR discussion was in what some commentators called a stalemate. After the failure of the UN Draft Norms, the positions of opponents and proponents seemed hardened, and moving ahead appeared difficult. However, the UN had escalated the BHR issue to the extent that abandoning it was not an option anymore, either. Thus, Ruggie's first critical task was to navigate the discussion out of the apparent impasse and lead it to a point where progress was possible again. The idea was to create a "focal point" in the discussion around which both progressives and skeptics within the debate could rally and which would catalyze a constructive dialogue. There is no doubt that the SRSG delivered on this point. The UNGPs have provided a focal point and they have created considerable momentum to propel the discussion forward.

Second, and perhaps most important, the SRSG contributed considerably to shifting the burden of proof from those who argue in favor of corporate human rights responsibility to those who argue against it. While he did not do so alone – but rather as a part of a long process that involved the efforts and work of many – his six-year mandate played a crucial part in fostering a consensus on the issue and, indeed, establishing it in the mainstream (Wettstein 2015). This was a tremendous achievement, considering how deeply engrained state-centrism had been in the human rights discourse. Nonetheless, much work lies ahead to turn this consensus into real and tangible impact on human rights policy on the one hand and business practice on the other. As Ruggie (2011a: 5) himself stated: The UNGPs will not bring BHR challenges to an end, but rather mark the end of the beginning.

Third, the work of the SRSG facilitated the first decisive steps in this transition from mere commitment to actual and tangible developments in policy and practice. The UNGPs in particular created considerable momentum, especially among governments, to discuss and adopt concrete measures to implement their duty to protect human rights from corporate abuse. As discussed in Chapter 12.3.1, a growing number of governments have adopted or are in the process of adopting NAPs on BHR, which outline prospective measures and activities to advance the BHR agenda domestically. Increasingly, governments are integrating BHR provisions into their procurement and other policies to create both pressure on and incentives for companies (Chapter 12.3.2). A number of countries have put in place binding legislation on BHR or BHR-related issues or have started concrete discussions around adopting such legislation (Chapter 12.4). Such developments are still at an early stage and their impact has yet to fully materialize. Thus, caution is advised when assessing the (prospective) impact of the UNGPs, but considering the progress made so far, there is reason for optimism.

10.3.2   Main Criticism

Like any initiative, the mandate of the SRSG more generally and the UNGPs specifically have received both praise and criticism. The critique has been wide-ranging and voiced by legal and non-legal scholars alike. Some of the more prominent points raised in the discussion are addressed below.

10.3.2.1   Principled Pragmatism: Accommodating Business to Achieve Consensus?

One persistent and recurring criticism has been that the SRSG accommodated businesses too much while compromising on making the UNGPs more forceful. One major reason for the failure of the UN Draft Norms was the fierce opposition of the private sector. Thus, avoiding the same fate for the UNGPs was critically dependent on generating sufficient buy-in among businesses and business associations. Critics argue that by starting the mandate on this premise, Ruggie was too "corporate friendly" at the outset. More generally, critics contend that by aiming at a consensus on the UN Framework and the UNGPs, the bottom-up approach chosen by the SRSG allowed for too much influence by powerful stakeholders such as the private sector and Western governments (Bilchitz & Deva 2013: 8–9), while granting too little representation and influence to vulnerable and marginalized stakeholder groups, such as victims, and giving little consideration to critics (Deva 2013: 83). The consequences of this are twofold.

First, the UNGPs are formulated using soft and business-compatible language. Terms that are most common and familiar in the human rights vocabulary were replaced by terms that cater more to business. For example, and as discussed in Chapter 4.1, rather than speaking of human rights "violations," the UNGPs refer to adverse human rights "impacts" or "risks." Similarly, the UNGPs do not refer to "victims" of human rights abuse, but rather to "affected stakeholders." As outlined above, the sphere of influence concept was replaced by HRDD and thus with terminology that has long been familiar to business.

> The impact terminology shifts the focus from the breach of obligations implicit in the notion of "violation" to companies merely affecting adversely the ability of a person to enjoy human rights. Furthermore, "impact" turns the attention away from the deviant behavior of companies to the fate of victims, which may be the result of multiple factors (Deva 2013: 97).

For some, it is precisely this use of business-related terminology that makes the UNGPs a stroke of genius (Buhmann 2013; Jägers 2013). For others, however, the softening and toning down of business responsibility and its underlying normativity comes at a cost and may end up undermining rather than advancing the BHR agenda in the long run (Deva 2013).

Second, some critics argue that the SRSG not only watered down the normativity of the UNGPs by adopting business-friendly language and concepts but also either bypassed contentious issues altogether or failed to take any clear stand on them (Bilchitz & Deva 2013: 16; Deva 2013: 86). Thus, the means to lead the BHR discussion out of the deadlock, as critics claim, was to steer it away from controversial issues and toward those issues on which agreement was most likely to be achieved. A case in point is the UNGPs' vague position on extraterritorial jurisdiction, which, as outlined in Chapter 10.2.1, Ruggie deliberately adopted in order not to jeopardize a possible consensus on the issue. This is the flipside of Ruggie's approach of principled pragmatism, critics contend, since swift and pragmatic progress may, at times, indeed be achievable only by not bringing up the more controversial questions at all.

10.3.2.2   Normative Foundation: Social Expectations or Ethical Principles?

Business ethicists and philosophers in particular (but not only) have criticized the lack of moral normativity of the UN Framework and the UNGPs (Arnold 2010; Cragg 2012; Bilchitz 2013; López 2013). Rather than building on a moral foundation, the SRSG argued that the corporate responsibility to respect human rights is grounded in social expectations (Chapter 10.1.2). Two major concerns have been voiced against this foundation.

First, social expectations are deemed inadequate as a normative foundation based on two arguments, one general and one specific. *The general argument* rejects social expectations as a foundation based on the claim of a naturalistic fallacy. Philosophers speak of a naturalistic fallacy when normative prescriptions are derived from factual circumstances – that is, if "ought" is derived from "is." In other words, just because people expect businesses to respect human rights does not automatically mean that they do indeed have such a responsibility. Social expectations can be illegitimate, even if they are widely shared and accepted unquestioningly (Chapter 6.3.2). There are countless examples of people's social expectations being unreasonable and even harmful and dangerous to others. Thus, social expectations themselves need to be justified in order to unfold normative force. This means that it is not social expectations that provide the missing foundation, but the moral principles that justify those expectations in the first place. *The specific argument* addresses Ruggie's claim that there is a "near-universal" expectation that businesses ought to respect human rights. The criticism here is not that normative prescriptions are derived from the fact of social expectations, but rather the assumption that the particular social expectations in place would limit corporate responsibility to merely respecting human rights. As López points out:

It can be said that limiting the formulation of corporate responsibilities to "respect" rights does not necessarily hold in many parts of the world, where businesses are also expected to contribute positively to the realization of rights (López 2013: 67).

Indeed, a vast majority of people around the world believe that companies have a responsibility to proactively address the pressing global challenges we face today through collaborative efforts (Edelman 2009: 3). Furthermore, as will be shown later on, the notion of respect itself may be interpreted in different ways and thus entail more than merely a non-violation requirement. While this observation does not negate Ruggie's view that a responsibility not to violate human rights enjoys near-universal recognition, it does put a question mark on his near-absolute limitation of corporate responsibility to this negative interpretation, while assigning all other responsibilities to governments at the outset. This point will be taken up again below. Some critics have raised doubts even about this alleged convergence of social expectations, pointing to widespread disagreements between governments, businesses, and civil society organizations on critical BHR questions. Even if there is a consensus regarding an abstract corporate responsibility to respect human rights, opinions differ widely in terms of giving more detailed content to this responsibility (Bilchitz 2013: 122).

Second, Ruggie was criticized for giving his reliance on social expectations an instrumental spin. Corporations ought to respect human rights, not because of a moral normativity derived from them, but because not doing so jeopardizes their social license to operate (Chapter 6.3.1). Not respecting human rights may subject them to the "courts of public opinion" and result in reputational losses and economic cost. Hence, at the core, Ruggie relies on the business case for corporate respect for human rights, which, as pointed out in Chapter 6.3.2, has clear normative and empirical shortcomings and thus can only serve in a very limited sense as a foundation to ground such responsibilities.

10.3.2.3   Enforcement Mechanisms: Hard Duties or Soft Responsibilities?

The SRSG was adamant that the UNGPs do not create any new legal rules. The state duty to protect, and the principles spelling this out in detail, "merely" restate what is already established in international law; the principles relating to the corporate responsibility to respect human rights, on the other hand, are a part of soft law and not meant to give rise to any legal obligations for business. As mentioned earlier, the SRSG deliberately differentiated between the terms "duty" and "responsibility" in order to emphasize this difference.

Three lines of critique have been advanced against the SRSG's stance on the soft nature of the corporate responsibility to respect human rights:

First, and not surprisingly, those pressing for hard regulation of corporations on human rights issues criticized Ruggie for abandoning the strategy of the UN Draft Norms, which aimed for a legally binding framework. They argued that previous soft-law approaches were rather unsuccessful and did not keep their promises in terms of achieving tangible impacts. Thus, for them it was time to change course and mandate respect for human rights through an international legal framework.

Second, critics argued that the question of whether or not corporations actually have legally binding human rights obligations to begin with is not as clear-cut as the SRSG made it seem. In fact, a considerable part of the BHR discussion is precisely about the question of whether or not businesses have such legal responsibilities and, if so, how far they potentially reach. This question is not merely academic; an increasing number of lawsuits against companies for the violation of human rights abroad aim to push jurisprudence to progressively embrace such obligations step by step. In short, whether or not corporations have binding human rights obligations is an ongoing discussion. However, by treating the question as if it was settled, the UNGPs may potentially serve as a roadblock to more progressive interpretations of international law in the future (Wettstein 2015).

Third, by putting governments in the driver's seat in regard to the enforcement of the corporate responsibility to respect human rights, Ruggie turned the root cause of the BHR problem into its solution. The root cause of the BHR predicament, as Ruggie pointed out, lies in the governance gaps that exist not least because of state inability or refusal to hold corporations to account. The very reason why the UNGPs were needed in the first place was that states did not live up to their responsibility in this regard. Thus, handing the responsibility to hold corporations accountable back to states based on the UNGPs seems like setting a thief to catch a thief (Wettstein 2015).

10.3.2.4   Distribution of Roles and Responsibilities: Clear Division or Blurred Lines?

Finally, some critics have taken issue with the rigid separation of duties and duty-bearers in the UNGPs. The solution proposed by the UNGPs is to assign diverse categories of responsibility to distinct agents. Thus, Ruggie saw the responsibilities of states and corporations as separate rather than overlapping, and as complementary rather than shared. As a reminder, the UN Draft Norms proposed an opposite model, in which corporations shared some of the same responsibilities as states. Two slightly different lines of critique can be distinguished in this regard.

First, while Ruggie's model is straightforward and appealing in terms of its clear division and distribution of tasks and responsibilities, it may fall short both normatively and empirically. Normatively, it is less than clear whether corporate responsibility can indeed be reduced to merely respecting human rights. As Chapter 7.3 showed, there are plausible arguments why corporations may have responsibilities in all three categories – to respect, protect, and fulfil human rights, particularly if argued from a non-legal perspective. Silent complicity, as argued in that same chapter, is a case in point, where corporate responsibilities in the realm of protecting human rights are widely acknowledged. Many human rights problems, as argued in Chapter 7.3.3, require dynamic, non-linear and complex solutions, which can only be achieved through collaborative settings (Wettstein 2012b). Within such settings, however, roles and tasks may not always be neatly separable, and corporations may have to do more than merely not violate human rights in order to make such collaborative initiatives work properly. The appreciation of such collaborative approaches requires a change of perspective: The goal is not that corporations replace governments by taking over their responsibilities, as Ruggie justifiably warned, but that they collaborate to strengthen and leverage state responsibilities within such settings. The goal is not that they undermine regulatory approaches or the provision of essential public goods, but that they promote and contribute to such approaches through effective collaboration. Corporate human rights responsibility – in all three categories – ought not to replace state responsibility but be interpreted as an essential part of strengthening it. As I have argued elsewhere:

> Such models of collaboration are inherently dynamic. They are defined not by separate but by shared responsibility. Thus, the real challenge at the heart of business and human rights is not how to divvy up responsibility but indeed how to share it between different agents and agencies without, however, conflating and undermining their assigned roles and purposes. The challenge is to cope with this new constellation in the global age, rather than to undo it through creating artificial dichotomies where none exist. In other words, the challenge at the heart of business and human rights is one of thinking responsibility anew, and with it the possible contributions of specific agents that are obligated by it (Wettstein 2015: 174).

Second, the very categories of responsibility may be overlapping rather than entirely distinct. The line between respecting and protecting human rights in particular is "tenuous and murky" (Nolan & Taylor 2009: 443), rather than clear and obvious, particularly with regard to social and economic human rights. Shue (1996: 59) has also affirmed that "the distinction between duties to avoid (I) and duties to protect (II), which is relatively clear in the abstract, blurs considerably in concrete reality." The very notion of respect entails more than mere non-violation of human rights. It includes an element of positive recognition, appreciation, and care for human beings and it requires that one is not indifferent about situations of despair and need (Karp 2014: 64). As such, the responsibility to respect itself may require more of companies than "do no harm". For example, can a pharmaceutical company stand by and watch a health crisis unfold in a poor country? Does passivity and indifference in such a situation amount to actual disrespect? As a consequence, would respect, in such a situation, require more of the company than mere noninfringement? And where is the line between such an understanding of respect and human rights protection? (Wettstein 2015: 172–173)

To conclude, Ruggie set out to assess the unique and distinctive responsibilities of corporations as economic institutions during his mandate. However, what he came up with in terms of corporate human rights responsibility seems hardly unique: On the contrary, the responsibility to respect is a general duty. We all have a responsibility to respect human rights, irrespective of who we are and what we do; individuals have it, NGOs have it, corporations have it, states have it. It is neither characteristic nor defining of corporations and corporate responsibility. As productive organizations, corporations fulfil their distinct role through the positive contributions they make to society. Thus, it seems intuitive to start looking for the *distinctive* responsibilities of corporations within these unique contributions. This, however, will inevitably and naturally take corporate human rights responsibility closer to the categories of protecting and fulfilling human rights again. Granted that corporations do have a responsibility to respect human rights and granted that it is an important and indeed the first human rights responsibility they have, but it may not be the only one.

STUDY QUESTIONS

1. What are the three pillars of the UN Framework/UNGPs and why is each important? Name a key principle for each pillar.
2. Which one of the pillars is legally binding and for which actor? What choice of terminology signals this in the UNGPs?
3. What does it mean to say that the corporate responsibility to respect human rights is independent of the state duty to protect human rights? Can you show the relevance of this with an example?
4. The SRSG decided on a fresh start for his mandate, rather than to build on the UN Draft Norms. What were his arguments for this decision?
5. What is "principled pragmatism" and why is it relevant to the UNGPs?
6. What is the UN Framework/UNGP's position on extraterritorial jurisdiction? How did the SRSG justify this position?

REFLECTION QUESTIONS

1. The UNGPs are considered "soft law." The corporate responsibility to respect human rights is not a legal norm and there is no direct enforcement attached to the UNGPs. Do you think the SRSG should have pursued a more forceful approach?

2. What does the SRSG mean by a "smart mix" of measures? Do you think that most states follow this approach today? If you were a government, what would your "smart mix" look like?

3. The SRSG has been criticized for catering too much to corporations to gain their support for the UNGPs. Others have praised him for succeeding in generating sufficient buy-in from the private sector. What is your opinion on this controversy? Did the SRSG compromise too much?

4. The UNGPs limit corporate human rights responsibility to "doing no harm." As such, they avoid overburdening companies and keep things manageable. However, there has been criticism that this model does not adequately reflect the complexity of human rights challenges. What is your opinion? Should the UNGPs have defined corporate human rights responsibility more broadly?

11 Further International Soft-Law Standards and Voluntary Initiatives

The UNGPs are the most prominent international framework to address the human rights conduct of business. However, besides the UNGPs, there are many international soft-law standards and initiatives that shape the BHR landscape. Such standards have different aims and serve different purposes. For example, some standards are principle-based and deliberately broad and general. They aim at providing orientation for companies without prescribing how they ought to be operationalized. Other standards are process-based and are much more detailed with regard to what procedures and instruments companies need to implement in order to meet the requirements of the standard. Such standards can be generic in their outlook and address the shared challenges that all companies face or they can be issue and industry-specific and thus be narrower in scope but more detailed with regard to their prescriptions. Industry-specific standards and initiatives are addressed in Chapter 14. This chapter introduces three more general international standards with a strong human rights component. These three standards are important for BHR students and scholars to know because of the impact they have had in shaping the human rights practices of business and the BHR field more generally. They are the OECD Guidelines for Multinational Enterprises, the UNGC, and ISO 26000. The introduction of these standards will be kept brief and will focus specifically on how they address human rights. For each of the three standards, their human rights-related content is outlined, followed by some reflections on how the standards are enforced and a summary of major criticism they have faced. In addition, the last subsection of this chapter (Chapter 11.4) takes a more general look at the role and significance of MSIs, which have become an important element of the larger governance landscape in BHR. There are hundreds of small and large MSIs that cover a wide range of issues, industries, and specific challenges. Accordingly, Chapter 11.4 will deal with MSIs in a more general, conceptual sense, rather than focusing on selected examples. Some examples of industry-specific MSIs will then be discussed in Chapter 14.

11.1   OECD Guidelines for Multinational Enterprises

In 1976, the Organisation for Economic Co-operation and Development (OECD) launched their Guidelines for Multinational Enterprises. The Guidelines are one of the oldest and most impactful international soft-law standards in the field of corporate responsibility and they contain some features that make them unique to this day in the landscape of such standards. While the Guidelines are often seen and used as a "free-standing" soft-law instrument, they are formally a part of the OECD Declaration and Decisions on International Investment and Multinational Enterprises. The Declaration is "a policy commitment by adhering governments to provide an open and transparent environment for international investment and to encourage the positive contribution multinational enterprises can make to economic and social progress" (OECD n.d.(a)).

11.1.1   Content

The OECD Guidelines address responsible conduct of multinational enterprises in a more comprehensive way than, for example, the UNGPs. Human rights are only one of several other "issue areas" covered by the OECD Guidelines. More concretely, the Guidelines are divided into a total of eleven sections, the first two of which address the Concept and Principles as well as General Policies. The remaining sections cover more specific issue areas such as disclosure, human rights, employment and industrial relations, environment, combating bribery, bribe solicitation and extortion, consumer interests, science and technology, competition, and taxation.

The content of the OECD Guidelines has evolved considerably over time. The Guidelines have gone through five iterations – 1979, 1984, 1991, 2000, and 2011 – since their inception in 1976. A more prominent focus on human rights was introduced only in 2000. A paragraph on human rights was placed within the section on General Policies encouraging companies to "respect the human rights of those affected by their activities" (Bernaz 2017: 201). The 2011 update added a whole section on human rights, specifying and expanding on the reference in the General Policies. The section is modeled on the UNGPs and is consistent with them in both content and in language. This means that the OECD Guidelines now require that companies have a human rights policy, conduct HRDD according to the UNGPs, and engage in the remediation of adverse impacts through legitimate processes where they caused or contributed to them through their activities. Using their leverage, companies should try to prevent or mitigate impacts to which they are linked through their business relationships, even if they have not contributed to them. The commentary to the human rights section specifies and contextualizes the recommendations by pointing to the UN Framework and the provisions of the UNGPs.

One of the most significant and unique features of the OECD Guidelines is that they are government-endorsed. They are "recommendations addressed by governments to multinational enterprises operating in or from adhering countries" (OECD 2011: 3). In other words, adhering governments are legally bound to implement the Guidelines. However, the Guidelines are not binding on companies (Daniel et al. 2015). Most importantly, each adhering government is asked to set up an NCP for the Guidelines. The NCP's role is to "further the effectiveness of the *Guidelines* by undertaking promotional activities, handling enquiries and contributing to the resolution of issues that arise relating to the implementation of the *Guidelines* in specific instances" (OECD 2011: 68). Thus, NCPs are an example of state-based, non-judicial grievance mechanisms and have served as an implementation and soft enforcement mechanism for the Guidelines. We will look at the role and workings of NCPs in Chapter 11.1.2. A total of forty-eight countries have adhered to the Guidelines, including the thirty-six OECD member nations and twelve additional non-member signatories.

11.1.2 Accountability Regime

The OECD Guidelines are voluntary and non-binding in nature. However, as pointed out in Chapter 11.1.1, by requiring states to set up NCPs they do contain a soft, nonjudicial enforcement mechanism, which makes them stand out from other international soft-law standards in the area of corporate responsibility.

NCPs were introduced in 1984 and continuously strengthened in subsequent updates of the Guidelines, requiring, for example, the implementation of a complaint mechanism in 2000 and the allotment of adequate personnel and financial resources as well as tougher transparency rules in 2011 (Bernaz 2017: 201). States have considerable flexibility in organizing their NCPs, though the Guidelines require a certain degree of "functional equivalence" between countries, meaning that NCPs ought to handle cases in a similar manner (Daniel et al. 2015: 10) and that they "operate in an impartial manner while maintaining an adequate level of accountability to the adhering government" (OECD 2011: 71).

The most significant task of the NCPs is their mandate to receive complaints (referred to as "specific instances") and to contribute to the resolution of issues that arise from the alleged non-implementation of the Guidelines. Complaints concerning an alleged breach of the Guidelines by a multinational company ought to be handled in three phases (Ochoa Sanchez 2015: 96):

- *Initial assessment*: The NCP determines if the issues raised merit further examination.
- *Offer of good offices*: The NCP seeks advice and facilitates access to consensual and non-adversarial means to resolve the issues.
- *Conclusion*: The NCP issues statements or reports on the outcome.

Importantly, NCPs ought to make the results of their dispute settlement procedures publicly available. In this vein, the NCP has to issue a) a statement if it decides to drop a case, containing a description of the issues raised and the reasons for not considering them further; b) a report if the parties have reached agreement on the issues raised, though the report will only include the specific content of the agreement if both parties consent to it; c) a statement if no agreement is reached or if a party is unwilling to participate in the procedures, including, where appropriate, the reasons why an agreement could not be reached, as well as recommendations on the implementation of the Guidelines.

Generally, the NCP of the country where a specific instance has occurred is responsible to deal with the respective issue, though it should consult also with the NCP of the home country of the company. If issues arise in non-adhering countries, the NCP of the home country should take steps to adequately deal with the issue. Exchange of information and close cooperation between all NCPs is encouraged and actively facilitated.

The alignment of the OECD Guidelines with the UNGPs in 2011 has led to an evolving discussion in the BHR field on the use of NCPs specifically to advance the BHR agenda (Nieuwenkamp 2014; Ochoa Sanchez 2015). The human rights chapter has been the most frequently cited chapter in special instances procedures since 2011 (Nieuwenkamp 2014). However, enhancing the effectiveness of NCPs in addressing human rights matters might necessitate stronger requirements regarding their independence as well as strengthening their enforcement power. Nevertheless, as Bernaz (2017: 203) states, "the NCP-run specific instances' proceedings remain the closest thing there is to an international mechanism to hold corporations accountable for human rights violations" to date (Box 14.2).

11.1.3   Critique

Since the content of the human rights chapter of the OECD Guidelines is closely aligned with the UNGPs, the respective substantive criticism applies here, as well. Further relevant criticism has been levelled specifically at the NCPs as the implementation and soft enforcement mechanism of the OECD Guidelines. A variety of aspects relating to NCP mediation have been subject to critique; however, since the specific organization of NCPs varies from country to country, not all criticisms apply to all NCPs across the board. The following paragraphs will briefly discuss the most relevant and most frequently stated critiques of NCPs, relying predominantly on a respective compilation by the prominent OECD-focused NGO, OECD Watch (Daniel et al. 2015).

Failure to improve access to remedy for victims: As state-based non-judicial grievance mechanisms, NCPs can be expected to make a positive difference for those whose rights were violated by corporations' breach of the OECD Guidelines. However, as OECD Watch concludes, out of a total of 250 cases filed by 2015, only

35 (14 percent) had led to beneficial results that included some measure of remedy. Most of those measures were limited to improvements of the companies' policies or procedures and acknowledgments of wrongdoing. However, none of the cases included actual compensation for harms and only three of them had led to directly improved conditions for the victims (Daniel et al. 2015: 19).

Lack of accessibility: The cost of accessing NCP mediation can be prohibitive, particularly for poor and marginalized communities. NCPs may charge translation fees, for example, and are not always willing to hold meetings in the home countries of the victims nor to pay for their travel costs if meetings take place outside of those countries (Daniel et al. 2015: 23). Other reported obstacles include excessively high standards of proof in the assessment stage of filing a complaint; there are also documented cases in which complainants were harassed by the company or even faced defamation lawsuits. Particularly for complainants with limited resources, so-called SLAPPs (Chapter 12.6.4) can cripple their attempts to get redress. NCPs have been criticized for not taking adequate measures to prevent and mitigate such risks for complainants (Daniel et al. 2015: 23–24).

Lack of independence: Many NCPs are housed in a single government ministry or department and composed of representatives only of that particular ministry. This may affect independence and unbiased decision-making, particularly if that same ministry is also tasked with promoting business interests (Daniel et al. 2015: 33). There are documented cases in which NCPs made decisions that heavily relied on or even simply restated company responses submitted to them in an undisclosed and confidential manner (Daniel et al. 2015: 35–36). From the standpoint of impartiality and independence, NCPs should ideally be set up across different government agencies and be composed of a variety of government officials and external stakeholders, selected through an open and transparent process.

Transparency: NCPs face the challenge of striking an adequate balance between transparency and confidentiality. While transparency is essential for maintaining public confidence in the accountability mechanism, a level of confidentiality may be required to facilitate open communication during the mediation process (Daniel et al. 2015: 37). However, NCPs have frequently been criticized for applying overly broad standards of confidentiality, which restrict the capacity of the public – and sometimes even the parties involved in the mediation – to access critical information on the proceedings and results of the mediation.

Resourcing and effectiveness: Besides the criticism mentioned above, NCPs have been criticized for delaying cases, for being understaffed and underfunded, for failing to use their investigative powers, and for failing to publish statements of non-compliance with the OECD Guidelines in cases of non-agreement between the parties or when companies refused to enter mediation (Daniel et al. 2015; Ochoa Sanchez 2015). Furthermore, critics say that NCPs do not do enough to persuade reluctant companies to enter into dialogue and do not adequately follow up on the implementation of agreements reached through mediation (Daniel et al. 2015: 25–28).

11.2 UN Global Compact

The UNGC is a principle-based initiative that encourages companies to adopt sustainable and socially beneficial business practices. It was initiated and launched in the year 2000 by then UN Secretary-General Kofi Annan. As pointed out earlier (Chapter 2.2), the UNGC was the first high-level international code to truly put the human rights responsibilities of companies center stage. While its concrete impact is contested, it has made a critical contribution to the advancement of the BHR agenda and can be considered a key initiative in the field.

With more than 13,000 signatories in 160 countries, the UNGC is the largest international soft-law initiative to date. It is open to all businesses, with only a few restrictions. The following are excluded from becoming members: companies that are subject to a UN sanction, listed on the UN Ineligible Vendors List for ethical reasons, engaged in the production, sale and/or transfer of antipersonnel landmines or cluster bombs, or in the production and/or manufacture of tobacco (UN Global Compact n.d. (a)).

Initially a "free-standing" corporate responsibility initiative within the UN system, it has recently been fully aligned with the UN Agenda 2030. As such, the larger objective of the UNGC is to contribute to the lasting, sustainable transformation of the global economy within the framework of the Sustainable Development Goals (SDGs) (Chapter 15.1) by harnessing corporations' potential to bring about positive change through partnership and innovation. In the process of this realignment, the UNGC has undergone substantial reorganization. However, its core content has remained unchanged.

11.2.1 Content

Similar to the OECD Guidelines, the UNGC covers more than just human rights. It consists of ten broad normative principles in the areas of human rights, labor, environment, and anti-corruption (Box 11.1). At the time of its launch, the UNGC only included nine principles; the anti-corruption requirement was added four years later, in 2004. Compared to other corporate responsibility standards, the UNGC remains general and broad. Its ten principles represent basic commitments to be upheld by adhering companies without specifying any particular implementation processes. However, the UNGC offers a host of different engagement opportunities for companies to collaborate with and learn from like-minded organizations. Such

BOX 11.1 (Context) Ten principles of the UN Global Compact

Human Rights

Principle 1: Businesses should: support and respect the protection of internationally proclaimed human rights; and

Principle 2: make sure that they are not complicit in human rights abuses.

Labour

Principle 3: Businesses should uphold: the freedom of association and the effective recognition of the right to collective bargaining;

Principle 4: the elimination of all forms of forced and compulsory labour;

Principle 5: the effective abolition of child labour; and

Principle 6: the elimination of discrimination in respect of employment and occupation.

Environment

Principle 7: Businesses should: support a precautionary approach to environmental challenges;

Principle 8: undertake initiatives to promote greater environmental responsibility; and

Principle 9: encourage the development and diffusion of environmentally friendly technologies.

Anti-Corruption

Principle 10: Businesses should work against corruption in all its forms, including extortion and bribery.

collaborative engagement is organized around key focus areas aligned with the ten principles and the SDGs. Furthermore, the UNGC is organized in countless national networks that allow for regular and close interaction with and between signatory companies. As a key element of the SDGs, collaborative engagement has become a signature focus of the UNGC in recent years. Companies commit to the principles of the UNGC voluntarily by signature of the CEO and large companies pay an annual fee in addition. Doing so, they pledge to 1) uphold the ten principles of the UNGC, 2) engage in partnerships to advance the goals of the UN more generally, and 3) report annually on their progress in realizing the principles in their operations. The UNGC offers different levels of engagement to signatory organizations, ranging from low-level support (e.g. through implementation guidance tools) to more active training and advisory services, to engagement in collaborative initiatives and high-level policy dialogues, among other things.

The UNGC devotes the first two principles to human rights. Principle 1 commits signatory businesses to "support and respect the protection of internationally proclaimed human rights", while Principle 2 asks them to "make sure that they are not complicit in human rights abuses". Thus, the UNGC adheres to the common distinction between direct and indirect human rights violations as introduced earlier (Chapter 4); while Principle 1 deals with direct impacts, Principle 2 addresses indirect ones. Importantly, the UNGC separates human rights commitments from labor conditions, which are covered in Principles 3–6, signaling clearly that corporations have human rights responsibilities beyond the decent treatment of their employees and workers. While this may be commonplace today, at the time of the UNGC launch, corporate human rights responsibility, if acknowledged at all, was often perceived to be limited to workers' rights issues. Hence, the UNGC made an important contribution to promoting a more comprehensive understanding of corporate human rights responsibility.

The UNGC's human rights principles were broadly aligned with the UNGPs after their publication in 2011 and make direct reference to them. However, there are important differences. For one, the UNGC goes beyond what the UNGPs require. While the UNGC also asks companies to adopt HRDD to avoid infringing on human rights, it encourages companies to take action to proactively support human rights in addition to and beyond merely respecting them:

> Supporting human rights involves making a positive contribution to human rights, to promote or advance human rights. Socially responsible organizations will typically have a broader capability and often desire to support the promotion of human rights within their sphere of influence especially in ways that link strategically to their core business activities. The business case for supporting human rights can be as strong as the business case for respecting human rights. Likewise, stakeholder expectations often extend to the belief that organizations can and should make a positive contribution to the realization of human rights where they are in a position to do so (UN Global Compact n.d. (b)).

The UNGC lists four specific areas in which a company can typically make a positive difference in terms of promoting and supporting human rights. They are 1) through their core activities, 2) through strategic social investment and philanthropy, 3) through advocacy and public policy engagement, and 4) through partnership and collective action.

Principle 2 is closely aligned with the UNGPs' definition of complicity. In particular, it includes not only instances in which the company actively contributes to human rights violations but also cases in which it is merely linked to them through their products, services, or business relationships. Furthermore, the UNGC emphasizes that complicity does not refer only to situations in which the company may be held legally liable, but applies also to a broader range of circumstances such as when companies may benefit from human rights abuse. In such situations, as the

UNGC points out, it may be appropriate for companies to take on an advocacy role (see also Wettstein 2012c). Accordingly, the UNGC distinguishes between direct, beneficial, and silent complicity as defined earlier (Chapter 4.3).

As pointed out above, the UNGC separates its human rights principles from the principles on labor conditions. Nevertheless, those principles bear direct relevance from a human rights perspective, too. Principle 3 commits businesses to uphold workers' freedom of association and their right to collective bargaining. This includes: respecting their right to form and join trade unions without fear of intimidation; and non-interference with their role as workers' representatives. Principle 4 asks companies to work toward the elimination of all forms of forced and compulsory labor. Forced labor is commonly characterized by a lack of consent and the threat of a penalty; the UNGC refers to different forms of forced labor such as slavery, bonded labor, or debt-bondage. Legitimate businesses – which members of the UNGC are assumed to be – commonly become associated with forced labor through their business relations with suppliers and other companies. The UNGC recommends a number of measures that companies can take in the workplace to counteract forced labor, such as prohibiting business partners from charging recruitment fees (Chapter 5.5.2). Beyond the workplace, the UNGC recommends that businesses engage in industry-wide approaches to tackle the issue and have actors from other sectors join the effort. For an in-depth look at the issue of forced labor and modern slavery, see Chapter 5.2.3.

Principle 5 aims at the effective abolition of child labor (Chapter 5.2.1). The UNGC advises companies to provide viable alternatives if occurrences of child labor are identified. This may include enrolling the children for school or providing income-generating alternatives for parents. However, it cannot simply mean terminating the relationship with affected children, since this may force them into even more dire circumstances (UN Global Compact n.d. (c)). Finally, Principle 6 aims at the elimination of discrimination in respect of employment and occupation. The UNGC points out that discrimination, be it based on gender, nationality, race, religion, or other grounds, is a human rights issue that can occur both with regard to gaining access to work and to the treatment of employees during a work relationship (UN Global Compact n.d. (c)). The UNGC notes that discrimination often occurs indirectly, "where rules or practices have the appearance of neutrality but in fact lead to exclusions" (UN Global Compact n.d. (c)) and advises companies to assign responsibility for discrimination and equal employment issues at a high level, to issue clear policies, and to facilitate trainings for management and employees, among other things.

Principles 7–9 cover the company's environmental footprint. They ask companies to take a precautionary approach (Box 11.2) with regard to their impacts on the environment. Human rights are not mentioned explicitly, though as shown in Chapter 5.4 and Chapter 15.2, environmental degradation and climate change are

BOX 11.2 (Context) Precautionary principle

In a nutshell, the precautionary principle means that decision-makers must not use the absence of clear and certain scientific evidence regarding environmental and human rights risks to justify delays in adopting effective and proportionate measures in response to such potential risks (Shelton 2010: 249). In other words, decision-makers must err on the side of caution in situations in which they lack full information and knowledge about the implications and consequences of their decisions. The precautionary approach was introduced in Principle 15 of the 1992 Rio Declaration, which states that "where there are threats of serious or irreversible damage, lack of full scientific certainty shall not be used as a reason for postponing cost-effective measures to prevent environmental degradation" (UN Global Compact n.d. (g)). Principle 7 of the UNGC applies a corporate lens to the precautionary principle, stating that companies ought to adopt a precautionary approach to environmental challenges (Box 11.1).

directly linked to human rights violations. The same goes for Principle 10 on anti-corruption: While this principle is not explicitly presented in human rights terms, corruption affects human rights in manifold ways, for example, by diverting funds from public goods and services into private pockets and by undermining public governance and the rule of law more generally, which are critical elements of effective human rights protection.

11.2.2 Accountability Regime

When the UNGC was launched in 2000, it was based fully on the idea of dialogue and peer learning and contained no real accountability mechanism. Not surprisingly, this led to harsh criticism – particularly from NGOs. The UNGC responded to the critique by adding a soft accountability regime consisting of three parts:

Learning platforms and local networks: The UNGC is first and foremost thought to be a platform for dialogue, learning, and collaboration. It provides a forum for companies to share good practices and to learn from each other behind closed doors. Similarly, it also provides a variety of possibilities for organizations from other sectors – such as unions and labor organizations, government agencies, and NGOs – to engage and collaborate with member companies. Local networks are an integral part of this strategy; they are independent, self-governed, and self-managed entities at the country level that aspire to "help companies understand what responsible business means within different national, cultural and language contexts and facilitate outreach, learning, policy dialogue, collective action and partnerships" (UN Global Compact n.d. (d)). While this arguably adds little accountability toward the outside, the safe space provided by the UNGC can lead companies to address dilemmas and issues in open and constructive ways and it can provide at least a level of peer pressure and accountability toward the inside.

Annual Communication on Progress (COP): In 2003, the UNGC introduced a new requirement for member companies to report annually on the progress they have made on implementing the ten principles. The format of the COP is flexible. However, it must, at minimum, include: 1) a statement by the CEO, expressing the company's continued support for the UNGC and renewing its commitment to uphold the ten principles; 2) a description of measures and practical actions that the company has taken or plans to take to implement the ten principles in each of the four areas; and 3) a measurement of outcomes (UN Global Compact n.d. (e)). The reports are publicly available on the UNGC website, which adds a layer of accountability to the broader public, though assessing the reports and putting them into context is arguably difficult for many interested parties. Companies failing to report on their progress adequately within the specified time frame of one year will be listed as "non-communicating." Non-communicating participants who fail to meet COP requirements also in the subsequent year, will be expelled from the UNGC (UN Global Compact 2013). The UNGC makes the list of expelled companies publicly available on its website.

Dialogue facilitation mechanism: The UNGC does not routinely assess a company's commitment and adherence to the ten principles nor its performance in implementing them beyond the COP. However, complaints against particular companies for not living up to their commitment can be launched under the UNGC's dialogue facilitation mechanism. The UNGC will then encourage and facilitate a dialogue between the company and the complainant. Complaints are restricted to matters of systematic or egregious abuse of the UNGC principles that put a company's basic commitment to the UNGC's mission in question, such as, for example, serious human rights abuses (UN Global Compact n.d. (f)). Companies that refuse to respond to such complaints risk being listed as non-communicating and thus being delisted eventually.

11.2.3   Critique

The first years of the UNGC in particular were accompanied by frequent and at times harsh criticism. The UNGC responded to many of the points of contention and implemented measures to address them. This has not made the critique disappear entirely, but it has eased some of the more fundamental opposition against the UNGC. The most important recurring points of critique voiced against the UNGC include the following:

"Blue-washing": Particularly in the early years of the UNGC, but also today still, there remains a concern that companies with less than stellar corporate responsibility track records would use the UNGC as a tool to enhance their public image,

while changing little about their actual business practices and thereby benefiting from the lax governance and accountability regime of the UNGC. The term "blue-washing" alludes to the official color of the UN and was used in analogy to the more familiar term "green-washing." As a response, the UNGC implemented a policy on the use of their logo by signatory companies. However, the larger concern underlying this criticism was one of corrupting the UN system. The UNGC is often credited with heralding a paradigm change with regard to the UN's relationship with the private sector. While in earlier times, the UN was perceived as critical or even hostile toward business, the UNGC relies on a partnership approach based not on top-down regulation but on dialogue and mutual learning. For many critics, opening the doors to the private sector crossed a red line, making the UN vulnerable to being captured by powerful private interests.

Lack of teeth: Despite the adjustments made by the UNGC to its accountability regime, the most common and recurring criticism is that the UNGC still lacks any effective mechanisms to ensure that companies follow through and implement their commitment to the ten principles. The broad normative principles, as the criticism goes, provide too much leeway for companies' own interpretation and thus cannot be effectively enforced. This increases the risk that companies sign up to the UNGC without any firm intention of changing anything about their conduct. Supporters of the UNGC tend to perceive the criticism as dishonest and unfair, because the UNGC was never meant to be a regulatory instrument and thus was not designed with a view on enforcement and respective sanctions in the case of non-compliance (Rasche 2013).

Lack of impact and effectiveness: While for some the large number of signatory companies is a sign of the success of the UNGC, critics have pointed to the discrepancy between this number of signatories and the concrete impact of UNGC on their actual conduct (see, e.g., Sethi & Schepers 2014). While there is most certainly a number of companies that have made great efforts in implementing the ten principles, there are differing views on how significantly the UNGC has influenced the policies and operations of adhering companies overall and thus whether it truly succeeded in improving business conduct on average.

While criticism has never fully subsided, the UNGC arguably achieved a number of things. Given that the UNGC's impact on the policies and conduct of individual companies may be debatable, it can nevertheless be credited with initiating a broad and sustained discussion on responsible business conduct at the turn of the millennium, and contributing to raising awareness on the subject both within the private sector and in the broader public. Second, the UNGC helped restore the private sector's trust in the UN, which had suffered during the lengthy and tense discussions on the UN Draft Code (Bernaz 2017: 180). Third, the UNGC's contribution to shaping a context in which new and more far-reaching initiatives such as the UNGPs became possible again, particularly after the failure of the UN Draft Norms, is not to be underestimated. Overall, the UNGC had an important signaling effect for the broader BHR movement: Not only was the UN ready and willing to engage critically with businesses on their social and environmental impacts but it also recognized corporations' relevance to the broader human rights movement and, importantly, their significance for human rights beyond employment and labor relations (Wettstein 2012a).

11.3   ISO 26000

The final standard discussed in this chapter is ISO 26000. A number of more specific standards and initiatives will be touched on in the discussion of specific industries (Chapter 14) and the broader SDGs will be addressed in Chapter 15.1.

ISO 26000 is the International Organization for Standardization's (ISO) CSR standard. ISO is an independent international NGO that specializes in the development of standards. Founded in 1947 with the goal of coordinating and harmonizing industry standards internationally, it is based in Geneva and consists of 164 national standard bodies, making it the world's largest developer of standards. The organization has published 22,844 standards and related documents to date, which address almost every industry imaginable. The organization's standards generally enjoy considerable authority (Henriques 2012: 8).

ISO 26000 is the first ISO standard that comprehensively addresses corporate responsibility and sustainable development. Given ISO's reach and significance in the "world" of standardization, its launch was significant and widely noted (Henriques 2012). ISO 26000 was launched in 2010 after five years of negotiations. It was developed and drafted by a designated Working Group for Social Responsibility, consisting of 450 experts from eighty countries and representing a variety of different stakeholder groups (industry; labor; consumers; NGOs; government; service; support; research; and others). Each national standard body was allowed to nominate up to six such experts for the working group (Hahn & Weidtmann 2016: 104). The negotiations included more representatives from the Global South than from the North (Henriques 2012), which is significant not only because the impacts of corporate irresponsibility are often felt most strongly in the Global South but also because the lack of representation from the Global South has been one of the most frequently raised criticisms of the ISO in the past.

11.3.1   Content

The purpose of ISO 26000 is to provide guidance not only to business but to all kinds of organizations on their social responsibility (Henriques 2012: 11). It addresses organizations of all sizes and from all geographic areas, operating in or focusing on any industry. It covers seven core subjects: organizational governance; human rights; labor practices; environment; fair operating practices; consumer issues; and community involvement and development. Each subject is divided in a number of issues for which the standard formulates certain expected actions and measures (Henriques 2012: 14).

The human rights core subject is divided in eight issues: due diligence; human rights risk situations; avoidance of complicity; resolving grievances; discrimination and vulnerable groups; civil and political rights; economic, social, and cultural rights; fundamental principles and rights at work. Similar to the OECD Guidelines or the UNGC, the different core subjects and issues are interdependent and overlapping. Other subject areas, such as labor practices or environment, may have human rights implications as well, both in direct and indirect ways. Accordingly, "respect for human rights" is listed also as one of the overarching principles of social responsibility, which guide behavior regarding all core subjects. The other core principles are: accountability; transparency; ethical behavior; respect for stakeholder interests; respect for the rule of law; and respect for international norms of behavior.

Companies are asked to integrate social responsibility throughout their organization, consisting of the following steps: Making social responsibility integral to their policies, organizational culture, strategies and operations; building internal competencies for social responsibility; undertaking internal and external communication on social responsibility; and regularly reviewing these actions and practices related to social responsibility (ISO 2018: 17). In 2018, ISO 26000 counted approximately 70,000 corporate members in 114 countries (Idowu 2019), making it a highly successful standard in terms of sheer numbers. However, since the standard does not include any measurable requirements or indicators, there is no guarantee that the respective companies actually comply with the standard.

The human rights chapter of ISO 26000 aligns with the UNGPs. However, interestingly, the notion and concept of a company's "sphere of influence" still features rather prominently in the standard, while the SRSG eliminated it from the vocabulary of the UN Framework and the UNGPs deliberately due to its perceived vagueness (Chapter 10.1.2). John Ruggie did urge the ISO 26000 working group to reconsider the use of the concept in the lead-up to the standard's publication; as a response, the working group adjusted its definition of the concept to align it better with the impact-based outlook of the UNGPs. However, ISO 26000 advances a more extensive and demanding understanding of corporate human rights responsibility, which is not limited to non-violation, but includes a positive responsibility to promote and defend human rights. The clause on general principles of CSR urges companies to "respect and, where possible, promote" human rights; the human rights clause calls on them to promote and defend the overall fulfilment of human rights, promote gender equality, contribute to disabled people's enjoyment of dignity, autonomy, and full participation in society, promote respect for the rights of migrant workers, and make efforts to advance vulnerable groups and eliminate child labor (Wood 2012: 71). Worth mentioning, too, are the Standard's provisions on corporate political involvement. According to ISO 26000, corporations ought to refrain from efforts to control politicians or activities that may otherwise undermine the political process; they should also abstain from engaging in misinformation, intimidation, or threats (Wood 2012: 71).

In sum, ISO 26000 is another example of a standard that embraces a more expansive, both negative and positive understanding of corporate human rights responsibility. While the negative dimension largely corresponds to the understanding advanced in the UNGPs and the OECD Guidelines, the positive dimension is more akin to the notion of responsibility advanced by the UNGC (Wood 2012). From an ethical point of view, such a more expansive notion certainly aligns more with a holistic understanding of corporate human rights responsibility as outlined in Chapter 7.3. However, once we factor in an accountability perspective, particularly with a view on the legalization of corporate human rights responsibility, problems may arise in terms of the proper determination and delimitation of such expansive accounts. This is reflected in the accountability regime – or lack thereof – of ISO 26000, which will be addressed in section 11.3.2.

11.3.2   Accountability Regime

ISO is commonly known for its certification standards. Certification is thought to provide a layer of accountability by attesting the compliance of a company with a standard through an independent certification body. However, ISO 26000 does not provide certification nor any requirements for which compliance could be measured; this makes it difficult to assess a company's conformity with the standard (Henriques 2012: 17). Accordingly, the standard does not contain any verification, monitoring, or even enforcement mechanism.

While the option of certification was on the table early in the process of developing the standard, the aim of working toward certification was later dropped amid controversial stakeholder positions on the issue (Balzarova & Castka 2012: 267). Interestingly, opposition to certification came from two sides in the development process. Industry argued against it on cost-related grounds and because they feared it would lead to a compliance and box-ticking culture, rather than one based on values. Similar concerns are discussed today with regard to new BHR legislation at the domestic level (Chapter 12.4). Labor organizations, on the other hand, were skeptical of certification because of the inherent difficulty of making social issues measurable; they feared that this might lead to the unintended consequence of excluding stakeholders from the assessment of such contentious issues, reducing them to mere technicalities that could be outsourced to uninvolved consultancies (Henriques 2012: 18).

11.3.3 Critique

Some have praised ISO 26000 for its high legitimacy based -on representation of different stakeholder groups and geographic areas in the expert group (Hahn & Weidtmann 2016). However, for others, the broad inclusion of different groups has watered down the standard, making it vague, non-committal and political (Entine 2012). The literature on ISO 26000 commonly discusses two major points of criticism, which derive at least partly from the perceived non-committal nature of the standard.

First, and as pointed out above, ISO 26000 does not contain any certification or verification scheme. As with the UNGC, critics argue that corporations can tout their use of the standard without actually having to change anything about their conduct. The lack of a certification scheme may reduce the incentive for companies to put sufficient effort into the standard's implementation; and even those who want to invest in its operationalization may find it difficult to justify their engagement to shareholders without being able to point to the benefit of certification (Henriques 2012: 23). On the other hand, since ISO is known for its certification standards, people may not commonly be aware that ISO 26000 does not contain a verification and certification scheme, which may lead them to believe that companies using the standard are assessed and certified by ISO.

Second, ISO 26000 is not a management system standard like other well-known ISO standards. Granted, it outlines a number of management practices that can help companies implement and integrate CSR throughout their organizations, but it does not contain a formal approach to management, which has been a signature feature of ISO standards in the past; that is, it does not address how to manage CSR and sustainable development in a systematic way (Henriques 2012: 15). The lack of a formal mechanism or a management system for the implementation of the standard, according to some critics (Henriques 2012: 4), is a missed opportunity and dilutes the power of the standard.

More conservative critics perceive ISO 26000, along with other similar standards, as an instrument to foster protectionism and to hamper innovation and economic growth. Some also fear that voluntary standards such as ISO 26000 serve as a gateway to stricter transnational and domestic regulation of multinational business (Entine 2012).

11.4 The Role and Purpose of Multi-stakeholder Initiatives

MSIs started to emerge in the 1990s as a response to the increasing governance challenges posed by accelerating globalization processes and the growing dissatisfaction of civil society with self-regulation schemes of companies as a response to these challenges (Baumann-Pauly, Nolan, van Heerden, & Samway 2016: 774). As a consequence, they quickly became indispensable tools also in addressing corporate human rights challenges. In a nutshell, MSIs are collaborative initiatives that bring together private and public actors from different sectors representing different stakeholder groups to collaborate and work toward holistic solutions for human rights challenges that are too complex and multifaceted to be solved by any one actor alone. Besides companies, participating stakeholders can include NGOs, trade unions, business associations, investors, academic organizations, and government agencies, among others. Thus, the basic assumption underlying MSIs is that such holistic and viable solutions are possible only if all relevant actors come together and find a common understanding of how to tackle the underlying challenges. MSIs often thereby serve multiple functions, ranging from operational guidance and support to accountability platforms and fully fledged governance instruments.

At the operational level, participation in MSIs is part of companies' broader implementation strategy in discharging their human rights responsibilities. Active collaboration in MSIs enhances both the effectiveness and the legitimacy of corporate responses to human rights challenges and often enables companies to learn from each other and to share best practices. MSIs can thus serve as important spaces not only for learning and deliberation but also for contestation and resolution of conflicts (Arenas, Albareda, & Goodman 2020). Furthermore, MSIs often contain some form of monitoring and accountability mechanism to make sure that participants live up to their commitments. One possible accountability tool is certification for companies that commit to and effectively implement certain standards of operation. There is a large range of possible accountability measures used by MSIs, ranging from the weak and rather symbolic to the strong and effective. However, it is generally assumed that the stronger the accountability mechanisms, the more legitimacy an MSI can claim with the larger public. Finally, MSIs are a partial response to the governance gaps that the SRSG has identified as the key problem in the BHR space. Often, MSIs provide standards and guidance with regard to how specific issues and challenges ought to be addressed and how its participants should go about it. As such, they fulfil important governance functions in well-defined issue areas.

There is a wide variety of MSIs. They can differ dramatically in size and form, in their governance and accountability structure, and with regard to their focus and purpose. For example, the UNGC, at its core, is an MSI of enormous size. In contrast, there are MSIs consisting of only a handful of actors. Accordingly, MSIs vary also in terms of corporate engagement. Four levels of corporate engagement have been distinguished in this regard (Mena & Palazzo 2012: 536): **1)** MSIs provide learning platforms for corporations to engage in dialogue, learn from each other, exchange best practices, and communicate commitment; **2)** MSIs develop guidelines, codes of conduct, standards, and rules for companies to adhere to; **3)** MSIs develop monitoring, auditing, and compliance mechanisms to make sure companies meet such standards; 4) MSIs may issue certification and labels to confi-rm and signal companies' compliance.

MSIs are often set up to tackle industry-specific issues, convening companies from the same industry and other actors from civil society and the public sector to agree on common standards and responses to human rights challenges. Such industry-specific MSIs ought to fulfil three functions (Baumann-Pauly, Nolan, Labowitz, & van Heerden 2016: 112): *First*, they need to define human rights standards in a specific industry context; *second*, they should operationalize the standard into measurable benchmarks in order to assess member companies' performance; *third*, they should establish processes to sanction non-compliance and provide access to remedy for those who get harmed. As such, industry-specific MSIs can play important roles in creating a level playing field around improved standards within a given industry. Examples of industry-specific MSIs will be provided in Chapter 14.

MSIs offer a few distinct benefits, but have also been subject to criticism. One of the main advantages of MSIs is that they pull together crucial expertise from a variety of sectors and players and thus can facilitate solutions that are more holistic and may enjoy broader support across those sectors. Particularly among companies, MSIs can generate broader buy-in than it is commonly the case for public regulation. On the other hand, this raises questions concerning the possible coopting and overall legitimacy of such initiatives. This point will be addressed shortly. Another advantage of MSIs is their often flexible set-up, which makes it possible to adapt them to changing circumstances much more quickly than is the case, for example, with regulatory and legislative approaches. Accordingly, they can generate impact in a relatively short time and make it possible to respond swiftly to unfolding situations or crises. Nevertheless, MSIs and legislative and regulatory approaches should not be seen as opposites or adversaries. Rather, it is one of the benefits of MSIs that they can complement existing regulation in very targeted ways – for example, by specifying certain requirements and providing guidance in terms of their operationalization and implementation and generally by enhancing their impact on the ground (Baumann-Pauly, Nolan, Labowitz, & van Heerden 2016: 110; Schrempf-Stirling & Wettstein 2021).

MSIs are often criticized for inadequate representation. This mostly concerns an alleged overrepresentation of companies, while NGOs and civil society more generally are underrepresented; in particular, affected communities and victims of human rights abuse are often entirely missing. Companies often provide the lion's share of the funding to such initiatives and as such hold substantial power in determining their set-up, accountability, and monitoring structures. NGOs, on the other hand, often face severe budgetary constraints to participate adequately in such initiatives (Baumann-Pauly, Nolan, Labowitz, & van Heerden 2016: 119). Furthermore, they may fear losing independence or credibility with their main constituents if they team up with companies to tackle human rights problems, rather than calling them out.

Hence, MSIs are often criticized for being vulnerable to distortions by large power differentials between participating parties, which puts into question their overall legitimacy. This criticism is compounded by what is often perceived as lacking or inadequate monitoring and accountability mechanisms that would ensure that companies meet the commitments and requirements of the initiative. At a more general level, the increasing significance of MSIs as private governance mechanisms without a democratic mandate and without being embedded in democratic processes have caused unease and concern among some critics. It has been argued that in order to overcome this democratic deficit, MSIs must ensure inclusivity of stakeholders, procedural fairness of deliberations, a consensual orientation among stakeholders, and transparency of the MSIs' structures and processes (Mena & Palazzo 2012: 536). The significance of MSIs in the BHR space will likely increase despite, or perhaps because, of the current trend toward BHR legislation. Thus, these discussions on the proper role and place of MSIs as well as their legitimacy and respective safeguards will remain relevant.

STUDY QUESTIONS

1. Can you name three key aspects that distinguish the OECD Guidelines for Multinational Enterprises from other international corporate responsibility standards? What makes them unique?
2. What are NCPs? Can you name the four aspects of NCPs that have been subject to critique and explain their relevance?
3. How does the UNGC engage with the topic of human rights? Why has the UNGC been important for BHR despite the critique that its impact is limited?
4. Is ISO 26000 a private or a public standard? How does it embrace both negative and positive understandings of corporate human rights responsibility?
5. What are MSIs and what is their significance for BHR? What are some of the advantages and potential disadvantages of MSIs?

REFLECTION QUESTIONS

1. Imagine you have recently been invited to provide guidance on the latest iteration of the OECD Guidelines for Multinational Enterprises. In their current form, how are the Guidelines relevant to the broader discussion on BHR? How could they be adapted to better respond to human rights concerns?
2. How can MSIs be made more accountable? If you had to set up an MSI, how would you design its accountability mechanism, if any? How would you ensure adequate representation and what would you do to prevent undue influence by any particular stakeholder group?

3. Do you believe that hard law and regulation or MSIs are more effective and likely to enact change?
4. How does the UNGC ensure the accountability of its members? In your opinion, are these accountability measures enough? And if not, how could they be improved?
5. Imagine you work as a BHR consultant and are approached by a company for advice. Which one of the three more general international standards (OECD Guidelines for Multinational Enterprises, the UNGC, or ISO 26000) would you advise the company to implement? Would you ask them to implement all three?

12 | Home-State Solutions

International initiatives and standards are important reference points in holding corporations accountable for their human rights conduct. However, they tend to contain only soft enforcement and accountability mechanisms at best. Therefore, the most significant developments regarding corporate human rights accountability have happened at the state level in recent years, though many of those developments have been inspired by and framed with reference to the UNGPs.

Given its role at the center of the political and legal international human rights regime, the state has an obligation to make sure that people's fundamental rights are not violated by economic actors and processes. Protecting human rights from corporate abuse is a basic obligation of the state, which exists parallel to and independent of the corporation's own responsibility to respect human rights; as such, the state is an integral and indeed a central part of the BHR agenda. In fact, while a managerial view on BHR naturally focuses on the company as the central subject of concern, a legalistic view tends to move the state and its obligation to protect human rights center stage. This is one crucial reason why there has been a chasm between legal and non-legal discussions in the BHR field that makes it appear as if legal and non-legal scholars, despite working in the same field, speak different languages and are having entirely different conversations (Chapter 1.4).

This section explores states' obligation to hold companies incorporated within their jurisdiction accountable for human rights impacts. In doing so, it focuses squarely on the home states' obligation to increase accountability for companies operating abroad and possible ways of doing this. While the regulation of the domestic conduct of companies is of similar importance, the critical open questions and issues in BHR arise predominantly with regard to companies' extraterritorial conduct. Indeed, discussions around such "home-state solutions" have become a signature feature of the BHR discussion. Therefore, this chapter will first explore the state duty to protect, and extraterritorial obligations in particular, from a more general perspective. It will then assess different instruments that states can make use of to meet such obligations in the policy, legislative, and adjudicative spaces. The discussion on legislative approaches will provide an overview and assessment of different types of BHR laws with extraterritorial effects that various states have adopted in recent years. The subsection on adjudicative approaches will provide a brief introduction to BHR litigation and an overview of recent seminal cases in various jurisdictions. The chapter will conclude with a discussion of several criticisms that have been voiced against such extraterritorial state measures.

12.1 The State Duty to Protect Human Rights

States are commonly seen as the key actors and primary duty-bearers for human rights. Accordingly, they have the full range of obligations in regard to the threefold structure of human rights. This includes an obligation to respect, protect, and to fulfil human rights. From a BHR perspective, the key focus is on the duty to protect human rights from negative impacts and violations committed by third parties, including companies. This means that the state has an obligation to make use of its available means to make sure that private parties respect human rights. It must take preventive measures to ensure that prevailing human rights risks do not materialize. Furthermore, the duty to protect human rights includes an obligation to hold perpetrators accountable in case human rights violations do occur, and to enable victims of such human rights abuse to have access to adequate remedies (De Schutter 2014: 427).

The state duty to protect human rights is the central pillar in the UN Framework and the UNGPs (Chapter 10.1.1) and it is well established in both treaty-based and customary international law (Ruggie 2013: 84). For example, Article 2 of the ICCPR (Chapter 3.3.3 and Chapter 3.3.4) requires states both to avoid infringing on human rights directly and to ensure that other social actors, such as companies, do not infringe on human rights (Ruggie 2013: 84). It reiterates the twofold interpretation of the duty to protect mentioned above, whereby states ought to take preventive measures against human rights violations by third parties (Article 2[2]), as well as remedial measures in case such violations have occurred (Article 2[3]) (Chirwa 2004). Other core human rights treaties, among them the ICESCR, as well as key regional human rights covenants, include similar provisions (Chirwa 2004; Baughen 2015: 8). While the focus of the state duty to protect human rights was traditionally on armed rebel groups as relevant third parties, it has shifted to include a broader range of public and private actors, including, more recently, business enterprises (Ruggie 2013: 83).

Having a duty to protect means that the state is not allowed to remain passive in the face of situations in which the rights of individuals are threatened by private actors (De Schutter 2014: 428). Thus, if certain business models, situations, or contexts are seen as inherently threatening to the human rights of people, states must make use of all available and necessary means to provide protection to them. This basic obligation is neither arguable nor controversial. Whether or not multinational corporations are subjects of international law and have international law-based human rights responsibilities themselves (Chapter 6.2), is mostly irrelevant from this perspective. Thus, by focusing on the state's duty to protect, BHR does not require that we abandon state-centrism. This is why legal BHR scholars, in particular, have focused heavily on spelling out in detail what this state obligation entails and how it can and ought to be discharged appropriately.

However, even states are not capable of guaranteeing the full protection of all human rights at all times. Such a guarantee would require absolute surveillance and monitoring, as well as correspondingly tight restrictions on the conduct of all potential perpetrators. Particularly in liberal democracies, such far-reaching control by the state would conflict with the basic freedoms that people ought to enjoy. Thus, there is a certain trade-off between individual freedom and the extent of protection a state can provide. Therefore, the state duty to protect human rights is commonly not interpreted as an absolute obligation of the state, but rather as a standard of conduct. This means that, while states cannot guarantee protection from all potential threats at all times, they ought to take appropriate steps to prevent, investigate, punish, and redress such abuse (Ruggie 2013: 84). Alternatively, this has been called an *obligation of means*, as opposed to an *obligation of result* (De Schutter 2014: 477).

The obligation to protect amounts to a due diligence obligation of the state in relation to the conduct of third parties within, and possibly beyond (Chapter 12.2), its own jurisdiction (Baughen 2015: 7). As the Inter-American Court of Human Rights (Chapter 3.2.2) stated in the landmark case *Velasquez Rodriguez* v. *Honduras*, a state can be held responsible for violations by private actors if it fails to exercise due diligence in preventing and responding to the violation (Chirwa 2004). In this particular case, the state was seen to be responsible not because the human rights violation itself was attributable to the state – as in that case we would be dealing with the state's own responsibility to respect human rights – but rather because of a lack of due diligence to prevent the violation or to adequately respond to it (Chirwa 2004). In order for a state to breach its duty to protect human rights, it is thus not sufficient that the violation occurred; in addition, it must be shown that the state failed to take certain reasonable measures that could have prevented the event from occurring (De Schutter 2014: 428). However, what such reasonable measures should consist of and what level of protection can be deemed appropriate is up for discussion in each specific case. It is, not least, dependent on the available resources of the state.

As a standard of conduct, the duty to protect human rights from third-party abuse does not presuppose any particular list of measures that must be in place. However, the state must take reasonable and serious steps and make use of all the effective means at its disposal to protect human rights. This can and should include legislative, regulatory, policy, and administrative instruments. Such instruments can be adopted in combination to achieve the most effective results – recall the UNGPs' recommendation that states adopt a "smart mix" of measures to provide the most effective protection to human rights (Chapter 10.2.2). Similarly, states can make use both of judicial and non-judicial mechanisms to hold companies accountable and to provide access to effective remedies in case human rights have been violated. This chapter will look at some of the available instruments within the policy, legislative and judicative domains in more detail. However, before doing so, a contentious question needs to be addressed – namely, whether or not, or to what degree, the state duty to protect human rights applies extraterritorially, that is, beyond a state's own territorial borders.

12.2   Extraterritorial Obligations

Whether states have an obligation to protect human rights from corporate abuse is unarguable. However, whether or to what extent such an obligation applies to extraterritorial situations, that is, whether states have an obligation to make sure "their" companies do not violate human rights abroad, is a more controversial issue. This is despite the fact that the use of measures with extraterritorial implications by states is quite common in many regulatory areas, particularly as it pertains to transnational crimes such as terrorism, corruption, money laundering, or trafficking (Zerk 2010). That there is controversy around the extraterritorial obligations of states is due to state sovereignty being a key principle of international law and thus the fear that extraterritorial measures may interfere with the domestic affairs of another state.

Things are more clear-cut in regard to the state's duty to respect human rights. States ought to make sure that their own conduct does not violate human rights, either at home or abroad. Accordingly, the state duty to respect human rights also applies extraterritorially. Such constellations are typically discussed with regard to a state's security or military operations on foreign territory (Salomon & Seiderman 2012: 459). However, whether the state duty to protect human rights applies also to the extraterritorial conduct of third parties is still a somewhat open question, particularly as it pertains to legal rather than to natural persons (De Schutter 2006).

Generally, it is a principle of international law that states have jurisdiction over the acts or omissions of third parties within their own territory and the territory that is under their control. Therefore, their organs commonly perform state functions only within their own territory. The exercise of jurisdiction beyond their own state territory and thus in the territory of another state is the exception to this rule (Bernaz 2013: 495). Some treaties contain jurisdictional clauses, which explicitly limit jurisdiction to a state's own territory. Others, such as the ICESCR, leave it open (Bernaz 2013: 504). The Committee on Economic Social and Cultural Rights has argued in several of its comments that the ICESCR gives rise also to extraterritorial obligations to protect human rights. For example, in General Comment 14 on the right to health, the Committee argues:

> To comply with their international obligations in relation to article 12, States parties have to respect the enjoyment of the right to health in other countries, and to prevent third parties from violating the right in other countries, if they are able to influence these third parties by way of legal or political means, in accordance with the Charter of the United Nations and applicable international law (Committee on Economic, Social and Cultural Rights 2000: 11).

Hence, the extraterritorial application of the state duty to protect human rights is possible – at least in principle. In order to perform this duty, the state must assert jurisdiction over the foreign conduct of a company. This raises the question about the scope of such extraterritorial jurisdiction. For this purpose, three general kinds of jurisdiction can be distinguished (Zerk 2010: 13; Bernaz 2013: 495): *Prescriptive jurisdiction* refers to the state's authority to adopt legislation that sets the norms for appropriate behavior and conduct. *Adjudicative jurisdiction* refers to the state's authority to determine the rights of parties under its law in a particular case. *Enforcement jurisdiction* refers to the state's authority to ensure compliance with its laws, for example, by setting up police forces. Hence, extraterritoriality can be assessed with regard to each of these three kinds of jurisdiction. Accordingly, extraterritorial prescriptive jurisdiction refers to legislation that regulates the conduct of companies outside of the state's territory; extraterritorial adjudicative jurisdiction means that the state adjudicates in domestic courts violations that were committed abroad; extraterritorial enforcement jurisdiction would apply to situations where a state enforces compliance directly on the territory of another state (De Schutter 2006: 9–10).

However, what counts as extraterritorial is not always clear-cut and we are dealing here more with a spectrum than with a binary matter (Ruggie 2010: 11). For this purpose, two basic kinds of extraterritorial actions of the state can be distinguished. This distinction has been adopted also by the UNGPs.

- *"Domestic measures with extraterritorial implications"* (Ruggie 2010: 11; Zerk 2010) do not technically amount to extraterritorial action of a state in a narrow sense. Rather than regulating the conduct of foreign subsidiaries on foreign territory directly, the state is prescribing domestic norms to domestic actors, but with the intention of impacting their conduct or the conduct of their subsidiaries abroad. Such measures come in a variety of different shapes and forms and are frequently made use of by states. One example, which will be discussed in more detail below (Chapter 12.3), is when governments tie procurement contracts or export credits to human rights criteria. Thus, in order to benefit from such opportunities, companies then have to show that they have adequate protective measures in place to prevent human rights violations from occurring in their extraterritorial operations. Vice versa, the government may put import bans on products that were produced under conditions that violated human rights (Zerk 2010: 15). Another example are regulatory measures that require companies to report on the human rights conduct of their foreign subsidiaries. While such legislation mandates reporting only for companies "at home," its intention is that increased transparency would prompt those companies to implement tighter controls and monitoring also over their subsidiaries abroad. Reporting laws and other types of legislation with extraterritorial effects will be discussed in more detail below (Chapter 12.4). Most measures that are referred to as extraterritorial fall in this category. As these examples show, many of them are prescriptive in nature. Nevertheless, the category is not limited to prescriptive jurisdiction but can also include adjudication or enforcement.

- *"Direct extraterritorial jurisdiction"* (Ruggie 2010: 11; Zerk 2010) means that a state directly addresses the conduct of an actor on foreign territory. For example, if companies violate the human rights of foreign nationals on foreign territory, the victims may decide to sue the company not in the country in which the violations occurred (host state), but in the country in which the company, or its parent company, is registered (home state). In this regard, states exercise direct extraterritorial jurisdiction if domestic courts adjudicate matters that have at least partly taken place within the territory of a different state (Bernaz 2013: 495). However, if such litigation solely refers to actions or omissions of the parent company that took place within the home state, rather than in the country where the harm occurred, we are dealing with litigation that yields extraterritorial effects, rather than with direct extraterritorial jurisdiction (Zerk 2010: 14). The reason for this is evident: The state does not assert direct jurisdiction over the *foreign conduct* of the company, but over its domestic actions. Such "foreign direct liability" will be discussed extensively in Chapter 12.5.

Evidently, the extraterritorial actions of states become more controversial as we move from the first to the second category and from merely prescriptive to enforcement jurisdiction. Accordingly, the question about the role, scope, and legitimacy of direct extraterritorial adjudicative jurisdiction has become one of the key discussions in the BHR field in recent years, particularly as it pertains to civil, rather than criminal, cases.

The UNGPs take a cautious position on the question of extraterritoriality, noting that states are not required by international law to regulate and adjudicate the extraterritorial activities of businesses headquartered in their jurisdictions, but that they are not prohibited from doing so either (Ruggie 2013: 85; similar: De Schutter

2006). De Schutter (2006: 22–24) distinguishes four classical and widely accepted bases for the exercise of extraterritorial jurisdiction. States can address extraterritorial activities of third parties, if:

a. they have a substantial, direct, and foreseeable effect on or in its national territory;
b. either the potential offender or the potential victim of the human rights violation are nationals of the respective state: In the first case, the state addresses the conduct of its nationals abroad (active personality principle), while the second case is aimed at protecting its nationals abroad (passive personality principle);
c. persons, property, or acts abroad constitute a threat to the fundamental national interests of a state, such as its security or creditworthiness;
d. it addresses particularly heinous crimes, which under the principle of universality and in the name of the international community are commonly agreed to be subject to prosecution by any state, whether or not they have a connection to the crime: This is commonly referred to as "universal jurisdiction."

That international law permits states to exercise extraterritorial jurisdiction over the conduct of their companies abroad is broadly accepted (Cassell & Ramasastry 2016: 46). However, the opinion that states have an actual *obligation* at least to regulate the extraterritorial conduct of companies where they are in a position to do so and where such conduct impacts negatively on human rights seems to have gained broad currency among UN treaty bodies, with UN experts, and in the BHR discourse more generally (Salomon & Seiderman 2012: 460; Cassell & Ramasastry 2016: 46). The Committee on Economic, Social and Cultural Rights – the treaty body of the ICESCR (Chapter 3.3.3 and Chapter 3.3.4) – for example, is much more resolute in its position. In its widely noted General Comment No. 24, it asserts that, at least with regard to the rights covered by the ICESCR, states parties' obligations do not stop at their territorial borders and that they are required to "take steps to prevent and redress infringements of Covenant rights that occur outside their territories due to the activities of business entities over which they can exercise control, especially in cases where the remedies available to victims before the domestic courts of the State where the harm occurs are unavailable or ineffective" (Committee on Economic, Social and Cultural Rights 2017: 10). This explicitly includes requiring corporations to deploy their best efforts to make sure that their foreign subsidiaries, business partners, suppliers, and other business entities whose conduct they influence do not violate Covenant rights, either. For this purpose, the Committee suggests that states impose due diligence obligations on companies domiciled in their territory or jurisdiction and engage in effective cross-border cooperation to improve accountability and access to remedy for victims of corporate abuse (Committee on Economic, Social and Cultural Rights 2017: 11). Indeed, for the Committee, "it would be contradictory [. . .] to allow a State to remain passive where an actor domiciled in its territory and/or under its jurisdiction, and thus under its control or authority, harmed the rights of others in other States, or where conduct by such an actor may lead to foreseeable harm being caused" (Committee on Economic, Social and Cultural Rights 2017: 8–9). Accordingly, the Committee sees the state's duty to protect under the Covenant breached if a violation of Covenant rights could have been prevented through the adoption of reasonable measures by the state (Committee on Economic, Social and Cultural Rights 2017: 10). The UNGPs seem to agree insofar as they argue that, even in the absence of a clear obligation, "there are strong policy reasons for home States to set out clearly the expectation that businesses respect human rights abroad" (Ruggie 2011a: 7). As a consequence, states seem to interpret their duty to protect increasingly progressively, that is, as including at least an extraterritorial component; how extensive that component is or ought to be, however, remains a matter of controversy.

12.3 Policy Measures

Governments issue targeted policies to regulate, guide, and incentivize responsible business conduct in countless domains. Examples include policies on health and safety at work, on product safety, and on emission and pollution control. Such policies frequently lead to heated discussions between their opponents and proponents. However, the legitimacy of governments making use of such policies is rarely questioned in principle. More controversial are policies whose intended effects unfold abroad. Nevertheless, governments frequently adopt such policies not only with regard to responsible business but also in other domains. Similarly, they have a variety of policy options to incentivize and encourage companies headquartered in their jurisdiction to respect human rights abroad and they are increasingly making use of them. The focus of this chapter is specifically on such policies with extraterritorial effects in the BHR domain. The following subsections will outline some of the more popular emerging policy options in this regard.

12.3.1 National Action Plans on BHR

The most prominent policy measure that governments have adopted in the BHR space in recent years are NAPs. NAPs are policy tools that are known from other policy areas and were adapted to the BHR realm after the publication of the UNGPs in 2011. NAPs are comparable to implementation plans; their purpose is to outline priorities and specific measures and activities to implement state obligations and policy commitments (Methven O'Brien, Mehra, Blackwell, & Poulsen-Hansen 2016: 118). As of May 2021, twenty-four countries have adopted NAPs for the implementation of the UNGPs, thirty-two countries have been in the process of developing them or have taken concrete steps in the direction of doing so, and three countries have included a BHR chapter in their NAPs on human rights (OHCHR n.d. (c)). This proliferation of NAPs in the BHR domain is due not least to the call of the European Commission to its member states to develop NAPs in order to implement the UNGPs shortly after their publication (Cantú Rivera 2019: 216–217; De Felice & Graf 2015: 42). In 2014, the HRC echoed this call (Methven O'Brien, Mehra, Blackwell, & Poulsen-Hansen 2016). The UK and the Netherlands were the first two nations to publish their respective NAPs in 2013. By 2021, a little more than half of the EU's member countries as well as various nations outside of the EU had published NAPs. The UNWG later provided much-needed guidance on the nature and requirements of NAPs in the BHR domain (UNWG 2016). A NAP, according to the UNWG, is an "evolving policy strategy developed by a State to protect against adverse human rights impacts by business enterprises in conformity with the UN Guiding Principles on Business and Human Rights (UNGPs)" (UNWG 2016: 3). As such, NAPs provide the strategic orientation and outline the specific activities of a government in addressing BHR (UNWG 2016: 3). As a part of this task, NAPs should identify needs and gaps in the current infrastructure of human rights protection which require further policy action on the part of the government (Cantú Rivera 2019). In accordance with the UNGPs, the UNWG (2016: ii) suggests that NAPs should outline a "smart mix" of both voluntary and mandatory, domestic and international measures that allow governments to effectively address the adverse human rights impacts of businesses. Thus, importantly, NAPs are not policy instruments to directly address companies; rather, they address the executive branch of the government.

The UNWG sees the value of NAPs as implementation tools in several dimensions (UNWG 2016: 1): They can help foster better coordination and coherence within governments; provide an inclusive process to identify effective policy measures and priorities; provide transparency and predictability within the policy process; lead toward continuous monitoring, evaluation, and measurement of policy implementation; offer a platform for ongoing multi = stakeholder dialogues on BHR; and facilitate international cooperation and coordination on BHR policy measures. In order to do so, they should meet four essential criteria. They must 1) be founded upon the UNGPs; 2) respond to specific challenges of the national context; 3) be developed and implemented through an inclusive and transparent process; and 4) be regularly reviewed and updated (UNWG 2016: 3). While NAPs focus first and foremost on governments' responses to BHR challenges on their own territory, the UNWG explicitly points out that the extraterritorial conduct of companies domiciled in their territory should be taken into consideration, as well (UNWG 2016: 12).

NAPs have been acknowledged as instruments that effectively commit governments to put and keep BHR on their policy agenda. As such, the ongoing process of governments developing, drafting, and updating NAPs can be considered an important element of keeping up the momentum that the publication of the UNGPs created in 2011. As Methven O'Brien, Mehra, Blackwell, & Poulsen-Hansen (2016: 115) state: "Every NAP process affirms the UNGPs' essential tenet that human rights apply within the business sector and indicates a political commitment to bring domestic laws, policies and practices into alignment with this norm."

However, NAPs have also been subject to criticism. Most NAPs developed so far have been declaratory in nature, predominantly outlining existing measures and policies, rather than committing to new ones (Methven O'Brien, Mehra, Blackwell, & Poulsen-Hansen 2016: 118). Furthermore, despite the UNWG's recommendation that NAPs should outline a smart mix of mandatory and voluntary measures, governments have been reluctant to formally commit to new hard regulations in their NAPs. Accordingly, they have largely focused on soft measures, dismissing the need for new legislation. A notable exception is the German NAP, which contains a commitment to implement mandatory HRDD rules, if by 2020 voluntary UNGP implementation would not reach a threshold of 50 percent of companies based in Germany. A respective baseline study conducted in 2020 revealed that not even one-fifth of German companies met the required implementation level (BHRRC 2020). As a consequence, Germany announced that it would follow through and adopted mandatory HRDD legislation in 2021. Against the background of this reluctance of governments to commit to the full range of voluntary and mandatory measures, there has been concern in the BHR space that governments may use NAPs as a smokescreen to create a perception of vague commitment to the BHR agenda, while not changing anything concrete about their policy priorities. Cantú Rivera (2019) takes a differentiated view and argues that NAPs can be effective policy tools to raise awareness and foster horizontal policy coherence. As such, they can be important implementation tools, at least as they pertain to the respective Article 8 of the UNGPs, which refers to policy coherence between different departments in a government's administration as an important element of human rights protection. However, they are insufficient in terms of implementing states' actual international obligations in this realm and thus also insufficient in ensuring corporate respect for human rights.

12.3.2 Public Procurement

Governments not only regulate markets but also often act as market participants themselves. In order to be able to operate and function properly, the public sector depends on the purchase of large amounts of goods and services through public procurement processes (Methven O'Brien, Mehra, Andrecka, & Vander Meulen 2016: 9). It is estimated that on a worldwide scale, governments procure products and services of €2 trillion annually. Procurement spending of the US government alone amounts to $350 billion–$500 billion annually, which makes it the largest single purchaser in the global economy (Stumberg, Ramasastry, & Roggensack 2014: 4).

BOX 12.1 (Context) Practical guidance on NAPs

The Danish Institute for Human Rights (DIHR) and the International Corporate Accountability Roundtable have developed a practical toolkit that can guide the development of NAPs (Muñoz Quick & Wrzoncki 2017). In addition to guiding the development process, for example, with regard to the inclusion of stakeholders or the allocation of responsibilities, the toolkit outlines six more substantive criteria with regard to the prospective scope, content, and priorities of NAPs:

(1) *Address the full scope of the UNGPs*: NAPs should address all identified major gaps with regard to the implementation of the UNGPs and indicate how the measures outlined are designed to address those gaps.
(2) *Address the state's full scope of jurisdiction*: NAPs should consider regulating the actions of businesses to prevent, address, and remedy the negative impacts on human rights deriving therefrom, both at home and abroad.
(3) *Prioritize actions to address major gaps and challenges*: NAPs should focus on relevant thematic or sector-specific human rights issues that emerge from systematic baseline assessments and stakeholder consultations.
(4) *Include a particular focus on marginalized and at-risk groups*: NAPs should identify such groups and outline specific measures to be taken to address business impacts on them.
(5) *Comprise action points that are specific, measurable, achievable, relevant, and time-specific (SMART)*: NAPs should address relevant issues based on the UNGPs, be specific with regard to the measures it proposes to address the issues, make sure that progress on such issues can be measured, include a timeline for their realization, and thereby be realistic in terms of the allocation of time and resources to addressing the issues.
(6) *Ensure that NAP action points are coherent with other relevant frameworks*: NAPs should include references to other related frameworks and initiatives where they can contribute to the successful implementation of the UNGPs and, vice versa, where NAP actions can make a contribution to their adoption and implementation.

In the OECD, governments spend 12 percent of their GDP annually on public procurement; in the EU, they spend 16 percent and worldwide even 20 percent on procurement. Needless to say, governments hold considerable leverage to push for and advance respect for human rights and the implementation of the UNGPs among contracting companies by integrating respective requirements into their procurement policies and contracts (Martin-Ortega 2018: 76).

However, the focus of the international public procurement regime, established through the World Trade Organization (WTO)'s Plurilateral Agreement on Government Procurement, has been on the prevention of anti-competitive and discriminatory behavior, rather than on the promotion of sustainable practices and the respect of human rights (Methven O'Brien, Mehra, Andrecka, & Vander Meulen 2016: 16). The narrow aim of promoting free trade and competition allows for the consideration of social objectives only in very limited ways (Martin-Ortega 2018: 77; Methven O'Brien, Mehra, Andrecka, & Vander Meulen 2016: 16). Accordingly, procurement laws and practices in many countries are currently undermining rather than promoting the inclusion of human rights considerations in procurement decisions and processes (Methven O'Brien, Mehra, Andrecka, & Vander Meulen 2016: 11). Nevertheless, the WTO rules only apply to those members who have explicitly chosen to accede to them. In recent years, new legislation in a variety of jurisdictions has started to create space for the inclusion of social objectives and a number of laws have explicitly mandated the consideration of social and sustainability criteria in governments' sourcing decisions (Martin-Ortega 2018: 77f.). In 2010, the European Commission published the first edition of its *Guide to Taking Account of Social Consideration in Public Procurement* (European Commission 2021), encouraging member states to introduce human rights criteria into their public procurement policies (Bernaz 2017: 247). It reiterated this call to use public procurement as an instrument to promote responsible business conduct in its *Communication on Corporate Social Responsibility* in 2011 (European Commission 2011). In 2014, these recommendations were formalized in the Directive on Public Procurement, which requires member states to ensure that the companies they contract comply with applicable social, environmental, and labor obligations, as defined by the Directive. The Directive does not directly refer to human rights, however. At the domestic level, the UK Modern Slavery Act (Chapter 12.4.1.1) also requires public buyers to report on their efforts to prevent modern slavery, human trafficking, and forced labor in their supply chains (Martin-Ortega 2018: 78). The Federal Acquisition Regulation in the US prohibits forced child labor and human trafficking and asks for fair pay and safe workplaces in relation to federal contracts sourced abroad (O'Brien, Mehra, Andrecka, & Vander Meulen 2016: 15). One more example can be found in Switzerland, where a reform of public procurement regulation effective 2021 has created considerably more space for the inclusion particularly of social and sustainability considerations and objectives in the procurement process. Overall, however, few regional or national procurement regulations explicitly refer to human rights, and if they do they tend to limit their scope to specific issues, such as child labor or trafficking. Similarly, only a limited number of NAPs (Chapter 12.3.1) make public procurement a policy priority for human rights protection (Methven O'Brien, Mehra, Andrecka, & Vander Meulen 2016: 53f.). Thus, the potential of this policy option is far from being met and there is much room for improvement.

Generally, three rationales for the inclusion of HRDD requirements in public sourcing and procurement decisions can be distinguished. *First*, governments' duty to protect human rights, according to the UNGPs, requires them to use "the full range of permissible preventative and remedial measures" (Ruggie 2011a: 7) available to them to make sure that companies domiciled or operating in their territory respect human rights. Principle 6 of the UNGPs asks governments directly to "promote respect for human rights by business enterprises with which they conduct commercial transactions" (Ruggie 2011a: 10) and specifically mentions procurement activities in the respective commentary. Considering the significant purchasing power and thus the leverage they hold through their procurement decisions, not making use of the "unique opportunities to promote awareness of and respect for human rights" (Ruggie 2011a: 10) through public procurement could be seen as conflicting with this duty. *Second*, where states are economic actors themselves, they operate at the intersection of their duty to protect human rights from infringements by third parties and their own duty to respect human rights. In other words, as economic actors they have the same responsibility to respect human rights that the UNGPs demand of commercial actors. Ensuring that government procurement decisions are not associated with human rights violations in their supply chains is thus a matter of their very own HRDD obligation. *Third*, because of the large volumes of goods and services purchased through public procurement, governments are able to send powerful market signals with their procurement decisions. As Methven O'Brien, Mehra, Andrecka, & Vander Meulen (2016: 13) put it, "within specific sectors, the scale of public procurement can create or define a market." As such, governments can have a powerful impact on markets for sustainable goods and services and are of key importance in reaching a tipping point in the mainstreaming of BHR.

12.3.3   Export Credit and Investment Guarantees

Export credits are another domain besides public procurement in which governments hold significant leverage over companies that make use of such services. Export credit agencies support cross-border business, trade, and investment activity by providing finances to exporting companies. They are "meant to help companies' exports by guaranteeing they will be paid for the goods or services they have invested to produce or provide, and also by providing credit when the overseas buyers wish to wait for the goods to be delivered before paying for them" (Bernaz 2013: 500). Such agencies were originally put in place to maintain and support trade flows and to secure jobs in exporting sectors, particularly during economic downturns. As such, they played a critical role in helping to maintain trade and investment flows also during the most recent global financial crisis of 2008 (Evans 2011: 64). Even before the financial crisis, export credits within the OECD were at a substantial $66 billion annually (Bollen 2011: 61).

Yet despite these economically useful attributes, export credits have been under scrutiny for their unwanted effects for some time. Not only have they often been perceived as state-sponsored trade distortions, but in the 1990s NGOs in particular argued that export credits contributed to the rising debt of countries in the Global South. Furthermore, they raised concerns that export contracts sponsored by official export credits could be connected to bribery and negative environmental impacts. As a consequence, in the 1990s the OECD started to adopt measures in order to promote a common international approach to export credit provision in order to mitigate such impacts (West 2011: 22–23). The ensuing integration of civil society issues, and particularly the environmental screening and appraisal of projects and businesses applying for export credits, was called the most fundamental shift in the export credit agenda of the OECD (Crick 2011: 64). It eventually led to the 2003 OECD *Recommendation on Common Approaches on the Environment and Export Credits* (Crick 2011: 65).

Subsequently, the OECD continuously strengthened its assessments of member states' efforts to deter bribery and to review social and environmental impacts on their export credit activities (Evans 2011: 67). The 2007 revision of the 2003 *Recommendation on Common Approaches* asked export credit agencies to screen projects for their potential environmental and social impacts and benchmark them against international standards, such as the IFC Performance Standards (Chapter 14.2.2) (Evans 2011: 68). Hence, more and more, export credits have come to be seen as a powerful instrument for the promotion of responsible business conduct, particularly if export credit agencies are working together and adopt common standards (Evans 2011: 67).

Following the progress made on including environmental and social criteria into export credit provision, the integration of human rights requirements based on the UNGPs seemed to be a logical next step. Accordingly, John Ruggie called on the OECD to include human rights in the *Recommendation on Common Approaches* and on export credit agencies to integrate human rights standards into their assessments and, accordingly, to exclude companies from export credit schemes if they were involved in severe human rights abuses (Evans 2011: 69).

The OECD recommendations were renamed the OECD *Recommendation of the Council on Common Approaches for Officially Supported Export Credits and Environmental and Social Due Diligence* in 2012. Their most recent update in 2016 integrated human rights on a broad basis (OECD n.d. (b)). Principle 4.iv. of the recommendations suggests that adherents should "encourage protection and respect for human rights, particularly in situations where the potential impacts from projects or existing operations pose risks to human rights" (OECD 2016b) and refer to human rights as a criterion for the screening, assessment, and classification of applications for export credits. Where the likelihood of human rights impacts is high, the recommendations ask for the use of HRDD by export credit agencies

(OECD 2016b). While the recommendations are not binding, they make it clear that the integration of human rights into export credit assessments are a policy expectation on adhering states today.

The implementation of such policy options, be it conditional procurement or export credit contracts, raises practical questions and challenges regarding the assessment and monitoring of corporate human rights performance and the resources, costs, and competencies required for such new tasks (Bernaz 2013: 498). However, there is little doubt about the considerable influence that such policies can have on the conduct of businesses.

12.4   Legislative Measures

Despite, or perhaps because of, the reluctance to introduce binding BHR measures that many governments have expressed in their NAPs (Chapter 12.3.1), there has been a push, particularly by civil society, for binding BHR legislation. As a result, a growing number of countries have adopted such laws in different forms or are at various stages in the process. The predominant aim of this legislation is to increase the accountability of companies for adverse human rights impacts along their global value chains. This chapter is particularly interested in those laws that are designed to address the extraterritorial dimension of corporate human rights conduct. It provides a brief overview and introduction to some of the most important and emblematic current examples of such laws. For this purpose, three categories of BHR legislation can be distinguished:

1. *Transparency and disclosure legislation on BHR*: Such laws require companies to report on their processes and measures to address certain BHR issues, such as modern slavery or child labor. However, they typically do not prescribe that companies address such issues in a specific, predetermined way; they commonly do not even require that companies adopt any measures at all, as long as they are transparent about it. The aim underlying such legislation is that heightened transparency will lead to more pressure on companies to adopt stringent measures to address BHR. This chapter will discuss the European Non-Financial Reporting Directive, the UK Modern Slavery Act of 2015, and the Australian Modern Slavery Act of 2019, as well as the California Transparency in Supply Chains Act as examples of such reporting and disclosure laws.

2. *Disclosure legislation with HRDD obligations*: These are essentially also reporting laws; however, they leave less leeway to companies than the laws in the previous category. More concretely, these laws contain an explicit obligation for companies to adopt certain specific HRDD mechanisms and processes and report on them. Typically, companies that do not put the respective mechanisms

in place can be fined under such laws; thus, they do not leave it to the discretion of the company to decide whether or not it intends to adopt any measures at all. This chapter will look at Dodd-Frank Act Section 1502, the European Conflict Minerals Regulation, and the Dutch Child Labor Due Diligence Law as examples in this category. A further example, the German Supply Chain Act, will be covered in Box 12.2.

3. *HRDD legislation with corporate liability provisions*: These laws may or may not contain disclosure provisions as in the previous two categories. However, their key feature is an HRDD obligation, which is supported by a liability provision. This means that the victims of a human rights violation can sue the company if such a violation is connected to the company's failure to meet the HRDD obligation. Thus, while the previous two categories of disclosure laws may foresee sanctions for the violation of the law, they do not provide opportunities for victims of human rights abuse to seek remedy. There is currently only one example that squarely falls within this category, which is the groundbreaking French Duty of Vigilance Law. However, with the standard being set by this law, it is likely that other countries will follow suit in the near future. Discussions for similar legislation are currently underway at the level of the EU.

12.4.1 Accountability by Reporting: Transparency and Disclosure Legislation

Transparency and reporting requirements ask companies to disclose information on how they address certain non-financial issues, commonly without prescribing any specific measures, processes, or policies. Companies may not even be required to take any particular steps at all, as long as they are transparent about not adopting any. An increasing number of countries have adopted such non-financial disclosure requirements in recent years. The respective laws vary in scope and focus. While some zoom in on human rights or even more narrowly on particular issue areas relating to BHR (for example, modern slavery), others keep a broad view on CSR measures more generally. Such reporting laws often pursue two interrelated aims. First, they aim at enhancing transparency and the availability of information around corporations' efforts to ensure respect for human rights. Second, they often also pursue a social-engineering goal (Buhmann 2018). Hence, a desired side-effect of such legislation is that it can also shape corporate behavior more substantively (Ewing 2016: 291). They are thus based on the assumption that transparency can drive accountability. By having to disclose their approaches to address human rights issues, companies are subjected to public scrutiny and pressure, which may lead them to improve their record (Sinclair & Nolan 2020: 164). At the very least, due to such reporting requirements, many companies have to seriously consider their human rights impact for the first time (Ewing 2016: 291).

Policy-makers and companies often prefer such disclosure laws over more substantive regulation because they are less intrusive and softer in terms of market interference. Furthermore, they leave more leeway to managers to pursue measures and approaches that are tailored to their specific business and the sector and context in which they operate. Leaving room for maneuver and to pursue tailored approaches may turn out to be more effective than strict mandates, in their opinion. On the other hand, the relative lack of substantive prescriptions and the softness of such disclosure laws have been subject to widespread critique, as well. Four recurring points of critique are of particular relevance; some will be elaborated on again in connection with the specific laws discussed below:

- The laws tend to be too broad and unspecific with regard to what disclosures they require. They often neither specify in sufficient detail what exactly needs to be disclosed nor establish how the information ought to be reported. As a result, reporting by companies is often vague and general and fails to provide detailed information.
- Such laws typically come with weak, if any, enforcement mechanisms and a lack of sanctions in the case of non-compliance. Accordingly, the compliance rate is often moderate.
- The mandate of such laws typically applies only to the actual disclosure of information. It does not commonly include any verification of the accuracy of such information nor a requirement that a company is actually addressing the underlying issue (e.g. modern slavery). In other words, as long as a company discloses its inactivity, it can be compliant with such laws, even if it does not address the issue at all. Similarly, poor performance on the issue (such as documented cases of forced labor in the value chain) does not mean that a company is non-compliant with the law.
- As a consequence, to date, it is not obvious whether existing reporting rules have had a positive effect on companies' actual human rights performance (Buhmann 2018: 26). While they may be important in terms of making certain expectations toward responsible company behavior explicit and can be a stepping stone for more far-reaching policies and legislation, in and of themselves they may have little impact on the ground.

In the following subsections, we will focus on disclosure laws specifically in the domain of BHR. Most of these reporting laws focus on specific issues or problem areas, such as modern slavery and forced labor (UK and Australia) or conflict minerals (US and EU).

12.4.1.1 UK Modern Slavery Act and Australian Modern Slavery Act

Slavery is not a thing of the past but remains a global problem of alarming proportions (Chapter 5.2.3). To respond to the persistence of this challenge, the UK enacted the UK Modern Slavery Act in 2015, with the aim of consolidating and expanding existing legislation to criminalize and combat modern slavery in the UK. It also increases sentences for offenders and establishes an Independent Anti-Slavery Commissioner, who is tasked with encouraging good practice in the prevention, detection, investigation, and prosecution of offenses as well as the identification of victims (Mantouvalou 2018: 1021).

The Act addresses modern slavery comprehensively with one specific section of it (Section 54) devoted to corporate supply chains. Section 54 is largely modeled on the 2010 California Transparency in Supply Chains Act. The section asks companies – both domestic and foreign – doing business in the UK and with an annual turnover exceeding £36 million to produce and publish a statement that details the measures that they have adopted in order to eliminate modern slavery and human trafficking from their operations and global supply chains. Statements must be signed by a company director, approved by the company board, and made publicly available on the company website. It is estimated that about 12,000 companies may fall within the scope of this provision (Craig 2017: 22).

In terms of content, the statements ought to describe all steps that a company has taken to tackle modern slavery and human trafficking. However, companies are largely free to decide on the form and detail of such descriptions. Furthermore, as a pure reporting mandate, the UK Modern Slavery Act does not require companies to take any substantive action to combat modern slavery:

> The Act therefore leaves companies discretion not to deal with forced labour or slavery in their supply chains at all, since companies can be compliant with the law without taking any steps to prevent or address forced labour, so long as they publish a statement (LeBaron & Rühmkopf 2017: 20).

Accordingly, Section 54 of the UK Modern Slavery Act neither establishes any extraterritorial liability for potential incidences of modern slavery (LeBaron & Rühmkopf 2017: 16) nor does it enable access to remedies for victims (Mantouvalou 2018: 1041). Rather, the rationale behind the law is that the pressure of publicity will lead companies to implement suitable measures to improve their record, thereby leaving sufficient flexibility for the companies to tailor their strategies closely to the context in which they operate. However, the Act has been criticized for not putting some of the critical conditions in place for such a publicity-based approach to work: For example, there is no comprehensive list of all companies that are supposed to issue a modern slavery statement and there is no monitoring of whether such companies actually end up publishing a statement, making it difficult for watchdogs to identify and track laggards. To compensate for the government's lack of monitoring, the BHRRC has set up a Modern Slavery Registry, which collects and makes accessible all modern slavery statements in one place. There are no sanctions or penalties for non-disclosure in place, either, although the duty to issue a statement can be enforced by the Secretary of State through an injunction issued by the High Court (LeBaron & Rühmkopf 2017: 18; Mantouvalou 2018: 1039).

As a consequence, the compliance rates have remained rather low (Mantouvalou 2018: 1042) and companies publishing statements tend to keep them rather generic and superficial. According to the Modern Slavery Registry, only 23 percent of all companies in the scope of the Act meet all three of its minimum requirements (published on the company's website; signed by director; approved by company board); only 62 percent of companies publish an actual statement on their website (BHRRC n.d. (c)). Furthermore, according to an assessment conducted by the BHRRC, the majority of the Financial Times Stock Exchange (FTSE) 100 company reports did not show how they actually attempt to tackle modern slavery (BHRRC 2017; Mantouvalou 2018: 1043). There is also a danger that reporting is outsourced or that companies approach the task purely mechanically, without any deeper engagement with the substance matter (Mantouvalou 2018: 1042). Consistent with this finding, another study found that many corporate statements evolve only marginally from year to year (Ergon Associates 2018). Accordingly, LeBaron & Rühmkopf (2017: 23) have noted that the UK Modern Slavery Act has done little so far to change corporate behavior. Nevertheless, it has put modern slavery firmly on the political agenda in the UK and thus provides leverage for campaigners and a basis upon which further steps can be built (Craig 2017: 17).

On January 1, 2019, a Modern Slavery Act similar to the one in the UK took effect also in Australia, after nearly two years of public consultations (Sinclair & Nolan 2020: 165). The Australian Modern Slavery Act applies to entities (including civil society organizations and universities) based or operating in Australia with consolidated annual revenues of at least AUD 100 million. The Australian Modern Slavery Act is modeled closely on its UK equivalent, but includes a number of specific mandatory reporting criteria in order to make statements more consistent and comparable across entities. It also features a federal registry that collects and makes available the modern slavery statements. However, Australia, too, has abstained from attaching financial penalties to non-reporting, making critics fear that compliance rates will turn out to be similarly low to those in the UK. Furthermore, there is no detailed list that indicates which entities are within the scope of the law and thus ought to report, making it difficult for watchdogs to monitor compliance (Sinclair & Nolan 2020: 167–168). Thus, while the Australian Modern Slavery Act corrects some of the shortcomings of its UK equivalent, it leaves others unaddressed, leading to similar criticism as outlined above.

12.4.1.2 California Transparency in Supply Chains Act

The California Transparency in Supply Chains Act was enacted in 2010 and went into effect in January 2012. Its aim is to provide consumers and the public with adequate information on large retailers' and manufacturers' efforts in tackling slavery and human trafficking in their supply chains. The assumption behind the law is that providing transparency to consumers leads to more informed and responsible buying decisions, which will put irresponsible companies at a disadvantage in the market. The law applies to retailers and manufacturers that are doing business in California and whose annual global gross revenues exceed $100 million. Companies within the scope of the law must inform consumers on their efforts to combat slavery and human trafficking in their supply chains on their website so that it is clearly visible and easy to find. The scope of the law includes only the first tier of the supply chain; suppliers, contractors, and subcontractors further upstream are not included. Companies must report on their approach to supply-chain verification, their engagement in supplier audits, certification of delivered products by suppliers, internal accountability systems with regard to slavery and trafficking, and training offered and given to management and employees with direct responsibility for supply-chain management (State of California Department of Justice 2021). While they must report on their efforts in those five categories, they enjoy discretion with regard to how they address them. Similar to the UK Modern Slavery Act, the law does not require companies to actually implement effective measures to tackle slavery and human trafficking, nor does it prohibit them from working and continuing to work with suppliers who accommodate the use of forced labor (Koekkoek, Marx, & Wouters 2017: 524). Rather, companies must simply disclose any effort that they make. This applies also – and perhaps particularly – to companies that have not adopted any specific measures in this regard. Accordingly, similar to the UK Modern Slavery Act, companies cannot be sued for not adopting any effective measures – the law precludes civil action by private citizens. However, a number of companies have been sued on the basis of the Unfair Competition Law, the Truth in Advertising Law, and the Consumer Legal Remedy Act for providing false or incomplete information under the California Transparency in Supply Chains Act (Koekkoek, Marx, & Wouters 2017: 525). However, all such cases were later dismissed (Koekkoek, Marx, & Wouters 2017: 525). Thus, the enforcement mechanism of the Act has been described as very weak (Prokopets 2014: 364). There are no penalties or possibilities of civil action for non-compliance. Solely the Attorney General of California can file a civil action for injunctive relief against companies who are supposed to disclose information but fail to do so (Harris 2015: 4).

It is reported that both the number of companies that fail to comply as well as those who go well beyond what is required by the Act is rather small. Thus, overall compliance with the mandate is quite high (Birkey et al. 2018). However, the bulk of companies only meet the minimum requirements and their reporting is rather superficial and written in vague and general language (Koekkoek, Marx, & Wouters 2017: 525, 527; Birkey, Guidry, Islam, & Patten 2018). Thus, while the Act's rationale is that companies may start paying more attention to slavery and human trafficking due to the disclosure requirements, it seems that the concern about investor and client perceptions rather leads managers to keep their statements vague and general instead (Birkey, Guidry, Islam, & Patten 2018: 828).

This holds particularly for companies that may not already be exposed to heightened scrutiny due to increased supply-chain risks (Birkey, Guidry, Islam, & Patten 2018: 837). Accordingly, it has been alleged that the Act has not led to significant behavioral changes on either side, as neither companies nor consumers have significantly adjusted their operations and consumption (Koekkoek, Marx, & Wouters 2017: 525). This is compounded by the fact that companies are only obligated to report once. That is, it is not a recurring annual obligation as is the case for the UK Modern Slavery Act. The Act has also been criticized for not making sure that the information provided by the companies is true and verified (Koekkoek, Marx, & Wouters 2017: 526); that the way such information is disclosed makes it unlikely that it will get embedded into the purchasing decisions of customers (Prokopets 2014: 365–369); and for applying only to very large companies, while many smaller and medium-sized retailers and manufacturers fall through the cracks (Prokopets 2014: 358).

12.4.1.3   EU Non-Financial Reporting Directive

The EU Non-Financial Reporting Directive (2014/95/EU) asks public-interest companies incorporated or listed in the EU and with more than 500 employees to include a statement on non-financial matters in their annual reports. Public-interest entities are defined as companies of significant public relevance, including, among others, listed companies, credit institutions, and insurance companies. There are about 6,000 such companies across the EU that are covered by the Directive (Buhmann 2018: 28). In addition to publishing the statement in the annual report, it must be made publicly available on the company's website. The Directive was adopted by the European Commission in 2014 as an amendment to the EU Accounting Directive. It asks member states to implement the laws, regulations, and administrative provisions necessary to ensure compliance by December 2016. Companies within the Directive's scope had to report for the first time in 2018. At minimum, they have to report on environmental, social and employee matters, respect for human rights, anti-corruption and bribery, and board diversity. The report should detail the companies' policies, risks, and due diligence processes, as well as key performance indicators in those areas. Where relevant and proportionate, it should also provide information on the corporations' value and subcontracting chains. From a management perspective, this means that in order to properly report, companies ought to set up appropriate management and reporting processes in the respective areas. Ideally, this includes mechanisms "to collect, measure and analyse non-financial data; to identify, evaluate and manage both risks and opportunities related to sustainability issues; to introduce policies, set targets and implement adequate measures; to promote skills and incentives to drive better decision-making, performance, transparency and accountability" (Hallensleben & Harrop 2015: 4).

The goals of the Directive are twofold: First, it aims at making companies' reporting on non-financial matters more relevant, more consistent, and comparable. Second, as with any reporting law, the goal and assumption underlying it is that increased transparency will lead to a continuous improvement of such mechanisms and eventually to a change of practices that can have a real impact on the situation on the ground (Buhmann 2018: 28). The process of gathering information on impacts and processes and of communicating it toward the outside is meant to trigger and maintain a learning process inside the organization that leads toward organizational change (Buhmann 2018: 39).

The Directive adopts a "comply or explain" approach – that is, companies that do not have the relevant policies in place in the respective areas must provide an explanation for the lack thereof. Furthermore, companies enjoy ample flexibility and leeway in regard to how they wish to address and report on those issues. The European Commission has issued guidelines on how to report, but they are not binding. As a result, some first analyses identify shortcomings in the quality of company reporting. With respect to human rights, more than 80 percent of companies report on human rights policies, but only 22 percent describe their HRDD process and only 20 percent describe how human rights are integrated into their day-to-day activities and operations. Only 7 percent state a commitment to provide remedy to victims of human rights harm. Furthermore, while 56 percent report on human rights risks, only 27 percent disclose policies designed to address them and only 19 percent report on specific measures and actions taken to respond to such risks. Only 4 percent report on examples and indicators that illustrate the management of such issues. Similarly low are the number of companies that report on actual negative human rights impacts (15 percent) (Alliance for Corporate Transparency 2019: 18–19). With regard to supply chains, 29 percent report on supplier audits, but only 20 percent disclose the results of audits and only 14 percent report on follow-up actions (Alliance for Corporate Transparency 2019: 20). Thus, critics have described the information reported as largely inadequate. The formulation of possible consequences for non-compliance is left to the discretion of member states. Despite aiming to have an impact on the ground, as some commentators argue, the Directive puts little emphasis on what processes might actually stimulate organizational change, and instead focuses narrowly on compliance with the reporting obligation. Audits merely focus on whether a report has been provided and sanctions, if adopted by member states, are foreseen only in cases of non-reporting. Whether or not the information provided is consistent and accurate or whether the processes reported on are plausible and effective does not play any role, as it is meant to be subject to scrutiny by the critical public (Buhmann 2018: 29). As a consequence, critics are skeptical as to whether the mere reporting mandate can indeed drive lasting change in business conduct (European Coalition for Corporate Justice 2019: 3).

12.4.2 Accountability by Process: Disclosure and Mandatory Human Rights Due Diligence Legislation

Some disclosure laws are more restrictive in terms of the obligations they put on companies to address the issues of concern. While "pure" disclosure and transparency provisions commonly do not obligate companies to adopt any particular measures to address these issues, the laws discussed in this section contain an explicit obligation to implement an HRDD process. Thus, rather than merely disclosing what measures, if any, companies are adopting in order to combat modern slavery, for example, they must follow a HRDD process that the law may specify to varying degrees. Accordingly, sanctions commonly do not merely apply to non-disclosure, but also to non-implementation of the HRDD measures. However, in contrast to the laws discussed in Chapter 12.5, these laws do not sanction the actual adverse impacts that companies may have on human rights and thus do not offer any possibilities for the victims of human rights violations to seek redress.

There has been a push toward substantive HRDD legislation (with or without liability provisions) starting shortly after the publication of the UNGPs. As one of the most significant developments in this regard, the European Commissioner of Justice announced that the European Commission commits to introducing mandatory HRDD rules, including sanctions for violations. As he noted, "A regulation without sanctions is not a regulation" (quoted in Burrow & Blumer 2020). This announcement follows previous calls by several other European institutions in support of mandatory HRDD.

Critics of HRDD obligations fear that such laws may shift human rights responsibility within companies from CSR departments to the compliance divisions and thus suspect that substantive engagement with BHR issues will turn into a mere tick-box exercise (Chapter 12.6.3). Rather than making sure the underlying problems are addressed adequately, company lawyers will be content with the fulfilment of the legal requirement – irrespective of how effective they are in actually combating the problems at hand. Proponents, on the other hand, argue that only mandatory rules will make sure that human rights will not be ignored by a large majority of companies that may face little public scrutiny and for whom reputational risks are low.

The following subsections will discuss three signature pieces of legislation in this category: Section 1502 of the Dodd-Frank Act in the US, the EU Conflict Minerals Regulation and the Dutch Child Labor Due Diligence Law.

12.4.2.1 Dodd-Frank Act, Section 1502, and EU Conflict Minerals Regulation

In 2010, as a response to the global financial crisis, the US enacted the Wall Street Reform and Consumer Protection Act, or in short, the so-called Dodd-Frank Act, named after the then Senate banking committee chairman Chris Dodd and financial services committee chairman Barney Frank. Section 1502 of this Act requires companies to disclose whether the products they manufacture or have manufactured by contractors contain conflict minerals sourced in the Democratic Republic of the Congo (DRC) or in any of the countries sharing an internationally recognized border with it. It does not apply to retailers who do not manufacture or contract for manufacturing (Philips, LeBaron, & Wallin 2018: 13). Countries within the scope of the section include Angola, Burundi, the Central African Republic, Republic of the Congo, Rwanda, South Sudan, Tanzania, Uganda, and Zambia. Conflict minerals include tantalum, tin, tungsten, and gold (the so-called 3TG minerals). The underlying purpose of Section 1502 is to motivate companies to conduct due diligence in regard to the origins of the minerals contained in their products and, ultimately, to prevent their sourcing of those minerals fueling and contributing to ongoing conflicts and the violation of human rights in the DRC region.

Section 1502 came into effect with some delay after the Securities and Exchange Commission (SEC) passed the final rule for its implementation in 2012. According to the final rule, all manufacturing companies that file reports with the SEC and whose products contain conflict minerals for their functionality must disclose to the SEC and publicly on their company website whether or not those minerals originate from one of the countries mentioned above. For this purpose, they have to conduct a "reasonable country of origin inquiry." Companies that cannot rule out that their conflict minerals originate from the designated region must file a so-called Conflict Minerals Report with the SEC (Taylor 2015: 205), outlining the measures taken by the company to exercise due diligence on the source and chain of custody of the respective minerals. In that sense, the law contains a conditional due diligence obligation, which is specified in the final rule for implementation. The report requires attestation by an independent private sector auditor. However, even if the companies do find that their minerals originate from the DRC or one of the adjoining countries, Section 1502, as a "mere" reporting provision, still allows them to continue to source those minerals. There is no ban or penalty on the use of conflict minerals sourced from the DRC region (Philips, LeBaron, & Wallin 2018: 13). By disclosing their due diligence process, companies must show that they are handling the sourcing from this region with proper care. If they do not, they may be subject to potential market reactions by consumers and investors, or suffer from reputational damage more generally. While companies cannot be sued for the use of conflict minerals originating in the DRC region, they can be subject to liability for fraudulent or false reporting on conflict minerals (LeBaron & Rühmkopf 2017: 18).

Section 1502 of the Dodd-Frank Act has been subject to various legal challenges over the years. For example, the SEC suspended enforcement of the rule under the

Trump administration. The suspension was opposed and lobbied against by many companies as well as a powerful coalition of investors – a move that can be interpreted as a manifestation of corporate political advocacy and responsibility (Chapter 6.1.1 and Chapter 7.3.2.2; Wettstein & Baur 2016).

There are conflicting views on the benefits and drawbacks of Section 1502. Some have argued that the presence of armed groups controlling mines in the DRC region has decreased significantly as a result of the law and that it has led to a shrinking of the black market for conflict minerals, which is a major driver of conflict, violence, and human rights violations (Whitney 2015). However, others emphasize negative economic impacts on local populations (Taylor 2015: 209). They argue that the law makes Western companies reconsider investing in the DRC at all, which may make people worse off than before and may lead to the rise of illegal activity such as smuggling among artisanal miners. Furthermore, the livelihoods of many people are negatively affected by the eradication of black markets (Whitney 2015: 191) and by what they call a de facto embargo on mineral trade from the region (see Koch & Burlyuk 2019: 8-9). While there is little hard evidence on the impacts of Section 1502 on the ground in general, the different narratives seem to point to an opening gap between those who benefit from the loosening of the grip of armed groups and those who primarily pay the price for the slowing Western demand for conflict minerals from the region. What the controversy shows clearly, however, is that for any law, it is important to assess carefully the various ways in which it may shift behaviors – of managers, local populations, consumers, regulators in other countries, etc. – and the potential unintended consequences that such behavioral shifts may have.

Following the US's lead, the EU passed similar regulation on the responsible trade of minerals originating in the DRC in 2017, which came into force in January 2021. The scope of the regulation is wider than Section 1502 with regard to the countries covered, but narrower for the companies to which it is applicable. Since it targets conflict minerals per se, it covers not only the DRC region but also all countries that can be considered conflict-affected or high-risk. The global scope is thought to prevent a specific region, such as the DRC, being singled out and put at a disadvantage (Koch & Burlyuk 2019: 13). However, as opposed to Dodd-Frank Section 1502, the EU regulation only applies to direct importers of raw materials and only above a certain threshold-volume of imports, rather than to all actors in the supply chain. Hence, a car manufacturer, for example, would only be covered by the EU regulation if it engaged directly in the import of raw materials rather than already processed components containing such minerals (Partzsch 2018: 483). As such, it directly covers 600–1,000 importers across Europe (European Commission 2020). As a comparison, around 6,000 stocklisted companies are covered directly by Dodd-Frank Section 1502 (Koch & Burlyuk 2019: 8).

The legislation asks EU importers to follow the five-step due diligence procedure laid down by the *OECD Due Diligence Guidance for Responsible Supply Chains from Conflict-Affected and High-Risk Areas* (OECD 2016a). In this regard the EU regulation does contain a binding due diligence obligation that goes beyond a mere reporting mandate. Nevertheless, the creation of transparency within the supply chains of importers remains the primary stated goal of the legislation (Nowrot 2018: 23).

Concerning transparency, importers must provide a list of the countries from which they source conflict minerals and the quantities of sourced materials by country. They also need to include the names and addresses of their suppliers. In case the minerals come from conflict-affected areas and high-risk countries, they must also include information on: the mines from which the minerals came; where the minerals were consolidated, traded, and processed; and the taxes, fees, and royalties paid. Enforcement of the regulation is handled by each member state individually. However, as of 2021, the legislation does not provide a basis for member states to impose penalties for non-compliance. Thus, it is much softer than Section 1502 when it comes to enforcement, which has been subject to criticism. Another point of contention is the narrow focus on a small number of importers, while leaving the rest of the value chain, as well as the import of products and product parts containing conflict minerals all but untouched. A first review and potential adjustment of the regulation is scheduled for 2023.

12.4.2.2   Dutch Child Labor Due Diligence Law

The Dutch Child Labor Due Diligence Law was adopted by the Dutch Senate in May 2019. The government is in the process of elaborating its General Administrative Order (GAO), which specifies and determines the modalities of implementation. Initially, the law was planned to enter into force on January 1, 2020, but the timeline has been delayed substantially. It is likely to enter into force in 2022.

The law requires affected companies to conduct due diligence in order to assess whether child labor exists in their supply chains. If there is a reasonable presumption that there is child labor in their supply chains, companies must draw up and implement an action plan to address it. The stated goal of the law is to protect Dutch consumers from having to purchase products manufactured using child labor. However, the law does not require that no child labor occurs in the supply chains of the respective companies. Rather, the companies must show that they have done what can reasonably be expected of them to address the problem (MVO Platform 2019).

The law applies to all companies registered in the Netherlands, as well as to foreign companies that deliver their products to the Dutch market more than once a year. Companies have to submit a statement declaring that appropriate due diligence mechanisms are in place and provide a plan of action to address potential cases of child labor in their value chains. The content and form of the statement have not been specified at the time of writing, though the law refers to the International Labor Organization's and International Organisation of Employers' child labor guidance tool for orientation (ILO & IOE 2015; MVO Platform 2019). Furthermore, action plans to address child labor ought to be in line with international guidelines, namely the UNGPs and the OECD *Guidelines for Multinational Enterprises* (MVO Platform 2019). The GAO is expected to further specify the requirements. The statements are published in a central public registry and – in contrast to most other reporting laws, which require annual reporting – companies have to issue their statement only once. The statements will be due six months after the law comes into effect. Companies that fail to carry out due diligence, fail to produce a statement or an action plan, or whose statement or action plan are inadequate can be subject to fines ranging from €4,100 to €750,000 or 10 percent of the company's annual turnover. Authorities will become active on the basis of reasonable complaints by third parties, if such complaints were filed directly with the company prior to addressing the authorities and were not considered adequately by the company within a given time. Companies that fail to comply twice within five years may become subject to criminal charges for which the responsible directors of the company may face imprisonment for up to two years. The Dutch law is the first such law to introduce criminal sanctions for violations (Hoff 2019).

The often-voiced criticism that binding rules may undermine the existing voluntary commitments of companies was raised also in the lead-up to the Dutch law. More specifically, some opponents of the law criticized it for undermining the Dutch Agreements for International Responsible Business Conduct (IRBC Agreements). The IRBC Agreements are agreements between various industries, the government, unions, and the civil society sector on principles of responsible business for a variety of industries. Interestingly, in the case of the Dutch law, twenty-two companies, among them important brands such as Nestlé Netherlands, Heineken, Cargill, and Barry Callebaut, wrote an open letter to the members of the parliament in support of the law and opposing such criticism. They argued that voluntary initiatives and self-regulation needed to be complemented and supported by legally binding frameworks and that the law would not impose any unreasonable or unattainable requirements on companies. Their demonstrated political responsibility (Chapter 6.1.1 and Chapter 7.3.2.2) and leadership may indeed have made a critical contribution to pave the way toward the adoption of the law.

BOX 12.2 (Context) German Supply Chain Act

The German Supply Chain Act ("Lieferkettengesetz") was adopted by the German parliament in June 2021 and will enter into force in 2023. The law formulates a due diligence obligation with regard to human rights and a limited scope of environmental impacts for German companies of more than 3,000 employees (in 2024, the threshold will be reduced to 1,000 employees) and for foreign companies that have a branch office in Germany with the equivalent number of employees (Initiative Lieferkettengesetz 2021: 4). The due diligence obligation applies to the company's own activities, including those of its subsidiaries, as well as to direct first-tier suppliers. However, it does not systematically include indirect suppliers along the value chain unless the company has substantiated knowledge that abuses are taking place, in which case it ought to conduct ad hoc due diligence beyond the first tier (Initiative Lieferkettengesetz 2021: 4). The due diligence obligation includes a requirement to adopt mitigating measures and report on them to the Federal Office for Economic Affairs and Export Control (BAFA), if actual or potential adverse impacts are identified. It has been pointed out that by limiting the due diligence obligation to first-tier suppliers, the German Supply Chain Act falls behind the HRDD requirement of the UNGPs.

The law enables negatively affected parties to authorize German trade unions and NGOs to bring lawsuits based on existing legal provisions to German courts on their behalf, but it does not provide for a new civil liability clause. Hence, potential victims of human rights violations cannot sue companies based on the Supply Chain Act. The law does not improve the legal basis on which such lawsuits rest (ECCHR 2021), which means that even once the law has entered into force, it will remain exceedingly difficult for victims to receive justice in German courts (Initiative Lieferkettengesetz 2021: 4). However, adversely affected parties can notify the BAFA about actual or potential negative human rights impacts resulting from a company's failure to comply with its due diligence obligation. The BAFA must then investigate the matter and order the company to eliminate the harmful impacts (Initiative Lieferkettengesetz 2021: 3). The BAFA can also conduct risk-based inspections at its own initiative, if deemed to be warranted based on the company's reporting (ECCHR 2021). Companies that are in violation of the Act can be fined at least €175,000 and up to 2 percent of their annual turnover and be excluded from public procurement (ECCHR 2021; Initiative Lieferkettengesetz 2021: 3).

A first cross-partisan proposal foresaw a much more rigid accountability regime for the law, but pressure by business associations and corporate lobby groups led the parliament to adopt a weaker compromise.

Discussion Questions:

(1) Is a sanction regime based on fines preferable to one based on civil litigation? What are its relative advantages and disadvantages?

(2) The German Supply Chain Act does not apply to small and medium-sized companies. Is there justification for their exclusion? What are arguments in favor of and against making them subject to the law?

12.4.3 Accountability by Impact: Mandatory Human Rights Due Diligence and Liability Legislation

Substantive HRDD legislation with liability provisions not only counts on the indirect effects of disclosure and transparency to reduce adverse impacts on the ground or prescribe a process to address them but also renders the adverse impacts themselves subject to sanctions, be it through administrative fines or liability provisions.

Not surprisingly, the liability risk for companies has been subject to ongoing critique, particularly by the private sector and business associations. They argue that the avoidance of liability risk may do more harm than good and undermine companies' voluntary initiatives to address the issues of concern. The liability provisions may make it too risky for companies to engage with affected communities and thus lead to the elimination rather than the expansion of their existing CSR programs and initiatives. Proponents of rigid enforcement and liability regimes, on the other hand, point to the modest achievements made by decades of voluntary engagement and the respective need to increase the stakes for corporations that fail to act with proper care.

This subsection will have a closer look at the first piece of mandatory HRDD legislation to include a liability provision, which was adopted in 2017 in France. The French Duty of Vigilance Law is considered to be groundbreaking in the global movement for corporate human rights accountability and has provided further momentum for ongoing initiatives in other countries.

12.4.3.1 French Duty of Vigilance Law

The French Duty of Vigilance Law, which consists of two new articles in the French Commercial Code, came into effect in 2017. It is the first piece of legislation worldwide that essentially puts the UNGPs into binding law across all industries. A challenge to the Vigilance Law by 120 legislators was struck down by the French Constitutional Court. However, the court did rule that a civil fine, which was meant to sanction non-compliance with the duty of care, was unconstitutional (Cossart, Chaplier, & Beau De Lomenie 2017: 318).

The law applies to companies established in France with more than 5,000 employees in France or 10,000 worldwide and in relation to all human rights and the environment. Estimates as to how many companies are covered by these criteria range from 100 to 300. The law establishes a binding duty for such companies to identify and prevent human rights abuses and environmental damage resulting from their own activities, the activities of companies under their control, or from suppliers and subcontractors with which they maintain an established business relationship. French law defines an established commercial relationship as "a stable, regular commercial relationship, taking place with or without a contract, with a certain volume of business, and under a reasonable expectation that the relationship will last" (Cossart, Chaplier, & Beau De Lomenie 2017: 320). For this purpose, companies ought to draw up, effectively implement, and report on a so-called annual vigilance plan. Both the vigilance plan and the reporting on its implementation are public and must be included in the company's annual report. According to Article 1 of the law, the plan must outline:

> the reasonable vigilance measures to allow for risk identification and for the prevention of severe violations of human rights and fundamental freedoms, serious bodily injury or environmental damage or health risks resulting directly or indirectly from the operations of the company and of the companies it controls within the meaning of Article L.233–16, II, as well as from the operations of the subcontractors or suppliers with whom it maintains an established commercial relationship, when such operations derive from this relationship.

Reasonable vigilance measures, as outlined in the law, include: 1) a mapping that identifies, analyzes and ranks risks; 2) procedures to regularly assess the situation of subsidiaries, subcontractors, or suppliers with whom the company maintains an established commercial relationship; 3) appropriate action to mitigate risks or prevent serious violations; 4) an alert mechanism that collects reporting of existing or actual risks; and 5) a monitoring scheme that follows up on the measures implemented and assesses their efficiency. Essentially, the law mandates HRDD as stipulated in the UNGPs.

Companies that fail to set up and publish a vigilance plan according to the legislation or to effectively implement one may be subject to a two-stage enforcement mechanism. At the first stage, any interested party can serve the company with a formal notice to comply. If, after three months, the company has not made satisfactory adjustments to its vigilance plan, the complainant can file a lawsuit with the responsible district court. The company can then be ordered by the court to comply with the obligation or else may face penalties (such penalties are different from the civil fines that were ruled unconstitutional). As of January

2020, there were five cases for which formal notices to comply had been served to companies by interested groups; two of them, both concerning the oil company Total SA, had advanced to court, after the company did not use the three-month period to make suitable improvements. The court will have to decide if the company complied with its vigilance obligations in the particular incidents and, if not, how it wants the company to comply, potentially under a periodic penalty payment (Brabant & Savourey 2020). The two cases are outlined in more detail in Box 12.3.

In addition to this enforcement mechanism, the law also includes a remediation mechanism. If the failure to comply with the legal obligation causes damage, affected parties can sue the company for compensation. However, the bar for compensation is high: Compensation can only be granted if the damage that occurred can be causally linked to the company's non-compliance with the vigilance obligation. The burden of proof is on the shoulders of the victims; a proposal to reverse the burden of proof was eliminated in the parliamentary negotiation process (Cossart, Chaplier, & Beau De Lomenie 2017: 317). Proving such a causal link will be difficult and companies that have adequately met their vigilance obligation will not be liable, even if damage has occurred. Whether or not a vigilance plan and its implementation can be considered adequate must be decided by the judge.

The first vigilance plans were published by companies subject to the law in 2018. Some first assessments (Renaud et al. 2019) of the published reports revealed that most plans are insufficient; they are imprecise, contain gaps, and are often hard to read. Risk identification methods and the mapping of such risks were found to be inadequate in most cases. The measures and actions to address, mitigate, and prevent adverse impacts often lack detail and a clear connection to the identified risks. A study by the BHR consulting agency Shift, assessed the second year of reporting and came to a similar conclusion (Shift 2019). The Duty of Vigilance Radar, a NGO coalition that monitors implementation of the law, reports that a quarter of all companies within the scope of the law have not published a vigilance plan at all (Sherpa, Terre Solidaire, & BHRRC. n.d.). As mentioned above, the enforcement mechanism has been triggered in a limited number of cases. These cases will show how effective the mechanism will turn out to be and whether it is likely to be relied on more frequently in the future.

While, at the time of writing, France is still the only country to have adopted a law in this third category of BHR legislations, a proposal for a similar law, but with a different liability mechanism, was discussed and voted on in Switzerland. The initiative, which was narrowly rejected in a national referendum in 2020, is briefly touched on in Box 12.4.

BOX 12.3 (Context) French Duty of Vigilance Law litigation cases against Total SA

There are two ongoing litigation cases against the French oil giant Total SA, based on the French Duty of Vigilance Law.

In the first case, fourteen French authorities along with five French NGOs allege that Total's vigilance plan does not adequately deal with climate risk and fails to include sufficiently detailed information on how the company would go about reducing emissions (Brabant & Savourey 2020; BHRRC n.d. (h)). While it does address climate change, it does so from a general perspective, rather than relating it directly to the company's own activities. Accordingly, as the parties argued, the vigilance plan fails to identify appropriate preventive and mitigation measures for Total's climate impacts and is not aligned with the objectives of the Paris Agreement (Brabant & Savourey 2020). Total is responsible for more than two-thirds of France's greenhouse gas emissions and one of the top twenty emitters globally. Since the Vigilance Law does not specify which court is to be considered competent in a case (Savourey 2020), Total launched a jurisdictional challenge to have the case handed over to a commercial court. Commercial courts in France are composed of former company directors for the purpose of serving justice in managerial and commercial matters (Chatelain 2021). In February 2021, the civil court ruled against Total's request (BHRRC n.d. (h)). The jurisdictional ruling to have the case heard in the civil court is considered a first victory for the claimants. Total has announced that it will appeal the decision.

The second case was brought against Total in January 2020 by two French NGOs and four Ugandan NGOs, alleging that Total's vigilance plan failed to properly identify human rights, health and safety, and environmental risks associated with an oil exploration and exploitation project and a pipeline development project in Uganda. The claimants point to concrete ecological risks in protected natural areas, risks associated with large-scale land acquisition requiring resettlements and involving inadequate compensation, and risks to freshwater resources and biodiversity (Brabant & Savourey 2020). After an initial review, the civil court in Nanterre found itself incompetent to rule on the case, handing it over to a commercial court. The claimants appealed this decision, but the Court of Appeal rejected their appeal, which meant that the commercial court would rule on the merits of the case (BHRRC n.d. (i)). However, upon further appeal by the claimants, the French Supreme Court finally ruled to give jurisdiction to the civil court, which will proceed to examine the case on the merits. If the civil court agrees with the claimants, it can force the company, potentially by imposing financial penalties, to adjust its vigilance plan and order it to take action to prevent further human rights violations and environmental damage (BHRRC n.d. (i)).

BOX 12.4 (Context) Swiss Responsible Business Initiative

After unsuccessfully petitioning the Swiss parliament to introduce mandatory HRDD legislation in 2014, a coalition of ultimately more than 120 NGOs, unions, and advocacy groups launched a popular initiative in 2015 to include such a provision in the Swiss constitution. The Swiss Responsible Business Initiative (RBI) was voted on in a national referendum in November 2020 and was rejected narrowly. While it won the popular vote, it failed to also win approval by majority of cantons, which is a requirement for popular initiatives. However, the strong campaign by the 120 organizations led the parliament to formulate a counterproposal to the initiative, which was to be put into law if the initiative was rejected. The counterproposal, which is now set to become mandatory for large Swiss companies, is significantly weaker than the initiative. It consists of a reporting mandate with an HRDD obligation in regard to child labor and conflict minerals. The law will not include a liability provision.

The RBI, on the other hand, sought to establish a much stricter accountability regime, consisting of the following key elements:

(a) It demanded an HRDD obligation along companies' entire value chain. Included in its scope were large Swiss companies and certain SMEs in high risk sectors.

(b) It proposed civil liability for damages brought about in breach of international human rights norms or international environmental standards by Swiss companies' own conduct or by the conduct of companies under their de facto control. Thus, a company would be liable by default for its own subsidiaries and, under certain circumstances, for suppliers the company controls through its contractual relationships.

(c) It included an exoneration clause through which the company could free itself from liability if it were to show that the damage occurred despite it having properly fulfilled its HRDD obligation.

(d) It contained a mandatory overriding rule that would have established application of the RBI provisions (i.e. Swiss law) to extraterritorial cases by default.

Discussion Questions:

(1) Do you think holding parent companies liable for the conduct of their foreign subsidiaries by default is desirable from a BHR perspective or would such a provision go too far, considering that their separation is well established in company law? What are arguments in favor and against such a provision?

(2) Some argue that applying HRDD as a possibility of exoneration for companies gives companies too much leeway to escape liability. Others see it as an adequate mechanism to incentivize companies to truly engage in substantive, rather than merely cosmetic, HRDD. Where do you stand on the debate?

(3) Do you think the RBI provisions could set an example of how existing HRDD laws could be improved? Which elements of the RBI should be broadly adopted and in what regard does the RBI itself require improvements?

(4) How would you answer questions 1–3 after reading Chapter 12.5 on foreign direct liability?

12.5   Adjudicative Measures: Foreign Direct Liability

The state obligation to protect human rights from corporate abuse includes an obligation to provide access to remedy where violations have occurred. Whether or not, or to what extent, this obligation holds extraterritorially and if home states have an international legal obligation to make their domestic courts available to foreign victims of corporate human rights abuse is subject to controversial discussions. As pointed out earlier (Chapter 12.2), the UNGPs take the position that international law permits such extraterritorial jurisdiction but does not prescribe it, whereas the Committee on Economic, Social and Cultural Rights assumes that states do have such extraterritorial obligations.

Mandatory HRDD laws that include liability clauses (Chapter 12.4.3) provide avenues for victims of corporate human rights violations to bring lawsuits against multinational companies in the companies' home states. As these laws develop, it is to be expected that such lawsuits will become a much more frequent occurrence. Even beyond specialized laws, a number of jurisdictions – particularly in common law countries – have for many years and to varying degrees allowed civil and in some cases criminal action against companies for their extraterritorial human rights conduct. However, most of such cases, even though they are commonly seen as BHR cases and in substance and intention aim at the remedial of human rights violations, do not refer directly to human rights or human rights law, but to personal injury or property damage based on domestic tort or criminal law (Bernaz 2017: 257). In other words, "although the cases can be seen through a human rights lens, they are not really human rights cases as such" (Bernaz 2017: 283). Exceptions are, for example, lawsuits brought under the ATCA as discussed below (Chapter 12.5.3) or based on the French Duty of Vigilance Law as discussed above (Chapter 12.4.3.1). Both pieces of legislation allow for lawsuits with direct reference to the violation of international human rights. A company's own activities abroad may be subject to such lawsuits but more common and from a BHR perspective more challenging are lawsuits against parent companies whose foreign subsidiaries are or were involved in human rights abuse.

Section 12.5.1 will briefly outline the reasons why plaintiffs decide to sue parent companies in their home states rather than local subsidiaries in the host state. Section 12.5.2 will then explore some common elements of these lawsuits across different jurisdictions, in order to build a general understanding of the nature and shape of such extraterritorial human rights litigation. Generally, each jurisdiction handles cases differently, according to its own tort and criminal laws and its respective case history. However, there are a number of common conceptual challenges that characterize all such foreign direct liability cases, irrespective of the jurisdiction, in which they are negotiated. After addressing those challenges, this chapter will provide an overview of a number of different jurisdictions, their respective laws and some emblematic cases that have set important precedents or shaped the discussion on foreign direct liability decisively. Specifically, it will cover the US, UK, Canada, and a number of civil law jurisdictions such as the Netherlands, Germany, and Italy. After some brief elaborations on corporate criminal liability for human rights abuse, the chapter will conclude by assessing some of the common criticisms against extraterritorial human rights liability.

12.5.1   Reasons for Human Rights Litigation against Parent Companies

The reasons why victims of corporate human rights abuse decide to sue parent companies in their home countries rather than go after the subsidiary in the country in which the violation occurred are manifold. Often, such violations occur in contexts of weak, failing, or entirely absent institutions where victims have little or no possibility of legal redress. In such cases, litigating against the parent companies in their respective home states may be the only possibility for the victims to find justice. Furthermore, local subsidiaries may be undercapitalized and there may be little prospect of being compensated adequately in the host state. Targeting parent companies thus increases the chances of receiving adequate compensation, possibly by reaching a settlement. Finally, a court in the home country of the parent company is more likely to accept jurisdiction over the parent company than over the foreign subsidiary directly, so if plaintiffs decide to sue abroad sueing the parent company may have a better chance of success. Nevertheless, there is, to date, only one partially successful extraterritorial case against a parent company for human rights violations of its foreign subsidiary (Chapter 12.5.6.1). Most of such cases were dismissed by the courts or resulted in settlements. However, some recent advancement particularly in cases in the UK and in the Netherlands (Chapter 12.5.4 and Chapter 12.5.6.1) nurture the hope that more successful verdicts can be achieved in the near future. Such breakthroughs would be important not least because in most cases, settlements between companies and victims hardly compensate for the damage and harm that the victims suffered. For example, in *Wiwa* v. *Shell*, a lawsuit brought in the US on the basis of the ATCA (Chapter 12.5.3), the parties settled for $15.5 million. Similarly, in 2015 Shell settled a lawsuit brought to a London court by the Nigerian Bodo community for £55 million. While such amounts are, of course, far better than no compensation at all, they are nowhere close to representative of the devastation that occurred in the respective regions and communities. Beyond the limited compensation, settlements commonly do not include any admission of guilt on the part of the company. This makes them an attractive and affordable way for companies to rid themselves of lengthy and potentially risky lawsuits, as well as a tool to stall the development of the law and to undermine the progression toward a precedence (Simons & Macklin 2014: 255).

Nevertheless, even without any judicial precedence and with many cases dismissed before they could even be heard in court, there can be benefits to such lawsuits beyond the potential settlements. It has been shown that most companies that have faced lawsuits started to adopt measures to address human rights responsibility during or shortly after the court proceedings. Among such measures are the participation in designated MSIs, the adoption of responsibility standards and codes of conduct, and the implementation of human rights trainings for staff (Schrempf-Stirling & Wettstein 2017). While the impact of such measures on the ground is always arguable, they show clearly that human rights lawsuits have an effect beyond the legal dimension.

12.5.2 Common Characteristics and Challenges

Before looking at more specific developments in various jurisdictions, this subsection will approach foreign direct liability from a more general, conceptual angle in order to understand better what characteristics and challenges are defining for most such cases, no matter where they are brought to court.

12.5.2.1 Jurisdiction

Jurisdiction has two dimensions, one deriving from public international law and one from private international law (Zerk 2006: 132). From the **perspective of public international law**, jurisdiction defines the spatial or geographical limits of the state's regulatory power. These geographical limits are commonly seen to be set by the territorial principle. With some exceptions, this principle generally prohibits states from imposing direct regulation on companies abroad. However, recent years have heralded an increasing awareness of the need and importance of regulation with extraterritorial effects, including in the BHR domain. As the previous sections on BHR policy (Chapter 12.3) and legislation (Chapter 12.4) have shown, states are increasingly willing to regulate the headquarters of multinational companies at home in ways that have indirect extraterritorial effects on the operations of foreign subsidiaries. Thus, while the principles of territoriality and non-interference have traditionally been interpreted rather restrictively, the ongoing trend toward BHR regulation is consolidating the rapidly changing perceptions in this regard. As a consequence, the legitimacy of such regulation is now measured not solely by the territorial principle but also by the requirements of effective human rights protection.

From the *perspective of private international law*, jurisdiction defines the power of domestic courts to decide on matters of private law, such as tort-based or contractual disputes between private parties. Private international law does not follow the territorial principle of jurisdiction; rather, jurisdiction is a function of various other factors:

> Broadly speaking, whereas the scope of public law tends to be understood in spatial terms, civil jurisdiction in the private law sphere tends to be defined by reference to connecting factors between the parties, the subject matter of the dispute and the state (Zerk 2006: 113).

To what extent domestic courts have jurisdiction in civil cases against multinational corporations and which law – domestic or foreign – is to apply in a specific case of extraterritorial human rights violations depends on the country and how the respective courts interpret the above-mentioned criteria in the specific case. In the EU, rules on jurisdiction have been harmonized in the so-called Brussels Regulation. Hence, when victims of corporate human rights abuse decide to bring lawsuits to a domestic court in the parent company's home country, the court will first have to decide on whether or not to assert jurisdiction over the case. Once jurisdiction is established, the case can move on to the trial phase. However, overcoming the jurisdictional stage has proven to be a formidable challenge in and of itself and most cases never advance to the trial stage. This illustrates a fundamental conflict between the way international law is set up to protect the interests of states and the basic underlying aim of human rights to put the individual at the center of attention. The rules of jurisdiction are designed first and foremost to safeguard the territorial sovereignty of states, even if they are opposed to the aim of granting justice to people whose human rights have been violated. Not only from an ethical point of view, but also from the perspective of human rights law, this prioritization of state interests over the human rights of individuals is problematic (Zerk 2006: 135).

12.5.2.2   Forum Non Conveniens

Even if a court has jurisdiction in principle, this does not provide a guarantee that it will be exercised. Some common law countries allow courts to dismiss a case on the grounds of the *forum non conveniens* doctrine, which expresses the view that another court – most likely in the country in which the damage occurred – provides a more appropriate venue to deal with the matter. *Forum non conveniens* needs to be raised by the defendant, since judges will not apply the doctrine on their own (Joseph 2004: 87). The US is the most significant country that allows courts to dismiss cases based on the *forum non conveniens* principle. The UK, too, allowed for the application of the doctrine before it was ruled inconsistent with the Brussels regulation of the EU. Whether the withdrawal of the UK from the EU may also revive the discussions to bring back *forum non conveniens* is to be seen.

The application of the *forum non conveniens* doctrine in different countries varies. In the US, in order for a court to claim *forum non conveniens*, a two-step test will be applied. In the first step, judges assess whether there is an adequate alternative forum outside of the US to hear the case. Adequacy depends not least on whether or not the state itself was involved in the alleged violation of human rights. Bringing a case to the court of a state, which was itself a perpetrator in the abuse, would seem unreasonable, particularly if the abuse was egregious and systematic (Joseph 2004: 91). In the second step, If adequacy can be established, the court will weigh the private interests of both parties and public interests for and against the alternative forum in order to decide whether it is the more convenient or appropriate location for the litigation (Joseph 2004: 88; Zerk 2006: 120ff.; Bernaz 2017: 266).

Corruption, a lack of independence, or other institutional shortcomings are common reasons to deny adequacy of an alternative forum. Reasons for an alternative court to be considered more convenient or appropriate may include certain procedural issues such as convenience of access to evidence and witnesses or the general logistics of the proceedings, but also public policy and the public interest considerations of hearing the case in one forum or the another. A controversial public policy reason is international comity. Courts may decline jurisdiction based on *forum non conveniens* in order to avoid offending the host country in which the damage occurred. The assumption here is that adjudicating the case in the home state of the multinational company may be deemed paternalistic or otherwise put strains on the relationship between the countries. Courts often argue also that host states have a stronger public interest in hearing the case than home states. In the UK, such public interest considerations played less of a role when *forum non conveniens* was still common practice; rather, what mattered regarding whether an alternative forum was deemed appropriate was that substantive justice was served (Zerk 2006: 124–125). In Australia, the defendant has to show not that another court is more appropriate than the Australian court in which the lawsuit was filed, but that the Australian court is clearly inappropriate to hear the case. This means that even if there is a more appropriate forum elsewhere, the Australian court can retain jurisdiction unless it is shown to be clearly unsuitable (Zerk 2006: 126). Hence the bar for *forum non conveniens* arguments is higher in Australia, which provides a better chance for foreign plaintiffs to have their cases heard in Australian courts.

As opposed to the US and Australia, EU member states are prohibited from applying the *forum non conveniens* doctrine. The so-called Brussels I regulation (Box 12.5) prescribes for EU member states that persons – including corporations –

> ## BOX 12.5 (Context) Brussels I Regulation (EC Regulation No. 44/2001)
>
> The Brussels I Regulation of 2001 and its amended recast of 2012 (Council Regulation No. 1215/2012; Brussels I Recast) harmonize the rules on jurisdiction within the EU for civil liability claims against defendants domiciled in the EU. The regulation establishes that EU-domiciled defendants are to be sued in the courts of their country of domicile (Article 2). For companies, this is the country in which it has its statutory seat, central administration, or principal place of business (Article 60). In the landmark case *Owusu* v. *Jackson and Others*, the European Court of Justice established in 2005 that the courts of EU member states cannot decline to exercise the jurisdiction that Brussels I confers on them on the basis of *forum non conveniens* (Marx, Bright, & Wouters 2019: 34; Palombo 2019b: 61–63).

domiciled in a member state must be sued in the courts of that member state, irrespective of where the damage occurred and the nationality of the plaintiffs. This does not mean, of course, that there are not other jurisdictional challenges to overcome, but the elimination of *forum non conveniens* considerably strengthens the position of plaintiffs. After all, the doctrine has repeatedly been used as an effective legal strategy for companies to avoid accountability and often with devastating consequences for victims, since such cases are rarely relitigated in the potential alternative forum (Joseph 2004: 88).

12.5.2.3   Choice of Law

Determining jurisdiction and overcoming a potential *forum non conveniens* challenge of the defendants is only the first step in foreign direct liability cases. Once jurisdiction of a domestic court is confirmed, it must then determine which law – foreign or domestic – ought to be applied in order to decide on the case. In EU law and in most international tort litigation cases, the place where the harm, injury, or damage occurred provides the most natural choice of law. In the EU, Article 4(1) of the so-called Rome II regulation (Box 12.6) states as a general rule (Bernaz 2017: 281):

> The law applicable to a non-contractual obligation arising out of a tort/delict shall be the law of the country in which the damage occurs irrespective of the country in which the event giving rise to the damage occurred and irrespective of the country or countries in which the indirect consequences of that event occur (European Parliament & Council of the European Union 2007).

BOX 12.6 (Context) Rome II Regulation (EC Regulation No. 864/2007)

In European private international law, the issue of applicable law is governed by the Rome II Regulation. Rome II establishes that the applicable law for torts is the law of the country in which the damage or harm occurred. Hence, what is relevant is where the damage materialized, rather than where the event occurred that gave rise to the damage (Palombo 2019b: 64). The regulation excludes environmental damage from this rule by allowing the person suffering the damage to choose the law of the country in which the event giving rise to the damage occurred. This provides additional protection to victims of environmental degradation (Palombo 2019b: 65). A further exception to this rule is if both the claimant and the defendant have their domicile in the same country at the time when the damage occurred, in which case the law of that country of domicile ought to apply. Furthermore, if the tort is more closely connected with another country than the one in which the damage occurred, the law of that country shall apply. Finally, the parties can reach an agreement on which law should be applied to the case. The court can deviate from this rule and apply the law of the forum if: a) an overriding provision of its domestic law calls for it (Article 16); and b) the application of the foreign law would be manifestly inconsistent with its public policy (Article 26) (Marx, Bright, & Wouters 2019: 34–35; Palombo 2019b: 63–66).

Hence, under this rule, if a UK parent company faces a lawsuit in a UK domestic court for damage done in South Africa, the case would be assessed based on South African law. However, Article 26 of Rome II grants courts the possibility of refusing the application of the foreign law if its application would be "manifestly incompatible with the public policy of the forum" (Bernaz 2017: 282). In the US, too, foreign law ought not to be applied if it contradicts important public policy considerations within the forum (Joseph 2004: 75). Such considerations may include situations in which the foreign law shields corporations from being liable for egregious human rights abuses (Joseph 2004: 75; Zerk 2006: 129).

Generally, matters are much more complicated in the US, where different states apply different rules for choice of law. Some states choose the law of the jurisdiction with the most significant relationship to the case and its parties (Joseph 2004: 74). For this purpose, a number of factors ought to be considered by the respective courts in addition to where the damage occurred, such as "the needs of the international system, the regulatory policies of interested states, expectations of the parties, certainty, predictability and uniformity" (Zerk 2006: 130). For some of these factors, answers may not be clear-cut. For example, the location of the wrong that caused the damage may not be clear; is it the local implementation of a particular company policy in the host country that counts or the decision that led to the adoption of the policy at the headquarters in the home country (Joseph 2004: 75)? Other US states simply apply the law of the forum, if it has an interest in the outcome of the case. In some states, combinations of such rules are applied. In sum, choice of law in the US is decided case-by-case (Joseph 2004: 75).

12.5.2.4 Attribution

Once jurisdiction is established and a potential *forum non conveniens* claim overcome, a case can proceed to be heard in court. However, since most foreign direct liability cases target the parent company rather than the foreign subsidiary, another challenge is waiting for the plaintiffs: attributing the tort to the parent company. From a management perspective, this may appear to be a small obstacle, since it tends to look at multinational corporations as single entities that ought to be managed across jurisdictions. However, from a legal perspective, attributing the activities of a subsidiary to its parent company has in the past been a close to insurmountable challenge. The reason lies in the legal structure of multinational companies and the separation of the company from its shareholders. The aim of this separation is precisely to shield shareholders from liability for corporate activities beyond their initial investment. No difference is being made in this regard between individual and corporate shareholders. This means that parent companies are commonly shielded from liability for the activities of the subsidiaries of which they hold stocks. This legal separation of the parent company from its subsidiaries is commonly referred to as the "corporate veil." Overcoming this separation is possible only under special circumstances. There are a number of different routes to overcome the attribution challenge, but essentially there are two broad categories:

1. *Indirect parent liability/enterprise liability*: In this first category, the activities of the subsidiary are attributed to the parent company based on its relation to the subsidiary. We can call this "indirect parent liability" since the parent company is held indirectly liable for the actions of the subsidiary. This strategy requires that the corporate veil is lifted or "pierced." That is, the separation between parent company and subsidiary is eliminated and they are regarded as one single entity. More technically, the parent company would be held strictly liable for the activities of the subsidiary based on the control relationship between them (Zerk 2006: 229). Again, from a management perspective, this may seem like an adequate way to look at multinational companies. After all, multinational companies tend to be run and managed in a consolidated way as an overarching entity. Furthermore, this perspective is also adopted in competition and antitrust laws, with which managers are intimately familiar. However, for the purposes of holding companies liable for tort, such a move would require exceptional

circumstances and would pose obstacles to litigants that are hard to overcome. This discrepancy between the principle of separate legal personality and the economic realities of managing multinational enterprises has been subject to recurring critiques, which claim that something akin to a corporate group liability principle would capture the nature of today's multinationals more adequately (see, e.g., Joseph 2004: 138ff.). Essentially, enterprise liability would require a relationship between the parent company and the subsidiary that is so close and characterized by control so all-encompassing that the parent company could be seen as acting through the subsidiary and turn the subsidiary into a mere instrument without its own identity. Courts are extremely reluctant to apply enterprise liability because lifting the veil is seen to be in conflict with the basic principles of company law. Therefore, such a move could realistically be expected only, if at all, if the subsidiary ought to be regarded as a sham, which is fraudulently set up for the mere purpose of escaping liability and if such arrangements result in grave injustice (Joseph 2004: 130).

 A special case of enterprise liability is vicarious liability. It means that parent companies are being held strictly liable for actions of the subsidiary, based on the idea that the subsidiary acts as an agent of and thus on behalf of the parent company. Many jurisdictions apply vicarious liability to the relationship between employer and employees, but it is less common to extend it to the relation between the parent company and its subsidiary. However, courts in at least some states of the US have accepted vicarious liability as a basis to bring lawsuits against parent companies under the ATCA (Zerk 2013: 46). The lines between direct and indirect liability are blurred with regard to vicarious liability and some courts may be more inclined to count it as a direct form of liability. Since the actions of the subsidiary are carried out on behalf of the parent company, however, there certainly is an element of attribution of those actions to the parent, which goes beyond a mere duty of care on the parent company's part.

2. *Direct parent liability*: "Direct parent liability" (Joseph 2004: 134ff.) means that the parent company is not being held accountable for the actions of the subsidiary, but for its own actions and omissions, if they can be tied to the harm that occurred. In such cases, the actions of the subsidiary do not need to be attributed to the parent company and thus the corporate veil is left untouched. There are two bases of direct parent liability that are commonly discussed in the literature: breach of a duty of care and aiding and abetting.

 • *Duty of care*: Suing parent companies based on a breach of a potential duty of care is by far the most common way of litigating against parent companies in domestic courts. In order to do so, plaintiffs must be able to show that the parent company had – and breached through its own actions – a duty of care toward the victims that derives from its direct operational influence and control. Two scenarios are possible in this regard, one active and one passive.

In the *active scenario*, the parent company is seen as the orchestrator of the subsidiary's harmful activities. Thus, it neglected due care in its active interaction with and direction of the subsidiary, which can be seen as a cause of or causal contribution to the human rights violation. In the *passive scenario*, the parent company does not actively get involved, but rather neglects to take control over the harmful actions of the subsidiary. That is, it is negligent in terms of exercising its general supervision over the subsidiary's activities (Zerk 2006: 218). However, generally, direct liability requires affirmative actions by the parent company and thus a substantial degree of operational involvement and control. In other words, mere omission or negligence to intervene based on a parent company's strategic control over a subsidiary may not be enough to establish a duty of care (Joseph 2004: 136–137). Similarly, parent companies do not generally have a duty of care toward, for example, the employees of a subsidiary simply *qua* being the parent company. To illustrate this with an example, a parent company may not be liable "merely" for not intervening with the decision of a subsidiary to hire "rogue" security forces, which then engage in human rights abuse. However, it may face liability for actively promoting such a decision through its own actions (Joseph 2004: 138). The practical problem or paradox to which this can lead on the ground is that it sets an incentive for parent companies to avoid liability risk by following a hands-off approach precisely in those contexts in which the risk for human rights abuse may be highest and the involvement of the parent company most needed. Zerk summarizes the relevant conditions for direct parent liability based on a duty of care as follows:

> In summary, to succeed in a "primary liability" claim against a parent company for damage arising from the activities of its foreign affiliates, it seems that the foreign plaintiffs would need to be able to show, at a minimum, (a) that the parent had detailed knowledge of the health and environmental risks posed by the relevant activities, processes or technology; (b) that the parent had had particularly close involvement in the day-to-day operations of the foreign affiliate; (c) that the parent failed to exercise the level of due diligence that would have been appropriate given all the circumstances; and (d) that those failures were a direct cause of the injury or damage, even if they were not the only cause (Zerk 2006: 222).

- *Aiding and abetting*: The second form of direct parent liability is what Zerk (2006: 225ff.; 2013: 47) calls "secondary parent liability." In such cases, the parent company is aiding and abetting the commission of the tort by the subsidiary. Thus, secondary liability neither presupposes a duty of care nor that the parent company's actions or omissions were the primary cause of the tort. Rather, what is required is a knowing contribution to the commission of the tort that is substantial in the sense that the tort would not have been committed if not for the parent's assistance. This strategy has been significant in ATCA cases in the US, but has not been utilized in other jurisdictions. Therefore, it will be elaborated on more closely below in Chapter 12.5.3.1.

Having outlined the general features of such extraterritorial litigation cases against parent companies, the following subsections will now have a closer look at the main jurisdictions in which such cases have been brought to court. This will allow for a discussion of some of the specificities of these jurisdictions and some of their seminal cases beyond the general features outlined above.

12.5.3   US: Alien Tort Claims Act

Most of the relevant extraterritorial BHR litigation cases brought to domestic courts of home states have happened in the US on the basis of a specific piece of legislation called the Alien Tort Claims Act (ATCA). The ATCA allows foreign plaintiffs to bring actual human rights cases, that is, cases referring to international human rights law, rather than having to resort to regular domestic tort law. However, two recent Supreme Court decisions, which will be discussed below, have restricted the scope of the ATCA to a degree that renders it inapplicable to most potential cases. As a consequence, there has been an increase of BHR litigation in other countries in recent years.

Nevertheless, the ATCA is a seminal piece of legislation whose importance for the BHR movement can hardly be overstated. This is despite the fact that no parent company has ever been convicted under ATCA for human rights violations abroad. In fact, most ATCA cases were either dismissed, for example, on grounds of *forum non conveniens*, before they could be heard in court, or were settled outside of court. Nevertheless, despite its limited success, the ATCA made it possible to bring the first BHR cases to the courts of home states and allowed the BHR movement to build and develop a respective practice and infrastructure to litigate selected cases, which is now enabling and benefiting lawsuits in other jurisdictions.

12.5.3.1   Main Features

The ATCA allows foreign nationals to sue for compensation for torts that amount to violations of international law. It consists of one single paragraph as follows:

> The district courts shall have original jurisdiction of any civil action by an alien for a tort only, committed in violation of the law of nations or a treaty of the United States (28 USC § 1350).

As the text implies, the ATCA was not initially meant to provide a basis for BHR litigation. It was enacted in 1789 with the purpose of protecting foreign diplomats from breaches of customary international law. However, the ATCA was predominantly dormant and hardly used until it was rediscovered two centuries later in the now famous *Filartiga* v. *Peña-Irala* case in 1980. In *Filartiga*, two Paraguayan residents of the US brought a suit alleging the torture and murder of a family member by a former Paraguayan police chief who also resided in the US. The case was first dismissed, but later overturned by a court of appeal. The *Filartiga* case showed ATCA's potential to hold individuals accountable for egregious breaches of human rights even if they occurred abroad (Zerk 2006: 207). Similarly decisive from a BHR perspective was *Doe* v. *Unocal* in 1997, which was the first time that the ATCA was applied to private corporations. In the *Unocal* case, a Burmese villager accused the company of complicity in human rights abuses such as forced labor, forced relocation, rape, and murder committed by military and police forces in relation to a pipeline project that involved the Californian energy company Unocal and the French company Total (Bernaz 2017: 261–262). While the case survived all motions to dismiss (for example based on *forum non conveniens*), it was ultimately settled out of court before it had a chance to go to trial. Nevertheless, for the first time, a federal court recognized that corporations could, in fact, violate international law (Bernaz 2017: 262). Henceforth, ATCA was predominantly used as a basis for bringing human rights litigations against multinational companies and about 130 such cases had been filed by 2013 (Bernaz 2017: 262).

Two specifications are important: First, "law of nations" is what customary international law was called at the time of the enactment of the ATCA (Bernaz 2017: 260). The ATCA refers to both customary international law and *jus cogens* norms (Chapter 3.3.2), as well as to international treaties that have been ratified by the US. In other words, companies can be sued for breaches with direct reference to human rights law, rather than "merely" based on general domestic tort law. Second, companies can become implicated in and thus liable for such breaches on three possible grounds: **a)** if their own conduct violates norms that are applicable directly to the company under customary international law. This is the case for a small amount of *jus cogens* norms. For all other violations of customary law, companies can only be held liable based on the involvement of the state. This is the case, **b)** if they violate relevant norms based on "state action," and, **c)** by way of complicity, that is, if they aid and abet state actors. The following paragraphs will briefly specify the respective grounds.

- *Direct company violations*: As shown earlier, international human rights law does not commonly confer human rights obligations on non-state actors (Chapter 6.2). The exception to this rule are a number of egregious international crimes, which apply directly to individuals and potentially to companies. Thus, under the ATCA companies can be directly liable without the requirement of "state action" (see below) or any other kind of involvement of the state for a small number of violations within the scope of international customary law. Those violations predominantly pertain to *jus cogens* norms (Chapter 3.3.2) and include, among others, genocide, war crimes, piracy, slave trading, and forced labor (Zerk 2006: 211). Against this background, cases of ATCA litigation against companies violating human rights through their own conduct as a private actors are rare. Litigation based on "state action" or "aiding and abetting" has been much more common.

- *Direct company violations under "state action"*: For customary law norms that do not fall in the category of *jus cogens*, companies can be liable only in connection with the state, that is, by aiding and abetting the state (see below), or by "state action." Under the doctrine of "state action," corporations directly violate applicable norms through their own conduct, rather than merely contributing to them as it is the case for aiding and abetting. However, their actions are carried out "under the colour of governmental authority" (Joseph 2004: 33), for example, if the violation occurs while carrying out an official state mandate, or if the company acted under specific instructions of the state. Courts have applied a number of different "tests" that outline the contours of "state action": First, if the company exercises public functions that are traditionally assigned exclusively to the state ("public function" test); second, if the company is compelled by the state ("state compulsion" test); third, if the relation between the two is so close that the actions of one can count as the actions of the other ("nexus" test); fourth, if both parties are willful participants in a partnership in whose realm the abuse is committed ("joint action" test); fifth, if the company exercises control over the state's abuse ("proximate cause" test).
- *Indirect company violations through aiding and abetting*: Most ATCA cases have been brought forward based on corporations' complicity with abusive governments, that is, based on their aiding and abetting violations committed by host governments. Direct complicity (Chapter 4.3.1) is most likely to trigger ATCA liability, while passive forms of complicity such as beneficial and silent complicity are rather unlikely to meet the necessary threshold. Courts have applied varying standards to aiding and abetting liability under the ATCA. In particular, while some relied on the purpose standard for the required *mens rea* in aiding and abetting liability, others have regarded the knowledge standard as sufficient (Chapter 4.3.3) (Dodge 2019: 136). The former presupposes that the company acted for the purpose of facilitating the abuse, while the latter merely presupposes that the company knew, or should have known, about the abuse, but did not act with the purpose, or even the intent, of contributing to it (Bernaz 2017: 271–273).

As mentioned above, most ATCA cases have been dismissed before they could proceed to be judged by their merits. *Forum non conveniens* provides the most common, but not the only, grounds for dismissal. Courts can deny jurisdiction also if cases raise thorny political issues that courts are ill-equipped to address and which are more properly dealt with by the executive branch of the government ("political questions" doctrine); if hearing a case would involve judging official governmental acts of foreign states ("act of state" doctrine), which could undermine US foreign policy interests and negatively affect US international relations; or, if hearing a case goes against the legitimate policy interests of a foreign state ("international comity" doctrine) (Zerk 2006: 213–214). Nevertheless, the ATCA served as by far the most frequently used basis globally for human rights litigation against corporations up to the two Supreme Court decisions on *Kiobel* and *Jesner*, which have severely curtailed the scope of the ATCA and brought an abrupt halt to this trend.

12.5.3.2 *Curtailing ATCA I: Kiobel v. Royal Dutch Petroleum Co.*

The Supreme Court decision on the *Kiobel* case unexpectedly redefined the parameters of ATCA litigation in 2013. The case was brought by lead plaintiff Esther Kiobel against a Nigerian subsidiary of Royal Dutch Petroleum Co. (Shell) on claims of complicity in extrajudicial killing, torture, crimes against humanity, and prolonged arbitrary arrest and detention. Esther Kiobel is the widow of the late Dr. Barinem Kiobel, who was tortured and executed by the Abacha regime in 1995, along with Ken Saro-Wiwa and eight other Ogoni activists (the "Ogoni 9") (Chapter 2.1).

The case was filed in 2002 in New York. In 2006, Shell filed an interlocutory appeal, which was granted by the second circuit court. In an unprecedented move, the appellate court decided in 2010 that the ATCA was not applicable to corporations. The basis for this decision was provided in an ambiguous formulation in footnote 20 of *Sosa* v. *Alvarez-Machain*, which aimed at distinguishing norms that require state action from norms that do not, but was interpreted by the court as a negation of corporate liability under international law altogether (Dodge 2019: 132). The plaintiffs subsequently filed a petition for *certiorari* (a petition for judicial review) on this question to the Supreme Court in June 2011. Oral arguments as to whether corporations are immune from tort liability for international law violations started in February 2012. The Supreme Court then decided that the case would be reargued with a focus on extraterritoriality, which happened in October 2012. In April 2013, the Supreme Court reached a decision and established a presumption against extraterritoriality for the ATCA, arguing that the text of the ATCA does not contain "a clear indication of extraterritorial reach." This means that cases brought by aliens particularly against foreign companies for damage or harm that was committed outside of the US are presumed to be outside of the scope of ATCA, unless they "touch and concern the territory of the United States … with sufficient force to displace" this presumption. The mere presence of a company (through one of its subsidiaries) in the US was explicitly stated not to be sufficient to displace the presumption. The presumption was ruled to apply to the Kiobel case, which essentially confirmed the decision of the appellate court.

The implications of this decision for ATCA litigation practice were momentous. It overturned the long-lasting practice that companies with a presence in the US could effectively be sued on the basis of the ATCA. For the case at hand, this meant that before the ruling, Shell could be sued for the actions of its Nigerian subsidiary, based on its presence in the US through its US subsidiary. After the ruling, only cases against American companies seem to be able to touch on American interests with the force necessary to overcome the presumption against extraterritoriality. However, some courts held that even US nationality is not sufficient, if the relevant conduct occurs outside of the US (Dodge 2019: 136). Thus, a large part of traditional ATCA cases involving foreign companies with a presence in the US was no longer possible after *Kiobel*. Not surprisingly, most cases in which the "touch and concern" test was applied ended up being dismissed (Dodge 2019: 136).

Shell came under criticism for its legal strategy to confront the lawsuit. It was alleged that rather than defending itself based on the facts of its particular case, Shell successfully aimed at undercutting the underlying statute and thus weakening the basis for countless victims of human rights abuse to bring lawsuits in other cases, as well. In his issues brief on *Kiobel*, John Ruggie commented on Shell's questionable role as follows:

> But what would the corporate responsibility to respect human rights involve in a case like Kiobel? [. . .] Of course, the company must be free to argue, in the courts and elsewhere, that it met both the law and its wider responsibilities to respect human rights whenever it believes that to be the case. Yet questions remain. Should the corporate responsibility to respect human rights remain entirely divorced from litigation strategy and tactics, particularly where the company has choices about the grounds on which to defend itself? Should the litigation strategy aim to destroy an entire juridical edifice for redressing gross violations of human rights, particularly where other legal grounds exist to protect the company's interests? Or would the commitment to socially responsible conduct include an obligation by the company to instruct its attorneys to avoid such far-reaching consequences where that is possible? And what about the responsibilities of the company's legal representatives? Would they encompass laying out for their client the entire range of risks entailed by the litigation strategy and tactics, including concern for their client's commitments, reputation, and the collateral damage to a wide range of third parties? (Ruggie 2012: 6).

John Ruggie's point makes it clear that the corporate responsibility to respect human rights ought not to be interpreted in an overly narrow relational sense only, but also in regard to the larger political implications of a corporation's activities (Chapter 6.1.1 and Chapter 7.3.2.2). Respecting human rights for a corporation is not commensurable with activities that undermine the general infrastructure of human rights protection, even if such activities may not be in immediate and direct violation of anyone's human rights.

12.5.3.3   *Curtailing ATCA II: Jesner* v. *Arab Bank*

While the presumption against extraterritoriality established in *Kiobel* left open the possibility of suing foreign companies at least in principle, this option was eliminated in a second momentous Supreme Court decision five years later, in 2018. In *Jesner* v. *Arab Bank*, the Supreme Court ruled that "foreign corporations may not be defendants in suits brought under the ATS [Alien Tort Statute]" altogether. The plaintiffs in this case accused Arab Bank of funneling money through its New York branch to finance terrorist attacks in Israel, the West Bank, and Gaza. The district court rejected the case, arguing, based on circuit precedent, that the ATCA is not applicable to corporations, and this was held up by the appeals court (Dodge 2019: 132). Eventually, the Supreme Court had to decide on this question again, after dodging it in the *Kiobel* decision. However, only a minority held that the ATCA was not applicable to corporations, while a majority believed this to be the case only in regard to foreign companies. Another minority held that the ATCA was applicable to both foreign and American companies (Dodge 2019: 132). Nevertheless, after *Jesner*, plaintiffs now must be able to show not only that the violation at stake occurred through the activities of a US company, but likely also that there was sufficient conduct in the US to satisfy the "touch and concern" requirement established in *Kiobel*. Thus, while corporations remain liable under the ATCA in principle, the threshold for mounting a lawsuit against them has become exceedingly high:

> So, while corporations continue to be subject to customary international law norms of human rights law, the prospects of holding them liable for violating those norms in US courts have faded nearly to vanishing point (Dodge 2019: 137).

How high the threshold has indeed become was shown in the Supreme Court decision on *John Doe I et al.* v. *Nestlé et al.* The case, which was brought in 2005, was dismissed in June 2021 based on the presumption against extraterritoriality (Chapter 14.5.1). Against this background, it is not surprising that attention has shifted to other jurisdictions after *Kiobel* and particularly after *Jesner*. While the US has become increasingly restrictive on human rights litigation in recent years, there has been an opposite development outside of the US. The following sections will provide a brief overview over some key developments and milestones in this regard.

12.5.4   UK: Common-Law Duty of Care

With the US becoming more restrictive on human rights lawsuits, the UK has turned into the most promising alternative jurisdiction for human rights litigation against companies in recent years. One important reason for this is that under Brussels I the *forum non conveniens* doctrine no longer applies in the UK. Therefore, the UK offers the advantages of a common law country, without mounting the obstacle of *forum non conveniens*.

Legal action can be brought against English companies as well as foreign companies if they maintain a presence in the UK, for example, through a branch office or a subsidiary that acts as an agent of the parent company (Zerk 2006: 118). Furthermore, cases can be brought based on customary international law, which is accepted as a part of English common law (Joseph 2004: 115), or based on the Private International Law Miscellaneous Provisions Act, which grants English courts jurisdiction over torts committed abroad (Joseph 2004: 115). The former commonly requires "act of state," which is applied more restrictively in the UK than in the US (Joseph 2004: 121). Thus, human rights cases are commonly brought as torts committed abroad. In such cases, parent companies are sued for the alleged violation of a duty of care toward the victims of human rights abuse.

In such "duty of care" litigation, a parent company would be liable, under the following conditions: a) the English court confirms jurisdiction; b) the parent company had a duty of care toward the victims; c) the breach of the duty of care resulted in harm. However, the burden of proof has been so high that no parent company has been held liable in an extraterritorial case to date. Nevertheless, the recent cases outlined below mark further progress toward corporate accountability. Before discussing them, the three conditions will be touched upon in some more detail.

a. *Jurisdiction*: On matters of jurisdiction, the UK is bound by Brussels I (Box 12.5), which grants jurisdiction to domestic courts for cases against companies incorporated in the UK. This holds irrespective of whether the tort occurred within our outside of UK territory. As mentioned above, Brussels I bans *forum non conveniens* as a possibility to stay the proceedings. Nevertheless, to date, all such cases in English courts have been decided on jurisdictional grounds or settled before they could be heard on the merits (Palombo 2019a: 271). *Okpabi* v. *Royal Dutch Shell Plc*, which will be discussed below, could become the first such case to be argued on the merits.

b. *Duty of care*: Whether or not the parent company owes a duty of care to the tort victims has commonly been assessed based on three aspects as established in *Caparo Industries Plc* v. *Dickman* and *Chandler* v. *Cape Plc*: First, that the harm was foreseeable; second, that there is sufficient proximity between the parties; third, that it is reasonable to impose the duty of care (Meeran 2013: 387). In regard to the second point, the relationship both to the victims and to the subsidiary that committed the tort tends to be relevant. In *Chandler* v. *Cape Plc*, the court established that the proximity between the parent company and the tort victims can derive from the proximity between the parent company and the subsidiary that committed the tort. In other words, the parent company can owe a duty of care to the victims based solely on the quality of the relationship with its subsidiary (Palombo 2019a: 273). However, the parent company does not owe a duty of care merely by virtue of being the parent company. Rather, the question is whether it engaged in actions that imply that it took on a duty of care (Meeran 2013: 390–391). There are no set criteria to assess proximity. In *Chandler* v. *Cape Plc*, the court ruled that such proximity was given based on the cumulation of various elements, such as the exchange of information between parent and subsidiary; group-wide empirical research on asbestos in the factories of the corporate group; guidance given by the parent company to the subsidiary; and the fact that the parent company set up the asbestos business and subsequently sold it to the subsidiary (Palombo 2019a: 274). Importantly, Cape Plc employed a medical and scientific officer who was responsible for overseeing health and safety across the group, which can be interpreted as an assumption of responsibility for the employees also of subsidiaries and thus as giving rise to a respective duty of care (Meeran 2013: 390). *Chandler* v. *Cape Plc* was seminal because it confirmed that parent companies can incur a duty of care over their subsidiaries. However, as Chandler was a domestic case specifically concerning employees of the subsidiary as victims, it remained unclear, first, whether or not such a duty of care can arise in transnational cases and, second, if and under what circumstances non-employee victims can be considered in a sufficiently proximate relationship to give rise to a duty of care for the parent company. The recent decision in *Vedanta Resources Plc* v. *Lungowe* (see below for details) has confirmed both aspects. Furthermore, it has broadened the proximity criteria that can lead a parent company to incur a duty of care far beyond what Chandler would imply to be valid considerations.

c. *Harm*: Tort cases against parent companies are based on the allegation of harm caused by negligence arising from the violation of a duty of care (Meeran 2013: 379). The duty of care of the parent company is interpreted as containing a due diligence obligation to oversee its subsidiaries and make sure they do not harm any of their stakeholders (Palombo 2019a: 270). Thus, plaintiffs must show that the parent company violated its duty of care by not meeting its due diligence obligation and that this failure to conduct due diligence resulted in harm. To prove a violation of the parent company's duty of care, plaintiffs must often also demonstrate the responsibility of the subsidiary that committed the tort (Palombo 2019a: 270). In such cases, UK courts will deliberate not only the case against the parent company, but also the case against the subsidiary. *Vedanta Resources Plc* v. *Lungowe*, which will be discussed in Chapter 12.5.4.1, is a case in point.

12.5.4.1   *Vedanta Resources Plc* v. *Lungowe*

The *Vedanta* case was brought to the High Court in London in 2015 by 1,826 Zambian villagers. The lawsuit was based on the claim that Vedanta's Zambian subsidiary Konkola Copper Mines (KCM) polluted soil and water through its local mining operations at the Nchanga copper mine, which resulted in health consequences as well as loss of income and livelihood for the villagers. The claimants argued that, based on its control over KCM, Vedanta should have taken adequate precautions to prevent the pollution from occurring and, by failing to do so, committed a tort of negligence against the plaintiffs.

What may strike some as unusual in the *Vedanta* case is that it was not only the British parent company but also the Zambian subsidiary that was on trial in the British court. It was on this basis that the defendants appealed the lawsuit based on jurisdictional grounds, alleging that the UK was not the proper place to bring claims against KCM. The appeal went all the way to the Supreme Court of the UK. The Supreme Court agreed in principle with the defendants that Zambia would be the proper place to hear the case, but argued that substantial justice would not be available to the plaintiffs in Zambia due to a lack of financial resources and legal expertise. As a consequence, the Supreme Court dismissed the final appeal in 2019 and ruled that the case could be heard in English courts. However, before the case proceeded to be argued in court, Vedanta Resources and Konkola Copper Mines agreed to settle the claims in January 2021. The settlement was without admission of liability. While this settlement can be considered a rare and important victory of communities harmed by corporate activities, not advancing the case to the merits stage also means missing out on the opportunity of potentially establishing an important precedent on the substance of the case.

Nevertheless, the Supreme Court decision to let the case continue in English courts contains a number of important implications:

First, because the Zambian subsidiary was a part of the case, the Supreme Court had to consider, at least in principle, if Vedanta might have a duty of care toward the claimants, that is, if there was an arguable claim against the parent company. This is because the claim against the parent company "anchors" the lawsuit in the UK and without a valid claim against Vedanta, there would be no basis to claim jurisdiction over the foreign subsidiary. The reason why the foreign subsidiary can be tried in the UK to begin with is based on judgment coherence and efficiency; since the court will have to assess the conduct of the subsidiary, as well, in order to reach a decision on the parent company's potential breach of a duty of care, it can claim jurisdiction also over the subsidiary in order to avoid irreconcilable judgments in two parallel proceedings. The subsidiary is then considered a "necessary and proper party" to the case and can be tried in UK courts. In other words, the Supreme Court had to consider the question of whether or not Vedanta might have incurred a duty of care toward the Zambian villagers already at the preliminary jurisdictional stage of the case and, at least in principle, it did not reject this possibility. This yields two further implications.

Second, while relying on *Chandler* v. *Cape Plc* in arguing that the parent company can owe a duty of care to those affected by the activities of its subsidiaries, the *Vedanta* case sends an important signal with regard to the validity of such claims being raised in a transnational setting. Furthermore, it assumes that such a potential duty of care holds not only toward employees of the foreign subsidiary but also toward third parties who are adversely affected by the affiliate's activities.

Third, breaking with *Chandler*, the Supreme Court argued that incurring a parent company duty of care does not presuppose exceptional circumstances, but should be assessed under ordinary principles of tort law. As a consequence, the Supreme Court established that a duty of care of the parent company can derive from a broader set of conditions, which include not only situations in which the parent company actively intervenes, takes over, or controls relevant activities of the subsidiary but also when it "merely" supervises and advises the management of the relevant operations (Roorda & Leader 2021). This includes situations in which a parent company sets flawed group-wide policies or where it creates a public impression of exercising control but fails do so in reality (Roorda & Leader 2021). This argumentat not only lowers the bar for courts' assessments of jurisdictional questions but also broadens the scope for the decisions on the merits of potential future cases.

In the concrete case, Vedanta argued that a parent company could not incur a duty of care simply on the basis of issuing group-wide policies and the expectation that a subsidiary would comply with them. The Supreme Court rejected this claim and instead outlined three general "routes" under which group-wide policies might indeed give rise to a duty of care (Croser, Day, Van Huijstee, & Samkalden 2020: 133). These are now known as the "*Vedanta* routes" (Roorda & Leader 2021). Accordingly, a duty of care can arise if a parent company (Holly 2019):

- has set down group guidelines that contain systemic errors that cause harm to third parties; or
- has taken active steps to implement guidelines in the operations of its subsidiary; or
- has represented that it has a relevant degree of supervision and control (even if this may not actually be the case).

Internationally, there seems to be an increasing trend to argue for proximity based on group-wide responsibility policies. In a recent case in Canada, *Choc* v. *Hudbay Minerals Inc.*, the court similarly accepted the company's public statements on due diligence standards and principles as an element of proximity between the parent company and the subsidiary (Redecopp 2020: 29). In *Garcia* v. *Tahoe Resources Inc.*, also in Canada, the plaintiffs argued in a similar way, though this argument has not been considered by the court at the time of writing (Redecopp 2020: 29). This trend may have positive and negative implications for future cases. One could see it as a positive that, increasingly, companies may be held accountable for the commitments that they make voluntarily. A danger that comes with this is that in the future companies may be more cautious of becoming closely involved with subsidiaries in corporate responsibility matters. In order to avoid accountability, they may pursue a hands-off approach or at least be less transparent about such engagements.

The implications of *Vedanta* have started to impact further cases already. While in the initial ruling on *Okpabi* v. *Royal Dutch Shell Plc*, the court dismissed the plaintiffs' claim for a parent company duty of care on the basis of the existence of group-wide environmental and safety policies, this decision was overturned by the Supreme Court in 2021 with reference to *Vedanta*. As a result, the *Okpabi* case can proceed to be tried in English courts, as discussed below.

12.5.4.2 *Okpabi* v. *Royal Dutch Shell Plc*

In *Okpabi*, inhabitants of the Ogale and Bille communities in Nigeria accused Royal Dutch Shell and its Nigerian subsidiary Shell Petroleum Development Company of Nigeria Ltd (SPDC) of contaminating their land and water, by failing to maintain their pipelines properly. The claimants argued that Royal Dutch Shell had a duty of care based on promulgating, monitoring, and enforcing group-wide health, safety, and environmental policies and standards (Roorda & Leader 2021). As in *Vedanta*, the claimants argued that SPDC was a "necessary and proper party" to the case and thus could be tried in a UK court as well.

The High Court dismissed these claims based on the argument that the claimants failed to make a convincing case why Royal Dutch Shell owed a duty of care to them and thus that there was no arguable case against Royal Dutch Shell as the parent company. Basing its decision on *Chandler*, it argued that the proximity criterion was not met, since the parent company was too far removed from the Nigerian subsidiary. As a "mere" holding company, such was the High Court's argument, Royal Dutch Shell only dealt with financial matters of the group and had no specialized knowledge in the operative business of oil exploration (Aristova 2017). As a consequence, the case against SPDC also had to be dismissed, since such a case against a foreign subsidiary would only be viable if it were "anchored" in the UK through an arguable case against the UK parent company. This decision was upheld by the Court of Appeal, which argued that even though Royal Dutch Shell designed, implemented, and monitored group-wide environmental and security policies, this was not sufficient to establish a level of control over the subsidiary that would meet the proximity criterion (Bernaz 2018).

The plaintiffs challenged this decision in the Supreme Court, which in February 2021 overturned the decision of the Court of Appeal. Relying on the *Vedanta* ruling, the Supreme Court argued that the plaintiffs did have an arguable case against Royal Dutch Shell and that the case could proceed in English courts as a consequence. Furthermore, the Supreme Court criticized the extent of the inquiry that the courts conducted to assess this question. In the Supreme Court's view, it was inappropriate to mount actual "mini trials" at the jurisdictional stage of a case, not least because crucial internal company documents are not subject to disclosure at that stage. Since plaintiffs cannot rely on disclosure rules at the preliminary stage of the case, they may not be able to present the full range of evidence if the courts engage in an extensive assessment of the merits at the jurisdictional stage (Bernaz 2018) – and this puts the plaintiffs at a disadvantage. Therefore, the Supreme Court was of the opinion that such a case should only be dismissed at the jurisdictional stage if it were demonstrably untrue or unsupportable (Roorda & Leader 2021). Similar arguments were made by scholars, who criticized the ruling of the Court of Appeal for confusing an "arguable" case with a "winnable" case. In their opinion, courts should avoid going too deeply into the merits of a case at the jurisdictional stage; it is not their task to assess whether the plaintiffs' argument is of the quality that will win the case, but merely whether their argument is sufficiently plausible to be heard (Bernaz 2018).

In sum, the *Okpabi* case represents another critical advance in foreign direct liability litigation in two regards. First, it reiterated and confirmed the broader perspective on the parent company duty of care applied in the *Vedanta* case, which improves both the prospects of claimants anchoring a case against a foreign subsidiary at the jurisdictional stage of a case and establishing a duty of care at the merits stage. Second, it lowered the evidentiary burden for claimants at the jurisdictional stage by clearly rejecting as inappropriate courts' practice of engaging in actual "mini trials":

> The Supreme Court makes it plain that courts cannot place unrealistic evidential burdens on claimants in parent company liability cases prior to trial, when so much of the evidence will turn on internal corporate documents which will only become available upon disclosure. Proving that a parent company exercised sufficient control over a subsidiary to incur a duty of care requires insight into the internal structure of a company, knowledge of decision-making procedures and governance frameworks, and how these have been applied in practice. Internal company documents are thus essential to making a case, which can only be obtained through disclosure proceedings (Roorda & Leader 2021).

On a more critical note, *Okpabi* again confirmed the problematic unintended consequence of incentivizing parent companies not to become closely and actively involved with the affairs of their subsidiaries. While it would be desirable for a parent company to exert influence and control to ensure its affiliates' compliance with group-wide human rights and environmental policies, the increased risk of litigation can lead them to do the opposite (Bernaz 2018). Depending on their design, mandatory HRDD laws (Chapter 12.4) could potentially be a solution to this dilemma, both by preventing such engagement being at the discretion of the company and also perhaps by including a provision that would allow companies to escape liability if they could show that they did, in fact, properly engage with the subsidiary on the ground.

12.5.5   Canada: Duty of Care Liability Continued

Canada is another common-law jurisdiction that has seen a small but steadily increasing number of BHR litigation cases (Simons 2015: 199). One reason for this is that Canada is home to a relatively large number of extractive companies that mine for metals and minerals both within and outside of Canada. Like *Vedanta* and *Okpabi* in the UK, Canada has its own recent breakthrough case, which the Canadian Supreme Court has allowed to proceed to the trial stage: *Araya* v. *Nevsun Resources*. However, like *Vedanta*, *Nevsun* was also eventually settled out of court. Some more elaboration on this case will be provided in Chapter 12.5.5.1.

Generally, Canada's BHR litigation experience is similar to that of the UK. To overcome the jurisdictional stage, plaintiffs must be able to show that there is a real and substantial connection of the case to the province in which the case is brought to court (Simons 2015: 199–200). Some Canadian provinces recognize the doctrine of forum of necessity, which allows courts to establish jurisdiction, even if that connection is not satisfied. Forum of necessity can be claimed if there is no other forum in which the plaintiffs could seek redress (Simons & Macklin 2014: 251). One significant difference to the UK is that, being located outside of Europe, Brussels I does not apply to Canada and thus the *forum non conveniens* doctrine is firmly in place.

Canadian courts, like their counterparts in other jurisdictions, are reluctant to pierce the corporate veil in human rights lawsuits against parent companies and consider it only in very limited circumstances in which subsidiaries act as agents of the parent company, or are entirely controlled by them while being used as a shield for fraudulent conduct (Simons 2015: 233). Hence, duty of care liability may be the most promising route to hold companies accountable for the human rights violations committed by their subsidiaries abroad also in Canada. Similar to the UK, plaintiffs have to establish a duty of care, prove that the violation of that duty caused harm, and establish that the chain of causation was not broken by the negligent acts of the subsidiary (Simons & Macklin 2014: 253–254). In order to assess the existence of a duty of care, Canadian courts apply the so-called "Anns test" deriving from *Anns* v. *Merton, London Borough Council* (1977). The Anns test requires a degree of proximity of and reasonable foreseeability for the parent company. Based on this, it asks whether there is a good reason not to impose such a duty of care (Redecopp 2020: 26). In the Canadian landmark case *Choc* v. *Hudbay Minerals Inc.* of 2013, the court argued at the jurisdictional stage that it was not plain and obvious that the test for foreseeability of the harm, proximity of the parties, and absence of policy reasons to restrict the duty would fail and allowed the lawsuit to proceed (Redecopp 2020: 26). The case has been ongoing at the time of writing (Box 12.7).

An interesting feature of the Canadian common law system is that customary international law norms are generally accepted as a part of Canada's common law. That is, while not pursued often in cases against private actors thus far, it is possible to bring cases directly for the violation of such norms, rather than only based on domestic tort law. *Araya* v. *Nevsun Resources* has set an important precedent in this regard. Hence, it is a landmark case not merely because it passed the jurisdictional stage, but because at least part of its claim is based on customary international law. Even more remarkably, perhaps, Nevsun's argument that customary international law does not apply to corporations and its subsequent motion to strike the respective claims in the case was rejected by the respective court of appeal and later by the Canadian Supreme Court. The momentousness of the case warrants a closer look, in Chapter 12.5.5.1. In addition, Box 12.7 provides a brief overview of two other important Canadian cases: *Garcia* v. *Tahoe Resources* and *Choc* v. *Hudbay Minerals*.

12.5.5.1 *Araya* v. *Nevsun Resources*

In 2014, three Eritrean refugees and former mine workers filed a lawsuit against British Columbia based mining company Nevsun for complicity in human rights abuses at its Bisha mine in Eritrea, which it exploited as a joint venture with the Eritrean government. The plaintiffs advanced their lawsuit based on common torts, but also based on the company's alleged breach of international customary law norms, such as forced labor, slavery, torture, inhumane or degrading treatment, and crimes against humanity, which are deemed a part of domestic common law in Canada. Nevsun advanced three grounds on which they sought to have the claims dismissed: a) *forum non conveniens*, b) act of state, and c) that customary international law would not apply to corporate actors. Both the British Columbia Supreme Court and the British Columbia Court of Appeal rejected all three arguments as valid grounds to dismiss the case. Nevsun then took b) and c) further to the Canadian Supreme Court, while dropping the *forum non conveniens* claim, after both courts argued that no real trial would be feasible in Eritrea (Redecopp 2020: 32). In a landmark ruling in February 2020, the Canadian Supreme Court upheld the British Columbia Court of Appeal decision, allowing the case to move on to the trial stage. The case was eventually settled out of court in October 2020, so no actual decision on the merits was made.

Most momentous about the Supreme Court's decision is its confirmation of customary international law as a potential basis for the claims against Nevsun. It confirmed, first, that as a part of domestic common law, the violation of customary international law norms is civilly actionable in domestic courts and, second, that customary international law norms that are binding on individuals are binding also on corporations (Yap 2020). Thus, while the merits of the plaintiffs' novel claims would still have to be deliberated, the Supreme Court at least confirmed that they

BOX 12.7 (Context) *Garcia* v. *Tahoe Resources* and *Choc* v. *Hudbay Minerals*

Garcia v. *Tahoe Resources* and *Choc* v. *Hudbay Minerals* were the first two extraterritorial BHR cases in Canada that overcame the jurisdictional and procedural obstacles and made it to the trial stage.

Garcia v. Tahoe Resources: The case against Tahoe Resources, a Canadian mining company, was brought in 2014 by seven Guatemalan villagers who were injured during a shooting while protesting the operations of Tahoe Resources at the Escobal silver mine in San Rafael de Las Flores in southeast Guatemala. The shooting was initiated by Tahoe's security personnel and ordered by Tahoe's security manager, for which he was later criminally charged in Guatemala, but fled the country before the proceedings could take place. The plaintiffs argued that the shooting was premeditated with the intention of suppressing local resistance against the mine and that the company ought to be held accountable for its negligence to prevent and stop it, despite knowing that local security personnel were routinely breaching the norms and standards to which the company had publicly committed. Thus, similar to *Vedanta* and *Okpabi* in the UK, the plaintiffs argued that Tahoe's public statements regarding oversight and mining standards on site, as well as the company's adoption of various soft-law initiatives such as the Voluntary Principles on Security and Human Rights created a level of proximity based on which a duty of care of the parent company could be established.

The British Columbia Supreme Court initially followed Tahoe's request to dismiss the case based on *forum non conveniens* in 2015. It declined jurisdiction, arguing that Guatemala would be the proper place to hear the case. The plaintiffs appealed this decision at the British Columbia Court of Appeal, which overturned the ruling in 2017, emphasizing the danger that a fair trial would not be possible in a Guatemalan court under current circumstances. This decision was again appealed by the company. However, the Canadian Supreme Court declined to hear the appeal, which meant that the case could go to trial. In 2019, the case was settled after the company was acquired by Pan American Silver, who also issued a public apology to the victims and the community.

Choc v. Hudbay Minerals: This case is representative for three related lawsuits addressing Hudbay Minerals' role in various human rights violations committed by its security personnel at its former Fenix mining site in Guatemala (the mine was sold to a Russian company in 2011). *Angelica Choc* v. *Hudbay Minerals Inc.* is about the brutal killing of community leader Adolofo Ich Chamán by the company's security personnel; *German Chub Choc* v. *Hudbay Minerals Inc.*

is about the shooting of German Chub Choc by company security personnel, which left him paralyzed; *Margarita Caal Caal* v. *Hudbay Minerals Inc.* is about the gang rape of eleven women by company security personnel during the forced eviction of their village. The lawsuits were filed with Ontario's Superior Court of Justice in 2010 and 2011.

Hudbay initially argued that the case should not be heard in Canada, but abandoned this line of defense in 2013, agreeing on Ontario as the forum for the case. Subsequently, the Ontario court ruled that Hudbay could indeed potentially be held liable for the alleged torts, clearing the way for the case to go to trial. At the same time, Hudbay's former chief of security at the Fenix mine, Mynor Padilla, was arrested and tried in Guatemala in front of a criminal court. He was initially acquitted of the charges, but this ruling was overturned by a Guatemalan court of appeal, sending the case to retrial. Active litigation against Hudbay in Ontario was briefly paused in 2018 in order to allow for settlement negotiations, but resumed in 2019. Noteworthy is Amnesty International Canada's intervention before the Ontario Superior Court of Justice, arguing that the court should draw on the UNGPs and other international standards endorsed by Canada in order to determine that Canadian companies owe a duty of care to those whose rights are adversely affected by the companies' operations abroad (Amnesty International 2017). Amnesty's intervention may foreshadow a generally enhanced role of widely endorsed soft-law standards and particularly the UNGPs in shaping legal proceedings in BHR litigation, particularly as it pertains to the definition and establishment of a duty of care for parent companies in the future. As such, it points to the wider trend of a "hardening" of soft law in the BHR field (Chapter 9.3). The three aforementioned lawsuits have been ongoing at the time of writing.

were far from baseless and might well succeed at the trial stage. In regard to Nevsun's claim that customary international law only applied to states, the Supreme Court stated the following:

> There is no doubt that in pursuing claims under CIL [Customary International Law], the plaintiffs face significant legal obstacles, including states' legitimate concerns about comity and equality and the role of the judiciary as opposed to that of the legislature. It is not necessarily the case, however, that the recognition of a CIL norm against torture as the basis for some type of private law remedy in this instance would bring the entire system of international law crashing down... If, as the Court suggested, the development of the law in this area should be gradual, it may be that an incremental first step would be appropriate in this instance. (*Araya* v. *Nevsun Resources Ltd.*, 2017, para. 196).

The *Nevsun* ruling is momentous not only because it sent the case, as one of only a handful of cases so far, to the trial stage. It also sends an important signal to Canadian companies that human rights norms may indeed become directly relevant in the future when it comes to their accountability for the impacts of their operations abroad (Yap 2020). Thus, despite having ultimately been settled out of court, *Nevsun* has important implications for the broader BHR movement because it can be seen as another indication of a slow inching toward broad recognition of direct corporate human rights obligations. While the UNGPs (Chapter 10) have established such a responsibility at least as a soft norm, developments in the realm of hard law and litigation trace a trajectory toward recognition of such an obligation, as well. While this may not yet be explicitly reflected in a potential new treaty on BHR (Chapter 13.2), the discussion during the drafting stage about whether or not to include direct corporate obligations clearly shows that state exclusivity with regard to human rights responsibility is at least not sacrosanct as a principle anymore.

12.5.6   Various Civil-Law Jurisdictions

Most extraterritorial BHR cases so far have been filed in common law jurisdictions, with an overwhelming majority of cases based on the ATCA in the US. However, there are a number of relevant cases also in various civil-law countries. Furthermore, the number of cases and the relevance of civil-law jurisdictions for BHR litigation is likely to increase with new BHR legislation being put in place and the US becoming less attractive for litigation due to the diminished importance of the ATCA. The following subsections will briefly touch on some relevant developments in the Netherlands, Germany, and Italy. While in France the new Duty of Vigilance Law provides a novel avenue for human rights litigation (Chapter 12.4.3.1), most cases outside of this new law so far have been based on criminal charges, which will be dealt with in Chapter 12.5.7.

12.5.6.1   The Netherlands

In the Netherlands, it is possible to pursue human rights claims against companies both through criminal and civil action. Criminal law does not differentiate between natural and legal persons and allows for the prosecution of corporations for all crimes. However, not all human rights violations are criminally actionable; it is only possible to prosecute for human rights violations to the extent that they have been defined as crimes in Dutch law. This explicitly includes international crimes such as genocide, crimes against humanity, war crimes, and torture, which are all codified under Dutch law. Criminal liability may arise also (and perhaps first and foremost) from complicity in such crimes (see International Commission of Jurists 2010: 6–9). The jurisdictional scope for extraterritorial criminal cases is narrow in the Netherlands and may be most promising in regard to such international crimes (International Commission of Jurists 2010: 20). Dutch civil law contains a noteworthy provision that makes the violation of a rule of unwritten law pertaining to proper social conduct civilly actionable. Leaving the interpretation of such rules largely to the courts, this provides an avenue also to bring human rights lawsuits against companies (International Commission of Jurists 2010: 12–15).

There have been a small number of civil liability cases in BHR in the Netherlands, of which two seem of particular relevance and moment, both concerning Royal Dutch Shell: *Four Nigerian Farmers and Milieudefensie* v. *Shell* and *Kiobel* v. *Royal Dutch Shell*. A third pathbreaking climate litigation case, *Milieudefensie et al.* v. *Shell*, will be elaborated on in Chapter 15.2.

Four Nigerian Farmers and Milieudefensie v. *Shell*: *Four Nigerian Farmers* is representative for three separate lawsuits around the same incidents in three different Nigerian villages. The three lawsuits are *Friday Alfred Akpan* v. *Royal Dutch Shell*, *Fidelis Ayoro Oguru* v. *Royal Dutch Shell, Oguru and Ofanga* v. *Royal Dutch Shell*. The cases were brought to the District Court of The Hague in 2009 by four Nigerian villagers and the NGO Friends of the Earth Netherlands (Milieudefensie) against Royal Dutch Shell, as well as its Nigerian subsidiary Shell Petroleum Development Company of Nigeria (SPDC). Similar to the *Vedanta* case in the UK, both the parent company and its Nigerian subsidiary are part of this lawsuit. The claimants accused the Nigerian subsidiary of poor maintenance of pipelines and wells and inadequate handling of leakages and spills, which resulted in the pollution of their land, water, and fishing grounds, and the parent company of negligence in making sure that the subsidiary operated properly and safely. Shell denied these allegations, arguing that the spills resulted from sabotage and that they had done what was in their power to prevent such acts from occurring. Since Royal Dutch Shell is incorporated in the Netherlands, the Dutch court established mandatory jurisdiction based on Brussels I (Box 12.5). In addition, the Dutch Code of Civil Procedure allows the merging of cases against two defendants if there is sufficient coherence between them and if it is expedient to hear them together, even if one of the defendants lies outside the jurisdiction (International Commission of Jurists 2010: 24; Roorda 2019: 148). Similar to *Vedanta*, the defendants argued that the case against Royal Dutch Shell had no basis and only served the purpose of anchoring the case against SPDC. The court rejected this argument and saw a sufficient connection between the two cases as given and thus considered the claim against SPDC as not entirely frivolous and cleared the way for the case to be heard, by application of Nigerian law. The court decided on the merits of the case in 2013.

The court was of the opinion that the plaintiffs' case for a duty of care of Royal Dutch Shell, modelled after *Chandler* (the reliance on UK precedent is due to the application of Nigerian common law), was not sufficiently supported, not least because its business is different and too far removed from the daily oil exploration business that SPDC was in. Thus, the case against Royal Dutch Shell was dismissed.

However, the court upheld one claim against SPDC. The court argued that while the leakages may indeed have been caused by sabotage, rather than a lack of maintenance, SPDC could be liable for negligence in taking reasonable precautions where such acts were foreseeable. It ruled that such conditions were given in the case of *Alfred Akpan*, while rejecting all other claims (Roorda 2019: 150). Both defendants and plaintiffs appealed the decision by the district court.

The court of appeal rejected the defendant's appeal on the question of jurisdiction in an interlocutory decision in 2015, and overturned the district court's decision on the two dismissed cases, arguing that under Nigerian law, SPDC was subject to strict liability for the damage caused by the respective oil spills (Roorda 2019: 150–152; Roorda & Leader 2021). Furthermore, it found SPDC's responses to the oil spills negligent, arguing that the installation of a leak-detection system would have enabled a faster response. On this particular point, the appeals court also argued that Royal Dutch Shell incurred a duty of care toward the victims, and ordered it to install such a system within a year. However, it denied a parent company duty of care both in regard to causing the spills and for the inadequate clean-up (Roorda 2021; Roorda & Leader 2021). The implications of this decision are notable far beyond the Netherlands: For the first time in Europe, a foreign direct liability case has resulted in an enforceable decision on the merits and for the first time a parent company was found to have incurred a duty of care towards third state claimants (Roorda 2021; Roorda & Leader 2021).

Kiobel v. *Royal Dutch Shell*: After the US Supreme Court rejected Esther Kiobel's lawsuit against Shell in the US based on a presumption against ATCA's extraterritorial application (Chapter 12.5.3.2), the lawsuit was refiled in the Netherlands in 2017. It alleges the complicity of Royal Dutch Shell in the Nigerian government's violent crackdown on protesters and the execution of Ken Saro-Wiwa and eight of his followers, among them Esther Kiobel's late husband, Dr. Barinem Kiobel. Like *Four Nigerian Farmers*, *Kiobel* concerns Royal Dutch Shell's Nigerian subsidiary, SPDC. In this case also, Royal Dutch Shell challenged the claims on jurisdictional grounds, but once again the Dutch court issued an interlocutory decision, arguing that the claims against the parent company, as an anchor of the case against the subsidiary, were not bound to fail at the outset and that there was sufficient connection between the cases to justify hearing them together. Subsequently, the court established jurisdiction over Royal Dutch Shell, its Nigerian subsidiary, SPDC, and two UK-based Shell subsidiaries. In this case, too, the parties agreed on the application of Nigerian law. However, after considering the merits of the case, the court rejected all claims of the plaintiffs except for one. It held that the allegations of complicity in the execution of "the Ogoni 9" were not sufficiently substantiated. The claimants alleged that Shell maintained informal contact with the prosecutor, bribed witnesses, and failed to use its influence for the benefit of "the Ogoni 9," among other things. Of those claims, only the one on Royal Dutch Shell's alleged bribing of witnesses was upheld. The court asked both parties to produce more evidence on this one claim before the trial could continue (Roorda 2019: 153–154). An interesting feature of the case is the claimants' allegation of Royal Dutch Shell's silent complicity (Chapter 4.3.2) in the execution of "the Ogoni 9" by arguing that the company should have taken a public stance against the executions and used its power to exert influence over the trial. The court dismissed this claim, arguing that Shell did not have an obligation to exert such influence beyond the silent diplomacy in which it engaged (Roorda 2019: 153–154). This illustrates the limited judiciability of passive complicity as outlined in Chapter 4.3.3. However, the court's negation of silent complicity does not mean that there was not a moral failure on the part of Royal Dutch Shell in this regard.

12.5.6.2 Germany

Germany has not been one of the major fora for bringing civil litigation cases against companies for their alleged breaches of human rights abroad. However, in 2015, a case against the German clothing retailer KiK received some international attention due to its role as a "test case" to chart the territory of legal accountability in Germany.

Jabir and others v. *KiK Textilien*: The case against KiK was filed by the European Center for Constitutional and Human Rights and four victims of a 2012 fire in the Baldia textile factory in Karachi, Pakistan, which cost 260 factory workers their lives and injured thirty-two more. The plaintiffs claimed that KiK, which was the main client of the factory, should bear responsibility for the deficient fire-safety measures at its supplier's factory, since not doing so would be a violation of their code of supplier engagement. The court accepted jurisdiction in 2016 based on Brussels I. Meanwhile, the ILO brokered a payment of $5.15 million by KiK to the victims and their families, which started to be paid out in monthly pensions in 2018 (BHRRC n.d. (d)). While KiK continued to deny any responsibility for the fire, the lawsuit against the company was eventually dismissed in 2019 on the grounds of the statute of limitations. The reason for this was that the court adopted Pakistani law for this case, which is subject to a two-year limitation period as opposed to three years under German law.

Another case, which is ongoing at the time of writing, is a climate litigation case. However, it may yield implications for human rights litigation, nevertheless. Box 12.8 contains a brief outline of the case.

It has proven difficult to establish extraterritorial human rights litigation cases in Germany and for the time being, also the new HRDD legislation, which was adopted in 2021, will not significantly improve the situation (Box 12.2).

BOX 12.8 (Context) *Lliuya* v. *RWE AG*

In 2015, Peruvian farmer Saúl Luciano Lliuya filed a lawsuit against the German energy company RWE in a German court, alleging that RWE's contribution to climate change threatened his home. The home was built in the floodpath of Palcacocha lake, which is fed by two rapidly melting glaciers. RWE is one of the major global emitters of carbon dioxide. Lliuya argued that the emissions of RWE's power plants contributed to the increasing local temperatures in the Andes, which put his property at risk from flooding or landslides (Agence France Press 2017). Lliuya sued RWE for compensation for a share of the costs he incurred in protecting his home against flooding. The share of the cost corresponds to RWE's estimated historical contribution to global-warming emissions. The estimate is based on calculations by the Institute of Climate Responsibility. The lawsuit was dismissed in 2016, which led to an appeal by Lliuya in 2017. Subsequently, the court of appeal considered the appeal to have merit and announced that it would hear the case and consult experts to measure RWE's contribution to the risks of flooding (BHRRC. n.d. (e)). The case is ongoing at the time of writing.

Discussion Questions:

(1) Can this case be framed as a human rights case? Were Lliuya's human rights violated and is there a connection between RWE's contribution to climate change and the potential violation?

(2) What should RWE's responsibility be in this case and what parameters or criteria does it depend on a) from a legal perspective and b) from an ethical perspective?

12.5.6.3   Italy

In Italy, a series of asbestos cases involving the Swiss company Eternit has received a good deal of attention in the BHR community. The former CEO of Eternit, Stephan Schmidheiny, was found guilty of involuntary manslaughter and sentenced to four years in prison in 2019, after a number of previous rulings with much more extensive sentences were overturned by the Italian Supreme Court. Since the case is based on criminal charges against the company's CEO and took place not in Eternit's home state but in its host state, it is of less interest for this section. However, there has been one extraterritorial civil litigation case in Italy so far, involving the oil company ENI. It is the first of its kind in Italy and thus may show a path for potential future litigation.

Ododo Francis v. *ENI and Nigerian Agip Oil Company (NAOC)*: The lawsuit against ENI was filed in 2017 by the Nigerian Ikebiri community and supported by Friends of the Earth for the contamination of creeks, fishing ponds, and trees through an oil spill in 2010. The oil spill resulted from a ruptured pipeline operated by ENI's subsidiary NAOC. NAOC initially offered the community 4.5 million Nigerian naira (in 2017 about €14,000), but the community was seeking compensation of €2 million (Friends of the Earth Europe 2018). The beginning of the trial was scheduled for 2018, but was postponed to give the parties more time to negotiate a settlement. Eventually, an agreement was reached. Specifically, ENI agreed to renew the community's electricity generator sets, renovate its health center, build a 2.5-mile (4km) concrete road, and provide electricity directly to the Ikebiri communities (Friends of the Earth Europe 2019).

12.5.7   Corporate Criminal Liability

Establishing corporate liability for human rights abuses based on criminal law can be an alternative to the civil lawsuits discussed above. Such criminal cases may commonly be framed as aiding and abetting liability, but also criminal liability based on duty of care violation or negligence is a possibility (Ryngaert 2018). Either way, criminal cases for human rights abuses against companies are still very rare and criminal liability in the BHR space generally is less well explored than tort liability. Some jurisdictions do not even allow for corporations to be held criminally liable – Germany is a case in point. Where criminal law does not provide for corporate criminal liability, it can at best be used to prosecute the individuals, such as the directors or top management, representing the company. Other jurisdictions may allow for corporate criminal liability, but only for a limited number of specified crimes, or with other limitations applying. In Switzerland, for example, corporate criminal liability only arises if it is not possible to mount a case for a particular crime against individual company representatives (Stewart 2014: 21). This was the case in the criminal investigation against the Swiss gold refinery Argor Heraeus in 2013, which was one of the first cases in which domestic criminal law was used to seek accountability for alleged extraterritorial human rights abuses by a company. The company was under investigation for money laundering in connection with pillaged gold in the DRC, but the investigation was closed in 2015, due to a lack of evidence showing that the company was aware of the criminal origins of the gold (BHRRC n.d. (f)).

Where criminal law is applicable to corporations, the burden of proof tends to be higher than for civil lawsuits. Beyond the lower burden of proof, the decisive advantage of civil action is that victims can mount their own lawsuits, while criminal law depends entirely on the willingness of the authorities to prosecute a company after a criminal complaint is filed. On the other hand, an advantage of criminal litigation is that as a public law response it does not depend on there being plaintiffs with sufficient resources to mount a lawsuit. Furthermore, the power imbalance between plaintiffs and the corporation is reduced in criminal proceedings where corporate power on one side is matched by the power of the state on the other (Clough 2005: 8–9). Another positive is that in most jurisdictions, international

BOX 12.9 (Context) Lafarge in Syria

In 2016, the French NGO Sherpa and the European Center for Constitutional and Human Rights, along with eleven former LaFarge employees, filed a criminal complaint against the French cement company Lafarge (after the merger with the Swiss cement company Holcim in 2015, the company became officially known as LafargeHolcim), for the funneling of money to the Islamic State (IS) and other armed groups by its subsidiary Lafarge Cement Syria in order to prevent it from having to shut down operations amid the conflict ravaging the country. The company allegedly paid a total of €13 million in exchange for safe passage of employees and products (BHRRC n.d. (g)). The Paris public prosecutor opened an investigation for financing terrorism and the Lafarge group, its Syrian subsidiary, and two senior executives and the former CEO were formally charged with complicity in crimes against humanity in 2018 (BHRRC n.d. (g)). It was the first time worldwide that a parent company was formally indicted for complicity in crimes against humanity (ECCHR 2018). The Paris Court of Appeal later decided to drop this particular charge. Going beyond a mere knowledge test to establish *mens rea* (Chapter 4.3.3), it argued that criminal accomplice liability would require the willingness of the defendant to take part in the perpetration of the crime, which it considered as not met. Importantly, however, it upheld the charges against Lafarge for financing a terrorist group, deliberately endangering the lives of its Syrian employees, and for violating a trade embargo. This indictment of the parent company is in addition to the charges against eight former executives, among them the former CEO of Lafarge. The plaintiffs appealed the court of appeal's decision on the crimes against humanity charges, which moved the case to the French Supreme Court (BHRRC n.d. (g)). In September 2021, the French Supreme Court overturned the Paris Court of Appeal's decision, meaning that the charges for complicity in crimes against humanity could be reinstated.

Discussion Questions:

(1) Was the Supreme Court's decision to overturn the dismissal of the crimes against humanity charge correct, in your opinion? Or was the appeals court right in applying a more restrictive test for *mens rea* than mere knowledge?

(2) If you were LaFargeHolcim's human rights manager, what would you do in order to prevent similar situations from happening in the future? What processes and instruments would you implement, and how?

crimes as defined by international criminal law are directly integrated into domestic criminal law and are thus directly relevant for corporate conduct (Stewart 2014: 40). In addition, some scholars have rightly raised the question whether seeking accountability based on tort law, particularly for severe violations of human rights, may not do justice to the severity of the harm (Stephens 1997; Stewart 2014: 53–54). While certainly important for victims, the exclusive emphasis on compensation payments in civil litigation proceedings may allow corporations to "purchase massive human rights violations" (Stewart 2014: 54). Therefore, human rights violations risk becoming a mere cost-benefit calculation or a cost of doing business. In contrast, the punishment and condemnation based on criminal law and the stigma attached to it may be more fitting when dealing with egregious abuses and atrocities. Thus, the underlying question is a deeply moral one: Do we want to merely put a price tag on corporate human rights violations or is their criminalization a more adequate response?

Criminal litigation as an alternative to civil litigation has gained traction in recent years, not least because the UNGPs explicitly encourage governments to establish "criminal regimes that allow for prosecutions based on the nationality of the perpetrator no matter where the offence occurs" (Smith & Lepeuple 2018). There have been a few cases in various jurisdictions to date. Most were dismissed, but some are ongoing at the time of writing. However, none have led to a company being found guilty of the respective criminal charges as yet. The most promising ongoing case in this regard is the case against Lafarge in France, which is described in Box 12.9.

12.6   Home-State Solutions: Criticisms and Responses

Many of the key developments in BHR in recent years have involved the extraterritorial application of policy, legislation, or adjudication by multinational corporations' home states. Yet this has not always been received with approbation. While proponents of this approach have applauded and some put much of their hope for multinational companies' improved human rights accountability into such developments, critics have rejected them as counterproductive and illegitimate. This section will present and briefly assess some of the key criticisms of home-state solutions.

12.6.1   Imperialism

One of the often-voiced, recurring criticisms is that extraterritorial home-state solutions amount to a new form of imperialism by Western states over the Global South. Critics lament that by extending their law, policies, and adjudication beyond their own territory, Western states are forcing their values and their legal systems upon other nations and thus are infringing on their sovereignty and their ability to autonomously design policies and regulation they deem appropriate to spur economic development in their own country. Two responses are commonly put forth against such criticism.

Universality of human rights: What such criticism seems to ignore is that at their core, home-state solutions aim at the protection of human rights, which are internationally recognized standards of universal validity. The key proposition behind the notion of human rights is that there should be limits to the sovereignty of the state. Thus, autonomy and self-determination should always be interpreted within the boundaries of respecting and protecting human rights to begin with. In fact, the autonomy and self-determination of human beings is dependent on human rights being respected in the first place. Thus, it is not about the imposition of domestic laws and values on foreign countries, but about the utilization of national legal, regulatory, and adjudicative tools to promote accountability for international standards.

Home companies: Home-state solutions aim at the regulation or adjudication of the conduct of parent companies, which are incorporated in the home state. This is not about telling other countries how they ought to treat their own companies, but rather about home states accepting responsibility for their own companies and making sure that they apply acceptable standards in their operations both at home and abroad. Not doing so would undermine the integrity of the home-state legal system, which would essentially allow multinational companies to operate based on a double-standard: While human rights have to be respected at home, they can be ignored abroad, at the discretion of the companies.

This raises the question of whether such solutions are an instrument not to advance but to curtail the imperialism that emanates from unchecked economic expansion and exploitation by multinational companies. Maintaining corporate impunity in the face of human rights violations seems to fit the narrative of imperialism much more closely than opening up domestic courts for alien plaintiffs in order to hold such companies to account.

12.6.2   Unintended Consequences

Critics of extraterritorial home-state solutions often argue that while such measures may be well-meant, their impact on the ground can be precisely the opposite of what the law or the policy intends. For example, one argument is that the laws and policies in question may increase the reputational or litigation risks for companies in doing business in certain parts of the world, which is why these laws and policies can lead them to withdraw completely from certain regions. This, in turn, may cause the local populations to be worse off than before, since they lose jobs, infrastructure, business opportunities, and other positive spillovers often connected to the presence of multinational companies. In addition, it is argued, once companies pull out of a certain region other ones coming in may have even worse environmental and social records, so making the situation worse than it was before. This criticism was touched on in connection with Dodd-Frank Act Section 1502 above (Chapter 12.4.2.1).

Proponents respond that it is precisely the point of human rights to define a minimum standard whose violation cannot be tolerated for the sake of economic gain. Even if a particular law leads to the decrease of foreign direct investment, maintaining economic activity at the expense of human rights is not a legitimate option. Furthermore, there is certainly a danger that the void will be filled by even less responsible companies moving in. But in and of itself, this does not make it acceptable for companies to be complacent with regard to their own environmental and human rights records. The standard cannot be merely to be better than the worst violators in the industry.

Furthermore, the withdrawal of investment and business also provides an opportunity for other companies willing to take a risk and build more sustainable business models and markets in the respective regions. For example, while some have criticized the withdrawal of businesses from the DRC region due to the provisions on conflict minerals of the Dodd-Frank Act (Chapter 12.4.2.1), others have pointed to the resulting increase of sustainable mineral exports.

12.6.3   Compliance over Engagement

Related to the previous point, those arguing for voluntary initiatives over mandatory laws and policies often state that the latter will increase the risk for companies genuinely engaging with local communities and other affected parties, since the closeness, active engagement, and interaction may expose them to litigation if things go wrong. We have seen above that in some lawsuits such as *Vedanta* (Chapter 12.4.5.1), courts may interpret corporate responsibility policies and engagement as a manifestation of influence and proximity, leading to an increased exposure to litigation risk for parent companies. As a consequence, companies may stop engaging and focus more on minimizing their own compliance risks. The focus, as they argue, then shifts from assessing the impacts on the ground to primarily ticking the necessary boxes in order to reduce the risk of non-compliance.

While this risk seems real, it is not necessarily an argument against legislation and regulation per se. Rather, it is an argument against legislation that does not carefully take account of such unintended consequences. In fact, specifically designed legislation may reduce rather than increase the risk of companies avoiding true and effective engagement. For example, an exoneration provision that allows parent companies to free themselves from liability if they can show that a particular incidence and violation occurred despite their acting with appropriate care and engagement can set an incentive in favor of, rather than against, company engagement. The more extensive a company's engagement, the more plausible its argument that it did what it could to avoid human rights violations. Hence, the critique does not discredit legislation and regulation as such, but is to be taken seriously by lawmakers and policy-makers, who want to set the correct incentives.

12.6.4 Frivolous Litigation

One of the most frequently voiced criticisms of BHR laws, particularly those including specific litigation clauses, is that they will lead to a flood of litigation cases and expose companies to the risk of being arbitrarily pulled into court proceedings despite doing little or nothing wrong. Such a critique is often voiced by business associations or the corporations themselves. The assumption is that business-savvy lawyers might find a lucrative new source of income in suing corporations for alleged human rights breaches abroad, which might lead to frivolous legal action for the sake of boosting the profits of law firms. As a consequence, companies would be tied up in costly, time- and resource-intensive legal proceedings over years even if the respective cases against them had only a slim chance of succeeding. Moreover, the sharply increasing litigation risk would negatively impact corporations' willingness to take risks, to innovate, and to expose themselves, which would stifle economic development and growth precisely in those areas where it is most needed.

Two responses can be given to this critique. First, any law that provides avenues to hold companies accountable for their human rights impacts ought to do so not only on paper but must also lead to actual legal action in practice. It is the very purpose of such laws that corporations will be sued in case of human rights abuses. Thus, the mere argument that corporations will likely be sued a lot more is not an argument against but in favor of such laws, since this seems to show the very need for them. Second, where the concern indeed relates only to potential frivolous lawsuits, the past two decades of human rights litigation practice seems not to confirm such a tendency. Even the ATCA, which was for a long time the only and most effective legal base on which to launch human rights lawsuits against multinational companies in any jurisdiction, has not led to the "flood" of litigation cases that critics are warning of. Mounting such lawsuits requires substantial resources and has not in the past proven to be the lucrative business that critics allege. As a consequence, most lawsuits are still brought with the support of nonprofit organizations, which do not have the capacity and resources to engage in arbitrary, frivolous litigation. Rather, they often have to focus on the most egregious cases, while other corporate human rights violations remain unaddressed due to a lack of resources.

What we have seen in recent years, instead, is a reverse trend: Corporations suing NGOs and human rights defenders strategically in order to intimidate them, tie them up in court proceedings, and thus to effectively silence them. Such so-called SLAPPs have become a notorious – some would say frivolous – instrument of large and potent companies to retaliate against human rights defenders who criticize them. As the BHRRC notes in a report on the topic:

SLAPPs drain the resources of those they target, often causing acute financial and psychological stress. Lawsuits can last for years, and the lingering threat of losing your savings or your home can be devastating. As HRDs [Human Rights Defenders] are diverted to deal with the threat of SLAPPs, the impact of their work is undermined. Companies often accompany SLAPPs with smear campaigns that destroy the reputations of HRDs and judge them guilty in the "court of public opinion," while making the HRD's colleagues afraid to associate with them for fear of being targeted. SLAPPs also put a significant strain on public resources, forcing national courts to waste their time and resources on superfluous legal processes (Zorob 2020: 3).

The BHRRC reported 2,152 attacks on human rights defenders worldwide between 2015 and 2019, of which 40 percent constituted judicial harassment. Such cases increased with an average rate of 48 percent every year (Zorob 2020: 3). In other words, frivolous lawsuits are indeed turning into a problem, but rather for human rights defenders than for companies.

STUDY QUESTIONS

1. What does it mean to say that the state's obligation to protect human rights is an obligation of means rather than of results? Can you illustrate it with an example?
2. What are NAPs and what are the four essential criteria that they must meet, according to the UNWG? What is the role of NAPs for the BHR movement?
3. What are three general types of BHR laws? Can you give an example for each one? Compared to other BHR laws, what makes the French Duty of Vigilance Law unique?
4. Why do human rights lawsuits increasingly target parent companies in their home states? Can you explain the difference between direct and indirect parent liability in this regard?
5. What is *forum non conveniens*? What role has it played in the past in BHR litigation?
6. What is the Alien Tort Claims Act and what is its significance for the BHR movement? How have the two cases *Kiobel* v. *Shell* and *Jesner* v. *Arab Bank* changed ATCA litigation?
7. What is frivolous litigation? What are SLAPPs and why are they of concern for the BHR movement?
8. In what regard can *Vedanta Resources Plc* v. *Lungowe* be considered a breakthrough case? How did it advance BHR litigation?
9. What is the significance of *Okpabi* v. *Royal Dutch Shell Plc* for BHR litigation at the jurisdictional stage?

REFLECTION QUESTIONS

1. BHR reporting laws have often been criticized for being ineffective. How would you design such a law to make it more impactful?

2. Can you describe the French Duty of Vigilance Law's enforcement and liability mechanism? What are the strengths of this mechanism and what are its potential weaknesses? What would you change about it to improve its effectiveness?

3. Some legal scholars have proposed a "corporate group liability principle" in order to overcome some of the difficult challenges in parent-company liability. What problem would this principle address? Are you in favor of or against such a solution?

4. There has been some concern that BHR litigation could lead companies to not invest anymore in certain high-risk areas, which could have counterproductive effects on those regions. It could also lead to even less responsible companies to fill the void. Do you share these concerns? What could be done to mitigate such unintended consequences of BHR litigation?

5. Some scholars have raised the question of whether tort law is an adequate avenue to litigate severe human rights violations, alleging that its emphasis on compensation payments risks turning human rights violations into a mere cost-benefit calculation for businesses. Do you share their view that criminalization of corporate human rights violations would be more adequate? What are arguments in favor of and against criminal law as an avenue for dealing with corporate human rights violations?

13 International Law-Based Solutions

After the previous chapters looked at the corporate accountability mechanisms of home states as well as corporate accountability in the domain of international soft-law initiatives, this chapter concludes the part on accountability by assessing international law-based solutions. While Chapter 6.2 assessed whether and to what extent international human rights law can accommodate for non-state actors and particularly for corporations, this chapter assesses more concrete solutions beyond the status quo. The negotiations by the HRC on a binding international treaty on BHR is the most significant development in this regard. This chapter will take a detailed look at the idea and prospect of such a binding legal framework. However, before doing so, some other potential accountability mechanisms in the realm of international law will be assessed, namely, international investment law and international arbitration.

13.1 International Investment Law and International Arbitration

International investment law regulates how states ought to treat individual and corporate investors who invest in their territory. Its purpose is to create a stable and predictable environment for international investors, most commonly multinational corporations. The main instruments of international investment law are so-called International Investment Agreements (IIAs). IIAs are agreements between countries on the terms and conditions under which companies or individuals from one country can invest in the other. Such agreements can have an international, a regional, or a bilateral character. Bilateral Investment Treaties (BITs) are among the most common IIAs. They are binding international contracts (i.e. treaties) between two states covering how each should treat investors from the other country. There are more than 3,300 IIAs, including BITs and free trade agreements with investment chapters (Columbia Center on Sustainable Development & UNWG 2018: 6).

While the protection of property and investment can be seen as an important element in the protection of the rule of law and the rights of investors, international investment law has come under increasing scrutiny for prioritizing the economic interests of foreign investors over the protection of the human rights of other, sometimes vulnerable, stakeholders in host countries. This is because states depend ever more on international investment to drive development and economic growth. Therefore, they are often willing to offer favorable investment conditions to international investors at the expense of social and environmental protections. Thus, while IIAs grant investors extensive rights and protections, very few also impose social and environmental obligations on them. In the past, hardly any of the thousands of IIAs imposed any obligations to respect human rights in the host state on investors (Simons & Macklin 2014: 340). More recently, a growing number of agreements have started to include human rights and sustainable development as policy objectives. However, such mentions still remain rather non-committal and tend to be located in the preamble rather than being formulated as actual obligations of investors (Deva 2018).

Among the protections for investors laid out in most IIAs are the so-called investor–state dispute settlement (ISDS) mechanisms. Such mechanisms allow investors to call on an ad hoc tribunal in case of alleged breaches of the treaty by the host state. This can be problematic from a BHR angle, because it can lead to conflicts between the host nation's obligation to protect human rights and its obligation to honor the investment treaty it has signed. For example, states may be taken to arbitration by international investors for imposing new social or environmental policies, which may restrict investment opportunities. In other instances, multinational companies have sued states, for example, over the requirement of plain packaging for tobacco products, over court decisions that held companies accountable for damage caused through their operations, or over measures adopted to address local opposition to investment projects (Columbia Center on Sustainable Development & UNWG 2018: 6). Thus, host states' policy space may be severely restricted by the conditions of IIAs and these conditions may limit the possibilities for progressive human rights politics for years and sometimes decades to come. With ISDS mechanisms, companies have an instrument with which to challenge the measures and regulations of states directly. One may object that it is the free choice of host states to sign these agreements, but such a view underestimates the economic pressures that poor countries in particular face when it comes to negotiating access to capital and markets. The power differential between the parties to IIAs can be vast, which is often reflected in the one-sided terms and conditions of such agreements.

Two kinds of possible solutions to address BHR issues are commonly discussed with regard to international investment law: The first is to integrate human rights provisions into IIAs; the second, to change the rules of international arbitration in order to put it at the service of human rights protection.

13.1.1 Integrating Human Rights into International Investment Agreements

Integrating human rights principles into IIAs is the most obvious and direct way of protecting human rights through international investment law. Host states that seek to attract investment should pursue a holistic approach; rather than pursuing investment narrowly for the sake of boosting economic growth, they should channel investment to build more sustainable and more equitable economies. This means that the powerful home states of investors in particular should not use their bargaining power to negotiate investment treaties that undercut the ability of host nations to protect human rights. The UNGPs ask states to ensure policy coherence in regard to human rights protection, which ought to apply also to the negotiation of IIAs. Principle 9 of the UNGPs even addresses IIAs head on. It asks governments to "maintain adequate domestic policy space to meet their human rights obligations when pursuing business-related policy objectives with other States or business enterprises, for instance through investment treaties or contracts" (Ruggie 2011a: 12). With regard to integrating human rights into IIAs, we can distinguish a defensive and an offensive approach.

A *defensive approach* makes sure that policy coherence is maintained and that IIAs are aligned with human rights law, do not conflict with human rights protections, and leave sufficient policy and regulatory space for governments to implement social and environmental regulations. This would mean, for example, that states abstain from including provisions into IIAs that help investors enforce so-called stabilization or exclusion clauses (Columbia Center on Sustainable Development & UNWG 2018: 16). Stabilization or exclusion clauses are provisions in investor–state contracts that prohibit states from imposing new regulations on the investors for a defined number of years. Often, such clauses are negotiated for durations of up to several decades. Governments ought to conduct holistic human rights impact assessments when negotiating IIAs in order to assess their compatibility with human rights law (UNWG 2017a: 22).

An *offensive approach* aims at directly integrating human rights responsibilities for investors into IIAs. They could, for example, entail provisions on how investors ought to conduct HRDD, or on how to set up grievance mechanisms for local communities that are affected by their projects. They could even go so far as to allow stakeholders that are negatively impacted by investors to bring claims against them. In 2016, Morocco and Nigeria signed an IIA that contained an explicit obligation for investors to respect human rights. It was the first time worldwide that any such agreement included an explicit human rights obligation for investors and it remains the only one to date (Krajewski 2020: 114). More common are statements in IIAs that investors should meet international standards on human rights and corporate responsibility on a voluntary basis (Krajewski 2020: 118).

The UNWG outlines three implications for human rights-compatible IIAs, which are aligned with the three pillars of the UNGPs (OHCHR n.d. (d)): First, based on Pillar I, IIAs must leave adequate regulatory space for governments and maintain a balance between attracting investment and promoting responsible business conduct; second, aligned with Pillar II, IIAs ought to include and spell out the responsibility of investors to respect human rights in all their investment activities; third, based on Pillar III, IIAs should provide access to remedy to individuals and communities who are negatively impacted by investment-related activities covered under a IIA.

13.1.2   Human Rights-Compatible Investor–State Dispute Settlement Mechanisms

The above-described current approach to dispute settlement arising from IIAs between states and investors has been subject to ongoing criticism mainly for three reasons.

First, it exacerbates the aforementioned problem of diminishing policy space for governments, not only because it allows investors (rather than their home state) to sue governments directly, but also because the dispute settlement mechanisms tend to be favorable to the interests and claims of investors. Over the last 30 years (1987–2019), as the UN Conference on Trade and Development (UNCTAD) has reported, 61 percent of all dispute settlement cases were decided in favor of investors (UNCTAD 2020: 5). The average amount of their claims was $504 million. Overall, investors have sued states more than 800 times through ISDS (Columbia Center on Sustainable Development & UNWG 2018: 6).

Second, and closely related to the first point, the choice and qualification of arbitrators have been subject to ongoing criticism. In ISDS, arbitrators are commonly chosen by the parties themselves, which has frequently raised questions about their independence and impartiality, as well as about potential unconscious biases and the conflicts of interests they may face. This problem is compounded if arbitrators are repeatedly appointed in different proceedings by the same party or by what is known as "double-hatting," that is, if arbitrators are serving as counsels or experts in other proceedings at the same time. This problem is widespread in international investment arbitration (Giorgetti et al. 2020). Furthermore, despite bringing highly specialized knowledge and expertise in the area of commercial conflicts to the table, they may lack the competence to judge broader aspects of international law if they arise.

Third, the dispute settlement mechanisms do not allow for third parties harmed by investment projects to bring claims against the investors, or participate in the proceedings. The third parties' only way of intervening is to submit *amicus* briefs in which they may address human rights (Krajewski 2019: 179; Steininger 2018: 35).

However, the acceptance and handling of such arguments is subject to the discretion of arbitrators and, accordingly, their impact on the proceedings remains unclear overall (Kube & Petersmann 2016: 91). As a result, negatively impacted communities frequently voice disappointment with ISDS mechanisms. For example, in an undisclosed case involving Indigenous communities in South America, a multinational mining company sued a state for revoking its mining concession. The local communities, which had protested against the company all along and whose rights were repeatedly violated, had no opportunity to participate and have a voice in the proceedings, even though their lives were going to be directly and immediately impacted by the decision:

> Community representatives were disheartened by the investment and dispute process, as they were left out of every stage of decision-making around the land and natural resources that they consider their sanctuary, their source of medicine, their place to pray, and, in some sense, their life (Columbia Center on Sustainable Development & UNWG 2018: 9).

Since third parties have no opportunity to bring claims, investment tribunals consider human rights claims in such proceedings only if either the investor bases their allegations on human rights, or, more commonly, if the host state bases its defense on human rights or raises human rights-based counterclaims against the investor. Furthermore, arbitrators can reference human rights without being prompted by the parties, for example, in cases in which the underlying IIA asks tribunals to consider "relevant principles of international law" for the interpretation and application of the IIA (Steininger 2018: 46). However, while there is a growing trend toward the referencing of human rights in investment arbitration (Steininger 2018: 35), such scenarios remain rather rare (Krajewski 2020: 121). Where human rights claims were raised in the past, investment tribunals were described as rather reluctant to accept such arguments and apply human rights instruments (Hirsh 2009: 109; Kube & Petersmann 2016: 86). The predominantly private character of investment tribunals and their emphasis on the private-commercial aspects of investment disputes have been identified as possible reasons for this reluctance (Hirsh 2009: 114). Symptomatically, investment tribunals are more inclined to pick up on (mostly property rights-based) human rights references if they are introduced by the investors, while they commonly reject references to other substantive human rights (e.g. Indigenous rights) raised by defendants based on a lack of jurisdiction or failure to substantiate such claims (Steininger 2018: 43; Kube & Petersmann 2016: 93–94). This illustrates the general critique that such tribunals tend to prioritize the interest of international investors over those of other groups.

Hence, ISDS is currently a tool to protect the rights of investors over any other party. Against this background, the lack of transparency and information around such proceedings and their outcomes has also been criticised, since it removes them from public accountability. While the awards are eventually made public, the

BOX 13.1 (Context) *Urbaser* v. *Argentina*

An often-discussed and potentially precedent-setting case in regard to the application of human rights in investment arbitration was *Urbaser* v. *Argentina*, which was decided in 2016 (see Kriebaum 2018: 26–29; Krajewski 2019, 2020). Urbaser S.A., a shareholder in a consortium in charge of water and sewage provision in Buenos Aires, sued Argentina for the termination of the concession for water and sewage services during the Argentinian financial crisis between 1998 and 2001. The government countered Urbaser's challenge by arguing that Urbaser failed to make the necessary investments in the concession, which was in violation of its commitment and obligations under international law based on the human right to water (Krajewski 2020: 123).

The tribunal confirmed its jurisdiction to hear the government's counterclaim, arguing that human rights were indeed part of the applicable law in the dispute, since the respective BIT contained a reference to "general principles of international law." Furthermore, the tribunal acknowledged that private companies may have international law-based human rights obligations, potentially opening the door for similar arguments in future cases. However, it denied that this implied that Urbaser had a human rights-based obligation to provide drinking water and sewage services in this particular case. Accordingly, the tribunal dismissed the government's counterclaim (Krajewski 2020: 124). Nevertheless, the tribunal did agree with the government that the concession agreement failed predominantly due to Urbaser's failure to make adequate investments. Accordingly, it denied Urbaser's claim for damages (Schacherer 2018).

For Kriebaum (2018: 29), "the case serves as an example for a tribunal finding that measures undertaken by a State to protect its local population against human rights violations caused by an investor's conduct did not violate investment protection standards" and that "in cases where the jurisdictional clause and the applicable law allow for it, a tribunal may be prepared to accept jurisdiction for counterclaims based on human rights abuses by investors." Generally, even though individuals cannot hold corporations accountable for alleged human rights breaches in front of investment arbitration tribunals, the identification of such violations by the tribunal can lead, under certain circumstances, to denial of investment protection, which can be an important deterrent (Kriebaum 2018: 39–40).

proceedings happen largely behind closed doors (Columbia Center on Sustainable Development & UNWG 2018: 17). This problem is inherent in arbitration, since confidentiality is one of the reasons why arbitration has become a standard mechanism for the resolution of commercial disputes.

Two principal solutions are commonly proposed to these issues of arbitration. The *first solution* is to drop investor–state arbitration from IIAs altogether. Brazil is one country that has done so and replaced ISDS with a state–state dispute settlement mechanism. Under such arrangements, investors cannot sue states directly anymore; only their home states can engage in arbitration. The *second solution* is to reform the existing approach to ISDS. In particular, a reformed process should be open and transparent, and it should allow third parties whose rights are affected by investment projects to have their voices heard and participate in the proceedings as a party. Aligning ISDS and IIAs more generally with human rights law would require also that arbitrators bring adequate expertise and qualifications in human rights to the table.

International arbitration has recently become a focus in the BHR field beyond international investment law, also. There has been discussion about the potential of international arbitration to provide access to remedy as an alternative dispute-resolution mechanism. This possibility will be briefly addressed in Chapter 13.1.3.

13.1.3   Arbitration for BHR Disputes Beyond Investor–State Dispute Settlement Mechanisms

International arbitration has been discussed as a possible way to provide a non-judicial, non-state-based remedy mechanism for BHR claims and disputes beyond the investment regime. The idea is that arbitration could provide an alternative forum for dealing with human rights violations, particularly in contexts in which judicial mechanisms are weak or non-existent. Generally, arbitration is a non-state-based mechanism commonly but not exclusively used for the settlement of commercial disputes between two parties who have agreed contractually to resolve their disputes through arbitration. Unlike mediation, arbitration does not aim at a consensual settlement of the dispute, but leads to a court-like judgment by the arbitration tribunal, which normally awards financial compensation to the winning party. The international enforcement of arbitral awards is governed by the New York Convention on the Recognition and Enforcement of Foreign Arbitral Awards. A unique characteristic of arbitration is that the parties choose the arbitrators themselves, which leads to one of the perceived advantages of arbitration for businesses seeking to resolve commercial disputes: Arbitrators have highly specialized expertise in commercial disputes, which judges are often said to be lacking. Furthermore, arbitration is relatively efficient in cost and time compared to lengthy legal proceedings.

Technically, whenever there is a contract between two parties, they can agree on arbitration as their primary way of settling potential conflicts and disputes. However, as discussed in connection with ISDS, the institutional set-up of current arbitration mechanisms does not lend itself to dealing with human rights claims. Among the frequently mentioned problems are: transparency and confidentiality issues; a general lack of alignment with human rights law; a lack of human rights competence in arbitrators; or that third parties, who get harmed without being a party of the contract, commonly do not have a voice in arbitration proceedings. Arbitration is largely designed for the settlement of private disputes and the public nature of BHR issues, clearly, can be at odds with this.

For this purpose, a working group has drafted the so-called "Hague Rules on Business and Human Rights Arbitration," an alternative set of rules specifically for the arbitration of disputes relating to the human rights impacts of businesses (Simma, Desierto, Doe Rodríguez et al. 2019: 3). Thus, any legal relationship (e.g. a contract) between any actors that includes an arbitration agreement can designate the Hague Rules as a basis for the respective proceedings. The Hague Rules build on the Arbitration Rules of the United Nations Commission on International Trade Law ("UNCITRAL Rules"), but adjust them with regard to their suitability to address human rights-related disputes. Specifically, as the Hague Rules outline in their preamble, the adjustments address:

> a) The particular characteristics of disputes related to the human rights impacts of business activities; b) The possible need for special measures to address the circumstances of those affected by the human rights impacts of business activities; c) The potential imbalance of power that may arise in disputes under these Rules; d) The public interest in the resolution of such disputes, which may require, among other things, a high degree of transparency of the proceedings and an opportunity for participation by interested third persons and States; e) The importance of having arbitrators with expertise appropriate for such disputes and bound by high standards of conduct; and f) The possible need for the arbitral tribunal to create special mechanisms for the gathering of evidence and protection of witnesses (Simma, Desierto, Doe Rodríguez et al. 2019: 13–14).

The Hague Rules are meant to be an instrument for companies to enforce the contractual BHR commitments of suppliers or business partners, but also an alternative means for victims of human rights abuse to access remedy (Simma, Desierto, Doe Rodríguez et al. 2019: 14).

However, despite these adjustments, not everyone agrees that arbitration provides a suitable and adequate platform for dealing with human rights claims. Some fear that while in commercial disputes between companies there may generally be a power balance between the parties to the dispute, large power differentials in BHR arbitration may be endemic no matter what the rules are. Others argue that, in line with the public character of human rights, they should not be subject to such private dispute settlement mechanisms per se, but only be dealt with in official courts.

13.2   Toward a Binding Treaty on BHR

Discussions around a binding global framework to hold corporations legally accountable for their human rights conduct have accompanied BHR since its beginnings. However, despite several such attempts, no binding international instrument has been adopted as yet. As outlined previously, an early attempt to introduce a binding code to regulate multinational companies at the international level was initiated in the 1970s and abandoned again two decades later. Shortly thereafter, the UN Sub-Commission on Human Rights proposed the so-called UN Draft Norms, which were rejected by the UN Commission on Human Rights in 2003 (Chapter 2.2). Both of those failed attempts had in common that they were supported predominantly by civil society organizations and countries from the Global South, but fiercely opposed by Western governments and the private sector. However, the momentum created by the publication of the UNGPs led to a new attempt to move toward a binding treaty on BHR. A drafting and negotiation process has been ongoing in the HRC since 2015.

Chapter 13.2.1 will first explore some of the key discussions around the possible contours of a potential BHR treaty. It will then consider some of the most common arguments for and against a BHR treaty and conclude with a brief outlook on the prospects of the ongoing treaty process in the HRC.

13.2.1   Elements of a Binding Treaty on BHR

A BHR treaty would be a novelty in human rights law. Human rights treaties commonly establish the rights of individuals or of vulnerable groups, most commonly against the state. However, a BHR treaty would not outline new entitlements of people, but rather deal with the regulation of corporations as non-state actors (Bilchitz 2017: 185).

A possible treaty on BHR could take many different shapes and forms. There are a few key elements around which the discussions tend to evolve. We will briefly touch on some of these elements, broadly distinguishing between those that concern the scope of the treaty and those that concern sanctions and enforcement.

13.2.1.1   Scope

With regard to the possible scope of a binding treaty, three elements are commonly viewed as being of particular importance. Those concern the subjects of treaty obligations, the kinds of corporations addressed, and the rights and violations covered.

- *State or corporate obligations:* Generally, there are two basic possibilities for setting up such a binding instrument. The first, more traditional option would be to stick to the state-centrism that characterizes international human rights law by not stipulating any direct obligations for companies in the treaty. Instead, the treaty would be limited to outlining and specifying the duties of states to protect human rights from corporate abuse and to make sure that companies are being held accountable for potential human rights violations.

This could be called an *"indirect model"* of a BHR treaty (Bilchitz 2017: 186). While states already have a binding duty to protect human rights at least within their territory, the task of such a treaty would be to specify such obligations in more detail and to address and clarify governments' extraterritorial human rights obligations in particular (Chapter 12.2), including the provision of access to remedy for victims of extraterritorial corporate human rights abuses. The second, more progressive possibility would be to abandon state-centrism and to assign direct international law-based human rights obligations to companies through the treaty. Such a *"direct model"* of a BHR treaty would essentially settle one of the key questions that has coined the BHR discussion all along, which is if or to what extent international human rights law gives rise to direct obligations for corporations.

- *Multinational or all companies?* Another key question with regard to the scope of the treaty is whether such an instrument should address all companies, small and large, domestic and transnational, or only apply to multinational companies. An argument for the latter possibility is that a key purpose of a BHR treaty is precisely to correct an imbalance between the regulatory reach of national governments and the transnational structure unique to multinational companies. From that point of view, the rationale underlying the treaty is predominantly connected to the transnational operations and character of multinationals. Opposing this is the former possibility, which argues that not only multinational but all companies can violate human rights, and not all governments are willing to meet or capable of meeting their own obligation to hold such companies accountable. In the case of the current negotiations by the HRC, however, the discussion of this question is political, rather than normative: Countries of the Global South tend to favor a limitation of the scope to multinational companies based on the concern that their domestic companies may be burdened unreasonably by treaty obligations; countries of the Global North, on the other hand, push for the inclusion of all companies, since multinationals are predominantly headquartered in their territory (Deva 2017). Surya Deva proposes a hybrid approach, which would regulate all companies but include special provisions tailored specifically to the characteristics of multinational corporations, such as a state obligation to regulate the extraterritorial conduct of multinationals (Deva 2017: 172–173). Irrespective of which approach is chosen, any treaty on BHR must pay particular attention to transnational value chains and the role of parent companies in ensuring respect for human rights along them.
- *Which human rights and human rights violations?* Another question would be whether to limit the scope to particularly egregious violations of human rights or to include all possible human rights violations. An argument for a narrow scope would be that a political consensus might be easier to achieve. Alternatively, an argument for a wider scope would be that focusing only on gross or especially

egregious human rights violations would put many corporate human rights impacts beyond the scope of any potential treaty. It is possible that even very common violations with corporate involvement, such as land grabs or forced displacement of local communities for mining and development projects (Chapter 5.3.1) would fall outside of the scope, if "gross violations" were interpreted narrowly (Deva 2017: 174–176). A narrow scope on gross violations would simultaneously limit the list of relevant human rights. The broader scope would include all human rights in principle. The question then is, which human rights instruments should act as the reference point for such a broad interpretation? Options here would be to focus either on the International Bill of Human Rights (Chapter 3.3.3), on all human rights treaties, or even to go beyond treaties to include also non-binding declarations and other human rights documents of particular relevance to corporate impacts such as the Declaration on the Rights of Indigenous Peoples or the ILO conventions (Deva 2017: 176–178).

13.2.1.2   Sanctions and Enforcement

If a binding treaty rather than a mere declaration on corporate human rights obligations is to be pursued, then such obligations ought to be enforced (López 2017: 316). There are several options for sanctioning non-compliance with a treaty, which can be included both cumulatively or separately. Possibilities include penalties, but also civil or criminal liability, which can arise both 1) for non-compliance, for example, with stipulated HRDD provisions, and 2) for actual violations of human rights that result from such non-compliance. Such a mechanism could be similar to the one laid down in the French Duty of Vigilance Law (Chapter 12.4.3.1).

With regard to the level of enforcement, a number of possibilities are commonly discussed. At the *domestic level*, a treaty should stress the obligation of all states to provide for adequate accountability mechanisms for corporate human rights violations in their territory. The most likely and realistic option to delegate the enforcement to the domestic level would be to include in the treaty an obligation for states to enact legal liability for companies that breach the norms stated in the treaty. However, knowing that institutions are weak and inadequate in some states, a treaty should clarify the extraterritorial obligations of multinational corporations' home states (Chapter 12.2). Without such home-state mechanisms (Chapter 12), remedy provision for many victims of corporate human rights abuse will remain unachievable; home-state litigation is currently the only realistic option and will remain important even if international mechanisms can be established. Thus, a treaty would have to include provisions for holding parent companies liable in their home states for the violations committed abroad by their subsidiaries and potentially their suppliers (Stephens 2017: 428). For that purpose, the treaty could presume a duty of care of parent companies for the activities of their subsidiaries and potentially include the possibility of exculpation in cases where adequate HRDD was conducted by the parent company (Stephens 2017: 429). This resembles the mechanism envisioned by the Swiss RBI (see Box 12.4). In addition, a treaty could mandate domestic legal reform to enable criminal prosecutions of companies for grave human rights violations and require that states allocate sufficient resources for such investigations and prosecutions (Stephens 2017: 431).

At the *international level*, a treaty body could be established to monitor whether governments and multinational companies meet their treaty obligations and to accept complaints from third parties (Cassel & Ramasastry 2016: 3032). Another more ambitious option, which is frequently discussed, is to expand jurisdiction of the ICC to include the prosecution of corporate crimes (Stephens 2017: 432). It could define the crimes that warrant criminal prosecution and clarify and harmonize jurisdiction over such crimes (Stephens 2017: 431). In fact, such a proposal was made by France in the lead-up to the ICC, but a majority of states were against such an extension of the ICC's jurisdiction. Perhaps even more ambitious would be to work toward the establishment of an all new International Human Rights Court with the competence and jurisdiction to investigate and hear cases of corporate human rights abuse (see Box 13.2), or an international civil court with particular focus on corporate human rights violations (Hamdani & Ruffing 2017:46; Stephens 2017: 433), that is, a specialized international BHR court (Cassel & Ramasastry 2016: 32–33). Another option would be to create an international arbitration tribunal to resolve treaty-based human rights disputes (Cassel & Ramasastry 2016: 34–35; Stephens 2017: 433). The potential advantages and disadvantages of such a solution are discussed in Chapter 13.1.3. Since the capacities of international courts and tribunals are necessarily limited and only a relatively small number of cases could be heard in such forums, they are to be seen less as an alternative than as a complement to domestic jurisdiction (Cassel & Ramasastry 2016: 45).

BOX 13.2 (Context) Toward a World Court of Human Rights?

In 2010, human rights scholars Julia Kozma, Manfred Novak, and Martin Scheinin (Kozma, Novak, & Scheinin 2010) presented a draft statute for a world court of human rights. The three authors did not do so based on an official mandate, meaning that the draft statute was meant predominantly as a conversation starter. Since currently human rights courts only exist at the regional level (Chapter 3.2.2), such a court would close the resulting gaps by elevating enforcement to the global level. Hence, the main focus of the court remains on the improvement of the enforcement infrastructure vis-à-vis states. However, a major innovation of their proposal was the extension of the court's jurisdiction to other entities, such as international organizations and certain non-state actors, among them most notably multinational corporations. Such entities would have to recognize jurisdiction of the court through a respective declaration. Since the proposal was not based on the existence of a BHR treaty, the different entities' declarations would also have to specify which human rights treaties they recognize for their conduct. Thus, similar to state consent in traditional international law, jurisdiction of the court is defined by what those actors voluntarily accept (Scheinin 2012: 489). The court would operate similarly to regional courts and accept complaints by individuals, groups of individuals, or NGOs, once internal and domestic remedies were exhausted. "Internal" remedies refer to a non-state entity's internal remedy mechanisms. This would set an incentive for corporations to build up effective internal remedy structures that could prevent potential cases being escalated to the court (Scheinin 2012: 489).

Discussion Questions:
(1) What do you think about the idea of establishing such a world court of human rights?
(2) What do you think about extending jurisdiction of such a court to multinational companies? What benefits and challenges do you see in doing so?
(3) Where do you see advantages or disadvantages to the fact that the proposed statute does not presuppose a specific BHR treaty?
(4) Is it realistic to assume that multinational companies would subject themselves to the court's jurisdiction voluntarily? What mechanisms could support this process?

13.2.2 Arguments For and Against a Binding Treaty on BHR

Even within the BHR community, there are differing views on the necessity or desirability of a binding international treaty on BHR. Some of the most common arguments in favor include the following:

- The most obvious argument in favor of a binding treaty is that voluntary frameworks alone hardly suffice to hold corporations accountable for their human rights impacts (Chapter 9.4). The imbalance in international law that tends to favor the interests and rights of companies over the human rights of affected individuals, as Simons (2017: 65) points out, cannot be corrected by a soft-law framework like the UNGPs, but rather requires respective rules at the level of formal international law. While the UNGPs may have achieved more than any previous soft standard, their uptake by both states and businesses is still far from what it ought to be (Simons 2017: 61–63), as, for example, a survey conducted in the context of Germany's NAP clearly showed (Chapter 12.3.1).
- At their core, corporate human rights violations are global or transnational problems that require a transnational solution. While states can address the

conduct of companies in their own territory, their extraterritorial reach is limited. Furthermore, governments have proven to be reluctant to embrace such measures, whether due to a lack of capacity or failure of political will. Accordingly, a system that exclusively builds on domestic approaches will inevitably remain a patchwork and leave ample room for companies to evade regulation. A global framework could regulate transnational companies directly, or at least make sure that all states were required to put respective rules and policies in place. It could create mutual assurance among states and companies alike and eliminate the incentive to free-ride on the commitment of others, and effectively create a level playing field. Furthermore, it could establish a system of mutual assistance and cooperation between states with regard to judicial proceedings, whether about the collection of evidence or the enforcement of judgments (Deva 2017:163)

- A treaty could work not only toward filling gaps in the international policy arena but also toward the harmonization of different national approaches, and thus create policy coherence both at the national and international levels (Leader 2017). For example, a treaty could address the above-described conflicts between international investment law and human rights by requiring that the interpretation of IIAs would have to consider their potential impact on human rights (Leader 2017: 82).

However, not everyone in the BHR field is automatically in favor of a binding international treaty. Caveats against a binding international instrument are commonly expressed along the following lines:

- One general argument against a BHR treaty, which is often leveled also against proposals for domestic legislation, is that such legalistic approaches may undermine voluntary commitments and initiatives in the BHR domain (Chapter 12.6.3). Specifically, in the context of the current treaty negotiations in the HRC (Chapter 13.2.3), the argument has been that working toward a binding instrument would stall the implementation of the UNGPs at both state and company levels. The new and lengthy negotiations, critics argue, create uncertainty for states and companies that their UNGPs implementation efforts may be futile due to the looming new rules. Thus, they may take advantage of the situation to wait and observe the situation, rather than to press forward with implementing the UNGPs, for example through new domestic policies and legislation. As John Ruggie has warned:

> [States] tend to evoke ongoing treaty negotiations as a pretext for not taking other significant steps, including changing national laws under pressure from domestic groups – arguing that they would not want to preempt the ultimate treaty outcome (Ruggie 2013: 59).

- For the former SRSG, John Ruggie, an overarching, all-encompassing treaty for BHR would be too broad to be effective and would inevitably remain a largely symbolic gesture. This is not to say that he was against the legalization of BHR at the domestic or even at the international levels. However, he argued that the international community should not strive for an all-encompassing BHR treaty, but rather for narrowly crafted international legal instruments as "precision tools complementing and augmenting existing institutional capacities" (Ruggie 2007: 839) and targeting specific problems and governance gaps in the BHR domain. His view was that such an approach would be both more effective and more likely to garner support and consensus among states.

- Finally, opponents of an international BHR treaty often point to the impossibility of enforcement. Some possible enforcement mechanisms were outlined above, but such suggestions are argued to be unrealistic in light of the fact that to this day states have not even come up with an effective system to enforce international human rights law in general (Ruggie 2013: 62–65). Even the task of monitoring the large number of transnational companies by a treaty body is deemed a close to impossible task (Ruggie 2013: 64). Without effective enforcement, such a treaty threatens to become merely cosmetic rather than leading to substantive change on the ground.

Having touched on some of the main arguments in favor and against a BHR treaty, this chapter will be concluded with a brief look at the HRC's current treaty negotiations.

13.2.3   Outlook and Prospect of (Current) Treaty Negotiations

In 2014, on the petition of the UN delegations of Ecuador and South Africa and co-sponsored by Bolivia, Cuba, and Venezuela, the HRC adopted a resolution to establish an Open-Ended Intergovernmental Working Group on Transnational Corporations and other Business Enterprises with Respect to Human Rights (OEIWG). The OEIWG was mandated to "elaborate an international legally binding instrument to regulate, in international human rights law, the activities of transnational corporations and other business enterprises" (UN Human Rights Council 2014: 2). The OEIWG was tasked with engaging in "constructive deliberations on the content, scope, nature and form of the future international instrument" (UN Human Rights Council 2014: 2) during the first two sessions taking place in 2015 and 2016 and to prepare "elements for the draft legally binding instrument for substantive negotiations" (UN Human Rights Council 2014: 2) in the third.

The compilation of possible elements of such a treaty, which was published by the OEIWG in 2017, foresaw extensive direct human rights obligations for multinational corporations. However, these were dropped altogether in the first complete draft of the treaty – the so-called "zero draft" – in 2018. The opposition against an approach that would break with the state-centric paradigm of international human rights law was too strong. Instead, the draft treaty focused on the obligations of states to hold corporations accountable for their human rights impacts. It addressed both the obligations of states to protect human rights in their own territory and their extraterritorial obligations to regulate corporate human rights impacts abroad and to provide access to judicial remedies for victims of corporate human rights abuse. The revised draft of 2019 and the second revised draft of 2020 left this approach intact and abstained from formulating direct corporate obligations.

The early negotiations were characterized by fierce disagreement over the scope of the treaty. While the EU in particular insisted on the inclusion of domestic companies by blocking and threatening to derail the negotiations at various points, Global South countries argued for the limitation of its scope to multinational companies. Furthermore, reservations and resistance against the process in general loomed large, particularly among Western governments and business actors, who feared that the process would slow down and undermine the implementation of the UNGPs. These concerns were shared by the former SRSG and author of the UNGPs, John Ruggie.

The latest draft of the treaty focuses on all businesses, rather than only on multinationals, and it covers all internationally recognized human rights emanating from the UDHR, the international human rights core treaties, the ILO conventions to which the respective state is party, and from customary international law. States must ensure that corporations conduct adequate HRDD and that non-compliance will be sanctioned. Furthermore, they must provide "for a comprehensive and adequate system of legal liability of legal and natural persons conducting business activities, domiciled or operating within their territory or jurisdiction, or otherwise under their control, for human rights abuses that may arise from their own business activities, including those of transnational character, or from their business relationships" (OEIWG 2020: Art. 8). This includes both civil liability, but also criminal liability for human rights abuses that amount to criminal offenses under international human rights law, customary international law, or their domestic law.

After six years of negotiations, the prospects of the potential treaty on BHR are still up in the air. The current constellation between those parties pushing the process forward and those stalling it mirrors the experiences with previous initiatives: Global South countries are largely supportive of the process, while Western countries have been critical of it and generally reluctant to engage constructively. There are hardly any provisions within the draft that are not subject to disagreements and controversies. Thus, divergencies between the different parties still dominate the process, which makes the ultimate outcome highly uncertain. While it can be seen as a success that the negotiation process is still ongoing, it is built on a fragile foundation. It is still far from evident whether the process will eventually result in a binding treaty and, if so, how strong such a treaty would end up being.

STUDY QUESTIONS

1. Why is the way that international investment law is structured problematic from a BHR perspective? How do ISDS mechanisms contribute to this problem?

2. There is a defensive and an offensive approach to solving the problems identified in (1). Can you explain both approaches and how they address human rights?

3. What does it mean to say that ISDS mechanisms are compromising governments' policy space? What other criticism is often voiced against ISDS from a human rights perspective? How could the problem be addressed?

4. Can you explain the difference between the "direct" and the "indirect" models of a BHR treaty? Which is the more traditional approach?

5. Why was the former SRSG critical of an overarching BHR treaty? What are three common arguments in favor of and against an international treaty for BHR?

REFLECTION QUESTIONS

1. Is arbitration an adequate remedy mechanism for corporate human rights violations? What are arguments in favor of and against it?

2. Should a potential international BHR treaty contain direct human rights obligations for corporations?

3. In your opinion, what impact would an international BHR treaty have on corporate human rights accountability? What would it depend on? Is a BHR treaty the proverbial "silver bullet" for which the BHR movement is looking?

PART V
Selected Industries and Emerging Discussions

14 Industry-Specific Issues and Challenges

After the clarification of the conceptual foundations both of corporate human rights responsibility and accountability in Part III and Part IV of this book, the emphasis of the current chapter will be on particular BHR issues and challenges as they arise in different industries, how those industries deal with them, and what specific policy instruments have been put in place to address those issues. The brief overviews provided do not aim at being comprehensive, but rather at giving short introductions to the prevailing challenges and solutions in some of the industries that are most exposed to human rights risks and impacts.

14.1 Extractive Sector

The extractive sector is perhaps the most notorious one when it comes to negative impacts on human rights. A survey conducted by the SRSG in 2008 showed that 28 percent of corporate human rights violations on record are associated with the extractive sector (Ruggie 2013: 25). The sector includes companies mining minerals and metals or extracting crude oil, but also companies further down the commodities value chain, such as traders, smelters, and refineries. Many of the persistent human rights issues in the sector occur directly at the mining sites, which is why this section will focus predominantly on mining and extraction-related human rights challenges. However, trading companies, refineries, and other companies further downstream are connected to such human rights issues through their activities and business relationships. They have a responsibility to identify such impacts through their HRDD processes and to adopt measures and use their leverage to prevent and mitigate them to the best of their ability.

There are various reasons why the extractive sector is particularly exposed to human rights risks. First, mining and oil extraction are long-term undertakings that require large investments in host countries and promise revenues, jobs, and economic development. This prospect can make governments unscrupulous, for example, in clearing mining sites of local communities and quelling opposition to such projects. Second, the large amounts of money and capital involved and the direct ties of such projects to the government officials who grant the concessions and set the terms and conditions under which mining can take place makes such projects particularly vulnerable to corruption and bribery. Corruption and bribery undermine democratic governance, the rule of law, and countries' ability to protect and fulfil human rights across the board. Third, resource-rich areas have often been subject to armed conflicts and violence, not least over who controls the resources. Such contexts of conflict are a breeding ground for human rights violations and for businesses it is often impossible to operate in such areas without being connected to or being implicated in the conflicts. Some minerals, such as tin, tungsten, tantalum, and gold, which are found in many consumer electronics, cell phones, and cars, are commonly referred to as "conflict minerals" because they are particularly prone to originate from conflict areas (Chapter 5.3.3). Similarly, notorious conflicts around diamond mines have led to a large part of the diamond trade being called "blood diamonds."

14.1.1   Issues and Challenges

Mining sites cover large areas of land and take a heavy toll on nature and the environment, often leading to irreparable damage. Destruction and large-scale contamination and pollution of land, soil, water, and air is endemic in the industry and can severely impact the health of local populations and negatively affect their livelihoods by destroying fishing grounds and agricultural land (Chapter 5.4.1). For this reason, mining and extraction projects are often accompanied by protests in concerned local communities. Such protests are frequently met with violent crackdowns by government forces and many communities face forced evictions and resettlement to make space for mining projects. Forced evictions are particularly problematic, if they concern Indigenous communities (Chapter 5.5.1). The UN Declaration on the Rights of Indigenous Peoples stipulates that any use of Indigenous lands requires FPIC of such communities. Forcing them off their territory without their voluntary consent amounts to a violation of their human rights.

Despite these challenges, mining projects also generate benefits for communities. They provide stable jobs and income, lead to improvements in the local infrastructure such as roads, hospitals or schools, and foster environments in which local shops and suppliers can thrive. However, the benefits are often distributed unequally. While some benefit from the opportunities that these projects bring to the area, others suffer the consequences of their heavy environmental toll. This can lead to inequality and conflict within the communities and undermine their social cohesion. Mining companies' investments in local infrastructure can also lead to increasing dependencies and diminish communities' autonomy. Furthermore, mining towns often experience a heavy influx of people, which changes not only their social fabric, but often leads to an increase in crime, violence, and other associated problems (Sovacool 2019).

A particular challenge in the mining industry is posed by artisanal or small-scale mining (ASM). Artisanal miners are individuals or small groups of individuals who engage of their own accord in the mining of minerals with very basic means, often by digging narrow and unstable tunnels into the ground through which they access the minerals. They do so often in informal and sometimes illegal settings, under dangerous and precarious conditions and without adequate equipment and safety gear. There are frequent, often grave, accidents, particularly when tunnels collapse and the miners are exposed to dust and chemicals that have a heavy impact on their health. Child labor (Chapter 5.2.1) is rampant in ASM. Because ASM still takes place predominantly in the informal economy, there are no adequate protections and child laborers are vulnerable to exploitation and often subject to violence and abuse. For some minerals, such as gold or cobalt, ASM is very common: 12–15 percent of the world's gold supply is mined by 10–15 million artisanal miners, of whom 4–5 million are women and children (UNEP n.d. (a)). Overall, artisanal mining provides a key source of income for approximately 150 million people in more than 120 countries (Much 2020). Considering the size and extent of the ASM sector, researchers and civil society advocates agree that any viable solution to the problems associated with it must point in the direction of formalizing ASM and making it safer and less precarious, rather than eliminating it altogether.

14.1.2   Sector-Specific Standards and Initiatives

A host of standards and initiatives specifically address the particular human rights challenges and issues in the extractive sector. Such initiatives can complement more general standards, such as the UNGPs (Chapter 10) or the OECD Guidelines for Multinational Enterprises (Chapter 11.1), in order to provide more targeted and specific guidance on such characteristic industry-related problems. Such standards and initiatives exist both for specific commodity types such as copper or cobalt and for particular issues faced at mining sites.

The OECD (2016a) has created due diligence guidance particularly for companies sourcing minerals from conflict areas. The *OECD Due Diligence Guidance for Responsible Supply Chains of Minerals from Conflict-Affected and High-Risk Areas* is the product of a multi-stakeholder effort involving governments, international organizations, industry, and civil society and lays particular emphasis on companies' responsibility to ensure that their sourcing practices do not contribute to ongoing conflicts at extractive sites. The OECD *Guidance* is also an important tool for companies to make sure that they comply with regulation concerning conflict minerals such as Section 1502 of the Dodd Frank Act or the EU Conflict Minerals Regulation (Chapter 12.4.2.1). The *Responsible Mining Initiative* shares this goal and provides companies with instruments that enable more responsible sourcing of minerals from conflict-affected areas. In particular, it offers third-party audits of the sourcing practices of smelters and refiners. An early initiative with a similar aim but with particular focus on the trade in conflict diamonds is the so-called *Kimberly Process*. It was established in 2003 and is based on a certification scheme that asks states to implement certain safeguards for the rough diamond trade and to conduct such exchanges only with other certified partners.

A couple of other standards address the role of private security companies in the extractive sector. The *Voluntary Principles on Security and Human Rights* ask companies that make use of the services of private security providers to conduct comprehensive risk assessments to make sure that their security providers do not violate human rights. The *International Code of Conduct for Private Security Service Providers (ICoC)* addresses private security companies directly and asks them to respect human rights in their business endeavors. Thus, the ICoC addresses the private security sector more generally, but bears direct relevance also for its intersection with the extractive sector.

A final initiative worth mentioning here is the *Extractive Industries Transparency Initiative (EITI)*. While this initiative does not directly address the human rights conduct of extractive companies, it asks both companies and extractive states to be transparent about the financial flows between governments and companies. By increasing the transparency of financial flows in the extractive sector, the initiative aims at the detection and elimination of corruption, which has contributed significantly to the industry's dismal human rights record.

14.1.3   Solutions and Best Practice

Despite the many standards and initiatives that address the problems and challenges the sector is faced with, the industry's impact on human rights remains problematic. As Meyersfeld (2017) argues, the living conditions for local communities often worsen during mining operations, despite the promises of the industry to create jobs and infrastructure. Meyersfeld calls this the "myth of mining." One of the key drivers to make mining more respectful of human rights and more beneficial for local communities is to protect and increase the agency of the local communities in the lead-up to projects and during their implementation and thus to distribute power between local people and the companies more equally (Meyersfeld 2017). The effective involvement and engagement of local communities is key when it comes to respecting human rights at mining sites. This means that local communities need to be integrated in every step of such projects and have real decision power beyond merely being consulted on certain issues. For example, they must have a real say in the negotiation of impact and benefit agreements, which set out the benefits that the mining project is supposed to generate for local people, and they must be an integral part of the facilitation and implementation of human rights impact assessments and grievance mechanisms (Kaufman & McDonnell 2015: 129–130). Furthermore, it has been argued that HRDD mechanisms should be enhanced and made more sensitive in order to identify and respond to conflict dynamics early on and to prevent their

BOX 14.1 (Short case) Formalizing artisanal mining in the DRC: Entreprise Générale du Cobalt

Throughout the DRC's history, mining has been critical to Congolese livelihoods. Its importance has been further amplified in recent times due to the increasing interest in cobalt as demand for electric vehicles and consumer electronics has accelerated (Chapter 14.3.1).

With an estimated 20 percent of the DRC's total cobalt output mined by the country's more than 2 million artisanal miners, significant efforts have been made to formalize the sector in order to combat exploitation and improve its safety and human rights record. Designated "Zones d'Exploration Artisanales" (ZEAs) were initially created under the Congolese Mining Code so that artisanal miners could legally mine in areas not suited for industrial exploration (Democratic Republic of Congo 2002). However, a lack of accessible sites kept hampering that effort. As a result, artisanal miners continued to invade mining sites belonging to private companies, risking retribution at the hands of private security companies and the police, or worked on private concessions where they had to accept exploitative conditions set by internal marketplaces that had monopolies on purchasing their cobalt (Nkumba 2020: 297).

Despite revisions to the Congolese Mining Code in 2018, there remained concerns surrounding the traceability of cobalt, and the mixing of artisanally mined cobalt with large-scale mined cobalt. In an effort to alleviate these concerns, the Entreprise Générale du Cobalt (EGC) was established in November 2019 and launched in April 2021 as a subsidiary of the state-owned mining enterprise Gécamines, with the aim of supporting the commercialization of responsibly sourced artisanal cobalt in the DRC (Trafigura n.d. (b); Entreprise Générale du Cobalt 2021). EGC aims to purchase, process, and sell all artisanally mined cobalt in the DRC, in order to improve transparency and accountability within the cobalt supply chain (Entreprise Générale du Cobalt 2021). For this purpose, it will assume total control over the artisanal cobalt sector and establish a monopoly right to buy all cobalt production and tie it to a responsible sourcing standard (Home 2021; Reuters 2021). EGC's state monopoly aims to combat exploitative conditions of private cobalt buyers and allows the government to keep control over artisanal cobalt output and thus to prevent cobalt prices from slipping, as happened in 2019 (Home 2021). To accomplish this enormous undertaking, EGC partnered with Trafigura and Pact, an international NGO, which have piloted a similar but private project at the Mutoshi mine (Box 10.1). A concern that has been raised is EGC's weak enforcement capacity (Reuters 2021).

Discussion Questions:

(1) In your opinion, what is the potential of the DRC's approach to formalizing the artisanal cobalt sector? What advantages to you see and what risks?

(2) If you were to manage the project of establishing EGC, what would you consider critical success factors that need to be in place to make it work?

(3) How would you bring artisanal miners on board with the agenda of EGC? How would you secure the goodwill of private mining and trading firms in the country?

escalation and the respective increase of human rights risks that comes along with it (Graf & Iff 2017). Crucially, communities must retain the power to say "no" altogether to extractive projects that they deem undesirable and not welcome.

Importantly, however, addressing human rights issues connected to the extraction of commodities requires a broader focus on the context in which mining operations take place. The root causes of many mining-related human rights abuses, particularly as they pertain to the situation of artisanal miners, lie in the poverty and often desperate living conditions of people, the lack of viable alternative forms of work, and the general social and economic vulnerability of the population. Any solution to the human rights challenges of the extractive sector must address this context in order to be sustainable. This includes the formalization of ASM and the provision of viable and safe ways for artisanal and small miners to mine. However, creating alternatives for local people to make a living beyond mining and thus decreasing their dependency on the sector must be as much a part of the solution as the direct improvement of working and living conditions at the mines.

14.2   Finance and Banking Sector

Doing business requires capital and funding. For example, extractive companies (Chapter 14.1) require large amounts of funding for heavy machinery, equipment, and materials, personnel on the ground, security and logistics, as well as for other key services connected to starting and maintaining such projects. The same goes for trading companies that buy and sell extracted commodities. Transporting and shipping large amounts of raw materials such as oil or minerals and metals around the world are tremendous undertakings, posing complex logistical challenges connected not only to the transport, but also to the storage and protection of the materials, as well as equipping, staffing, and insuring vessels. Another example is that of large development projects run by both private and public agencies, such as large dam projects, or wind and solar farms, which are highly capital-intensive and require large investments at the outset. Such projects, activities, and business models are only possible with banks and other financial institutions in the background to provide the loans and capital required during the start-up phase and throughout the projects' lifespan.

The funding activities of the financial sector have come under increasing scrutiny with regard to their human rights record in recent years. While the financial sector's indirect contributions and links to human rights violations have often been overlooked in the past, banks in particular are increasingly recognized as key institutions when it comes not only to contributing to problematic business practices but also to facilitating holistic, systemic solutions.

14.2.1   Issues and Challenges

The above examples already show that the banking and finance sector is closely connected to potential adverse human rights impacts that may occur within and through the projects and businesses they fund and support. More generally and in line with the UNGPs (Chapter 10), we can distinguish between human rights violations that the banking and finance sector causes, is contributing to, or to which it is directly linked through its business relationships. A 2017 working paper by a coalition of banks known as the "Thun Group of Banks" stirred some controversy when it claimed that banks generally do not contribute through their financial services to human rights violations emanating from their clients' operations. The paper argued that banks are at best indirectly linked to such impacts (Thun Group of Banks 2017). This provoked strong opposing reactions, including from the former SRSG, John Ruggie. The backlash eventually made the group rethink its position and revise the paper accordingly, acknowledging that under certain circumstances, banks' financing activities can indeed *contribute* to human rights violations. According to the OHCHR (2017: 7), such circumstances arise if a bank facilitates and incentivizes human rights violations through the provision of funding and finances, acknowledging that the difference between merely being linked to human rights violations and actually contributing to them is often not clear-cut (OHCHR 2017: 7). Generally, it is now widely accepted that banks, like any other company, can cause, contribute to, and be linked to human rights violations.

Banks can cause human rights violations directly within and through their core business, for example, through discriminatory lending practices (De Felice 2015b; BSR 2020). There have been cases in various contexts in which people have been denied access to credit and finance altogether or in which they were subject to predatory lending practices based on their race, religion, or gender. For example, during the subprime mortgage crisis, which later spiraled into the global financial crisis of 2008, marginalized groups were specifically targeted for loans they were unable to afford in the long term and which resulted in a large number of foreclosures on real estate in the US. Algorithmic bias (Chapter 14.3.1) in the financial models underlying banks' lending practices is often prone to perpetuate, exacerbate, or mask such discriminatory practices (BSR 2020). In addition to such core business-related causation of human rights violations, a bank may violate the human rights of its employees, for example, through abusive or discriminatory work or hiring practices (OHCHR 2017: 5). In this regard, a bank is no different to other businesses and is subject to the same risk of direct causation of human rights violations.

Perhaps even more pervasive than direct violations are the banking and finance sector's indirect contributions and links to negative human rights impacts through their financing and lending practices, as mentioned above. A concrete example is the financing of the Dakota Access Pipeline, a 1,172-mile (1,886km)-long pipeline project in the US which has been fiercely opposed by the Standing Rock Sioux, whose reservation the pipeline crosses. The pipeline project may impact water sources and threatens the integrity of Indigenous sacred grounds. The right to FPIC of the Indigenous tribe has allegedly not been observed. Seventeen banks have loaned $2.5 billion for the project, thereby facilitating rather directly the construction of the pipeline and thus contributing to the violation of human and Indigenous rights associated with it (BankTrack 2017: 4). Credit Suisse's involvement in the financing of the pipeline was subject to a complaint at the Swiss NCP (Chapter 11.1.2). The case is briefly outlined in Box 14.2.

According to the UNGPs, when a bank is linked to human rights violations through its financing, it has a responsibility to use its leverage to work toward the improvement of the situation. Banks are often seen as being in particularly influential positions in this regard and thus may be able to have a significant impact when tying their lending requirements to human rights criteria (De Felice 2015b: 331–332). This is one reason for the heightened attention that the financial sector has received in the BHR discussion in recent years.

14.2.2   Sector-Specific Standards and Initiatives

One of the most influential and widely known standards in the banking and finance sector are the *Equator Principles*. The Equator Principles focus specifically on project financing through banks. They address one of the most significant areas of human rights impacts emanating from banking and finance. They provide a risk management framework for banks to assess and manage human rights and other social risks as well as environmental risks in this domain. However, they point out explicitly that banks' human rights responsibility does not stop there but includes other areas of their business, which the standard is not meant to address. The Equator Principles reference the UNGPs (Chapter 10) as well as the SDGs (Chapter 15.1) directly. Special emphasis is put on community engagement and

BOX 14.2 (Context) Financing the Dakota Access Pipeline

On April 24, 2017, the Society for Threatened Peoples, a Swiss NGO, filed a complaint with the Swiss NCP (Chapter 11.1.2) targeting Credit Suisse's business relations and financial investment with companies involved in the construction of the Dakota Access Pipeline (DAPL) (OECD Watch n.d.).

The nearly $4 billion DAPL project acts as a key conduit for connecting oil wells in Bakken Shale – a region in eastern Montana and western North Dakota in which fracking had accessed billions of gallons of new oil – to valuable consumer markets in the Gulf Coast, Midwest, and East Coast of the US (Worland 2016). Designed with the aim of transporting up to 570,000 barrels of crude oil daily, the pipeline crosses the region of Standing Rock, a reserve of the Indigenous Sioux people (Society for Threatened Peoples n.d.). The project raised concern about threats to the main source of drinking water of the Indigenous communities, significant environmental damage in case of leaks, and the destruction of Indigenous sanctuaries. It prompted significant protests, bringing together thousands of people, including many Indigenous community members, as well as water and climate activists (Society for Threatened Peoples n.d.).

The complaint of the Society for Threatened Peoples with the Swiss NCP alleged that Credit Suisse's business relations with its clients violated its own internal policies and breached the OECD Guidelines for Multinational Enterprises (Chapter 11.1) by failing to carry out HRDD and to actively encourage its clients to prevent and mitigate adverse human rights impacts emanating from the project (OECD Watch n.d.).

The Swiss NCP saw itself competent to handle the case, since the main part of the case was about company policies issued by the company headquarters in Switzerland, but stated that it would handle the case in close consultation and collaboration with the US NCP (OECD Watch n.d.). The complaint was resolved after a two-year mediation process between Credit Suisse and the Society for Threatened Peoples, facilitated by the NCP (Mair 2019). The process resulted in Credit Suisse agreeing to update its internal guidelines on direct project financing in the oil and gas, mining and forestry, and agribusiness sectors in alignment with the key objectives of the IFC Performance Standard 7 on Indigenous Peoples (Chapter 14.2.2), which include the principles of FPIC (Chapter 5.5.3). The parties also agreed that the Swiss NCP would follow up with Credit Suisse to ensure implementation of its commitment (Mair 2019; BankTrack n.d.). Commentators welcomed the agreement as a step in the right direction, if only a small one. It remains to be seen what impact Credit Suisse's policy adjustment will have on its future project-financing activities.

Discussion Questions:

(1) The NCP case "targeted" Credit Suisse's financing activities, rather than the companies directly involved in the DAPL project. In your opinion, what are the advantages and disadvantages in addressing financial institutions rather than the companies operating on the ground?

(2) The mediation process between the Society for Threatened Peoples and Credit Suisse resulted in the latter agreeing to include FPIC with Indigenous communities in its internal project financing guidelines. What would this look like if implemented correctly within the context of the DAPL?

(3) There were mixed reactions to the agreement reached through the NCP mediation process. What is your take on the outcome? Do you consider it a success or a defeat for the BHR movement? What strengths and what weaknesses of NCP mediation are revealed through the agreement reached?

consultation with local and Indigenous communities as well as the importance of effective grievance mechanisms (Chapter 8.1.3.3).

The *IFC Performance Standards* also address project financing. They outline the social and environmental criteria to which clients of the International Finance Corporation (IFC) must adhere in order to receive funding from the IFC. The IFC is the private-sector lending arm of the World Bank Group. Among others, the IFC Performance Standards refer to the responsibility to respect human rights and establish some of the most far-reaching requirements regarding local community engagement and FPIC (Chapter 5.5.1). This is directly connected to the IFC's focus on large-scale development projects, for which FPIC and community engagement are core concerns from a human rights perspective. Because of their stringency, the IFC Performance Standards have also become implicit and sometimes explicit reference points outside of direct IFC investments. For example, private or public actors may refer to the IFC Performance Standards when formulating their own policies or their code of engagement with suppliers or strategic partners, or they may be used as a reference and as an interpretive guide to define the scope and content of other standards, such as e.g. the above-discussed Equator Principles. Not least because of their broader use, the IFC Performance Standards have become important reference points in the discussion on responsible finance more generally.

Perhaps the most widely known standard in the banking and finance sector are the *Principles for Responsible Investment (PRI)*. The principles were created by a group of institutional investors convened by the UN. However, the standard is independent and not a part of the UN organization. The PRI are a set of six principles (Box 14.3) aiming at the incorporation of ESG considerations into the

BOX 14.3 (Context) Principles for Responsible Investment

Principle 1: We will incorporate ESG issues into investment analysis and decision-making processes.

Principle 2: We will be active owners and incorporate ESG issues into our ownership policies and practices.

Principle 3: We will seek appropriate disclosure on ESG issues by the entities in which we invest.

Principle 4: We will promote acceptance and implementation of the Principles within the investment industry.

Principle 5: We will work together to enhance our effectiveness in implementing the Principles.

Principle 6: We will each report on our activities and progress towards implementing the Principles.

investment decisions of institutional investors and at the promotion of such responsible investment practices through the network of PRI signatories. Thus, the standard does not focus exclusively or even explicitly on human rights, but entails a broader perspective on social impacts. However, responsible investment has become a significant driver also of the BHR agenda and its importance will further grow in the coming years. By 2020, the standard counted close to 3,000 signatories, who sign up to it on a voluntary basis (Principles for Responsible Investment n.d.).

14.2.3   Solutions and Best Practice

As mentioned above, responsible investment has become a significant driver of responsible business practices more generally and of the BHR agenda specifically (Chapter 9.4.2). Generally, responsible investors use three different but complementary strategies to drive the agenda:

- *Negative screening*: The most basic strategy is to exclude harmful industries and firms from the investment portfolio. For example, tobacco, arms or the pornographic industry are commonly blacklisted from responsible investment portfolios.
- *Positive screening*: Positive screening goes a step further and only includes industries or companies in the investment portfolio that proactively pursue responsible business models and strategies and play leadership roles in promoting responsible business practices in their respective industries.
- *Impact investing*: Impact investing is even more targeted than positive screening. The aim is to fund specific projects and often start-up companies with a strong focus on responsible practices. As opposed to more general positive

screening strategies, impact investing must achieve a direct and measurable social impact. Impact investors often directly influence the projects and companies they fund.

While responsible investment has increased significantly and entered the mainstream over the past years (Park 2018: 237), a specific human rights lens is often still missing. This can be significant, since the positive social impacts generated through responsible and impact investments often do not guarantee that all human rights are respected (Park 2018). In order for this to happen, specific evaluative frameworks based on human rights are necessary.

Responsible practices in the banking and finance sector can have a ripple effect on the entire economy, since as an intermediary the sector provides liquidity, credit, and financing for the economy and so has significant leverage to drive the BHR agenda through the standards and requirements it ties to the provision of financial services. Financial data also provides a unique insight into business models and practices, which banks may use for targeted interventions. For example, human trafficking and modern slavery often leave distinct financial traces, which can help in detecting and prosecuting these practices. Salary payments, which are first transferred in and later out of victims' accounts can be red flags that point to modern slavery and trafficking. Banks can implement systems to detect such traces and train their staff, particularly those interacting directly with retail clients, to look out for such indicators (Van Dijk, De Haas, & Zandvliet 2018). They can then adopt measures not only to prevent their own services from being used to facilitate such crimes but also to report and combat such practices. As Van Dijk, De Haas, & Zandvliet (2018: 105) argue, "the banking sector is uniquely positioned to contribute to the abolition of human trafficking" and so has a responsibility to do this.

14.3   Information and Communication Technology Sector

The way we live our lives today would be unthinkable without the support and integration of digital technology. It has fundamentally altered the way we interact, communicate, and organize our personal, social, and professional lives. While the advent of this technology has brought tremendous advantages to our lives, the disruptions it causes also pose serious challenges at the same time. For example, control over the access and flow of information and over a rapidly growing amount of user data is increasingly in the hands of a few large companies in the tech sector. As a result, tech giants such as Google and Facebook have become exceptionally powerful institutions on a global scale. A third of all human beings use services and applications owned by Facebook. Google, on the other hand, accounts for about

90 percent of global search engine use (Amnesty International 2019: 5). This yields potentially large implications also from a human rights perspective.

The economy in general has become increasingly data-driven in recent years. Information about people's personal and social lives, about their preferences, routines, or tastes, enables businesses to design ever more effective, personalized marketing campaigns, to create tailor-made products, or even to develop entire business models running on such data. Not surprisingly, data has even been called "the new oil" of our digital economy. It is the fuel on which an ever larger part of the economy is running. To extract such data, companies access our lives ever more extensively. They track our activities on the internet and social media, they equip us with self-tracking devices such as cell phones, step-counters, or sleep-cycle trackers, which quantify our lives and provide a basis for their commercialization by businesses. Thereby, human beings are turned into mere "data subjects" by and for companies (Ebert, Busch, & Wettstein 2020: 9), their business models being based not only on consumers demanding their goods but also on the same customers providing their data. At the heart of this datafication of peoples' lives is a subtle but profound instrumentalization of human beings for business purposes, a dehumanization that risks undermining our autonomy and thus our dignity as human beings (Chapter 3.1.4.1). This raises a plethora of specific human rights challenges (Ebert, Busch, & Wettstein 2020: 9).

14.3.1   Issues and Challenges

Similar to the banking and finance sector (Chapter 14.2), information and communication technology (ICT) has come to play a key role in facilitating business interactions. Today, technology-based and data-driven solutions support almost all areas of business. Accordingly, the use of ICT can facilitate and potentially accentuate and aggravate certain business-related human rights impacts; simultaneously, the use and development particularly of nascent digital technologies pose all-new human rights challenges that are often difficult to identify and to which adequate responses are only starting to be discussed and developed. The following paragraphs outline just a small sample of possible issues and challenges connected particularly to the rise of "big data" and the emergence of artificial intelligence (AI). They can be clustered in four broad categories of human rights challenges relating to the human right to privacy, freedom of expression, non-discrimination, and labor and employment issues.

Surveillance and privacy: Our human right to privacy is protected under Article 12 of the UDHR and Article 17 of the ICCPR. The threat to privacy is perhaps the most immediate and intuitive human rights concern emanating from the datafication of the economy. The extensive tracking of our activities, as well as the collecting, storing, sharing, and trading of our data by companies pose new and previously unknown risks to our privacy. What is now known as the "Cambridge

Analytica scandal" provided a glimpse of the dimensions of this problem. Cambridge Analytica obtained data from Facebook on millions of its users in order to target them with political messages and thus to influence their voting behavior in the 2016 US presidential elections. The case made it clear how unprotected online user data is from access by third parties and how such data can be used not only for private interests but also for influencing the way we think and behave in subtle ways. Depending on who will get access to such data, the consequences of privacy breaches can be disastrous. One famous case, which is now seen as a "tipping point for public concern over the Internet and risks of corporate complicity" (Samway 2016: 137) involved the tech company Yahoo!. In 2004, Yahoo! complied with a request to provide the Chinese government with user account data of the Chinese dissident Shi Tao, who was subsequently jailed as a political prisoner for ten years (Samway 2016: 137). The sophisticated possibilities of identifying, tracking, and surveilling people that new digital technologies are offering provide new opportunities for authoritarian governments to get an ever tighter grip on their populations.

Yet it is not only governments that are using such technology for surveillance. Companies also increasingly rely on ever more intrusive tech solutions to track the work performance and productivity of their employees, for example, by constantly monitoring their keyboard activity. Some authors have been speaking of an age of "surveillance capitalism" in this regard (Zuboff 2015, 2019). The use of technology for such purposes raises new challenges for the companies developing and offering it. For example, companies developing facial recognition technology or other tracking devices may be linked to human rights violations if the technologies are used for problematic purposes. Therefore, the due diligence efforts of such companies must increasingly account for the potential use of their products and services to undermine human rights and democracy.

Hate propaganda and freedom of expression and information: Social media, messaging services, and chat platforms have been used to spread discriminatory and hate propaganda, for stalking purposes, and for cyberbullying, in some cases with fatal consequences. They have also facilitated the rise and rapid spread of so-called "fake news," that is, systematic misinformation campaigns with the aim of undermining and delegitimizing fact-based policy and decision-making and of mobilizing crowds based on populist propaganda. Previously, platform and social media companies have argued that they are not responsible for the content that is posted and spread through their services. However, this position has increasingly been criticized, because the problematic consequences of the unmonitored and unrestricted use of such media have become visible. As a consequence, social media companies and platforms have stepped up their efforts to moderate the content, but the sheer volume of items to control poses unprecedented challenges. In addition, there is a fine line that tech companies ought to navigate between restricting harmful and discriminatory content and interfering with people's freedom of expression. There is no standard answer as to where this line needs to be drawn; it requires careful deliberation on a case-by-case basis. Again, this raises a challenge of capacity, resources, and not least the human rights expertise of companies. Some of them, such as Facebook, have responded to the challenge by creating human rights positions and implementing human rights oversight boards that review content moderation decisions.

Bias and discrimination: However, it is not only the use of new technologies for problematic purposes that poses human rights challenges. Solutions and applications based on AI technology often run on algorithms, which contain systematic biases and lack an integration of human rights considerations. For example, intelligent technology used to support law enforcement and predictive policing, which attempts to identify trends and forecasts in crime, may be based on historic crime datasets that are systematically biased against certain demographics. Similar biases, for example, against minorities or women, can be built into software that supports companies' recruiting processes (Ebert, Busch, & Wettstein 2020: 12). Similarly, if occupational health and safety measures are designed on the basis of historical data predominantly relating to male employees and their respective physiognomy and health features, it can result in measures that offer suboptimal protection for women (Criado Perez 2019). More generally, AI models that run on historic training data are prone to replicate and consolidate pre-existing injustices and power imbalances and thus potentially perpetuate rather than combat existing human rights challenges.

Labor and employment issues: A broader problem connected to the ICT sector relates to the implications of new technologies for labor and work more generally. The advancement of AI and automation creates new opportunities for companies in various sectors to reorganize their value and supply chains and potentially replace workers, particularly in labor-intensive industries, with automated systems. This threatens the livelihoods of millions of low-wage workers, particularly – but not only – in the Global South. Further technology-driven disruptions of labor relations occur in the so-called "gig economy," where platform organization has enabled tech companies to circumvent labor regulations and designate workers as independent contractors in order to deny them basic employment protections and benefits.

Finally, the tech industry is facing human rights challenges not only in regard to its design and use of software but also in regard to the conditions of production and disposal of hardware. For example, most electronic devices and batteries in particular contain cobalt, which is mined predominantly in the DRC often under precarious and dangerous conditions (Chapter 14.1.1). Thus, the supply chains of most electronic products are inherently connected to human rights issues in the mines in which the minerals and metals, which will find their way into electronic devices, are extracted. Problems occur also with regard to the disposal of such products. "Electronic waste" is often shipped for disposal to countries in the Global South, where it is dumped in vast landfills. Local people have come to find an opportunity in disassembling such electronic waste in the search for the precious metals contained in them. The extraction of such metals exposes them to poisonous gases and substances that can severely impact their health.

14.3.2   Sector-Specific Standards and Initiatives

A number of standards and initiatives have been developed with the aim of addressing the specific challenges facing the ICT sector. The most prominent one certainly is the *Global Network Initiative* (*GNI*). A further interesting initiative worth mentioning here is the *Partnership on AI*. Finally, the *OECD AI Principles* are the first AI standard that addresses governments.

The *GNI* is a multi-stakeholder platform put in place in 2008 in response to the mounting challenges that tech companies faced with governments requesting user data, censoring content, or restricting user access to their services and to the internet. Thus, GNI is an industry initiative aspiring to set a global standard for responsible company decision-making, emphasizing respect of digital rights and privacy, and the promotion of freedom of expression in challenging contexts. Members include some of the largest and most influential tech and social media companies as well as civil society and academic organizations, human rights advocacy groups, and investors. GNI is based on four pillars: 1) foster accountability to generate trust; 2) provide a framework to enable responsible decision-making; 3) enable learning to shape best practices; 4) empower policy that promotes human rights. At the heart of the initiative are the GNI principles, which outline company responsibilities in the areas of privacy protection, promotion of freedom of expression, responsible decision-making, and stakeholder collaboration, as well as governance, accountability, and transparency. In addition, the GNI provides more concrete implementation guidelines for these principles. Implementation of the principles is periodically assessed by independent assessors (Samway 2016).

The *Partnership on AI* is a multi-stakeholder initiative bringing together tech companies, civil society organizations, and academic institutions to foster and explore AI's potential as a source of benefit for people and society. The initiative is not focused specifically on human rights issues, but adopts a broader perspective on security, privacy, transparency, and fairness. However, many of the thematic areas and issues addressed by the Partnership deal with human rights at their core. The initiative pursues four specific goals: 1) develop and share best practices with regard to the inclusivity, fairness, transparency, and generally the ethics of AI technology; 2) advance the wider public understanding and awareness of AI through thought leadership and the facilitation of dialogue; 3) provide an open and inclusive platform for multi-stakeholder discussion and engagement; 4) identify

BOX 14.4 (Context) Global Network Initiative Principles

(1) *Freedom of expression*

- Participating companies will respect and work to protect the freedom of expression of their users by seeking to avoid or minimize the impact of government restrictions on freedom of expression, including restrictions on the information available to users and the opportunities for users to create and communicate ideas and information, regardless of frontiers or media of communication.
- Participating companies will respect and work to protect the freedom of expression rights of users when confronted with government demands, laws, and regulations to suppress freedom of expression, remove content, or otherwise limit access to communications, ideas, and information in a manner inconsistent with internationally recognized laws and standards.

(2) *Privacy*

- Participating companies will employ protections with respect to personal information in all countries where they operate in order to work to protect the privacy rights of users.
- Participating companies will respect and work to protect the privacy rights of users when confronted with government demands, laws, or regulations that compromise privacy in a manner inconsistent with internationally recognized laws and standards.

(3) *Responsible company decision-making*

- Participating companies will ensure that the company board, senior officers, and others responsible for key decisions that impact freedom of expression and privacy are fully informed of these Principles and how they may be best advanced.
- Participating companies will identify circumstances where freedom of expression and privacy may be jeopardized or advanced, and integrate these Principles into their decision-making in these circumstances.
- Participating companies, when implementing these Principles, will always seek to ensure the safety and liberty of company personnel who may be placed at risk.
- Participating companies will implement these Principles when they have operational control. When they do not have operational control, participating companies will use best efforts to ensure that business partners, investments, suppliers, distributors, and other relevant related parties follow these Principles.

(4) *Multi-stakeholder collaboration*
- Participants will take a collaborative approach to problem-solving and explore new ways in which the collective learning from multiple stakeholders can be used to advance freedom of expression and privacy.
- Individually and collectively, participants will engage governments and international institutions to promote the rule of law and the adoption of laws, policies, and practices that protect, respect, and fulfil freedom of expression and privacy.

(5) *Governance, accountability, and transparency*
- Participants will adhere to a collectively determined governance structure that defines the roles and responsibilities of participants, ensures accountability, and promotes the advancement of these Principles.
- Participants will be held accountable through a system of (a) transparency with the public and (b) independent assessment and evaluation of the implementation of these Principles.

and foster aspirational efforts and areas of untapped opportunity in AI for socially beneficial purposes.

In 2019, the *OECD Principles on AI* were launched. The OECD Principles are, in contrast to the above-mentioned initiatives, government-backed and endorsed. They have been endorsed by OECD member countries as well as a number of non-members. The OECD Principles on AI promote AI solutions that respect human rights and democratic values. More specifically, they ask governments to facilitate public and private investment in the development of trustworthy AI, to create an environment conducive to the development of trustworthy AI, foster accessibility of AI ecosystems, ensure a policy environment that is favorable to trustworthy AI, make sure people will have the rights skills as well as cooperate across borders to advance trustworthy AI.

14.3.3   Solutions and Best Practice

The tech sector has entered the BHR discourse with some delay. However, growing awareness regarding the sector's heightened exposure to human rights issues and risks have led to an accelerating discussion in recent years. As a consequence, tech companies have started to address both the risks and the positive potential connected to their operations.

Addressing negative impacts: In order to address the various negative human rights impacts that can result from the production and use of ICT, tech companies ought to implement specific human rights policies and tailored due diligence processes. Importantly, such HRDD processes must address all stages of the technology life cycle, from technology design and development and its production all the way to its usage, and it must involve critically affected rights-holders along all the different stages of the technology life cycle (Ebert, Busch, & Wettstein 2020). Accordingly, institutions such as The Danish Institute for Human Rights (2020), as well as Shift & Institute for Human Rights and Business (2013c) have issued much-needed tailored guidance for HRIAs of digital activities as well as the implementation of the UNGPs in the ICT sector more generally.

Unlocking positive potential: The development, design, and use of new technologies not only comes with BHR risks but also provides potential solutions to some of the prevailing BHR issues and challenges, as the focus of *Partnership on AI* particularly shows. For example, blockchain technology is said to have the potential to provide new and effective solutions for enhancing traceability within complex corporate value chains. The technology can enhance reliability in the tracking of the materials that are contained in end products to their source and thus increase consumers' knowledge about the potential human rights impacts that are connected to the production of such products. While these applications and solutions are still in their infancy, they may eventually contribute an important piece to the puzzle of enhanced value chain transparency. This may help companies to comply more effectively, for example, with HRDD legislation or with recent conflict minerals regulations (Chapter 12.4) and thus enhance the impact of such policy instruments on the ground.

New digital communication technology has also equipped rural communities in the Global South to access critical information, services, and markets. For example, they have enabled mobile banking services or remote access to health records and to learning and information (Shift & Institute for Human Rights and Business 2013c: 8). Information on weather patterns can enable them to tap into new possibilities of increasing yields and outputs in farming, among other things. Enhancing the information literacy of rural communities can also make them more resilient and better equipped to defend their rights against the economic interests of companies and the government.

14.4   Garment and Footwear Sector

In the 1990s, garment and footwear companies were among the very first organizations to be confronted with the growing public concern over business impacts on human rights. Nike, in particular, was on the end of a public backlash over exploitative labor relations in its overseas factories, where the shoes and sports attire with the famous swoosh icon were produced. Nike has since done much to address and improve labor conditions in its supply chain and has become one of the leading companies in the industry when it comes to the promotion of human rights (Box 6.1).

However, the concern over exploitation and grave human rights violations in the sector have remained. Factory fires and building collapses that kill and injure hundreds of workers still occur with painful regularity and NGO reports keep exposing labor rights violations in the value chains of large fashion and sportswear brands. The collapse of the Rana Plaza factory building in 2013 in Bangladesh that killed more than 1,000 workers and left hundreds more severely injured has become a symbol for the human rights challenges that plague this industry (Box 14.5). Bangladesh has become a major "hub" for low-wage garment production with about 6,000 such factories employing up to 4 million people. But also other Southeast Asian and some African countries such as Ethiopia depend on the garment sector, which has been a major force of social and economic development (Nolan 2016: 279).

The root cause of these problems lies in the business models and structure of the industry, which are based on ever faster fashion cycles, combined with shrinking margins and accelerating cost pressure. Fashion trends change at an ever faster pace, which increases time pressure along the supply chains; this phenomenon has come to be known as "fast fashion." As a consequence, suppliers in the first tier of the supply chain of global brands often pass on the orders to an opaque network of subcontractors who operate in a largely unmonitored and unregulated space since this allows them to take on more and much larger orders than their production capacity would allow. Those subcontractors may themselves pass on some of the orders to yet another layer of subcontractors, and so on. In other words, supply chains get ever longer and more complex. Often, subcontractors in the lower tiers of the supply chains operate in the informal economy under precarious working conditions. At the same time, the clothing and footwear brands increase their margins by increasing the pressure to cut production costs. Suppliers thus end up in a situation of having to produce ever faster at decreasing cost. This pressure is eventually being passed on to the workers, who will work longer hours for less money and under dismal working conditions.

14.4.1   Issues and Challenges

Garment and footwear production is rife with human rights challenges. The structural root causes and systemic nature of such violations illustrate the complexity of BHR issues. The human rights challenges facing the industry can roughly be divided in two stages: first, raw materials production and second, processing, in which garments and other materials are turned into clothing and footwear.

The garment value chain starts in the cotton fields – for example, of Uzbekistan, Turkmenistan, or Azerbaijan – where cotton pickers often work long hours collecting bags of cotton for little pay and under physically demanding conditions. Forced labor has been described as endemic to the cotton industry (Box 4.2) and there are reported instances of child labor as well. Cotton is often produced with the heavy

BOX 14.5 (Short Case): Rana Plaza factory collapse

On April 24, 2013, Rana Plaza – an industrial complex in Dhaka, Bangladesh – collapsed, killing 1,134 clothing workers and injuring an estimated 2,500 (Barrett, Baumann-Pauly, & Gu 2018: 5). It was the worst industrial accident globally since Bhopal in 1984 (Box 2.3) (Nolan 2016: 27). The complex was home to five local ready-made garment (RMG) factories on eight floors, which produced clothes for thirty-one Western multinational corporations (Chowdhury 2017: 938). Yet despite sending shockwaves around the world, the incident was unfortunately not a surprise for many.

One day prior, on April 23, 2013, large structural cracks were discovered in the Rana Plaza building (Clean Clothes Campaign n.d. (b)). While the shops and bank on the lower floors closed immediately, garment factory managers ignored the warnings and pressured thousands of workers to return to work the following day (Clean Clothes Campaign n.d. (b)). Just a few hours after their return, the factory collapsed, burying thousands under debris and rubble, in countless cases with devastating consequences (Clean Clothes Campaign n.d. (b)).

The Rana Plaza incident was unprecedented in its magnitude and scale, but not with regard to the nature of the incident. Rather, it fits within a long history of tragic incidents related to workplace safety in the RMG industry in Bangladesh. Only five months prior, an estimated 112 RMG workers lost their lives in a tragic accident at the Tazreen Factory (Nolan 2016: 27), when workers became trapped inside the burning building because factory managers prevented workers from fleeing when the fire alarm went off (Banerji 2019).

Although efforts have been made in recent years to improve the conditions of RMG factories at the heart of the fast fashion industry, through changes to the Bangladeshi labor code and the creation of several multi-stakeholder initiatives, there remain many challenges with regards to the proper enforcement of regulations and payment of compensation (International Labour Organization n.d. (c)).

Discussion Questions:

(1) Based on the above case, imagine that you are the head of CSR for a large multinational fast fashion retailer and you have been tasked with selecting a new supplier in Bangladesh to produce clothing. What criteria would you look for when selecting a supplier, in order to ensure that the human rights of workers are respected?

(2) As a part of your evaluations as head of CSR, you find that the factory safety record for some of your existing suppliers is worrying. How are you going to deal with them? What kind of action plan would you implement?

> **(3)** Since the rise of globalization and the expansion of the fast fashion industry in Bangladesh from 400 to about 6,000 factories with more than 4 million workers (Nolan 2016: 27) between 1990 and 2016, a growing number of incidents have occurred within the Bangladeshi garment sector, hinting at underlying structural issues. In your opinion, what efforts could the governments both of Bangladesh and of home states of fashion brands take to improve the working conditions in garment factories?

use of pesticides, which contaminate soil and water and affect the health of workers and nearby communities. Biodiversity, too, is negatively affected by contamination through pesticides. Furthermore, cotton is one of the most water-intensive of crops. Irrigation often requires the diversion of waterways, which affects communities and the entire ecosystem surrounding them.

The focus of BHR in the garment sector commonly is put on the manufacturing stage. The sector has been notorious for exploitative working conditions at clothing and footwear factories. Subcontracting often shifts production into the informal sector, with little or no control and monitoring. Accordingly, production sites frequently maintain sweatshop conditions (Chapter 5.2.2); workers work long shifts, often without being allowed to take breaks; they earn very low wages – trafficking and forced labor are frequent occurrences, too – hardly get any time off and are put under considerable physical and mental pressure. Factories are often crowded and poorly ventilated and workers exposed to dust and toxic substances used in the dying and coloring process of the garments (Stanwick & Stanwick 2015: 41). Factory doors are frequently locked, preventing workers from getting outside. This has had particularly devastating consequences in factory fires, when workers were trapped inside and could not escape. Factory fires and building collapses occur regularly, since investment in facilities and equipment and their proper maintenance are often lacking and they are operated in poor and unsafe conditions.

In an industry in which most workers are female, discrimination, harassment, and physical and sexual abuse are similarly common. Furthermore, workers' unions are often barred in garment-producing countries and are actively opposed and undermined by garment and footwear manufacturers. This is in and of itself a violation of workers' rights and effectively serves to keep workers in weak positions without the possibility of confronting their employers over such conditions and demanding change.

Finally, pollution is a massive problem in the garment sector. Carbon pollution and the release of toxic chemicals into the environment are big problems at the production stage. The apparel and footwear industry accounts for more than 8 percent of global climate impact, which is more than all international airline flights and maritime shipping trips combined (Clean Clothes Campaign n.d. (a)). Furthermore, a large part of the clothing sold on the global markets will be discarded and end up in landfills within one year of production. This, too, is one of the endemic problems of "fast fashion."

14.4.2   Sector-Specific Standards and Initiatives

In the aftermath of the Rana Plaza factory collapse, the global garment industry launched two large-scale multi-stakeholder initiatives involving businesses, the Bangladeshi authorities, trade unions, NGOs, and the ILO, with the aim of improving factory safety standards and working conditions in Bangladesh's garment sector. More than 170 apparel companies, mainly based in Europe, joined the *Accord on Fire and Building Safety in Bangladesh*, which committed the brands to improving factory safety by having them audited by independent factory safety inspectors and requiring necessary renovations and repairs (Stanwick & Stanwick 2015: 41). The Accord was initiatially limited to five years. In 2018, the brands signed the Transition Accord to extend the period to June 2021, when the work was supposed to be handed over to a national regulatory body, supported by the ILO. In June 2021, the period was extended for another three months. Within those three months a new agreement was negotiated between garment brands and global unions that builds and expands on the core elements of the Accord. The new agreement, called "International Accord for Health and Safety in the Textile and Garment Industry", took effect on September 1, 2021. In parallel to the Accord, more than twenty American brands and garment businesses joined the *Alliance for Bangladesh Worker Safety*, which largely mirrored the provisions of the Accord, but with less binding force. The Alliance, too, was limited to five years and ceased operations in 2018. The two initiatives were widely hailed for their potential to make a real difference in the garment sector in Bangladesh. However, there has also been criticism that the initiatives only covered a fraction of factories in Bangladesh and that precisely those factories that tend to commit the worst offenses generally were outside of the initiatives' scope (Labowitz & Baumann-Pauly 2014). Furthermore, the two initiatives left the responsibility to fund the necessary renovations and repairs to the factory owners themselves, who often were not in a position to come up with the finances required to do so (Labowitz & Baumann-Pauly 2014: 40)

The *Fair Labor Association (FLA)* is a multi-stakeholder initiative addressing labor conditions in the factories of large retail brands. It has been widely hailed as one of the most progressive and most effective initiatives in this regard. It is not focused exclusively on the apparel and footwear sector, though it originated as a response to the sweatshop and child labor controversy that emerged in the sector in the 1990s. It was set up in 1999 as a monitoring and auditing body for what was then the Apparel Industry Partnership, whose purpose was to make sure that suppliers of signatory companies complied with a newly designed workplace code of conduct (van Heerden 2016: 129). The code of conduct formulates requirements in the areas of non-discrimination, forced and child labor, harassment and abuse, freedom of association, and generally on decent working conditions. Today, the FLA still focuses heavily on apparel and sportswear, but counts major companies from other sectors, such as Apple and Nestlé, among its participants, as well. Participating companies hand in a list of their factories to the FLA, which then draws a random, risk-weighted sample of 5 percent for independent external monitoring (van Heerden 2016: 131). Companies must work with audited suppliers to develop plans to remedy identified shortcomings. Such remedy plans require approval by the FLA, and companies have to update the FLA on the progress of implemented measures. The FLA, in turn, engages in spot checks to verify progress and reports on its website on company monitoring and assessment results (van Heerden 2016: 131). The FLA also contains a third-party complaint mechanism through which persistent failures to comply with the workplace code of conduct can be reported. Companies that fail to meet remedial requirements within a given time will be placed under special review and risk expulsion.

The *Clean Clothes Campaign (CCC)* is a grassroots network that consists of NGOs and unions but not of companies. Founded as an advocacy group as early as 1989, its mission is to lobby companies and government for better labor conditions and empower workers in the garment and sportswear supply chains. Thus, the CCC aims at raising awareness and mobilizing people around both structural reforms and the confrontation of companies in concrete cases of rights violations. In 1999 the CCC, together with a Dutch union, founded the *Fair Wear Foundation*, which works with more than a hundred brands to transform the garment sector. The Fair Wear Foundation is organized as a multi-stakeholder organization. Its work is based on third-party checks not only of factories but also of the management decisions and business practices of the brands, which often generate the pressure that lead to rights violations further up the value chain. Furthermore, it engages directly with garment workers and offers complaint helplines for them to seek support. At the factory level, the Fair Wear Foundation offers training for factory managers and workers on their Fair Wear Code of Labour Practices.

14.4.3 Solutions and Best Practice

In the aftermath of the Rana Plaza disaster, at least partly based on the commitment of the brands to stay in Bangladesh, the Bangladeshi government increased the minimum wage for garment workers and improved other labor protection and safety regulations (Nolan 2016: 28). However, sustainable change requires that the underlying structural issues, particularly the sourcing practices of global brands, will be addressed and changed at a fundamental level. The root cause of workers' rights abuses in the garment and footwear supply chains are the fast fashion cycles combined with the tight margins caused by increasing cost pressure at the brand level and the lack of transparency in the global supply chains. Brands often engage in what is called "indirect sourcing." They work with purchasing agents, who place their orders and ensure a turnaround at the fastest pace and lowest cost. Thus, brands rarely have an overview, or even an idea, of what their supply chains look like in detail. The fast cycles lead to an ever-changing network of contractors and subcontractors that is impossible to control or even understand.

Thus, the key to more sustainability within the sector is to move from "fast fashion" to "slow fashion," combined with a switch from indirect to direct sourcing models, in which brands work directly with their suppliers to build value chains based on stable, predictable long-term relationships (Labowitz & Baumann-Pauly 2014). Such long-term relations would provide suppliers with the prospect and security to invest in the safety of the facilities, in training and labor conditions, and enable brands to commit to building capacity at the facilities of their suppliers. In the current model of ever-changing short-term supplier relations, there is little incentive for either brands or suppliers to make costly capacity-building investments. Furthermore, a model built on long-term relationships with suppliers would reduce brands' dependence on a system of factory audits, which has long been criticized as ineffective (Chapter 8.1.5.6). Mutual trust and engagement, rather than monitoring and control, may be the key to more sustainability in the sector. While some brands, such as Nike or H&M, have started to move in this direction, this model of organizing supply chains is not only relevant for the garment and footwear sector but could lead other industries characterized by short product cycles and long and complex supply chains on a path toward more transparency and sustainability.

14.5   Food, Beverage, and Agribusiness Sector

In 2015, the Swiss food giant Nestlé made headlines by publicly admitting that an internal investigation showed the existence of forced labor in its seafood supply chains in Thailand. For some, this admission came as a confirmation of the unscrupulous and irresponsible business practices of large multinationals and as a symbol of all that is wrong with the way global businesses operate today. But many human rights groups praised the move as a first step toward solving the underlying problems. The fact that a large multinational such as Nestlé openly admitted to not being able to keep full oversight and control over its supply chains, despite its resources and expertise, says much about the complexity of the task at hand. Understanding and admitting to this complexity may indeed open the possibility for constructive collaboration and it may be the first step toward developing holistic and sustainable solutions. From a legal perspective, such admissions are risky, as they may lead to new litigation or be used in ongoing court cases. This is one major reason why companies are reluctant to openly address the problems they face in their supply chains and it illustrates one of the key dilemmas on the way to lasting improvements: Increasing litigation risk may not only have positive impacts but can also stifle companies' engagement in the search of holistic and lasting solutions. On the other hand, litigation is a key avenue for victims of human rights abuse to seek justice and remedy for what they have experienced and, generally, such avenues are still underdeveloped and in need of becoming more effective.

14.5.1 Issues and Challenges

Much of the food we regularly consume is not grown locally but imported from faraway places, often as ingredients in processed food. Fruit, spices, tea, meat, or seafood from all corners of the world are freshly delivered to grocery stores worldwide day by day. But the fruit has to be grown and harvested, the seafood caught, the tea leaves picked; and they have to be transported and delivered over great distances before they appear in the aisles of the grocery stores. Many of these activities and stages along the various food and beverage supply chains are associated with distinct human rights risks. Even the food itself and its advertising and marketing to potential consumers often raise human rights issues. The following elaborations will distinguish between risks and impacts that occur upstream, where it is grown, harvested or caught, and those associated with downstream activities, such as the processing, advertising, marketing, and sale of the products.

Child and forced labor (Chapter 5.2) are among the most pertinent human rights risks occuring **upstream** in the food and beverage sector supply chains. Trafficking and forced labor are widespread, for example, in the fishing and seafood industry in Southeast Asia, as pointed out above. Migrant laborers have been found to work on high seas vessels under gruesome conditions for months at a time without setting foot on mainland. Their passports are often confiscated by their employers, so they have no chance of leaving; furthermore, the employment fees they may have paid to receive their jobs may have put them in debt towards their employer, which can take years to pay off, again, preventing them from moving on. Violence and abuse are common features of such working conditions and safety measures are often inadequate to mitigate the dangers of the occupation. Child labor has also been reported to be particularly widespread, for example, in the cocoa supply chains in Côte d'Ivoire and other countries. According to the Food and Agriculture Organization of the UN (FAO), nearly 70 percent of child labor occurs within agriculture and thus in the supply chains of large food companies, involving approximately 108 million children globally (FAO 2021). Lawsuits have been filed against food and chocolate companies for doing too little to improve the situation (Box 4.1). One case, *John Doe I et al.* v. *Nestlé et al.*, which was brought in 2005 on the basis of ATCA (Chapter 12.5.3) was dismissed by the US Supreme Court in June 2021. In the case,

Nestlé USA and Cargill were accused of aiding and abetting child slavery by providing financial support, training, and supplies to cocoa farmers in Côte d'Ivoire (Dufresne 2021). However, the Supreme Court ruled that the case did not meet the "touch and concern" requirement, since nearly all of the alleged unlawful conduct occurred in Côte d'Ivoire and the mere approval of such conduct by the headquarters in the US was not sufficient to overcome the presumption against extraterritoriality established in the the ruling on *Kiobel* (Chapter 12.5.3.2).

The use of natural resources is another big problem associated with the food and beverage industry. For example, beverage companies have been accused of "water grabbing," that is, of using up the water resources of local communities for the production and sale of their beverage products, and thus of undermining the human right to clean water. Similarly, deforestation has accelerated to make space for farmland and monocultures. Palm oil production has become the center of attention of global campaigns and raised public awareness of the ramifications of such production models. While deforestation destroys natural habitats and threatens biodiversity, the large fires that are used to clear forests create massive smoke pollution that negatively impacts the health of people (Chapter 5.4.2). Land-grabbing (Chapter 5.3.1) for large monocultures and the use of toxic pesticides that severely impact the health of workers and communities have been further persistent problems in the supply chain of food and beverage companies. Such issues are similarly connected to large agribusinesses, which produce and promote fertilizers, often without making sufficiently sure that users have the necessary precautions in place to protect their health. Large agribusinesses have come under increasing scrutiny also for monopolizing seed markets, land, and water resources to the detriment of small farmers.

Human rights issues occur also *downstream* in the food and beverage value chain. High-sugar drinks and ultra-processed food containing large amounts of salt, sugar, transfats, and preservatives can be linked to obesity, particularly among children and youths, and to other non-communicable diseases such as diabetes and cardiovascular diseases that have turned into major public health concerns across the globe (Buse, Tanaka, & Hawkes 2017). These risks and ramifications are often exacerbated by a lack of information and transparency about the health impacts of such products. Furthermore, aggressive and often deceptive advertising and marketing campaigns – often targeting children – create demand for such products without adequately informing consumers of the health risks. Nestlé's aggressive and deceptive marketing of its baby formula product in the 1970s is a particularly egregious example of such practices. Their marketing campaign convinced mothers in the Global South to abandon breastfeeding and instead use Nestlé's baby formula to feed their babies. However, many of them could not afford the expensive product and watered it down too much to stretch their supply, leading to grave undernourishment of the babies. Other mothers mixed the formula with contaminated water since they did not have access to sources of clean water. The health ramifications for countless babies were disastrous. However, manipulative and deceptive marketing practices – for example appealing to and associating products with consumers' desires, ideals, or emotional states – continue to be used today. New technology and social media (Chapter 14.3) have made it easier for companies to target consumers in personalized and highly effective ways.

14.5.2   Sector-Specific Standards and Initiatives

The food and beverage sector is characterized by a large diversity of different value chains. Agricultural products such as coffee, cocoa, or tea pose various challenges to be addressed and such challenges and their potential solutions can be very different from those experienced, for example, in seafood supply chains. Accordingly, the standards and initiatives governing the sector also tend to be specific and tailored to the different value chains. Therefore, this subsection will focus on a few more general standards that address a range of problems and products and have reached a level of prominence. Again, the elaborations distinguish between standards and initiatives that address downstream and those that address upstream activities.

Perhaps the best-known standards in the food and beverage industry that address a range of issues across a large variety of products and ingredients are the *Fairtrade International* standards. Fairtrade International is a non-profit multi-stakeholder organization that operates through three regional producer networks and twenty-five national Fairtrade organizations. Products that meet Fairtrade requirements can be certified and carry the well-known Fairtrade label. The main aim of Fairtrade is to ensure more equitable and fair terms of trade between international buyers and farmers in the Global South. The initiative includes payment of minimum prices high enough to cover the average costs of sustainable production; provision of an additional premium, which can be invested at the community level in projects that enhance social, economic, and environmental development; pre-financing for producers; the facilitating of long-term trading partnerships and the enabling of greater producer control over the trading process; the setting of clear requirements to ensure that the conditions of production and trade are fair and responsible (Fairtrade International n.d.). The standards include provisions on issues such as child and forced labor, gender equality, climate change, and workers' and human rights more generally. One recurring criticism of the Fairtrade movement is that the price premium that is paid to producers will create a disincentive for them to diversify into potential higher value products, activities, or even economic sectors. However, such criticism overlooks the fact that such changes come at significant risk and cost for local producers, who lack the economic means to make such transitions possible. Thus, empirical results show the opposite – that is, that Fairtrade-certified producers often manage to diversify into producing more highly processed goods for export precisely because the fair trade system provides them with the stability and means for investment and long-term planning (Smith 2013).

Another well-known multi-stakeholder initiative is the **Rainforest Alliance**. The Rainforest Alliance aims to protect the human rights of farming and forest communities in the Global South. It is based on the belief that the conservation of forests, soil, and waterways is a critical component of protecting local communities. It runs a certification program, which is based on the continuous improvement of business practices with regard to such conservation. For this purpose, producers are assessed by independent third-party auditors. Assessment criteria include the protection of forests, climate, and of the human rights and sustainable livelihoods of rural communities. In addition to certification, the Rainforest Alliance also provides training, technical assistance, and sustainable financing to producers.

The **International Food and Beverage Alliance (IFBA)** addresses some of the human rights problems associated with downstream activities of food and beverage companies. It was founded in 2008 and counts twelve of the largest companies in the industry among its members. Its aim is to tackle the public health concerns associated with ultra-processed food by reducing sodium or sugar as ingredients and to promote responsible marketing, particularly that aimed at children. A similar aim is pursued by the **Sydney Principles**. The Sydney Principles are a set of guiding principles drafted by the World Obesity Task Force, with the aim of improving the protection of children from the commercial promotion of foods and beverages. They are based on the insight that such marketing practices are a major driver of the obesity epidemic. The principles essentially promote a rights-based approach to public regulation of the commercial marketing of foods and beverages to children.

14.5.3 Solutions and Best Practice

Some 80 percent of the food consumed every day is produced by the more than 570 million farms across the globe; 90 percent of those farms are run by individuals and families. More than 1 billion people, as Posner (2016: 173) points out, earn their livelihood in agriculture. These numbers alone show how daunting a task it is for global food and beverage brands to maintain oversight, let alone ensure respect for human rights across their global supply chains, which often stretch to the most remote corners of the planet. The numbers also show that sustainable solutions require real engagement and collaboration between various actors. With the livelihoods of millions of people depending on farm work, disengagement and withdrawal by global food and beverage brands cannot be a viable approach to these human rights challenges. The child labor challenge provides an illustrative and much-discussed example for this. As detrimental as child labor can be, it is often also critical as an income source for families in poverty-stricken areas in the Global South. Therefore, cutting ties can make the situation even worse for the affected families, who may lose an important source of income. More constructive are solutions that are based on a long-term vision with a view to both the rights of the children and the best interest of the families. From such a perspective, holistic approaches to dealing with child labor ensure access to education for the children, while covering the families' income loss. Furthermore, an effective feature of such approaches is a commitment to offering secure employment once the children reach working age. Thus, similar to the garment and footwear sector (Chapter 14.4), such collaborative solutions must be based on trusted relationships that evolve over time, and, similar to what we have noted in the context of the extractive sector (Chapter 14.1), the problems are hardly solved by "walking away" from them.

Before such measures can be adopted, however, companies must become aware of the problems in their supply chains and identify both the impacts their business activities and decisions have on the workers and communities in their supply chain and the potential measures they plan to adopt in response to those issues. Thus, particularly in long and complex value chains – such as those of food and beverage companies – having effective traceability and due diligence systems in place that allow the origins of sourced goods and the impacts of one's own business activities to be identified is a critical element. However, it must be seen as the starting point, rather than the essence, of such solutions.

STUDY QUESTIONS

1. What is artisanal or small-scale mining (ASM)? What BHR problems and challenges are associated with it?
2. What are the Equator Principles and with which sector are they associated? What is the importance of the IFC performance standards for BHR?
3. AI solutions often excacerbate existing inequalities and discriminations. Why is that? Can you explain the mechanism that makes AI solutions vulnerable to bias?
4. What is understood by "fast fashion" and what is the problem with it from a BHR perspective? How is "fast fashion" connected to subcontracting in the value chains of clothing brands?
5. Can you describe some of the BHR challenges that occur upstream in the supply chains of global food and beverage companies? What problems arise downstream?
6. What are Fairtrade standards and how does the Fairtrade system work?

REFLECTION QUESTIONS

1. The Thun Group of Banks argued that banks are at best indirectly linked to their clients' potential human rights violations but do not contribute to them through their financial services and products. Do you agree or disagree with this position?

Can you formulate a *precise* argument for why you think that banks do or do not contribute to such violations? Can you relate your answer to the case of Credit Suisse's financing of the DAPL project discussed in Box 14.2?

2. The case of Yahoo! providing user data of a Chinese dissident to the Chinese government led to widespread criticism. How should ICT companies handle such data requests by governments from a BHR perspective? What role can collaborative initiatives such as the Global Network Initiative play in supporting them?

3. It has become increasingly clear that platform and social media companies have a responsibility to moderate the content posted on their websites in order to prevent the spread of hate propaganda, fake news, and bullying. However, where and how should they draw the line between restricting content and allowing for people's freedom of expression? What mechanisms should they put in place to deal with such thorny issues?

4. The structure of "fast fashion" has known adverse impacts on human beings and the environment. What do you do with this information? How does it affect your own purchasing behavior as a consumer? Can you make a difference in the fashion industry, and how?

5. Food and beverage companies often argue that consumers have the agency to make the "right" decisions when it comes to healthy food choices. They argue that by selling junk food, they are not harming people, but simply provide them with choices. Do you agree with this statement? How does this logic connect a BHR perspective on the topic?

15 | Emerging Discussions and Narratives

BHR is a fast-evolving interdisciplinary field and naturally its focus expands over time and as new subdiscussions start to emerge. Such new discussions often appear at the intersection between BHR and other fields. It is typical of scholarship that the most significant scholarly innovations tend to happen within and through these types of interlinkages. This chapter briefly outlines four emerging discussions within the BHR field, all of which will likely gain in significance in the coming years.

15.1 BHR and the UN Sustainable Development Goals

In 2000, the UN adopted the so-called Millennium Development Goals (MDGs), a framework to coordinate sustainable development efforts around eight specific goals that aimed to cut extreme poverty by 2015. The MDGs were succeeded by the Sustainable Development Goals (SDGs), which the UN General Assembly adopted in 2015 as a part of its 2030 Agenda for Sustainable Development (UN General Assembly 2015). The SDGs are more comprehensive than the MDGs, consisting of seventeen objectives, which are specified by a total of 169 targets as well as a set of indicators that aim to make progress measurable. They quickly became a powerful narrative and influential framework to coordinate the development efforts of governments, as well as of other public and private organizations. The goals address a variety of issues in the domain of sustainable development, such as ending poverty, reducing inequality in all its relevant dimensions, promoting health and education, providing access to clean water and sanitation, and addressing climate change.

Partnerships are seen as a critical means of achieving the SDGs. In this vein, the SDGs assign a prominent and critical role also to the private sector as a "key partner," not only in providing the necessary financial resources and investments but also in finding innovative solutions, generating jobs and economic growth, and transferring knowledge and technology, among other things. SDG 17, in particular, calls upon businesses to engage in partnerships for sustainable development and assist governments in addressing SDGs 1–16 (Buhmann, Jonsson, & Fisker 2019: 390). Businesses are asked "to apply their creativity and innovation to solving

BOX 15.1 (Context) Seventeen Sustainable Development Goals

Goal 1:   End poverty in all its forms everywhere

Goal 2:   End hunger, achieve food security and improved nutrition and promote sustainable agriculture

Goal 3:   Ensure healthy lives and promote well-being for all at all ages

Goal 4:   Ensure inclusive and equitable quality education and promote lifelong learning opportunities for all

Goal 5:   Achieve gender equality and empower all women and girls

Goal 6:   Ensure availability and sustainable management of water and sanitation for all

Goal 7:   Ensure access to affordable, reliable, sustainable, and modern energy for all

Goal 8:   Promote sustained, inclusive, and sustainable economic growth, full and productive employment, and decent work for all

Goal 9:   Build resilient infrastructure, promote inclusive and sustainable industrialization, and foster innovation

Goal 10:   Reduce inequality within and among countries

Goal 11:   Make cities and human settlements inclusive, safe, resilient, and sustainable

Goal 12:   Ensure sustainable consumption and production patterns

Goal 13:   Take urgent action to combat climate change and its impacts

Goal 14:   Conserve and sustainably use the oceans, seas, and marine resources for sustainable development

Goal 15:   Protect, restore, and promote sustainable use of terrestrial ecosystems, sustainably manage forests, combat desertification, halt and reverse land degradation, and halt biodiversity loss

Goal 16:   Promote peaceful and inclusive societies for sustainable development, provide access to justice for all, and build effective, accountable, and inclusive institutions at all levels

Goal 17:   Strengthen the means of implementation and revitalize the global partnership for sustainable development

sustainable development challenges" (UN General Assembly 2015: 29). Hence, with businesses directly and explicitly addressed, the SDGs quickly became a second prominent UN framework influencing and shaping corporate responsibility efforts. This raises the question of how these two high-profile initiatives – the UNGPs and the SDGs – relate to each other. Questions have been raised particularly about their coherence and whether the respective requirements formulated in and through them are truly compatible with each other.

A major point of contention is that the SDGs formulate a positive role for corporations as partners and providers of development, while the UNGPs emphasize their potential to negatively impact human rights through their business activities and relationships. While some see in this aspect the complementary potential of the two frameworks, others have feared that the SDGs may evolve as a prominent and powerful counternarrative to the UNGPs by providing an alternative, more lenient framework that may undermine the accountability focus of the UNGPs. Therefore, they may provide corporations with a platform to showcase their positive contributions and initiatives, while potentially distracting from corporate human rights violations that lie hidden in their value chains. Such concerns may be reinforced by the fact that references to corporate accountability and its respective regulatory regimes, which were included in earlier drafts of the SDGs, were dropped later on in the process (Jägers 2020: 165). Furthermore, a growing number of international bodies and initiatives have started to prominently refer to and integrate the SDGs and encourage businesses to contribute to them (Deva, Ramasastry, Wettstein, & Santoro 2019: 206). For example, the UNGC has put the SDGs at the very center of its strategy for 2021–2023 (Jägers 2021).

While the SDGs framework mentions companies as relevant actors, it does not formulate any specific *responsibility* for any actor – neither for companies nor for governments – with regard to the achievement of or contribution to any SDG (Pogge & Sengupta 2016). Accordingly, it does not contain any real accountability mechanisms, either (Zagelmeyer & Sinkovics 2019: 44). In this vein, the SDGs are perceived as providing too much leeway, enabling different actors to cherrypick when it comes to their implementation efforts (Ruggie 2016). They can establish and showcase initiatives and projects addressing particular goals, for which they may incur little cost or for which they see promising win-win potentials (Chapter 6.3.2), while avoiding others whose achievement would require more complicated and costly partnerships with little evident gains for business. Symptomatically, the win-win rhetoric features prominently in the discourses around the SDGs and is used as a means to motivate corporations to get engaged.

To address this concern, human rights scholars have increased their efforts to show that corporate human rights accountability is not an alternative to but a critical and necessary condition for the achievement of any of the seventeen SDGs. This is despite none of the seventeen SDGs explicitly referring to human rights, let alone to BHR more specifically. However, the preamble to the General Assembly resolution that passed Agenda 2030 clearly denotes the realization of the human rights of all as a superior aim of the SDGs (UN General Assembly 2015). Hence, they are said to at least implicitly integrate human rights principles and reflect human rights language. Accordingly, their implementation would contribute substantially to the realization of human rights. For example, working toward SDG 2 to end hunger is directly related to the fulfilment of the human right to food. SDG 3, which aims at ensuring healthy lives and promoting well-being, contributes to the fulfilment of the right to health. The Danish Institute for Human Rights has shown that more than 90 percent of the SDG targets can be linked to human rights and labor standards (Morris, Wrzoncki, & Andreasen Lysgaard 2019: 6). As a consequence, human rights treaty bodies (Chapter 3.2.1) and other human rights organizations have started to embrace the SDGs as a means to further and advance human rights goals, emphasizing and stressing the need for a human rights-based approach to the implementation of the SDGs (Jägers 2020: 154). This is in contrast to their predecessors, the MDGs, which were said to be at least partly at odds with and diverge from the human rights regime (Jägers 2020: 151). Nevertheless, as Jägers (2020: 155) summarizes:

> The jury is still out whether there is true convergence between the agendas of those dealing with the SDGs and those dealing with human rights. There clearly is a commonality of interests and synergies, but statements that the SDGs are grounded in human rights have to be approached with some caution.

BHR scholars, in particular, have pointed out the need to ensure that partnerships involving the private sector must be based on respect for human rights as outlined in the UNGPs. The General Assembly resolution contains a passing reference to the UNGPs, emphasizing the importance of the protection of "labor rights, environmental and health standards in accordance with relevant international standards and agreements and other ongoing initiatives in this regard, such as the Guiding Principles for Business and Human Rights" (UN General Assembly 2015: 29). However, other than that, the general impression is that the SDGs "seem to have largely ignored the parallel UN-level debates on the link between transnational business and human rights" (Zagelmeyer & Sinkovics 2019: 42). The UNWG, on the other hand, makes it clear that both businesses and governments must put human rights at the center of their pursuit of and contribution to the SDGs, stating that the most powerful contribution that companies can make to sustainable development "is to embed respect for human rights across their value chains" (UNWG 2017b: 3). Additionally, John Ruggie (2016) left no doubt that "for business to fully realize its contribution to sustainable development, it must put efforts to advance respect for human rights at the heart of the people part of sustainable development." If such an integration indeed takes place, the SDGs can become an important catalyzer for the BHR agenda, too (Morris, Wrzoncki, & Andreasen Lysgaard 2019: 12–14). They can provide motivation and urgency to address the major global challenges of our time and unlock critical new investments and finances; they can also provide an alternative language for addressing human rights challenges, for example, in regions and places where human rights are perceived with suspicion or for companies that struggle with human rights language, which some businesses still see as rather abstract and conceptual (Obara & Peattie 2018):

> Actors who are unfamiliar with or have a somewhat narrow or politicised understanding of what human rights entail may find that the 2030 Agenda provides an alternative avenue to introduce human rights concepts. It provides multiple entry points with time bound goals and targets, which are relatable and understandable to all actors, including business" (Morris, Wrzoncki, & Andreasen Lysgaard 2019: 13).

Despite the evident links between the SDGs framework and the BHR agenda, only a very few governments explicitly connect the SDGs with BHR more generally or the UNGPs specifically as yet. This becomes evident in the national reports that governments have handed in so far on their implementation and progress on the SDGs (Jägers 2020: 169–171). Accordingly, the UNWG (2017b: 2) observes that "much work remains to be done, however, to translate the SDGs into action by States and businesses in a manner that is consistent with international human rights standards. This includes ensuring that partnership activities involving the business sector are based on respect for human rights."

15.2   BHR and Climate Change

The more visible the real impacts of climate change become, the more it is perceived to be a genuine human rights issue. Climate change has already had devastating impacts on people's lives and livelihoods – particularly, though not exclusively, in the Global South. As the OHCHR (n.d. (b)) comments:

> The negative impacts of climate change are disproportionately borne by persons and communities already in disadvantageous situations owing to geography, poverty, gender, age, disability, cultural or ethnic background, among others, that have historically contributed the least to greenhouse gas emissions. In particular, persons, communities and even entire States that occupy and rely upon low-lying coastal lands, tundra and Arctic ice, arid lands, and other delicate ecosystems and at risk territories for their housing and subsistence face the greatest threats from climate change.

Droughts and floods impact agricultural lands and threaten to make certain regions uninhabitable. Typhoons and hurricanes of ever greater magnitude leave unprecedented devastation, wildfires destroy ever larger areas of land, and rising sea levels threaten to swallow up entire islands and shorelines. Thus, the effects of climate change are wide-ranging and can have similarly wide-ranging impacts on human well-being and development, on food and water security, on health, and on physical infrastructure and economic activity, among other things (Tuana 2014: 410). For Kristian Toft (2020: 7) it is "indisputable that the very basic human rights of life, liberty and security are at stake, and that these are certainly inseparable from a more expansive list of rights including social, economic and cultural rights." Among such affected rights are the right to safe drinking water and sanitation, the right to housing and shelter, the right to food, the right to health, and the right to self-determination (OHCHR n.d. (b)).

From this insight, it is only a small step to the conclusion that climate change is not only a human rights issue but also a BHR issue more specifically. Richard Heede has shown that only ninety corporations, predominantly in the oil, gas, coal, and cement industries – the so-called Carbon Major companies – are responsible for two-thirds of historic emissions driving climate change (Heede 2014). Chevron alone is responsible for 3.5 percent of such emissions. In 2015, the Human Rights Commission of the Philippines was petitioned to launch an investigation against fifty Carbon Majors for possible human rights violations. The Commission presented its findings in 2019, concluding that there is clear evidence that the Carbon Majors contributed significantly to anthropogenic climate change and thus can be held morally and legally liable for human rights violations resulting therefrom (Center for International Environmental Law 2019). Accordingly, the Commission recommended that appropriate mechanisms should be put in place for victims of climate impacts to bring lawsuits to domestic courts and possibly also for the criminal prosecution of Carbon Majors in circumstances involving obstruction, deception, and fraud (Center for International Environmental Law 2019).

Against this background, it is not surprising that climate-related lawsuits have been on the rise in recent years (Macchi 2021: 94). In a landmark decision on *Milieudefensie et al.* v. *Shell* in May 2021, a district court in The Hague ordered Royal Dutch Shell to reduce its global carbon emissions by 45 percent by 2030, relative to 2019. The ruling was handed down based on a class action filed in April 2019 by six Dutch NGOs, accusing Shell of not taking adequate and sufficient action to reduce its carbon emissions and of having misled the public about the sustainability of its operations (Macchi 2021: 95–96). In its judgment, the court referenced the European Convention on Human Rights as well as the ICCPR. Furthermore, it cited the UNGPs as an authoritative and internationally endorsed soft-law instrument, whose stipulation of the corporate responsibility to respect human rights denotes a global standard of expected conduct for all corporations, wherever they operate and irrespective of whether or not they endorse them explicitly. The UNGPs, as the court argued, are clear about the measures that corporations ought to take to prevent and mitigate human rights impacts. As such, the court followed the argument of the plaintiffs that, based on the UNGPs, the company would have to account for climate change impacts on human rights in its HRDD process (Macchi 2021: 95–96).

The ruling on Shell essentially extends the conclusions of an earlier case, *State of the Netherlands* v. *Urgenda Foundation*, to a private actor (Macchi 2021: 96). In

2015, the Urgenda Foundation took the government of the Netherlands to court to force an adjustment of the country's climate targets, which, by the standards of climate science, were shown to be inadequate and insufficiently ambitious to contribute appropriately to the goal of keeping the average global rise of temperatures below 2 degrees Celsius. Among other legal bases, the case referred to the European Convention on Human Rights (Chapter 3.3.5) and argued that the country's lack of ambitious targets constituted a violation of its human rights obligations, particularly as they pertain to Article 2 (protection of the right to life) and Article 8 (protection of the right to private life, family life, home, and correspondence) of the European Convention. This was confirmed by The Hague Court of Appeal in 2018 and, in a seminal ruling in December 2019, by the Dutch Supreme Court, implying that "climate law and environmental law principles are to be read as integral elements of the due diligence obligations that states have under international human rights law" (Macchi 2021: 102–103). This conclusion was essentially echoed in *Milieudefensie et al.* v. *Shell*. Similar lawsuits have also been filed against other countries in Europe. In another historic judgment in March 2021, the German constitutional court ruled that Germany's Climate Change Act did not sufficiently specify measures to reduce emissions beyond 2030. As such, the Act was found to be incompatible with the fundamental rights of future generations. Germany was ordered to present a new and improved roadmap to reduce greenhouse gas emissions by the end of 2022.

Another important early court case against a corporation that connects climate change with corporate HRDD was brought against Total under the French Duty of Vigilance Law (Chapter 12.4.3.1). Total, which is responsible for 1 percent of the world's total greenhouse gas emissions and for two-thirds of France's emissions, was accused of climate inaction in the lawsuit. The plaintiffs argue that identifying climate risks and reducing carbon emissions is a key part of a corporation's duty of vigilance and that the company failed to include respective objectives and measures in its vigilance plan (Macchi 2021: 96–97). A more detailed description of the case is provided in Box 12.3. As Chiara Macchi summarizes in relation to current climate change litigation and NCP cases:

> The cases (before both judicial and non-judicial bodies) . . ., albeit still embryonic, show some features of an emerging notion of climate due diligence requiring corporations to assess and address risk, as well as to integrate the climate change dimension into vigilance planning, corporate reporting, external communication and investment decisions (Macchi 2021: 101).

Thus, the way climate change relates to the current BHR regime and what responsibilities ought to be derived from it for both states and corporations is emerging as one of the key discussions within the broader BHR field. The UNGPs do not refer to climate change explicitly. However, this does not mean that climate-related human rights impacts are not included at all in their provisions. The UNGPs' aim is to address all adverse human rights impacts to which corporations contribute or are linked through their activities and business relationships. This means that at least implicitly, this includes the human rights impacts that corporations have through their contribution to climate change. Thus, it is increasingly clear that climate-induced human rights violations must be an integral part of corporations' HRDD processes and, accordingly, of states' duty to protect human rights also with regard to the contributions of corporations to climate change. It is precisely the point of an HRDD process to identify and deal with human rights impacts that may not be obvious and readily noticeable. Hence, climate-related human rights impacts require a deliberate and specific assessment in corporations' HRDD processes and climate targets should be a part of corporate human rights policy commitments (Macchi 2021: 114).

Importantly, climate-related HRDD is not achieved simply by an assessment of a company's carbon emissions, but also includes, for example, an assessment of the specific vulnerabilities of rights-holders such as workers, communities, or human rights defenders to specific climate-related impacts. Corporations may compound these impacts with their business activities. For example, logging and deforestation may accelerate climate-induced erosion processes and desertification and compound climate-related threats to the livelihoods of local people. Furthermore, financial institutions may be linked to or contribute to climate-related impacts through their investment and financing activities (Chapter 14.2), without causing any major emissions themselves. Such indirect links and contributions must naturally be a part of any serious impact assessment.

From a moral point of view, a corporation's retrospective responsibility to remedy climate-induced harm may be a function not only of its contribution but also of its "culpable knowledge," as well as its past actions and engagements to counteract such impacts (Toft 2020: 11). In other words, it depends on the degree to which corporations knowingly contributed to climate change without adopting any mitigating measures in the past. Corporations that have deliberately obscured their contributions, distracted from their responsibilities, and even silenced critics, rather than being transparent in their actions and communications, arguably incur larger remedial responsibilities than those who have been transparent about problematic practices and proactively worked toward their improvement (Toft 2020: 16). However, it is acutely evident that coping with the current climate crisis and averting the collapse of our planet will require more of governments and businesses than merely not making things worse. While the individual contribution of companies such as the Carbon Majors is significant and may give rise to liability, for companies with much smaller contributions, retrospective liability regimes may do little to change their conduct. It is precisely one of the difficulties of large-scale global problems such as the climate crisis that they are the cumulative results of small contributions by a large number of actors. Such contributions may not be readily quantifiable. While holding major contributors accountable is an essential part of overall solutions, coping with such global challenges in a holistic way requires the proactive engagement of all companies, irrespective of the significance of their respective contributions. Such forward-looking responsibilities may be less dependent on how much a corporation contributes to climate change than a function of other parameters such as its leverage and power to influence the future trajectory of climate change (Young 2006; Wettstein 2012b; Toft 2020). Chapter 7.3.2.2 elaborates on forward-looking human rights responsibilities more generally.

15.3   Gender Perspectives on BHR

Women and girls tend to be disproportionately exposed to human rights abuse emanating from business activities. Furthermore, their experience of adverse human rights impacts is often different and unique. For example, the contamination of water sources can affect women and girls in two ways. Together with the rest of the community, they suffer from the direct impact of being denied access to clean water. However, additionally, since they tend to be the ones in charge of fetching water, it may force them to travel longer distances to the nearest clean water source, making it physically more demanding and requiring additional time. The BHR field has long paid insufficient attention to such gender-specific impacts of business activities and the respective need for gender-specific responses to resulting human rights violations. However, recent years have heralded a growing awareness and an emerging discussion on the implication of a gender perspective on BHR.

Gender-specific issues can be divided in two broad categories. In the *first category* are violations committed against women and girls specifically based on their gender. Among such violations are all kinds of discrimination against women, for example, with regard to equal pay, equal opportunity, or general workplace conditions. Cases of physical, mental, and sexual harassment, abuse, and violence at the workplace and beyond fall in this category, too, as well as human trafficking and forced labor, which affects women disproportionately. Of the 40.3 million people in modern slavery, 71 percent are women and girls, who are overrepresented in instances of forced labor (59 percent), forced marriage (84 percent), and forced sexual exploitation (99 percent) (Bryant 2017). Modern slavery (Chapter 5.2.3) is particularly prevalent among female domestic workers, with many of them reporting extreme overwork, lack of rest, and abusive and degrading treatment, as well as the confiscation of their passports, which places them in challenging and vulnerable situations (Amnesty International 2020). Women still experience widespread and pervasive disadvantages, underrepresentation, and discrimination in various dimensions of their daily lives due to discriminatory social norms, gender stereotypes, and male-dominated power structures (UNWG 2019: 50).

The *second category* consists of more general adverse human rights impacts, which, however, are compounded by the often vulnerable socioeconomic positions that women occupy in global value chains as well as in the communities that are affected by business activities. The contamination of water sources mentioned above is an example of such an instance. Women are also disproportionately represented in the informal sector, which is characterized by a lack of economic and social security, often dismal workplace safety, substandard working conditions and a heightened exposure to abuse and exploitation. In addition, they are over-represented in casual and part-time work and provide most of the care work, for example, for children and for the elderly, which tends to be undervalued, underpaid, and underrecognized in society (UNWG 2019: 51). Thus, in such positions, they are not only disproportionately affected by adverse impacts, but experience additional obstacles and barriers when it comes to their access to potential remedies. The disadvantaged positions that women experience in both categories can be worsened by further compounding factors. For example, women of color may be exposed to both gender and racial discrimination and be affected by marginalization and underrepresentation to an even larger degree. Thus, gender issues are often paired with other intersecting forms of marginalization based on race, religion, age, disability, Indigenous status, etc. A gender lens on BHR needs to pay sufficient attention to such issues of intersectionality, in order to avoid inadvertently making the situation of certain subsets of women and girls worse by glossing over diversity and difference within gender categories.

The UNGPs acknowledge the need to pay specific attention to the differentiated impacts that business activities may have on women and girls (OHCHR n.d. (e)):

- The commentary on Principle 3 calls on states to provide appropriate guidance on issues of "gender, vulnerability and/or marginalization".
- Principle 7 points to the "heightened risks of abuses" and particularly of "gender-based and sexual violence" for businesses operating in conflict-affected areas.
- The commentary on Principle 18 advises businesses to "pay special attention to any particular human rights impacts on individuals from groups or populations that may be at heightened risk of vulnerability or marginalization, and bear in mind the different risks that may be faced by women and men."
- Principle 20 calls on businesses to "make particular efforts to track the effectiveness of their responses to impacts on individuals from groups or populations that may be at heightened risk of vulnerability or marginalization" and to use "gender-disaggregated data where relevant."

The UNWG has specified and deepened such gender-based recommendations. In its 2019 report, it proposed a three-step gender framework based on 1) gender-responsive assessment, 2) gender-transformative measures, and 3) gender-transformative remedies:

> The assessment should be responsive: it should be able to respond to differentiated, intersectional and disproportionate adverse impacts on women's human rights as well as to discriminatory norms and patriarchal power structures. The consequent measures and remedies should be transformative in that they should be capable of bringing change to patriarchal norms and unequal power relations that underpin discrimination, gender-based violence and gender stereotyping (UNWG 2019: 63).

Based on this framework, the UNWG provides gender-specific guidance and recommendations for all thirty-one principles of the UNGPs (see UNWG 2019: 8–45). One key recommendation is that "business enterprises ensure meaningful participation of potentially affected women, women's organizations, women human rights defenders and gender experts in all stages of human rights due diligence" (UNWG 2019: 68). Yet, what sounds like a straightforward recommendation is often difficult to implement in practice. For example, female representation in community consultations by extractive companies is often low, due to the patriarchal structures of the local communities and cultures. The result is that even though "community concerns" are being taken seriously, they do not necessarily represent the experiences of women within those communities and, as such, may not provide an adequate basis for company responses that address the unique human rights impacts on women (Götzmann, Kristiansson, & Hillenbrand 2019: 14). Best practices in gender-responsive community engagement range from training community relations teams on gender issues, to ensuring gender balance in on-site community relations teams, to leading women-only consultations for which meeting times and conditions are adapted to the specific schedules of women, including, for example, the provision of childcare during the consultation (Götzmann, Kristiansson, & Hillenbrand 2019: 15–18).

Not least due to the efforts of the UNWG, gender perspectives on BHR and particularly on the UNGPs have become more prominent. However, we are still far from seeing comprehensive gender approaches informing implementation efforts both at the corporate and at the state levels (Götzmann, Wrzoncki, Kristiansson, & Heydari 2018). Addressing this gap will be key not only for the protection specifically of women's rights but also for the BHR agenda in general, not least because women play key roles for the well-being of entire communities. Protecting their rights more effectively will go a long way in strengthening the rights of all other community members, as well.

15.4   BHR in (Post-) Conflict and Transitional Justice Contexts

The most egregious business-related human rights violations tend to occur in the context of violent conflict (Ruggie 2011b: 3). In order to avoid becoming implicated in such human rights abuse when operating in conflict-affected areas, it has been suggested that businesses should engage in enhanced HRDD (Paul & Schönsteiner 2014: 80–81). The UNGPs emphasize the enhanced challenge that contexts of conflict raise for human rights protection, but they provide little in the way of detail as to what an enhanced HRDD process could look like in this regard. To fill this gap, the UNWG (2014: 14) proposed to integrate conflict-sensitive business practice into HRDD. This requires a much more contextualized approach to HRDD, which widens the lens from more narrow human rights impacts to broader societal dynamics and a deeper and more extensive understanding of social relations and how they can be affected by corporate activities (Graf & Iff 2017).

However, contexts of conflict do more than simply raise the question of what businesses should do in order to prevent becoming complicit in human rights abuse when operating in conflict zones. They also raise the issue of how to deal with businesses that were involved in systematic and egregious violations committed in past conflicts and of the role of business in transitional contexts – that is, in societies transitioning from long and protracted conflicts into a more stable and peaceful future. The UNGPs make no reference to such post-conflict or transitional contexts and have been criticized for not paying sufficient attention to conflict and post-conflict contexts in general (Pietropaoli 2020). As a consequence, a small, but growing discussion on how business relates to such contexts and to transitional justice more specifically has emerged within the BHR field.

Beyond the BHR field, there has been an established discussion on transitional justice since the 1980s (Pietropaoli 2020). Transitional justice, as a concept, practice, and movement is commonly understood to comprise processes and mechanisms specifically designed to support a society's coming to terms with its legacy of large-scale and systematic abuse, and facilitate its transition from past conflict to democracy, rule of law, and respect for human rights. In other words, "transitional justice has to confront the past and simultaneously think forward to decide how to construct the future" (Sánchez 2014: 115). Thus, transitional justice mechanisms commonly aim at ensuring accountability, recognition of victims, reconciliation, and building strong democratic institutions and governance to prevent falling back into old patterns of violence. In particular, dealing with the past in a holistic manner is perceived as a crucial condition for creating a context for a peaceful future. This is a key defining element of transitional justice and gives rise to a broader and more diverse set of mechanisms than are commonly used in more conventional justice settings. Generally, four key elements define a transitional justice approach (Sandoval, Filippini, & Vidal 2014; Pietropaoli 2020):

- *Justice:* The purpose of justice mechanisms in transitional justice settings is to investigate and prosecute perpetrators, bring them to justice, and punish them for their involvement in past atrocities if found guilty.

- *Truth:* The role of truth processes, often carried out by so-called truth and reconciliation commissions, is to fully investigate, collect evidence, and, accordingly, establish facts and uncover the truth about past crimes and atrocities. Where the emphasis is on reconciliation, testimonies by victims and perpetrators may aim at healing more than at fact finding – meetings between victims and perpetrators may be a part of such a healing process (Haas 2014: 130–131).
- *Reparation:* Remedy and reparation processes serve to acknowledge victims and compensate and redress them for the harm they suffered. Reparation is understood more holistically in transitional justice settings; in addition to financial compensation it often entails elements aimed at a broader rehabilitation of victims.
- *Institutional reform:* Institutional reform processes aim at preventing the reoccurrence of such patterns of violence. This can encompass reformation of the security infrastructure including army and police forces as well as a broader move toward democratization of institutions and the rule of law. An important element are so-called guarantees of non-repetition, that is, guarantees for victims that there will not be a reoccurrence of such violent acts. These guarantees must be accompanied by institutional reform if they are to be more than just a statement.

Interestingly, while the discussions on both BHR and transitional justice have gained traction in the 1990s and since, the links between the two had hardly been explored until very recently (Michalowski 2014: 1). Transitional justice mechanisms and processes commonly do not deal with the role of business as a facilitator, contributor, or instigator of violence and abuse. They have almost exclusively focused on state actors as well as on members of paramilitary and other armed groups. This may strike some as peculiar, since economic actors have been shown to not only be peripherally involved in past conflicts, but have often played key roles at their very core (Payne, Pereira, & Bernal-Bermúdez 2020: 9–10). However, despite such key involvements, some have argued that there is a trade-off between achieving peace and the requirement of justice. In this sense, giving priority to achieving peace may require focusing on the prosecution only of those who committed the most serious violations. Furthermore, peace requires economic stability and prosperity, which may be undermined by a systematic prosecution of corporate actors (Sandoval, Filippini, & Vidal 2014: 15). On the other hand, precisely such fragile transitional contexts lend themselves to undue corporate influence aimed at extending corporate impunity for their involvement in conflict-related crimes (Paul & Schönsteiner 2014: 85). Nevertheless, as Michalowski & Carranza (2014: 254) point out, where transitional justice mechanisms exist, it is important that corporate accountability for crimes and human rights violations that occurred in contexts of conflict are addressed within and not separate from such mechanisms:

Indeed, to the extent that corporations played a role in the occurrences of the past, attempts to address corporate accountability need to be approached with the needs and specificities of the transitional justice process in mind, to prevent corporate accountability measures from running counter to and possibly undermining the aims of transitional justice (Michalowski & Carranza 2014: 254).

Accordingly, truth commissions in a number of post-conflict settings, such as South Africa, Liberia, and Argentina, have started to contemplate, if only peripherally, the role of business in facilitating, prolonging, or contributing to conflict-based violence (Pietropaoli 2020). As a consequence, a scholarly discussion of the role and justification of corporate accountability as a part of transitional justice settings emerged in the early 2000s. However, most questions relating to the inclusion of corporations in such processes are still unanswered. For example, how does the involvement and inclusion of corporations in transitional justice processes relate to other accountability mechanisms? Does their participation in truth processes, for example, lead to the exoneration of their directors from criminal prosecution and liability? How should corporations be involved in truth processes to begin with? Should there be a designated, separate process for dealing with corporate complicity or should this be dealt with as a part of the "regular" truth process (Sandoval, Filippini, & Vidal 2014: 18–19)? How do the private grievance and remedy mechanisms of corporations relate to public transitional justice reparation processes and how can they be used without leading to incoherence and potential new divisions and conflicts (Paul & Schönsteiner 2014: 87)? Another important issue is how to deal with the historic responsibility of businesses for their involvement in long-past atrocities, particularly in situations in which both the leadership and ownership of a respective company has changed in the meantime (Paul & Schönsteiner 2014: 88; Schrempf-Stirling, Palazzo, & Philipps 2016).

Reparation processes, too, can be unique and different in transitional justice contexts. Transitional justice settings often deal with large-scale violence that requires reparations of much larger proportion and much broader efforts of healing and rebuilding. Thus, beyond holding companies accountable for their involvement in specific incidences with defined damage to distinct groups of victims, there is the question of what role corporations can and ought to play in more general, societal, and communal reparation processes, with regard to both the material and the immaterial healing of communities. It has been argued, for example, that corporations should contribute to special reparations funds or pay reparation taxes, which would aim at the broader reconstruction of a country (Sandoval, Filippini, & Vidal 2014: 21). A corporate trust fund was implemented, for example, in South Africa to support and finance reparations for the damage caused through and during the apartheid era (Sandoval, Filippini, & Vidal 2014: 22).

Another suggestion is to involve companies in the provision of symbolic reparations such as the creation of memorial sites, holding of commemoration ceremonies, or offering official apologies. Symbolic reparations are an important instrument to assist victims and their families in dealing with a traumatic past, to find a sense of closure, and eventually to direct their attention to the future. However, symbolic reparations have almost exclusively been viewed as entirely state-sponsored, while corporate involvement has hardly been contemplated, studied, and conceptualized as yet (Vives, Cotrina, & Zarama 2019).

Beyond establishing the facts about past crimes and atrocities and holding companies accountable for their possible contributions, transitional justice is also about rebuilding and indeed transitioning into a more stable, predictable, and more democratic future. In particular, the boundaries between general reparations processes aiming at broader reconstruction and institutional rebuilding and reform processes can be fluid. Corporations can also be critical actors in this rebuilding and reform process by providing resources, work, and in more general terms development, which contributes to and fosters stability and prospects for the future. Furthermore, guarantees of non-repetition and institutional reform can be relevant also for corporate actors involved in the violence. Linking transitional justice to BHR, such institutional reform for corporations would involve not only a replacement of company leadership, for example, but also the implementation of effective BHR measures such as HRDD processes (Chapter 8.1) and grievance mechanisms, as well as a broader transformation of business cultures (Chapter 8.2).

STUDY QUESTIONS

1. What are the SDGs and how do they relate to the BHR agenda? Are they equivalent to, complentary to, or conflicting with the UNGPs?
2. How is climate change related to BHR? Can you give some examples of how climate change may impact human rights? Why is retrospective responsibility not enough to address climate-related harm? What are Carbon Major companies and what is their responsibility with regard to climate change?
3. Why is it necessary to put particular focus on human rights violations committed against women and girls? How do the UNGPs address gender? And what steps has the UNWG taken to build upon the UNGPs gender-based recommendations?
4. Why are community consultations often not representative of the full community? What can be done to make community engagement more gender-responsive?
5. What are the four key elements that define a transitional justice approach? Why has there been little intersection between BHR and the transitional justice

discussion in the past? Why is it important to deal with corporate human rights violations within and not outside of transitional justice processes in post-conflict settings?

REFLECTION QUESTIONS

1. Some scholars fear that the SDGs may draw away attention from human rights accountability and thus undermine, rather than strengthen, the UNGPs implementation process. Do you share this concern? Can you support your position with evidence?

2. The SDGs do not specify the responsibility of any actor, and as a result lack a real accountability mechanism. Would it be desirable to strengthen the SDGs in this regard? How could they be made more forceful?

3. Gender-based discrimination and violence occurs at work and at home. Imagine that you are a gender expert for a large multinational company. How would you advise it to address this issue? How should the company get started on its journey to become more gender-responsive?

4. Should corporations be involved in truth processes? What are advantages of involving them in such processes and what are the dangers? Considering these risks and benefits, should there be a designated, separate process for dealing with corporate complicity or should this be dealt with as a part of the "regular" truth process?

16 | Conclusion: Building Back Better

In the 1990s, when BHR emerged as a broad international movement and a focus of scholarly discussion, human rights and business were commonly still seen as two entirely separate domains. Human rights were viewed as the concern of states and while corporations started broadly to embrace the idea of having social responsibilities beyond merely maximizing profits, human rights were commonly not perceived as a part of these responsibilities. Human rights, in other words, were seen as the business of states, rather than as of concern to the state of business.

Three decades later, the situation is profoundly different. The UNGPs, enabled by years of tireless work by BHR advocates, have shifted public perception and led to a broad consensus that businesses do have a responsibility to at least respect human rights. Given the deeply rooted state-centrism that has informed human rights scholarship and practice in the past, this is a profound development. Symptomatically, this shifting consensus has set the ground for significant advances during the first decade of UNGPs implementation. There is now a broad international trend toward the adoption of domestic HRDD legislation (Chapter 12.4). The EU will no doubt play a key role in consolidating this trend and establishing mandatory HRDD as the international standard.

Notwithstanding these developments in the policy and legislative space both at the international and domestic levels, and despite companies coming to terms with ever more extensive and enforceable HRDD obligations, one can safely say that not enough has changed yet for those for whom it matters the most: rights-holders and victims of corporate human rights abuse on the ground. Rights-holders still struggle to assert their rights when they conflict with powerful business interests, human rights defenders still face tremendous risks if they confront corporate human rights abuse, and victims of human rights violations committed by businesses still face almost insurmountable obstacles to access justice, despite recent advances in home-state litigation (Chapter 12.5). Thus, the undisputed achievements in BHR policy and practice over the past three decades have yet to translate into real and tangible improvements, particularly for the most vulnerable and exposed populations on the ground.

The global environment for human rights protection has become more, rather than less, challenging in recent years. Two developments can briefly be pointed out in this regard.

First, the rise of right-wing populism has put human rights and democratic movements under pressure everywhere. Nationalist sentiments have been on the rise and international cooperation has suffered as a consequence. Large-scale disinformation campaigns and the spread of "fake news" have discredited and undermined democratic institutions and supported broad human rights skepticism. This has emboldened authoritarian regimes to tighten their grip on their populations and has set the ground also in Western liberal democracies for a backsliding on human rights – for example, with regard to immigration policies or restriction of the free press.

Second, the COVID-19 pandemic that struck the world in 2020 has further increased the exposure of vulnerable groups and laid bare the massive inequalities in the world both within and between populations. This represents a tremendous human rights challenge in and of itself. Yet within this context and against the background of the massive disruptions the pandemic has caused to local and global economies, maintaining and advancing the BHR agenda may become less of a priority for governments, which are squarely focused on economic recovery and may find a welcome narrative to delegitimize ongoing BHR initiatives by framing them as obstacles that prevent businesses from regaining productivity and competitive advantage.

However, these developments have also offered glimpses of hope and windows of opportunity for BHR. In a world backsliding on human rights, businesses have repeatedly positioned themselves as progressive forces confronting and speaking up against harmful government policies, supporting democratic movements, and taking a stand against the rise of xenophobia, racism, and other hate-driven forms of harassment, marginalization, and discrimination. Such corporate activism has become a more frequent phenomenon in recent years (Wettstein & Baur 2016). For example, businesses have voiced support for LGBTQ communities around the world, have been progressive forces in addressing the marginalization of transgendered people and have pushed governments on gay-rights issues such as marriage equality. They have confronted governments' politics of stalling climate change action and voiced protest over harsh immigration restrictions and the treatment of refugees. Similarly, not all businesses have opposed and combated the movement for BHR legislation. In almost all countries in which such movements and initiatives were launched, there have been companies that have actively and vocally supported them. While the number of such corporate supporters is exceedingly small compared to the vast majority of companies overtly or covertly opposed to such legislation, their proactive support can send an important signal to policy-makers, legislators, and to the larger public and thus make a decisive difference toward the potential adoption of such laws. Thus, businesses have increasingly been willing to use their leverage to push for pro-social and human rights issues, embracing not only their political stature (Chapter 6.1.1), but also a conception of responsibility that entails more than just "do no harm" (Chapter 7.3).

BHR has had a tendency to focus rather narrowly on instruments and policies to prevent negative human rights impacts emanating from corporate activities. The potential positive contribution of businesses to addressing large-scale structural human rights issues such as poverty and inequality has been a relative blind spot of the discussion. HRDD will go a long way in improving respect for human rights in global value chains. But it may do little to address the underlying structural root causes that expose vulnerable populations to such human rights risks in the first place. However, businesses can and ought to be a force for good also with regard to such necessary structural transformation and some of them seem to be slowly embracing such extended roles and responsibilities of human rights protection and fulfilment.

This is not to say that the political engagement of companies does not raise new and potentially difficult questions and challenges to be addressed. After all, the jury is still out on what truly drives the companies' corporate political engagement. While it seems that for some companies support of pro-social causes, policies, and legislation grows from genuine concern, commitment, and a long track-record of engagement, others may be jumping on the bandwagon based on purely opportunistic reasons. Their support may reflect the desire to boost their reputation and image among a customer base that is shifting toward more conscious buying behavior (Chapter 9.4.1). Furthermore, amid the changing public perception toward corporate accountability it may simply be more beneficial for such companies to actively shape and influence the respective discussions rather than try to block them altogether. Perhaps the rationale is simply that by vocally supporting weaker policy and legislative proposals, they can prevent more far-reaching initiatives and legislation proposed by civil society organizations from gaining sufficient traction (Wettstein 2021). Rather than an expression of a progressive corporate mindset, such political engagement would have to be seen as a display of corporate capture in such cases. Fairly little is known as yet on the internal mechanisms and processes driving such engagement by businesses; this area of scholarship certainly is worth more thorough exploration as BHR progresses and expands as a discussion.

As national economies have suffered tremendously and the vulnerabilities of our interdependent economic systems have become obvious throughout the COVID-19 pandemic, governments and businesses alike have vowed to "build back better" after the crisis subsides. In a time of unprecedented public awareness of the stark discrepancies between privilege on the one side and disadvantage and despair on the other, this momentum ought to be used to push the BHR agenda. "Building back better" cannot merely mean to build stronger and more resilient economic systems, but must include making them more equitable and more just. Time and again, contexts of crisis have provided opportunities for ethical renewal, for unlearning the old and learning the new. Transformation often runs up against privilege, complacency, and vested interests in established systems. Yet when crises shake such systems up, alter perceptions, and open a window of raised consciousness and awareness, change can become possible. Students of BHR: Change happens through engagement; you are the authors of the BHR story of the next generation. What will it look like?

Helpful Online Resources and Blogs on BHR

This overview contains selected online resources that provide BHR students, teachers, and researchers with helpful BHR-related information and knowledge. The list is limited to resources whose primary aim is to provide BHR-related information.

General BHR Information

- Access Now (BHR Section): www.accessnow.org/issue/business-and-human-rights/
- BHR and Tech Resource Hub by Global Partners Digital: www.gp-digital.org/bhr-and-the-tech-sector-resource-hub/
- Business & Human Rights Resource Centre: www.business-humanrights.org/en/
- *Business and Human Rights Journal* (BHRJ): www.cambridge.org/core/journals/business-and-human-rights-journal
- Business and Human Rights Scholars Association (free membership for BHR scholars): https://bhrscholarsassociation.org/
- Institute for Human Rights and Business: www.ihrb.org/
- OHCHR Business and Human Rights: www.ohchr.org/en/issues/business/pages/businessindex.aspx
- Teaching Business and Human Rights Forum (free membership for BHR teachers to access information): https://teachbhr.org/

Information on BHR Practice

- Corporate Human Rights Benchmark: www.corporatebenchmark.org/
- DCAF ICRC Knowledge Hub: www.securityhumanrightshub.org/
- Global Business Initiative on Human Rights (GBI) Practice Portal: https://gbihr.org/business-practice-portal
- Human Rights and Business Dilemmas Forum: http://hrbdf.org/
- The Danish Institute for Human Rights (BHR Division): www.humanrights.dk/business-human-rights

Information on BHR Accountability

- BankTrack: www.banktrack.org/
- BHRRC Case Profiles: www.business-humanrights.org/en/big-issues/corporate-legal-accountability/case-profiles/
- BHRRC Lawsuits Database: www.business-humanrights.org/en/from-us/law suits-database/
- Business and Human Rights in Law: www.bhrinlaw.org/
- Corporate Justice Coalition: https://corporatejusticecoalition.org/
- Environmental Justice Atlas: https://ejatlas.org/
- ETO Consortium: www.etoconsortium.org/en/
- European Center for Constitutional and Human Rights (ECCHR): www.ecchr.eu/en/
- International Federation for Human Rights (FIDH) Interactive Accountability Guide: https://corporateaccountability.fidh.org/
- Know the Chain: https://knowthechain.org
- National Action Plans on Business and Human Rights: https://globalnaps.org/
- OECD Watch Complaints Database: www.oecdwatch.org/complaints-database/
- Ranking Digital Rights: https://rankingdigitalrights.org/
- The Multi-Stakeholder Initiative (MSI) Database: https://msi-database.org/

BHR Blogs

- *Business and Human Rights Journal* (BHRJ) Blog: www.cambridge.org/core/blog/tag/bhrj/
- Business and Human Rights Resource Centre Blog: www.business-humanrights.org/en/blog/
- Corporate Accountability Lab Blog: https://corpaccountabilitylab.org/blog
- Doing Business *Right* Blog: www.asser.nl/doingbusinessright/blog
- OpenGlobalRights (Business): www.openglobalrights.org/topics/business/
- OpinioJuris (International Human Rights Law Section): http://opiniojuris.org/category/topics/international-human-right-law/
- Rights as Usual Blog: https://rightsasusual.com

References of Court Cases

Anns v. *Merton London Borough Council* [1977] UKHL 4, [1978] AC 728

Araya v. *Nevsun Resources Ltd.* [2017] BCCA 401

Caparo Industries plc v. *Dickman and Others* [1990] 2 AC 605

Cardona, Doe, Henao Montes et al. v. *Chiquita* [2014, Eleventh Circuit] Case No. 12-14898

Chandler v. *Cape plc* [2012] EWCA (Civ) 525

Choc v. *Hudbay Minerals Inc.* [2013] ONSC 1414

Citizens United v. *Federal Election Commission* [2010] 558 U.S. 310

Doe v. *Unocal Corp.* [1997] 963 F. Supp. 880; [2002, Ninth Circuit] 395 F.3d 932

Filártiga v. *Peña-Irala* [1980, Second Circuit] 630 F.2d 876; [1984, D.N.Y.] 577 F. Supp. 860

Four Nigerian Farmers and Milieudefensie v. *Royal Dutch Shell Plc (also known as Milieudefensie et al.* v. *Royal Dutch Shell Plc)* [2021] The Hague Court of Appeal, ECLI:NL:GHDHA:2021:132 (*Oruma*), ECLI:NL:GHDHA:2021:133 (Goi) and ECLI:NL:GHDHA:2021:134 (*Ikot Ada Udo*)

Friends of the Earth and others v. *Total SA* [2020] Cour d'appel de Versailles (Versailles Court of Appeal) No. RG 20/01692

Garcia v. *Tahoe Resources Inc.* [2015] BCSC 2045

Jabir and others v. *KiK Textilien und Non-Food GmbH* [2019] Landgericht (Regional Court) Dortmund, Case No. 7 O 95/15

Jesner v. *Arab Bank* [2018] 138 S Ct 1386

John Doe I et al. v. *Nestlé USA et al.* [2021] 593 U. S.

Kiobel v. *Royal Dutch Petroleum Co. (Shell)* [2013] 569 U. S. 108

Lliuya v. *RWE AG* [2018] Az. 5 U 15/17 Oberlandesgericht (OLG) Hamm

Notre Affaire à Tous and Others v. *Total SA* [2021] Le tribunal administratif (Paris Administrative Court). No. 1904967, 1904968, 1904972, 1904976/4-1

Ododo Francis v. *ENI and Nigerian Agip Oil Company (NAOC) (also known as Ikebiri Community* v. *ENI)* closed in 2019 by the Italian Court due to reached settlement amongst the parties

Okpabi and others v. *Royal Dutch Shell Plc and another* [2021] UKSC 3

Owusu v. *Jackson and Others* [2005] ECR I-1383, Case C-281/02

Santa Clara County v. *Southern Pacific Railroad Company* [1886] 118 U. S. 394

Sherpa and the ECCHR v. *Lafarge/Syria*

Sosa v. *Alvarez-Machain* [2004] 542 U. S. 692

State of the Netherlands v. *Urgenda Foundation* [2019] Supreme Court of the Netherlands, No. 19/00135

Urbaser S.A. and Consorcio de Aguas Bilbao
   Bizkaia, Bilbao Biskaia Ur Partuergoa
   v. *The Argentine Republic* [2016] ICSID
   Case No. ARB/07/26
Vedanta Resources Plc v. *Lungowe* [2019]
   UKSC 20

Velásquez Rodríguez v. *Honduras*
   [1988] Inter-American Court of
   Human Rights (Series C)
   No. 4
Wiwa v. *Royal Dutch Petroleum Co. (Shell)*
   [2009] 48 ILM 972

Glossary

3TG minerals Tantalum, Tin, Tungsten and Gold

AI Artificial intelligence

ASEAN Association of South-East Asian Nations

ASM Artisanal or small-scale mining

ATCA Alien Tort Claims Act

AUD Australian Dollar

BAFA Bundesamt für Wirtschaft und Ausfuhrkontrolle (Federal Office for Economic Affairs and Export Control)

BHR Business and Human Rights

BHRJ *Business and Human Rights Journal*

BHRRC Business and Human Rights Resource Centre

BITs Bilateral Investment Treaties

CAT Committee Against Torture

CCC Clean Clothes Campaign

CCPR Human Rights Committee

CED Committee on Enforced Disappearances

CEDAW Committee on the Elimination of Discrimination Against Women

CERD Committee on the Elimination of Racial Discrimination

CESCR Committee on Economic, Social and Cultural Rights

CMW Committee on Migrant Workers

COP Annual Communication on Progress

COPINH Consejo Cívico de Organizaciones Populares e Indígenas de Honduras (Civic Council of Popular and Indigenous Organisations of Honduras)

CRC Committee on the Rights of the Child

CRPD Committee on the Rights of Persons with Disabilities

CSR Corporate Social Responsibility

DAPL Dakota Access Pipeline

Desa Desarrollos Energéticos SA

DIHR Danish Institute for Human Rights

DRC Democratic Republic of the Congo

ECHR European Convention on Human Rights

ECCHR European Center for Constitutional and Human Rights

Eds. Editors

EGC Entreprise Générale du Cobalt

EITI Extractive Industries Transparency Initiative

EU European Union

ESG Environmental, Social and Governance

FAO Food and Agriculture Organisation of the UN

FLA Fair Labor Association

FPIC Free, prior and informed consent

FTSE Financial Times Stock Exchange

GAO General Administrative Order

GBI Global Business Initiative on Human Rights

GBP British pound sterling

GNI Global Network Initiative

GRI Global Reporting Initiative

HRC UN Human Rights Council

HRDs Human rights defenders

HRDD Human rights due diligence

HRIAs Human rights impact assessments

ICC International Criminal Court

ICCPR International Covenant for Civil and Political Rights

ICESCR International Covenant on Economic, Social and Cultural Rights

ICJ International Court of Justice

ICoC International Code of Conduct for Private Security Service Providers

ICRC International Committee of the Red Cross

ICT Information and Communication Technology

IFBA International Food and Beverage Alliance

IFC International Finance Corporation

IHRB Institute for Human Rights and Business

IIAs International Investment Agreements

ILO International Labour Organisation

IOE International Organisation of Employers

IRBC Agreements Dutch Agreements for International Responsible Business Conduct

IS Islamic State

ISDS Investor–state dispute settlement mechanisms

ISO International Organisation for Standardization

KCM Konkola Copper Mines

LGBTQ Lesbian, Gay, Bisexual, Transgender, and Queer

MDGs Millennium Development Goals

MOSOP Movement for the Survival of the Ogoni People

MSC Marine Stewardship Council

MSIs Multi-stakeholder initiatives

NAOC Nigerian Agip Oil Company

NAPs National Action Plans

NCPs National Contact Points

n.d. No date

NGOs Non-governmental Organizations

OAS Organisation of American States

OECD Organisation for Economic Co-operation and Development

OEIWG Open-Ended Intergovernmental Working Group on Transnational Corporations and other Business Enterprises with Respect to Human Rights

OHCHR Office of the High Commissioner for Human Rights

PRI Principles for Responsible Investment

RAFI Human Rights Reporting and Assurance Framework Initiative

RBI Swiss Responsible Business Initiative

RMG Ready-made garment

RWE Rheinisch-Westfälisches Elektrizitätswerk (German Energy Company)

SDGs Sustainable Development Goals

SEC Securities and Exchange Commission

SLAPPs Strategic Lawsuits Against Public Participation

SMEs Small and medium-sized enterprises

SPDC Shell Petroleum Development Company of Nigeria Ltd.

SPT Subcommittee on Prevention of Torture

SRSG UN Special Representative on Business and Human Rights

UCC Union Carbide Corporation

UCIL Union Carbide India Ltd

UDHR Universal Declaration of Human Rights

UK United Kingdom

UN United Nations

UNCITRAL UN Commission on International Trade Law

UNCRC UN Convention on the Rights of the Child

UNCTAD UN Conference on Trade and Development

UNDP UN Development Programme

UN Draft Norms Norms on the
Responsibility of Transnational
Corporations and Other Business
Enterprises with Regard to Human Rights

UNEP UN Environment Programme

UNESCO UN Educational, Scientific and
Cultural Organization

UN Framework UN Protect, Respect and
Remedy Framework

UNGC UN Global Compact

UNGPs UN Guiding Principles on Business
and Human Rights

UNICEF UN Children's Fund

UNWG UN Working group on the issue of
human rights and transnational
corporations and other business
enterprises

UNPFII UN Permanent Forum on
Indigenous Issues

US/USA United States of America

WHO World Health Organisation

WTO World Trade Organisation

ZEAs Zones d'Exploration Artisanale
(Artisanal Exploration Sites)

References

Abbott, Kenneth W. 2012. Engaging the public and the private in global sustainability governance. *International Affairs* 88/3: 543–564.

Abbott, Kenneth W. & Snidal, Duncan. 2000. Hard and soft law in international governance. *International Organization* 54/3: 421–456.

Agence France Press. 2017. German court to hear Peruvian farmer's climate case against RWE. *The Guardian*, November 30, 2017. www.theguardian.com/ environment/2017/nov/30/german-court-to-hear-peruvian-farmers-climate-case-against-rwe

Alexander, Peter. 2013. Marikana, turning point in South African history. *Review of African Political Economy* 40/138: 605–619.

Alexander, Larry & Moore, Michael. 2020. Deontological ethics. In Zalta, Edward N. (ed.), *The Stanford Encyclopedia of Philosophy.* https://plato.stanford.edu/ archives/win2020/entries/ethics-deontological/

Alliance for Corporate Transparency. 2019. The Alliance for Corporate Transparency 2019 Research Report: An Analysis of the Sustainability Reports of 1000 Companies Pursuant to the EU Non-Financial Reporting Directive. https:// allianceforcorporatetransparency.org/

Amnesty International. 2016a. *Malabo Protocol: Legal and Institutional Implications of the Merged and Expanded African Court.* London: Amnesty International. www.refworld .org/pdfid/56a9ddcf4.pdf

Amnesty International. 2016b. Trafigura: A toxic journey. www.amnesty.org/en/ latest/news/2016/04/trafigura-a-toxic-journey/

Amnesty International. 2017. Angelica Choc v. Hudbay Minerals. www.amnesty.ca/ legal-brief/angelica-choc-v-hudbay-minerals

Amnesty International. 2019. *Surveillance Giants: How the Business Model of Google and Facebook Threatens Human Rights.* London: Amnesty International. www.amnesty.org/en/documents/ pol30/1404/2019/en/

Amnesty International. 2020. *"Why Do You Want to Rest?" Ongoing Abuse of Domestic Workers in Qatar.* London: Amnesty International. www.amnesty .org/en/documents/mde22/3175/2020/ en/

Amnesty International. 2021. *"Like We Were Enemies in a War." China's Mass Internment, Torture and Persecution of Muslims in Xinjiang.* London: Amnesty International. www .amnesty.org/en/documents/asa17/ 4137/2021/en/

Amnesty International. n.d. Qatar World Cup of Shame. www.amnesty.org/en/latest/ campaigns/2016/03/qatar-world-cup-of-shame/

Amnesty International & AfreWatch. 2016. *"This Is What We Die For" – Human Rights Abuses in the Democratic Republic of the Congo Power the Global Trade in Cobalt.* London: Amnesty International. www.amnesty.org/en/documents/afr62/3183/2016/en/

Anderson, Sarah & Cavanagh, John. 2000. *Top 200: The Rise of Corporate Global Power.* Washington: Institute for Policy Studies.

Arenas, Daniel, Albareda, Laura & Goodman, Jennifer. 2020. Contestation in multi–stakeholder initiatives: Enhancing the democratic quality of transnational governance. *Business Ethics Quarterly* 30/2: 169–199.

Aristova, Ekaterina. 2017. Suing TNCs in the English Courts: The challenge of jurisdiction. February 1, 2017. http://conflictoflaws.net/2017/suing-tncs-in-the-english-courts-the-challenge-of-jurisdiction/

Arnold, Denis. 2010. Transnational corporations and the duty to respect basic human rights. *Business Ethics Quarterly* 20/3: 371–399.

Asia Pacific Forum of National Human Rights Institutions. 2012. *Promoting and Protecting the Rights of Migrant Workers: The Role of National Human Rights Institutions.* Sydney: Asia Pacific Forum of National Human Rights Institutions. www.asiapacificforum.net/resources/manual-on-migrant-workers/

Baglayan, Basak, Landau, Ingrid, McVey, Marisa & Wodajo, Kebene. 2018. Good business: the economic case for protecting human rights. Business and Human Rights Young Researchers Summit; Frank Bold; ICAR. https://icar.squarespace.com/publications/2018/11/26/good-business-the-economic-case-for-protecting-human-rights

Baker, Mallen. 2016. Nike and child labour – how it went from laggard to leader. February 29, 2016. https://mallenbaker.net/article/clear-reflection/nike-and-child-labour-how-it-went-from-laggard-to-leader

Baker-Smith, Katelyn & Miklos Attila, Szocs B. 2016. What is land grabbing? A critical review of existing Definitions. Eco Ruralis. www.farmlandgrab.org/uploads/attachment/EcoRuralis_WhatIsLandGrabbing_2016.pdf

Balch, Oliver. 2021. Mars, Nestlé and Hershey to face child slavery lawsuit in US. *The Guardian*, February 12, 2021. www.theguardian.com/global-development/2021/feb/12/mars-nestle-and-hershey-to-face-landmark-child-slavery-lawsuit-in-us

Balzarova, Michaela A. & Castka, Pavel. 2012. Stakeholders' influence and contribution to social standards development: The case of multiple stakeholder approach to ISO 26000 development. *Journal of Business Ethics* 111: 265–279.

Banerji, Annie. 2019. Factbox: Grief and neglect – Ten factory disasters in South Asia. *Reuters*, December 10, 2019. www.reuters.com/article/us-india-fire-workers-factbox-idUSKBN1YE1PT

BankTrack. 2017. Human rights briefing paper: how banks contribute to human rights violations. BankTrack.

www.banktrack.org/download/how_banks_contribute_to_human_rights_abuses/180416_how_banks_contribute_human_rights_1.pdf

BankTrack. n.d. Overview: Closed Complaints on Banks. www.banktrack.org/campaign/overview_closed_complaints_on_banks

Bansal, Pratima & Song, Hee-Chan. 2017. Similar but not the same: Differentiating corporate sustainability from corporate responsibility. *Academy of Management Annals* 11/1: 105–149.

Barrett, Paul M., Baumann-Pauly, Dorothée & Gu, April. 2018. *Five Years After Rana Plaza: The Way Forward.* New York: NYU Stern Center for Business and Human Rights.

Bartley, Tim. 2018. *Rules Without Rights: Land, Labor, and Private Authority in the Global Economy.* Oxford: Oxford University Press.

Baughen, Simon. 2015. *Human Rights and Corporate Wrongs: Closing the Governance Gap.* Cheltenham; Northhampton, MA: Edward Elgar.

Baumann-Pauly, Dorothée. 2020. Making Mining Safe and Fair: Artisanal Cobalt Extraction in the Democratic Republic of the Congo. World Economic Forum White Paper. Geneva: World Economic Forum.

Baumann-Pauly, Dorothée, Nolan, Justine, Labowitz, Sarah & van Heerden, Auret. 2016. Setting and enforcing industry-specific standards for human rights: the role of multi-stakeholder initiatives in regulating corporate conduct. In Baumann-Pauly, Dorothée & Nolan, Justine (eds.), *Business and Human Rights: From Principles to Practice,* 107–127. London; New York: Routledge.

Baumann-Pauly, Dorothée, Nolan, Justine, van Heerden, Auret & Samway, Michael. 2016. Industry-specific multi-stakeholder initiatives that govern corporate human rights standards: Legitimacy assessment of the Fair Labor Association and the Global Network Initiative. *Journal of Business Ethics* 143: 771–787.

Baxi, Upendra. 1986a. From human rights to the right to become human: Some heresies. *India International Journal* 13: 185–200.

Baxi, Upendra (ed.). 1986b. *Inconvenient Forum and Convenient Catastrophe: The Bhopal Case.* Bombay: N M Tripathi Pvt. Ltd.

Baxi, Upendra. 2016. Human rights responsibility of multinational corporations, political ecology of injustice: Learning from Bhopal thirty plus? *Business and Human Rights Journal* 1/1: 21–40.

Baxi, Upendra & Dhanda, Amita (eds.). 1986. *Mass Disasters and Multinational Liability: The Bhopal Case.* Bombay: N M Tripathi Pvt. Ltd.

BBC. 2021. Who are the Uighurs and why is China being accused of genocide? March 26, 2021. www.bbc.com/news/world-asia-china-22278037

Benson, Thor. 2018. From Whole Foods to Amazon, invasive technology controlling workers is more dystopian than you think. *Salon,* February 24, 2018. www.salon.com/2018/02/24/from-whole-foods-to-amazon-invasive-technology-controlling-workers-is-more-dystopian-than-you-think_partner/

Bernaz, Nadia. 2013. Enhancing corporate accountability for human rights violations: Is extraterritoriality the magic potion? *Journal of Business Ethics* 13: 493–511.

Bernaz, Nadia. 2017. *Business and Human Rights: History, Law and Policy – Bridging the Accountability Gap.* London; New York: Routledge.

Bernaz, Nadia. 2018. Okpabi v. Shell on Appeal: Foreign Direct Liability in Troubled Waters. Rights as Usual Blog, February 23, 2018. https://rightsasusual .com/?p=1194

BHRRC. 2017. First Year of FTSE 100 Reports Under the UK Modern Slavery Act: Towards Elimination? Business & Human Rights Resource Centre. www .business-humanrights.org/sites/default/ files/FTSE%20100%20Report%20FINAL %20%28002%291Dec2017.pdf.

BHRRC. 2020. Germany: Monitoring of the National Action Plan on Business & Human Rights. Business & Human Rights Resource Centre, August 14, 2020. www.business-humanrights.org/ en/latest-news/germany-monitoring-of-the-national-action-plan-on-business-human-rights/

BHRRC. n.d. (a). Chiquita Lawsuits (re Colombia, Filed in USA by Colombian Nationals). www.business-humanrights .org/en/latest-news/chiquita-lawsuits-re-colombia/

BHRRC. n.d. (b). Human Rights Defenders & Civic Freedoms. www.business-humanrights.org/en/big-issues/human-rights-defenders-civic-freedoms/

BHRRC. n.d. (c). Modern Slavery Registry. www.modernslaveryregistry .org/

BHRRC. n.d. (d). KiK Lawsuit (re Pakistan). www.business-humanrights.org/en/ latest-news/kik-lawsuit-re-pakistan/

BHRRC. n.d. (e). RWE Lawsuit (re Climate Change). www.business-humanrights .org/en/latest-news/rwe-lawsuit-re-climate-change/

BHRRC. n.d. (f). Argor-Heraeus Investigation (re Dem. Rep. of Congo). www.business-humanrights.org/en/latest-news/argor-heraeus-investigation-re-dem-rep-of-congo/

BHRRC. n.d. (g). Lafarge Lawsuit (re Complicity in Crimes Against Humanity in Syria). www.business-humanrights .org/en/latest-news/lafarge-lawsuit-re-complicity-in-crimes-against-humanity-in-syria/

BHRRC. n.d. (h). Total Lawsuit (re Climate Change, France). www.business-humanrights.org/en/latest-news/total-lawsuit-re-climate-change-france/

BHRRC. n.d. (i). Total Lawsuit (re Failure to Respect French Duty of Vigilance Law in Operations in Uganda). www .business-humanrights.org/en/latest-news/total-lawsuit-re-failure-to-respect-french-duty-of-vigilance-law-in-operations-in-uganda/

BHRRC. n.d. (j). Union Carbide/Dow Lawsuit (re Bhopal, Filed in the US). www .business-humanrights.org/en/latest-news/union-carbidedow-lawsuit-re-bhopal-filed-in-the-us/

BHRRC. n.d. (k). Trafigura Lawsuit (re Hazardous Waste Disposal in Côte d'Ivoire, Filed in UK). www.business-humanrights.org/en/latest-news/ trafigura-lawsuit-re-hazardous-waste-disposal-in-c%C3%B4te-divoire-filed-in-uk/

Biesheuvel, Thomas. 2020. Glencore Makes U-turn to Back Artisanal Mining of Cobalt. Bloomberg, August 24, 2020. www.bloomberg.com/news/articles/2020-08-24/glencore-makes-u-turn-to-back-artisanal-mining-of-cobalt

Bilchitz, David. 2013. A Chasm between "Is" and "Ought"? A Critique of the Normative Foundations of the SRSG's Framework and the Guiding Principles. In Deva, Surya & Bilchitz, David (eds.), *Human Rights Obligations of Business: Beyond the Corporate Responsibility to Respect?* 107–137. Cambridge, UK: Cambridge University Press.

Bilchitz, David. 2017. Corporate Obligations and a Treaty on Business and Human Rights: A Constitutional Model? In Deva, Surya & Bilchitz, David (eds.), *Building a Treaty on Business and Human Rights: Context and Contours*, 185–215. Cambridge, UK: Cambridge University Press.

Bilchitz, David & Deva, Surya. 2013. The Human Rights Obligations of Business: A Critical Framework for the Future. In Deva, Surya & Bilchitz, David (eds.), *Human Rights Obligations of Business: Beyond the Corporate Responsibility to Respect?* 1–26. Cambridge, UK: Cambridge University Press.

Birkey, Rachel N., Guidry, Ronald P., Islam, Mohammad A. & Patten, Dennis M. 2018. Mandated social disclosure: An analysis of the response to the California Transparency in Supply Chains Act of 2010. *Journal of Business Ethics* 152: 827–841.

BlackRock. 2021. Our Approach to Engagement with Companies on their Human Rights Impacts. www.blackrock.com/corporate/literature/publication/blk-commentary-engagement-on-human-rights.pdf

Blair, Margaret M. 2013. Corporate personhood and the corporate persona. *University of Illinois Law Review* 2013/3: 785–820.

Blair, Margaret M. 2015. Of corporations, courts, personhood, and morality. *Business Ethics Quarterly* 25/4: 415–431.

Bollen, Nicole P. F. 2011. Building Bridges: From Aircraft to Sustainable Lending. In OECD (ed.), *Smart Rules for Fair Trade: 50 Years of Export Credits*, 59–61. Paris: OECD Publishing.

Bonnitcha, Jonathan & McCorquodale, Robert. 2017. The concept of "due diligence" in the UN Guiding Principles on Business and Human Rights. *The European Journal of International Law* 28/3: 899–919.

Borras Jr., Saturnino M., Franco, Jennifer C., Gómez, Sergio, Kay, Cristóbal & Spoor, Max. 2012. Land grabbing in Latin America and the Caribbean. *The Journal of Peasant Studies* 39/3-4: 845–872.

Brabant, Stéphane & Savourey, Elsa. 2020. All Eyes on France – French Vigilance Law First Enforcement Cases (1/2): Current Cases and Trends. *Business and Human Rights Journal* Blog, January 24, 2020. www.cambridge.org/core/blog/2020/01/24/all-eyes-on-france-french-vigilance-law-first-enforcement-cases-1-2-current-cases-and-trends/#_edn13

Brenkert, George. 2009. Google, human rights, and moral compromise. *Journal of Business Ethics* 85: 453–478.

Bryant, Katharine. 2017. Global Estimates of Modern Slavery: We Need to Talk about Gender. Guest Blog from Walk Free Foundation, October 30, 2017. https://plan-uk.org/blogs/global-estimates-of-modern-slavery-we-need-to-talk-about-gender

BSR. 2020. 10 Human Rights Priorities for the Financial Sector. www.bsr.org/reports/BSR_Primer_Human_Rights_Finance_Sector.pdf

Buergenthal, Thomas. 1982. The Inter-American Court of Human Rights. *The American Journal of International Law* 76/2: 231–245.

Buhmann, Karin. 2013. Navigating from "Train Wreck" to Being "Welcomed": Negotiation Strategies and Argumentative Patterns in the Development of the UN Framework. In Deva, Surya & Bilchitz, David (eds.), *Human Rights Obligations of Business: Beyond the Corporate Responsibility to Respect?* 29–57. Cambridge, UK: Cambridge University Press.

Buhmann, Karin. 2018. Neglecting the proactive aspect of human rights due diligence? A critical appraisal of the EU's Non-Financial Reporting Directive as a pillar one avenue for promoting pillar two action. *Business and Human Rights Journal* 3/1: 23–45.

Buhmann, Karin, Jonsson, Jonas & Fisker, Mette. 2019. Do no harm and do more good too: Connecting the SDGs with business and human rights and political CSR theory. *Corporate Governance* 19/3: 389–403.

Burrow, Sarah & Bloomer, Phil. 2020. Something for Europeans to Celebrate – A New Social Contract Begins to Emerge? Open Democracy, May 4, 2020. www.opendemocracy.net/en/can-europe-make-it/something-for-europeans-to-celebrate-a-new-social-contract-begins-to-emerge/

Buse, Kent, Tanaka, Sonja & Hawkes, Sarah. 2017. Healthy people and healthy profits? Elaborating a conceptual framework for governing the commercial determinants of non-communicable diseases and identifying options for reducing risk exposure. *Globalization and Health* 13/34: 1–12.

Cafaggi, Fabrizio. 2011. New foundations of transnational private regulation. *Journal of Law and Society* 38/1: 20–49.

Calvão, Filipe, McDonald, Catherine E. A. & Bolay Matthieu. 2021. Cobalt mining and the corporate outsourcing of responsibility in the Democratic Republic of Congo. *The Extractive Industries and Society:* forthcoming.

Cantú Rivera, Humberto. 2019. National action plans on business and human rights: Progress or mirage? *Business and Human Rights Journal* 4/2: 213–237.

Carraro, Valentina. 2019. Electing the experts: Expertise and independence in the UN human rights treaty bodies. *European Journal of International Relations* 25/3: 826–851.

Carrington, Michal J., Neville, Benjamin A. & Whitwell, Gregory J. 2014. Lost in translation: Exploring the ethical consumer intention–behavior gap. *Journal of Business Research* 67: 2759–2767.

Cassell, Doug & Ramasastry, Anita. 2016. White paper: Options for a treaty on business and human rights. *Notre Dame*

Journal of International & Comparative Law 6/1: 1–50.

Center for International Environmental Law. 2019. Groundbreaking Inquiry in Philippines Links Carbon Majors to Human Rights Impacts of Climate Change, Calls for Greater Accountability. December 9, 2019. www.ciel.org/news/groundbreaking-inquiry-in-philippines-links-carbon-majors-to-human-rights-impacts-of-climate-change-calls-for-greater-accountability/

Chatelain, Lucie. 2021. First Court Decision in the Climate Litigation against Total: A Promising Interpretation of the French Duty of Vigilance Law. Business & Human Rights Resource Centre, March 25, 2021. www.business-humanrights.org/en/blog/first-court-decision-in-the-climate-litigation-against-total-a-promising-interpretation-of-the-french-duty-of-vigilance-law/

Chirwa, Danwood M. 2004. The doctrine of state responsibility as a potential means of holding private actors accountable for human rights. _Melbourne Journal of International Law_ 5/1.

Choudhury, Barnali. 2017. Hardening Soft Law Initiatives in Business and Human Rights. In du Plessis, Jean J. & Low, Chee K. (eds.), _Corporate Governance Codes for the 21st Century_, 189–208. Cham, Switzerland: Springer.

Choudhury, Barnali. 2018. Balancing soft and hard law for business and human rights. _International & Comparative Law Quarterly_ 67/4: 961–986.

Chowdhury, Rashedur. 2017. The Rana Plaza disaster and the complicit behavior of elite NGOs. _Organization_ 24/6: 938–949.

Clapham, Andrew. 2004. State Responsibility, Corporate Responsibility, and Complicity in Human Rights Violations. In Bomann-Larsen, Lene & Wiggen, Oddny (eds.), _Responsibility in World Business: Managing Harmful Side-Effects of Corporate Activity_, 50–81. Tokyo: United Nations University Press.

Clapham, Andrew. 2006. _Human Rights Obligations of Non-State Actors_. Oxford; New York: Oxford University Press.

Clapham, Andrew & Jerbi, Scott. 2001. Categories of corporate complicity in human rights abuses. _Hastings International and Comparative Law Review_ 24: 339–349.

Clean Clothes Campaign. n.d. (a). Waste and Pollution. https://cleanclothes.org/fashions-problems/waste-and-pollution

Clean Clothes Campaign. n.d. (b). Rana Plaza. https://cleanclothes.org/campaigns/past/rana-plaza

Clough, Jonathan. 2005. Not-so-innocents abroad: Corporate criminal liability for human rights abuses. _Australian Journal of Human Rights_ 11/1: 1–32.

Coase, Ronald. 1937. The nature of the firm. _Economica_ 4/16: 386–405.

Columbia Center on Sustainable Development & UNWG. 2018. Impacts of the International Investment Regime on Access to Justice. Roundtable Outcome Document. www.ohchr.org/Documents/Issues/Business/CCSI_UNWGBHR_InternationalInvestmentRegime.pdf

Committee on Economic, Social and Cultural
Rights. 2000. General Comment No. 14
(2000): The Right to the Highest
Attainable Standard of Health (Article
12). E/C.12/2000/4. https://undocs.org/
E/C.12/2000/4

Committee on Economic Social and Cultural
Rights. 2017. General Comment No. 24
(2017) on State Obligations under the
International Covenant on Economic,
Social and Cultural Rights in the
Context of Business Activities. E/C.12/
GC/24. www.refworld.org/docid/
5beaecba4.html

Cossart, Sandra, Chaplier, Jérôme & Beau de
Lomenie, Tiphaine. 2017. The French
Law on Duty of Care: A historic step
towards making globalization work for
all. *Business and Human Rights Journal*
2/2: 317–323.

Cotula, Lorenzo. 2014. Addressing the
Human Rights Impacts of "Land
Grabbing". Directorate-General for
External Policies of the Union Study.
EXPO/B/DROI/2014/06. Brussels:
European Union. www.europarl.europa
.eu/RegData/etudes/STUD/2014/
534984/EXPO_STU(2014)534984_EN
.pdf

Cragg, Wesley. 2012. Ethics, enlightened
self-interest, and the corporate
responsibility to respect human rights:
A critical look at the justificatory
foundations of the UN Framework.
Business Ethics Quarterly 22/1: 9–36.

Craig, Gary. 2017. The UK's modern slavery
legislation: An early assessment of
progress. *Social Inclusion* 5/2: 16–27.

Cranston, Maurice. 1983. Are there any
human rights? *Daedalus* 112/4: 1–17.

Criado Perez, Caroline. 2019. *Invisible
Women: Exposing Data Bias in a World
Designed for Men*. New York City:
Vintage Publishing.

Crick, Bob. 2011. Reflections on Export
Credits in the OECD. In OECD (ed.),
*Smart Rules for Fair Trade: 50 Years of
Export Credits*, 62-65. Paris: OECD
Publishing.

Croser, Marilyn, Day, Martyn, Van Huijstee,
Mariëtte & Samkalden, Channa. 2020.
Vedanta v. Lungowe and Kiobel
v. Shell: The implications for parent
company accountability. *Business and
Human Rights Journal* 5/1: 130–136.

Daniel, Caitlin, Wilde-Ramsing, Joseph,
Genovese, Kris & Sandjojo, Virginia.
2015. Remedy Remains Rare: An
Analysis of 15 Years of NCP Cases and
their Contribution to Improve Access to
Remedy for Victims of Corporate
Misconduct. Amsterdam: OECD Watch.
www.oecdwatch.org/wp-content/
uploads/sites/8/2015/06/Remedy-
Remains-Rare.pdf

The Danish Institute for Human Rights.
2020. *Guidance on Human Rights
Impact Assessment of Digital
Activities*. Copenhagen: The Danish
Institute for Human Rights. www
.humanrights.dk/publications/
human-rights-impact-assessment-
digital-activities

Davies, Nick. 2015. Marikana Massacre: The
untold story of the strike leader who
died for workers' rights. *The Guardian*,
May 19, 2015. www.theguardian.com/
world/2015/may/19/marikana-
massacre-untold-story-strike-leader-
died-workers-rights

De Felice, Damiano. 2015a. Business and human rights indicators to measure the corporate responsibility to respect: Challenges and opportunities. *Human Rights Quarterly* 37/2: 511–555.

De Felice, Damiano. 2015b. Banks and human rights due diligence: A critical analysis of the Thun Group's discussion paper on the UN Guiding Principles on Business and Human Rights. *The International Journal of Human Rights* 19/3: 319–340.

De Felice, Damiano & Graf, Andreas. 2015. The potential of national action plans to implement human rights norms: An early assessment with respect to the UN Guiding Principles on Business and Human Rights. *Journal of Human Rights Practice* 7/1: 40–71.

DeGeorge, Richard T. 2010. *Business Ethics*. Seventh edition. Upper Saddle River, NJ: Prentice Hall.

Deloitte. 2016. The 2016 Deloitte Millennial Survey: Winning Over the Next Generation of Leaders. www2.deloitte .com/content/dam/Deloitte/global/ Documents/About-Deloitte/gx-millenial-survey-2016-exec-summary .pdf

Dembour, Marie-Bénédicte. 2010. What are human rights? Four schools of thought. *Human Rights Quarterly* 32/1: 1–20.

Democratic Republic of Congo. 2002. Law No. 007/2002 of July 11, 2002 Relating to the Mining Code. https://goxi.org/ sites/default/files/2019-06/Democractic %20Republic%20of%20the%20Congo %20%28DRC%29%2C%20Law%20of% 202002%20Relating%20to%20the% 20Mining%20Code.pdf

Demuijnck, Geert & Fasterling, Björn. 2016. The social license to operate. *Journal of Business Ethics* 136: 675–685.

Derber, Charles. 1998. *Corporation Nation: How Corporations Are Taking Over Our Lives and What We Can Do About It*. New York: St. Martin's Griffin.

De Schutter, Olivier. 2006. Extraterritorial Jurisdiction as a Tool for Improving the Human Rights Accountability of Transnational Corporations. https:// media.business-humanrights.org/ media/documents/df31ea6e492084 e26ac4c08affcf51389695fead.pdf

De Schutter, Olivier. 2014. *International Human Rights Law*. Second edition. Cambridge, UK: Cambridge University Press.

Deva, Surya. 2013. Treating Human Rights Lightly: A Critique of the Consensus Rhetoric and the Language Employed by the Guiding Principles. In Deva, Surya & Bilchitz, David (eds.), *Human Rights Obligations of Business: Beyond the Corporate Responsibility to Respect?* 78–104. Cambridge, UK: Cambridge University Press.

Deva, Surya. 2014. *Regulating Corporate Human Rights Violations: Humanizing Business*. London; New York: Routledge.

Deva, Surya. 2016. Bhopal: The Saga Continues 31 Years On. In Baumann-Pauly, Dorothée & Nolan, Justine (eds.), *Business and Human Rights: From Principles to Practice*, 22–26. London; New York: Routledge.

Deva, Surya. 2017. Scope of the Proposed Business and Human Rights Treaty: Navigating through Normativity, Law and Politics. In Deva, Surya & Bilchitz, David (eds.), *Building a Treaty on Business and Human Rights: Context and Contours*, 154–182. Cambridge, UK: Cambridge University Press.

Deva, Surya. 2018. Managing States' "Fatal Attraction" to International Investment Agreements. UNCTAD Investment Policy Hub Blog, August 13, 2018. https://investmentpolicy.unctad.org/blogs/75/managing-states-fatal-attraction-to-international-investment-agreements-

Deva, Surya, Ramasastry, Anita, Wettstein, Florian & Santoro, Michael. 2019. Business and Human Rights Scholarship: Past Trends and Future Directions. *Business and Human Rights Journal* 4/2: 201–212.

Dodge, William. 2019. Corporate liability under the US Alien Tort Statute: A comment on Jesner v. Arab Bank. *Business and Human Rights Journal* 4/1: 131–137.

Donaldson, Thomas. 1989. *The Ethics of International Business.* New York; Oxford: Oxford University Press.

Donaldson, Thomas. 1996. Values in tension: Ethics away from home. *Harvard Business Review* 74/5: 48–62.

Drucker, Peter F. 1993 [1946]. *Concept of the Corporation.* New Brunswick, NJ; London: Transaction Publishers.

Dufresne, Alexandra. 2021. Nestlé Ruling Shows Supply Chain Human Rights Flaws. Law 360, June 18, 2021. www.law360.com/articles/1395335

Ebert, Isabel, Busch, Thorsten & Wettstein, Florian. 2020. Business and Human Rights in the Data Economy.

A Mapping and Research Study. Berlin; St. Gallen: Deutsches Institut für Menschenrechte and Institute for Business Ethics. www.institut-fuer-menschenrechte.de/publikationen/detail/business-and-human-rights-in-the-data-economy

ECCHR. 2018. Landmark Decision in Lafarge Case. Company Lafarge Indicted – Complicity in Crimes Against Humanity Included. www.ecchr.eu/en/press-release/landmark-decision-in-lafarge-case/

ECCHR. 2021. Corporate Due Diligence Laws and Legislative Proposals in Europe: Comparative Table. https://corporatejustice.org/publications/comparative-table-corporate-due-diligence-laws-and-legislative-proposals-in-europe/

The Economist. 2021. Free to Quit, at Last: Foreign Workers in Qatar Get Some Basic Rights, May 6, 2021. www.economist.com/middle-east-and-africa/2021/05/06/foreign-workers-in-qatar-get-some-basic-rights

Edelman. 2009. Edelman Trust Barometer Executive Summary. www.edelman.com/sites/g/files/aatuss191/files/2018-10/2009-Trust-Barometer-Executive-Summary.pdf.

Entine, Jon. 2012. ISO 26000: Sustainability as Standard? Reuters Events, July 11, 2012. www.reutersevents.com/sustainability/business-strategy/iso-26000-sustainability-standard

Entreprise Générale du Cobalt. 2021. Official Launch of Entreprise Générale du Cobalt in the Democratic Republic of the Congo. March 31, 2021.

www.egcobalt-rdc.com/official-launch-of-entreprise-generale-du-cobalt-in-the-democratic-republic-of-the-congo/

Ergon Associates. 2018. Modern Slavery Reporting: Is there Evidence of Progress? London: Ergon Associates. https://ergonassociates.net/wp-content/uploads/2018/10/Ergon_Modern_Slavery_Progress_2018_resource.pdf

European Coalition for Corporate Justice. 2019. *A Human Rights Review of the EU Non-Financial Reporting Directive.* Brussels: European Coalition for Corporate Justice. https://corporatejustice.org/publications/a-human-rights-review-of-the-eu-non-financial-reporting-directive/

European Commission. 2011. A Renewed EU Strategy 2011–14 for Corporate Social Responsibility. http://eur-lex.europa.eu/LexUriServ/LexUriServ.do?uri=COM:2011:0681:FIN: EN:PDF

European Commission. 2020. The Regulation Explained. https://ec.europa.eu/trade/policy/in-focus/conflict-minerals-regulation/regulation-explained/

European Commission. 2021. Buying Social – A Guide to Taking Account of Social Considerations in Public Procurement. Second edition. C(2021) 3573. https://ec.europa.eu/docsroom/documents/45767

European Parliament & Council of the European Union. 2007. Regulation (EC) No 864/2007 of the European Parliament and of the Council of 11 July 2007 on the Law Applicable to Non-contractual Obligations (Rome II).

https://eur-lex.europa.eu/legal-content/EN/TXT/PDF/?uri=CELEX:32007R0864&from=en

Evans, John. 2011. Human Rights and Labour Standards: The Duty of Export Credit Agencies. In OECD (ed.), *Smart Rules for Fair Trade: 50 Years of Export Credits*, 66–70. Paris: OECD Publishing.

Ewing, Anthony P. 2016. Mandatory Human Rights Reporting. In Baumann-Pauly, Dorothée & Nolan, Justine (eds.), *Business and Human Rights: From Principles to Practice*, 284–298. London; New York: Routledge.

Ewing, Anthony P. 2021. Promoting business and human rights education: Lessons from Colombia, Ukraine, and Pakistan. *Business and Human Rights Journal* 6/3: 607–615.

Fagan, Andrew. 2014. Philosophical Foundations of Human Rights. In Cushman, Thomas (ed.), *Handbook of Human Rights*, 9–21. London; New York: Routledge.

Fairtrade International. n.d. Aims of the Fairtrade Standards. www.fairtrade.net/standard/aims

FAO. 2021. Call for Action: Ending Child Labour in Agriculture with the Help of Agricultural Stakeholders. April 21, 2021. www.fao.org/rural-employment/resources/detail/en/c/1396235/

Fasterling, Björn. 2017. Human rights due diligence as risk management: Social risk versus human rights risk. *Business and Human Rights Journal* 2/2: 225–247.

Fasterling, Björn & Demuijnck, Geert. 2013. Human rights in the void? Due diligence in the UN Guiding Principles on Business and Human Rights. *Journal of Business Ethics* 116: 799–814.

Feinberg, Joel. 1973. *Social Philosophy.* Englewood Cliffs, NJ: Prentice-Hall.

Flowers, Nancy (ed.). n.d. Human Rights Here and Now: Celebrating the Universal Declaration of Human Rights. Minneapolis: University of Minnesota Human Rights Resource Center. http:// hrlibrary.umn.edu/edumat/hreduseries/ hereandnow/Part-1/default.htm

Forst, Michel. 2017. Situation of Human Rights Defenders. Report by the Special Rapporteur on the Situation of Human Rights Defenders. A/72/170. https:// undocs.org/en/A/72/170

Friends of the Earth Europe. 2018. ENI and the Nigerian Ikebiri Case. www .foeeurope.org/sites/default/files/ extractive_industries/2018/foee-eni- ikebiri-case-briefing-update.pdf

Friends of the Earth Europe. 2019. Ikebiri Reach Settlement with Company, Niger Delta Still Awaits Justice. https:// friendsoftheearth.eu/news/ikebiri- reach-settlement-with-company-niger- delta-still-awaits-justice/

Fremuth, Michael-Lysander. 2015. *Menschenrechte: Grundlagen and Dokumente.* Bonn: Bundeszentrale für politische Bildung.

French, Peter A. 1979. The corporation as a moral person. *American Philosophical Quarterly* 16/3: 207–215.

Frey, Barbara A. 1997. The legal and ethical responsibilities of transnational corporations in the protection of international human rights. *Minnesota Journal of Global Trade* 6: 153–188.

Friedman, Milton. 1962. *Capitalism and Freedom.* Chicago: University of Chicago Press.

Friedman, Milton. 1970. The Social Responsibility of Business Is to Increase its Profits. The New York Times Magazine, September 13, 1970.

Front Line Defenders. n.d. Case History: Berta Cáceres. www.frontlinedefenders .org/en/case/case-history-berta-c% C3%A1ceres

Fuchs, Doris. 2007. *Business Power in Global Governance.* Boulder, CO: Lynn Rienner Publishers.

Gaja, Giorgio. 2003. First Report on Responsibility of International Organizations. A/CN.4/532. http://legal .un.org/ilc/documentation/english/a_ cn4_532.pdf.

Garriga, Elisabet & Melé, Domènec. 2004. Corporate social responsibility theories: Mapping the territory. *Journal of Business Ethics* 53: 51–71.

Garthoff, Jon. 2019. Decomposing legal personhood. *Journal of Business Ethics* 154: 967–974.

GBI. 2017a. Making a Policy Commitment. https://gbihr.org/business-practice- portal/making-a-policy-commitment

GBI. 2017b. Identifying Human Rights Impacts. https://gbihr.org/business- practice-portal/identifying-human- rights-impacts

GBI. 2017c. Engaging Stakeholders. https:// gbihr.org/business-practice-portal/ engaging-stakeholders

GBI. 2017d. Raising Awareness, Training and Capacity Building. https://gbihr .org/business-practice-portal/training- and-capacity-building

Gewirth, Alan. 1996. *The Community of Rights.* Chicago; London: University of Chicago Press.

Giorgetti, Chiara, Ratner, Steven, Dunoff, Jeffrey, Hamamoto, Shatoro, Nottage, Luke, Schill, Stephan W. & Waibel, Michael. 2020. Independence and impartiality of adjudicators in investment dispute settlement: Assessing challenges and reform options. *Journal of World Investment and Trade* 21/2-3: 441–474.

Giuliani, Elisa, Macchi, Chiara & Fiaschi Davide. 2014. Corporate Social Irresponsibility in International Business. In Van Tulder, Rob, Verbeke, Alain & Strange, Roger (eds.), *International Business and Sustainable Development*, 141–171. Bingley: Emerald.

Giuliani, Elisa, Santangelo, Grazia & Wettstein, Florian. 2016. Human rights and international business research: A call for studying emerging market multinationals. *Management and Organization Review* 12/3: 1–7.

Global Witness. 2016. *On Dangerous Ground.* London: Global Witness. www .globalwitness.org/en/campaigns/ environmental-activists/dangerous- ground/

Goldstein, Jacob. 2014. To Increase Productivity, UPS Monitors Drivers' Every Move. NPR, April 17, 2014. www.npr.org/sections/money/2014/ 04/17/303770907/to-increase- productivity-ups-monitors-drivers- every-move

Götzmann, Nora. 2017. Human rights impact assessment of business activities: Key criteria for establishing meaningful practice. *Business and Human Rights Journal* 2/1: 87-108.

Götzmann, Nora, Wrzoncki, Elin, Kristiansson, Linnea & Heydari, Evina. 2018. *Women in Business and Human Rights: A Mapping of Topics for State Attention in United Nations Guiding Principles on Business and Human Rights Implementation Processes.* Copenhagen: The Danish Institute for Human Rights. www.humanrights.dk/ sites/humanrights.dk/files/media/ document/women%20in%20business .pdf

Götzmann, Nora, Kristiansson, Linnea & Hillenbrand, Julia. 2019. *Towards Gender-Responsive Implementation of Extractive Industries Projects.* Copenhagen: The Danish Institute for Human Rights. www.humanrights.dk/ sites/humanrights.dk/files/media/ migrated/gender_and_extractives_ report_sept2019.pdf

Graf, Andreas & Iff, Andrea. 2017. Respecting human rights in conflict regions: How to avoid the "conflict spiral." *Business and Human Rights Journal* 2/1: 109–133.

Griffin, James. 2008. *On Human Rights.* Oxford: Oxford University Press.

Griffin, James. 2012. Human Rights: Questions of Aim and Approach. In Ernst, Gerhard & Heilinger, Jan- Christoph (eds.), *The Philosophy of Human Rights*, 3–16. Berlin; Boston: De Gruyter.

Haas, Michael. 2014. *International Human Rights: A Comprehensive Introduction.* Second edition. London; New York: Routledge.

Haefele, Mark, Smiles, Simon & Carter, Matthew. 2017. Millennials – the Global Guardians of Capital. www.ubs.com/global/en/wealth-management/chief-investment-office/our-research/discover-more/2017/millennials.html

Hall, Ruth. 2011. Land grabbing in Southern Africa: The many faces of the investor rush. *Review of African Political Economy* 38/128: 193–214.

Hallensleben, Natalie & Harrop, Bernard. 2015. EU Non-Financial Reporting Directive. Implications for Business Travel Reporting. Global Business Travel Association/atmosfair. www.atmosfair.de/wp-content/uploads/hintergrundpapier-nicht-finanzielle-berichterstattung.pdf

Hamann, Ralph. 2019. Disconnect between Business and State Contributed to Marikana Massacre. The Conversation, August 15, 2019. https://theconversation.com/disconnect-between-business-and-state-contributed-to-marikana-massacre-121507

Hamdani, Khalil & Ruffing, Lorraine. 2017. Lessons from the UN Centre on Transnational Corporations for the Current Treaty Initiative. In Deva, Surya & Bilchitz, David (eds.), *Building a Treaty on Business and Human Rights: Context and Contours*, 27–47. Cambridge, UK: Cambridge University Press.

Harris, Kamala D. 2015. The California Transparency in Supply Chains Act: A Resource Guide. California Department of Justice. https://oag.ca.gov/sites/all/files/agweb/pdfs/sb657/resource-guide.pdf

Heede, Richard. 2014. Tracing anthropogenic carbon dioxide and methane emissions to fossil fuel and cement producers, 1854–2010. *Climatic Change* 122: 229–241.

Henderson, Rebecca & Hsieh, Nien-hê. 2016. Putting the Guiding Principles into Action: Human Rights at Barrick Gold (A). Harvard Business School Case 315–108. https://hbsp.harvard.edu/product/315108-PDF-ENG?Ntt=Henderson%20Hsieh

Hahn, Rüdiger & Weidtmann, Christian. 2016. Transnational governance, deliberative democracy, and the legitimacy of ISO 26000: Analyzing the case of a global multistakeholder process. *Business & Society* 55/1: 90–129.

Henriques, Adrian. 2012. *Standards for Change? ISO 26000 and Sustainable Development.* London: International Institute for Environment and Development.

Himma, Kenneth E. 2002. Inclusive Legal Positivism. In Coleman, Jules & Shapiro, Scott (eds.), *The Oxford Handbook of Jurisprudence & Philosophy of Law*, 125–165. Oxford: Oxford University Press.

Hirsh, Moshe. 2009. Investment Tribunals and Human Rights: Divergent Paths. In Dupuy, Pierre-Marie, Petersmann, Ernst-Ulrich & Francioni, Francesco (eds.), *Human Rights in International Investment Law and Arbitration*, 97–114. Oxford: Oxford University Press.

Hiskes, Richard P. 2014. Environmental Human Rights. In Cushman, Thomas (ed.), *Handbook of Human Rights*, 399–409. London; New York: Routledge.

Hoff, Anneloes. 2019. Dutch Child Labour Due Diligence Law: A Step Towards Mandatory Human Rights Due Diligence. OxHRH Blog, June 10, 2019. http://ohrh.law.ox.ac.uk/dutch-child-labour-due-diligence-law-a-step-towards-mandatory-human-rights-due-diligence

Holly, Gabrielle. 2019. Zambian Farmers Can Take Vedanta to Court over Water Pollution. What Are the Legal Implications? Business & Human Rights Resource Centre, April 10, 2019. www.business-humanrights.org/en/blog/zambian-farmers-can-take-vedanta-to-court-over-water-pollution-what-are-the-legal-implications/

Home, Andy. 2021. Column: Cobalt, Congo and a Mass Artisanal Mining Experiment. Reuters, May 13, 2021. www.reuters.com/business/energy/cobalt-congo-mass-artisanal-mining-experiment-andy-home-2021-05-13/

Hongbo, Wu. 2015. Foreword to the State of the World's Indigenous Peoples. In UN Permanent Forum on Indigenous Issues (ed.), *State of the World's Indigenous Peoples*. Second volume, iv–v. New York and Geneva: United Nations. www.refworld.org/docid/55c89dac4.html

Hsieh, Nien-hê. 2015. Should business have human rights obligations? *Journal of Human Rights* 14/2: 218–236.

Hsieh, Nien-hê. 2017. Business responsibilities for human rights. *Business and Human Rights Journal* 2/2: 297–309.

Hsieh, Nien-hê, Toffel, Michael W. & Hull, Olivia. 2019. Global Sourcing at Nike. Harvard Business School Case 619-008. https://hbsp.harvard.edu/product/619008-PDF-ENG?additionSource=Item%20Detail%20Page&dialog=teaching-note&parentProductId=619008-PDF-ENG

Human Rights Watch. 1999a. *The Enron Corporation: Corporate Complicity in Human Rights Violations*. New York: Human Rights Watch.

Human Rights Watch. 1999b. *The Price of Oil: Corporate Responsibility and Human Rights Violations in Nigeria's Oil Producing Communities*. New York: Human Rights Watch.

Human Rights Watch. 2020. Q&A: The International Criminal Court and the United States. www.hrw.org/news/2020/09/02/qa-international-criminal-court-and-united-states#1

Idowu, Samuel O. 2019. ISO 26000 – A Standardized View of Corporate Social Responsibility Practices, Cases and Facts: An Introduction. In Idowu, Samuel O., Sitnikov, Catalina & Moratis, Lars (eds.), *ISO 26000 – A Standardized View on Corporate Social Responsibility*, 1–10. Cham, Switzerland: Springer.

IHRB. 2016. IHRB Briefing: Recruitment Fees. Institute for Human Rights and Business. www.ihrb.org/uploads/briefings/2016-05%2C_IHRB_Briefing%2C_Recruitment_Fees.pdf

IHRB. 2018. *The Commodity Trading Sector Guidance on Implementing the UN Guiding Principles on Business and Human Rights.* Bern: FDFA/SECO. www.ihrb.org/uploads/reports/Commodities_Trading_UNGPs_Guidance_-_Nov_18.pdf

Initiative Lieferkettengesetz. 2021. Not There Yet, but Finally at the Start: What the New Supply Chain Act Delivers – and What It Doesn't. https://corporatejustice.org/wp-content/uploads/2021/06/Initiative-Lieferkettengesetz_Analysis_What-the-new-supply-chain-act-delivers.pdf

International Commission of Jurists. 2010. Access to Justice: Human Rights Abuses Involving Corporations: The Netherlands. Geneva: International Commission of Jurists. www.icj.org/access-to-justice-human-rights-abuses-involving-corporations-2/

International Council on Human Rights Policy. 2002. Beyond Voluntarism: Human Rights and the Developing International Legal Obligations of Companies. Versoix: International Council on Human Rights Policy.

International Court of Justice. n.d. The Court. www.icj-cij.org/en/court

International Criminal Court. n.d. (a). The States Parties to the Rome Statute. https://asp.icc-cpi.int/en_menus/asp/states%20parties/pages/the%20states%20parties%20to%20the%20rome%20statute.aspx

International Criminal Court. n.d. (b). How the Court Works. www.icc-cpi.int/about/how-the-court-works/Pages/default.aspx#legalProcess

International Labour Office. 2004. *Child Labour: A Textbook for University Students.* Geneva: International Labour Organization. https://resourcecentre.savethechildren.net/node/8335/pdf/wcms_067258.pdf

International Labour Office. 2007. Eradication of Forced Labour. Report of the Committee of Experts on the Application of Conventions and Recommendations (articles 19, 22 and 35 of the Constitution). ILC96-III(1B)-2007-02-0014-1-En. Geneva: International Labour Office. www.ilo.org/wcmsp5/groups/public/–ed_norm/–relconf/documents/meetingdocument/wcms_089199.pdf

International Labour Office. 2014. *Profits and Poverty: The Economics of Forced Labour.* Geneva: International Labour Organization. www.ilo.org/wcmsp5/groups/public/–ed_norm/–declaration/documents/publication/wcms_243391.pdf

International Labour Office. 2017. *Global Estimates of Child Labour: Results and Trends, 2012–2016.* Geneva: International Labour Organization. www.ilo.org/wcmsp5/groups/public/–dgreports/–dcomm/documents/publication/wcms_575499.pdf

International Labour Organization. 1999. Worst Forms of Child Labour Convention (No. 182). www.ilo.org/dyn/normlex/en/f?p=NORMLEXPUB:12100:0::NO::P12100_ILO_CODE:C182

International Labour Organization, Regional Office for Arab States. 2017.

Employer-Migrant Worker Relationships in the Middle East: Exploring Scope for Internal Labour Market Mobility and Fair Migration. Beirut: International Labour Organization. www.ilo.org/wcmsp5/groups/public/–arabstates/–ro-beirut/documents/publication/wcms_552697.pdf

International Labour Organization. n.d. (a). History of the ILO. www.ilo.org/global/about-the-ilo/history/lang–en/index.htm

International Labour Organization. n.d. (b). How the ILO Works. www.ilo.org/global/about-the-ilo/how-the-ilo-works/lang–en/index.htm

International Labour Organization. n.d. (c). The Rana Plaza Accident and its Aftermath. www.ilo.org/global/topics/geip/WCMS_614394/lang–en/index.htm

ILO & IOE. 2015. *Child Labour Guidance Tool for Business: How to Do Business with Respect for Children's Right to Be Free from Child Labour.* Geneva: International Labour Organization.

International Labour Organization & United Nations Children's Fund. 2020. *COVID-19 and Child Labour: A Time of Crisis, a Time to Act.* New York: ILO & UNICEF, New York, 2020. www.ilo.org/wcmsp5/groups/public/–ed_norm/–ipec/documents/publication/wcms_747421.pdf

International Labour Office & Walk Free Foundation. 2017. *Global Estimates of Modern Slavery: Forced Labour and Forced Marriage.* Geneva: International Labor Organization & Walk Free Foundation. www.ilo.org/wcmsp5/groups/public/@dgreports/@dcomm/documents/publication/wcms_575479.pdf

International Land Coalition. 2011. *Tirana Declaration: Securing Land Access for the Poor in Times of Intensified Natural Resources Competition.* Rome: International Land Coalition. https://d3o3cb4w253x5q.cloudfront.net/media/documents/Tirana_Declaration_2011_EN.pdf

ISO. 2018. *Discovering ISO 26000.* Geneva: International Organization for Standardization.

Jägers, Nicola. 2013. Will Transnational Private Regulation Close the Governance Gap? In Deva, Surya & Bilchitz, David (eds.), *Human Rights Obligations of Business: Beyond the Corporate Responsibility to Respect?* 295-328. Cambridge, UK: Cambridge University Press.

Jägers, Nicola. 2020. Sustainable development goals and the business and human rights discourse: Ships passing in the night? *Human Rights Quarterly* 42/1: 145–173.

Jägers, Nicola. 2021. UN Guiding Principles at 10: Permeating narratives or yet another silo? *Business and Human Rights Journal* 6/2: 198–211.

Jalloh, Charles C., Clarke, Kamari M. & Nmehielle, Vincent O. 2019. Preface. In Jalloh, Charles C., Clarke, Kamari M. & Nmehielle, Vincent O. (eds.), *The African Court of Justice and Human and Peoples' Rights in Context: Development and Challenges*, xix-xxii. Cambridge, UK: Cambridge University Press.

Jee, Charlotte. 2021. Amazon's system for tracking its warehouse workers can automatically fire them. *MIT Technology Review*, April 26, 2021. www.technologyreview.com/2019/04/26/1021/amazons-system-for-tracking-its-warehouse-workers-can-automatically-fire-them/

Joas, Hans. 2015. *Sind die Menschenrechte westlich?* München: Kösel.

Jonker, Jan. 2005. CSR Wonderland: Navigating between movement, community, and organization. *Journal of Corporate Citizenship* 20: 19–22.

Joseph, Sarah. 2004. *Corporations and Transnational Human Rights Litigation*. Oxford; Portland, OR: Hart Publishing.

Kamminga, Menno T. & Zia-Zarifi, Saman. 2000. Liability of Multinational Corporations Under International Law: An Introduction. In Kamminga, Menno T. & Zia-Zarifi, Saman (eds.), *Liability of Multinational Corporations Under International Law*. The Hague; London; Boston: Kluwer Law International.

Kant, Immanuel. 1996 [1797]. *The Metaphysics of Morals*. Translated by Mary Gregor. Cambridge, UK; New York: Cambridge University Press.

Karp, David J. 2014. *Responsibility for Human Rights: Transnational Corporations in Imperfect States*. Cambridge, UK: Cambridge University Press.

Katsos, John. 2020. Business, human rights and peace: Linking the academic conversation. *Business and Human Rights Journal* 5/2: 221–240.

Kaufman, Jonathan & McDonnell, Katherine. 2015. Community-driven operational grievance mechanisms.

Business and Human Rights Journal 1/1: 125–132.

Keller, Helen & Ulfstein, Geir. 2012. Introduction. In Keller, Helen & Ulfstein, Geir (eds.), *UN Human Rights Treaty Bodies: Law and Legitimacy*, 1–15. Cambridge, UK: Cambridge University Press.

Kelly, Annie. 2020. "Virtually entire" fashion industry complicit in Uighur forced labour, say rights groups. *The Guardian*, July 23, 2020. www.theguardian.com/global-development/2020/jul/23/virtually-entire-fashion-industry-complicit-in-uighur-forced-labour-say-rights-groups-china

Kerr, Steven. 1975. On the folly of rewarding A, while hoping for B. *Academy of Management Journal* 18/4: 769–783.

Khokhar, Tariq & Eshragh-Tabary, Mahyar. 2016. Five Forest Figures for the International Day of Forests. World Bank Blogs, March 21, 2016. https://blogs.worldbank.org/opendata/five-forest-figures-international-day-forests

Kinley, David & Tadaki, Junko. 2004. From talk to walk: The emergence of human rights responsibilities for corporations at international law. *Virginia Journal of International Law* 44/4: 931–1023.

Kline, John M. 2005. *Ethics for International Business*. New York; London: Routledge.

Kline, John M. 2010. *Ethics for International Business: Decision-Making in a Global Political Economy*. Second edition. New York; London: Routledge.

Knox, John H. 2018. Framework Principles on Human Rights and the Environment. UN Human Rights Special Procedures;

UNEP; Raoul Wallenberg Institute; Sida. www.ohchr.org/Documents/Issues/Environment/SREnvironment/FrameworkPrinciplesUserFriendly Version.pdf

Knuckey, Sarah & Jenkin, Eleanor. 2015. Company-created remedy mechanisms for serious human rights abuses: A promising new frontier for the right to remedy? *The International Journal of Human Rights*, 19/6: 801–827.

Kobrin, Stephen J. 2009. Private political authority and public responsibility: Transnational politics, transnational firms, and human rights. *Business Ethics Quarterly* 19/3: 349–374.

Koch, Dirk-Jan & Burlyuk, Olga. 2019. Bounded policy learning? EU efforts to anticipate unintended consequences in conflict minerals legislation. *Journal of European Public Policy*, 27/10: 1441–1462.

Koekkoek, Marieke, Marx, Axel & Wouters, Jan. 2017. Monitoring forced labor and slavery in global supply chains: The case of the California Act on Transparency in Supply Chains. *Global Policy* 8/4: 522–529.

Kolb, Robert. 2013. *The International Court of Justice*. Oxford; Portland, OR: Hart Publishing.

Kolk, Ans. 2016. The social responsibility of international business: From ethics and the environment to CSR and sustainable development. *Journal of World Business* 51: 23–34.

Kozma, Julia, Nowak, Manfred & Scheinin, Martin. 2010. A World Court of Human Rights – Consolidated Statute and Commentary. www.eui.eu/Documents/DepartmentsCentres/Law/Professors/Scheinin/ConsolidatedWorldCourtStatute.pdf

Krajewski, Markus. 2019. Human Rights in International Investment Law: Recent Trends in Arbitration and Treaty-Making Practice. In Sachs, Lisa, Johnson, Lise & Coleman, Jesse (eds.), *Yearbook on International Investment Law & Policy 2017*, 177–193. Oxford: Oxford University Press.

Krajewski, Markus. 2020. A nightmare or a noble dream? Establishing investor obligations through treaty-making and treaty-application. *Business and Human Rights Journal* 5/1: 105–129.

Kriebaum, Ursula. 2018. Human Rights and International Investment Law. In Radi, Yannick (ed.), *Research Handbook on Human Rights and Investment*, 14–40. Cheltenham; Northampton, MA: Edward Elgar.

Kube, Vivian & Petersmann, E. U. 2016. Human rights law in international investment arbitration. *Asian Journal of WTO and International Health Law and Policy* 11/1: 65–114

Kurasawa, Fuyuki. 2014. Human Rights as Cultural Practices. In Cushman, Thomas (ed.), *Handbook of Human Rights*, 155–163. London; New York: Routledge.

Labowitz, Sarah & Baumann-Pauly, Dorothée. 2014. *Business as Usual Is Not an Option: Supply Chains and Sourcing after Rana Plaza*. New York: NYU Stern Center for Business and Human Rights.

Lakhani, Nina. 2021. Berta Cáceres assassination: ex-head of dam company found guilty. *The Guardian*, July 5, 2021. www.theguardian.com/

world/2021/jul/05/berta-caceres-assassination-roberto-david-castillo-found-guilty

Leader, Sheldon. 2017. Coherence, Mutual Assurance and the Rationale for a Treaty. In Deva, Surya & Bilchitz, David (eds.), *Building a Treaty on Business and Human Rights: Context and Contours*, 79–101. Cambridge, UK: Cambridge University Press.

LeBaron, Genevieve. 2020. *Combatting Modern Slavery*. Cambridge, UK: Polity.

LeBaron, Genevieve & Rühmkopf, Andreas. 2017. Steering CSR through home state regulation: A comparison of the impact of the UK Bribery Act and Modern Slavery Act on global supply chain governance. *Global Policy* 8/3: 15–28.

LeBaron, Genevieve, Howard, Neil, Thibos, Cameron & Kyritsis, Penelope. 2018. Confronting Root Causes: Forced Labour in Global Supply Chains. Sheffield: OpenDemocracy & Sheffield Political Economy Research Institute (SPERI). https://cdn-prod .opendemocracy.net/media/documents/ Confronting_Root_Causes_Forced_ Labour_In_Global_Supply_Chains.pdf

López, Carlos. 2013. The "Ruggie Process": From Legal Obligations to Corporate Social Responsibility? In Deva, Surya & Bilchitz, David (eds.), *Human Rights Obligations of Business: Beyond the Corporate Responsibility to Respect?* 58–76. Cambridge, UK: Cambridge University Press.

López, Carlos. 2017. Human Rights Legal Liability for Business Enterprises: The Role of an International Treaty. In Deva, Surya & Bilchitz, David (eds.), *Building a Treaty on Business and*

Human Rights: Context and Contours, 299–317. Cambridge, UK: Cambridge University Press.

Macchi, Chiara. 2021. The climate change dimension of business and human rights: The gradual consolidation of a concept of "climate due diligence." *Business and Human Rights Journal* 6/ 1: 93–119.

MacIntyre, Alasdair. 1981. *After Virtue: A Study in Moral Theory*. Notre Dame, IN: University of Notre Dame Press.

Mair, Vibeka. 2019. Credit Suisse Includes Protection of Indigenous Rights in Project Finance Guidelines. Responsible Investor, October 24, 2019. www .responsible-investor.com/articles/ credit-suisse-includes-protection-of-indigenous-rights-into-project-finance

Mantouvalou, Virginia. 2018. The UK Modern Slavery Act 2015 three years on. *The Modern Law Review* 81/6: 1017–1045.

Marikana Commission of Inquiry. 2015. Report on Matters of Public, National and International Concern Arising out of the Tragic Incidents at the Lonmin Mine in Marikana, in the North West Province. www.sahrc.org.za/home/21/ files/marikana-report-1.pdf

Marmor, Andrei. 2002. Exclusive Legal Positivism. In Coleman, Jules & Shapiro, Scott (eds.), *The Oxford Handbook of Jurisprudence & Philosophy of Law*, 104–124. Oxford: Oxford University Press.

Martin-Ortega, Olga. 2014. Human rights due diligence for corporations: From voluntary standards to hard law at last. *Netherlands Quarterly of Human Rights* 31/4: 44–74.

Martin-Ortega, Olga. 2018. Public procurement as a tool for the protection and promotion of human rights: A study of collaboration, due diligence and leverage in the electronics industry. *Business and Human Rights Journal* 3/1: 75–95.

Marx, Axel, Bright, Claire & Wouters, Jan. 2019. *Access to Legal Remedies for Victims of Corporate Human Rights Abuses in Third Countries*. EP/EXPO/B/DROI/FWC/2013-08/Lot4/07. Brussels: European Union. www.europarl.europa.eu/thinktank/en/document.html?reference=EXPO_STU(2019)603475

Mason Meier, Benjamin & Brás Gomes, Virgínia. 2018. Human Rights Treaty Bodies: Monitoring, Interpreting, and Adjudicating Health-Related Human Rights. In Mason Meier, Benjamin & Gostin, Lawrence O. (eds.), *Human Rights in Global Health: Rights-Based Governance for a Globalizing World*, 509–536. Oxford: Oxford University Press.

Matharu, Hardeep. 2016. Saudi Arabian women banned from Starbucks after collapse of gender segregation wall. *The Independent*, February 4, 2016. www.independent.co.uk/news/world/middle-east/saudi-arabian-women-banned-starbucks-after-collapse-gender-segregation-wall-a6852646.html

Matten, Dirk & Crane, Andrew. 2005. Corporate citizenship: Toward an extended theoretical conceptualization. *Academy of Management Review* 30/1: 166–179.

McCorquodale, Robert. 2009. Corporate social responsibility and international human rights law. *Journal of Business Ethics* 87: 385–400.

McCorquodale, Robert, Smit, Lise, Neely, Stuart & Brooks, Robin. 2017. Human rights due diligence in law and practice: Good practices and challenges for business enterprises. *Business and Human Rights Journal* 2/2: 195–224.

Meeran, Richard. 2013. Access to Remedy: The United Kingdom Experience of MNC Tort Litigation for Human Rights Violations. In Deva, Surya & Bilchitz, David (eds.), *Human Rights Obligations of Business: Beyond the Corporate Responsibility to Respect?* 378–402. Cambridge, UK: Cambridge University Press.

Mehra, Amol & Blackwell, Sara. 2016. The Rise of Non-Financial Disclosure: Reporting on Respect for Human Rights. In Baumann-Pauly, Dorothée & Nolan, Justine (eds.), *Business and Human Rights: From Principles to Practice*, 276–284. London; New York: Routledge.

Mena, Sébastien & Palazzo, Guido. 2012. Input and output legitimacy of multi-stakeholder initiatives. *Business Ethics Quarterly* 22/3: 527–556.

Merrills, J. G. 1993. *The Development of International Law by the European Court of Human Rights*. Manchester: Manchester University Press.

Methven O'Brien, Claire, Mehra, Amol, Blackwell, Sara & Poulsen-Hansen, Cathrine B. 2016. National action plans: Current status and future prospects for a new business and human rights governance tool. *Business and Human Rights Journal* 1/1: 115–226.

Methven O'Brien, Claire, Mehra, Amol, Andrecka, Marta & Vander Meulen, Nicole. 2016. Public Procurement and Human Rights: A Survey of Twenty Jurisdictions. International Learning Lab on Public Procurement. https://issuu.com/_icar_/docs/public_procurement_and_human_rights_37d25528011462/7

Meyersfeld, Bonita. 2017. Empty promises and the myth of mining: Does mining lead to pro-poor development? *Business and Human Rights Journal* 2/1: 31–53.

Michalowski, Sabine. 2014. Introduction. In Michalowski, Sabine (ed.), *Corporate Accountability in the Context of Transitional Justice*, 1–6. London: Routledge.

Michalowski, Sabine & Carranza, Ruben. 2014. Conclusion. In Michalowski, Sabine (ed.), *Corporate Accountability in the Context of Transitional Justice*, 247–254. London: Routledge.

Midgley, Mary. 1981. *Heart and Mind: The Varieties of Moral Experience.* New York: St. Martin's Press.

Minderoo Foundation, WikiRate, Business & Human Rights Resource Centre & Australian National University. 2019. Beyond Compliance in the Hotel Sector: A Review of Modern Slavery Act Statements. https://media.business-humanrights.org/media/documents/files/2632_MSA-statements.V8_FNL.pdf

Mohan, Mahdev. 2017. A domestic solution for transboundary harm: Singapore's haze pollution laws. *Business and Human Rights Journal* 2/2: 325–333.

Molin, Anna. 2012. IKEA Regrets Cutting Women From Saudi Ad. The Wall Street Journal, October 1, 2012. www.wsj.com/articles/SB10000872396390444459240457803027420038136

Morris, Daniel, Wrzoncki, Elin & Andreasen Lysgaard, Signe. 2019. *Responsible Business Conduct as a Cornerstone of the 2030 Agenda – A Look at the Implications. A Discussion Paper.* Copenhagen: The Danish Institute for Human Rights. www.humanrights.dk/sites/humanrights.dk/files/media/document/~%2019_02922-15%20responsible_business_conduct_as_a_cornerstone_of_the_2030_agenda_dihr_2019%20-%20fd%20461990_1_1.pdf

Much, Laura. 2020. Artisanal and Small-Scale Mining: Addressing Challenges in Global Supply Chains. Alliance for Responsible Mining Blog. www.responsiblemines.org/en/2020/01/small-scale-mining-adressing-challenges-in-global-supply-chain2/

Muchlinski, Peter. 2001. Human rights and multinationals: Is there a problem? *International Affairs* 77/1: 31–47.

Muñoz Quick, Paloma & Wrzoncki, Elin. 2017. National Action Plans on Business and Human Rights Toolkit. 2017 edition. The Danish Institute for Human Rights and the International Corporate Accountability Roundtable. www.humanrights.dk/sites/humanrights.dk/files/media/migrated/dihr_icar_nap_toolkit_2017_edition.pdf

MVO Platform. 2019. Update: Frequently Asked Questions about the New Dutch Child Labour Due Diligence Law. www.mvoplatform.nl/en/frequently-asked-questions-about-the-new-dutch-child-labour-due-diligence-law/

Nieri, Federica & Giuliani, Elisa. 2018. International Business and Corporate Wrongdoing: A Review and Research Agenda. In Castellani, Davide, Narula, Rajneesh, Nguyen, Quyen T. K., Surdu, Irina & Walker, James T. (eds.), *Contemporary Issues in International Business: Institutions, Strategy and Performance*, 35–54. Cham, Switzerland: Palgrave Macmillan.

Nieuwenkamp, Roel. 2014. *OECD's Human Rights Grievance Mechanism as a Competitive Advantage*. London: Institute for Human Rights and Business. www.ihrb.org/other/ governments-role/oecds-human- rights-grievance-mechanism-as-a- competitive-advantage

Nisen, Max. 2013. How Nike Solved Its Sweatshop Problem. Business Insider, May 10, 2013. www.businessinsider .com/how-nike-solved-its- sweatshop-problem-2013-5?r=US& IR=T

Nkumba, Emmanuel U. 2020. How to reduce conflicts between mining companies and artisanal miners in the province of Lualaba: Overcoming the policy and systemic barriers to a model that respects human rights. *Business and Human Rights Journal* 5/2: 296–302.

Nolan, Justine. 2016. Rana Plaza: The Collapse of a Factory in Bangladesh and its Ramifications for the Global Garment Industry. In Baumann-Pauly, Dorothée & Nolan, Justine (eds.), *Business and Human Rights: From Principles to Practice*, 27–30. London; New York: Routledge.

Nolan, Justine & Taylor, Luke. 2009. Corporate responsibility for economic,

social and cultural rights: Rights in search of a remedy? *Journal of Business Ethics* 87: 433–451.

Nowrot, Karsten. 2018. The 2017 EU Conflict Minerals Regulation: An effective European instrument to globally promote good raw materials governance? *Rechtswissenschaftliche Beiträge der Hamburger Sozialökonomie, Heft* 20. www.wiso .uni-hamburg.de/fachbereich-sozoek/ professuren/nowrot/archiv/heft-20- nowrot-conflict-minerals.pdf

NPR. 2021. Alleged Mastermind Convicted in the Killing of Environmental Activist Berta Cáceres. NPR, July 5, 2021. www .npr.org/2021/07/05/1013216856/ alleged-mastermind-convicted-in-the- killing-of-environmental-activist- berta-cace

Nussbaum, Martha C. 2002. Capabilities and Human Rights. In De Greiff, Pablo & Cronin, Ciaran P. (eds.), *Global Justice and Transnational Politics: Essays on the Moral and Political Challenges of Globalization*, 117–149. Cambridge, MA; London: The MIT Press.

Nussbaum, Martha C. 2006. *Frontiers of Justice: Disability, Nationality, Species Membership*. Cambridge, MA; London: Belknap Press of Harvard University Press.

Obara, Louise. 2017. "What does this mean?": How UK companies make sense of human rights. *Business and Human Rights Journal* 2/2: 249–273.

Obara, Louise J. & Peattie, Ken. 2018. Bridging the great divide? Making sense of the human rights-CSR relationship in UK multinational companies. *Journal of World Business* 53/6: 781–793.

Ochoa Sanchez, Juan C. 2015. The roles and powers of the OECD National Contact Points Regarding Complaints on an alleged breach of the OECD Guidelines for Multinational Enterprises by a transnational corporation. *Nordic Journal of International Law* 84/1: 89–126.

O'Connor, Casey & Labowitz, Sarah. 2017. *Putting the "S" in ESG: Measuring Human Rights Performance for Investors.* New York: NYU Stern Center for Business and Human Rights. https://issuu.com/nyusterncenterforbusinessandhumanri/docs/final_metrics_report_march_16_2017?e=31640827/54952687

OECD. 2011. *OECD Guidelines for Multinational Enterprises.* Paris: OECD Publishing. www.oecd.org/corporate/mne/1922428.pdf

OECD. 2016a. *OECD Due Diligence Guidance for Responsible Supply Chains of Minerals from Conflict-Affected and High-Risk Areas.* Third edition. Paris: OECD Publishing. www.oecd-ilibrary.org/governance/oecd-due-diligence-guidance-for-responsible-supply-chains-of-minerals-from-conflict-affected-and-high-risk-areas_9789264252479-en

OECD. 2016b. Recommendation of the Council on Common Approaches for Officially Supported Export Credits and Environmental and Social Due Diligence (The "Common Approaches"). OECD/Legal/0393. https://legalinstruments.oecd.org/en/instruments/OECD-LEGAL-0393

OECD. n.d. (a) OECD Declaration and Decisions on International Investment and Multinational Enterprises. www.oecd.org/daf/inv/mne/oecddeclarationanddecisions.htm

OECD. n.d. (b). Environmental and Social Due Diligence. www.oecd.org/trade/topics/export-credits/environmental-and-social-due-diligence/

OECD Watch. n.d. Society for Threatened Peoples vs. Credit Suisse. www.oecdwatch.org/complaint/society-for-threatened-peoples-vs-credit-suisse/

OEIWG. 2020. Legally Binding Instrument to Regulate, in International Human Rights Law, the Activities of Transnational Corporations and Other Business Enterprises. OEIGWG Chairmanship Second Revised Draft, August 6, 2020. www.ohchr.org/Documents/HRBodies/HRCouncil/WGTransCorp/Session6/OEIGWG_Chair-Rapporteur_second_revised_draft_LBI_on_TNCs_and_OBEs_with_respect_to_Human_Rights.pdf

O'Flaherty, Kate. 2020. Microsoft's New Productivity Score and Workplace Tracking: Here's the Problem. Forbes, November 29, 2020. www.forbes.com/sites/kateoflahertyuk/2020/11/29/microsofts-new-productivity-score-what-does-it-mean-for-you/?sh=2991d5b31d6f

OHCHR. 2012. *The Responsibility to Respect Human Rights: An Interpretive Guide.* New York; Geneva: United Nations.

OHCHR. 2016. Ten Years On, the Survivors of Illegal Toxic Waste Dumping in Côte d'Ivoire Remain in the Dark. www.ohchr.org/EN/NewsEvents/Pages/DisplayNews.aspx?NewsID=20384

OHCHR. 2017. OHCHR Response to Request from BankTrack for Advice Regarding the Application of the UN Guiding Principles on Business and Human Rights in the Context of the Banking Sector. www.banktrack.org/download/ letter_from_ohchr_to_banktrack_on_ application_of_the_un_guiding_ principles_in_the_banking_sector/ banktrack_response_final.pdf

OHCHR. n.d. (a). Human Rights Bodies. www .ohchr.org/en/hrbodies/Pages/ HumanRightsBodies.aspx

OHCHR. n.d. (b). The Impacts of Climate Change on the Effective Enjoyment of Human Rights. www.ohchr.org/EN/ Issues/HRAndClimateChange/Pages/ AboutClimateChangeHR.aspx

OHCHR. n.d. (c). National Action Plans on Business and Human Rights. www .ohchr.org/en/issues/business/pages/ nationalactionplans.aspx

OHCHR. n.d. (d). International Investment Agreements (IIAs) and Human Rights. www.ohchr.org/EN/Issues/Business/ Pages/IIAs.aspx

OHCHR. n.d. (e). Gender Lens to the UNGPs. www.ohchr.org/EN/Issues/Business/ Pages/GenderLens.aspx

Open Society Justice Initiative. 2013. Factsheet – African Court of Human and Peoples' Rights. www.justiceinitiative .org/uploads/adae7b0b-8b4d-46ec-9ce1- af01e395aa2b/fact-sheet-african-court- human-peoples-rights-20130627.pdf

Organization of American States. n.d. What is the IACHR? www.oas.org/en/iachr/ mandate/what.asp

Orlitzky, Marc, Schmidt, Frank L. & Rynes, Sara L. 2003. Corporate social and financial performance: A meta-
analysis. *Organization Studies* 24/3: 403–441.

Osiatynski, Wiktor. 2016. The Historical Development of Human Rights. In Sheeran, Scott & Rodley, Nigel (eds.), *Routledge Handbook of International Human Rights Law*, 9–24. Abingdon; New York: Routledge.

Ouma, Stefan. 2012. Land Grabbing. In Marquart, Nadine & Schreiber, Verena (eds.), *Ortsregister: Ein Glossar zu Räumen der Gegenwart*, 171–177. Bielefeld: transcript Verlag.

Paine, Lynn S. 1994. Managing for organizational integrity. *Harvard Business Review* (March–April): 106–117.

Paine, Lynn S. 2000. Does ethics pay? *Business Ethics Quarterly* 10/1: 319–330.

Palombo, Dalia. 2019a. The duty of care of the parent company: A comparison between French law, UK precedents and the Swiss proposals. *Business and Human Rights Journal* 4/2: 265–286.

Palombo, Dalia. 2019b. *Business & Human Rights: The Obligations of the European Home States*. Oxford; London: Hart Publishing.

Park, Stephen K. 2018. Social bonds for sustainable development: A human rights perspective on impact investing. *Business and Human Rights Journal* 3/2: 233–255.

Partzsch, Lena. 2018. The new EU Conflict Minerals Regulation: Normative power in international relations? *Global Policy* 9/4: 479–488.

Pasqualucci, Jo M. 2013. *The Practice and Procedure of the Inter-American Court of Human Rights*. Second edition.

Cambridge, UK: Cambridge University Press.

Pattison, Pete, McIntyre, Niamh, Mukhtar, Imran, et al. 2021. Revealed: 6,500 migrant workers have died in Qatar since World Cup awarded. *The Guardian*, February 23, 2021. www .theguardian.com/global-development/ 2021/feb/23/revealed-migrant-worker-deaths-qatar-fifa-world-cup-2022

Paul, Geneviève & Schönsteiner, Judith. 2014. Transitional Justice and the UN Guiding Principles on Business and Human Rights. In Michalowski, Sabine (ed.), *Corporate Accountability in the Context of Transitional Justice*, 71–92. London: Routledge.

Payne, Leigh A., Pereira, Gabriel & Bernal-Bermúdez, Laura. 2020. *Transitional Justice and Corporate Accountability from Below*. Cambridge, UK: Cambridge University Press.

Phillips, Nicola, LeBaron, Genevieve & Wallin, Sara. 2018. Mapping and Measuring the Effectiveness of Labour-Related Disclosure Requirements for Global Supply Chains. International Labour Office Research Department Working Paper No. 32. International Labour Office. www.ilo.org/wcmsp5/ groups/public/–dgreports/–inst/ documents/publication/wcms_632120 .pdf

Pietropaoli, Irene. 2020. Business, Human Rights, and Transitional Justice. Abingdon; New York: Routledge.

Pogge, Thomas. 2002. *World Poverty and Human Rights*. Cambridge, UK: Polity Press.

Pogge, Thomas & Sengupta, Mitu. 2016. Assessing the sustainable development goals from a human rights perspective.

Journal of International and Comparative Social Policy 32/2: 83–97.

Posner, Michael. 2016. Standard Setting for Agriculture. In Baumann-Pauly, Dorothée & Nolan, Justine (eds.), *Business and Human Rights: From Principles to Practice*. 172–174. London; New York: Routledge.

Principles for Responsible Investment. n.d. About the PRI. www.unpri.org/pri/ about-the-pri

Prokopets, Alexandra. 2014. Trafficking in information: Evaluating the efficacy of the California Transparency in Supply Chains Act of 2010. *Hastings International and Comparative Law Review* 37/2: 351–375.

Quelch, John A. & Jocz, Katherine E. 2010. Google in China (A). *Harvard Business School Case* 510-071. https://hbsp .harvard.edu/product/510071-PDF-ENG

RAFI. 2015. The UN Guiding Principles Reporting Framework. Shift Project Ltd & Mazars LLP. www.ungpreporting.org/ wp-content/uploads/ UNGPReportingFramework_ withguidance2017.pdf

Ramasastry, Anita. 2002. Corporate complicity: From Nuremberg to Rangoon. An examination of forced labor cases and their impact on the liability of multinational corporations. *Berkeley Journal of International Law* 20: 91–159.

Ramasastry, Anita. 2013. Closing the Governance Gap in the Business and Human Rights Arena: Lessons from the Anti-Corruption Movement. In Deva, Surya & Bilchitz, David (eds.), *Human Rights Obligations of Business: Beyond the Corporate Responsibility to Respect?*

162–189. Cambridge, UK: Cambridge University Press.

Ramasastry, Anita. 2015. Corporate social responsibility versus business and human rights: Bridging the gap between responsibility and accountability. *Journal of Human Rights* 14/2: 237–259.

Rasche, Andreas. 2013. The United Nations and Transnational Corporations: How the UN Global Compact Has Changed the Debate. In Lawrence, Joanne & Beamish, Paul W. (eds.), *Globally Responsible Leadership: Managing According to the UN Global Compact*, 33–50. Thousand Oaks, CA: Sage.

Ratner, Stephen R. 2001. Corporations and human rights: A theory of legal responsibility. *The Yale Law Journal* 111/3: 443–545.

Raz, Joseph. 2010. Human Rights without Foundations. In Besson, Samantha & Tasioulas, John (eds.), *The Philosophy of International Law*, 321–337. Oxford: Oxford University Press.

Redecopp, Angie. 2020. With power comes responsibility: Incremental progress in Canada on parent company human rights liability. *Journal of Leadership, Accountability and Ethics* 17/1: 18–42.

Renaud, Juliette, Quairel, Françoise, Gagnier, Sabine, Elluin, Aymeric, Bommier, Swann, Burlet, Camille & Ajaltouni, Nayla. 2019. The Law on Duty of Vigilance of Parent and Outsourcing Companies. Year 1: Companies Must Do Better. Actionaid et al. https://vigilance-plan.org/wp-content/uploads/2019/06/2019.06.14-EN-Rapport-Commun-Companies-must-do-better.pdf

Reuters. 2021. Congo Launches State Artisanal Cobalt Buyer to Meet Booming Demand. Reuters, March 31, 2021. www.reuters.com/world/middle-east/congo-launches-state-artisanal-cobalt-buyer-meet-booming-demand-2021-03-31/

Rights and Resources Initiative. 2015. *Who Owns the World's Land? A Global Baseline of Formally Recognized Indigenous and Community Land Rights*. Washington, DC: RRI. https://rightsandresources.org/wp-content/uploads/GlobalBaseline_complete_web.pdf

Rogers, Jean. 2016. Millennials and Women Redefine What It Means to Be a Reasonable Investor. Institutional Investor, October 20, 2016. www.institutionalinvestor.com/article/b14z9p1fn9ynvw/millennials-and-women-redefine-what-it-means-to-be-a-reasonable-investor

Rogge, Malcolm. 2021. What BlackRock Gets Right in its Newly Minted Human Rights Engagement Policy. Harvard Law School Forum on Corporate Governance, May 5, 2021. https://corpgov.law.harvard.edu/2021/05/05/what-blackrock-gets-right-in-its-newly-minted-human-rights-engagement-policy/

Roorda, Lucas. 2019. Jurisdiction over Foreign Direct Liability Claims against Transnational Corporations in EU Member States. PhD Thesis. Utrecht University.

Roorda, Lucas. 2021. Wading through the (Polluted) Mud: The Hague Court of Appeals Rules on Shell in Nigeria. Rights as Usual Blog, February 2, 2021. https://rightsasusual.com/?p=1388

Roorda, Lucas & Leader, Daniel. 2021. Okpabi v Shell and four Nigerian farmers v Shell: Parent company liability back in court. *Business and Human Rights Journal* 6/2: 368–376.

Rose, Nick. 2016. A Starbucks in Saudi Arabia Bans Women After a "Gender Wall" Collapses. Vice, February 3, 2016. www.vice.com/en/article/pgv4am/a-starbucks-in-saudi-arabia-bans-women-after-a-gender-wall-collapses

Rost, Katja & Ehrmann, Thomas. 2017. Reporting Biases in Empirical Management Research: The Example of Win-Win Corporate Social Responsibility. *Business & Society* 56/6: 840–888.

Ruggie, John G. 2007. Business and human rights: The evolving international agenda. *American Journal of International Law* 101: 819–840.

Ruggie, John G. 2008. Protect Respect and Remedy. A Framework for Business and Human Rights. A/HRC/8/5. https://undocs.org/en/A/HRC/8/5

Ruggie, John G. 2010. Business and Human Rights: Further Steps Toward the Operationalization of the "Protect, Respect and Remedy" Framework. A/HRC/14/27. https://ap.ohchr.org/documents/dpage_e.aspx?si=A/HRC/14/27

Ruggie, John G. 2011a. Guiding Principles on Business and Human Rights: Implementing the United Nations "Protect, Respect and Remedy" Framework. www.ohchr.org/documents/publications/guidingprinciplesbusinesshr_en.pdf

Ruggie, John G. 2011b. Business and Human Rights in Conflict-Affected Regions: Challenges and Options towards State

Responses. A/HRC/17/32. www.ohchr.org/Documents/Issues/TransCorporations/A.HRC.17.32.pdf

Ruggie, John G. 2012. Kiobel and Corporate Social Responsibility: An Issues Brief by John Ruggie, September 4, 2012. https://media.business-humanrights.org/media/documents/files/media/documents/ruggie-kiobel-and-corp-social-resonsibility-sep-2012.pdf

Ruggie, John G. 2013. *Just Business: Multinational Corporations and Human Rights*, New York, London: W. W. Norton & Co.

Ruggie, John G. 2016. Making Globalization Work for All: Achieving the SDGs through Business Respect for Human Rights. https://shiftproject.org/making-globalization-work-for-all-achieving-the-sustainable-development-goals-through-business-respect-for-human-rights/

Ruggie, John G. 2017. Multinationals as global institution: Power, authority and relative autonomy. *Regulation & Governance* 12: 317–333.

Ruggie, John G. 2021. Corporate Purpose in Play: The Role of ESG Investing. In Rasche, Andreas, Bril, Herman & Kell, Georg (eds.), *Sustainable Investing: A Path to a New Horizon*, 173–190. London: Routledge.

Ryngaert, Cedric. 2018. Accountability for corporate human rights abuses: Lessons from the possible exercise of Dutch national criminal jurisdiction over multinational corporations. *Criminal Law Forum* 29: 1–24.

Salomon, Margot E. & Seiderman, Ian. 2012. Human rights norms for a globalized world: The Maastricht Principles on

Extraterritorial Obligations of States in the area of economic, social and cultural rights. *Global Policy* 3/4: 458–462.

Samway, Michael. 2016. The Global Network Initiative: How Can Companies in the Information and Communications Technology Industry Respect Human Rights? In Baumann-Pauly, Dorothée & Nolan, Justine (eds.), *Business and Human Rights: From Principles to Practice*, 136–147. London; New York: Routledge.

Sánchez, Nelson C. 2014. Corporate Accountability, Reparations, and Distributive Justice in Post-Conflict Societies. In Michalowski, Sabine (ed.), *Corporate Accountability in the Context of Transitional Justice*, 114–130. London: Routledge.

Sandler, Rachel. 2020. Microsoft Makes Changes To Productivity Score Tool After Privacy Backlash. Forbes, December 1, 2020. www.forbes.com/ sites/rachelsandler/2020/12/01/ microsoft-makes-changes-to-productivity-score-tool-after-privacy-backlash/?sh=74e1e8017270

Sandoval, Clara, Filippini, Leonardo & Vidal, Roberto. 2014. Linking Transitional Justice and Corporate Accountability. In Michalowski, Sabine (ed.), *Corporate Accountability in the Context of Transitional Justice*. 9–26, London: Routledge.

Santoro, Michael A. 2000. *Profits and Principles: Global Capitalism and Human Rights in China*. Ithaca, NY: Cornell University Press.

Santoro, Michael A. 2009. *China 2020. How Western Business Can – and Should –*

Influence Social and Political Change in the Coming Decade. Ithaca, NY: Cornell University Press.

Santoro, Michael A. 2010. Post-Westphalia and its discontents: Business, globalization, and human rights in political and moral perspective. *Business Ethics Quarterly* 20/2: 285–297.

Savourey, Elsa. 2020. All Eyes on France – French Vigilance Law First Enforcement Cases (2/2): The Challenges Ahead. Business and Human Rights Journal Blog, January 24, 2020. www.cambridge.org/core/blog/2020/ 01/24/all-eyes-on-france-french-vigilance-law-first-enforcement-cases-2-2-current-cases-and-trends/

Scarpa, Silvia. 2018. Contemporary Forms of Slavery. Directorate-General for External Policies of the Union Study. EP/EXPO/B/COMMITTEE/FWC/2013-08/Lot8/23. Brussels: European Union. www.europarl.europa.eu/RegData/ etudes/STUD/2018/603470/EXPO_STU(2018)603470_EN.pdf

Schabas, William. 2011. *An Introduction to the International Criminal Court*. Fourth edition. Cambridge, UK: Cambridge University Press.

Schaber, Peter. 2012. Human Rights without Foundations? In Ernst, Gerhard & Heilinger, Jan-Christoph (eds.), *The Philosophy of Human Rights*, 61–72. Berlin; Boston: De Gruyter.

Schacherer, Stefanie. 2018. Urbaser v Argentina. In Bernasconi-Osterwalder, Nathalie & Brauch, Martin D. (eds.), *International Investment Law and Sustainable Development: Key Cases from the 2010s*, 25–30. Winnipeg:

The International Institute for Sustainable Development. www.iisd.org/system/files/publications/investment-law-sustainable-development-ten-cases-2010s.pdf

Schein, Edgar H. 2010. *Organizational Culture and Leadership.* Fourth edition. San Francisco: Jossey-Bass.

Scheinin, Martin. 2012. International organizations and transnational corporations at a World Court of Human Rights. *Global Policy* 3/4: 488–491.

Scherer, Andreas G. & Palazzo, Guido. 2007. Toward a political conception of corporate responsibility: Business and society seen from a Habermasian perspective. *Academy of Management Review* 32/4: 1096–1120.

Scherer, Andreas G. & Palazzo, Guido. 2011. A new political role of business in a globalized world: A review and research agenda. *Journal of Management Studies* 48/4: 899–931.

Schrempf-Stirling, Judith, Palazzo, Guido & Philipps, Robert A. 2016. Historic corporate social responsibility. *Academy of Management Review* 41/4: 700–719.

Schrempf-Stirling, Judith & Wettstein, Florian. 2017. Beyond guilty verdicts: human rights litigation and its impact on corporations' human rights policies. *Journal of Business Ethics* 145: 545–562.

Schrempf-Stirling, Judith & Wettstein, Florian. 2021. Public and Private Governance in Business and Human Rights: A Dynamic Model of Mutual Influences. Academy of Management Proceedings. 2021/1.

Schwarz, Katarina & Allain, Jean. 2020. *Antislavery in Domestic Legislation: An Empirical Analysis of National Prohibition Globally.* Nottingham: University of Nottingham. https://antislaverylaw.ac.uk/wp-content/uploads/2021/01/Antislavery-in-Domestic-Legislation-report-120320.pdf

Sen, Amartya. 1985. *Commodities and Capabilities.* Amsterdam; New York; Oxford: North-Holland.

Sen, Amartya. 1997. *Human Rights and Asian Values. Sixteenth Morgenthau Memorial Lecture on Ethics & Foreign Policy.* New York: Carnegie Council on Ethics and International Affairs. www.carnegiecouncil.org/publications/archive/morgenthau/254/_res/id=Attachments/index=0/254_sen.pdf&lang=en

Sen, Amartya. 2004. Elements of a theory of human rights. *Philosophy and Public Affairs* 32/4: 315–356.

Sethi, S. Prakash & Schepers, Donald H.. 2014. United Nations Global Compact: The promise-performance gap. *Journal of Business Ethics* 122: 193–208.

Shelton, Dinah L. 2010. Tatar C. Roumanie. *American Journal of International Law* 104/2: 247–253.

Shelton, Dinah L. 2014. *Advanced Introduction to International Human Rights Law.* Cheltenham; Northampton, MA: Edward Elgar.

Sherpa, Terre Solidaire & BHRRC. n.d. Duty of Vigilance Radar. https://vigilance-plan.org/duty-of-vigilance-radar/

Shift. 2014. *Remediation, Grievance Mechanisms, and the Corporate Responsibility to Respect Human*

Rights. New York: Shift. https://shiftproject.org/resource/remediation-grievance-mechanisms-and-the-corporate-responsibility-to-respect-human-rights/

Shift. 2019. *Human Rights Reporting in France: Two Years In: Has the Duty of Vigilance Law led to more Meaningful Disclosure?* New York: Shift.

Shift & Institute for Human Rights and Business (IHRB). 2013a. Oil and Gas Sector Guide on Implementing the UN Guiding Principles on Business and Human Rights. European Commission. https://op.europa.eu/en/publication-detail/-/publication/e05fc065-f35c-4c0d-91e9-7e500374ee0f

Shift & Institute for Human Rights and Business (IHRB). 2013b. Employment and Recruitment Agencies Sector Guide on Implementing the UN Guiding Principles on Business and Human Rights. European Commission. https://op.europa.eu/en/publication-detail/-/publication/7fa3f4c2-9f0f-46df-b698-cdd627cabe31

Shift & Institute for Human Rights and Business (IHRB). 2013c. ICT Sector Guide on Implementing the UN Guiding Principles on Business and Human Rights. European Commission https://op.europa.eu/en/publication-detail/-/publication/ab151420-d60a-40a7-b264-adce304e138b

Shue, Henry. 1996. *Basic Rights: Subsistence, Affluence, and US Foreign Policy.* Second edition. Princeton: Princeton University Press.

Simma, Bruno, Desierto, Diane, Doe Rodríguez, Martin, et al. 2019. *The Hague Rules on Business and Human Rights Arbitration.* The Hague: Center for International Legal Cooperation. www.cilc.nl/cms/wp-content/uploads/2019/12/The-Hague-Rules-on-Business-and-Human-Rights-Arbitration_CILC-digital-version.pdf

Simons, Penelope. 2015. Canada's enhanced CSR strategy: Human rights due diligence and access to justice for victims of extraterritorial corporate human rights abuses. *The Canadian Business Law Journal* 56/2: 167–207.

Simons, Penelope. 2017. The Value-Added of a Treaty to Regulate Transnational Corporations and Other Business Enterprises: Moving Forward Strategically. In Deva, Surya & Bilchitz, David (eds.), *Building a Treaty on Business and Human Rights: Context and Contours*, 48–78. Cambridge, UK: Cambridge University Press.

Simons, Penelope & Audrey Macklin. 2014. *The Governance Gap: Extractive Industries, Human Rights, and the Home State Advantage.* London; New York: Routledge.

Sinclair, Amy & Nolan, Justine. 2020. Modern slavery laws in Australia: Steps in the right direction? *Business and Human Rights Journal* 5/1: 164–170.

Smith, Alastair M. 2013. Fair Trade and "The Economist's Critique". Open Democracy, February 28, 2013. www.opendemocracy.net/en/openeconomy/fair-trade-and-economists-critique/

Smith, Andrew & Lepeuple, Alice. 2018. Holding Companies Criminally Liable for Human Rights Abuses. CorkerBinning Blog, August 17, 2018.

https://corkerbinning.com/holding-companies-criminally-liable-for-human-rights-abuses/

Society for Threatened Peoples. n.d. No Business Without Human Rights. www.gfbv.ch/en/campaigns/no-business-without-human-rights/#overview

Sovacool, Benjamin. 2019. The precarious political economy of cobalt: Balancing prosperity, poverty, and brutality in artisanal and industrial mining in the Democratic Republic of the Congo. *The Extractive Industries and Society* 6/3: 915–939.

Stanwick, Peter & Stanwick, Sarah. 2015. The garment industry in Bangladesh: A human rights challenge. *Journal of Business & Economic Policy* 2/4: 40–44.

State of California Department of Justice. 2021. The California Transparency in Supply Chains Act. https://oag.ca.gov/SB657

Steininger, Silvia. 2018. What's human rights got to do with it? An empirical analysis of human rights references in investment arbitration. *Leiden Journal of International Law* 31: 33–58.

Stephens, Beth. 1997. Conceptualizing violence under international law: Do tort remedies fit the crime? *Albany Law Review* 60/3: 579–606.

Stephens, Beth. 2017. Making Remedies Work: Envisioning a Treaty-Based System of Effective Remedies. In Deva, Surya & Bilchitz, David (eds.), *Building a Treaty on Business and Human Rights: Context and Contours*, 408–438. Cambridge, UK: Cambridge University Press.

Stewart, James G. 2014. The turn to corporate criminal liability for international crimes: Transcending the Alien Tort Statute. *New York University Journal of International Law and Politics* 47. https://ssrn.com/abstract=2354443 or http://dx.doi.org/10.2139/ssrn.2354443

Strange, Susan. 1988. *States and Markets*. London: Pinter Publishers.

Strange, Susan. 1996. *The Retreat of the State: The Diffusion of Power in the World Economy*. Cambridge, UK: Cambridge University Press.

Stumberg, Robert, Ramasastry, Anita & Roggensack, Meg. 2014. *Turning a Blind Eye? Respecting Human Rights in Government Purchasing*. The International Corporate Accountability Roundtable (ICAR). https://icar.squarespace.com/publications/2017/1/4/turning-a-blind-eye-respecting-human-rights-in-government-purchasing

Tasioulas, John. 2012. On the Nature of Human Rights. In Ernst, Gerhard & Heilinger, Jan-Christoph (eds.), *The Philosophy of Human Rights*, 17–59. Berlin; Boston: De Gruyter.

Taylor, Celia R. 2015. Using securities disclosures to advance human rights: A consideration of Dodd-Frank Section 1502 and the Securities and Exchange Commission Conflict Minerals Rule. *Journal of Human Rights* 14: 201–217.

Thirlway, Hugh. 2016. *The International Court of Justice*. Oxford: Oxford University Press.

Thompson, Benjamin. 2017. Determining criteria to evaluate outcomes of businesses' provision of remedy:

Applying a human rights-based approach. *Business and Human Rights Journal* 2/1: 55–85.

Thun Group of Banks. 2017. Paper on the Implications of UN Guiding Principles 13b & 17 in a Corporate and Investment Banking Context. https://media .business-humanrights.org/media/ documents/files/documents/2017_12_ Thun_Group_of_Banks_Paper_UNGPs_ 13b_and_17.pdf

TNI Agrarian Justice Programme. 2013. The Global Land Grab: A Primer. Transnational Institute. www.tni.org/ files/download/landgrabbingprimer-feb2013.pdf

Toft, Kristian H. 2020. Climate change as a business and human rights issue: A proposal for a moral typology. *Business and Human Rights Journal* 5/ 1: 1–27.

Trafigura. n.d. (a). The Probo Koala Case in 13 Questions. www.trafigura.com/ probo-koala/

Trafigura. n.d. (b). Our Agreement with Entreprise Générale du Cobalt. www .trafigura.com/responsibility/ responsible-sourcing/our-agreement-with-entreprise-generale-du-cobalt/

Tuana, Nancy. 2014. Climate Change and Human Rights. In Cushman, Thomas (ed.), *Handbook of Human Rights*, 410–418. London; New York: Routledge.

Ulrich, Peter. 2008. *Integrative Economic Ethics. Foundations of a Civilized Market Economy.* Cambridge, UK: Cambridge University Press.

United Nations. n.d. Universal Declaration of Human Rights. www.un.org/en/about-us/universal-declaration-of-human-rights

United Nations. 2002. Rome Statute of the International Criminal Court. https:// treaties.un.org/doc/Treaties/1998/07/ 19980717%2006-33%20PM/volume-2187-I-38544-English.pdf

UN Commission on Human Rights. 2005. Human Rights and Transnational Corporations and other Business Enterprises. Human Rights Resolution 2005/69. E/CN.4/RES/ 2005/69. www.refworld.org/docid/ 45377c80c.html

UNCTAD. 2020. Investor-State Dispute Settlement Cases Pass the 1,000 Mark: Cases and Outcomes in 2019. IIA Issues Note, Issue 2, July 2020. https://unctad .org/system/files/official-document/ diaepcbinf2020d6.pdf

UNEP. n.d. (a) Artisanal and Small-Scale Gold Mining (ASGM). https://web.unep .org/globalmercurypartnership/our-work/artisanal-and-small-scale-gold-mining-asgm

UNEP. n.d. (b). Berta Cáceres – Inspiration and Action Award. www.unep.org/ championsofearth/laureates/2016/ berta-caceres

UN General Assembly. 2015. Transforming Our World: The 2030 Agenda for Sustainable Development. Resolution adopted by the General Assembly on 25 September 2015. A/Res/70/1. www .un.org/en/development/desa/ population/migration/generalassembly/ docs/globalcompact/A_RES_70_1_E .pdf

UN Global Compact. 2013. UN Global Compact Policy on Communicating Progress. https://d306pr3pise04h

.cloudfront.net/docs/communication_ on_progress%2FCOP_Policy.pdf

UN Global Compact. n.d. (a). Frequently Asked Questions. www .unglobalcompact.org/about/faq

UN Global Compact. n.d. (b). Principle One: Human Rights. www.unglobalcompact .org/what-is-gc/mission/principles/ principle-1

UN Global Compact. n.d. (c). Principle Five: Labour. www.unglobalcompact.org/ what-is-gc/mission/principles/ principle-5

UN Global Compact. n.d. (d). Engage Locally. www.unglobalcompact.org/engage- locally

UN Global Compact. n.d. (e). The Communication on Progress (CoP) in Brief. www.unglobalcompact.org/ participation/report/cop

UN Global Compact. n.d. (f). Integrity Measures. Frequently Asked Questions. https://d306pr3pise04h.cloudfront.net/ docs/about_the_gc%2FIntegrity_ measures%2FFAQ_EN.pdf

UN Global Compact. n.d. (g). Principle Seven: Environment. www .unglobalcompact.org/what-is-gc/ mission/principles/principle-7

UN Human Rights Council. 2008. Resolution 8/7. Mandate of the Special Representative of the Secretary General on the issue of human rights and transnational corporations and other business enterprises. A/HRC/ RES/8/7. http://ap.ohchr.org/ documents/E/HRC/resolutions/A_HRC_ RES_8_7.pdf

UN Human Rights Council. 2011. Resolution 17/4. Human Rights and Transnational Corporations and other Business

Enterprises. A/HRC/RES/17/4. www .undocs.org/en/A/HRC/RES/17/4

UN Human Rights Council. 2014. Elaboration of an International Legally Binding Instrument on Transnational Corporations and Other Business Enterprises with Respect to Human Rights. A/HRC/RES/26/9. https:// undocs.org/A/HRC/RES/26/9

UN News. 2020. Convention on Worst Forms of Child Labour Receives Universal Ratification, August 4, 2020. https:// news.un.org/en/story/2020/08/1069492

UN Permanent Forum on Indigenous Issues. 2015. Introduction. In UN Permanent Forum on Indigenous Issues (ed.), *State of the World's Indigenous Peoples, 2015.* Second volume, 2–9. New York, Geneva: United Nations. www.refworld .org/docid/55c89dac4.html

UN Permanent Forum on Indigenous Issues. n.d. Factsheet 'Who are Indigenous Peoples?' United Nations. www.un.org/ esa/socdev/unpfii/documents/5session_ factsheet1.pdf

UN Sub-Commission on the Promotion and Protection of Human Rights. 2013. Draft Norms on the Responsibilities of Transnational Corporations and Other Business Rnterprises with Regard to Human Rights. E/CN.4/Sub.2/2003/12. https://digitallibrary.un.org/record/ 498842?ln=en

UNWG. 2013. Report of the United Nations Working Group on the Issue of Human Rights and Transnational Corporations and Other Business Enterprises. A/68/ 279. https://undocs.org/A/68/279

UNWG. 2014. Report of the United Nations Working Group on the Issue of Human Rights and Transnational Corporations and Other Business Enterprises. A/69/ 263. https://undocs.org/A/69/263

UNWG. 2016. *Guidance on National Action Plans on Business and Human Rights.* Geneva: UN Working Group on Business and Human Rights. www .ohchr.org/Documents/Issues/Business/ UNWG_NAPGuidance.pdf

UNWG. 2017a. Report of the United Nations Working Group on the Issue of Human Rights and Transnational Corporations and Other Business Enterprises. A/72/ 162. https://undocs.org/A/72/162

UNWG. 2017b. The Business and Human Rights Dimension of Sustainable Development: Embedding "Protect, Respect and Remedy" in SDGs Implementation. Information Note, June 30, 2017. www.ohchr.org/ Documents/Issues/Business/Session18/ InfoNoteWGBHR_ SDGRecommendations.pdf

UNWG. 2019. *Gender Dimensions of the Guiding Principles on Business and Human Rights.* Geneva: UN Human Rights Special Procedures & UN Development Programme. www.ohchr .org/Documents/Issues/Business/ BookletGenderDimensionsGuiding Principles.pdf

Van Dijk, Maria A., De Haas, Marijn & Zandvliet, Ruben. 2018. Banks and Human Trafficking: Rethinking Human Rights Due Diligence. *Business and Human Rights Journal* 3/1: 105–111.

Van Heerden, Auret. 2016. The Fair Labor Association: Improving Workers' Rights in Global Supply Chains. In Baumann-Pauly, Dorothée & Nolan, Justine (eds.), *Business and Human Rights: From Principles to Practice,* 128–135. London; New York: Routledge.

Velasquez, Manuel. 1983. Why corporations are not morally responsible for anything they do. *Business & Professional Ethics Journal* 2/3: 1–18.

Vinciguerra, Venusia. 2011. How the Daewoo Attempted Land Acquisition Contributed to Madagascar's Political Crisis in 2009. Land Deal Politics Initiative. www .future-agricultures.org/wp-content/ uploads/pdf-archive/Venusia% 20Vinciguerra.pdf

Vives, Jordi, Cotrina, Laura & Zarama, Germán. 2019. Between Solidarity and Obligation: Challenges for the Participation of Businesses in Symbolic Reparations. Bogotá; St. Gallen: CREER & Institute for Business Ethics.

Vogel, David. 2005. *The Market for Virtue: The Potential and Limits of Corporate Social Responsibility.* Washington DC: Brookings Institution Press.

Votaw, Dow. 1961. The politics of a changing corporate society. *California Management Review* 3/3: 105–118.

Waddock, Sandra & Rasche, Andreas. 2012. *Building the Responsible Enterprise: Where Vision and Values Add Value.* Stanford: Stanford University Press.

Walk Free Foundation. 2018. Global Slavery Index 2018. www .globalslaveryindex.org/resources/ downloads/

Weissbrodt, David & Kruger, Muria. 2003. Norms on the responsibilities of transnational corporations and other business enterprises with regard to human rights. *American Journal of International Law* 97: 901–922.

Weissbrodt, David. 2005. Corporate human rights Responsibilities. *Zeitschrift für Wirtschafts- und Unternehmensethik* 6/3: 279–297.

Werhane, Patricia. 2015. Corporate moral agency and the responsibility to respect human rights in the UN Guiding Principles: Do corporations have moral rights? *Business and Human Rights Journal* 1/1: 5–20.

West, Janet. 2011. Export credits and the OECD. In OECD (ed.), *Smart Rules for Fair Trade: 50 Years of Export Credits*, 20–34. Paris: OECD Publishing.

Wettstein, Florian. 2009. *Multinational Corporations and Global Justice: Human Rights Obligations of a Quasi-Governmental Institution.* Stanford: Stanford University Press.

Wettstein, Florian. 2010. The duty to protect: Corporate complicity, political responsibility, and human rights advocacy. *Journal of Business Ethics* 96: 33–47.

Wettstein, Florian. 2012a. CSR and the debate on business and human rights: Bridging the great divide. *Business Ethics Quarterly* 22/4: 739–770.

Wettstein, Florian. 2012b. Corporate responsibility in the collective age: Toward a conception of collaborative responsibility. *Business and Society Review* 117/2: 155–184.

Wettstein, Florian. 2012c. Silence as complicity: Elements of a corporate duty to speak out against the violation of human rights. *Business Ethics Quarterly* 22/1: 37–61.

Wettstein, Florian. 2013. Making Noise About Silent Complicity: The Moral Inconsistency of the "Protect, Respect and Remedy" Framework. In Deva, Surya & Bilchitz, David (eds.), *Human Rights Obligations of Business: Beyond the Responsibility to Respect?* 243–268. Cambridge, UK: Cambridge University Press.

Wettstein, Florian. 2015. Normativity, ethics, and the UN Guiding Principles on Business and Human Rights: A critical assessment. *Journal of Human Rights* 14/2: 162–182.

Wettstein, Florian. 2016. From Side Show to Main Act: Can Business and Human Rights Save Corporate Responsibility? In Baumann-Pauly, Dorothée & Nolan, Justine (eds.), *Business and Human Rights: From Principles to Practice*, 78–87. London; New York: Routledge.

Wettstein, Florian. 2020. The History of "Business and Human Rights" and its Relationship with "Corporate Social Responsibility." In Deva, Surya & Birchall, David (eds.), *Research Handbook on Human Rights and Business*, 23–45. Cheltenham: Edward Elgar.

Wettstein, Florian. 2021. Betting on the wrong (Trojan) horse: CSR and the implementation of the UN Guiding Principles for Business and Human Rights. *Business and Human Rights Journal* 6/2: 312–325.

Wettstein, Florian & Baur, Dorothea. 2016. "Why should we care about marriage equality?" – Political advocacy as a part of corporate responsibility. *Journal of Business Ethics* 138: 199–213.

Wettstein, Florian, Giuliani, Elisa, Santangelo, Grazia D. & Stahl, Günter K. 2019. International business and human rights: A research agenda.

Journal of World Business 54/1: 54–65.

Whitney, Toby. 2015. Conflict minerals, black markets, and transparency: The legislative background of Dodd-Frank Section 1502 and its historical lessons. *Journal of Human Rights* 14: 183–200.

Whoriskey, Peter & Siegel, Rachel. 2019. Cocoa's child laborers. *The Washington Post*, June 5, 2019. www .washingtonpost.com/graphics/2019/ business/hershey-nestle-mars-chocolate-child-labor-west-africa/? utm_term=.c32b36c30bf3

Winograd, Morley & Hais, Michael. 2014. *How Millennials Could Upend Wall Street and Corporate America.* Washington, DC: The Brookings Institution. www.brookings.edu/wp-content/uploads/2016/06/Brookings_ Winogradfinal.pdf

Wood, Stepan. 2012. The case for leverage-based corporate human rights responsibility. *Business Ethics Quarterly* 22/1: 63–98.

Worland, Justin. 2016. What to Know About the Dakota Access Pipeline Protests. Time, October 28, 2016. https://time .com/4548566/dakota-access-pipeline-standing-rock-sioux/

World Bank. 2016. Why Forests are Key to Climate, Water, Health, and Livelihoods. March 18, 2016. www .worldbank.org/en/news/feature/2016/ 03/18/why-forests-are-key-to-climate-water-health-and-livelihoods

Wright, Michael. 2008. Corporations and Human Rights: A Survey of the Scope and Patterns of Alleged Corporate-Related Human Rights Abuse. John F. Kennedy School of Government.

https://media.business-humanrights .org/media/documents/files/reports-and-materials/Ruggie-scope-patterns-of-alleged-abuse-Apr-2008.pdf

WWF. n.d. Deforestation and Forest Degradation. www.worldwildlife.org/ threats/deforestation-and-forest-degradation

Xu, Vicky X., Cave, Danielle, Leibold, James, Munro, Kelsey & Ruser, Nathan. 2020. Uyghurs for Sale. Australian Strategic Policy Institute. www.aspi.org.au/ report/uyghurs-sale

Yap, James. 2020. Nevsun Resources Ltd. v. Araya: What the Canadian Supreme Court Decision Means in Holding Canadian Companies Accountable for Human Rights Abuses Abroad. Canadian Lawyers for International Human Rights Blog, April 23, 2020. http://claihr.ca/2020/04/23/nevsun-resources-ltd-v-araya-what-the-canadian-supreme-court-decision-means-in-holding-canadian-companies-accountable-for-human-rights-abuses-abroad/

Yeomans, Jon. 2017. Lonmin "Regrets" Marikana Massacre as Protestors Call for Action. The Telegraph, January 26, 2017. www.telegraph.co.uk/business/ 2017/01/26/lonmin-regrets-marikana-massacre-protestors-call-action/

Young, Iris M. 2006. Responsibility and global justice: A social connection model. *Social Philosophy and Policy* 23/1: 102–130.

Young, Iris M. 2011. *Responsibility for Justice.* Oxford: Oxford University Press.

Zagelmeyer, Stefan & Sinkovics, Rudolf R. 2019. MNEs, human rights and the

SDGs – the moderating role of business and human rights governance. *Transnational Corporations* 26/3: 33–62.

Zerk, Jennifer A. 2006. *Multinationals and Corporate Social Responsibility: Limitations and Opportunities in International Law*. Cambridge, UK: Cambridge University Press.

Zerk, Jennifer A. 2010. Extraterritorial Jurisdiction: Lessons for the Business and Human Rights Sphere from Six Regulatory Areas. Corporate Social Responsibility Initiative Working Paper No. 59. Cambridge, MA: John F. Kennedy School of Government, Harvard University

Zerk, Jennifer A. 2013. Corporate Liability for Gross Human Rights Abuses. Towards a Fairer and More Effective System of Domestic Law Remedies. A Report Prepared for the Office of the UN High Commissioner for Human Rights. www.ohchr.org/Documents/Issues/Business/DomesticLawRemedies/StudyDomesticeLawRemedies.pdf

Zorob, Maysa. 2020. Defending Defenders: Challenging Malicious Lawsuits in Southeast Asia. Business & Human Rights Resource Centre. www.business-humanrights.org/sites/default/files/documents/2020%20CLA%20Annual%20Briefing_SLAPPs%20SEA_FINAL.pdf

Zuboff, Shoshana. 2015. Big other: Surveillance capitalism and the prospects of an information civilization. *Journal of Information Technology* 30/1: 75–78.

Zuboff, Shoshana. 2019. *The Age of Surveillance Capitalism: The Fight for a Human Future at the New Frontier of Power*. New York: PublicAffairs.

Index

Abacha, Sani, 14
absolute rights, 53–54
absolutism, 32
Accord on Fire and Building
    Safety in Bangladesh,
    339
accountability mechanisms
  certification, by consumers,
    179
  by civil society organizations,
    182–183
  consumers as, 178–180
    conscious consumption,
    178–179
    Marine Stewardship
    Council, 179
    transparency of, 179–180
  for corporate social
    responsibility, 5
  investors, 180–181
    environmental, social and
    governance criteria, 180,
    182
    Principles for Responsible
    Investment, 180
  in ISO 26000, 220
  labels as, by consumers, 179
  in nation-states, legislative
    measures for, 241–258
  in OECD Guidelines for
    Multinational
    Enterprises, 208–209
    dispute settlement
    mechanisms, 208–209
    National Contact Points in,
    208–209
  soft, 178–183
    by civil society
    organizations, 182–183
  theoretical approach to,
    171–172
  in UN Global Compact,
    215–216
    Communication on
    Progress, 216

dialogue facilitation
    mechanisms, 216
learning platforms,
    215–216
local networks in, 215–216
under UN Guiding Principles,
    196–197
active complicity, in indirect
    human rights violations,
    70–71
  direct complicity, 71
  indirect complicity, 71
actus reus, 73
adjudicative jurisdiction, 230
Africa. See also Nigeria
  Côte d'Ivoire
    human rights violations in,
    69–70
    toxic waste dumping in,
    89–90
  regional human rights
    conventions in, 61
  South Africa, during
    apartheid era, 12–13
    Sullivan Principles as
    response to, 12–13
African Commission on Human
    and Peoples' Rights,
    51–52
African Court of Human and
    Peoples' Rights, 51–52,
    61
  Malabo Protocol, 52
agribusiness sector, corporate
    human rights
    responsibilities in. See
    food, beverage and
    agribusiness sector
aiding and abetting, 268–269
Alien Tort Claims Act (ATCA),
    US, 12, 20–21, 269–274
  direct company violations,
    270–271
  under state action,
    271

indirect company violations,
    271
international law and, 270
Jesner v. Arab Bank, 274
jus cogens norms, 270
Kiobel v. Royal Dutch
    Petroleum Co., 272–273
  main features of, 269–272
  Ruggie on, 273
  under law of nations, 270
Alliance for Bangladesh Worker
    Safety, 339
Annan, Kofi, 16–17
anti-corruption principles, in
    UN Global Compact, 212
Arab Charter of Human Rights,
    61–62
Arab States
  kafala system in, 95
  regional human rights
    conventions in, 61–62
Araya v. Nevsun Resources,
    282–285
arbitration. See international
    arbitration
artisanal mining (ASM), 319
  in Democratic Republic of the
    Congo, 321
ASEAN. See Association of
    South-East Asian
    Nations
ASM. See artisanal mining
Association of South-East
    Asian Nations (ASEAN),
    62
ATCA. See Alien Tort Claims
    Act
audits, for human rights due
    diligence, 163
Australian Modern Slavery Act
    (2019), 154, 240,
    242–244
autonomy, human rights and, 40
  internal autonomy of the
    state, 43

Bangladesh
  Accord on Fire and Building
    Safety in Bangladesh,
    339
  Alliance for Bangladesh
    Worker Safety, 339
banking and finance sector,
    corporate human rights
    responsibilities in,
    322–328
  best practices, 327–328
    impact investing,
    327–328
    through screening
    strategies, 327
  challenges in, 323–326
  Dakota Access Pipeline,
    financing of, 325
  human rights initiatives,
    324–327
  in lending practices, 324
  sector-specific standards,
    324–327
    Equator Principles,
    324–326
    IFC Performance
    Standards, 326
    Principles for Responsible
    Investment, 180,
    326–327
  Thun Group of Banks, 323
Barrick Gold mining company,
  158
Beitz, Charles, 42
beneficial complicity, 71
Bentham, Jeremy, 28–29
beverage sector, corporate
    human rights
    responsibilities in. See
    food, beverage and
    agribusiness sector
Bhopal gas disaster, 22–23
BHR. See business and human
    rights
BHRRC. See Business and
    Human Rights Resource
    Centre
bias and discrimination
  in information and
    communication
    technology sector, 331
  against women, 356–357
Bilateral Investment Treaties
  (BITs), 298

Bill of Rights
  in England, 27
  US, 27–28
binding treaty on business and
    human rights, 305–313
  arguments against/for,
    310–312
  elements of, 306–310
  enforcement mechanisms,
    308–310
    at domestic level, 308–309
    at international level, 309
  future outlook for, 312–313
  in Global South, 313
  Ruggie on, 312–313
  sanctions under, 308–310
  scope of, 306–308
  World Court of Human
    Rights, 309–310
BITs. See Bilateral Investment
    Treaties
BlackRock, new human rights
    approach at, 181
blue-washing, 216–217
Brandeis, Louis, 107–108
Brenkert, George, 133
Brussels I Regulation (2001),
  264
Burke, Edmund, 29
business and human rights
    (BHR). See also binding
    treaty on business and
    human rights; corporate
    social responsibility;
    ethical obligations of
    businesses; nation-
    states; specific countries;
    specific topics
  as academic discipline,
    xvii–xviii, 21–23
  climate change and, 352–356
    Carbon Major companies,
    353
    in Global South, 352
    human rights due diligence
    processes, 355–356
    legal cases and, 353–354
    under French Duty of
    Vigilance Law, 354
  corporate social
    responsibility as distinct
    from, 4
  definition and scope of, 1
  evolution of, xvii

  IKEA and, 37
  maturation of movement,
    from 2011-present,
    19–21
    at domestic level, 20–21
    at global level, 19–20
    National Action Plans, 20
    UN Working Group,
    19–20
  methodological approach to,
    6–7
  from 1945-1995, 11–15
    in apartheid-era South
    Africa, 12–13
    Nuremberg trials, 11–12
    OECD Guidelines, 15
    for oil extraction in
    Nigeria, 13–15
    Sullivan Principles,
    12–13
    under Alien Tort Claims
    Act (U.S.), 12, 20–21
  from 1995-2005, 15–17
    multi-stakeholder
    initiatives, 15–16
    UN Commission on Human
    Rights, 16–17
    UN Draft Norms for,
    16–17, 77
    under UN Global Compact,
    16
  overview of, 364–367
  in post-conflict contexts,
    358–362
  Ruggie and, 2, 17
  Starbucks and, 37
  Teaching Business and
    Human Rights Forum,
    xvii
  in transitional justice
    contexts, 358–362
  from 2005-2011, 18–19
    phases of, 18–19
    under UN Framework,
    16–18
    under UN Global Compact,
    18–19
  UN Forum on Business and
    Human Rights, xvii
  UN Sustainable Development
    Goals, 348–352
Business and Human Rights
    Resource Centre
    (BHRRC), 15

human rights defenders and, 97

business case, for corporate human rights responsibility, 118–121
negative business case, 119–120
positive business case, 120–122

Cáceres, Berta, 98
California Supply Chain Transparency Act, US (2010), 143, 244–246
UK Modern Slavery Act influenced by, 243
Cambridge Analytica scandal, 329–330
Canada, duty of care liability in, 281–285
Araya v. *Nevsun Resources*, 282–285
Choc v. *Hudbay Minerals*, 283–284
Garcia v. *Tahoe Resources*, 283
international law norms and, 282
Carbon Major companies, 353
CAT. *See* Committee Against Torture
Categorical Imperative, 28
CED. *See* Committee on Enforced Disappearances
CEDAW. *See* Committee on the Elimination of Discrimination against Women
CERD. *See* Committee on the Elimination of Racial Discrimination
certification, accountability through, by consumers, 179
CESCR. *See* Committee on Economic, Social and Cultural Rights
child labor
corporate human rights violations of, 80–81
as indirect human rights violation, 69–70
International Labour Organization and, 80–81

under Dutch Child Labor Due Diligence Law, 251–252
Children's Fund, UN (UNICEF). *See* United Nations
China
corporate human rights responsibility in, 132
indirect human rights violations in, 74
Choc v. *Hudbay Minerals*, 283–284
civil law jurisdictions. *See also specific countries*
adjudicative measures in, for human rights, 285–290
civil society organizations, accountability mechanisms by, 182–183
Clean Clothes Campaign, 327–340
climate change, business and human rights and, 352–356
in Global South, 352
human rights due diligence processes, 355–356
legal cases and, 353–354
under French Duty of Vigilance Law, 354
CMW. *See* Committee on Migrant Workers
Committee Against Torture (CAT), 48–49, 59
Committee on Economic, Social and Cultural Rights (CESCR), 48–49
Committee on Enforced Disappearances (CED), 48–49
Committee on Migrant Workers (CMW), 48–49
Committee on the Elimination of Discrimination against Women (CEDAW), 48–49, 59
Committee on the Elimination of Racial Discrimination (CERD), 48–49
Committee on the Rights of Persons with Disabilities (CRPD), 48–49, 60
Committee on the Rights of the Child (CRC), 48–49, 59

Common Law Duty of Care, UK, 274–280
duty of care, 275–276
jurisdiction of, 275
Okpabi v. *Royal Dutch Shell Plc*, 279–280
tort cases, 276
Vedanta Resources Plc v. *Lungowe*, 276–279
common law traditions. *See* domestic laws; *specific countries*
Communication on Progress (COP), 216
community-driven operational-level grievance mechanisms, 151
compliance, by nation-states, for human rights responsibilities, 294
complicity
in indirect human rights violations, 68
actus reus, 73
legal elements of, 72–76
mens rea, 73
moral elements of, 72–76
in UN Global Compact, 213–214
conscious consumption, 178–179
Constitution of 1787, US, 27–28
consumers, accountability for human rights by, 178–180
conscious consumption, 178–179
Marine Stewardship Council, 179
transparency for, 179–180
Convention on the Non-Applicability of Statutory Limitations of War Crimes and Crimes against Humanity, 60
Convention on the Prevention and Punishment of the Crime of Genocide, 60
COP. *See* Communication on Progress
corporate criminal liability, 290–291

corporate culture,
    implementation of
    human rights
    responsibility influenced
    by, 165–168
  corporate values and vision,
    166–167
  elements of corporate culture,
    166
  incentives and remuneration
    and, 167–168
  leadership and, 167
  recruitment strategies, 167
corporate human rights
    responsibility. *See also*
    implementation of
    human rights
    responsibility; *specific*
    industry sectors
  in China, 132
  common objections to,
    122–124
    as duplication of state
      responsibility, 123
    as legitimization of
      corporate power, 124
    as replacement for
      government
      responsibility, 123–124
  corporate power and, 107–110
    discursive, 109
    legitimization of, 124
    relational, 108
    social science and, 110
    structural, 108–109
  ethical imperatives of
    businesses, 103–106
    institutional rights
      approach, 107
    moral rights approach,
      106–107
  ethical obligations of
    businesses, 103–106
    corporations as political
      actors, 105–106
    Friedman on, 105
    moral agency of
      corporations, 104–105
    beyond profit
      maximization, 103–106
  fulfillment of human rights,
    138–140
    as obligation to rescue,
      138–139

    in public functions, 139
  as legal imperative, 113–116
    under state-centred
      doctrine, 114–116
  as legal obligations, 110–116
    at international level, for
      legal personhood of
      corporations, 112–113
    at national level, for legal
      personhood of
      corporations, 110–112
    under international law,
      112–113
  legal personhood, of
    corporations
    Citizens United case and,
      111
    at international level,
      112–113
    at national level, 110–112
  obligations in
    active, 127
    collaborative, 139–140
    duty to aid the deprived,
      129
    duty to avoid depriving,
      128–129
    duty to protect from
      deprivation, 128–129
    general/universal, 127
    imperfect, 128
    negative, 126–127
    passive, 126–127
    perfect, 128
    positive, 126–127
    for protection of human
      rights, 131–138
    to rescue, 138–139
    respect of/for human
      rights, 129–133
    special, 127
    typology of, 128–129
  pragmatic perspectives on,
    116–122
    business case for, 118–122
    Nike case, 121
    social license to operate,
      117–118
  protection of human rights,
    as corporate obligation,
      131–138
    conditions for, 134–135
    direct, relational contexts
      for, 133–136

    indirect, structural
      contexts for, 136–138
    Social Connection Model
      of responsibility,
      136–138
  Ruggie on, 117
  Santa Clara v. *Southern*
    Pacific, 111
  under International Bill of
    Human Rights, 115–116
  under ISO 26000, 220
  under UN Guiding Principles,
    130, 133–134
  under Universal Declaration
    of Human Rights, 115
corporate human rights
    violations
  against affected
    communities, 83–87
    conflict contexts, 85–87
    through displacement,
      85–99
    through land grabs, 85–99
    Marikana Massacre, 86–87
    against protesters, 85–87
    by security providers, 85–87
  direct company violations,
    270–271
    under state action, 271
  within employment relations,
    77–80
    discrimination issues,
      77–78
    harassment issues, 77–78
    monitoring issues, 78–80
    privacy issues, 78–80
    workplace surveillance
      cases, 79–80
  indirect company violations,
    271
  informed consent and, 84
  relating to environment,
    87–91
    contamination of, 88–90
    deforestation, 90–91
    toxic waste dumping,
      89–90
  supply chain workers and,
    80–83
    child labor, 80–81
    exploitation of, 82
    forced labor, 82–83
    modern slavery of, 82–83
    sweatshop labor, 82

against vulnerable groups, 91–100
  human rights defenders, 95–100
  Indigenous communities, 92–94
  migrant workers, 94–97
  in Qatar, 96–97
corporate power
  corporate human rights responsibility and, 107–110
  discursive power, 109
  as legitimization of power, 124
  relational power, 108
  as social science, 110
  structural power, 108–109
  historical development of, 107–108
  revenues as measurement of, 108
corporate social responsibility (CSR), 2–5
  as academic discipline, 21
  business and human rights as distinct from, 4
  challenges to traditional thinking about, 2–4
  as private responsibility, 3–5
  historical development of, 2–3
  human rights perspective on, 4–5
  moral relativism issues, 5
  as private responsibility, 4–5
  for public accountability, 5
  internationalization of, 3
"Corporation Nation," 108
corporations. *See also specific topics*
  moral agency of, 104–105
Côte d'Ivoire, 69–70
  toxic waste dumping in, 89–90
CPRD. *See* Committee on the Rights of Persons with Disabilities
CRC. *See* Committee on the Rights of the Child
CSR. *See* corporate social responsibility
cultural relativism, 32

Dakota Access Pipeline, financing of, 325
Danish Institute for Human Rights (DIHR), 236
Declaration of Independence, US, 27–28
Declaration of Rights, in France, 28–29
Declaration on Fundamental Principles and Rights and Work (ILO), 194
deforestation, 90–91
Democratic Republic of the Congo (DRC), 190
  artisanal mining in, 321
  Dodd-Frank Act and, 249–250
  EU Conflict Minerals Regulation, 250–251
Derber, Charles, 108
descriptive relativism, 32
descriptive universalism, 34
dialogue facilitation mechanisms, of UN Global Compact, 216
dignity, as element of human rights, 38
DIHR. *See* Danish Institute for Human Rights
direct company violations, under Alien Tort Claims Act, 270–271
  through state action, 271
direct complicity, 71
direct parent liability, 267
direct protection of human rights, as corporate obligation, 133–136
direct violations, of human rights, 66–67
disclosure legislation, 240–254. *See also specific legislation*
discrimination issues, 77–78
discursive corporate power, 109
dispute settlement mechanisms, in OECD Guidelines for Multinational Enterprises, 208–209
Dodd-Frank Act. *See* Wall Street Reform and Consumer Protection Act
dogmatism, absolutism and, 32

domestic laws. *See also specific countries; specific laws*
  human rights due diligence under, 143–144
  in France, 143
  in UK, 143
  in US, 143
DRC. *See* Democratic Republic of the Congo
Drucker, Peter, 108
Dutch Child Labor Due Diligence Law, Netherlands (2019), 251–252
duty of care liability
  in Canada, 281–285
    Araya v. *Nevsun Resources*, 282–285
    Choc v. *Hudbay Minerals*, 283–284
    Garcia v. *Tahoe Resources*, 283
    international law norms and, 282
  nation-states human rights measures
    adjudicative measures, 267–268
  under UK Common Law Duty of Care, 275–276
Duty of Vigilance law, France, 143, 254–258
  cases under, 257
  climate change under, 354
  enforcement mechanisms in, 255–256
  legal scope of, 255
  remedy mechanisms, 256
duty to aid the deprived, 129
duty to avoid depriving, 128–129
duty to protect from deprivation, 128–129

ECHR. *See* European Convention on Human Rights
EITI. *See* Extractive Industries Transparency Initiative
employment
  corporate human rights violations with, 77–80
  discrimination issues, 77–78

employment (cont.)
    harassment issues, 77–78
    monitoring issues, 78–80
    privacy issues, 78–80
    workplace surveillance
        cases, 79–80
    in information and
        communication
        technology sector,
        331–332
enforcement jurisdiction, 230
enforcement mechanisms
    in binding treaty on business
        and human rights,
        308–310
    at domestic level, 308–309
    at international level, 309
    in French Duty of Vigilance
        Law, 255–256
    in UN Guiding Principles,
        critical assessment of,
        201–202
England. See also United
        Kingdom
    Bill of Rights in, 27
    human rights in, 27
enterprise liability, 267–296
environmental, social and
        governance (ESG)
        criteria, 180, 182
environmental issues
    corporate human rights
        violations relating to,
        87–91
    contamination of
        environment, 88–90
    deforestation, 90–91
    toxic waste dumping,
        89–90
    gender perspectives on, 357
    in UN Global Compact
        guidelines, 212,
        214–215
equality, human rights and, 31
Equator Principles, for banking
        and finance sector,
        324–326
ESG criteria. See environmental,
        social and governance
        criteria
ethical imperatives of business,
        103–106
    institutional rights approach,
        107

moral rights approach,
        106–107
ethical obligations of business,
        103–106
    corporations as political
        actors, 105–106
    Friedman on, 105
    moral agency of
        corporations, 104–105
    as political actors, 105–106
    beyond profit maximization,
        103–106
    corporate moral agency,
        104–105
ethical relativism, 33
ethics, human rights due
        diligence and, 164
EU Conflict Minerals
        Regulation, 250–251
EU Non-Financial Reporting
        Directive, 246–247
    goals and scope of, 247
Europe. See also specific
        countries; specific
        legislation; specific
        topics
    regional human rights
        conventions in, 60–61
European Convention on
        Human Rights (ECHR),
        50, 60–61
European Court of Human
        Rights, 50, 60–61
export credit and investment
        guarantees, 238–240
Extractive Industries
        Transparency Initiative
        (EITI), 320
extractive sector, corporate
        human rights
        responsibilities in,
        317–322. See also
        specific companies
    artisanal mining, 319
        in Democratic Republic of
        the Congo, 321
    best practices, 320–321
    challenges with, 318–319
    human rights initiatives in,
        319–320
        Extractive Industries
        Transparency Initiative,
        320
        Kimberly Process, 319–320

OECD Due Diligence
        Guidance for
        Responsible Supply
        Chains of Minerals from
        Conflict-Affected and
        High-Risk Areas, 319
    Responsible Mining
        Initiative, 319–320
    issues within, 318–319
    sector-specific standards,
        319–320
        International Code of
        Conduct for Private
        Security Service
        Providers, 320
        Voluntary Principles on
        Security and Human
        Rights, 320
    under UN Declaration on the
        Rights of Indigenous
        Peoples, 318–319
extraterritorial regulation, 187
    by nation-states, human
        rights obligations of,
        229–233
    adjudicative jurisdiction,
        230
    direct extraterritorial
        jurisdiction, 231
    domestic measures with,
        230–231
    enforcement jurisdiction,
        230
    prescriptive jurisdiction,
        230
    under international law,
        229–230, 232–233

Fair Labor Association (FLA),
        339–340
Fair Wear Foundation, 327–340
Fairtrade International
        standards, 344–345
"fake news," 330–331
"fast fashion," 336
finance sector. See banking and
        finance sector
FLA. See Fair Labor Association
Flick, 11–12
food, beverage and agribusiness
        sector, corporate human
        rights responsibilities in,
        341–346
    best practices, 345–346

challenges within, 342–344
downstream issues, 343–344
human rights initiatives in,
    344–345
    International Food and
        Beverage Alliance, 345
    Rainforest Alliance, 345
land grabs, 343
Nestlé, 341–342
sector-specific standards,
    344–345
    Fairtrade International
        standards, 344–345
    Sydney Principles, 345
upstream issues, 342–343
footwear sector. *See* garment
    and footwear sector
forced labor, 82–83
Forced Labour Convention
    (No. 29), 83
foreign direct liability, 259–260
forum non conveniens doctrine,
    262–264
Forum on Business and Human
    Rights. *See* United
    Nations
foundationalist accounts, of
    human rights, 38–42
deontological approaches,
    39–40
rationalist approaches, 41–42
reconciliation of approaches
    in, 45
teleological approaches,
    38–39
Four Nigerian Farmers case,
    286–287
France
business and human rights
    in, 20
Declaration of Rights in, 28–29
Duty of Vigilance Law, 143,
    254–258
    climate change under, 354
    enforcement mechanisms
        in, 255–256
    legal scope of, 255
    remedy mechanisms, 256
human rights due diligence
    in, 143
free speech, in information and
    communication
    technology sector,
    challenges to, 330–331

Friedman, Milton, 105
frivolous litigation, 295–296

Garcia v. *Tahoe Resources*, 283
garment and footwear sector,
    corporate human rights
    responsibilities in,
    335–341
best practices, 340–341
challenges within, 336–339
    structure of industry as,
        336
    "fast fashion," 336
human rights initiatives,
    339–340
    Clean Clothes Campaign,
        327–340
    Fair Labor Association,
        339–340
    Fair Wear Foundation,
        327–340
Nike, 121, 336–339
Rana Plaza Factory Collapse,
    337–338
sector-specific standards,
    339–340
    Accord on Fire and
        Building Safety in
        Bangladesh, 339
    Alliance for Bangladesh
        Worker Safety, 339
gender perspectives, on BHR,
    356–358
discrimination and bias
    against women,
    356–357
environmental issues, 357
sexual abuse and harassment
    against women,
    356–357
under UN Guiding Principles,
    357–358
gender segregation, in Saudi
    Arabia, 37
generations of human rights, 53
German Supply Chain Act
    (2021), 253
Germany
corporate human rights
    violations in, 288
Flick, 11–12
I. G. Farben, 11–12
Jabir and others v. *KiK
    Textilien*, 288

Krupp, 11–12
Lliuya v. *RWE AG*, 289
Nuremberg trials, 11–12
Gewirth, Alan, 41–42
Global Network Initiative (GNI),
    332–334
Global North, 218
Global Reporting Initiative
    (GRI), 154
Global South
binding treaty on business
    and human rights in,
    313
climate change in, business
    and human rights and,
    352
information and
    communication
    technology sector in, 331
ISO 26000 and, 218
transnational governance in,
    172–173
globalization
human rights influenced by,
    2
transnational governance
    influenced by, 174
GNI. *See* Global Network
    Initiative
Google, corporate human rights
    responsibility of, 132
green-washing, 216–217
GRI. *See* Global Reporting
    Initiative
Griffin, James, 41
Grotius, Hugo, 28

Hague Rules on Business and
    Human Rights
    Arbitration, 305
harassment issues, 77–78
hard duties, in UN Guiding
    Principles, 201–202
hard law, transnational
    governance under,
    176–178
hate propaganda, 330–331
Heede, Richard, 353
Hobbes, Thomas, 27, 36
home states. *See* domestic laws;
    nation-states
HRC. *See* Human Rights Council
HRDD. *See* human rights due
    diligence

HRDs. *See* human rights
  defenders
human rights. *See also* human
  rights due diligence;
  human rights violations;
  international human
  rights law; international
  human rights systems;
  specific topics
Asian values and, 35–36
autonomy and, 40
  internal, of the state, 43
challenges to traditional
  thinking about, 1–2
  with globalization, 2
  as state-centric, 1–2
corporate social
  responsibility and, 4–5
  moral relativism issues
  with, 5
definition of, 30
elements of, 30–31
  equality, 31
  inalienability, 31
  indivisibility, 31
  universality of rights, 30
in England, 27
foundationalist accounts of,
  38–42
  deontological approaches,
  39–40
  rationalist approaches,
  41–42
  reconciliation of
  approaches in, 45
  teleological approaches,
  38–39
generations of, 53
history of thought of, 26–30
  criticism of human rights,
  28–29
  natural law, 26–27
  natural rights, 27–29
  United Nations and, role
  in, 29–30
  in Western world, 27–28
human dignity as element of,
  38
impacts on, 65–66
institutionalism and, 44
Kant on, 28
legal positivism and, 25–26
non-foundationalist accounts
  of, 42–45

constructivist approach,
  44–45
political approach, 42–44
pragmatist approach,
  44–45
realist approach, 42–44
reconciliation of
  approaches in, 45
normative agency and, 41
normativism and, 44
relativism of, 31–37
  cultural, 32
  descriptive, 32
  ethical, 33
  normative, 33
  universalism compared to,
  32–33
social contract and, 27–28
state duty to protect human
  rights, 187–188
types of, 53–54
under UN Global Compact,
  212–213
Universal Declaration of
  Human Rights, 29–30,
  35, 38, 55
universalism of, 30–37
  absolutism and, 32
  descriptive, 34
  normative, 34–35
  relativism compared to,
  32–33
in Western world
  in history of thought,
  27–28
  as Western concept,
  35–37
Westphalian international
  order and, 1–2
Human Rights Council (HRC),
  47–48
Open-Ended
  Intergovernmental
  Working Group on
  Transnational
  Corporations and other
  Business Enterprises
  with Respect to Human
  Rights, 312–313
UN Guiding Principles and,
  18–19
human rights defenders (HRDs)
Business and Human Rights
  Resource Centre and, 97

corporate human rights
  violations against,
  95–100
under UN Declaration on the
  Right and Responsibility
  of Individuals, Groups
  and Organs of Society to
  Promote and Protect
  Universally Recognized
  Human Rights and
  Fundamental Freedoms,
  98–99
human rights due diligence
  (HRDD), 142–145. *See
  also* human rights
  impact assessments
in business practices,
  144–145
in climate change contexts,
  355–356
critique of, 163–165
  from ethical point of view,
  164
  from legalistic point of
  view, 163–164
  from managerial point of
  view, 165
impacts of, actual and
  potential, 145
implementation of,
  challenges for, 159–163
  audits, 163
  collaborations in, 162–163
  community engagement,
  162
  as company-specific, 160
  dedicated processes in,
  160–161
  by industry, 160
  non-specific processes in,
  160–161
  prioritization, 161–162
  risk assessment in,
  161–162
  in small and medium-sized
  enterprises, 160
  supplier engagement and,
  163
in legislative measures, for
  human rights
  responsibilities,
  240–241, 248–258
negligence and,
  142–143

as ongoing process, 145–154
through policy measures, 238
policy statements for,
    145–147
    functions of, 147
purpose of, 143
risk to rights-holders, 145
UN Guiding Principles and,
    142, 144–147, 194
UN Protect, Respect and
    Remedy Framework and,
    189
under domestic laws,
    143–144
    in France, 143
    in UK, 143
    in US, 143
human rights impact
    assessments (HRIAs),
    147–159
human rights performance
    indicators, 151–153
    data quality, 152
    measurement challenges,
        153
    quality of approximations,
        152–153
operational-level grievance
    mechanisms, 148–151
    community-driven, 151
remedy mechanisms as result
    of, 154–158
    Barrick Gold mining
        company, 158
    independent third-party
        involvement in,
        156–157
    non-state-based non-
        judicial remedies, 150,
        155
    state-based judicial
        remedies, 155
    state-based non-judicial
        remedies, 155
    under UN Guiding
        Principles, 150
    under UN Working Group
        guidance, 157
    victim participation in,
        156
reporting of impact/corporate
    responses, 153–154
    Global Reporting Initiative,
        154

Reporting and Assurance
    Framework Initiative,
    154
structural processes of,
    147–148
    phases of, 147–148
human rights performance
    indicators, 151–153
    data quality, 152
    measurement challenges, 153
    quality of approximations,
        152–153
human rights policy statements
    human rights due diligence
        and, 145–147
    functions of, 147
human rights violations. See
    also corporate human
        rights violations;
        indirect human rights
        violations
    definition of, 65
    direct, 66–67
    impacts compared to, 65–66
Hume, David, 29

I. G. Farben, 11–12
ICC. See International Criminal
    Court
ICCPR. See International
    Covenant on Civil and
    Political Rights
ICESCR. See International
    Covenant on Economic,
    Social and Cultural
    Rights
ICJ. See International Court of
    Justice
ICRC. See International
    Committee of the Red
    Cross
IFC Performance Standards. See
    International Finance
    Corporation
    Performance Standards
IIAs. See International
    Investment Agreements
IKEA, 37
ILO. See International Labour
    Organization
impact investing, 327–328
impacts, on human rights,
    65–66
imperialism, 292–293

implementation of human
    rights responsibility, by
    corporations. See also
    human rights due
    diligence
    corporate culture as factor
        for, 165–168
    corporate values and
        vision, 166–167
    elements of, 166
    incentives and
        remuneration, 167–168
    leadership and, 167
    recruitment strategies,
        167
    theoretical approach to,
        142
inalienability, of human rights,
    31
Indigenous communities
    corporate human rights
        violations against,
        92–94
    under UN Declaration on the
        Rights of Indigenous
        Peoples, 93–94
indirect company violations,
    271
indirect complicity, 71
indirect human rights
    violations, 67–76
    active complicity in,
        70–71
        direct complicity, 71
        indirect complicity, 71
    child labor as, 69–70
    in China, 74
    complicity in, 68
        actus reus, 73
        legal elements of,
            72–76
        mens rea, 73
        moral elements of,
            72–76
    in Côte d'Ivoire, 69–70
    passive complicity in, 71
        beneficial complicity, 71
        silent complicity, 71–72
indirect liability, 267–296
indirect protection of human
    rights, as corporate
    obligation, 136–138
indivisibility, of human rights,
    31

information and communication
technology sector,
corporate human rights
responsibilities in,
328–335
best practices, 334–335
Cambridge Analytica
scandal, 329–330
challenges within, 329–332
bias and discrimination
issues, 331
for employment issues,
331–332
for free speech, 330–331
for hate propaganda,
330–331
for labor issues, 331–332
privacy and surveillance
issues, 329–330
"fake news," 330–331
in Global South, 331
human rights initiatives,
332–334
Global Network Initiative,
332–334
OECD Principles on AI,
332–334
Partnership on AI,
332–334
sector-specific standards for,
332–334
Yahoo!, 330
informed consent, violations of,
84
institutional rights approach, to
ethical imperatives of
businesses, 107
institutionalism, human rights
and, 44
Inter-American Commission on
Human Rights, 50–51
Inter-American Court on
Human Rights, 51, 61
international arbitration,
302–305
under Hague Rules on
Business and Human
Rights Arbitration, 305
International Bill of Human
Rights, 56–58
corporate human rights
responsibility under,
115–116

International Covenant for
Civil and Political
Rights, 53, 58
International Covenant on
Economic, Social and
Cultural Rights, 53,
58–59
Universal Declaration of
Human Rights, 29–30,
35, 38, 55–57
articles of, 57
International Code of Conduct
for Private Security
Service Providers, 320
International Committee of the
Red Cross (ICRC),
139–140
International Convention for
the Protection of All
Persons from Enforced
Disappearance, 60
International Convention on the
Elimination of All Forms
of Racial Discrimination,
59
International Convention on the
Protection of the Rights
of All Migrant Workers
and Members of their
Families, 59
International Convention on the
Protection of the Rights
of All Migrant Workers
and Members of Their
Families, 94
International Convention on the
Suppression and
Punishment and the
Crime of Apartheid, 60
International Court of Justice
(ICJ), 46–47
International Covenant on Civil
and Political Rights
(ICCPR), 53, 58–59
International Covenant on
Economic, Social and
Cultural Rights
(ICESCR), 53, 58–59
International Criminal Court
(ICC), 49–50
International Criminal
Tribunal for Rwanda,
49–50

International Criminal
Tribunal for the Former
Yugoslavia, 49–50
Nuremberg trials, 11–12,
49–50
Tokyo War Crimes Tribunal,
49–50
International Criminal Tribunal
for Rwanda, 49–50
International Criminal Tribunal
for the Former
Yugoslavia, 49–50
International Finance
Corporation (IFC)
Performance Standards,
326
International Food and
Beverage Alliance, 345
international human rights law,
52–62. *See also specific
conventions; specific
treaty bodies*
for absolute rights, 53–54
core treaties for, 58–60
for generations of human
rights, 53
historical development of,
52–53
International Bill of Human
Rights, 56–58
International Covenant for
Civil and Political
Rights, 53, 58–59
International Covenant on
Economic, Social and
Cultural Rights, 53,
58–59
Universal Declaration of
Human Rights, 29–30,
35, 38, 55–57
for negative rights, 54
for positive rights, 54
regional human rights
conventions, 60–62
in Africa, 61
in Arab states, 61–62
in Europe, 60–61
in North/South America,
61
in South-East Asian states,
62
for relative human rights,
53–54

sources of, 54–56
   customary law, 55
   general law principles, 56
   jus cogens, 55–56
   treaty law, 55
international human rights
      systems, 46–52. *See also*
      specific conventions;
      specific treaty bodies
   African Commission on
      Human and Peoples'
      Rights, 51–52
   African Court of Human and
      Peoples' Rights, 51–52
   Malabo Protocol, 52
   European Convention on
      Human Rights, 50
   European Court of Human
      Rights, 50
   Human Rights Council,
      47–48
   Inter-American Commission
      on Human Rights, 50–51
   Inter-American Court of
      Human Rights, 51
   International Court of Justice,
      46–47
   International Criminal Court,
      49–50
   Office of the High
      Commissioner for
      Human Rights, 47–48
   treaty bodies, 48–49
   United Nations' role in,
      46–49
International Investment
      Agreements (IIAs),
      298–304
   Bilateral Investment Treaties,
      298
   integration of human rights
      into, 300–301
      defensive approach to, 300
      offensive approach to, 300
   investor–state dispute
      settlement mechanisms,
      299, 301–311
   Urbaser v. *Argentina*, 303
international investment law,
      298–305
International Labour
      Organization (ILO), 46,
      48

child labor violations, 80–81
   Convention on Forced Labor,
      48
   Declaration on Fundamental
      Principles and Rights at
      Work, 194
   Freedom of Association and
      Protection of the Right
      to Organize, 48
international law
   Alien Tort Claims Act and,
      270
   corporate human rights
      responsibility under, as
      legal obligation,
      112–113
   duty of care liability and, in
      Canada, 282
   transnational governance
      under, 173
International Responsible
      Business Conduct (IRBC)
      Agreements, 252
International Standard
      Organization 26000 (ISO
      26000), 218–221
   accountability regimes for,
      220
   content of, 218–220
   corporate human rights
      responsibility under, 220
   critiques of, 221
   Global North and, 218
   Global South and, 218
   historical development of,
      218
   multi-stakeholder initiatives,
      221–224
      implementation strategies,
      222
      purpose of, 223
      representation imbalance
      in, 223–224
      varieties of, 222–223
   Ruggie on, 219–220
investors, accountability
      mechanisms and,
      180–181
   environmental, social and
      governance criteria, 180,
      182
   Principles for Responsible
      Investment, 180

investor–state dispute settlement
      (ISDS) mechanisms, 299,
      301–311
   Urbaser v. *Argentina*, 303
IRBC Agreements. *See*
      International
      Responsible Business
      Conduct Agreements
ISDS mechanisms. *See* investor–
      state dispute settlement
      mechanisms
ISO 26000. *See* International
      Standard Organization
      26000
Italy
   corporate human rights
      violations in, 289–290
   Ododo Francis v. *ENI and*
      Nigerian Agip Oil
      Company (NAOC),
      289–290

Jabir and others v. *KiK*
      Textilien, 288
Jesner v. *Arab Bank*, 274
Joas, Hans, 36
jurisdiction
   of nation-states, human
      rights responsibilities of,
      261–262
      adjudicative jurisdiction,
      230
      enforcement jurisdiction,
      230
      prescriptive jurisdiction, 230
   under international law
      private international law,
      262
      public international law,
      261–262
jus cogens norms, 55–56
   Alien Tort Claims Act and, 270

kafala system, in Middle
      Eastern states, 95
Kant, Immanuel
   Categorical Imperative, 28
   on human rights, 28
Kimberly Process, 319–320
Kiobel v. *Royal Dutch Petroleum*
      Co., 272–273, 287–288
Kozma, Julia, 309
Krupp, 11–12

labor principles. *See also* child
    labor
  in information and
      communication
      technology sector,
      331–332
  under UN Global Compact,
      212, 214
LaFarge, 291
land grabs
  by agribusiness sector, 343
  as corporate human rights
      violation, 85–99
law of nations, Alien Tort
      Claims Act under, 270
learning platforms, of UN
      Global Compact,
      215–216
legal imperatives, of corporate
      human rights
      responsibility, 113–116
  under state-centered
      doctrine, 114–116
legal personhood, of
      corporations
  Citizens United case and, 111
  at international level,
      112–113
  at national level, 110–112
legal positivism, 25–26
Leviathan (Hobbes), 27
Lliuya v. *RWE AG*, 289
Locke, John, 27–28, 36
  social contract and, 27–28

Malabo Protocol, 52
Marikana Massacre, 86–87
Marine Stewardship Council,
      179
McIntyre, Alasdair, 29
mens rea, 73
Middle Eastern States. *See* Arab
      States
Midgley, Mary, 33
migrant workers, 94–97
  International Convention on
      the Protection of the
      Rights of All Migrant
      Workers and Members
      of Their Families, 94
  under kafala system, in
      Middle Eastern states, 95
Milieudefensie v. *Shell*,
      286–287, 353

Mill, John Stuart, 29
Modern Slavery Act
  in Australia, 154, 240,
      242–244
  in UK, 143, 154, 237, 240,
      242–244
  California Supply Chain
      Transparency Act as
      influence on, 243
  monitoring of employees, as
      corporate human rights
      violation, 78–80
Montesquieu, 28
moral agency, 104–105
moral relativism, in corporate
      social responsibility, 5
moral rights approach, to
      ethical imperatives of
      businesses, 106–107
Movement for the Survival of
      the Ogoni People
      (MOSOP), 14
MSIs. *See* multi-stakeholder
      initiatives
multinational enterprises. *See
      also* OECD Guidelines
      for Multinational
      Enterprises
  transnational governance of,
      172–173
multi-stakeholder initiatives
      (MSIs), 15–16, 221–224
  Accord on Fire and Building
      Safety in Bangladesh,
      339
  Aliance for Bangladesh
      Worker Safety, 339
  Fair Labor Association,
      339–340
  implementation strategies,
      222
  Partnership on AI, 332–334
  purpose of, 223
  Rainforest Alliance, 345
  representation imbalance in,
      223–224
  varieties of, 222–223

National Action Plans (NAPs),
      20
  as policy measures,
      233–236
National Contact Points (NCPs),
      15

under OECD Guidelines for
      Multinational
      Enterprises
  accountability regime,
      208–209
  content of, 208
  critiques of, 209–211
nation-states, human rights as
      responsibility of, 1–2.
      *See also specific
      countries*; *specific laws*;
      specific measures
  adjudicative measures,
      259–291
  attribution factors,
      266–296
  choice of law, 264–266
  in civil law jurisdictions,
      285–290
  for corporate criminal
      liability, 290–291
  duty of care, 267–268
  for foreign direct liability,
      259–260
  forum non conveniens
      doctrine, 262–264
  against parent companies,
      260–261
  attribution factors, 266–269
  aiding and abetting,
      268–269
  direct parent liability, 267
  enterprise liability,
      267–296
  indirect liability, 267–296
  Brussels I Regulation, 264
  critiques of home-state
      solutions, 292–296
  compliance over
      engagement, 294
  frivolous litigation,
      295–296
  imperialism, 292–293
  unintended consequences,
      293–294
  extraterritorial obligations of,
      229–233
  adjudicative jurisdiction,
      230
  direct extraterritorial
      jurisdiction, 231
  domestic measures with
      extraterritorial effects,
      230–231

enforcement jurisdiction, 230

prescriptive jurisdiction, 230

under international law, 229–230, 232–233

jurisdictional issues, 261–262

adjudicative, 230

enforcement jurisdiction, 230

prescriptive, 230

under private international law, 262

under public international law, 261–262

through legislative measures, 240–258

accountability mechanisms in, 241–258

corporate liability provisions in, 241, 254–258

disclosure legislation, 240–254

human rights due diligence obligations, 240–241, 248–258

transparency legislation, 240–247

for parent companies, 293

through policy measures, 233–240

export credit and investment guarantees, 238–240

human rights due diligence in, 238

National Action Plans, 233–236

public procurement, 235–238

Rome II Regulation, 264–265

state duty to protect human rights, 187–188, 227–229

obligation of means in, 228

from third-party abuse, 228–229

in UN Guiding Principles, 227

in UN Protect, Respect and Remedy Framework, 227

UN Guiding Principles and, 234–235

natural law, human rights and, 26–27

natural rights

criticism of, 28–29

human rights and, 27–29

NCPs. *See* National Contact Points

negative business case, for corporate human rights responsibility, 119–120

negative human rights, 54

negligence, human rights due diligence and, 142–143

the Netherlands

Dutch Child Labor Due Diligence Law, 251–252

extraterritorial human rights cases in, 285–288

Four Nigerian Farmers and Milieudefensie v. *Shell*, 286–287

Kiobel v. *Royal Dutch Petroleum Co.*, 272–273, 287–288

Milieudefensie et al v. *Shell*, 353

State of Netherlands v. *Urgenda Foundation*, 353–354

Nigeria

Abacha in, 14

business and human rights in for oil extraction issues, 13–15

Shell Oil Company, 13–15

Ken Saro-Wiwa in, 14

Movement for the Survival of the Ogoni People, 14

Nike, 121, 336–339

non-foundationalist accounts, of human rights, 42–45

constructivist approach, 44–45

political approach, 42–44

pragmatist approach, 44–45

realist approach, 42–44

reconciliation of approaches in, 45

non-state-based non-judicial remedies, 150, 155

normative agency, 41

normative relativism, 33

normative universalism, 34–35

normativism, 44

North America. *See also* Canada; United States

regional human rights conventions in, 61

Novak, Manfred, 309

Nuremberg trials, 11–12, 49–50

obligations, for corporate human rights responsibility. *See* corporate human rights responsibility

Ododo Francis v. *ENI and Nigerian Agip Oil Company (NAOC)*, 289–290

OECD. *See* Organisation for Economic Co-operation and Development

OECD Due Diligence Guidance for Responsible Supply Chains of Minerals from Conflict-Affected and High-Risk Areas, 319

OECD Guidelines for Multinational Enterprises (OECD), 207–211

accountability regime, 208–209

dispute settlement mechanisms, 208–209

National Contact Points in, 208–209

content of, 207–208

National Contact Points, 208

critiques of, 209–211

development of, 207

National Contact Points

in accountability regime, 208–209

in content, 208

critiques of, 209–211

remedy mechanisms, 209–210

revisions of, 207

transparency for, 210

UN Guiding Principles and, 209

OEIWG. *See* Open-Ended Intergovernmental Working Group on Transnational

Corporations and other Business Enterprises with Respect to Human Rights

Office of the High Commissioner for Human Rights (OHCHR), 47–48

Okpabi v. *Royal Dutch Shell Plc*, 279–280

Open-Ended Intergovernmental Working Group on Transnational Corporations and other Business Enterprises with Respect to Human Rights (OEIWG), 312–313

operational-level grievance mechanisms, 148–151
community-driven, 151

Organisation for Economic Co-operation and Development (OECD), 15, 239–240. *See also* OECD Guidelines for Multinational Enterprises
human rights initiatives by, for extractive sector, 319

OECD Principles on AI, 332–334

Partnership on AI, 332–334

passive complicity, in indirect human rights violations, 71
beneficial complicity, 71
silent complicity, 71–72

Peace of Westphalia, 172. *See also* Westphalian international order

positive business case, for corporate human rights responsibility, 120–122

positive human rights, 54

positivism. *See* legal positivism

pragmatic perspectives, on corporate human rights responsibility, 116–122
business case for, 118–122
Nike case, 121
social license to operate, 117–118

precautionary principle, 215

prescriptive jurisdiction, 230

Principles for Responsible Investment (PRI), in banking and finance sector, 180, 326–327

privacy
corporate human rights violation of, 78–80
in information and communication technology sector, 329–330
protection of human rights, as corporate obligation, 131–138
conditions for, 134–135
direct, relational contexts for, 133–136
indirect, structural contexts for, 136–138
Social Connection Model of responsibility, 136–138

protest, as human right, corporate human rights violations of, 85–87

public procurement, 235–238

Qatar, 96–97

RAFI. *See* Reporting and Assurance Framework Initiative

Rainforest Alliance, 345

Rana Plaza factory collapse, 337–338

Rawls, John, 42

Raz, Joseph, 42

RBI. *See* Responsible Business Initiative

regional human rights conventions, 60–62
in Africa, 61
in Arab States, 61–62
in Europe, 60–61
in North/South America, 61
in South-East Asian states, 62

relational corporate power, 108

relativism, of human rights, 31–37
cultural relativism, 32
descriptive relativism, 32
ethical relativism, 33

normative relativism, 33
universalism compared to, 32–33

remedy mechanisms
from human rights impact assessments, 154–158
Barrick Gold mining company, 158
independent third-party involvement in, 156–157
non-state based non-judicial remedies, 150, 155
state-based judicial remedies, 155
state-based non-judicial remedies, 155
under UN Guiding Principles, 150
under UN Working Group guidance, 157
victim participation in, 156
in OECD Guidelines for Multinational Enterprises, 209–210
under French Duty of Vigilance Law, 256
under UN Guiding Principles
access to, 195–196
human rights impact assessments and, 150

Reporting and Assurance Framework Initiative (RAFI), 154

reporting mechanisms, for human rights impact assessments, 153–154
Global Reporting Initiative, 154
Reporting and Assurance Framework Initiative, 154

Responsible Business Initiative (RBI), Switzerland, 258

Responsible Mining Initiative, 319–320

risk assessment, in human rights due diligence, 161–162

risk to rights-holders, 145

Rome II Regulation, 264–265

Roosevelt, Eleanor, 46

Ruggie, John, 2, 17, 66–67, 77, 185–204. *See also* UN Guiding Principles
on Alien Tort Claims Act, 273
on binding treaty on business and human rights, 312–313
on corporate human rights responsibility, 117
on ISO 26000, 219–220
on transnational governance, 173

Safety in Bangladesh, 339
Santa Clara v. *Southern Pacific*, 111
Saro-Wiwa, Ken, 14–15
Saudi Arabia, gender segregation in, 37
Scheinin, Martin, 309–310
SDGs. *See* United Nations
Sen, Amartya, 36
sexual abuse and harassment, against women, 356–357
Shell Oil Company, 13–15
Shi Tao, 330
Shue, Henry, 128–129
silent complicity, 71–72
SLAPP. *See* Strategic Lawsuits Against Public Participation
small and medium-sized enterprises (SMEs), human rights due diligence by, 160
Social Connection Model of responsibility, 136–138
parameters of, 136–137
social contract, human rights as part of, 27–28
social license to operate, 117–118
soft accountability mechanisms, 178–183
by civil society organizations, 182–183
soft law, transnational governance under, 176–178
soft responsibilities, under UN Guiding Principles, 201–202

South Africa, business and human rights in, during apartheid era, 12–13
Sullivan Principles as response to, 12–13
South America. *See also specific countries*
regional human rights conventions in, 61
South-East Asian states. *See also specific countries*
regional human rights conventions in, 62
SPT. *See* Subcommittee on Prevention of Torture
Starbucks, 37
state duty to protect human rights, 187–188, 227–229
obligation of means in, 228
from third-party abuse, 228–229
in UN Guiding Principles, 227
UN Protect, Respect and Remedy Framework, 227
State of the Netherlands v. *Urgenda Foundation*, 353–354
state-based judicial remedies, 155
state-based non-judicial remedies, 155
Strategic Lawsuits Against Public Participation (SLAPP), 295–296
structural corporate power, 108–109
Subcommittee on Prevention of Torture (SPT), 48–49
Sullivan, Leon, 12–13
Sullivan Principles, 12–13
supply chain workers, corporate human rights violations and, 80–83
child labor, 80–81
exploitation of, 82
forced labor, 82–83
modern slavery, 82–83
sweatshop labor, 82
surveillance issues, in information and communication technology sector, 329–330

sweatshop labor, 82
Switzerland, Responsible Business Initiative, 258
Sydney Principles, 345
Syria, 291

Teaching Business and Human Rights Forum, xvii
third-party abuse, under state duty to protect human rights, protections from, 228–229
Tokyo War Crimes Tribunal, 49–50
toxic waste dumping, 89–90
Trafigura, toxic waste dumping by, 89–90, 190
transitional justice, business and human rights and, 358–362
transnational governance
domestic approaches to, 172–174
in Global South, 172–173
globalization of markets and, 174
hard law approaches to, 176–178
international approaches to, 172–174
of multinational companies, 172–173
Peace of Westphalia, 172
polycentric approaches to, 174–175
in post-Westphalian world, 173–174
private approaches to, 174–176
advantages of, 175
public approaches to, 174–176
Ruggie on, 173
soft-law approaches to, 176–178
under international law, 173
transparency
of consumers, as accountability mechanism, 179–180
legislative measures for, nation-states human rights responsibilities and, 240–247

transparency (cont.)
in OECD Guidelines for Multinational Enterprises, 210
under California Supply Chain Transparency Act, 143

UDHR. *See* Universal Declaration of Human Rights
UK. *See* United Kingdom
UN. *See* United Nations
UN Educational, Scientific and Cultural Organization (UNESCO). *See* United Nations
UN Global Compact (UNGC), 211–218
accountability regimes, 215–216
Communication on Progress, 216
dialogue facilitation mechanisms, 216
learning platforms, 215–216
local networks in, 215–216
business and human rights under, 16
content of, 211–215
anti-corruption principle, 212
complicity in, 213–214
environmental principles, 212, 214–215
human rights principles, 212–213
labor principles, 212, 214
precautionary principle, 215
critiques of, 216–218
blue-washing, 216–217
green-washing, 216–217
exclusions from, 211
scope of, 211
UN Guiding Principles (UNGP), on Business and Human Rights, 5, 19–20, 192–204. *See also* human rights due diligence; implementation of human rights responsibility

accountability regimes, 196–197
content of, 193–196
foundational principles, 193–196
operational principles, 193–196
corporate human rights responsibility under, 130, 133–134
critical assessment of, 197–204
of enforcement mechanisms, 201–202
of ethical principles, 200–201
of key achievements, 198
of principled pragmatism approach, 199–200
of social expectations, 200–201
Declaration on Fundamental Principles and Rights at Work, ILO, and, 194
development of, 185
gender and, 357–358
hard duties of, 201–202
HRC and, 18–19
human rights due diligence and, 142, 144–147, 194
for nation-states, human rights responsibilities of, 234–235
normative foundations of, 200–201
remedy mechanisms
access to, 195–196
human rights impact assessments and, 150
soft responsibilities of, 201–202
Sullivan Principles and, 12–13
UN Draft Norms and, 185–186
UN Guiding Principles on Business and Human Rights. *See* United Nations
UN Protect, Respect and Remedy Framework, 185–192
access to remedy, 191–192

corporate responsibility to respect human rights, 188–190
extraterritorial regulation, 187
human rights due diligence and, 189
policy coherence, 187–188
state duty to protect human rights, 187–188
UN Working Group. *See* United Nations
UNESCO. *See* United Nations
UNGC. *See* UN Global Compact; United Nations
UNGP. *See* UN Guiding Principles
UNICEF. *See* United Nations
United Kingdom (UK)
business and human rights in, 20–21
Common Law Duty of Care, 274–280
duty of care, 275–276
jurisdiction of, 275
Okpabi v. *Royal Dutch Shell Plc*, 279–280
tort cases, 276
Vedanta Resources Plc v. *Lungowe*, 276–279
human rights due diligence in, 143
Modern Slavery Act, 143, 154, 237, 240, 242–244
California Supply Chain Transparency Act as influence on, 243
United Nations (UN). *See also* UN Global Compact; UN Guiding Principles
business and human rights Commission on Human Rights, 16–17
Draft Norms on, 16–17, 77
Forum on Business and Human Rights, xvii
Prospect, Respect and Remedy Framework, 16–18
under Global Compact, 16
Working Group, 19–20
Children's Fund (UNICEF), 46

Declaration on the Right and
    Responsibility of
    Individuals, Groups and
    Organs of Society to
    Promote and Protect
    Universally Recognized
    Human Rights and
    Fundamental Freedoms,
    98–99
Declaration on the Rights of
    Indigenous Peoples,
    93–94, 318–319
Development Program
    (UNDP), 46
Draft Norms
    for business and human
    rights, 16–17, 77
    UN Guiding Principles and,
    185–186
Educational, Scientific and
    Cultural Organization
    (UNESCO), 46
international human rights
    systems and, role in,
    46–49
International Labour
    Organization and, 46, 48
    child labor, 80–81
    Convention on Forced
    Labor, 48
main/subsidiary organs, 46
Sustainable Development
    Goals, 348–352
Working Group
    human rights impact
    assessments and, 157
    National Action Plans and,
    234
    remedy mechanisms
    through, 157
United States (US). *See also*
    Alien Tort Claims Act

Bill of Rights, 27–28
business and human rights
    in, 20–21
California Supply Chain
    Transparency Act, 143,
    244–246
    UK Modern Slavery Act
    influenced by, 243
Constitution of 1787, 27–28
Declaration of Independence,
    27–28
Dodd-Frank Wall Street
    Reform and Consumer
    Protection Act, 143
human rights due diligence
    in, 143
Inter-American Court of
    Human Rights, 51, 61
Sullivan Principles, 12–13
Universal Declaration of Human
    Rights (UDHR), 29–30,
    35, 38, 55
corporate human rights
    responsibility under, 115
universalism, of human rights,
    30–37
    absolutism and, 32
    descriptive universalism, 34
    normative universalism,
    34–35
    relativism compared to,
    32–33
    responsibility of nation-
    states, 293
Urbaser v. *Argentina*, 303
US. *See* United States

Vedanta Resources Plc v.
    Lungowe, 276–279
Voluntary Principles on
    Security and Human
    Rights, 320

Votaw, Dow, 106
vulnerable groups, corporate
    human rights violations
    against, 91–100
    human rights defenders,
    95–100
    Indigenous communities,
    92–94
    migrant workers, 94–97
    in Qatar, 96–97

Wall Street Reform and
    Consumer Protection
    Act (Dodd-Frank Act),
    US (2010), 143, 249
    Section 1502, 249–250
Western world, human rights in
    history of thought, 27–28
    human rights as Western
    concept, 35–37
Westphalian international
    order, 1–2
WHO. *See* World Health
    Organization
women
    bias and discrimination
    against, 356–357
    sexual abuse and harassment
    against, 356–357
workplace surveillance cases,
    79–80
World Court of Human Rights,
    309–310
World Health Organization
    (WHO), 46
World Trade Organization
    (WTO), 237

Yahoo!, 330

Young, Iris Marion, 136–138
Zambia, 276–279